RADIOCARBON DATES

from samples funded by English Heritage and dated before 1981

RADIOCARBON DATES

from samples funded by English Heritage and dated before 1981

compiled by
David Jordan, David Haddon-Reece, and Alex Bayliss

ENGLISH HERITAGE

1994

Copyright © English Heritage 1994
First published 1994 by English Heritage, 23 Savile Row, London W1X 1AB

Printed by JW Offset Ltd.

A catalogue record for this book is available from the British Library

ISBN 1 85074 471 8

Text prepared for publication by Alex Bayliss, Robin Taylor, and Kate Macdonald

Designed by Karen Guffogg

Contents

Preface vii
Date list 1
Bibliography 243
Index 1: General index 250
Index 2: HAR numbers index 255
Index 3: Period index 261

Preface

This volume contains a list of radiocarbon age determinations carried out between 1970 and 1982 on behalf of the Ancient Monuments Laboratory, then part of the Inspectorate of Ancient Monuments and Historic Buildings, now part of English Heritage. It also contains supporting information about the samples and sites producing them and indexes which can be used for reference and analysis.

The list is as complete as possible. Given the complexities of the dating process and the long development of the English Heritage Dating Service (see below) some omissions and errors are inevitable. It is hoped that this volume will prove useful as a source for reference and research, and will at the same time stimulate debate on the applications of radiocarbon dating in English archaeology. While most submitters have found the dating useful, the cross-references of radiocarbon dates to their archaeological assumptions should provide food for thought.

The English Heritage dating service

The Laboratory of the Ministry of Public Works, which preceded the Ancient Monuments Laboratory, was amongst the first to sponsor radiocarbon dating programmes in Britain. The earliest dates were commissioned from the National Physical Laboratory in 1960. In 1970 English Heritage began to commission dating at the radiocarbon laboratory of the UK Atomic Energy Authority at Harwell. Only those projects in which the Inspectorate of Ancient Monuments and Historic Buildings had some formal interest were eligible for dating. Despite the stringent vetting arrangements which were established, samples appropriate for dating always exceeded capacity, and a backlog developed.

One of the more awkward limitations of conventional radiocarbon dating is that samples must contain enough carbon for nuclear decay counts to reach statistical significance. This determines the minimum size of sample that can be dated. Until the late 1970s this criterion of minimum size was enough to eliminate a large proportion of those samples submitted. Harwell tackled this problem by developing small gas-proportional counters which could produce reliable dates from much smaller samples. Development took rather longer than expected and, by the time small-sample dating became available, there was a long queue of samples.

This datelist includes only those dates submitted before March 1981 when small-counter dating was becoming available. From April 1981 to 1989 the Harwell Laboratory provided a dating service to English Heritage and all radiocarbon results produced between those years have been published in *Radiocarbon*. From 1987 onwards the smallest samples were submitted to the newly established Radiocarbon Accelerator Unit (AMS) at Oxford. Samples which Harwell could not deal with were dated there, providing a broader service to English Heritage and eliminating the backlog.

An addition to the range of the service was provided when the high-precision laboratory of Queens University, Belfast, started to offer commercial radiocarbon dating in 1989. The precision which the Belfast laboratory can achieve was a major advance, as was their ability to produce 'wiggle-match' dates which can tie floating tree-ring chronologies to a specific part of the radiocarbon calibration curve.

The Harwell laboratory accepted no further archaeological radiocarbon samples after 1989. Their backlog of dating was completed and the results submitted for publication in *Radiocarbon* by 1992. English Heritage subsequently arranged for samples to be submitted for standard dating to the radiocarbon laboratory of the Scottish Universities Research and Reactor Centre at East Kilbride (SURRC).

The current English Heritage Dating Service, located in the Ancient Monuments Laboratory, provides advice on all aspects of scientific dating, or information on where such advice may be sought. A total of about 200 samples are submitted for radiocarbon dating each year. Almost all of these come from projects in which English Heritage has an established interest, on the request of our colleagues in Conservation Group. The service can also help submitters with statistics, calibration, and publication of results. It also ensures that appropriate quality assurance is provided by the dating laboratories.

Compilation of the radiocarbon datelist

This datelist has been collated to give access to a large body of information which, although mostly published elsewhere, has never been accessible in a consistent form. When these dates were produced high-precision calibration was not possible; now that this is available (Stuiver and Pearson 1986; Pearson and Stuiver 1986), all dates have been converted. This has given the submitters the opportunity to review their dating results in the light of this calibration, and with hindsight.

The data was gathered by searching the Ancient Monuments Laboratory and dating laboratory archives covering the years in question and retrieving all records of samples submitted. These were then cross-checked and discrepancies reconciled. A note was made of relevant publications and submitters were asked to comment both on their sites and on the calibrated version of the dates provided. They were also asked to check the details of the samples which were taken from the original submission forms. All this information is in the datelist.

Much time and effort has been spent in removing errors and collecting comments from submitters. Some information could not be gathered, although in general we received a good response to our requests. This has made the final document more useful, although no effort has been made to amend the submitters' interpretation of their dating results. Consequently the reader is warned that some treatments of results and views about them may be inaccurate and reflect misunderstandings about radiocarbon dating, statistics, and calibration.

Furthermore, methods of radiocarbon dating advanced significantly during the time that the results listed here were produced. The accuracy of results obtained in a laboratory changes over time and varies according to the dating technique used and sample material provided. Thus the comparison of results and their statistical and archaeological interpretation is not simple (see for instance Baillie 1990).

There remains a large amount of raw additional information in the English Heritage Radiocarbon Dating Archive (now including the Harwell Radiocarbon Dating Archive). This archive is available for inspection and will be supplemented by a full computer database record of submissions and results.

Conventions

The conventions for quoting radiocarbon dates and supporting information used here conform to the international standard known as the Trondheim Convention, established by the international radiocarbon community in 1986 (Stuiver and Kra 1986). The uncalibrated results are given as radiocarbon years before present (BP) which has been fixed at 1950 AD. Calibrated dates are given as 'cal BC' or 'cal AD'.

All results in the text have been calibrated using the following curves:
- Stuiver and Pearson 1986 cal AD 1950 – 500 cal BC
- Pearson and Stuiver 1986 cal BC 500 – 2500
- Pearson *et al* 1986 cal BC 2500 – 5210

Bi-decadal weighted average of data from:
- Linick *et al* 1985
- Stuiver *et al* 1986   cal BC 5210 – 7210
- Kromer *et al* 1986

The datelist gives both the one and the two standard deviation ranges of the calibrated radiocarbon date. The probability of the true calendrical date of a sample lying within the one standard deviation range is only 68%, whereas the chance of it lying within the two standard deviation range is 95%. Normal scientific practice is to use the 95% range and it is strongly recommended that archaeological radiocarbon dates be quoted and used in this way (Pearson 1987).

We have chosen to present the calibration of the results as ranges (as recommended above) for reasons of space. At the time this publication was planned, the complex probability distributions caused by the irregularity of the calibration curve were not easily available. Now readers can calculate the graphs for themselves using the computer programs supplied, free of charge, by the University of Washington, Seattle, USA.

The calibration curve used here ends at 7210 cal BC; dates older than this have not been calibrated. Determinations which span the more recent past cannot be converted into calendar dates because of the effects of atmospheric ^{14}C produced in the atomic tests of the 1950s. This is indicated in the results as a calibrated value written 1955*. Calibrated ranges delimited by the year 0 cal AD/BC also occur: this is required by the calibration program, although according to convention this should be rendered as 1 AD/BC, there being no year 0.

Notes on the text

Bibliographic references within the datelist indicate occurrences of the date in question within the publication quoted. References to a site are general unless such a reference is followed by '(^{14}C)' when this indicates that a full listing of the dates from the datelist is cited in the publication. A full explanation of the final and preliminary phasing scheme used in the analysis of the Brook Street excavations in Winchester is provided in Biddle 1990, 14–21 and 1162–74. Readers requiring further background information on radiocarbon dating are referred to recent works that cover this topic in greater detail (eg Bowman 1990; Aitken 1990, 56–119).

Acknowledgements

The need for this datalist was originally recognised by the Panel for Science and Conservation. Its subsequent evolution has been the responsibility of various individuals, both present as well as past members of staff, at the Ancient Monuments Laboratory. In chronological order, these include Carole Keepax, Tony Clark, David Haddon-Reece, Andrew David, and David Jordan – the latter steering the project nearly to completion, a task now finalised by Alex Bayliss, his successor as Coordinator for Scientific Dating at English Heritage. A number of people have assisted in the task of collation, notably Alex Bayliss, Lyn Blackmore, Andrew Evans, Clare Jewess, and Jane Payne. Final editing has been greatly assisted by Robin Taylor, Val Horsler, and Kate Macdonald.

The efforts of all concerned – and of course not least of the staff at the various radiocarbon dating laboratories themselves – are warmly appreciated. Bob Otlet and Jill Walker, both formerly of the Harwell Laboratory, deserve special thanks. Most of the information in this volume, however, has been produced by the submitters of the samples dated. Without their help, and particularly their comments, the volume would be of much less value: we are very grateful for their time and interest.

The English Heritage Dating Service
Ancient Monuments Laboratory
September 1993

Supplementary bibliography to the preface

Aitken, M J, 1990 *Science-based dating in archaeology*, London

Baillie, M G L, 1990 Checking back on an assemblage of published radiocarbon dates, *Radiocarbon*, **32**, 361–6

Biddle, M, 1990 Object and economy in medieval Winchester, *Winchester studies*, **7ii Part 1**, Oxford

Bowman, S, 1990 *Radiocarbon dating*, London

Kromer, B, Rhein, M, Bruns, M, Schoch-Fischer, H, Münnich, K O, Stuiver, M, and Becker, B, 1986 Radiocarbon calibration data for the sixth to the eighth millennia BC, *Radiocarbon*, **28**, 954–60

Linick, T W, Suess, H E, and Becker, B, 1985 La Jolla measurements of radiocarbon in south German oak tree-ring chronologies, *Radiocarbon*, **27**, 20–32

Pearson, G W, 1987 Hope to cope with calibration, *Antiquity*, **61**, 98–103

—, Pilcher, *et al* 1986 High-precision ^{14}C measurement of Irish oaks to show the natural ^{14}C variations from AD 1840–5210 BC, *Radiocarbon*, **28**, 911–34

— and Stuiver, M, 1986 High-precision calibration of the radiocarbon time scale, AD 1950–600 BC, *Radiocarbon*, **28**, 805–38

Stuiver, M and Pearson, G W, 1986 High-precision calibration of the radiocarbon time scale, 500–2500 BC, *Radiocarbon*, **28**, 839–62

Stuiver, M and Kra, R S, 1986 Editorial comment, *Radiocarbon*, **28(2B)**, ii

Stuiver, M, Kromer, B, Becker, B and Ferguson, C W, 1986 Radiocarbon age calibration back to 13,300 years BP and the ^{14}C age-matching of the German oak and US bristlecone pine chronologies, *Radiocarbon*, **28**, 969–79

Abingdon: Ashville Trading Estate, Oxfordshire

Location: SU 483973
Lat. 51.40.19 N; Long. 01.18.05 W

Excavator: M Parrington (Oxford Archaeological Unit), 1974 – 6

Site: Iron Age settlement and a sequence of seven ditches, the latest of which was in use in the early Roman period (part of a larger complex of prehistoric and Roman features).

References: Parrington 1978, 39 (^{14}C)
Lambrick 1984

Objectives: to discover the duration and sequence of the Iron Age occupation and thereby the chronology of the ceramic assemblage; the only other dating evidence is a copper alloy La Tène brooch, which may have been used in the fourth century BC, and a sequence of pottery assemblages.

Comments:
G Lambrick: the calibrated dates add little to the interpretation of the site because the range is so large, especially at the 95% confidence interval. The dating has not refined significantly what was already known of the dating of Iron Age pottery groups, though it confirms widely held assumptions. For some of the periods considerably greater confidence could be placed on the pottery dating than on the two standard deviation range, and in some cases on the one standard deviation range. The sequence gives no confidence in the value of applying ^{14}C dating to Iron Age deposits where pottery groups are available.

M Parrington: apart from HAR-1248 and HAR-1249, the results agree with the accepted chronological framework for the Iron Age; it would appear that occupation started in the Early Iron Age and may have been continuous until the Roman period.

HAR-1100   2170 ± 70 BP

$\delta^{13}C$: –23.8 ‰

Sample: SAHMG37, submitted on 24 February 1975

Material: carbonised grain, recovered by sieving.

Initial comment: from pit 37 which was Iron Age and the earliest stratigraphic feature on the site, cut by feature 13 (HAR-1248 and HAR-1333).

Calibrated date: 1σ : cal BC 370 – 115
2σ : cal BC 390 – 40

Final comments:
G Lambrick: within the range for early Iron Age pottery.

HAR-1247   2470 ± 70 BP

$\delta^{13}C$: –24.8 ‰

Sample: SAHMG60, submitted on 22 July 1975

Material: carbonised grain and charcoal.

Initial comment: from pit 60 (Iron Age).

Calibrated date: 1σ : cal BC 785 – 410
2σ : cal BC 800 – 400

Final comments:
G Lambrick: within the range for early Iron Age pottery.

HAR-1248   3360 ± 130 BP

$\delta^{13}C$: –24.7 ‰

Sample: SAHMG13, submitted on 22 July 1975

Material: carbonised grain and charcoal, recovered by wet-sieving.

Initial comment: from house gully 13, which enclosed an Iron Age structure.

Calibrated date: 1σ : cal BC 1875 – 1520
2σ : cal BC 2020 – 1410

Final comments:
G Lambrick: see HAR-1333. This disagrees with the Iron Age pottery; it is unlikely that this feature is so much earlier than the others.

Harwell: an unsatisfactory result due to a low yield from a small sample.

HAR-1249   2970 ± 80 BP

$\delta^{13}C$: –24.1 ‰

Sample: SAHMG73, submitted on 22 July 1975

Material: carbonised grain and charcoal, recovered by wet-sieving.

Initial comment: from ditch 73, enclosing an Iron Age structure.

Calibrated date: 1σ : cal BC 1375 – 1055
2σ : cal BC 1420 – 940

Final comments:
G Lambrick: earlier than expected; possibly contaminated with material from the earlier Bronze Age occupation, or affected by variations in atmospheric carbon content; it is unlikely that this feature is so much earlier than the others.

HAR-1332   2050 ± 70 BP

$\delta^{13}C$: –22.5 ‰

Sample: SAMG32, submitted on 23 October 1975

Material: animal bone.

Initial comment: from ditch 32 (Iron Age).

Calibrated date: 1σ : cal BC 170 – 15 cal AD
2σ : cal BC 350 – 80 cal AD

Final comments:
G Lambrick: this conforms with middle Iron Age pottery groups and fits well with the site chronology.

HAR-1333   1870 ± 80 BP

$\delta^{13}C$: –22.4 ‰

Sample: SAMG13A, submitted on 23 October 1975

Material: animal bone.

Initial comment: from house gully 13 (sample submitted as a check on HAR-1248); this feature cuts pit 37 (HAR-1100), but is stratigraphically earlier than ditch 392 (HAR-1334).

Comment on uncalibrated date: this result is 1500 years younger than HAR-1248, which can be safely disregarded; a date in the first century AD is slightly anomalous, but is within one standard deviation of HAR-1334, which is stratigraphically later.

Calibrated date: 1σ : cal AD 60 – 235
2σ : cal BC 40 – 340 cal AD

Final comments:
G Lambrick: the 95% range gives a very broad date bracket; the pottery can be dated more closely than either of these date ranges.

HAR-1334 1900 ± 90 BP

$\delta^{13}C$: –21.9 ‰

Sample: SAMG392, submitted on 23 October 1975

Material: animal bone.

Initial comment: from Iron Age ditch 392, which is stratigraphically later than house gully 13 (HAR-1248 and HAR-1333).

Comment on uncalibrated date: when calibrated using the 5730 half-life this result is strengthened by the association with wheel-turned late Iron Age pottery.

Calibrated date: 1σ : cal AD 10 – 220
2σ : cal BC 110 – 335 cal AD

Final comments:
G Lambrick: this is consistent with the presence of late Iron Age or early Roman pottery (which is more closely datable than either of the calibrated date ranges).

Abingdon: Barton Court Farm, Oxfordshire

Location: SU 510978
Lat. 51.40.34 N; Long. 01.15.44 W

Excavator: D Miles (Oxford Archaeological Unit), 1972–7

Site: Neolithic, Iron Age, Romano-British, and Anglo-Saxon occupation just to the south of the Neolithic causewayed enclosure.

References: Miles 1984; 4, 8 (^{14}C)

HAR-1335 2200 ± 70 BP

$\delta^{13}C$: –23.7 ‰

Sample: ABBF311E, submitted on 23 October 1975

Material: carbonised grain.

Initial comment: from part of a cache of grain from the bottom of Iron Age pit 311.

Calibrated date: 1σ : cal BC 385 – 175
2σ : cal BC 400 – 100

HAR-1342 1830 ± 80 BP

$\delta^{13}C$: –22.9 ‰

Sample: ABBF725, submitted on 23 October 1975

Material: animal bone.

Initial comment: from Iron Age ditch 5.

Calibrated date: 1σ : cal AD 80 – 315
2σ : cal AD 10 – 390

HAR-2387 4030 ± 70 BP

$\delta^{13}C$: –23.3 ‰

Sample: 865/3

Material: bone.

Initial comment: from a Neolithic pit; the bones have been marked.

Comment on uncalibrated date: see HAR-2388.

Calibrated date: 1σ : cal BC 2855 – 2470
2σ : cal BC 2875 – 2405

HAR-2388 3910 ± 70 BP

$\delta^{13}C$: –23.6 ‰

Sample: 544

Material: antler.

Initial comment: from pit 544 (Neolithic).

Comment on uncalibrated date: HAR-2388 and HAR-2387 match ^{14}C dates from other Grooved Ware sites and seem to indicate the main period of Neolithic activity.

Calibrated date: 1σ : cal BC 2555 – 2315
2σ : cal BC 2580 – 2150

Alcester: Bulls Head Yard, Warwickshire

Location: SP 090575
Lat. 52.13.00 N; Long. 01.49.00 W

Excavator: J Greig (University of Birmingham), 1977

Site: a peat bog.

Objectives: to provide a date for a level of a pollen diagram; the pollen is post VIIb, but there is no clear archaeological dating evidence.

HAR-2257 1760 ± 60 BP

$\delta^{13}C$: –25.0 ‰

Sample: BM160, submitted on 1 June 1977

Material: peat.

Initial comment: from the base of a series of pollen samples collected from a JCB trench.

Calibrated date: 1σ : cal AD 215 – 345
2σ : cal AD 120 – 410

Final comments:
J Greig: it has been important to date this feature for two reasons, firstly because it may have provided a defence for Alcester that may have affected the siting of the settlement there, and secondly to provide a well-dated episode of Roman vegetational history.

Alcester: Pipeline Trench, Warwickshire

Location: SP 087560
Lat. 52.12.06 N; Long. 01.52.22 W

Excavator: D Ford (West Midlands Regional Excavation Unit), 1977

Site: sixteen east – west graves forming part of an unsuspected, apparently christian, cemetery beside a Roman road (Ricknield Street) one mile to the south of Alcester; the burials, which were cut by a trench for a water pipeline, lay between 2m and 40m from the road and between 0.4m and 1.5m below the topsoil, in pits dug into the red Keuper marl.

Objectives: in the absence of grave goods or other independent dating a ^{14}C measurement is required to date the graves; these are of interest in the context of early churches in the area, for which late Roman origins are suspected.

HAR-2732   1000 ± 80 BP

$\delta^{13}C$: –22.2 ‰

Sample: APT1015, submitted by R Lamb on 26 June 1978

Material: human bone.

Initial comment: from a burial; the date could be as early as AD 400 or as late as AD 1400.

Comment on uncalibrated date: the result is earlier than expected; the cemetery was thought to be contemporary with the nearby Boteler's Castle.

Calibrated date: 1σ : cal AD 975 – 1155
                     2σ : cal AD 890 – 1220

Final comments:
Harwell: a replacement for HAR-525 which failed; the excavator's comment is rather different from the original broad date range given.

HAR-3433   740 ± 70 BP

$\delta^{13}C$: –22.0 ‰

Sample: APT1017, submitted by R Lamb in 1979

Material: human bone.

Initial comment: as HAR-2732.

Calibrated date: 1σ : cal AD 1230 – 1285
                     2σ : cal AD 1170 – 1390

HAR-3434   880 ± 70 BP

$\delta^{13}C$: –21.0 ‰

Sample: APT1008, submitted by R Lamb in 1979

Material: human bone.

Initial comment: as HAR-2732.

Calibrated date: 1σ : cal AD 1035 – 1230
                     2σ : cal AD 1010 – 1270

Aldwincle, Northamptonshire

Location: SP 999801
Lat. 52.24.34 N; Long. 00.31.52 W

Excavator: D Jackson (Cambridge Excavation Fund), 1968

Site: a Roman bridge, which may have spanned an earlier course of the river Nene, on the alignment of the Huntingdon – Leicester road, for which evidence was also found; the first phase of construction (first century AD) was indicated mainly by fallen timbers, lying on the bottom of the watercourse, which were sealed by horizontal timbers associated with the final phase.

References: Jackson and Ambrose 1976; 46, 71 – 2 (^{14}C)

Objectives: to date the final phase of the bridge.

HAR-1186   1960 ± 80 BP

$\delta^{13}C$: –26.3 ‰

Sample: ALDWINCLE, submitted by H Keeley on 30 April 1975

Material: wood: *Quercus* sp. (C A Keepax), rings 30 – 40 (R Morgan).

Initial comment: from fallen timber 33 belonging to the first period of construction.

Comment on uncalibrated date: a single radiocarbon determination with a standard deviation of 80 years must be treated with the caution it deserves. It need not preclude the possibility that the bridge was a military construction of the first few decades of the Roman period.

Calibrated date: 1σ : cal BC 55 – 120 cal AD
                     2σ : cal BC 170 – 230 cal AD

Final comments:
D Jackson: this supports the suggestion that the final phase may have been military.

Aldwincle, Northamptonshire

Location: SP 996803
Lat. 54.24.40 N; Long. 00.30.20 W

Excavator: D Jackson (for the Department of the Environment), 1968

Site: a Neolithic mortuary enclosure comprising a rectangular ditched area within four concentric ditches with causeways. Two large pits, possibly postholes, were found at the centre of the complex, with two burials between them.

References: Jackson 1976, 13 – 29
               Radiocarbon **19**, 374 – 5 (^{14}C)

HAR-1411   4560 ± 70 BP

$\delta^{13}C$: –27.2 ‰

Sample: B18EAST

Material: charcoal, three bags combined.

Initial comment: from 0.3m from the base the inner of the two concentric ditches; expected date Neolithic.

Calibrated date: 1σ : cal BC 3370 – 3105
2σ : cal BC 3510 – 3040

Final comments:
D Jackson: earlier than expected.

Aldwincle, Northamptonshire

Location: TL 001805
Lat. 52.24.47 N; Long. 00.31.41 W

Excavator: D Jackson (Ministry of Public Buildings and Works), 1971

Site: a well which may have been part of an Anglo-Saxon settlement in the area. It lay 201m west of Harpers Brook which is assumed to have been the main course of the River Nene in the Roman period.

References: Jackson 1977, 47 (^{14}C)

HAR-1185   1180 ± 70 BP

$δ^{13}C$: −26.5 ‰

Sample: ALDWINCL, submitted on 30 April 1975

Material: soil.

Initial comment: from a wattle-lined timber structure set in a large oval pit; ?this well and a nearby pit also contained Anglo-Saxon pottery.

Calibrated date: 1σ : cal AD 770 – 955
2σ : cal AD 670 – 1000

Alfriston, East Sussex

Location: TQ 509036
Lat. 50.48.42 N; Long. 00.08.32 E

Excavator: P Drewett (Sussex Archaeological Field Unit), 1974

Site: a small, ploughed out, Bronze Age, oval barrow comprising a single dump of material derived from the two flanking ditches and containing a single central crouched inhumation; this is one of only twelve known third-millenium burial sites in East Sussex.

References: Drewett 1975

Comments:
Harwell: one small sample failed (ALF8), one withdrawn (ALF3), one not yet dated (ALF2).

AML: as only HAR-940 is consistent with the archaeology, all three dates from the central burial should be ignored.

HAR-940   4310 ± 110 BP

$δ^{13}C$: −22.5 ‰

Sample: ALF1, submitted on 26 November 1974

Material: antler.

Initial comment: from the primary silt of the south-east ditch, layer 6.

Calibrated date: 1σ : cal BC 3070 – 2710
2σ : cal BC 3340 – 2615

References: Drewett 1975, 151

HAR-942   2590 ± 90 BP

$δ^{13}C$: −23.5 ‰

Sample: ALF4, submitted on 26 November 1974

Material: human bone: leg bones.

Initial comment: from the central burial, a young female; the other leg was submitted as sample HAR-1811.

Comment on uncalibrated date: should be contemporary with HAR-940 and HAR-1811.

Calibrated date: 1σ : cal BC 830 – 610
2σ : cal BC 920 – 410

Final comments:
Harwell: dates from bone are generally reliable, but when they go wrong they are usually too old.

References: Drewett 1975, 151

HAR-1811   3190 ± 80 BP

$δ^{13}C$: −22.5 ‰

Sample: ALF12

Material: human bone.

Initial comment: from the primary burial; the other leg was submitted as sample HAR-942.

Comment on uncalibrated date: this result should be contemporary with HAR-942.

Calibrated date: 1σ : cal BC 1525 – 1410
2σ : cal BC 1670 – 1310

Alfriston: Winton Hill, East Sussex

Location: TQ 508038
Lat. 50.48.49 N; Long. 00.08.27 E

Excavator: T P O'Connor (Institute of Archaeology, London), 1975

Site: an unditched round barrow, 150m west of the Alfriston oval barrow (see above) and 1 mile east of the settlement at Black Patch (Alciston); the barrow contained a central burial disturbed by a later feature which was parallel to, and possibly contemporary with, a Saxon burial on the north side of the mound.

References: O'Connor 1976

Objectives: to ascertain whether the primary burial is Bronze Age or Anglo-Saxon.

HAR-1378   1060 ± 80 BP

$δ^{13}C$: −19.9 ‰

Sample: ALFIIA8, submitted on 28 November 1978

Material: human bone, not cleaned, just lifted and wrapped immediately in tinfoil.

Initial comment: from a bundle of human long bones in the infill of the robber trench which cut the primary burial; it could be Anglo-Saxon or earlier in date.

Calibrated date: 1σ : cal AD 890 – 1025
2σ : cal AD 780 – 1160

Final comments:
T P O'Connor: this result suggests that the bones are from an Anglo-Saxon secondary burial disturbed by a later feature – a surprising conclusion in view of the relationship of the cut to the barrow mound.

Alton: 10 Market Street, Hampshire

Location: SU 716395
Lat. 51.08.59 N; Long. 00.58.34 W

Excavator: M Millett (Alton Archaeological Committee), 1977

Site: part of a medieval street frontage and related structures, which were examined in advance of modernisation.

References: Millett 1983, M80 (^{14}C)

Objectives: to compare the ^{14}C result with the dendrochronological dates.

HAR-2536   650 ± 70 BP

$\delta^{13}C$: −25.3 ‰

Sample: ALT1, submitted by J Hillam on 21 February 1978

Material: wood: oak (*Quercus* sp.), years 11 – 26 of a sample with 122 rings.

Initial comment: from a structural timber in the cellar ceiling.

Comment on uncalibrated date: the sample forms part of a site dendrochronological mean curve (now absolutely dated) taken from years AD 1357 – 73.

Calibrated date: 1σ : cal AD 1275 – 1395
2σ : cal AD 1250 – 1420

Amesbury, Wiltshire

Location: SU 13154205
Lat. 51.10.37 N; Long. 01.48.43 W

Excavator: P Ashbee (for the Department of the Environment), 1960

Site: a single-ditched barrow (G39) approximately half a mile from Stonehenge. A central cremation on the old ground surface was sealed by a mound of loam with occupation debris; the grave goods were a jet button and jet and amber beads; earlier and later Neolithic pottery was found in the loam mound. This was the re-excavation of a barrow from which Wessex grave furniture had been obtained during the earlier nineteenth century.

References: Ashbee 1979 – 80; 9, 32 (^{14}C)

Objectives: to date the barrow and the associated grave goods.

HAR-1237   3620 ± 90 BP

$\delta^{13}C$: −25.2 ‰

Sample: AMESBO39, submitted on 16 July 1975

Material: wood: oak (*Quercus* sp.) (G W Dimbleby).

Initial comment: from an area of burning beneath the crown of the ploughed barrow, adjacent to the central cremation.

Comment on uncalibrated date: the result appears consonant with the middle and late Beaker phases, and significantly different from four of the later dates from three Camerton-Snowshill dagger graves of the Wessex culture, to which the grave furniture from barrow G39 is conventionally related.

The few dates available, to which this must be added, suggest that the expansion of the Wessex culture began in the late Beaker period, reaching a peak slightly later; deposition of grave goods may have continued longer than was formerly thought, and some sites may have an element of archaism.

Calibrated date: 1σ : cal BC 2135 – 1885
2σ : cal BC 2280 – 1750

Final comments:
P Ashbee: such single dates should be treated with reserve.

Harwell: the sample was less than the ideal size: three bags combined – G39, G39 west bank, G391AE.

Andover: Old Down Farm, Hampshire

Location: SU 356465
Lat. 51.08.14 N; Long. 01.32.18 W

Excavator: S M Davies (Test Valley Archaeological Committee), 1975 – 7

Site: Iron Age enclosure, with additional Neolithic, Roman, and early medieval features.

References: Davies 1981, 144 – 5 (^{14}C)

Objectives: to clarify the site chronology.

Comments:
AML: (A J Clark) the calibration, at the 68% confidence level, gives wide date brackets because of the fluctuations in the atmospheric radiocarbon during the period represented.

Although the calibrated ^{14}C dates and the archaeological dates for phases 4 and 5 overlap at the 68% confidence level, the median values diverge fairly steadily, with increasing age, from about 160 years for phase 5 to 690 years for phase 2.

This could be because either the timespan of the occupation was more compressed than proposed, or because of some technical problem with the material; even with the very wide brackets required for the 95% level of confidence, there is no overlap with the archaeological dates for phases 2 and 3.

HAR-3493   1980 ± 70 BP

$\delta^{13}C$: −23.5 ‰

Sample: 2420, submitted on 9 November 1978

Material: bone.

Initial comment: from a pit with a saucepan pot; middle Iron Age (phase 5).

Calibrated date: 1σ : cal BC 90 – 80 cal AD
2σ : cal BC 170 – 140 cal AD

HAR-3494 2000 ± 80 BP

$δ^{13}C$: –24.0 ‰

Sample: 1080, submitted on 9 November 1978

Material: bone.

Initial comment: from a pit, dating to the early Iron Age (phase 3).

Calibrated date: 1σ : cal BC 105 – 75 cal AD
2σ : cal BC 200 – 140 cal AD

HAR-3495 2040 ± 70 BP

$δ^{13}C$: –24.1 ‰

Sample: 937, submitted on 9 November 1978

Material: bone.

Initial comment: from a pit, dating to the early Iron Age (phase 2).

Calibrated date: 1σ : cal BC 160 – 120 cal AD
2σ : cal BC 340 – 90 cal AD

HAR-3496 2100 ± 80 BP

$δ^{13}C$: –24.7 ‰

Sample: 2664/2673, submitted on 9 November 1978

Material: bone.

Initial comment: from a pit, dating to the early Iron Age (phase 4).

Calibrated date: 1σ : cal BC 340 – 35
2σ : cal BC 380 – 70 cal AD

Ardleigh, Essex

Location: TM 055293
Lat. 51.55.25 N; Long. 00.59.20 E

Excavator: J Hinchliffe (Central Excavation Unit), 1980

Site: a Bronze Age barrow.

Objectives: dating was required to place the barrow within a chronological context as part of a wider landscape project.

Comments:
AML: five further samples were submitted after April 1981.

HAR-3908 3600 ± 80 BP

$δ^{13}C$: –26.1 ‰

Sample: 29-750, submitted by N Balaam on 15 July 1980

Material: charcoal: *Quercus* sp. from mature timber and *Corylus avellana* L. nutshell.

Initial comment: from a Bronze Age cremation.

Calibrated date: 1σ : cal BC 2125 – 1885
2σ : cal BC 2195 – 1750

Final comments:
J Hinchliffe: this date is in line with expectations.

Ashdown Forest: Millbrook, East Sussex

Location: TQ 441296
Lat. 51.02.50 N; Long. 00.03.21 E

Excavator: F C Tebbutt (Sussex Archaeological Society), 1980

Site: a middle Saxon iron smelting site comprising a single bowl furnace, with two associated hearths, and a shelter.

References: Tebutt 1982, 28 (^{14}C)
Clark *et al* 1988, 653 (^{14}C)

Objectives: to establish whether the site is Iron Age or Anglo-Saxon and to compare the results with the archaeomagnetic dating samples which were also taken (Clark *et al* 1988, 653).

HAR-4117 1220 ± 70 BP

$δ^{13}C$: –28.0 ‰

Sample: ASSHBL1, submitted by A J Clark on 14 October 1980

Material: soil and charcoal: oak (*Quercus* sp.), probably from mature timbers (C A Keepax).

Initial comment: from waste associated with the bloomery – either Iron Age or Saxon in date.

Calibrated date: 1σ : cal AD 685 – 890
2σ : cal AD 660 – 980

Final comments:
F C Tebbutt: the presence of soil in the sample, and the possible presence of older charcoal may account for an early bias in the ^{14}C result, for which combination with the archaeomagnetic date (*c* 860 ± 60) would compensate; the overlap indicates a date of *c* AD 800 – 835 for the site.

Ashley, Hampshire

Location: SU 371310
Lat. 51.04.36 N; Long. 01.28.13 W

Excavator: D Neal (Department of the Environment), 1977

Site: a series of ditched enclosures covering an area of about eight hectares; most surface traces had been removed through ploughing. The site lies about half a mile east of King's Somborne within a north-west salient of the Ashley parish boundary.

References: Neal 1979

HAR-2223 1640 ± 80 BP

$δ^{13}C$: –23.0 ‰

Sample: Ditch 87, submitted by N Balaam on 21 June 1977

Material: animal bone.

Initial comment: from the fill of a ditch which was believed to be Bronze Age, although all the other features on the site were Roman.

Calibrated date: 1σ : cal AD 265 – 530
2σ : cal AD 230 – 600

Final comments:
D Neal: the results were not included in the report since the feature also included Romano-British pottery recovered after the sample was taken.

Askham Bog, North Yorkshire

Location: SE 570480
Lat. 53.55.29 N; Long. 01.07.55 W

Excavator: J Greig (University of Birmingham), 1976

Objectives: to date part of a pollen diagram.

Comments:
J Greig: these results were not what would have been expected from the stratigraphic position of the samples, nor from the estimated dates for parts of the pollen diagram.

HAR-2256   2020 ± 70 BP

$\delta^{13}C$: –27.8 ‰

Sample: AB1/50, submitted on 1 June 1977

Material: peat.

Calibrated date: 1σ : cal BC 110 – 60 cal AD
2σ : cal BC 200 – 120 cal AD

Final comments:
J Greig: this result is unexpected.

HAR-2258   5150 ± 80 BP

$\delta^{13}C$: –27.9 ‰

Sample: AB2/36, submitted on 1 June 1977

Material: peat.

Calibrated date: 1σ : cal BC 4035 – 3820
2σ : cal BC 4225 – 3780

HAR-2259   410 ± 70 BP

$\delta^{13}C$: –28.9 ‰

Sample: AB1/25, submitted on 1 June 1977

Material: peat.

Calibrated date: 1σ : cal AD 1430 – 1615
2σ : cal AD 1400 – 1650

HAR-2614   1650 ± 60 BP

$\delta^{13}C$: –27.0 ‰

Sample: AB1/50, submitted on 21 March 1978

Material: peat: birch (*Betula* sp.) twigs, phragmites, and roots.

Initial comment: the sample was submitted to date a level of the pollen diagram following an unexpected date for HAR-2256.

Calibrated date: 1σ : cal AD 270 – 435
2σ : cal AD 240 – 540

Avebury: School Site, Wiltshire

Location: SU 105698
Lat. 51.25.36 N; Long. 01.51.20 W

Excavator: F J Vatcher (for the Department of the Environment), 1969

Site: a pit located 3m outside the foot of the bank on the south-west side of the henge. It cut through the first layer of soil which had been rainwashed off the bank, but was covered by a second layer and then by thick topsoil.

Objectives: to date the pit, which must be later than the bank (*c* 2500 – 2000 BC).

HAR-1696   1200 ± 80 BP

$\delta^{13}C$: –23.8 ‰

Sample: AVEGPIT2, submitted on 27 May 1976

Material: pit fill with carbonised grain: other seeds from the pit were identified as *Triticum aestivo-compactum* and possibly 6-row barley, with various weed seeds (AML-781187).

Initial comment: from a pit (1.1m deep, 1.51m × 1.0m across the oval top) containing carbonised grain, probably originally in a basket. This pit was 3m outside the foot of the bank of the Avebury henge monument, on the south-west side, and cut through the first layer of soil rainwashed off the bank, but was covered by a second layer of rainwash, and then by thick topsoil. The estimated date of the bank is between 2500 and 2000 BC.

Calibrated date: 1σ : cal AD 690 – 895
2σ : cal AD 660 – 1000

Final comments:
G Swanton: the pottery from the site, as a whole, ranges from the tenth to the thirteenth centuries; if there was any earlier Saxon material it is not now known where this came from. There was sub-Roman or early Saxon activity nearby however, while the church dates from *c* AD 1000, so that the radiocarbon dates for this pit may well be acceptable.

Harwell: no grain was apparent during pretreatment.

Balksbury, Hampshire

Location: SU 351466
Lat. 51.11.55 N; Long. 01.30.00 W

Excavator: G J Wainwright (Department of the Environment), 1973

Site: Iron Age hillfort excavated in advance of housing development.

References: Radiocarbon **19**, 408 (^{14}C)

Objectives: to date the construction of the hillfort.

HAR-442 2740 ± 170 BP

$\delta^{13}C$: −22.9 ‰

Sample: BC1-10, submitted by H Keeley on 10 October 1973

Material: antler.

Initial comment: from the base of the phase 1 rampart; the result should relate to the construction of the defences.

Calibrated date: 1σ : cal BC 1100 – 790
2σ : cal BC 1395 – 410

Final comments:
G J Wainwright: this date lies within the range suggested by other radiocarbon dates from other, similar, hillforts.

HAR-443 1310 ± 100 BP

$\delta^{13}C$: −25.3 ‰

Sample: 500-5/8, submitted by H Keeley on 10 October 1973

Material: charcoal.

Initial comment: a bulked sample from the floor of a bell-shaped storage pit 1.50m deep, associated with Iron Age pottery.

Calibrated date: 1σ : cal AD 640 – 790
2σ : cal AD 550 – 950

Final comments:
G J Wainwright: c 1000 years too late – the age was expected to be comparable with that of HAR-442; contamination of the bulked sample is suspected.

HAR-444 2140 ± 80 BP

$\delta^{13}C$: −25.2 ‰

Sample: 36/6, submitted by H Keeley on 10 October 1973

Material: charcoal.

Initial comment: from a bell-shaped storage pit, associated with pottery of middle Iron Age type.

Calibrated date: 1σ : cal BC 360 – 95
2σ : cal BC 390 – 20 cal AD

Final comments:
G J Wainwright: this date lies within the range obtained from dating similar remains elsewhere.

HAR-445 2000 ± 80 BP

$\delta^{13}C$: −24.1 ‰

Sample: 182/4, submitted by H Keeley on 10 October 1973

Material: charcoal and mud.

Initial comment: from a storage pit, as HAR-444.

Calibrated date: 1σ : cal BC 105 – 80 cal AD
2σ : cal BC 200 – 140 cal AD

Final comments:
G J Wainwright: as HAR-444.

HAR-446 2180 ± 150 BP

$\delta^{13}C$: −25.1 ‰

Sample: 106/4, submitted by H Keeley on 10 October 1973

Material: charcoal and mud.

Initial comment: from a storage pit, as HAR-444.

Calibrated date: 1σ : cal BC 400 – 40
2σ : cal BC 760 – 120 cal AD

Final comments:
G J Wainwright: as HAR-444.

Barham: BRH015, Suffolk

Location: TM 13455142
Lat. 52.07.10 N; Long. 01.07.05 E

Excavator: C Balkwill (Ipswich Museum) and E A Martin (Suffolk Archaeological Unit), 1978 – 9

Site: a late Bronze Age or early Iron Age settlement site on a hilltop flanking the Gipping valley.

Objectives: to date a pit containing the remains of an oven/furnace made out of large fragments of a late Bronze Age jar.

HAR-3610 2640 ± 70 BP

$\delta^{13}C$: −26.0 ‰

Sample: BARHAM1, submitted by P Murphy on 9 October 1979

Material: charcoal.

Initial comment: from two adjacent pits (pits 1 and 2) containing similar pottery.

Calibrated date: 1σ : cal BC 845 – 795
2σ : cal BC 920 – 610

Final comments:
C Balkwill: this date fits well with the pottery, which is of post-Deverel-Rimbury type.

Barnack: Gravel Pit, Lincolnshire

Location: TF 050069
Lat. 52.38.57 N; Long. 00.26.52 W

Excavator: P Donaldson (Nene Valley Research Committee and the Department of the Environment), 1974

Site: a multiphase round barrow containing 23 graves, on gravels 1km east of Stamford, and near Maxey and Fengate; the inner ditch was rapidly backfilled and replaced with a double ring of stakeholes centred on a rich, primary Wessex grave; outside this were two later ditches.

References: Donaldson 1977, 228 (^{14}C)
Lawson 1986a; 2, fig 1 (^{14}C)
Lawson *et al* 1981
Radiocarbon **21**, 371 (^{14}C)

Comments:
P Donaldson: comparison with the range of Beaker dates in Britain and Europe suggests that this result should be within the range 1850 – 1750 BC, but the coincident sequence of ^{14}C dates and stratigraphy at this site argue strongly that this result is archaeologically acceptable.

HAR-1156   3230 ± 100 BP

$\delta^{13}C$: −20.8 ‰

Sample: BGP1497, submitted by H Keeley on 30 April 1975

Material: human bone.

Initial comment: from burial 25.

Calibrated date: 1σ : cal BC 1630 – 1420
                    2σ : cal BC 1740 – 1310

HAR-1158   3800 ± 100 BP

$\delta^{13}C$: −21.4 ‰

Sample: BGP1496, submitted by H Keeley on 30 April 1975

Material: human bone.

Initial comment: from burial 7.

Calibrated date: 1σ : cal BC 2460 – 2050
                    2σ : cal BC 2565 – 1960

HAR-1205   3590 ± 80 BP

$\delta^{13}C$: −21.6 ‰

Sample: BGP1499, submitted by H Keeley on 30 April 1975

Material: human bone.

Initial comment: from burial 27.

Calibrated date: 1σ : cal BC 2115 – 1830
                    2σ : cal BC 2190 – 1740

HAR-1206   360 ± 90 BP

$\delta^{13}C$: −21.9 ‰

Sample: BGP1500, submitted by H Keeley on 30 April 1975

Material: human bone.

Initial comment: from an inhumation burial found in a barrow.

Calibrated date: 1σ : cal AD 1439 – 1645
                    2σ : cal AD 1410 – 1955*

HAR-1207   3400 ± 80 BP

$\delta^{13}C$: −21.6 ‰

Sample: BGP1501, submitted by H Keeley on 30 April 1975

Material: human bone.

Initial comment: from burial 37a.

Calibrated date: 1σ : cal BC 1870 – 1620
                    2σ : cal BC 1910 – 1520

HAR-1430   3450 ± 70 BP

$\delta^{13}C$: −22.4 ‰

Sample: BGP1498, submitted by H Keeley on 30 April 1975

Material: human bone.

Initial comment: from secondary burial 39a.

Calibrated date: 1σ : cal BC 1885 – 1685
                    2σ : cal BC 1750 – 1420

HAR-1612   3290 ± 80 BP

$\delta^{13}C$: −21.9 ‰

Sample: BGP2442, submitted by H Keeley on 1 April 1976

Material: human bone.

Initial comment: from burial 26, in a coffin (submitted as a check on HAR-1206).

Calibrated date: 1σ : cal BC 1680 – 1510
                    2σ : cal BC 1750 – 1420

HAR-1645   3570 ± 80 BP

$\delta^{13}C$: −24.8 ‰

Sample: BGP1450, submitted by H Keeley on 27 May 1976

Material: charcoal: *Quercus* sp. from large timbers (C A Keepax).

Initial comment: from beside burial 28, a primary grave associated with a Beaker, dagger, wristguard and pendant.

Calibrated date: 1σ : cal BC 2035 – 1780
                    2σ : cal BC 2170 – 1705

References: Lawson 1986c, 40

Barnard Castle: Moss Mire, County Durham

Location: NZ 0516 approx
              Lat. 54.32.21 N; Long. 01.55.22 W

Excavator: A Donaldson (University of Durham)

Objectives: as the samples from the clearance itself are rather small and from cores, HAR-3073 may more accurately put the whole clearance into its context; HAR-3075 is the latest datable sample to give a time scale to the upper part of the pollen diagram.

Comments:
AML: seven samples were dated after 1981, HAR-4747 (MM15), HAR-4748 (MM160), HAR-5070 (60-64CM), HAR-6804 (MM220), HAR-6805 (MM260), HAR-6845, and HAR-9028 (MM220).

HAR-3073   1550 ± 70 BP

$\delta^{13}C$: −27.8 ‰

Sample: MM130, submitted on 22 January 1979

Material: peat.

Initial comment: from near the beginning of a wooded period after the first major forest clearance.

Calibrated date: 1σ : cal AD 420 – 595
                       2σ : cal AD 350 – 640

HAR-3074   1430 ± 70 BP

$\delta^{13}C$: –27.4 ‰

Sample: MM100, submitted on 22 January 1979

Material: peat.

Initial comment: from the middle of the wooded period after the first major forest clearance.

Calibrated date: 1σ : cal AD 560 – 660
                       2σ : cal AD 450 – 690

HAR-3075   510 ± 80 BP

$\delta^{13}C$: –27.3 ‰

Sample: MM50, submitted on 22 January 1979

Material: peat.

Calibrated date: 1σ : cal AD 1320 – 1445
                       2σ : cal AD 1290 – 1610

Barnham: BNH009, Suffolk

Location: TL 866777
              Lat. 52.21.54 N; Long. 00.44.28 E

Excavator: E A Martin (Suffolk Archaeological Unit), 1978

Site: a trapezoidal, double-ditched Iron Age enclosure.

Objectives: to date the enclosure.

HAR-2902   2050 ± 80 BP

$\delta^{13}C$: –23.3 ‰

Sample: BARN0031, submitted by P Murphy on 27 October 1978

Material: charcoal: *Quercus* sp. from mature timber, also some unidentified fragments (C A Keepax).

Initial comment: from the primary fill of the inner ditch; an Iron Age date is expected.

Calibrated date: 1σ : cal BC 180 – 20 cal AD
                       2σ : cal BC 360 – 110 cal AD

Final comments:
E A Martin: the date is in keeping with the pottery evidence from the enclosure ditches.

Barrow: St Chad's, Humberside

Location: TA 074217
              Lat. 53.40.50 N; Long. 00.22.25 W

Excavator: J B Whitwell (Humberside County Council), 1979

Site: an Anglo-Saxon church and cemetery; most of the burials are to some degree disturbed, but some graves clearly predate the stone church; one of these, in a stone coffin with charcoal, may be a charcoal burial.

Objectives: the site has virtually no artefactual dating, but the layout of the foundations is generally agreed to be Saxon; ^{14}C dates are required to confirm this.

Comments:
J B Whitwell: the date of the church is thought to be eleventh-century on typological grounds, although this is in conflict with the tenth-century date, which is suggested by the ^{14}C dates for pre- and post-church burials. It is suggested that five dates are not sufficient to build a firm case for the earlier dating of the church.

HAR-3123   1030 ± 80 BP

$\delta^{13}C$: –26.8 ‰

Sample: BW78-60, submitted on 9 February 1979

Material: charcoal: *Quercus* sp. from mature timbers (C A Keepax).

Initial comment: from below a skeleton in a stone lined cist, which predates the foundations of the church.

Calibrated date: 1σ : cal AD 900 – 1035
                       2σ : cal AD 830 – 1170

HAR-3124   880 ± 80 BP

$\delta^{13}C$: –21.6 ‰

Sample: BW78-GRA, submitted on 9 February 1979

Material: human bone and clay.

Initial comment: from a burial, which may be contemporary with the church.

Calibrated date: 1σ : cal AD 1030 – 1245
                       2σ : cal AD 1000 – 1270

HAR-3125   1130 ± 80 BP

$\delta^{13}C$: –22.5 ‰

Sample: BW78-111, submitted on 9 February 1979

Material: human bone.

Initial comment: from the eastern extremity of the cemetery (?latest series).

Calibrated date: 1σ : cal AD 790 – 990
                       2σ : cal AD 680 – 1030

HAR-3126   1090 ± 70 BP

$\delta^{13}C$: –21.9 ‰

Sample: BW78-74b, submitted on 9 February 1979

Material: human bone.

Initial comment: from a burial either contemporary with, or earlier than, the church.

Calibrated date: 1σ : cal AD 885 – 1010
                       2σ : cal AD 780 – 1030

HAR-3127 970 ± 80 BP

$\delta^{13}C$: −20.5 ‰

Sample: BW78-23, submitted on 9 February 1979

Material: human bone.

Initial comment: from a burial either contemporary with, or earlier than, the church.

Calibrated date: 1σ : cal AD 990 – 1165
　　　　　　　　2σ : cal AD 890 – 1230

HAR-3128 1080 ± 80 BP

$\delta^{13}C$: −22.1 ‰

Sample: BW78-18, submitted on 9 February 1979

Material: human bone.

Initial comment: from a burial contemporary with, or earlier than, the church.

Calibrated date: 1σ : cal AD 890 – 1015
　　　　　　　　2σ : cal AD 780 – 1040

Barton-on-Humber: St Peter's Church, Humberside

Location: TA 03472195
　　　　　Lat. 53.41.01 N; Long. 00.25.59 W

Excavator: W Rodwell (Department of the Environment), 1978 – 81

Site: an Anglo-Saxon and medieval church.

References: Rodwell and Rodwell 1982
　　　　　　Radiocarbon **29**, 94 (¹⁴C)

Objectives: to date the timber elements in the Saxon/medieval tower and the attached western baptistry.

HAR-2863 720 ± 60 BP

$\delta^{13}C$: −25.5 ‰

Sample: BH05, submitted on 1 September 1978

Material: wood: *Quercus* sp. from large timbers (C A Keepax).

Initial comment: from the stump of one of the beams embedded in the belfry wall, which supported the former thirteenth- or fourteenth-century spire, probably contemporary with HAR-2864.

Calibrated date: 1σ : cal AD 1260 – 1290
　　　　　　　　2σ : cal AD 1220 – 1390

Final comments:
W Rodwell: this date conveniently confirms our deduction that the lost spire dated from *c* AD 1300 – 50.

References: Rodwell and Rodwell 1982, 305

HAR-2864 780 ± 80 BP

$\delta^{13}C$: −26.2 ‰

Sample: BH06, submitted on 1 September 1978

Material: wood: *Quercus* sp. from large timbers (C A Keepax).

Initial comment: from the central joist in the floor of the ringing chamber of the tower; probably contemporary with HAR-2863.

Calibrated date: 1σ : cal AD 1180 – 1280
　　　　　　　　2σ : cal AD 1040 – 1380

Final comments:
W Rodwell: while a date of *c* AD 1300 – 50 (as anticipated) is clearly within the calibrated range, it is possible that the beam was inserted in one of the earliest constructional campaigns of the late twelfth and early thirteenth centuries.

References: Rodwell and Rodwell 1982, 305

HAR-2865 570 ± 70 BP

$\delta^{13}C$: −25.0 ‰

Sample: BH03, submitted on 1 September 1978

Material: wood: *Quercus* sp. from large timber. (C A Keepax).

Initial comment: from one of the east – west timbers of the base frame of the former thirteenth- or fourteenth-century spire.

Calibrated date: 1σ : cal AD 1295 – 1425
　　　　　　　　2σ : cal AD 1280 – 1450

Final comments:
W Rodwell: the proposed date of *c* AD 1300 – 50 for the spire falls well within the range of this date. Could the observed date be influenced by wood preservative, pushing it slightly later than in reality?

References: Rodwell and Rodwell 1982, 297

HAR-3106 960 ± 70 BP

$\delta^{13}C$: −26.0 ‰

Sample: BH01, submitted on 1 September 1978

Material: wood: *Quercus* sp. from mature timber (C A Keepax).

Initial comment: part of one of two surviving joists which supported the floor and upper chamber in the Anglo-Saxon west annexe to the church (baptistry).

Calibrated date: 1σ : cal AD 1010 – 1165
　　　　　　　　2σ : cal AD 960 – 1230

Final comments:
W Rodwell: on architectural grounds this timber cannot be later than the early eleventh century, while a date around AD 975 is most likely. Again one wonders whether timber preservative has been applied in the past and influenced the dating.

Barton-under-Needwood: Catholme, Staffordshire

Location: SK 197163
　　　　　Lat. 52.44.37 N; Long. 01.42.29 W

Excavator: S Losco-Bradley (Trent Valley Research Committee), 1973 – 4

Site: Anglo-Saxon village 800m east of the Roman road from Wall (Letocetum) to Derby (Derventio), close to the River Trent and Needwood Forest; traces of Romano-British activity have also been found in the area.

References: Losco-Bradley and Wheeler 1984

Objectives: to date the development of the Saxon settlement.

Comments:
Harwell: the dates in the interim report were calibrated after Ralph *et al* 1973.

HAR-949 1580 ± 80 BP

$\delta^{13}C$: −26.4 ‰

Sample: CA74BF, submitted on 26 November 1974

Material: charcoal.

Initial comment: from a layer of brown, sandy soil *c* 0.10m deep within a sunken-featured building.

Calibrated date: 1σ : cal AD 400 – 560
 2σ : cal AD 255 – 640

Final comments:
S Losco-Bradley: this date fits within the expected range; suggesting that settlement developed simultaneously both inside and outside the enclosure.

References: Losco-Bradley and Wheeler 1984, 103 – 4

HAR-950 3410 ± 100 BP

$\delta^{13}C$: −25.5 ‰

Sample: CA74KA, submitted on 26 November 1974

Material: charcoal.

Initial comment: from grey-brown fine soil with charcoal, interpreted as a burnt post rotted *in situ*, set in a hole packed with light brown sandy soil.

Calibrated date: 1σ : cal BC 1880 – 1610
 2σ : cal BC 2010 – 1510

Final comments:
S Losco-Bradley: this date is anomalous, being much earlier than anticipated.

HAR-951 1440 ± 80 BP

$\delta^{13}C$: −26.6 ‰

Sample: CA74KC, submitted on 26 November 1974

Material: charcoal.

Initial comment: from a brown mixed sandy/loamy soil with flecks of clay and charcoal, interpreted as packing for posts set in a continuous wall trench.

Calibrated date: 1σ : cal AD 550 – 660
 2σ : cal AD 430 – 750

Final comments:
S Losco-Bradley: as HAR-949.

References: Losco-Bradley and Wheeler 1984, 103 – 4

HAR-952 1180 ± 70 BP

$\delta^{13}C$: −24.9 ‰

Sample: CA74LD, submitted on 26 November 1974

Material: charcoal.

Initial comment: from a burnt post set in a hole cut into natural sand and gravel, packed with a brown sandy soil and gravel.

Calibrated date: 1σ : cal AD 770 – 955
 2σ : cal AD 670 – 1000

Final comments:
S Losco-Bradley: the date fits with the constructional interpretation of 'post-in-trench' structures belonging to a later phase in the development of the enclosure.

References: Losco-Bradley and Wheeler 1984, 103 – 4

HAR-953 1450 ± 70 BP

$\delta^{13}C$: −26.2 ‰

Sample: CA74PO, submitted on 26 November 1974

Material: charcoal.

Initial comment: from a dark brown sandy/loamy soil, approximately 0.04m deep in a ditch cut into 'natural' sand and gravel; the sample was taken from an area of *c* 1.00m × 0.30m.

Calibrated date: 1σ : cal AD 550 – 655
 2σ : cal AD 430 – 680

Final comments:
S Losco-Bradley: this dates the outer ditch C, which marks the final point in the progressive expansion of the enclosure and is contemporary with dates obtained from structures; supporting the theory that the enclosure boundaries defined a group of associated buildings within the settlement.

References: Losco-Bradley and Wheeler 1984, 103 – 4

HAR-954 1480 ± 80 BP

$\delta^{13}C$: −26.0 ‰

Sample: CA74SQ, submitted on 26 November 1974

Material: charcoal.

Initial comment: from a layer of soil 0.5 – 0.8m deep in a small pit.

Calibrated date: 1σ : cal AD 460 – 650
 2σ : cal AD 410 – 670

Final comments:
S Losco-Bradley: this date is acceptable.

References: Losco-Bradley and Wheeler 1984, 103 – 4

HAR-1500 1060 ± 70 BP

$\delta^{13}C$: −25.7 ‰

Sample: CA75BHM, submitted on 6 February 1976

Material: charcoal: *c*<D 80% oak (*Quercus* sp.) with some birch (*Betula* sp.), willow (*Salix* sp.), and hazel (*Corylus* sp.) from small timbers (C A Keepax).

Initial comment: from a layer of dark grey soil in a Saxon hut.

Calibrated date: 1σ : cal AD 895 – 1020
2σ : cal AD 810 – 1155

References: Losco-Bradley and Wheeler 1984, 103 – 4

HAR-1501 5050 ± 70 BP

$\delta^{13}C$: –25.0 ‰

Sample: CA75BMT, submitted on 6 February 1976

Material: charcoal.

Initial comment: from wood burnt *in situ*, in a pit filled with sand.

Calibrated date: 1σ : cal BC 3970 – 3780
2σ : cal BC 4000 – 3700

HAR-1502 1130 ± 80 BP

$\delta^{13}C$: –25.9 ‰

Sample: CA75BCX, submitted on 6 February 1976

Material: charcoal.

Initial comment: from the fill of a shallow ditch (brown sandy soil).

Calibrated date: 1σ : cal AD 790 – 990
2σ : cal AD 680 – 1030

References: Losco-Bradley and Wheeler 1984, 103 – 4

HAR-1503 1390 ± 60 BP

$\delta^{13}C$: –25.9 ‰

Sample: CA75BGM, submitted on 6 February 1976

Material: charcoal: oak (*Quercus* sp.) from a large branch or trunk, also a few grams of acorns.

Initial comment: from wood burnt *in situ*, in a pit filled with potboilers.

Calibrated date: 1σ : cal AD 610 – 670
2σ : cal AD 550 – 760

References: Losco-Bradley and Wheeler 1984, 103 – 4

HAR-1506 1010 ± 70 BP

$\delta^{13}C$: –25.0 ‰

Sample: CA187BDD, submitted on 6 February 1976

Material: charcoal.

Initial comment: from brown soil in a pit.

Calibrated date: 1σ : cal AD 975 – 1040
2σ : cal AD 890 – 1170

References: Losco-Bradley and Wheeler 1984, 103 – 4

HAR-1507 1340 ± 80 BP

$\delta^{13}C$: –27.3 ‰

Sample: CA188BGL, submitted on 6 February 1976

Material: charcoal.

Initial comment: from wood burnt *in situ*, in a pit filled with potboilers.

Calibrated date: 1σ : cal AD 635 – 765
2σ : cal AD 560 – 880

References: Losco-Bradley and Wheeler 1984, 103 – 4

HAR-1591 3370 ± 100 BP

$\delta^{13}C$: –25.6 ‰

Sample: CA185A20, submitted on 6 February 1976

Material: charcoal.

Initial comment: from a concentration of charcoal in the initial silts at the base of a small ring ditch.

Calibrated date: 1σ : cal BC 1865 – 1530
2σ : cal BC 1930 – 1440

HAR-1621 20 ± 70 BP

$\delta^{13}C$: –26.5 ‰

Sample: CABQM, submitted on 6 February 1976

Material: charcoal.

Initial comment: from the remains of a large post which rotted *in situ* and was perhaps part of a Saxon granary.

Calibrated date: 1σ : cal AD 1890 – 1955
2σ : cal AD 1680 – 1955

HAR-2184 1290 ± 80 BP

$\delta^{13}C$: –25.7 ‰

Sample: CA205BHK, submitted on 6 February 1976

Material: charcoal: *c* 80% oak (*Quercus* sp.) with some birch (*Betula* sp.), willow (*Salix* sp.), and hazel (*Corylus* sp.) from twigs or small branches (C A Keepax).

Initial comment: from wood burnt *in situ*, in a pit filled with potboilers.

Calibrated date: 1σ : cal AD 655 – 790
2σ : cal AD 610 – 890

Final comments:
Harwell: replacement for HAR-1504.

References: Losco-Bradley and Wheeler 1984, 103 – 4

HAR-2347 110 ± 70 BP

$\delta^{13}C$: –26.3 ‰

Sample: CA75BQM, submitted on 6 February 1976

Material: charcoal, heavily iron stained: *Quercus* sp. from a fairly large timber.

Initial comment: from a post partially rotted *in situ*, possibly part of an Anglo-Saxon granary.

Calibrated date: 1σ : cal AD 1675 – 1955
2σ : cal AD 1650 – 1955

HAR-2446 1180 ± 70 BP

$\delta^{13}C$: –25.9 ‰

Sample: CA75BTN, submitted on 22 December 1977

Material: charcoal: *Quercus* sp. from large timber and *Corylus/Alnus* sp. from branch-sized and large timber; *c* 50% identified.

Initial comment: from burnt wood in the base of an Anglo-Saxon pit, cut into sand and gravel.

Calibrated date: 1σ : cal AD 770 – 955
2σ : cal AD 670 – 1000

References: Losco-Bradley and Wheeler 1984, 103 – 4

HAR-2448   200 ± 70 BP

$\delta^{13}C$: –25.4 ‰

Sample: CA76BZI, submitted on 24 January 1978

Material: charcoal: *Quercus* sp. from large timbers, *Prunus* sp. from branch-sized timbers, and ?Papillionaceae twigs; also Rosaceae, sub-family Pomoideae, *Salix/Populus* sp, *Corylus* sp. and *Ilex* sp.; *c* 25% identified.

Initial comment: from wood burnt in the middle silt of the latest phase of a recut Anglo-Saxon ditch.

Calibrated date: 1σ : cal AD 1645 – 1955
2σ : cal AD 1515 – 1950

HAR-2449   1050 ± 90 BP

$\delta^{13}C$: –25.7 ‰

Sample: CA76BY1, submitted on 22 December 1977

Material: charcoal: *Quercus* sp., *Corylus/Alnus* sp., *Salix/Populus* sp., and Rosaceae, sub-family Pomoideae; *c* 50% identified.

Initial comment: from a later deposit in an Anglo-Saxon sunken-featured building.

Calibrated date: 1σ : cal AD 890 – 1030
2σ : cal AD 780 – 1170

References: Losco-Bradley and Wheeler 1984, 103 – 4

HAR-2456   1280 ± 70 BP

$\delta^{13}C$: –25.4 ‰

Sample: CA76CAU, submitted on 22 December 1977

Material: charcoal: *Quercus* sp. from large timbers, *Corylus/Alnus* sp., and ?*Salix* sp.; *c* 25% identified.

Initial comment: from burnt wood which came from a sandy layer covering the central area in the bottom of an Anglo-Saxon sunken-featured building.

Calibrated date: 1σ : cal AD 665 – 790
2σ : cal AD 640 – 890

References: Losco-Bradley and Wheeler 1984, 103 – 4

HAR-2457   1290 ± 80 BP

$\delta^{13}C$: –25.0 ‰

Sample: CA76CAB, submitted on 24 January 1978

Material: charcoal: *Quercus* sp. from large timbers; c25% identified.

Initial comment: from wood burnt in a pit associated with the latest phase of a recut Anglo-Saxon ditch.

Calibrated date: 1σ : cal AD 655 – 790
2σ : cal AD 610 – 890

References: Losco-Bradley and Wheeler 1984, 103 – 4

HAR-2458   1210 ± 70 BP

$\delta^{13}C$: –26.5 ‰

Sample: CA75BSD, submitted on 22 December 1977

Material: charcoal: *Quercus* sp. from large timbers, *Corylus* sp. and ?*Prunus* sp. (mainly twiggy), and *Salix/Populus* sp..

Initial comment: from an area of burnt wood in an Anglo-Saxon ditch.

Calibrated date: 1σ : cal AD 690 – 890
2σ : cal AD 660 – 980

References: Losco-Bradley and Wheeler 1984, 103 – 4

HAR-2459   1880 ± 70 BP

$\delta^{13}C$: –27.0 ‰

Sample: CA76BZB, submitted on 22 December 1977

Material: charcoal: *Quercus* sp., *Corylus* sp., *Betula* sp., *Fraxinus* sp., and Rosaceae, sub-family Pomoideae, mainly large timbers with some twig- and branch-sized wood, also *Salix/Populus* sp.; *c* 25% identified.

Initial comment: burnt wood from a post-occupation layer in an Anglo-Saxon sunken-featured building.

Calibrated date: 1σ : cal AD 60 – 220
2σ : cal BC 40 – 320 cal AD

HAR-2507   1100 ± 80 BP

$\delta^{13}C$: –26.4 ‰

Sample: CA76BSE, submitted on 22 December 1977

Material: charcoal: *Quercus* sp., *Corylus/Alnus* sp., and Rosaceae, sub-family Pomoideae, mainly from twigs and branches; also *Prunus* sp..

Initial comment: from an area of burnt wood in the lowest silt of an Anglo-Saxon ditch, probably associated with a group of Anglo-Saxon buildings.

Calibrated date: 1σ : cal AD 880 – 1010
2σ : cal AD 725 – 1020

HAR-2508   1500 ± 60 BP

$\delta^{13}C$: –26.1 ‰

Sample: CA76BWE, submitted on 24 January 1978

Material: charcoal: *Quercus* sp. from large timbers; *c* 25% identified.

Initial comment: from wood burnt in a pit, probably associated with an Anglo-Saxon building.

Calibrated date: 1σ : cal AD 460 – 625
2σ : cal AD 420 – 660

References: Losco-Bradley and Wheeler 1984, 103 – 4

Beacon Hill: M40, site 12, Oxfordshire

Location: SU 722972
Lat. 51.40.13 N; Long. 00.57.14 W

Excavator: R A Chambers (Oxford Archaeological Unit), 1972

Site: rescue excavation of a cemetery of uncertain date on the Upper Icknield Way, which was discovered during the construction of a drainage ditch for the motorway.

References: Chambers 1973a
Chambers 1973b
Wilson *et al* 1973, 296
Chambers 1976a
Radiocarbon **19**, 412 (^{14}C)

Objectives: to date the cemetery to either the Late Roman or Anglo-Saxon period. The graves selected for dating were some distance apart from each other. Trench III revealed settlement evidence from Saxo-Norman times through to the post-medieval period.

HAR-506   1130 ± 70 BP

$\delta^{13}C$: −19.9 ‰

Sample: GRAVE14, submitted in 1974

Material: human bone.

Initial comment: from a burial (grave 14) in a chalk cut grave 0.75m below the topsoil. The grave fill was of hard packed chalk with some topsoil mixed in. This grave is of late Roman or Saxon date.

Comment on uncalibrated date: this date is acceptable.

Calibrated date: 1σ : cal AD 810 – 985
2σ : cal AD 715 – 1020

HAR-507   1090 ± 90 BP

$\delta^{13}C$: −20.7 ‰

Sample: GRAVE33, submitted in 1974

Material: human bone.

Initial comment: from a burial in a chalk cut grave 0.5m below topsoil. The grave fill was of hard packed chalk with some topsoil mixed in. The approximate date of this grave is Late Roman or Saxon.

Comment on uncalibrated date: this date is acceptable.

Calibrated date: 1σ : cal AD 880 – 1020
2σ : cal AD 715 – 1155

Beckford, Hereford and Worcester

Location: SO 984364
Lat. 52.01.01 N; Long. 00.33.57 W

Excavator: W Britnell, 1973

Site: Iron Age settlement.

Objectives: dating of the later phases of Middle Iron Age settlement.

HAR-1162   2260 ± 100 BP

$\delta^{13}C$: −24.4 ‰

Sample: BD272307, submitted on 30 April 1975

Material: charcoal: *Quercus* sp. from fairly large timbers; *c* 50% identified (C A Keepax).

Initial comment: from a pit cutting the upper layers in a small enclosure ditch; the estimated date is first or second century BC.

Calibrated date: 1σ : cal BC 400 – 200
2σ : cal BC 755 – 100

Beckford, Hereford and Worcester

Location: SP 984364
Lat. 52.01.01 N; Long. 00.33.57 W

Excavator: J Wills (Hereford and Worcester County Museum and the Department of the Environment), 1975

Site: an extensive Iron Age settlement densely spread over some 10 acres of a flat gravel terrace.

Comments:
AML: also submitted but not dated by 1981: HAR-3948, HAR-4439, HAR-4440, and HAR-4442.

HAR-1841   2400 ± 100 BP

$\delta^{13}C$: unknown

Sample: BD4865, submitted on 27 May 1976

Material: charcoal: hawthorn type (*Crataegus/Pyrus/Malus/Sorbus* sp.) and probably *Prunus* sp. (eg blackthorn) (C A Keepax).

Initial comment: from a shallow ditch, cut by Iron Age features including the main enclosure ditch and completely alien to the layout of the Iron Age settlement; it produced no pottery or other means of dating, but may possibly be of Late Bronze Age date, as a similar ditch was found in 1972.

Calibrated date: 1σ : cal BC 765 – 390
2σ : cal BC 800 – 233

Final comments:
Harwell: repeated as HAR-2157.

HAR-2157   2670 ± 80 BP

$\delta^{13}C$: −25.2 ‰

Sample: BD4865, submitted on 27 May 1976

Material: charcoal: hawthorn type (Rosaceae, sub-family Pomoideae) and *Prunus* sp. (eg blackthorn), not twiggy (C A Keepax).

Calibrated date: 1σ : cal BC 906 – 799
2σ : cal BC 1000 – 770

Final comments:
Harwell: repeat of HAR-1481.

HAR-3093   2370 ± 110 BP

$\delta^{13}C$: −26.0 ‰

Sample: BD5322, submitted on 9 February 1979

Material: charcoal: *Quercus* sp. from mature timbers (C A Keepax).

Initial comment: from a posthole building with inconclusive stratigraphical relationships to any other reliably dated feature within the Iron Age settlement.

Calibrated date: 1σ : cal BC 760 – 380
2σ : cal BC 800 – 190

HAR-3094   2270 ± 70 BP

$\delta^{13}C$: –25.9 ‰

Sample: BD65686, submitted on 9 February 1979

Material: charcoal: *Quercus* sp., *Corylus/Alnus* sp., and ?*Prunus* sp. (eg blackthorn) from mature timbers (C A Keepax).

Initial comment: from an Iron Age enclosure ditch.

Calibrated date: 1σ : cal BC 399 – 234
2σ : cal BC 410 – 180

HAR-3095   2080 ± 70 BP

$\delta^{13}C$: –26.6 ‰

Sample: BD65071, submitted on 9 February 1979

Material: charcoal: *Quercus* sp., *Corylus/Alnus* sp., and *Fraxinus* sp. from mature timbers (C A Keepax).

Initial comment: from a dump of burnt material including bone and loom weights, possibly from a Late Iron Age context.

Calibrated date: 1σ : cal BC 192 – 9
2σ : cal BC 362 – 70 cal AD

HAR-3096   4680 ± 80 BP

$\delta^{13}C$: –25.5 ‰

Sample: BD4846B, submitted on 9 February 1979

Material: charcoal: *Quercus* sp. from mature timbers (C A Keepax).

Initial comment: from a shallow ditch enclosing a round house belonging to an Iron Age settlement.

Calibrated date: 1σ : cal BC 3616 – 3359
2σ : cal BC 3640 – 3141

HAR-3097   2440 ± 90 BP

$\delta^{13}C$: –24.0 ‰

Sample: BD65448, submitted on 9 February 1979

Material: charcoal: *Quercus* sp. and *Corylus/Alnus* sp. from mature timbers, also Rosaceae, sub-family Pomoideae, from mature, branch-sized, and twig-sized wood (C A Keepax).

Initial comment: from an Iron Age gully enclosing a round house.

Calibrated date: 1σ : cal BC 778 – 400
2σ : cal BC 810 – 380

HAR-3944   2240 ± 70 BP

$\delta^{13}C$: –28.0 ‰

Sample: BD657192, submitted on 7 July 1980

Material: charcoal.

Initial comment: from lens of charcoal and earth in an enclosure ditch. Considered unlikely to be residual. The ditch forms part of the first phase of a large, perhaps long-lived, rectilinear enclosure system, asssociated with Iron Age occupation and 'duck-stamped' pottery.

Calibrated date: 1σ : cal BC 394 – 199
2σ : cal BC 410 – 120

HAR-3945   2330 ± 60 BP

$\delta^{13}C$: –27.3 ‰

Sample: BD657191, submitted on 7 July 1980

Material: charcoal.

Initial comment: as HAR-3944.

Calibrated date: 1σ : cal BC 407 – 383
2σ : cal BC 753 – 250

HAR-3947   2130 ± 80 BP

$\delta^{13}C$: –26.2 ‰

Sample: BD657834, submitted on 7 July 1980

Material: charcoal.

Initial comment: from a backfill of rubbish in a rectangular pit, which may have been for storage. The sample should date the associated occupation and give a *terminus ante quem* for the small enclosure cut by the pit.

Calibrated date: 1σ : cal BC 358 – 91
2σ : cal BC 390 – 20 cal AD

HAR-3950   2310 ± 110 BP

$\delta^{13}C$: –27.6 ‰

Sample: BD756181, submitted on 7 July 1980

Material: charcoal.

Initial comment: this sample dates the second major phase of an extensive, possibly long-lived, Iron Age enclosure system.

Calibrated date: 1σ : cal BC 486 – 235
2σ : cal BC 780 – 110

HAR-3951   2970 ± 130 BP

$\delta^{13}C$: –25.7 ‰

Sample: BD657881, submitted on 7 July 1980

Material: charcoal.

Initial comment: from a lens of charcoal and burnt material in a storage pit, shown to be *in situ* by the burning on the pit walls. The pit is one of a cluster associated with early Middle Iron Age pottery, within the Beckford settlement.

Calibrated date: 1σ : cal BC 1410 – 1000
2σ : cal BC 1520 – 840

HAR-3952 2140 ± 110 BP

$\delta^{13}C$: −27.1 ‰

Sample: BD658441, submitted on 7 July 1980

Material: charcoal.

Initial comment: from a posthole (possibly burnt *in situ*), forming part of a stratigraphically early structure within the Iron Age settlement.

Calibrated date: 1σ : cal BC 370 – 40
                    2σ : cal BC 400 – 80 cal AD

HAR-3953 1130 ± 70 BP

$\delta^{13}C$: −26.6 ‰

Sample: BD758381, submitted on 7 July 1980

Material: charcoal.

Initial comment: from a lens of charcoal-rich material in a ditch. Considered unlikely to be residual. The feature forms an early phase of a circular enclosure, associated with a major reorganisation of the site and with a distinctive Late Iron Age pottery style. Dating of this reorganisation, and of the inception of the Late Iron Age pottery style, is of major importance to an understanding of the site and of the chronology of regional pottery styles.

Calibrated date: 1σ : cal AD 810 – 986
                    2σ : cal AD 714 – 1020

HAR-3955 1990 ± 70 BP

$\delta^{13}C$: −28.9 ‰

Sample: BD743062, submitted on 7 July 1980

Material: charcoal.

Initial comment: from charcoal-rich layer sealed within a clay oven which is in turn sealed within the stratigraphy of a complex stone-floored round house.

Calibrated date: 1σ : cal BC 96 – 77 cal AD
                    2σ : cal BC 180 – 130 cal AD

HAR-4001 1130 ± 70 BP

$\delta^{13}C$: unknown

Sample: BD758382, submitted on 7 July 1980

Material: charcoal.

Initial comment: a reserve sample.

Calibrated date: 1σ : cal AD 810 – 986
                    2σ : cal AD 714 – 1020

HAR-4439 2320 ± 80 BP

$\delta^{13}C$: −26.5 ‰

Sample: BD65229, submitted on 14 August 1978

Material: charcoal: *Quercus* sp. and ?*Prunus* sp. from mature timber (C A Keepax).

Initial comment: from a pit in a sequence of ?Late Iron Age occupation.

Calibrated date: 1σ : cal BC 408 – 370
                    2σ : cal BC 760 – 200

HAR-4440 1870 ± 80 BP

$\delta^{13}C$: −25.5 ‰

Sample: BD54102, submitted on 9 February 1979

Material: charcoal: *Quercus* sp. from mature timbers and *Corylus/Alnus* sp. from twig or branch-sized timber (C A Keepax).

Initial comment: from a shallow ditch enclosing a round house belonging to an Iron Age enclosure settlement.

Calibrated date: 1σ : cal AD 55 – 234
                    2σ : cal BC 40 – 339 cal AD

HAR-4442 2180 ± 80 BP

$\delta^{13}C$: −25.0 ‰

Sample: BD65062, submitted on 14 August 1978

Material: charcoal: *Quercus* sp. from mature timbers. (C A Keepax).

Initial comment: from a possibly Late Iron Age posthole.

Calibrated date: 1σ : cal BC 379 – 116
                    2σ : cal BC 400 – 30

Beckford, Hereford and Worcester

Location: SO 984364
            Lat. 52.01.32 N; Long. 02.01.24 W

Excavator: S M Colledge, 1979

Objectives: to provide a *terminus ante quem* for a pollen diagram for samples taken from within the peat.

HAR-3624 1000 ± 70 BP

$\delta^{13}C$: −29.3 ‰

Sample: BD1-70, submitted on 9 October 1979

Material: organic silt.

Initial comment: from the layer at the boundary between alluvium and peat, the alluvium above being 700mm deep – a homogenous sticky clay. A pollen diagram will be prepared from samples within the peat.

Calibrated date: 1σ : cal AD 979 – 1150
                    2σ : cal AD 890 – 1180

HAR-3954 3750 ± 110 BP

$\delta^{13}C$: −30.5 ‰

Sample: BD1-130

Material: charcoal.

Initial comment: from the base of a peat deposit (lying on an eroded surface of Pleistocene sands and gravels) for which a pollen diagram is being prepared. The top of the peat has already been dated (HAR-3624) and gave an unexpectedly recent date, so it was decided to try to date the inception of the peat too.

Calibrated date: 1σ : cal BC 2340 – 2030
                      2σ : cal BC 2480 – 1890

Bedford: 20 – 24 St Johns Street, Bedfordshire

Location: TL 050500
              Lat. 52.08.16 N; Long. 00.27.56 W

Excavator: J Hassall (Bedford Museum), 1976

Site: two timber buildings close to the street frontage in the south-east area of the Saxon town, associated with some possible tenth-century pottery; numerous rubbish pits and a well-house lay to the rear of these structures, and Saxo-Norman and early medieval remains were also found.

References: Hassall 1979b, 119 – 20 (^{14}C)

Objectives: no absolute dates have been obtained for any of the early medieval sites in Bedford, and coin evidence is scanty; ^{14}C dates would aid both the interpretation of the site and the pottery chronology.

HAR-1896   1010 ± 70 BP

$δ^{13}C$: –25.9 ‰

Sample: BSJ76C1, submitted on 19 November 1976

Material: charcoal: mainly *Quercus* sp. from large timbers, some fragments of *Corylus* sp. and Rosaceae, sub-family Pomoideae (C A Keepax).

Initial comment: from a layer of dark brown loam in the largest rubbish pit (3.40m in diameter × 1.25m deep); the large amount of charcoal suggests that rubbish was thrown into the pit and burnt *in situ*; some Saxo-Norman pottery was found, but no absolute dating evidence.

Comment on uncalibrated date: this pit belongs to phase I which post-dated phase J (HAR-1897) stratigraphically. A mid tenth- to early eleventh-century date is therefore quite reasonable.

Calibrated date: 1σ : cal AD 975 – 1040
                      2σ : cal AD 890 – 1170

References: *Radiocarbon* **27**, 87

HAR-1897   1110 ± 70 BP

$δ^{13}C$: –26.2 ‰

Sample: BSJ76C3, submitted on 19 November 1976

Material: charcoal: mainly *Quercus* sp. from large timber, with some ?maple (*Acer* sp.) and hawthorn type (Rosaceae, sub-family Pomoideae) from large timbers, some *Fraxinus* sp. (branch-sized), and some *Corylus* sp. (twiggy) (C A Keepax).

Initial comment: from a layer of medium to dark brown fine, sandy, clayey loam in a small, deep, rubbish pit; probably contemporary with HAR-1896; the pit was full of domestic debris, but no dating evidence was found.

Comment on uncalibrated date: a late ninth- or early tenth-century date was anticipated for this earliest occupation phase (phase J).

Calibrated date: 1σ : cal AD 880 – 1000
                      2σ : cal AD 770 – 1030

References: *Radiocarbon* **27**, 87

HAR-1929   650 ± 70 BP

$δ^{13}C$: –26.7 ‰

Sample: BSJ76W5, submitted on 19 November 1976

Material: wood: *Quercus* sp. (C A Keepax).

Initial comment: from the same well as HAR-1930, submitted to give a check on HAR-1930.

Comment on uncalibrated date: stratigraphic and pottery evidence suggested a thirteenth- or fourteenth-century date.

Calibrated date: 1σ : cal AD 1275 – 1395
                      2σ : cal AD 1250 – 1420

Final comments:
J Hassall: the calibrated date appears to confirm the excavation evidence.

HAR-1930   480 ± 70 BP

$δ^{13}C$: –26.0 ‰

Sample: BSJ76W1, submitted on 19 November 1976

Material: wood: *Quercus* sp. (C A Keepax).

Initial comment: from one of four timbers surrounded by a thick, silty clay, outlining a square well; below the well housing, just above the present water-table; pottery of ?eleventh- or twelfth-century date was found above the silty clay, which contained no dating evidence.

Comment on uncalibrated date: this date is considerably later than that anticipated by excavation.

Calibrated date: 1σ : cal AD 1405 – 1455
                      2σ : cal AD 1305 – 1620

References: *Radiocarbon* **27**, 87

Bedford: 29 – 39 St Johns Street, Bedfordshire

Location: TL 050500
              Lat. 52.08.16 N; Long. 00.27.56 W

Excavator: J Hassall (Bedford Museum), 1974

Site: three trenches were opened stretching from St Johns Street to Kingsway. Trench III revealed settlement evidence from Saxo-Norman times through to the post-medieval period.

References: Hassall 1979b, 112 (^{14}C)

Objectives: to determine the extent of the Saxo-Norman and medieval occupation of the site and help with the pottery chronology.

HAR-987   790 ± 80 BP

$δ^{13}C$: –26.0 ‰

Sample: BSJ74IIIF6, submitted on 26 January 1974

Material: wood in organic matter.

Initial comment: from the base of a large rubbish pit, in a damp silty layer just above the water-table; no evidence for the construction date was found, but the upper fill contained sherds of eleventh- to thirteenth-century St Neots ware.

Calibrated date: 1σ : cal AD 1170 – 1280
2σ : cal AD 1030 – 1375

Final comments:
J Hassall: a date in the twelfth century is commensurate with the pottery evidence: a late thirteenth- or fourteenth-century date would not agree.

Bedford: Empire Cinema, Bedfordshire

Location: TL 04804982
Lat. 52.08.11 N; Long. 00.28.07 W

Excavator: J Hassall (Bedford Museum), 1978

Site: the Anglo-Saxon and early medieval town.

References: Hassall 1983, 50 (^{14}C)

Objectives: to determine the extent of Saxo-Norman and early medieval occupation and to locate town defences such as the bank and ditch, which were expected to occur on this site.

HAR-3436 850 ± 80 BP

$\delta^{13}C:$ –28.1 ‰

Sample: L782116, submitted on 1 July 1979

Material: organic matter.

Initial comment: from a waterlogged layer of mid brown sandy silt with twigs, at the base of a square, straight-sided well or cess pit cut into natural gravel. It is likely to be of Saxo-Norman or early medieval date.

Calibrated date: 1σ : cal AD 1045 – 1260
2σ : cal AD 1010 – 1280

Final comments:
J Hassall: this result confirms the pottery dating.

HAR-3437 900 ± 70 BP

$\delta^{13}C:$ –27.2 ‰

Sample: 782123, submitted on 1 July 1979

Material: organic matter.

Initial comment: from a blue – grey silty clay near the base of a waterfilled boundary or drainage ditch (1m wide × 1.5m deep) cut into natural gravel and fed by a natural spring flowing south towards the river Ouse (0.5 mile away); the ditch apparently silted up in the twelfth century.

Calibrated date: 1σ : cal AD 1030 – 1220
2σ : cal AD 1000 – 1270

Final comments:
J Hassall: this date confirms that suggested by the pottery; in the absence of pre-ninth- or tenth-century finds it seems unlikely that the ditch was open before 1050, although the sample may be residual in its context.

HAR-3438 1570 ± 70 BP

$\delta^{13}C:$ –27.8 ‰

Sample: 782124, submitted on 1 July 1979

Material: organic matter.

Initial comment: waterlogged primary ditch fill, a dark grey, silty soil (see HAR-3437).

Calibrated date: 1σ : cal AD 410 – 560
2σ : cal AD 265 – 630

Bedford: Midland Road, Trench II, Bedfordshire

Location: TL 050500
Lat. 52.08.16 N; Long. 00.27.56 W

Excavator: J Hassall (Bedford Museum), 1974

Site: rapid rescue excavations undertaken near the Midland Road street frontage in the north-west part of the Saxon town of Bedford uncovered settlement features dating from Saxo-Norman times to the post-medieval period.

References: Hassall 1979a, 91 (^{14}C)

Objectives: to determine the extent of the Saxo-Norman and medieval occupation of the site and help with the pottery chronology.

HAR-976 1000 ± 100 BP

$\delta^{13}C:$ –26.4 ‰

Sample: BMR74IIF18, submitted on 26 November 1978

Material: wood.

Initial comment: from a timber stake found upright in a medieval cess pit.

Calibrated date: 1σ : cal AD 960 – 1160
2σ : cal AD 810 – 1250

Final comments:
J Hassall: despite the apparent inadequacy of the sample, a date in the mid tenth century coincides with stratigraphic evidence.

Harwell: a small sample diluted to make up the deficiency of material accounts for the larger than normal error term.

Belling Law, Northumbria

Location: NY 788904
Lat. 55.11.10 N; Long. 02.19.50 W

Excavator: G Jobey (Newcastle University and the Department of the Environment), 1975

Site: Iron Age or Romano-British settlement comprising a series of timber-built huts, superceded by stone-built round houses and a medieval farmstead.

References: Jobey 1977; 13, 15 (^{14}C)

Objectives: C14 dating is required to fix the date of the earliest phase on this, and other ostensibly Romano-British native sites in the area which have produced no datable artefacts; this would also help to determine whether there was continuous occupation; there is first- to second-century Roman pottery in the latest phase.

HAR-1393 1670 ± 70 BP

$\delta^{13}C$: −25.6 ‰

Sample: LB7527, submitted on 28 November 1975

Material: charcoal: approximately equal amounts of *Fraxinus* sp. (fairly large timbers) and *Corylus* sp. (small branch or post): there were also some rootlets which were removed as far as possible (C A Keepax).

Initial comment: from well down in a posthole in the trench of a timber structure; the earliest in a sequence of four structures, overlain by the remains of a stone-built Romano-British round house.

Calibrated date: 1σ : cal AD 260 – 430
2σ : cal AD 220 – 540

HAR-1394 2110 ± 80 BP

$\delta^{13}C$: −26.3 ‰

Sample: LB7536, submitted on 28 November 1975

Material: charcoal: mainly *Quercus* sp. with a few fragments of ?*Alnus* sp.; all from large timbers: there were also some rootlets which were removed as far as possible (C A Keepax).

Initial comment: burnt stakes (as HAR-1393).

Calibrated date: 1σ : cal BC 350 – 40
2σ : cal BC 380 – 60 cal AD

Berkhamsted: Castle, Hertfordshire

Location: SP 995083
Lat. 51.45.51 N; Long. 00.33.29 W

Excavator: A Pacitto

HAR-847 880 ± 80 BP

$\delta^{13}C$: −26.9 ‰

Sample: 748290, submitted on 5 September 1974

Material: wood: *Quercus* sp. (not twiggy).

Initial comment: from stakes and piles.

Calibrated date: 1σ : cal AD 1030 – 1245
2σ : cal AD 1000 – 1270

Beverley: Highgate, Humberside

Location: TA 0440 approx
Lat. 53.50.44 N; Long. 00.25.09 W

Excavator: B Whitwell (Humberside County Council)

Site: houses fronting on to Highgate; the sample is from a peat layer commonly observed in excavations in the town.

References: Watkins and Williams 1983, 74 (^{14}C)

Objectives: sample submitted primarily to obtain dating for the associated biology; the flora and fauna are of considerable interest in relation to the site and in comparison with other urban sequences.

HAR-2736 920 ± 70 BP

$\delta^{13}C$: −28.4 ‰

Sample: BVH9A, submitted by H Kenward on 21 March 1978

Material: peat and plant fragments, washed in tap water, retaining the fraction over 300µ, boiled for 30 minutes to break down the finer silt, and dried at 105°C after the larger fragments had been removed.

Initial comment: 0.5 – 0.6m below the site datum, where the highest concentration of biological remains was found. Environmental analysis has shown it to be consistent with early medieval occupation.

Comment on uncalibrated date: this result compares well with the pottery from this layer and the date of a knife from a similar deposit on the Butchers Row site.

Calibrated date: 1σ : cal AD 1020 – 1210
2σ : cal AD 980 – 1260

Final comments:
Harwell: pretreated using the dessicator treatment.

Bidford-on-Avon, Warwickshire

Location: SP 09915197
Lat. 52.09.56 N; Long. 01.51.18 W

Excavator: S Hirst (Warwickshire Museum), 1978

Site: Site 1 – the bank.

References: Webster and Cherry 1980, 233

Objectives: to provide dates for these two contexts on a multiperiod site.

Comments:
S Hirst: the general similarity of the fills of the two contexts from which these samples were taken, strongly suggests that they are contemporary, and that the most likely date range is AD 790 – 970. Both appear to be similar to a group of nearby burials (cf HAR-3456 and HAR-8576).

HAR-2599 1070 ± 70 BP

$\delta^{13}C$: −25.8 ‰

Sample: F55a, submitted on 21 March 1978

Material: charcoal: *Quercus* sp., *Fraxinus* sp., and ?lime (*Tilia* sp.); all from fairly large timbers (C A Keepax).

Initial comment: from a ditch containing burnt daub and stone, with fragments of six rotary querns, animal bone, and charcoal, and two fragments of Roman tile.

Calibrated date: 1σ : cal AD 890 – 1020
2σ : cal AD 790 – 1150

HAR-2600 1290 ± 100 BP

$\delta^{13}C$: −26.2 ‰

Sample: D17b, submitted on 21 March 1978

Material: charcoal: *Quercus* sp. from large timber, and some unidentifiable fragments (C A Keepax).

Initial comment: from a pit containing an important group of iron (including a scythe), quern fragments, and a loom weight.

Comment on uncalibrated date: the loom weight can generally be dated to the Late Saxon period (ninth to twelfth centuries AD).

Calibrated date: 1σ : cal AD 650 – 860
2σ : cal AD 570 – 970

Bidford-on-Avon, Warwickshire

Location: SP 1051 approx
Lat. 52.09.24 N; Long. 01.51.14 W

Excavator: J Greig

Site: a layer of organic matter over gravel and Keuper marl beside the river Avon; sealed by a layer of stones, eighteenth-century build-up, and the slump of the collapsed river bank.

Objectives: a ^{14}C date would justify the study of the pollen, seeds, mollusca etc, for which the pollen only gives circumstantial evidence for a date.

HAR-3069 2270 ± 80 BP

$\delta^{13}C$: –27.2 ‰

Sample: BID1, submitted on 9 February 1979

Material: wood.

Initial comment: a layer of organic matter; the pollen suggests a date of *c* 2500 BC.

Calibrated date: 1σ : cal BC 400 – 210
2σ : cal BC 520 – 125

Final comments:
J Greig: this date, with the flora and fauna, provided more evidence of the possible climatic deterioration at this time which was suggested by the results of beetle analysis.

Bidford-on-Avon: Lloyd's Bank, Warwickshire

Location: SP 1051 approx
Lat. 52.09.24 N; Long. 01.51.14 W

Excavator: H Maclagan

HAR-3452 1210 ± 80 BP

$\delta^{13}C$: –21.5 ‰

Sample: BIDVII4A, submitted on 19 July 1979

Material: human bone.

Calibrated date: 1σ : cal AD 685 – 895
2σ : cal AD 660 – 990

HAR-3456 1960 ± 70 BP

$\delta^{13}C$: –22.5 ‰

Sample: BIDVII2A, submitted on 19 July 1979

Material: human bone.

Calibrated date: 1σ : cal BC 45 – 115 cal AD
2σ : cal BC 150 – 210 cal AD

Bilby, Nottinghamshire

Location: SK 638832
Lat. 53.20.30 N; Long. 01.02.30 W

Excavator: M Dolby (Doncaster Museum), 1976

Site: bridge spanning the river Ryton, near the deserted medieval village of Bilby; a seventeenth-century stone bridge spans the river some 100m west of the old timber bridge.

References: Howard *et al* 1985, 35 (^{14}C)
Radiocarbon **27**, 90 (^{14}C)

Objectives: a ^{14}C date is required to help locate possible matches for a 228 year tree-ring sequence from the bridge piers.

HAR-2261 480 ± 60 BP

$\delta^{13}C$: –26.1 ‰

Sample: BILBY1, submitted by R Morgan on 1 June 1977

Material: wood: the outer 20 heartwood rings.

Initial comment: from a bridge pier, recovered during maintenance work and not *in situ*.

Calibrated date: 1σ : cal AD 1405 – 1450
2σ : cal AD 1315 – 1490

Final comments:
M Dolby: the results of ^{14}C dating imply a later date for the structure than the tree-ring dates suggest, but nevertheless prove the existence of a medieval bridge crossing of the river Ryton at this location.

Billingborough Fen, Lincolnshire

Location: TF 126334
Lat. 52.53.09 N; Long. 00.19.35 W

Excavator: P Chowne (South Lincolnshire Archaeological Unit), 1977

Site: a settlement dating to the Bronze Age and Iron Age.

References: Chowne 1978
Chowne 1979

Comments:
P Chowne: these dates fit in well with the site phasing and the pottery sequence.

HAR-2483 2390 ± 70 BP

$\delta^{13}C$: –24.8 ‰

Sample: BFE77F98, submitted on 22 December 1977

Material: charcoal: *Quercus* sp. from a large timber; 25% identified (C A Keepax).

Initial comment: a charred post from a posthole.

Calibrated date: 1σ : cal BC 755 – 395
2σ : cal BC 780 – 370

References: Radiocarbon **29**, 84

HAR-2523   2410 ± 80 BP

δ*¹³C:* –26.1 ‰

Sample: BFE77F43C, submitted on 21 February 1978

Material: charcoal: mainly *Corylus/Alnus* sp. with some Rosaceae, sub-family Pomoideae, both mainly from fairly large timbers (C A Keepax).

Initial comment: from the upper levels of a silted up enclosure ditch.

Calibrated date: 1σ : cal BC 760 – 400
2σ : cal BC 800 – 370

References: Chowne 1980, 297
Radiocarbon **29**, 84

HAR-3101   2500 ± 100 BP

δ*¹³C:* –27.0 ‰

Sample: BFE78257, submitted on 9 February 1979

Material: charcoal: *Quercus* sp. and *Fraxinus* sp. from large timbers, and ?Rosaceae, sub-family Pomoideae (eg hawthorn) (C A Keepax).

Initial comment: from a pit cut into a Middle Bronze Age enclosure ditch.

Calibrated date: 1σ : cal BC 800 – 410
2σ : cal BC 840 – 390

References: Chowne 1980, 297

Billingborough: Car Dyke, Lincolnshire

Location: TF 1334 approx
Lat. 52.53.28 N; Long. 00.19.13 W

Excavator: B B Simmons, 1974

Site: a clear trend from open water through to reed swamp and terrestrialisation was apparent from the organic remains.

Objectives: this sample was submitted primarily in relation to the biology; it provides a rather crucial date for understanding the last phases of the usability of the dyke.

HAR-2810   1710 ± 70 BP

δ*¹³C:* –29.1 ‰

Sample: CD74/6, submitted on 21 March 1978

Material: organic silt, selected from large lumps with the outer layers washed off in tap water; rinsed in deionised water and dried at 105°C. The material contains inadequate particulate organic matter for this alone to be dated.

Initial comment: a probably well-sealed context free from contamination from later humates; the layer was quite distinct from those above and below, suggesting limited intermixture of organic matter.

Calibrated date: 1σ : cal AD 240 – 410
2σ : cal AD 130 – 450

Final comments:
Harwell: repeat of HAR-2655.

Bishopstone: Rookery Hill, East Sussex

Location: TQ 467008
Lat. 50.40.15 N; Long. 00.04.53 E

Excavator: M Bell (Institute of Archaeology, London), 1967 – 75

Site: Neolithic, Bronze Age, Iron Age, Romano-British, and Anglo-Saxon rural settlements.

References: Bell 1977; 9, 39, 63, 132, 215, 270 – 1, 291 (¹⁴C)

Objectives: to resolve the chronology of some of the key elements in the development of this multiphase site.

Comments:
AML: three small samples withdrawn: HAR-1660 (BI357L2), HAR-1661 (BI570), and HAR-? (BIJ2531I).

HAR-1086   2220 ± 80 BP

δ*¹³C:* –24.8 ‰

Sample: BIJ1143, submitted by P Drewett on 22 January 1975

Material: charcoal.

Initial comment: from *c* 0.45m deep in a probably Early Iron Age pit.

Calibrated date: 1σ : cal BC 390 – 185
2σ : cal BC 410 – 100

Final comments:
M Bell: this implies that this, apparently Middle Iron Age pit, postdated an adjacent earlier Iron Age enclosure ditch with a thermoluminescence date of 950 BC ± 300.

HAR-1662   4460 ± 70 BP

δ*¹³C:* –25.6 ‰

Sample: BI3574-7, submitted by P Drewett on 27 February 1976

Material: charcoal.

Initial comment: from pit F357 (layers 4 – 7), the most productive of the Neolithic pits, which contained an assemblage of artefacts and biota.

Calibrated date: 1σ : cal BC 3335 – 2940
2σ : cal BC 3360 – 2920

Final comments:
M Bell: this is in line with the earlier Neolithic artefact assemblage from the feature and may belong to the later part of the Early Neolithic occupation (mid fourth- to mid third-millennium BC).

References: *Radiocarbon* **27**, 82

HAR-1663   1630 ± 70 BP

$\delta^{13}C$: −26.2 ‰

Sample: BIKXXXV, submitted by P Drewett on 27 February 1976

Material: charcoal: *Quercus* sp. (C A Keepax).

Initial comment: from fairly large timbers of rectangular structure XXXV, thought to be Anglo-Saxon.

Calibrated date: 1σ : cal AD 340 – 530
2σ : cal AD 240 – 590

Final comments:
M Bell: this date does not resolve the question of whether this structure was Romano-British or Anglo-Saxon; however calibration makes an Early Saxon date more likely and this is confirmed by the associated pottery which could have been of some age when the building was constructed.

References: *Radiocarbon* **27**, 82

Black Patch, East Sussex

Location: TQ 495086
Lat. 50.51.25 N; Long. 00.07.28 E

Excavator: P Drewett (Sussex Archaeological Field Unit), 1977 – 9

Site: Bronze Age hut platforms and enclosures in a system of rectangular fields overlooked by round barrows; one of a series of broadly contemporary sites in the area.

References: Drewett 1982a; 342 – 3, 347, 391 (^{14}C)

Objectives: dating is crucial since the site appears to be later than the comparable settlement on Itford Hill; a definite range of dates for the pottery produced is required so that the site may be slotted into the Bronze Age or the Late Bronze Age – Early Iron Age transition.

Comments:
Drewett 1982: the three samples from pits 3 and 4 in hut 5 were all taken from the bottom of the pits and are therefore likely to relate to the final use of these pits, and thus, probably the hut. The probabilistic error limits do not render these dates incompatible - a date somewhere between 1000 and 900 BC appearing likely.

The same comments apply to the dates from huts 1 and 2, with a probable date of 1060 – 940 BC for these structures. It is possible that hut 1 slightly predates hut 4. In both cases the dates relate to the desertion of the site, not the occupation of it.

HAR-2939   2780 ± 80 BP

$\delta^{13}C$: −23.8 ‰

Sample: 1979282B, submitted on 29 November 1978

Material: carbonised grain.

Initial comment: from pit 5 (82) in hut 4.

Calibrated date: 1σ : cal BC 1025 – 840
2σ : cal BC 1160 – 800

Final comments:
P Drewett: later than expected, but this result may relate to the dumping of grain in old pits.

HAR-2940   3020 ± 70 BP

$\delta^{13}C$: −24.1 ‰

Sample: 1979250D, submitted on 29 November 1978

Material: carbonised grain.

Initial comment: from pit 4 (50) in hut 3.

Calibrated date: 1σ : cal BC 1400 – 1165
2σ : cal BC 1430 – 1040

Final comments:
P Drewett: the only one of HAR-2939 – HAR-2941 to fit the artefactual evidence.

Harwell: the difference in age between HAR-2940 and HAR-2939+HAR-2941 seems surprising, but experimental details do not suggest any error.

HAR-2941   2790 ± 70 BP

$\delta^{13}C$: −23.9 ‰

Sample: 1979283D, submitted on 29 November 1978

Material: carbonised grain.

Initial comment: from pit 4 (83) in hut 4.

Calibrated date: 1σ : cal BC 1025 – 845
2σ : cal BC 1155 – 810

Final comments:
P Drewett: later than expected. Further samples from this feature (F50) were dated by the British Museum.

HAR-3735   2970 ± 80 BP

$\delta^{13}C$: −24.5 ‰

Sample: 792P149C, submitted on 29 July 1980

Material: carbonised grain.

Initial comment: from the clean chalk floor of pit F49 in hut 1; the expected date was the latest part of the Bronze Age.

Calibrated date: 1σ : cal BC 1375 – 1055
2σ : cal BC 1420 – 940

Final comments:
P Drewett: the date range is not unreasonable.

HAR-3736   3080 ± 70 BP

$\delta^{13}C$: −24.2 ‰

Sample: 792P124B, submitted on 29 July 1980

Material: carbonised grain.

Initial comment: as HAR-3735.

Calibrated date: 1σ : cal BC 1430 – 1265
2σ : cal BC 1510 – 1135

Final comments:
P Drewett: this date is a little earlier than expected.

HAR-3737 2850 ± 70 BP

$\delta^{13}C$: −24.0 ‰

Sample: 792P124A, submitted on 29 July 1980

Material: carbonised grain.

Initial comment: as HAR-3735.

Calibrated date: 1σ : cal BC 1125 − 920
2σ : cal BC 1260 − 840

Final comments:
P Drewett: the date range is not unreasonable.

Black Patch, East Sussex

Location: TQ 495086
Lat. 50.51.25 N; Long. 00.07.28 E

Excavator: P Drewett (Sussex Archaeological Field Unit), 1979

Site: transects cut through eight of the eleven Bronze Age barrows on the hill crests surrounding the settlement at Black Patch.

References: Drewett 1982a

Objectives: to check the relationship of the barrows to the main settlement more precisely than is possible using the artefactual evidence alone.

Comments:
AML: two small samples (19792Y and 1979Z) were withdrawn.

HAR-3976 3830 ± 80 BP

$\delta^{13}C$: −23.0 ‰

Sample: 19792W, submitted on 29 July 1980

Material: human bone.

Initial comment: from an infant inhumation (barrow 3, pit 10).

Calibrated date: 1σ : cal BC 2460 − 2145
2σ : cal BC 2560 − 2040

Final comments:
P Drewett: a reasonable result, since the burial was associated with a Collared Urn.

Harwell: the difference between the dates produced by HAR-3976 and HAR-3977 is disturbing, but nothing in the experimental notes gives cause for concern, although the $\delta^{13}C$ values are rather negative for bone.

References: Drewett 1982a; 321, 352, 392

HAR-3977 2010 ± 80 BP

$\delta^{13}C$: −24.2 ‰

Sample: 19792X, submitted on 29 July 1980

Material: human bone.

Initial comment: from disturbed bone redeposited in what appeared to be the primary burial pit of the barrow.

Calibrated date: 1σ : cal BC 110 − 70 cal AD
2σ : cal BC 330 − 130 cal AD

Final comments:
P Drewett: in the light of this date, and in the absence of any artefact to the contrary, it appears that this is a secondary burial of Late Iron Age or Romano-British date; clearly neither barrow was related to the adjacent Late Bronze Age settlement (*c* 1200 BC).

Harwell: see above.

Bletchley: Magiovinium, Buckinghamshire

Location: SP 890335
Lat. 51.59.33 N; Long. 00.42.13 W

Excavator: D Neal (Central Excavation Unit), 1978 − 9

Site: a Romano-British site on Oxford clay.

References: Neal 1987, 22 (^{14}C)

HAR-2935 1660 ± 80 BP

$\delta^{13}C$: −21.6 ‰

Sample: 1 7-1H93364, submitted by N Balaam on 29 November 1978

Material: human bone.

Initial comment: from an area of Romano-British occupation, but possibly medieval.

Calibrated date: 1σ : cal AD 255 − 440
2σ : cal AD 210 − 560

HAR-3174 1550 ± 90 BP

$\delta^{13}C$: −21.8 ‰

Sample: 17-212, submitted by N Balaam on 26 November 1978

Material: bone.

Initial comment: from an area of Romano-British occupation, but possibly part of the medieval cemetery.

Calibrated date: 1σ : cal AD 410 − 605
2σ : cal AD 260 − 660

Final comments:
Harwell: repeat of HAR-2934.

Bognor: Hazel Road, West Sussex

Location: SU 92740082
Lat. 50.47.56 N; Long. 00.41.02 W

Excavator: M Pitts (Institute of Archaeology, London), 1975

Site: Iron Age occupation on the coastal plain; a rescue excavation.

References: Bedwin and Pitts 1978, 346 (^{14}C)

HAR-2276 2050 ± 70 BP

$\delta^{13}C$: −24.1 ‰

Sample: HRA2F1L2, submitted by P Drewett on 1 June 1977

Material: charcoal.

Initial comment: from ditch 1 (Fe.1, layer 2); see below.

Calibrated date: 1σ : cal BC 170 – 15 cal AD
2σ : cal BC 350 – 80 cal AD

Final comments:
M Pitts: this date is acceptable.

HAR-2277   2020 ± 70 BP

$\delta^{13}C$: –25.9 ‰

Sample: HRA2F1L2, submitted by P Drewett on 1 June 1977

Material: charcoal: *Quercus* sp., *Fraxinus* sp., and *Crataegus* sp. (C Cartwright).

Initial comment: from ditch 1 (Fe.1, layer 2); Iron Age as far as the ceramic evidence goes.

Calibrated date: 1σ : cal BC 110 – 60 cal AD
2σ : cal BC 200 – 120 cal AD

Final comments: M Pitts: this date is acceptable.

Boynton: High Easton Farm, Humberside

Location: TA 15687049
Lat. 54.06.59 N; Long. 00.13.53 W

Excavator: T G Manby (Yorkshire Archaeological Society), 1972

Site: round barrow (levelled by cultivation) surrounded by a ring ditch of linked quarry pits (22.0m internal diameter) which contained Peterborough ware in the secondary fill, and Beaker pottery in the upper fill; inside was a henge type feature (8.0m diameter) with opposed causeways, which had apparently not stood open for any length of time; the site is near the Grindale barrows (see below).

References: Manby 1980, 45 (^{14}C)
Radiocarbon **19**, 403 (^{14}C)

HAR-268   4840 ± 80 BP

$\delta^{13}C$: –27.2 ‰

Sample: Boynton 1, submitted on 7 March 1973

Material: charcoal.

Initial comment: from the fill of the inner 'henge'.

Calibrated date: 1σ : cal BC 3770 – 3525
2σ : cal BC 3790 – 3380

Final comments:
T G Manby: comparable with the dating from the Kilham long barrow, if not as old as Grindale barrow 1, phase 1 ditch.

Bradbourne: Springs Bridge, Derbyshire

Location: SK 205522
Lat. 53.03.59 N; Long. 01.41.39 W

Excavator: M Wildgoose (Department of Archaeology, University of Sheffield), 1977

Site: possible mill, one mile upstream from Bradbourne Mill.

References: Morgan *et al* 1980, 45 (^{14}C)
Morgan 1982b
Morgan 1983, 101 (^{14}C)
Radiocarbon **27**, 90 (^{14}C)

Objectives: to date the dendrochonological curve.

HAR-2260   100 ± 70 BP

$\delta^{13}C$: –27.7 ‰

Sample: BR1, submitted by R Morgan on 1 June 1977

Material: wood: *Quercus* sp., the outermost 20 sapwood rings.

Initial comment: from a ?base plate for a sluice gate.

Calibrated date: 1σ : cal AD 1675 – 1955
2σ : cal AD 1650 – 1955

Final comments:
M Wildgoose: unexpectedly late, but archaeologically possible; the date has now been confirmed dendrochonologically by a date of AD 1836 for the outermost growth ring; the associated medieval timbers were reused.

Bradwell Bury, Buckinghamshire

Location: SP 830396
Lat. 52.02.53 N; Long. 00.47.22 W

Excavator: D Mynard (Milton Keynes Development Corporation), 1974

Site: a mass burial of eight adult articulated cow skeletons, with two foeti.

Objectives: to date the burial.

Comments:
D Mynard: the date is surprisingly recent; the ceramic dating evidence was late fifteenth – sixteenth century, although clay pipes were found in the upper fill; these were thought to be intrusive, but conform with the late seventeenth-century radiocarbon date.

AML: one sample, HAR-1141, was abandoned.

HAR-1410   -20 ± 0 BP

$\delta^{13}C$: –22.0 ‰

Sample: 2DEDCOWS, submitted by R J Jones on 30 April 1975

Material: animal bone.

Initial comment: from a cow burial.

Final comments:
Harwell: the sample is too recent to calibrate.

HAR-1638   60 ± 70 BP

$\delta^{13}C$: −23.0 ‰

Sample: 2DEDCOWS, submitted by R J Jones on 30 April 1975

Material: animal bone.

Initial comment: from a cow burial.

Calibrated date: 1σ : cal AD 1690 – 1955
                    2σ : cal AD 1670 – 1955

Brandon, Suffolk

Location: TL 7886 approx
              Lat. 52.26.33 N; Long. 00.37.09 E

Excavator: R Carr (Suffolk Archaeological Unit), 1980

Site: Iron Age and Anglo-Saxon settlement on a terrace beside the Little Ouse river, directly adjacent to the flood plain; in the northern part of the excavation a section showing just over 0.50m of peat was exposed and sampled for pollen and plant macrofossils.

References: Carr *et al* 1988

Objectives: to provide a chronology for the environmental data and (using the archaeological evidence for phases of settlement), to describe a sequence of habitat change and land use.

HAR-4086   1350 ± 70 BP

$\delta^{13}C$: −26.4 ‰

Sample: BRD01820, submitted by P Murphy on 29 July 1980

Material: charcoal and peat.

Initial comment: from a layer of charcoal (mainly *Calluna* sp.) in the valley floor peat adjacent to the settlement (depth 0.20m).

Calibrated date: 1σ : cal AD 635 – 690
                    2σ : cal AD 565 – 790

Final comments:
R Carr: this date provides evidence for the burning of *Calluna* heath, perhaps related to Middle Saxon site clearance.

References: Carr *et al* 1988, 376

HAR-4087   1810 ± 80 BP

$\delta^{13}C$: −29.0 ‰

Sample: BRD01850, submitted by P Murphy on 29 July 1980

Material: peat.

Initial comment: from base of peat deposits in the valley floor adjacent to the settlement (depth 0.50 – 0.53m).

Calibrated date: 1σ : cal AD 115 – 330
                    2σ : cal AD 20 – 410

Final comments:
R Carr: this date indicates when peat formation began over the previously dry land surface.

Brixworth: Vicarage Garden, Northamptonshire

Location: SP 74647121
              Lat. 52.20.01 N; Long. 00.54.16 W

Excavator: P Everson (Brixworth Archaeological Rescue Committee), 1972

Site: Anglo-Saxon monastery with church, inhumation cemetery (eleven burials were excavated, all east – west aligned and lacking grave goods), and perhaps the *vallum monasterii*; Saxo-Norman features and later medieval buildings were also found.

References: Everson 1977, 73 – 4 (^{14}C)
                Radiocarbon **19**, 410 – 11 (^{14}C)

Objectives: to date the ditch and burials, which were not securely dated by associated finds or stratigraphy except as being before the later-medieval period.

Comments:
AML: two further samples were submitted by M Audouy after 1982.

HAR-483   1250 ± 80 BP

$\delta^{13}C$: −21.5 ‰

Sample: BRXABN or BX72JB and BX72JT, submitted by H Keeley on 1 June 1977

Material: animal bone.

Initial comment: from the primary fill of the major ditch.

Calibrated date: 1σ : cal AD 670 – 885
                    2σ : cal AD 640 – 970

Final comments:
P Everson: published as cal AD 700 – 720; mean 710 ± 80 (Ralph *et al* 1973); this result confirms the opinion that the feature was Saxon rather than pre-Roman, and that it was the boundary ditch of the Saxon monastic precinct.

HAR-484   1150 ± 70 BP

$\delta^{13}C$: −19.8 ‰

Sample: BRXS10 or BX72JF, submitted by H Keeley on 16 January 1974

Material: human bone.

Initial comment: from west – east burial 10 with no grave goods; cut into the natural subsoil and sealed by twelfth-century and later deposits.

Calibrated date: 1σ : cal AD 785 – 975
                    2σ : cal AD 680 – 1020

Final comments:
P Everson: published as cal AD 830 – 50; mean 840 ± 70 (Ralph *et al* 1973); this date confirms the relationship of the burials to the boundary ditch, and establishes that they belong to a monastic rather than a later parochial burial ground.

HAR-485 1200 ± 80 BP

$\delta^{13}C$: −20.0 ‰

Sample: BRXSK1 or BX72BM, submitted by H Keeley on 16 January 1974

Material: human bone.

Initial comment: from west – east burial 1, which was cut into the natural subsoil and was accompanied by no grave goods.

Calibrated date: 1σ : cal AD 690 – 900
2σ : cal AD 660 – 1000

Final comments:
P Everson: published as cal AD 770 – 90; mean 780 ± 80 (Ralph *et al* 1973).

Bromfield, Shropshire

Location: SO 485775
Lat. 52.23.34 N; Long. 02.45.25 W

Excavator: S C Stanford (University of Birmingham, Department of Extramural Studies), 1978

Site: Neolithic and Beaker occupation, Mid – Late Bronze Age cemetery.

References: Stanford 1982, 283 (^{14}C)

Objectives: to confirm the Neolithic occupation suggested by the pottery.

HAR-3968 4680 ± 80 BP

$\delta^{13}C$: −26.9 ‰

Sample: S163, submitted on 29 July 1980

Material: charcoal.

Initial comment: from the base of pit F247, one of the two earliest pits on the site, 0.25m deep in natural gravel; unweathered sherds from three or four Neolithic vessels were found on the top of this layer, probably derived from nearby hearths.

Calibrated date: 1σ : cal BC 3615 – 3360
2σ : cal BC 3640 – 3140

Final comments:
S C Stanford: satisfactory; the date is within the expected period.

Bullock Down Farm: Frost Hill, site 44, East Sussex

Location: TV 584964
Lat. 51.38.37 N; Long. 00.17.22 E

Excavator: D R Rudling (Field Archaeology Unit, Institute of Archaeology, London), 1978

Site: a beacon or post-mill represented by a complex of features with horizontal beams, pits and postholes, near to two Roman corn-drying ovens and a threshing floor.

References: Drewett 1982b, 130 (^{14}C)

Objectives: to ascertain whether the features relate to the nearby Roman settlement, or are of a different period; the pottery associated with the complex is all Roman, of third- to fourth-century date.

HAR-3970 1670 ± 70 BP

$\delta^{13}C$: −27.1 ‰

Sample: BD44E9, submitted on 29 July 1980

Material: charcoal.

Initial comment: from F6 (context 9), an enigmatic feature which produced no artefactual evidence.

Calibrated date: 1σ : cal AD 260 – 430
2σ : cal AD 220 – 540

Final comments:
D R Rudling: the calibrated date is consistent with that of the pottery finds associated with this group of features.

Burgh Castle, Suffolk

Location: TG 474045
Lat. 52.34.54 N; Long. 01.38.47 E

Excavator: C Green (for the Department of the Environment), 1960

Site: Saxon cemetery within the south-west corner of the Roman fort; the east – west graves were sealed by an eleventh-century motte with a timber tower and encircling ditch which disturbed much of the site.

References: Johnson 1983; 3, 111 – 12 (^{14}C)

Objectives: to have some clear indication of the date of the cemetery and to establish the date within the period AD 400-1100 to which it belonged.

Comments:
C Green: these results give a wide bracket for the general date range of the cemetery; HAR-3794 is later than expected, but spanned the eighth and ninth centuries if not longer.

HAR-3794 1040 ± 80 BP

$\delta^{13}C$: −21.8 ‰

Sample: INT37, submitted by S Johnson on 30 April 1980

Material: human bone.

Initial comment: from a mass of leg bones buried within grave 64, thought to be part of an earlier burial disturbed when grave 64 was inserted.

Calibrated date: 1σ : cal AD 900 – 1030
2σ : cal AD 810 – 1170

Final comments:
C Green: a surprisingly late result which suggests that either the cemetery had a very long life, or that the bone was not from the earlier grave, but in fact part of a later burial.

HAR-3795 1290 ± 70 BP

$\delta^{13}C$: −22.5 ‰

Sample: INT121, submitted by S Johnson on 30 April 1980

Material: human bone.

Initial comment: from burial 121, close to burial 122, both part of an apparently undisturbed series of regularly spaced graves at the western extremity of the cemetery.

Calibrated date: 1σ : cal AD 660 – 785
2σ : cal AD 630 – 890

HAR-3804   1230 ± 70 BP

$\delta^{13}C$: −21.3 ‰

Sample: INT122, submitted by S Johnson on 30 April 1980

Material: human bone.

Initial comment: as HAR-3795, found 0.45m below plough-soil.

Calibrated date: 1σ : cal AD 680 – 885
2σ : cal AD 660 – 970

Burghfield: Heron's House, Berkshire

Location: SU 66357008
Lat. 51.25.31 N; Long. 01.02.44 W

Excavator: J C Richards, 1977

Site: a Bronze Age ring ditch and cremation cemetery, on river gravel at 140m OD.

References: Bradley and Richards 1979 – 80, 5 – 6 (^{14}C)

Objectives: to confirm the presumed Bronze Age date of the monument.

HAR-2749   3030 ± 60 BP

$\delta^{13}C$: −25.5 ‰

Sample: HH77NECH, submitted on 12 July 1978

Material: charcoal: *Quercus* sp. and Rosaceae, sub-family Pomoideae, from mature timbers (C A Keepax).

Initial comment: from a 'clearance horizon' within ditch silts.

Comment on uncalibrated date: this result is statistically indistinguishable from HAR-2754.

Calibrated date: 1σ : cal BC 1400 – 1220
2σ : cal BC 1430 – 1100

HAR-2754   3050 ± 80 BP

$\delta^{13}C$: −27.2 ‰

Sample: HH77NEF8, submitted on 18 July 1978

Material: charcoal: *Prunus* sp. (eg blackthorn) and Rosaceae, sub-family Pomoideae (eg hawthorn) from large timbers, and *Corylus/Alnus* sp. and *Rhamnus catharticus* L. (buckthorn) from large and branch-sized timbers (C A Keepax).

Initial comment: feature 3, associated with a Deverel-Rimbury urn, which was cut into a partially silted ring ditch.

Calibrated date: 1σ : cal BC 1420 – 1220
2σ : cal BC 1510 – 1050

Burghfield: Knight's Farm, Berkshire

Location: SU 67906993
Lat. 51.25.26 N; Long. 01.01.24 W

Excavator: J C Richards

Site: the first Late Bronze Age occupation site excavated on the Kennet gravels and the first gravel and non-hillfort or heathland site within the upper and middle Thames region.

References: Bradley *et al* 1980

Objectives:

1. For comparison with those from a larger site 7km to the south and from Rams Hill in order to relate this site to others in area.

2. For internal comparison with dates from Early Iron Age pits in order to confirm the typological evidence of the sequence in the region.

3. To establish a better chronology for the important series of diagnostic pottery forms, which are post Middle Bronze Age (Deverel-Rimbury) and pre-Early Iron Age, but without close dating. The estimated date of the site is 1000 – 750 BC.

Comments:
AML: one sample, HAR-2928 (KF75F1), failed.

HAR-2929   3000 ± 70 BP

$\delta^{13}C$: −25.4 ‰

Sample: KF75F3, submitted on 1 June 1977

Material: charcoal.

Initial comment: from a large pit (possibly a pond) cutting F2, which contained a wooden plank or stake.

Calibrated date: 1σ : cal BC 1390 – 1130
2σ : cal BC 1420 – 1020

Burghfield: Knight's Farm, Berkshire

Location: SU 67906993
Lat. 51.25.26 N; Long. 01.01.24 W

Excavator: T W Gates (Berkshire Archaeological Committee), 1974

Site: pits, gully, and a pond excavated in advance of gravel quarrying.

References: Bradley *et al* 1980
Gates *et al* 1980, 263 (^{14}C)

Objectives: three charcoal samples were submitted from pits 5 and 12; the objective was to date the pits and the pottery in them.

HAR-1011   2690 ± 80 BP

$\delta^{13}C$: −25.7 ‰

Sample: P5L2A, submitted on 22 January 1975

Material: charcoal, the possibility of contamination is low.

Initial comment: from layer 2 in rubbish pit 5, associated with large quantities of presumed Early Iron Age pottery; the date should be the same as HAR-1012.

Calibrated date: 1σ : cal BC 915 – 805
2σ : cal BC 1010 – 780

Final comments:
T W Gates: this result places the site firmly in the Late Bronze Age rather than the Early Iron Age.

References: Longley 1980, 72

HAR-1012   2250 ± 80 BP

$δ^{13}C$: –26.3 ‰

Sample: P5L2B, submitted on 22 January 1975

Material: charcoal, the possibility of contamination is low.

Initial comment: from same context as HAR-1011, submitted to give a check on that date.

Calibrated date: 1σ : cal BC 400 – 200
2σ : cal BC 410 – 110

Final comments:
T W Gates: the suggested calibrations for HAR-1012 appear very late. The result for HAR-1011 is more consistent with the associated pottery.

References: Longley 1980, 72

HAR-1013   3050 ± 90 BP

$δ^{13}C$: –25.5 ‰

Sample: P12L2, submitted on 22 January 1975

Material: charcoal.

Initial comment: from a layer 2 of rubbish pit 12; the pottery is broadly similar to that from pit 5 and the expected date should be comparable to HAR-1011 and HAR-1012, although pit 12 had been recut at least twice so there is a risk that some material could be residual.

Calibrated date: 1σ : cal BC 1425 – 1215
2σ : cal BC 1520 – 1030

Final comments:
T W Gates: this result is slightly earlier than expected, though the calibrated date approaches that for HAR-1011 at the extreme of the two standard deviation range.

Harwell: HAR-1013 is not statistically similar to the other samples.

Burton Fleming, Humberside

Location: TA 096697
Lat. 54.06.41 N; Long. 00.19.24 W

Excavator: I M Stead (Department of the Environment), 1967 – 78

Site: extensive Iron Age cemetery (La Tène) with inhumations in square-ditched barrows; the earlier (north – south) burials were crouched, the later (east – west) burials were mainly flexed.

References: Dent 1982, 439 (^{14}C)
Stead 1976, 224 – 5 (^{14}C)
Radiocarbon **29**, 80 (^{14}C)

Objectives: to date the graves in the cemetery, which dates from the fourth century to the first century BC; the expected order of the graves is HAR-1130 (earliest), HAR-1058, HAR-1129, and HAR-1057.

HAR-1057   2600 ± 70 BP

$δ^{13}C$: –21.0 ‰

Sample: FAAM4, submitted on 22 January 1975

Material: human bone: one femur and one fibula.

Initial comment: from burial 182, an east – west grave with a sword; this date was expected to be later than the other three.

Calibrated date: 1σ : cal BC 825 – 780
2σ : cal BC 900 – 540

Final comments:
I M Stead: too early; a date before the first century BC is unlikely.

HAR-1058   2520 ± 70 BP

$δ^{13}C$: –21.1 ‰

Sample: FAAQ10, submitted on 22 January 1975

Material: human bone: one femur and one fibula.

Initial comment: from burial 180, which contained a flattened bow-brooch and a pot.

Calibrated date: 1σ : cal BC 800 – 530
2σ : cal BC 820 – 400

Final comments:
I M Stead: too early.

HAR-1129   2050 ± 80 BP

$δ^{13}C$: –20.7 ‰

Sample: FACM34, submitted on 22 January 1975

Material: human bone: one femur and one humerus.

Initial comment: from burial 143, which contained an involuted brooch and a pot, this bone was not coated with quent-glaze.

Calibrated date: 1σ : cal BC 180 – 20 cal AD
2σ : cal BC 360 – 110 cal AD

Final comments:
I M Stead: this is within the expected range.

HAR-1130   2150 ± 150 BP

$δ^{13}C$: –21.1 ‰

Sample: FABG7, submitted on 22 January 1975

Material: human bone: one femur and one humerus.

Initial comment: from burial 178, which contained a bow-brooch and a pot, this bone was painted with quent-glaze on the terminals.

Calibrated date: 1σ : cal BC 390 – 0 cal AD
2σ : cal BC 750 – 130 cal AD

Final comments:
I M Stead: within the expected range.

Harwell: this bone did not produce enough collagen for a completely satisfactory result; this accounts for the larger than normal error term.

Butley: Burrow Hill, Suffolk

Location: TM 39004853
              Lat. 52.04.58 N; Long. 01.29.19 E

Excavator: V Fenwick (Butley Excavation Group), 1978 – present

Site: Middle Saxon occupation with an associated cemetery on a former island (SMR BU1), subsequently dated by coins to the late seventh – mid ninth century.

References: Fenwick 1984; 37, 52 (^{14}C)

Objectives: to obtain a date for an early phase of the cemetery.

HAR-2897   1170 ± 80 BP

$\delta^{13}C$: −20.4 ‰

Sample: HB153, submitted on 27 October 1978

Material: human bone, dried naturally, not washed or treated: the sample included fragments of rib, vertebrae, humeri, ulnae, and pelvis.

Initial comment: first phase inhumation, buried in sandy humus

Calibrated date: 1σ : cal AD 770 – 970
                    2σ : cal AD 670 – 1020

Final comments:
V Fenwick: the result is consistent with settlement contexts closely dated by coins and an archaeomagnetic date for a kiln (D Tarling, Newcastle).

Butterbump, Lincolnshire

Location: TF 492724
              Lat. 53.13.38 N; Long. 00.14.07 E

Excavator: B M Beeby (Department of the Environment), 1972 – 5

Site: one of a group of eleven or more Late Neolithic or Early Bronze Age barrows, on a possible former island in the middle marsh. The primary cremation was in a pit covered by wooden planks, perhaps a bier; a probably contemporary pit 2m away contained a perforated whetstone and a bronze dagger in a wooden sheath. A number of secondary cremations were also found.

Objectives: to establish a fixed chronology for the site and the associated environment.

Comments:
J Grieg: these dates seem to show a fairly wide spread, which could reflect the use of the barrow over a long time period.

HAR-449   unknown

$\delta^{13}C$: unknown

Sample: CHAROL, submitted on 10 October 1973

Material: charcoal.

Final comments:
Harwell: there is no evidence that this material was ever actually dated. It may have presented experimental difficulties and been abandoned.

HAR-487   2590 ± 80 BP

$\delta^{13}C$: −26.2 ‰

Sample: BB72HA/C, submitted on 16 January 1974

Material: charcoal: *Quercus* sp. (H Keeley).

Initial comment: well stratified in a barrow.

Calibrated date: 1σ : cal BC 825 – 770
                    2σ : cal BC 910 – 510

HAR-488   3460 ± 130 BP

$\delta^{13}C$: −25.4 ‰

Sample: BB73GPC/C (NEQC1), submitted on 16 January 1974

Material: charcoal: *Betula* sp. (H Keeley).

Initial comment: from the fill of grave pit C.

Calibrated date: 1σ : cal BC 1950 – 1630
                    2σ : cal BC 2140 – 1465

References: Grieg 1982, 11

HAR-489   3070 ± 120 BP

$\delta^{13}C$: −26.9 ‰

Sample: BB73HC/C (NEQ3HC), submitted on 16 January 1974

Material: charcoal: *Betula* sp. (H Keeley).

Initial comment: from hearth C above and around grave C.

Calibrated date: 1σ : cal BC 1490 – 1165
                    2σ : cal BC 1620 – 1000

HAR-490   3700 ± 180 BP

$\delta^{13}C$: −26.0 ‰

Sample: BB73CGF/1-4, submitted on 16 January 1974

Material: charcoal: *Quercus* sp. and *Betula* sp. (H Keeley).

Initial comment: from the primary burial.

Calibrated date: 1σ : cal BC 2455 – 1880
                    2σ : cal BC 2590 – 1640

References: Grieg 1982, 11

HAR-491   3470 ± 80 BP

$\delta^{13}C$: −27.6 ‰

Sample: BB73FAC1-6, submitted on 16 January 1974

Material: charcoal.

Initial comment: combined samples from above and around feature A cremation.

Calibrated date: 1σ : cal BC 1895 – 1690
2σ : cal BC 2030 – 1610

References: Grieg 1982, 11

HAR-492   37600 ± 5460 BP

$\delta^{13}C$: –23.9 ‰

Sample: BB73CGOAUC, submitted on 16 January 1974

Material: charcoal: *Quercus* sp. (H Keeley).

Initial comment: from an occupation area with flintwork below the old ground surface under the barrow.

Final Comments:
Harwell: too old to calibrate.

Butterbump, Lincolnshire

Location: TF 492724
Lat. 53.13.38 N; Long. 00.14.07 E

Excavator: J Greig and B Beeby (Department of the Environment), 1972 – 5

Site: a peat-filled kettlehole *c* 100m from the above barrow.

References: Greig 1982, 12 (^{14}C)

Objectives: to provide a *terminus post quem* for a sequence of pollen samples showing an episode of forest clearance.

HAR-2255   4430 ± 90 BP

$\delta^{13}C$: –25.0 ‰

Sample: B95, submitted on 1 June 1977

Material: peat.

Initial comment: from the base of the profile.

Calibrated date: 1σ : cal BC 3330 – 2920
2σ : cal BC 3370 – 2900

Final comments:
J Greig and B Beeby: although useful, I should have dated the horizon with *Tilia* decline.

Caerwent, Gwent

Location: ST 470905
Lat. 51.36.21 N; Long. 02.46.47 W

Excavator: V L Gregory, 1973

Site: excavation outside the east gate of the Roman town of an inhumation cemetery and extra-mural building: also the outer defensive ditch of the Roman town.

References: Gregory 1973
Wilson *et al* 1975, 223 (^{14}C)

HAR-493   1090 ± 70 BP

$\delta^{13}C$: –20.1 ‰

Sample: HB97, submitted by H Keeley on 24 January 1974

Material: human bone.

Calibrated date: 1σ : cal AD 885 – 1010
2σ : cal AD 780 – 1030

HAR-494   1540 ± 70 BP

$\delta^{13}C$: –21.9 ‰

Sample: HB26, submitted by H Keeley on 24 January 1974

Material: human bone.

Calibrated date: 1σ : cal AD 425 – 600
2σ : cal AD 380 – 650

HAR-495   1410 ± 80 BP

$\delta^{13}C$: –21.3 ‰

Sample: HB34, submitted by H Keeley on 24 January 1974

Material: human bone.

Calibrated date: 1σ : cal AD 656 – 670
2σ : cal AD 450 – 770

HAR-496   1250 ± 80 BP

$\delta^{13}C$: –21.6 ‰

Sample: HB134, submitted by H Keeley on 24 January 1974

Material: human bone.

Calibrated date: 1σ : cal AD 670 – 885
2σ : cal AD 640 – 970

HAR-497   1460 ± 80 BP

$\delta^{13}C$: –21.4 ‰

Sample: HB111, submitted by H Keeley on 24 January 1974

Material: human bone.

Calibrated date: 1σ : cal AD 540 – 655
2σ : cal AD 420 – 680

Callis Wold, Humberside

Location: SE 832559
Lat. 53.59.32 N; Long. 00.43.51 W

Excavator: D Coombs (University of Manchester), 1974 – 5

Site: Neolithic long barrow (Mortimer 275) on the western edge of the Yorkshire Wolds, with ten crouched inhumations and cremations on a platform within a mortuary structure, covered by a low mound later enlarged with a turf stack.

References: Coombs 1976
Radiocarbon **21**, 376 (^{14}C)

Objectives: to provide a *terminus ante quem* for the original mound.

HAR-1448   3480 ± 80 BP

$\delta^{13}C$: –25.8 ‰

Sample: CW755229, submitted on 19 December 1975

Material: charcoal: mainly Rosaceae, sub-family Pomoideae with *Quercus* sp. and a little *Corylus* sp. (or *Alnus glutinosa* (L.) Gaertn.); *c* 20% identified (C A Keepax).

Initial comment: from a Beaker occupation layer on the edge of, and over, the first mound.

Calibrated date: 1σ : cal BC 1910 – 1695
2σ : cal BC 2030 – 1620

Final comments:
D Coombs: this result seems rather late for a Beaker horizon; the European evidence would suggest a date nearer 2000 BC.

Canterbury: Bridge By-pass, Kent

Location: TR 19165322
Lat. 51.14.10 N; Long. 01.08.31 E

Excavator: N Macpherson-Grant (Isle of Thanet Archaeological Unit), 1974

Site: a Late Bronze Age barrow with possible secondary cremations outside the mound, excavated in advance of road construction.

References: Macpherson-Grant 1980, 170 (^{14}C)
Radiocarbon **21**, 376 (^{14}C)

Objectives: to provide dates for the barrow and associated cremations, but particularly to provide a relative fixed-point for any future assessment of the dating of Late Bronze Age ceramics in east Kent.

Comments:
N Macpherson-Grant: both uncalibrated dates relate fairly well to the pottery styles, dating the barrow and both the internal and external cremations to the Late Bronze Age, a period which is not yet clearly understood in east Kent.

Harwell: the dates are published as a combined mean of 980 ± 60 BC.

HAR-1492   2880 ± 80 BP

$\delta^{13}C$: –25.1 ‰

Sample: SAMPLEA, submitted on 23 September 1975

Material: charcoal: *Quercus* sp., not twiggy; *c* 25% identified (C A Keepax).

Initial comment: from barrow 2, cremation 7.

Calibrated date: 1σ : cal BC 1255 – 930
2σ : cal BC 1370 – 850

Final comments:
N Macpherson-Grant: the result appears later than the supposed secondary burial (HAR-1493).

HAR-1493   2970 ± 80 BP

$\delta^{13}C$: –25.4 ‰

Sample: SAMPLEB, submitted on 23 September 1975

Material: charcoal: *Quercus* sp. (not twiggy), mainly too small for identification; *c* 25% identified (C A Keepax).

Initial comment: from cremation 5, outside the barrow; thought to be secondary to the cremations within the barrow; depth 0.35m.

Calibrated date: 1σ : cal BC 1375 – 1055
2σ : cal BC 1420 – 940

Final comments:
N Macpherson-Grant: although the upper limits for both the one and two standard deviation ranges fall close to, or within the range of, the combined mean, the earlier emphasis for this sample seems slightly anomalous.

Canterbury: St Pancras, Kent

Location: TR 155577
Lat. 51.16.37 N; Long. 01.05.25 E

Excavator: F Jenkins (for the Department of the Environment), 1974

Site: a Saxon church on a Roman site.

HAR-3710   1130 ± 90 BP

$\delta^{13}C$: –22.3 ‰

Sample: 5L3S2, submitted on 5 March 1980

Material: human bone.

Initial comment: from skeletal material below the buttress of the south porticus.

Comment on uncalibrated date: the porticus was previously thought to have been part of the Saxon church as first built.

Calibrated date: 1σ : cal AD 785 – 1000
2σ : cal AD 680 – 1040

Final comments:
Harwell: a very small sample.

HAR-3749   1650 ± 70 BP

$\delta^{13}C$: –25.9 ‰

Sample: 7AL4S1, submitted on 5 March 1980

Material: charcoal: medium size timber and twig with some soil.

Initial comment: from one of the layers of soil in a Roman rubbish disposal pit, associated with early fourth-century pottery sherds.

Calibrated date: 1σ : cal AD 265 – 440
2σ : cal AD 230 – 560

Final comments:
Harwell: a very small sample.

Carlisle: Grapes Lane, Cumbria

Location: NY 4015555948
Lat. 54.53.41 N; Long. 02.56.00 W

Excavator: P Clack (Department of the Environment, Carlisle City Council, and Durham University), 1975

Site: a small urban excavation which revealed a medieval stratigraphic sequence.

Objectives: to provide a date for the Roman well.

HAR-1894   1120 ± 90 BP

$\delta^{13}C$: −25.0 ‰

Sample: CAR75269, submitted on 1 September 1976

Material: wood: *Quercus* sp..

Initial comment: timber from a Roman well under a thirteenth-century or earlier garden.

Calibrated date: 1σ : cal AD 790 – 1010
2σ : cal AD 680 – 1040

Final comments:
M McCarthy: P Clack accepted the dates – dendrochronological dates which have been obtained from some timbers indicate a felling date in the late twelfth century (unpublished). The ^{14}C date is probably wrong.

Carlisle: Hodgson's Court, Cumbria

Location: NY 4016456056
Lat. 54.53.44 N; Long. 02.56.00 W

Excavator: P Gosling (Department of the Environment, Carlisle City Council, and Durham University), 1975

Site: a small excavation in an urban context – medieval garden deposits overlying a late first-century Roman building were revealed.

HAR-1895   1860 ± 100 BP

$\delta^{13}C$: −26.0 ‰

Sample: CAR75144, submitted on 1 September 1976

Material: wood: *Quercus* sp..

Initial comment: from a context under a medieval garden.

Calibrated date: 1σ : cal AD 30 – 250
2σ : cal BC 100 – 400 cal AD

Final comments:
P Gosling: the date is unhelpful.

Carmarthen: Llanstephen Castle, Dyfed

Location: SN 351101
Lat. 51.45.45 N; Long. 04.22.40 W

Excavator: G Guilbert (Clwyd-Powys Archaeological Trust), 1971 – 3

Site: a medieval castle of several phases, beginning in the twelfth century, constructed on a promontory, cut off by a complex series of earthworks thought to be of prehistoric date.

References: *Radiocarbon* **19**, 409 – 10 (^{14}C)

Comments:
G Guilbert: after calibration the results form an impressively complementary group; this was not expected on archaeological grounds since HAR-477 was from a different part of the site and the stratigraphy between HAR-475 and HAR-476 was broken by a Norman ditch when the castle was adapted;
it is now clear that the castle stands within an Iron Age hillfort although these levels produced no datable artefacts.

HAR-475   2450 ± 90 BP

$\delta^{13}C$: −25.3 ‰

Sample: L1042, submitted on 14 November 1975

Material: charcoal.

Initial comment: from a shallow ditch at the front of bank C, probably related to the original timber-revetted construction of that bank.

Calibrated date: 1σ : cal BC 785 – 400
2σ : cal BC 810 – 380

HAR-476   2460 ± 70 BP

$\delta^{13}C$: −25.0 ‰

Sample: L1068, submitted on 14 November 1975

Material: charcoal.

Initial comment: from the primary silt in the deep U-shaped ditch X, which is probably the earliest defensive line on the site; could be any date from Iron Age to early Norman (a sherd of second-century AD Roman pottery was found in the upper fill), but the result may be earlier than HAR-475.

Calibrated date: 1σ : cal BC 780 – 405
2σ : cal BC 800 – 400

HAR-477   2470 ± 70 BP

$\delta^{13}C$: −25.8 ‰

Sample: L7115, submitted on 14 November 1975

Material: charcoal.

Initial comment: from a charcoal-rich occupation deposit cut by postholes and sealed by the first phase of the twelfth-century castle defences.

Calibrated date: 1σ : cal BC 785 – 410
2σ : cal BC 800 – 400

Carn Euny, Cornwall

Location: SW 403288
Lat. 50.06.06 N; Long. 05.37.56 W

Excavator: P Christie (for the Department of the Environment)

References: Christie 1966
Christie 1973
Christie 1976
Christie 1978, 430 (^{14}C)
Christie 1983

Comments:
P Christie: The four samples submitted, with the possible exception of HAR-335, have given an extremely interesting, and generally satisfactory sequence for the site, which was occupied for over 600 years.

In the view of the shortage of radiocarbon determinations for the Cornish Iron Age, this sequence is of particular interest. It is also of great interest in relation to the series of radiocarbon dates for the Iron Age in Brittany which have been published over recent years, since there are strong cultural connections between these two regions.

HAR-237 1740 ± 70 BP

$\delta^{13}C$: −25.3 ‰

Sample: F122, submitted by S Limbrey on 28 December 1972

Material: charcoal: *Quercus* sp. (G C Morgan).

Initial comment: from the base of a thick charcoal layer below soil/stones, in a pit c 0.53m deep, sealed by c 0.50m accumulation of soil; to the south of courtyard house 1.

Comment on uncalibrated date: younger than expected but acceptable – this confirms the supected late date of the pit.

Calibrated date: 1σ : cal AD 220 – 390
 2σ : cal AD 120 – 430

References: Christie 1976, 72
 Radiocarbon **19**, 402

HAR-238 2370 ± 70 BP

$\delta^{13}C$: −26.2 ‰

Sample: F140, submitted by S Limbrey on 28 December 1972

Material: charcoal: *Quercus* sp. from a large timber (S Limbrey).

Initial comment: from a trench below the entrance to courtyard house 1, above an ash layer and sealed by c 0.45m of humic soil beneath paving stones and a further accumulation of soil.

Calibrated date: 1σ : cal BC 525 – 390
 2σ : cal BC 770 – 265

Final comments:
P Christie: this result is surprisingly early; in view of the context and association with decorated pottery of a type so far unknown on the site, it may be accepted as part of the earliest Iron Age occupation.

References: *Radiocarbon* **19**, 402
 Christie 1976, 72

HAR-334 2080 ± 80 BP

$\delta^{13}C$: −26.4 ‰

Sample: F134, submitted by S Limbrey on 3 May 1973

Material: charcoal: *Quercus* sp. (S Limbrey).

Initial comment: from black, greasy soil with many stones, to the east of the fogou entrance passage, associated with local decorated pottery.

Comment on uncalibrated date: most satisfactory.

Calibrated date: 1σ : cal BC 195 – 0 cal AD
 2σ : cal BC 370 – 80 cal AD

HAR-335 1860 ± 100 BP

$\delta^{13}C$: −23.4 ‰

Sample: F135, submitted by S Limbrey on 3 May 1973

Material: charcoal: *Quercus* sp. (S Limbrey).

Initial comment: from the brown earth fill of a bell-shaped storage pit containing decorated Iron Age sherds; sealed by a rab floor.

Calibrated date: 1σ : cal AD 30 – 250
 2σ : cal BC 100 – 400 cal AD

Final comments:
P Christie: too young even allowing a pottery survival factor, but the sample was very small; could just fall within the maximum margin.

Carngoon Bank, Cornwall

Location: SW 696131
 Lat. 49.58.22 N; Long. 05.12.49 W

Excavator: F McAvoy (Central Excavation Unit), 1979

Site: prehistoric occupation comprising a Mesolithic presence, Mid – Late Bronze Age house platforms, and Iron Age activity; finds from the Romano-British settlement include briquetage for salt production, associated with a structure which appears to have been in use until the sixth century AD.

References: McAvoy *et al* 1980, 33 (^{14}C)

HAR-3712 2990 ± 60 BP

$\delta^{13}C$: −25.9 ‰

Sample: 32-266, submitted by N Balaam on 19 March 1980

Material: charcoal: *Quercus* sp. from large timbers.

Initial comment: from pit 265, one of fifteen pits in Bronze Age hut platform 65.

Calibrated date: 1σ : cal BC 1375 – 1130
 2σ : cal BC 1410 – 1030

Catsgore, Somerset

Location: ST 342125
 Lat. 51.01.08 N; Long. 02.42.02 W

Excavator: R Leech (Yeovil Archaeological and Local History Society), 1973

Site: Romano-British settlement; a 'small village' comprising 5 – 12 farms occupied around AD 100 – 400.

References: Leech 1982, 132 (^{14}C)

Objectives: lead tin oxide (cubic PbSnO^3) has been described as a dating marker in north-west Europe; confirmation of a fourth-century date would make this the first specific Roman record of the use of lead tin oxide.

HAR-3197 1800 ± 90 BP

$\delta^{13}C$: −25.2 ‰

Sample: CATGF399, submitted by L Biek on 11 May 1979

Material: charcoal: *Acer* sp., twig (C A Keepax).

Initial comment: from the ditch fill which accumulated before and during the use of building 3.5 in the fourth century; found in association with pot sherds which had been reused as crucibles and which contained residues of opaque glass (AML-791278) coloured yellow with lead tin oxide.

Calibrated date: 1σ : cal AD 115 – 340
2σ : cal AD 10 – 420

Final comments:
AML: (L Biek) this places the actual melting of lead tin oxide glass in Britain firmly in the (?later) Roman period for the first and so far only time. However the proximity of the site to Iron Age glass production centres at Meare and Glastonbury (cf bead 6) raises the possibility of remelting here, as such glass is known to have been made there (Biek and Kay 1982).

Chanctonbury Ring, West Sussex

Location: TQ 139121
Lat. 50.43.48 N; Long. 00.22.49 W

Excavator: O Bedwin (Sussex Archaeological Field Unit), 1977

Site: a small, Early Iron Age, univallate hillfort, probably abandoned in the fourth century BC; with a Romano-British temple at the centre of the interior; some Neolithic and Bronze Age activity.

References: Bedwin 1980, 220 (^{14}C)

Objectives: although the site was a hillfort, the large scale excavations produced very little Iron Age material; this was the only material suitable for ^{14}C dating.

HAR-2703   2320 ± 80 BP

$\delta^{13}C$: −23.0 ‰

Sample: CR77B110, submitted by P Drewett on 6 December 1977

Material: animal bone.

Initial comment: from F110, Area B, one of the very few Iron Age features found.

Calibrated date: 1σ : cal BC 410 – 370
2σ : cal BC 760 – 200

Final comments:
O Bedwin: the date range is compatible with the pottery, and adds Chanctonbury to the Early Iron Age hillfort building horizon.

Chichester, West Sussex

Location: SU 861048
Lat. 50.50.09 N; Long. 00.46.38 W

Excavator: A Down, 1975

Site: Roman public baths.

References: Down 1978, 151

Objectives: samples submitted to check whether the water supply system was coeval with the latest phase of Roman development in Chichester.

Comments:
AML: one sample, HAR-3087 (CHIAJC1Z) from the same timber as HAR-2572, gave an unsatisfactory result.

HAR-2572   1610 ± 70 BP

$\delta^{13}C$: −26.4 ‰

Sample: CHIAJC1, submitted by A J Clark on 3 March 1978

Material: wood: *Quercus* sp., from the outer 10 rings of a large timber to ensure a result as contemporary as possible with the date of felling.

Initial comment: from part of the Roman water supply system (later timber than HAR-2580).

Calibrated date: 1σ : cal AD 380 – 540
2σ : cal AD 250 – 600

Final comments:
A Down: this result is consistent with the late phase.

Harwell: it was noted that the outer rings were considerably more contaminated than the inner rings, and in future samples will be taken from these, and adjusted by adding ring counts from the outer surface.

HAR-2580   1760 ± 70 BP

$\delta^{13}C$: −26.0 ‰

Sample: CHIAJC2, submitted by A J Clark on 3 March 1978

Material: wood: from the outer 7 rings.

Initial comment: from the Roman water supply system.

Calibrated date: 1σ : cal AD 145 – 370
2σ : cal AD 90 – 420

Final comments:
A Down: within the range expected.

Harwell: the $\delta^{13}C$ value is assumed.

HAR-3084   2070 ± 110 BP

$\delta^{13}C$: −25.6 ‰

Sample: CHIAJC1X, submitted by A J Clark on 9 February 1979

Material: wood: drillings from an oak (*Quercus* sp.) timber.

Initial comment: from same timber as HAR-2572.

Calibrated date: 1σ : cal BC 340 – 50 cal AD
2σ : cal BC 390 – 130 cal AD

Final comments:
A Down: not understood.

HAR-3085   1630 ± 80 BP

$\delta^{13}C$: −22.3 ‰

Sample: CH78E13, submitted by A J Clark on 9 February 1979

Material: human bone: two femurs.

Initial comment: from burial 13, submitted for comparison with the late timbers from the bath-house site.

Calibrated date: 1σ : cal AD 270 – 525
2σ : cal AD 230 – 600

Final comments:
A Down: the date bracket is too wide to be useful.

HAR-3086   1950 ± 70 BP

$\delta^{13}C$: −26.5 ‰

Sample: CHIAJCY, submitted by A J Clark on 9 February 1979

Material: wood.

Initial comment: from same timber as HAR-2572.

Calibrated date: 1σ : cal BC 35 – 120 cal AD
2σ : cal BC 110 – 220 cal AD

Final comments:
A Down: HAR-2572 falls within the likely date range.

Chichester: Eastgate, West Sussex

Location: SU 867050
Lat. 50.50.15 N; Long. 00.46.07 W

Excavator: A Down, 1978

Site: a Roman cemetery.

References: Down 1981, 95 (^{14}C)

Objectives: to exclude an Early Saxon date for the cemetery.

Comments:
A Down: the combined mean of these results is 320 ± 65; due to the uncertain reliability of ^{14}C dates in the Late Roman period however, this can only provide an exclusion of a later, pagan Saxon date.

HAR-3653   1630 ± 80 BP

$\delta^{13}C$: −21.2 ‰

Sample: CH78E13A, submitted by A J Clark on 30 January 1980

Material: human bone.

Initial comment: from burial 13, associated with the latest phase of Romano-British activity.

Calibrated date: 1σ : cal AD 270 – 535
2σ : cal AD 230 – 600

Final comments:
A Down: this date bracket is too wide to be useful.

HAR-3654   1620 ± 90 BP

$\delta^{13}C$: −25.0 ‰

Sample: CH78E13B, submitted by A J Clark on 30 January 1978

Material: human bone.

Initial comment: from burial 13.

Calibrated date: 1σ : cal AD 270 – 545
2σ : cal AD 230 – 620

HAR-3655   1710 ± 60 BP

$\delta^{13}C$: −21.2 ‰

Sample: CH78E13C, submitted by A J Clark on 30 January 1978

Material: human bone.

Initial comment: from burial 13.

Calibrated date: 1σ : cal AD 245 – 405
2σ : cal AD 145 – 440

Chippenham: Water Hall Farm, Cambridgeshire

Location: TL 67176665
Lat. 52.16.20 N; Long. 00.27.01 E

Excavator: E A Martin (for the Department of the Environment), 1973

Site: a Bronze Age round barrow – one of two natural mounds into which five graves had been inserted, one with Beaker grave goods; the latter (grave II) was a multiple grave containing at least three adult females and two children.

References: Lawson *et al* 1981
Lawson 1986a; 2, fig 1 (^{14}C)
Martin 1976
Martin and Murphy 1988, 357 (^{14}C)

Objectives: to date the burials.

HAR-3880   3520 ± 70 BP

$\delta^{13}C$: −23.1 ‰

Sample: CHIPINHU, submitted by P Murphy on 30 April 1980

Material: human bone.

Initial comment: from Grave II, cut into the summit of the mound.

Calibrated date: 1σ : cal BC 1950 – 1750
2σ : cal BC 2090 – 1680

Final comments:
E A Martin: the date obtained fits closely with the dates from other Bronze Age barrows in the vicinity (cf Martin and Murphy 1988).

Christchurch: Bargates, site X17, Dorset

Location: SZ 15759305
Lat. 50.44.11 N; Long. 01.46.36 W

Excavator: K Jarvis (Poole Museums Service), 1969 – 80

Site: traces of Late Neolithic occupation with Grooved Ware pottery, two Bronze Age ring ditches, Early Iron Age occupation, and a seventh-century pagan Saxon cemetery with 30 graves.

References: Jarvis 1982, 140 (^{14}C)

Objectives: to date the Late Neolithic Grooved Ware occupation.

HAR-2907   4170 ± 80 BP

$\delta^{13}C$: −25.8 ‰

Sample: X17101:X17102, submitted on 27 October 1978

Material: charcoal and nuts: *Quercus* sp., Rosaceae, sub-family Pomoideae, *Corylus/Alnus* sp., and *Ilex* sp., all from fairly mature timbers; *c* 25% identified (C A Keepax).

Initial comment: from a layer *c* 0.20m thick, containing burnt flint, in a pit with Grooved Ware pottery; interpreted as occupation debris from a settlement. The natural was extensivly root-disturbed sand.

Calibrated date: 1σ : cal BC 2890 − 2615
    2σ : cal BC 2920 − 2500

Final comments:
K Jarvis: the result is the earliest so far for a pit containing only Grooved Ware pottery, but it is consistent with the emerging evidence for the wide time span of this ceramic type; the date is considered acceptable, although in view of the fragmentary nature of the sample the possibility that earlier charcoal was included cannot be ruled out.

Harwell: the seed submitted from the same pit had fresh organic contents and is therefore a modern contaminant.

Cirencester, Gloucestershire

Location: SP 02130415
    Lat. 51.44.08 N; Long. 01.58.09 W

Excavator: A McWhirr (Cirencester Excavation Committee), 1969 − 76

Site: a Romano-British cemetery outside the south-west or Bath gate of the Roman town of Corinium Dobunnorum. Between 1969 and 1974, and in 1976, 453 individuals (inhumation and cremation) were excavated in an area bordering the Fosse way, in response to building development and the construction of a dual carriageway bypass.

References: McWhirr *et al* 1982, MG11 (^{14}C)

Objectives: the dates are required to supplement coin and stratigraphic evidence; HAR-1010 would assist the stratigraphic analysis of the site; HAR-1009 would help establish the date for the final use of the cemetery.

HAR-992   1730 ± 90 BP

$\delta^{13}C$: −19.7 ‰

Sample: BUR57, submitted on 26 November 1974

Material: human bone.

Initial comment: from burial 57 (site code ref 71 CS XVII layer 2).

Calibrated date: 1σ : cal AD 215 − 410
    2σ : cal AD 80 − 540

Final comments:
A McWhirr: estimated date third − fourth century AD.

HAR-1006   1680 ± 70 BP

$\delta^{13}C$: −19.4 ‰

Sample: BUR28, submitted on 26 November 1974

Material: human bone.

Initial comment: from burial 28 (site code ref 70 CS II layer 1), estimated date late fourth or early fifth century AD.

Calibrated date: 1σ : cal AD 255 − 425
    2σ : cal AD 210 − 540

HAR-1009   1640 ± 80 BP

$\delta^{13}C$: −21.0 ‰

Sample: BURIALF, submitted on 26 November 1974

Material: human bone.

Initial comment: from burial F (site code ref 69 CT 4/5, layer 1).

Calibrated date: 1σ : cal AD 265 − 530
    2σ : cal AD 230 − 600

Final comments:
A McWhirr: on the evidence of a coin of Honorius beneath the middle spinal vertabrae, an early fifth-century date was expected.

HAR-1010   5250 ± 90 BP

$\delta^{13}C$: −17.1 ‰

Sample: BUR293, submitted on 26 November 1974

Material: soil, charcoal, and cremated human bone.

Initial comment: from a burial which had been cremated *in situ* in a wooden coffin (site code ref: 73 CS 88 IV, layer 7).

Calibrated date: 1σ : cal BC 4230 − 3990
    2σ : cal BC 4340 − 3820

Final comments:
A McWhirr: quite unexpected; the estimated date was second century AD.

Harwell: the measurement was checked with HAR-1116 but cremated bone may contain mineral carbon giving a falsely old date.

HAR-1116   5130 ± 80 BP

$\delta^{13}C$: −15.9 ‰

Sample: BUR293, submitted on 26 November 1974

Material: soil, charcoal, and small fragments of cremated human bone.

Initial comment: from burial 293 (site code ref 73 CS 8 IV, layer 7).

Calibrated date: 1σ : cal BC 4030 − 3815
    2σ : cal BC 4230 − 3720

Final comments:
A McWhirr: see HAR-1010.

Harwell: this result confirms that of HAR-1010 being a replicate of HAR-1010, starting again from pretreated sample material.

Clophill: Cainhoe Castle, Bedfordshire

Location: TL 098373
Lat. 52.01.30 N; Long. 00.24.15 W

Excavator: P J Woodward and A F Taylor (Bedfordshire County Council), 1973

Site: a Saxon stake and wattle structure, below earthworks, to the east of the motte and bailey castle, which was excavated in advance of proposed roadworks.

References: Taylor and Woodward 1975; 41, 51 (^{14}C)
Radiocarbon **19**, 417 (^{14}C)

Objectives: to date the assumed Saxon stake and wattle structure.

HAR-715   1450 ± 70 BP

$\delta^{13}C$: −26.6 ‰

Sample: 735: stake B, submitted on 21 June 1974

Material: wood: *Quercus* sp..

Initial comment: from a stake preserved in a peaty soil (?part of an animal pen); the few associated finds include flint tools and Roman and early medieval pottery.

Calibrated date: 1σ : cal AD 550 – 655
2σ : cal AD 430 – 680

Final comments:
P J Woodward and A F Taylor: acceptable, although early.

Coddenham, Suffolk

Location: TM 11695281
Lat. 52.07.57 N; Long. 01.05.36 E

Excavator: the late E Owles (Ipswich Museum), 1973

Site: an Iron Age well, within a large Roman settlement.

References: HMSO 1974, 58 – 9

Objectives: to date construction of the well – confirm pre-Roman?

Comments:
Harwell: from all dates only a mean of HAR-508, HAR-509, HAR-607-II, and HAR-607-III should be taken; this is the same as HAR-607-I.

HAR-508   2075 ± 59 BP

$\delta^{13}C$: −27.9 ‰

Sample: SPL2, submitted by the late J Fletcher on 15 January 1974

Material: wood: *Quercus* sp.: growth allowance 33 ± 10 years.

Initial comment: from plank 7-B-73, which was cut/sawn by the through and through method; the rings are therefore not radial but slanted away from the oldest; there was no softwood, the likely date of felling is 20 – 25 years after the latest ring. The fill of the well contained a quantity of Belgic pottery, a La Tène III brooch, and a silver Iceni coin.

Calibrated date: 1σ : cal BC 180 – 30
2σ : cal BC 350 – 50 cal AD

HAR-509   2103 ± 62 BP

$\delta^{13}C$: −28.5 ‰

Sample: SPL1, submitted by the late J Fletcher on 15 January 1974

Material: wood: *Quercus* sp.: growth allowance 25 ± 10 years.

Initial comment: from plank 7-B-7.

Calibrated date: 1σ : cal BC 200 – 50
2σ : cal BC 365 – 20 cal AD

HAR-510   2248 ± 54 BP

$\delta^{13}C$: unknown

Sample: SPL3, submitted by the late J Fletcher on 15 January 1974

Material: wood: *Quercus* sp..

Calibrated date: 1σ : cal BC 395 – 210
2σ : cal BC 400 – 180

HAR-607-I   1995 ± 46 BP

$\delta^{13}C$: unknown

Sample: SPL5c, submitted by the late J Fletcher on 8 May 1974

Material: wood.

Calibrated date: 1σ : cal BC 60 – 60 cal AD
2σ : cal BC 110 – 85 cal AD

HAR-607-II   2030 ± 70 BP

$\delta^{13}C$: unknown

Sample: SPL5c, submitted by the late J Fletcher on 8 May 1974

Material: wood.

Initial comment: from plank 7-B-73, growth allowance 55 ± 10 years.

Calibrated date: 1σ : cal BC 150 – 50 cal AD
2σ : cal BC 330 – 110 cal AD

HAR-607-III   2020 ± 60 BP

$\delta^{13}C$: unknown

Sample: SPL5c, submitted by the late J Fletcher on 8 May 1974

Material: wood.

Initial comment: from plank 7-B-73, growth allowance 55 ± 10 years.

Calibrated date: 1σ : cal BC 105 – 50 cal AD
2σ : cal BC 190 – 90 cal AD

Colwick: Colwick Hall Gravel Pit, Nottinghamshire

Location: SK 605388
 Lat. 52.56.34 N; Long. 01.05.59 W

Excavator: C R Salisbury (Nottingham Historical Arts Society), 1973

Site: medieval weir or fish trap in a meander of the River Trent.

References: Losco-Bradley and Salisbury 1979, 20 (^{14}C)
 Salisbury *et al* 1984, 196 (^{14}C)
 Radiocarbon **19**, 413 (^{14}C)

Objectives: to date the structure in the absence of other archaeological finds; documentary sources suggest that this may have been one of many obstacles placed across the river in the fourteenth century by Sir R Byron to divert water into his mill and fish traps.

HAR-552   820 ± 70 BP

$\delta^{13}C$: −26.8 ‰

Sample: SAMPLE1, submitted on 1 March 1974

Material: wood: compressed, decayed oak (*Quercus* sp.), although it resembles *Betula* sp..

Initial comment: from one of hundreds of posts (*c* 2.0m long and 0.10 – 0.15m diameter) buried *c* 5.0m below the surface of the gravel pit.

Calibrated date: 1σ : cal AD 1160 – 1270
   2σ : cal AD 1030 – 1280

Final comments:
C R Salisbury: although the dating did not confirm that this was Lord Byron's fishweir, it suggests that the weir was probably the fishery mentioned in the Domesday entry for Colwick.

HAR-846   860 ± 60 BP

$\delta^{13}C$: −28.6 ‰

Sample: 748280, submitted on 5 September 1980

Material: wood: ?*Salix* sp..

Initial comment: from a wattle panel *c* 3.0m below the surface of the gravel pit; these panels were supported by the posts to form a fence which deflected eels towards catching baskets or nets.

Calibrated date: 1σ : cal AD 1050 – 1245
   2σ : cal AD 1020 – 1270

Final comments:
C R Salisbury: the closeness of the ^{14}C dates confirms the archaeological evidence that the posts and panels were exactly contemporary.

Condicote: Henge, Gloucestershire

Location: SP 15382841
 Lat. 51.57.13 N; Long. 01.46.34 W

Excavator: A Saville (Committee for Rescue Archaeology in Avon, Gloucestershire, and Somerset), 1977

Site: a section through the inner ditch of the henge.

References: Saville 1978
 Saville 1983; 31, 46 (^{14}C)
 Radiocarbon **29**, 95 (^{14}C)

Objectives: to provide an indication of the date at which the henge monument was in use.

Comments:
A Saville: HAR-3067 and HAR-3064 are in close agreement and probably relate to the same, early phase of secondary ditch silting, reflecting the main period of henge use. Two points should however be noted. Firstly, the samples were taken from mature timbers, and the dates may be substantially previous to the actual date of the deposit in which they were incorporated; secondly, the samples were not from primary positions in the ditch fill, and the dates may only be related to the use of the monument, not its construction.

HAR-3064   3720 ± 80 BP

$\delta^{13}C$: −28.0 ‰

Sample: CH77/C6/9A, submitted on 9 February 1979

Material: charcoal: Rosaceae, sub-family Pomoideae, and *Corylus/Alnus* sp. from mature timbers (C A Keepax).

Initial comment: an amalgamated sample of all the charcoal fragments from the ditch fill (layer 9A), which contained a possibly deliberate deposit of domestic rubbish from the henge; the pottery has possible Beaker affinities.

Calibrated date: 1σ : cal BC 2280 – 2030
   2σ : cal BC 2455 – 1910

Final comments:
A Saville: an acceptable date range for the type of monument and for the Beaker-related pottery.

HAR-3067   3670 ± 100 BP

$\delta^{13}C$: −26.1 ‰

Sample: CH77/C1/14, submitted on 9 February 1979

Material: charcoal: *Quercus* sp. from mature timbers (C A Keepax).

Initial comment: from the penultimate phase of the lower silting layer 14, which contained substantial pieces of burnt timber in the north-west corner of the ditch section.

Calibrated date: 1σ : cal BC 2200 – 1920
   2σ : cal BC 2450 – 1770

Final comments:
A Saville: the result indicates an acceptable date range for the type of monument.

Cookley, Hereford and Worcester

Location: SO 836798
 Lat. 52.24.56 N; Long. 02.14.28 W

Excavator: S Limbrey (University of Birmingham), 1978

Site: 3.0m of peaty sediments revealed in a section cut across the valley of the River Stour for the new Birmingham water main.

Objectives: to help establish a chronological framework for the alluvial stratigraphy and the study of pollen, plant macrofossils, insect remains etc from this exposure.

Comments:
AML: also one mini sample, which has not been dated.

HAR-3109   1260 ± 80 BP

$\delta^{13}C$: −28.4 ‰

Sample: CKL-140, submitted on 9 February 1979

Material: wood: *Alnus* sp.; bark, not identified, but probably also *Alnus* sp. (S Limbrey).

Initial comment: from 0.14m above site datum (34m OD) at the point where the pollen column was taken.

Calibrated date: 1σ : cal AD 666 – 880
2σ : cal AD 640 – 960

Cowdery's Down, Hampshire

Location: SU 657532
Lat. 51.16.25 N; Long. 01.03.29 W

Excavator: M Millett (Hampshire County Museum Service), 1978 – 81

Site: multiperiod site including an Anglo-Saxon village.

References: Millett and James 1983, 197 – 200 (^{14}C)

Objectives: to provide dating in the almost complete absence of cultural material from phase 4.

Comments:
M Millett: the results confirm the sixth- to seventh-century date of the structures, suggested by other buildings similar to those in phase C; the phase date for structure A2 is 580 ± 67 (after Ward and Wilson 1978); the phase date for structure C9 is 609 ± 57 (after Ward and Wilson 1978).

AML: two small samples were withdrawn – HAR-3788 (B79938) and HAR-3789 (B79465): one was abandoned – HAR-4448 (1017).

HAR-3720   1480 ± 60 BP

$\delta^{13}C$: −26.1 ‰

Sample: B79929, submitted on 5 March 1980

Material: charcoal: *Quercus* sp..

Initial comment: from a posthole (possibly a large timber), interlaminated with soil, structure A2 (929).

Calibrated date: 1σ : cal AD 540 – 640
2σ : cal AD 430 – 660

Final comments:
M Millett: dates for this structure, at the one standard deviation confidence range, are consistent with evidence from other sites of this type.

HAR-3721   1560 ± 70 BP

$\delta^{13}C$: −26.4 ‰

Sample: B79826, submitted on 5 March 1980

Material: charcoal: *Quercus* sp., much rootlet and soil penetration.

Initial comment: from a posthole (probably a small timber), structure A2 (926).

Calibrated date: 1σ : cal AD 415 – 590
2σ : cal AD 340 – 640

Final comments:
M Millett: as HAR-3720.

HAR-3764   1620 ± 70 BP

$\delta^{13}C$: −26.9 ‰

Sample: B79559, submitted on 5 March 1980

Material: charcoal: *Quercus* sp., small fragments with soil and chalk; too small to assess the size of the tree.

Initial comment: from a building slot, structure C9 (559F).

Calibrated date: 1σ : cal AD 350 – 535
2σ : cal AD 250 – 600

Final comments:
M Millett: at the one standard deviation level of confidence the dates for this stucture are difficult to accept at face value, since this building is stratigraphically later than A2 (HAR-3720); if account is taken of the size of the structural timbers used, the date is consistent with the stratigraphy and is comprehensible.

References: *Radiocarbon* **30**, 333

HAR-3767   1630 ± 80 BP

$\delta^{13}C$: −26.3 ‰

Sample: B79633F, submitted on 5 March 1980

Material: charcoal: *Quercus* sp. probably from a large timber.

Initial comment: from a building slot, structure C9 (633F).

Calibrated date: 1σ : cal AD 270 – 535
2σ : cal AD 230 – 600

Final comments:
M Millett: as HAR-3764.

HAR-3768   1700 ± 90 BP

$\delta^{13}C$: −25.0 ‰

Sample: B79634, submitted on 5 March 1980

Material: charcoal: *Quercus* sp. probably from a large timber.

Initial comment: from a building slot, structure C9 (1016).

Calibrated date: 1σ : cal AD 235 – 425
2σ : cal AD 120 – 550

Final comments:
M Millett: as HAR-3764.

HAR-4447   1490 ± 90 BP

$\delta^{13}C$: −23.8 ‰

Sample: 1037, submitted on 14 February 1981

Material: charcoal: *Quercus* sp. from mature timbers (C A Keepax).

Initial comment: a sample from a plank from a side wall of structure C12 which was burnt *in situ*.

Calibrated date: 1σ : cal AD 440 – 650
                    2σ : cal AD 390 – 680

Final comments:
M Millett: as HAR-3764.

HAR-4449   1490 ± 80 BP

$\delta^{13}C$: –24.7 ‰

Sample: 1016, submitted on 14 February 1981

Material: charcoal: *Quercus* sp. from mature timbers (C A Keepax).

Initial comment: a sample from a plank from a side wall of structure C12 which was burnt *in situ*.

Calibrated date: 1σ : cal AD 450 – 645
                    2σ : cal AD 400 – 670

Final comments:
M Millett: as HAR-3764.

Crawley: Broadfields, West Sussex

Location: TQ 258353
              Lat. 51.06.10 N; Long. 00.12.11 W

Excavator: the late J Gibson-Hill (Crawley Archaeological Group), 1970 – 4

Site: Iron Age and Romano-British ironworking settlement of some 30 acres, with over 40 furnaces; the most north-westerly and largest such site to be excavated in the Weald, providing the opportunity to study early iron technnology, the evolution of smelting techniques, and the structural development of the furnaces.

Objectives: to establish a relative sequence of dates for three or four different types of furnace (one non-AML sample gave a date of 1900 ± 60 BP, which is the earliest for a shaft type smelting furnace in Britain) and to compare the results with archaeomagnetic dates which were also obtained.

HAR-970   2010 ± 60 BP

$\delta^{13}C$: –25.1 ‰

Sample: 1042, submitted on 26 November 1974

Material: charcoal.

Initial comment: from the shaft of the furnace (2:FC:2:602).

Calibrated date: 1σ : cal BC 100 – 60 cal AD
                    2σ : cal BC 180 – 110 cal AD

HAR-971   2140 ± 80 BP

$\delta^{13}C$: –25.7 ‰

Sample: 1043, submitted on 26 November 1974

Material: charcoal.

Initial comment: from the shaft of the furnace (607:2:FC:5).

Calibrated date: 1σ : cal BC 360 – 95
                    2σ : cal BC 390 – 20 cal AD

HAR-972   1840 ± 80 BP

$\delta^{13}C$: –24.7 ‰

Sample: 1044, submitted on 26 November 1974

Material: charcoal.

Initial comment: from the shaft of the furnace (2:FC:16).

Calibrated date: 1σ : cal AD 80 – 250
                    2σ : cal AD 0 – 380

HAR-973   1920 ± 70 BP

$\delta^{13}C$: –25.0 ‰

Sample: 1044CD, submitted on 26 November 1974

Material: charcoal.

Initial comment: from the shaft of the furnace (2:FC:16).

Calibrated date: 1σ : cal AD 10 – 135
                    2σ : cal BC 100 – 240 cal AD

HAR-974   1920 ± 70 BP

$\delta^{13}C$: –24.8 ‰

Sample: 1045AB, submitted on 26 November 1974

Material: charcoal.

Initial comment: from the shaft of the furnace (2:FC:8).

Calibrated date: 1σ : cal AD 10 – 135
                    2σ : cal BC 100 – 240 cal AD

HAR-975   1920 ± 70 BP

$\delta^{13}C$: –26.0 ‰

Sample: 1046, submitted on 26 November 1974

Material: charcoal.

Initial comment: from the shaft of the furnace (hearth 1:2).

Calibrated date: 1σ : cal AD 10 – 135
                    2σ : cal BC 100 – 240 cal AD

Curbridge: Coral Springs, Oxfordshire

Location: SP 337089
              Lat. 51.46.38 N; Long. 01.30.41 W

Excavator: R A Chambers (Oxford Archaeological Unit), 1975

Site: Romano-British cemetery overlying an earlier Romano-British rural settlement; the site is important in that it contains some 'head between the legs' burials; the cemetery demonstrates the later Romano-British change from north – south to west – east burial, and suggests the imposition or adoption of christian practices alongside continuing pagan ritual.

References: Chambers 1976b
                Chambers 1978, 252 (^{14}C)

Objectives: to establish the period of deposition.

Comments:
R A Chambers: the ^{14}C dates suggest that this part of the underlying settlement was deserted before the fourth century; this agrees with the recorded changes in burial practice.

HAR-2005   1840 ± 80 BP

$\delta^{13}C$: −21.4 ‰

Sample: GRAVEF27, submitted on 1 April 1976

Material: human bone.

Initial comment: from grave 27; expected date range Late Roman or Anglo-Saxon.

Calibrated date: 1σ : cal AD 80 – 250
                     2σ : cal AD 0 – 380

Final comments:
R A Chambers: at two standard deviations the range is acceptable: the archaeological evidence suggests that the cemetery is no earlier than the third century AD.

HAR-2006   1640 ± 70 BP

$\delta^{13}C$: −21.9 ‰

Sample: GRAVEF8, submitted on 1 April 1976

Material: human bone.

Initial comment: from grave 8; the expected date range is Late Roman or Anglo-Saxon.

Calibrated date: 1σ : cal AD 270 – 450
                     2σ : cal AD 240 – 560

Final comments:
R A Chambers: this result is quite acceptable.

Danebury, Hampshire

Location: SU 323377
              Lat. 51.08.14 N; Long. 01.32.18 W

Excavator: B Cunliffe (University of Oxford and the Department of the Environment), 1969 – 88

Site: a densely occupied Iron Age hillfort, the first extensively excavated 'developed' hillfort in southern Britain, with over 1100 pits and numerous buildings with ancillary structures, excavated in advance of tree-planting; contemporary sites in the area include Balksbury and Winklebury (see above and below).

References: Cunliffe 1984; 7, 12, 45 – 6, 96, 146, 172 – 3, 179, 190 – 8, 233 – 4, 242, 258, 314, 316, 325, 482, 549 – 50, M7 (^{14}C)
Orton 1983

Objectives: to obtain as close a chronology as possible for the ceramic sequence; the potential of the site was such that the dating programme was designed to demonstrate the degree of reliability of ^{14}C dating in late first-millennium BC contexts.

The samples were selected according to the following well-defined criteria:

1. the sample had to be well sealed and related to either a distinctive ceramic assemblage or clearly defined structural phase; preference was given to samples from stratified sequences.

2. where possible different types of material were selected for dating from a single context.

3. as many samples as possible were taken from closed contexts containing the same style of pottery.

Comments:
B Cunliffe: the suite of 65 acceptable dates from this site has been commented on at length in the excavation report (Cunliffe 1984, 190-8); the salient points only are summarised here.

Comparative measurements: the tests included two replicate measurements from the same charcoal samples, and twelve pairs of different sample types from the same features (charcoal/bone × 9; grain/charcoal × 1; grain/bone × 2). The former both fell within a statistically acceptable range of variation. Of the latter, in the two cases where the bone and charcoal samples gave widely differing results, the charcoal gave the more acceptable result; the number of paired grain/bone and grain/charcoal samples was too small to assess which is the more reliable.

Measurements of samples from the stratified sequence: nineteen samples from the sequence excavated 1977 – 8 were submitted (phases a – e; f; h – l), of which the four samples from phase k were from a single structure. Comments on these samples are included below.

The dating of the ceramic phases: statistical analysis of 54 of the total samples sumitted confirmed the dating of nine distinct ceramic phases, with nine dates each in ceramic phases 1 – 3 and ceramic phases 4 – 5, twelve dates in ceramic phase 6, and 24 in ceramic phase 7. Attempts to refine the dating of each ceramic phase using the 'maximum likelihood estimation technique' together with 'poor' estimation (proportion outside of range) are summarised and discussed (Cunliffe 1984, 193-8).

Calibration and chronology: calibration of the dates after Clark (1975) made little difference to the fit between the dates and the ceramic phases, but this relationship improved if the dates were calibrated after Suess (1970) or Ralph *et al* (1973); the results of this work are discussed (Cunliffe 1984, 195-8).

The finds and dating suggest that occupation of the site may have begun as early as the seventh century BC, although only one date is available for phases a – e. The dates for the rampart are of little help in dating the rampart sequence, but the available evidence suggests that phase 4 commenced at the beginning of the fourth century BC. The latest dates indicate that occupation probably ceased *c* 100 BC. How does the new calibration fit?

AML: in addition to those listed below seven samples were too small for dating by the standard process: HAR-967 (P574, layer 4), HAR-1439 (P860, layer 5), HAR-1441 (P829, layer 3), HAR-4326, HAR-4465 (P1135), HAR-4467 (P1040), and HAR-4469 (layer 472).

HAR-963   2180 ± 70 BP

$\delta^{13}C$: −25.2 ‰

Sample: DA70/4806, submitted on 26 November 1974

Material: charcoal.

Initial comment: from posthole 61, period 6 gate – trench 11, layer 81 (see also HAR-2030, HAR-4206, and HAR-4208).

Calibrated date: 1σ : cal BC 375 – 125
2σ : cal BC 400 – 50

Final comments:
B Cunliffe: this result is of little use in dating the entrance sequence due to the possible reuse of timbers. The expected date is in the second century BC.

HAR-964   2230 ± 70 BP

$\delta^{13}C$: −21.8 ‰

Sample: DA74/4807, submitted on 26 November 1974

Material: carbonised grain.

Initial comment: from pit P675, layer 6 (ceramic phase 6); associated with 362 sherds comprising a typical middle period pit group (mainly jars, with a few early saucepan pots).

Calibrated date: 1σ : cal BC 392 – 196
2σ : cal BC 400 – 110

Final comments:
B Cunliffe: the date lies within the expected range. Note: a number of samples were taken from pits producing pottery of only ceramic phase 6 to compare with those producing pottery of ceramic phase 7 to see if, statistically, ceramic phase 6 can be distinguished from ceramic phase 7. The results showed that, while there were some overlaps, the two phases could be separated.

HAR-965   2210 ± 70 BP

$\delta^{13}C$: −22.9 ‰

Sample: DA74/4808, submitted on 26 November 1974

Material: carbonised grain.

Initial comment: from a pit in association with pottery of the middle group – pit P757, layer 4 (ceramic phase 6).

Calibrated date: 1σ : cal BC 390 – 185
2σ : cal BC 400 – 100

Final comments:
B Cunliffe: the date is within the expected range.

HAR-966   3520 ± 70 BP

$\delta^{13}C$: −18.3 ‰

Sample: DA74/4809, submitted on 26 November 1974

Material: carbonised grain.

Initial comment: from a pit, associated with a group of decorated saucepan pots, which are typical of the later ceramic assemblage – pit P604, layer 2.

Calibrated date: 1σ : cal BC 1950 – 1750
2σ : cal BC 2090 – 1680

Final comments:
B Cunliffe: carbonate contamination was not totally removed. This result should be ignored.

Harwell: the $\delta^{13}C$ value is suspiciously low and reduces the reliability of this result; the sample was contaminated by geological material, probably chalk.

HAR-968   2140 ± 80 BP

$\delta^{13}C$: −23.7 ‰

Sample: DA74/4810, submitted on 26 November 1974

Material: carbonised grain.

Initial comment: from a pit, in association with plain saucepan pottery – pit P589 (ceramic phase 7); submitted to compare the result with HAR-4366.

Calibrated date: 1σ : cal BC 360 – 95
2σ : cal BC 390 – 20 cal AD

Final comments:
B Cunliffe: the date lies within the expected range. Note: this is one of the cases in which charred grain and charcoal were collected separately from one context for comparison.

Harwell: laboratory notes indicate some chalk nodules in the combusted material, but the $\delta^{13}C$ value gives no cause for concern.

HAR-1425   2040 ± 80 BP

$\delta^{13}C$: −26.7 ‰

Sample: DA75/450, submitted on 19 December 1975

Material: charcoal: *Quercus* sp., cf *Prunus* sp., and *Corylus/Alnus* sp. from twigs and small branches; c20% identified (C A Keepax).

Initial comment: from the fill of pit P802, layer 7.

Calibrated date: 1σ : cal BC 170 – 50 cal AD
2σ : cal BC 355 – 120 cal AD

Final comments:
B Cunliffe: this is just within the expected range but towards the later end; possible contamination from rootlets.

Harwell: some rootlets were present; they were removed as far as possible.

HAR-1426   1760 ± 80 BP

$\delta^{13}C$: −22.3 ‰

Sample: DA75/530, submitted on 19 December 1975

Material: charred cereal remains: mainly grain (C A Keepax).

Initial comment: from pit P858, layer 3 (ceramic phases 1 – 3).

Calibrated date: 1σ : cal AD 140 – 380
2σ : cal AD 80 – 430

Final comments:
B Cunliffe: an anomalous result (replicated with HAR-1801).

HAR-1440   2160 ± 70 BP

$\delta^{13}C$: −24.7 ‰

Sample: DA75/460+498, submitted on 19 December 1975

Material: charcoal: *Corylus/Alnus* sp., small branches with woodworm attack.

Initial comment: from small branches in the fill of pit P813, layer 10 (ceramic phase 7); associated with 202 sherds comprising a typical late group.

Calibrated date: 1σ : cal BC 365 – 110
2σ : cal BC 390 – 30

Final comments:
B Cunliffe: this is exactly within the expected range.

HAR-1442   2090 ± 90 BP

$\delta^{13}C$: –27.1 ‰

Sample: DA75/452, submitted on 19 December 1975

Material: charcoal: *Corylus/Alnus* sp. and hawthorn type from twigs or small branches; *c* 20% of three bags identified (C A Keepax).

Initial comment: from pit P809, layer 4 (ceramic phase 6).

Calibrated date: 1σ : cal BC 340 – 0 cal AD
2σ : cal BC 380 – 80 cal AD

Final comments:
B Cunliffe: this is within the expected range.

Harwell: the sample was a little smaller than the ideal size.

HAR-1801   1870 ± 90 BP

$\delta^{13}C$: –22.1 ‰

Sample: DA75/4811, submitted on 19 December 1975

Material: charred grain.

Initial comment: from pit P858, layer 3 (ceramic phases 1 – 3).

Calibrated date: 1σ : cal AD 30 – 240
2σ : cal BC 90 – 370 cal AD

Final comments:
B Cunliffe: this is outside the expected range (550 – 400 BC).

Harwell: repeat of HAR-1426.

HAR-2028   1980 ± 80 BP

$\delta^{13}C$: –25.3 ‰

Sample: DA76/4811, submitted on 15 February 1977

Material: charcoal: *Quercus* sp. and *Betula* sp., from large timbers; *c* 25% identified (C A Keepax).

Initial comment: from pit P891, layer 7 (ceramic phase 7), ?in association with pottery; submitted to the compare result with HAR-3743.

Calibrated date: 1σ : cal BC 95 – 90
2σ : cal BC 190 – 210

Final comments:
B Cunliffe: the expected range is 350 – 50 BC. The second date, HAR-3743, is a far better fit suggesting that this is anomalous.

HAR-2029   2530 ± 110 BP

$\delta^{13}C$: –25.1 ‰

Sample: DA76/1653, submitted on 15 February 1977

Material: charcoal: all *Quercus* sp. from large timbers; *c* 25% identified (C A Keepax).

Initial comment: from pit P868, layer 2 (ceramic phases 1 – 3).

Calibrated date: 1σ : cal BC 810 – 425
2σ : cal BC 910 – 390

Final comments:
B Cunliffe: this brackets the expected date range.

Harwell: a small sample accounts for the larger than normal error term.

HAR-2030   2290 ± 60 BP

$\delta^{13}C$: –25.3 ‰

Sample: DA76/1658, submitted on 15 February 1977

Material: charcoal: *Ulmus* sp., *Quercus* sp., and *Fraxinus* sp. from large timbers; *c* 25% of one of two bags identified (C A Keepax).

Initial comment: from layer 357 (ceramic phase 4), equivalent to second rampart extension of gatephase 4 (see also HAR-963, HAR-4206, and HAR-4208); submitted to compare the result with HAR-4372.

Calibrated date: 1σ : cal BC 400 – 265
2σ : cal BC 410 – 200

Final comments:
B Cunliffe: within the date bracket expected for the phase; however, the sample probably contained heartwood from a large tree, therefore making detailed argument about the date irrelevant.

HAR-2031   2030 ± 70 BP

$\delta^{13}C$: –23.0 ‰

Sample: DA76/1642, submitted on 15 February 1977

Material: charred grain.

Initial comment: from an Iron Age pit, P925, layer 8 (ceramic phase 7).

Calibrated date: 1σ : cal BC 150 – 50 cal AD
2σ : cal BC 330 – 110 cal AD

Final comments:
B Cunliffe: this is within the expected date range towards the more recent end.

HAR-2032   2370 ± 80 BP

$\delta^{13}C$: –25.5 ‰

Sample: DA76/1661, submitted on 15 February 1977

Material: charcoal: *Corylus/Alnus* sp., *Quercus* sp., *Fraxinus* sp., *Ulmus* sp., and hawthorn type (Rosaceae, sub-family Pomoideae), all from large timbers; *c* 20% of one bag of two identified (C A Keepax).

Initial comment: from pit P906, layer 7 (ceramic phases 1 – 3); associated with 248 sherds from bowls and jars.

Calibrated date: 1σ : cal BC 750 – 390
2σ : cal BC 780 – 250

Final comments:
B Cunliffe: this brackets the expected date range.

Harwell: repeated as HAR-2085.

HAR-2033   2460 ± 60 BP

δ¹³C: −25.5 ‰

Sample: DA76/1656, submitted on 15 February 1977

Material: charcoal: cf *Salix* sp. (twig- and branch-sized timbers), *Ulmus* sp. (large timbers), *Corylus/Alnus* sp. (twig- and branch-sized timbers), *Quercus* sp. (large timbers), and possibly *Ilex* sp. and hawthorn type (Rosaceae, sub-family Pomoideae); 25% of one bag of two identified (C A Keepax).

Initial comment: from pit P875, layer 3 (ceramic phases 1 – 3); submitted to compare the result with HAR-3726.

Calibrated date: 1σ : cal BC 770 – 410
                     2σ : cal BC 800 – 400

Final comments:
B Cunliffe: this brackets the expected date range.

HAR-2034   2200 ± 80 BP

δ¹³C: −24.5 ‰

Sample: DA76/1660, submitted on 15 February 1977

Material: charcoal: *Corylus/Alnus* sp. (twig- and branch-sized wood), *Quercus* sp. and *Fraxinus* sp. (twig-sized to large timbers), and cf *Salix* sp. (large timbers); *c* 20% identified (C A Keepax).

Initial comment: from pit P901, layer 5 (ceramic phase 7); submitted to compare the result with HAR-3733.

Calibrated date: 1σ : cal BC 390 – 170
                     2σ : cal BC 400 – 50

Final comments:
B Cunliffe: this is exactly within the expected date range.

HAR-2035   2260 ± 80 BP

δ¹³C: −25.4 ‰

Sample: DA76/1657, submitted on 15 February 1977

Material: charcoal: *Quercus* sp. from large timbers, and twiggy *Corylus/Alnus* sp.; 100% of one bag of two identified (C A Keepax).

Initial comment: from pit P885, layer 2 (ceramic phase 7); submitted to compare the result with HAR-3899.

Calibrated date: 1σ : cal BC 400 – 205
                     2σ : cal BC 490 – 120

Final comments:
B Cunliffe: this is exactly within the expected date range.

HAR-2036   2100 ± 90 BP

δ¹³C: −24.8 ‰

Sample: DA76/1667, submitted on 15 February 1977

Material: charcoal: *Quercus* sp. from large timbers, and *Corylus/Alnus* sp., twiggy; *c* 25% of one of two bags identified (C A Keepax).

Initial comment: from pit P925, layer 8 (ceramic phase 7).

Calibrated date: 1σ : cal BC 350 – 10
                     2σ : cal BC 390 – 80 cal AD

Final comments:
B Cunliffe: this brackets the expected date range.

HAR-2037   2060 ± 80 BP

δ¹³C: −27.4 ‰

Sample: DA76/1649, submitted on 15 February 1977

Material: charcoal: *Fraxinus* sp. (small branch), *Quercus* sp. (small branch and larger timber), and cf *Salix* sp. (large timber); *c* 20% of one bag of four identified (C A Keepax).

Initial comment: from pit P866, layer 2 (ceramic phase 6).

Calibrated date: 1σ : cal BC 190 – 15 cal AD
                     2σ : cal BC 360 – 90 cal AD

Final comments:
B Cunliffe: the one standard deviation ¹⁴C range is not within the expected period of *c* 350 – 250 BC. It could be a ceramic phase 7 pit without the diagnostic sherds.

HAR-2038   2090 ± 70 BP

δ¹³C: −25.2 ‰

Sample: DA76/1663, submitted on 15 February 1977

Material: charcoal: *Quercus* sp., *Fraxinus* sp., and *Betula* sp. from large timbers; twiggy hawthorn type (Rosaceae, sub-family Pomoideae) and *Corylus/Alnus* sp.; *c* 20% identified (C A Keepax).

Initial comment: from pit P912, layer 3 (ceramic phase 6).

Calibrated date: 1σ : cal BC 195 – 35
                     2σ : cal BC 365 – 60 cal AD

Final comments:
B Cunliffe: the one standard deviation ¹⁴C range is not within the expected period of *c* 350 – 250 BC. It could be a ceramic phase 7 pit without the diagnostic sherds.

HAR-2039   2420 ± 80 BP

δ¹³C: −25.0 ‰

Sample: DA76/1662, submitted on 15 February 1977

Material: charcoal: *Ulmus* sp., from a large timber; *Quercus* sp. and hawthorn type (Rosaceae, sub-family Pomoideae), twiggy; *c* 20% of one of two bags identified (C A Keepax).

Initial comment: from pit P878, layer 5 (ceramic phases 1 – 3), possibly in association with pottery.

Calibrated date: 1σ : cal BC 765 – 400
                     2σ : cal BC 800 – 380

Final comments:
B Cunliffe: this brackets the expected date range.

Harwell: the δ¹³C value is assumed.

HAR-2040   1830 ± 70 BP

δ¹³C: −24.8 ‰

Sample: DA76/1652, submitted on 15 February 1977

Material: charcoal: *Quercus* sp. from large timber and *Corylus/Alnus* sp., twiggy; *c* 20% identified (C A Keepax).

Initial comment: from pit P878, layer 8 (ceramic phase 7).

Calibrated date: 1σ : cal AD 90 – 250
2σ : cal AD 20 – 375

Final comments:
B Cunliffe: this gives a second-century AD date for a context which should be no earlier than the second century BC.

HAR-2085 2440 ± 70 BP

$\delta^{13}C$: –25.5 ‰

Sample: DA76/1661, submitted on 15 February 1977

Material: charcoal: *Corylus/Alnus* sp., *Fraxinus* sp. *Quercus* sp. *Ulmus* sp. and hawthorn type (Rosaceae, sub-family Pomoideae), all from large timbers; *c* 20% identified.

Initial comment: from pit P906, layer 7 (ceramic phases 1 – 3).

Calibrated date: 1σ : cal BC 770 – 405
2σ : cal BC 800 – 390

Final comments:
B Cunliffe: this brackets the expected date range.

Harwell: a replicate check on HAR-2032.

HAR-2564 2300 ± 70 BP

$\delta^{13}C$: –25.2 ‰

Sample: DA77/1738, submitted on 15 March 1977

Material: charcoal: apparently from large timbers.

Initial comment: from pit P978, layer 1 (ceramic phase 7).

Calibrated date: 1σ : cal BC 405 – 265
2σ : cal BC 750 – 200

Final comments:
B Cunliffe: the expected date lies within this range.

HAR-2567 2210 ± 60 BP

$\delta^{13}C$: –23.4 ‰

Sample: DA77/1762, submitted on 15 March 1977

Material: charcoal: from a single piece of wood.

Initial comment: from pit P944, layer 1 (ceramic phases 1 – 3).

Calibrated date: 1σ : cal BC 385 – 190
2σ : cal BC 400 – 110

Final comments:
B Cunliffe: the expected date would be *c* 550 – 400 BC. It is possible that the radiocarbon date is acceptable and that the diagnostic sherds of ceramic phases 4 – 7 were not present, suggesting an earlier archaeological date.

HAR-2568 2090 ± 60 BP

$\delta^{13}C$: –24.9 ‰

Sample: DA77/1744, submitted on 15 March 1977

Material: charcoal: apparently from large timbers.

Initial comment: from timbers from F40 (ceramic phase 7); from the stratified sequence, phase l (see HAR-2573, HAR-2970, and HAR-4337).

Calibrated date: 1σ : cal BC 190 – 40
2σ : cal BC 360 – 20 cal AD

Final comments:
B Cunliffe: this is within the expected date range.

HAR-2571 2110 ± 80 BP

$\delta^{13}C$: unknown

Sample: DA77/1739, submitted on 15 March 1977

Material: charcoal.

Initial comment: from pit P955, layer 2 (ceramic phase 7).

Calibrated date: 1σ : cal BC 350 – 40
2σ : cal BC 380 – 60 cal AD

Final comments:
B Cunliffe: this is exactly within the expected date range.

HAR-2573 2060 ± 70 BP

$\delta^{13}C$: –24.1 ‰

Sample: DA77/1752, submitted on 15 March 1977

Material: charcoal: apparently from large timbers.

Initial comment: from pit P393 (ceramic phase 7); from the stratified sequence, phase l (see HAR-4337 from the same context, HAR-2568, and HAR-2970).

Calibrated date: 1σ : cal BC 180 – 10 cal AD
2σ : cal BC 355 – 80 cal AD

Final comments:
B Cunliffe: this is consistent with HAR-2568, HAR-2970, and HAR-4337 and within the expected range.

HAR-2581 2160 ± 80 BP

$\delta^{13}C$: –25.0 ‰

Sample: DA77/1728, submitted on 15 March 1977

Material: charcoal: apparently from large timbers.

Initial comment: from pit P945, layer 1 (ceramic phases 1 – 3).

Calibrated date: 1σ : cal BC 370 – 105
2σ : cal BC 400 – 0 cal AD

Final comments:
B Cunliffe: this is later than would be expected (*c* 550 – 400 BC). It could be that the pit was later than ceramic phases 1 – 3 and that the distinctive pottery was absent.

Harwell: the $\delta^{13}C$ value is assumed.

HAR-2585 2330 ± 60 BP

$\delta^{13}C$: –24.0 ‰

Sample: DA77/1724, submitted on 15 March 1977

Material: charcoal: apparently from large timbers.

Initial comment: from pit P936, layer 4 (ceramic phases 1 – 3).

Calibrated date: 1σ : cal BC 405 – 385
2σ : cal BC 755 – 250

Final comments:
B Cunliffe: this date is just within the expected range.

HAR-2586 2490 ± 60 BP

$δ^{13}C:$ −25.2 ‰

Sample: DA75/1749, submitted on 15 March 1977

Material: charcoal.

Initial comment: from layer 313.

Calibrated date: 1σ : cal BC 790 – 515
2σ : cal BC 800 – 400

Final comments:
B Cunliffe: this is acceptable.

HAR-2969 2120 ± 70 BP

$δ^{13}C:$ −23.5 ‰

Sample: DA78/1826, submitted on 29 November 1978

Material: carbonised grain.

Initial comment: from pit P1089, layer 5 (ceramic phase 7); submitted to compare the result with HAR-2975.

Calibrated date: 1σ : cal BC 350 – 90
2σ : cal BC 380 – 20 cal AD

Final comments:
B Cunliffe: this is exactly within the expected range.

HAR-2970 2060 ± 60 BP

$δ^{13}C:$ −24.9 ‰

Sample: DA78/1904, submitted on 29 November 1978

Material: charcoal: *Quercus* sp., *Fraxinus* sp., and ?*Prunus* sp. from mature timbers; *Corylus/Alnus* sp. from twigs; *c* 25% identified.

Initial comment: from layer 522 (ceramic phase 7); from the stratified sequence, phase l (see HAR-2568, HAR-2573, and HAR-4337).

Calibrated date: 1σ : cal BC 170 – 0 cal AD
2σ : cal BC 340 – 70 cal AD

Final comments:
B Cunliffe: this is consistent with comparable dates and within the expected range.

HAR-2971 2110 ± 70 BP

$δ^{13}C:$ −24.1 ‰

Sample: DA78/1908, submitted on 29 November 1978

Material: charcoal: *Quercus* sp. from mature timbers, *c* 25% identified (C A Keepax).

Initial comment: from posthole 3619 (ceramic phase 6).

Calibrated date: 1σ : cal BC 340 – 50
2σ : cal BC 380 – 20 cal AD

Final comments:
B Cunliffe: this is within the expected range.

HAR-2972 2170 ± 70 BP

$δ^{13}C:$ −25.6 ‰

Sample: DA78/1942, submitted on 29 November 1978

Material: charcoal: *Quercus* sp. and *Populus/Salix* sp. from mature timbers; *Corylus/Alnus* sp., twig of 10 years growth (C A Keepax).

Initial comment: from pit P1078, layer 10 (ceramic phase 7); submitted to compare the result with HAR-2974.

Calibrated date: 1σ : cal BC 370 – 115
2σ : cal BC 390 – 40

Final comments:
B Cunliffe: this is within the expected range, but see HAR-2974.

HAR-2973 2000 ± 70 BP

$δ^{13}C:$ −24.4 ‰

Sample: DA78/1898, submitted on 29 November 1978

Material: charcoal: *Quercus* sp. from mature timbers; *c* 25% of four bags identified (C A Keepax).

Initial comment: from layer 450 (ceramic phase 7).

Calibrated date: 1σ : cal BC 100 – 70 cal AD
2σ : cal BC 190 – 130 cal AD

Final comments:
B Cunliffe: this is within the latter part of the expected range.

HAR-2974 1990 ± 70 BP

$δ^{13}C:$ −22.4 ‰

Sample: DA78/1943, submitted on 29 November 1978

Material: charcoal, grain, and soil.

Initial comment: from pit P1078, layer 10 (ceramic phase 7); submitted to compare the result with HAR-2972.

Calibrated date: 1σ : cal BC 95 – 75
2σ : cal BC 180 – 130

Final comments:
B Cunliffe: this is just within the expected range, but see HAR-4972.

HAR-2975 2370 ± 70 BP

$δ^{13}C:$ −26.2 ‰

Sample: DA78/1827, submitted on 29 November 1978

Material: charcoal: *Quercus* sp. from mature timbers; *c* 50% identified (C A Keepax).

Initial comment: from pit P1089, layer 5 (ceramic phase 7); submitted to compare the result with HAR-2969.

Calibrated date: 1σ : cal BC 525 – 390
2σ : cal BC 770 – 265

Final comments:
B Cunliffe: the range at two standard deviations of confidence includes the expected date range.

HAR-3021   2210 ± 70 BP

$\delta^{13}C$: −25.0 ‰

Sample: DA78/1901, submitted on 29 November 1978

Material: charcoal: *Quercus* sp., *Fraxinus* sp., and ?*Prunus* sp. from mature timbers; *Corylus/Alnus* sp. from twig-sized wood; *c* 25% identified (C A Keepax).

Initial comment: from layer 478 (ceramic phase 6), which was deposited some considerable time after the quarry had been dug; from the stratified sequence, phase h (see HAR-4339 from the same context).

Calibrated date: 1σ : cal BC 390 − 185
                    2σ : cal BC 400 − 100

Final comments:
B Cunliffe: one of the earliest dates for this layer (see HAR-3022). This is within the expected range. The bone date for this context, HAR-4439, is not acceptable − it is too old.

HAR-3022   2210 ± 70 BP

$\delta^{13}C$: −24.9 ‰

Sample: DA78/1903, submitted on 29 November 1978

Material: charcoal: *Quercus* sp. and *Corylus* sp. from mature and twig-sized wood; Rosaceae, sub-family Pomoideae, twig-sized wood only; *c* 25% identified (C A Keepax).

Initial comment: from layer 511 (ceramic phase 6); from a layer deposited some considerable time after the quarry had been dug; from the stratified sequence, phase h (see HAR-4343).

Calibrated date: 1σ : cal BC 390 − 185
                    2σ : cal BC 400 − 100

Final comments:
B Cunliffe: this is one of the earliest dates for this layer (see HAR-3021). This is within the expected range. The bone date for this context, HAR-4343, is not acceptable − it is too old.

HAR-3026   2450 ± 80 BP

$\delta^{13}C$: −25.1 ‰

Sample: DA26/1946, submitted on 29 November 1978

Material: charcoal: mainly *Ulmus* sp. with *Fraxinus* sp., *Acer* sp., and Rosaceae, sub-family Pomoideae, from mature timbers; *c* 25% identified (C A Keepax).

Initial comment: from pit P1131, layer 6 (ceramic phases 1 − 3); from the stratified sequence, phases a − e (see HAR-4470). The sample was obtained after flotation in water.

Calibrated date: 1σ : cal BC 780 − 405
                    2σ : cal BC 800 − 390

Final comments:
B Cunliffe: this brackets the expected range. It is from an earlier context that HAR-4970 but in the same stratified sequence.

HAR-3027   2130 ± 60 BP

$\delta^{13}C$: −24.8 ‰

Sample: DA78/1932-36, submitted on 29 November 1978

Material: charcoal: *Quercus* sp. from mature and twig-sized wood, *Fraxinus* sp. from mature timber, and *Corylus/Alnus* sp. from twig-sized wood (C A Keepax).

Initial comment: from pit P1115 (6, 7, 8, 10, and 13) (ceramic phase 7 from the same context); from the stratified sequence, phase i (see HAR-3901).

Calibrated date: 1σ : cal BC 350 − 100
                    2σ : cal BC 380 − 10

Final comments:
B Cunliffe: this is exactly within the expected range.

HAR-3726   2270 ± 70 BP

$\delta^{13}C$: −23.0 ‰

Sample: DA76/4811, submitted on 26 March 1980

Material: bone.

Initial comment: from pit P875, layer 3 (ceramic phases 1 − 3); submitted to compare the result with HAR-2033.

Calibrated date: 1σ : cal BC 400 − 235
                    2σ : cal BC 410 − 180

Final comments:
B Cunliffe: this is later than expected. The charcoal date from the same context, HAR-2033, is entirely acceptable.

HAR-3733   2170 ± 70 BP

$\delta^{13}C$: −23.8 ‰

Sample: DA76/4812, submitted on 26 March 1980

Material: bone.

Initial comment: from pit P901, layer 5 (ceramic phase 7); submitted to compare the result with HAR-2034.

Calibrated date: 1σ : cal BC 370 − 115
                    2σ : cal BC 390 − 40

Final comments:
B Cunliffe: this is within the expected range. It compares well with the charcoal date HAR-2034.

HAR-3743   2120 ± 70 BP

$\delta^{13}C$: −22.2 ‰

Sample: DA76/4813, submitted on 26 March 1980

Material: bone.

Initial comment: from pit P891, layer 7 (ceramic phase 7); submitted to compare the result with HAR-2028.

Calibrated date: 1σ : cal BC 350 − 90
                    2σ : cal BC 380 − 20 cal AD

Final comments:
B Cunliffe: this is within the expected range. The charcoal date, HAR-2028, just overlaps and is at the late extremity of what was expected.

HAR-3899   1900 ± 60 BP

$\delta^{13}C$: −23.1 ‰

Sample: DA76/4814, submitted on 26 March 1980

Material: bone.

Initial comment: from pit P885, layer 2 (ceramic phase 7); submitted to compare the result with HAR-2035.

Calibrated date: 1σ : cal AD 30 – 140
2σ : cal BC 40 – 240 cal AD

Final comments:
B Cunliffe: the expected range would be 350 – 50 BC. This date is much too late.

HAR-3901   2040 ± 70 BP

$\delta^{13}C$: –23.0 ‰

Sample: DA78/4815, submitted on 26 March 1980

Material: bone.

Initial comment: from pit P1115, layers 4 and 6 (ceramic phase 7 from same context); from the stratified sequence, phase i (see HAR-3027).

Calibrated date: 1σ : cal BC 160 – 20 cal AD
2σ : cal BC 340 – 90 cal AD

Final comments:
B Cunliffe: this is within the expected range. The comparison with the charcoal date, HAR-3027, is acceptable but not close.

HAR-4206   2400 ± 70 BP

$\delta^{13}C$: –27.1 ‰

Sample: DA70/1290

Material: charcoal, stored with a card label next to the charcoal: *Quercus* sp. from mature timbers.

Initial comment: from posthole 23, period 6 gate (trench 10, layer 20); see also HAR-963, HAR-2030, and HAR-4208.

Calibrated date: 1σ : cal BC 755 – 400
2σ : cal BC 790 – 380

Final comments:
B Cunliffe: of little value in dating the entrance sequence due to possible reuse of the timber. The expected date would be in the second century BC.

HAR-4207   2650 ± 120 BP

$\delta^{13}C$: –25.8 ‰

Sample: DA70/1291

Material: charcoal, stored with a card label next to the charcoal: all *Quercus* sp. from mature timbers; 23.5g out of 33.8g was identified.

Initial comment: from trench 11, layer 30, ph 20.

Calibrated date: 1σ : cal BC 920 – 780
2σ : cal BC 1060 – 410

Final comments:
B Cunliffe: this is too early.

Harwell: a small sample – only a third of the optimum size, therefore there is a larger error term than usual.

HAR-4208   2380 ± 70 BP

$\delta^{13}C$: –25.2 ‰

Sample: DA70/1292

Material: charcoal: *Quercus* sp. from mature timbers; many pieces had rotted to some extent.

Initial comment: from posthole 16, period 6 gate (trench 11, layer 28); see also HAR-963, HAR-2030, and HAR-4206.

Calibrated date: 1σ : cal BC 750 – 395
2σ : cal BC 770 – 270

HAR-4243   2250 ± 70 BP

$\delta^{13}C$: –25.1 ‰

Sample: DA78/1910, submitted on 14 February 1981

Material: charcoal: *Quercus* sp. from mature timber; *c* 25% of two out of three bags was identified (C A Keepax).

Initial comment: from posthole 3627 (ceramic phase 6), part of a five-post structure (PS1); very likely to represent the remains of the actual structure (see also HAR-4243, HAR-4244, and HAR-4278); from the stratified sequence, phase k.

Calibrated date: 1σ : cal BC 395 – 205
2σ : cal BC 410 – 125

Final comments:
B Cunliffe: this date is within the expected range of *c* 400 – 300 BC: see comment for HAR-4279.

HAR-4244   2120 ± 80 BP

$\delta^{13}C$: –24.8 ‰

Sample: DA78/1912, submitted on 14 February 1981

Material: charcoal: *Quercus* sp. from mature timbers; *c* 50% of two out of five bags identified (C A Keepax).

Initial comment: from subrectangular posthole 3629 (ceramic phase 6), part of a five-post structure (PS1); very likely to represent the remains of the actual structure (see also HAR-4243, HAR-4278, and HAR-4279); from the stratified sequence, phase k.

Calibrated date: 1σ : cal BC 355 – 50
2σ : cal BC 390 – 50 cal AD

Final comments:
B Cunliffe: the date is within the expected range: see comment for HAR-4279.

HAR-4278   2470 ± 90 BP

$\delta^{13}C$: –24.6 ‰

Sample: DA78/1911, submitted on 14 February 1981

Material: charcoal: *Quercus* sp. from large timbers; *c* 50% identified (C A Keepax).

Initial comment: from posthole 3628 (ceramic phase 6), part of a five-post structure (PS1); very likely to represent the remains of the actual structure (see also HAR-4243, HAR-4244, and HAR-4279); from the stratified sequence, phase k.

Calibrated date: 1σ : cal BC 795 – 405
2σ : cal BC 820 – 390

Final comments:
B Cunliffe: this is too early: see comment for HAR-4279.

HAR-4279 2280 ± 70 BP

$\delta^{13}C$: −25.9 ‰

Sample: DA78/1909, submitted on 14 February 1981

Material: charcoal: *Quercus* sp. from large timber, possibly part of the actual structure; also some *Corylus/Alnus* sp. twig; c 50% of 2 bags of 3 were identified.

Initial comment: from subrectangular posthole 3624 (ceramic phase 6), part of a five-post structure (PS1); the hazel/alder charcoal may possibly represent the remains of charred wattles, but could be unrelated to the structure; from the stratified sequence phase k (see also HAR-4243, HAR-4244, and HAR-4278).

Calibrated date: 1σ : cal BC 400 – 250
    2σ : cal BC 490 – 180

Final comments:
B Cunliffe: this lies within the expected range. The four dates, HAR-4243, HAR-4244, HAR-4278, and HAR-4279 are all for timber of a single structure. Their range is possibly the result of old timbers being reused.

HAR-4325 2270 ± 90 BP

$\delta^{13}C$: −28.2 ‰

Sample: DA74/311, submitted on 30 March 1981

Material: charcoal: *Quercus* sp., from mature and twig-sized wood.

Initial comment: from pit P554, layer 9 (ceramic phase 5).

Calibrated date: 1σ : cal BC 400 – 205
    2σ : cal BC 750 – 110

Final comments:
B Cunliffe: this is exactly within the expected range.

HAR-4327 2120 ± 80 BP

$\delta^{13}C$: −25.4 ‰

Sample: DA71/1287, submitted on 30 March 1981

Material: charcoal: *Quercus* sp., from mature timbers with very closely spaced rings (one has 20 rings, another 35); *Corylus/Alnus* sp. (two twigs, 6- and 7-year-old); *Corylus/Alnus* sp. small branches and twiggy material (two twigs, 4- and 5-year-old).

Initial comment: from pit P35, layer 2 (ceramic phase 4).

Calibrated date: 1σ : cal BC 350 – 90
    2σ : cal BC 380 – 20 cal AD

Final comments:
B Cunliffe: this is later than expected. It is possible that the pit belongs to a later ceramic phase and is lacking diagnostic sherds.

HAR-4328 2330 ± 90 BP

$\delta^{13}C$: −26.5 ‰

Sample: DA70/1289, submitted on 30 March 1981

Material: charcoal: *Quercus* sp. mainly from mature timbers.

Initial comment: from pit P19, layer 51 (ceramic phase 5); associated with 241 sherds, the latest of which include bipartite jars.

Calibrated date: 1σ : cal BC 490 – 370
    2σ : cal BC 770 – 190

Final comments:
B Cunliffe: this is exactly within the expected range.

HAR-4329 2270 ± 90 BP

$\delta^{13}C$: unknown

Sample: DA77/1289, submitted on 30 March 1981

Material: charcoal: *Quercus* sp. from mature timbers.

Initial comment: from pit P932, layers 5 and 9 (ceramic phase 5).

Calibrated date: 1σ : cal BC 400 – 205
    2σ : cal BC 750 – 110

Final comments:
B Cunliffe: this is within the expected range.

HAR-4330 2580 ± 80 BP

$\delta^{13}C$: unknown

Sample: DA77/1734-35, submitted on 30 March 1981

Material: charcoal: *Quercus* sp. from mature timbers.

Initial comment: from pit P969, layers 1 and 3 (ceramic phase 4).

Calibrated date: 1σ : cal BC 820 – 610
    2σ : cal BC 900 – 420

Final comments:
B Cunliffe: this is too early; it is inconsistent with the other dates from the same phase.

HAR-4331 2340 ± 100 BP

$\delta^{13}C$: −24.7 ‰

Sample: DA71/1285, submitted on 30 March 1981

Material: charcoal.

Initial comment: from pit P51, layer 3 (ceramic phase 4).

Calibrated date: 1σ : cal BC 520 – 370
    2σ : cal BC 790 – 190

Final comments:
B Cunliffe: this is exactly within the expected range.

HAR-4337 2150 ± 70 BP

$\delta^{13}C$: −25.6 ‰

Sample: DA77/4816, submitted on 14 February 1981

Material: bone.

Initial comment: from layer 393 (ceramic phase 6); from the stratified sequence, phase l (see HAR-2573 from the same context, HAR-2568, and HAR-2970).

Calibrated date: 1σ : cal BC 360 – 105
    2σ : cal BC 390 – 10

Final comments:
B Cunliffe: this is within the expected range.

Harwell: the $\delta^{13}C$ is very negative for bone.

HAR-4339   2380 ± 90 BP

$\delta^{13}C$: −22.7 ‰

Sample: DA78/4818, submitted on 30 February 1981

Material: bone.

Initial comment: from layer 478 (ceramic phase 6); from the stratified sequence, phase h (see HAR-3021 from the same context).

Calibrated date: 1σ : cal BC 755 − 390
                    2σ : cal BC 790 − 235

Final comments:
B Cunliffe: this is not acceptable at the one standard deviation range: it is too early.

HAR-4343   2520 ± 80 BP

$\delta^{13}C$: −22.5 ‰

Sample: DA78/4818, submitted on 14 February 1981

Material: bone.

Initial comment: from layer 511 (ceramic phase 6); from the stratified sequence, phase h (see HAR-3022 from the same context).

Calibrated date: 1σ : cal BC 800 − 520
                    2σ : cal BC 830 − 400

Final comments:
B Cunliffe: this is inconsistent with the other dates from the same phase. It is not acceptable; it is too early.

HAR-4366   2320 ± 100 BP

$\delta^{13}C$: unknown

Sample: DA74/4819, submitted on 14 February 1981

Material: charcoal.

Initial comment: from pit P589 (ceramic phase 7); submitted to compare the result with HAR-968.

Calibrated date: 1σ : cal BC 485 − 260
                    2σ : cal BC 770 − 170

Final comments:
B Cunliffe: this date brackets the expected range but the grain date, HAR-968, fits better within the expected range.

HAR-4372   2300 ± 90 BP

$\delta^{13}C$: unknown

Sample: DA76/4820, submitted on 14 February 1981

Material: bone.

Initial comment: from layer 357 (ceramic phase 4); submitted to compare the result with HAR-2030.

Calibrated date: 1σ : cal BC 410 − 250
                    2σ : cal BC 760 − 170

Final comments:
B Cunliffe: this is consistent with the charcoal date, HAR-2030, and just within the expected range at the one standard deviation level of confidence.

Harwell: the $\delta^{13}C$ is very negative for bone.

HAR-4464   2300 ± 70 BP

$\delta^{13}C$: unknown

Sample: 1951, submitted on 30 March 1981

Material: charcoal: *Quercus* sp., *Ulmus* sp., *Prunus* sp., *Alnus* sp., and *Ilex aquifolium* L. (all mature timber); *Acer* sp., *Corylus* sp., and Rosaceae, sub-family Pomoideae, or *Crataegus* sp. (mixture of mature and twiggy wood).

Initial comment: from pit P1131, layer 4 (ceramic phases 1 − 3).

Calibrated date: 1σ : cal BC 405 − 265
                    2σ : cal BC 750 − 200

Final comments:
B Cunliffe: this is within the expected range at two standard deviations of confidence (550-450 BC).

HAR-4466   2220 ± 90 BP

$\delta^{13}C$: unknown

Sample: 1906, submitted on 30 March 1981

Material: charcoal: *Quercus* sp. (mature) and Rosaceae, sub-family Pomoideae, or *Crataegus* sp. (twiggy).

Initial comment: layer 568 (ceramic phase 6); from the stratified sequence, phase h.

Calibrated date: 1σ : cal BC 395 − 180
                    2σ : cal BC 410 − 50

Final comments:
B Cunliffe: this is exactly within the expected range.

Harwell: a small sample accounts for the larger than normal error term.

HAR-4468   2330 ± 70 BP

$\delta^{13}C$: unknown

Sample: 1907, submitted on 30 March 1981

Material: charcoal: *Quercus* sp., mainly of moderate maturity but varying from twiggy to mature.

Initial comment: from posthole 3613, layer 1 (ceramic phase 6).

Calibrated date: 1σ : cal BC 410 − 380
                    2σ : cal BC 760 − 210

Final comments:
B Cunliffe: this is exactly within the expected range.

HAR-4470   2180 ± 90 BP

$\delta^{13}C$: unknown

Sample: 1902, submitted on 30 March 1981

Material: charcoal: *Quercus* sp. (mainly mature with one twig), *Corylus* sp. (large twig/small trunk), and *Acer* sp. (mainly twiggy).

Initial comment: from F49, layer 497 (ceramic phases 4 − 5); from the stratified sequence, phases a − e (see HAR-3026).

Calibrated date: 1σ : cal BC 385 – 110
2σ : cal BC 400 – 0 cal AD

Final comments:
B Cunliffe: this is within the expected range for ceramic phases 4 – 5 (ie 450 – 350 BC).

Dorchester: Wollaston House, Dorset

Location: SY 6990 approx
Lat. 50.42.30 N; Long. 02.26.21 W

Excavator: D Batchelor (Central Excavation Unit), 1977

Site: Roman baths.

Objectives: to date an early robbing phase.

Comments:
AML: one sample, HAR-2857 (16-780), has been returned.

HAR-2856   1620 ± 70 BP

$\delta^{13}C$: –20.4 ‰

Sample: 16-486, submitted by N Balaam on 9 October 1978

Material: human bone.

Initial comment: from a human skeleton found on a burnt occupation layer, in the midst of the robbed material, associated with a second phase room.

Calibrated date: 1σ : cal AD 350 – 535
2σ : cal AD 250 – 600

Final comments:
D Batchelor: the pottery and coin evidence, recovered from the stratigraphic sequence associated with this deposit, suggests a date in the first half of the fifth century AD.

Droitwich: Friar Street, Hereford and Worcester

Location: SO 89746349
Lat. 52.16.09 N; Long. 02.09.01 W

Excavator: A Hunt (Hereford and Worcester County Museum), 1975

Site: Iron Age salt production; Roman domestic occupation; possible Saxo-Norman industrial activity; medieval and post-medieval domestic occupation.

References: Radiocarbon **27**, 91 (^{14}C)

Objectives: to cross confirm with the dendrochronological date for comparison with similar structures on this and other sites in Droitwich.

HAR-2263   1950 ± 70 BP

$\delta^{13}C$: –27.1 ‰

Sample: DF1, submitted by R Morgan on 1 June 1977

Material: wood: *Quercus* sp., outermost 20 sapwood growth rings of waterlogged board 262/112 – very close to felling year; the rings have now been dated absolutely to AD 19 – 45.

Initial comment: from a board deposited with broken stakes (730), second-century AD pottery and briquetage in the ashy fill of a pit lined with timber and clay, possibly a brine storage and settling tank; the board may have been part of the superstructure of the pit. Expected date is first to second century AD.

Calibrated date: 1σ : cal BC 35 – 120
2σ : cal BC 110 – 220 cal AD

HAR-2264   800 ± 70 BP

$\delta^{13}C$: –27.2 ‰

Sample: DF2, submitted by R Morgan on 1 June 1977

Material: wood: outermost 15 sapwood rings – close to year of felling .

Initial comment: from a young stake (444) driven into the base of a cess pit with waterlogged fill containing eleventh- or twelfth-century pottery.

Calibrated date: 1σ : cal AD 1170 – 1270
2σ : cal AD 1040 – 1290

Final comments:
A Hunt: this result supports the archaeological evidence.

Droitwich: Old Bowling Green, Hereford and Worcester

Location: SO 897635
Lat. 52.16.09 N; Long. 02.09.03 W

Excavator: J Sawle (Hereford and Worcester County Museum), 1977 – 9

Site: Iron Age and Roman salt production site.

Objectives: the date is for comparison with similar structures on this and other sites in Droitwich.

Comments:
AML: sixteen further samples from the other barrels submitted in 1983.

HAR-4084   1770 ± 70 BP

$\delta^{13}C$: –27.2 ‰

Sample: 600-1102, submitted on 29 July 1980

Material: wood.

Initial comment: from part of a wooden barrel stave (one of five barrels, now being conserved).

Calibrated date: 1σ : cal AD 140 – 345
2σ : cal AD 80 – 420

Final comments:
J Sawle: this result agrees with other dating methods.

Durham: Saddler Street, Sutton Sale Rooms, County Durham

Location: NZ 275424
Lat. 54.46.36 N; Long. 01.34.21 W

Excavator: M Carver (University of Durham), 1974

Site: early medieval town with a stratified sequence of sand and midden deposits c 3.0 – 6.0m below the present ground surface, sealing very well preserved wattle fences.

References: Carver 1979; 13, table 3, fig 11 (^{14}C)

Objectives:

1. to obtain independent dating for the earliest and latest activities on the site.

2. to date the principle structures which were not associated with finds.

3. to date the two principal groups of pottery which have no direct parallels.

HAR-599   900 ± 80 BP

$\delta^{13}C:$ –27.3 ‰

Sample: L1574, submitted on 27 April 1974

Material: wood.

Initial comment: from leather working debris over a stone platform, which contained the second pottery group; the estimated date is twelfth century.

Calibrated date: 1σ : cal AD 1025 – 1225
2σ : cal AD 980 – 1270

HAR-601   1090 ± 130 BP

$\delta^{13}C:$ –24.0 ‰

Sample: L1574, submitted on 27 April 1974

Material: leather.

Initial comment: as HAR-599.

Calibrated date: 1σ : cal AD 790 – 1030
2σ : cal AD 660 – 1220

Final comments:
Harwell: a small sample accounts for the larger than normal error term.

HAR-602   970 ± 80 BP

$\delta^{13}C:$ –27.6 ‰

Sample: L1562, submitted on 27 April 1974

Material: wood.

Initial comment: from brushwood debris; the estimated date is tenth century.

Calibrated date: 1σ : cal AD 990 – 1165
2σ : cal AD 890 – 1230

HAR-826   920 ± 80 BP

$\delta^{13}C:$ –27.1 ‰

Sample: DC741591, submitted on 12 September 1974

Material: wood: hazel (*Corylus* sp.) and birch (*Betula* sp.).

Initial comment: from one of three wattle fences built over the fill of a possible storm drain (1796); the estimated date is tenth century or earlier.

Calibrated date: 1σ : cal AD 1020 – 1220
2σ : cal AD 970 – 1270

HAR-827   1010 ± 70 BP

$\delta^{13}C:$ –28.5 ‰

Sample: DC741625, submitted on 12 September 1974

Material: wood, supplied wet and muddy: *Salix* sp..

Initial comment: from the brushwood fence lining of a shallow scoop; the estimated date is tenth century or earlier.

Calibrated date: 1σ : cal AD 975 – 1040
2σ : cal AD 890 – 1170

HAR-828   740 ± 70 BP

$\delta^{13}C:$ –29.3 ‰

Sample: DC741689, submitted on 12 September 1974

Material: wood, smaller of two pieces supplied.

Initial comment: from a wattle-lined pit, cutting organic debris (1574); the latest feature on the site. The estimated date is thirteenth century.

Calibrated date: 1σ : cal AD 1230 – 1285
2σ : cal AD 1170 – 1390

HAR-829   1010 ± 80 BP

$\delta^{13}C:$ –28.6 ‰

Sample: DC741757, submitted on 12 September 1974

Material: wood, supplied wet and muddy.

Initial comment: from a wattle wall; the estimated date is tenth century or earlier.

Calibrated date: 1σ : cal AD 970 – 1150
2σ : cal AD 880 – 1210

HAR-830   830 ± 80 BP

$\delta^{13}C:$ –27.0 ‰

Sample: DC741783, submitted on 12 September 1974

Material: wood.

Initial comment: from a pit fill; the estimated date is tenth century or earlier.

Calibrated date: 1σ : cal AD 1060 – 1270
2σ : cal AD 1020 – 1290

Final comments:
M Carver: this date suggests that this badly stratified posthole belongs to structure S3 or S4, likely to be late eleventh century at the latest.

HAR-831   1490 ± 100 BP

$\delta^{13}C:$ –26.8 ‰

Sample: DC741796, submitted on 12 September 1974

Material: wood and charcoal, pieces picked out from the material supplied.

Initial comment: from the fill of a shallow scoop cut into natural – interpreted as a storm drain; the estimated date is tenth century or earlier.

Calibrated date: 1σ : cal AD 430 – 650
2σ : cal AD 350 – 690

Final comments:
M Carver: the wood appears to have been already 300 years old when discarded in the storm drain.

Eaton, Leicestershire

Location: SK 762265
Lat. 52.49.49 N; Long. 00.52.08 W

Excavator: P Clay (Leicestershire Museums Archaeological Unit), 1979

Site: Bronze Age multiphase ring ditch.

References: Clay 1981c, 44 (^{14}C)

Objectives: to provide a date for the enlargement of the burial mound.

HAR-3941   3450 ± 70 BP

$δ^{13}C$: –26.5 ‰

Sample: 34F1134, submitted on 7 July 1980

Material: charcoal, found in association with cremated human bone: *Corylus/Alnus* sp., mainly twig and branch (C A Keepax).

Initial comment: from the third central cremation burial which postdates two others and so may be a later insertion, connected with the later enlargement phase of the monument.

Calibrated date: 1σ : cal BC 1885 – 1685
2σ : cal BC 1950 – 1610

Final comments:
P Clay: within the expected date range.

HAR-3942   3430 ± 80 BP

$δ^{13}C$: –26.8 ‰

Sample: 11F19, submitted on 7 July 1980

Material: charcoal: *Corylus/Alnus* sp., ?elder (*Sambucus nigra* L.), *Quercus* sp., *Fraxinus excelsior* L., conifer (?yew, *Taxus baccata* L.); some twig/branch but mainly from large timbers (C A Keepax).

Initial comment: from a hearth feature in the partially silted second barrow ditch; after the initial construction of the mound, but before the subsequent enlargements of the Bronze Age multi-ring barrow.

Calibrated date: 1σ : cal BC 1880 – 1675
2σ : cal BC 1950 – 1530

Final comments:
P Clay: within the expected date range: very useful for comparison with similar sites in the area.

Elton, Cambridgeshire

Location: TL 083961
Lat. 52.33.06 N; Long. 00.24.09 W

Excavator: A F Taylor (Cambridgeshire Archaeological Committee), 1978

Site: cropmark site of a possible Neolithic henge.

Objectives: to date the monument: there were no finds in the layer from which the sample was taken, but the soil just above contained pottery and worked flints which are most probably of Neolithic date.

HAR-3111   4050 ± 110 BP

$δ^{13}C$: –27.0 ‰

Sample: ELTON1(5), submitted on 9 February 1979

Material: charcoal: all *Quercus* sp. from mature timbers (C A Keepax).

Initial comment: from a dark layer almost at the bottom of the henge ditch, *c* 1.0m below the present ground surface (the site has been ploughed for many years).

Calibrated date: 1σ : cal BC 2870 – 2470
2σ : cal BC 2910 – 2300

Final comments:
A F Taylor: acceptable and very useful.

Harwell: the small size of the sample accounts for the larger than normal error term.

Exeter: Cathedral Close, Devon

Location: SX 926920
Lat. 50.43.02 N; Long. 03.31.17 W

Excavator: P T Bidwell (?Exeter Museum)

Site: an early fifth- to eighth-century cemetery overlying the Roman basilica; the burials, apparently part of a planned cemetery, were aligned with the head to the north-west and feet to the south-east.

References: Bidwell 1979, 111 (^{14}C)

Objectives: the burials can only be dated archaeologically to a wide time span, but the samples submitted, although not necessarily contemporary, must on archaeological evidence lie within the period of a generation; more precise dating would

1. provide a *terminus ante quem* for the demolition of the basilica which formerly occupied the site

2. suggest a date for the establishment of a religious community on or near the site

3. help to construct a chronology for the history of Exeter in the post-Roman period.

HAR-1611   880 ± 70 BP

$δ^{13}C$: –20.7 ‰

Sample: OB485, submitted on 27 June 1976

Material: human bone.

Initial comment: from an extended inhumation, in a grave cut through the floor of the basilica.

Calibrated date: 1σ : cal AD 1035 – 1230
2σ : cal AD 1010 – 1270

Final comments:
P T Bidwell: the result is clearly anomalous and should be discounted.

Harwell: the result is rather different from HAR-1613 and HAR-1614, but no reason is apparent in the experimental notes.

HAR-1613 1460 ± 80 BP

δ¹³C: –21.4 ‰

Sample: OB486, submitted on 27 June 1976

Material: human bone.

Initial comment: from an extended inhumation, in a grave cut through the floor of the basilica.

Calibrated date: 1σ : cal AD 540 – 655
2σ : cal AD 420 – 680

HAR-1614 1530 ± 70 BP

δ¹³C: –21.4 ‰

Sample: OB278, submitted on 27 June 1975

Material: human bone.

Initial comment: from an extended inhumation, in a grave cut through the floor of the basilica.

Calibrated date: 1σ : cal AD 430 – 605
2σ : cal AD 390 – 650

Farmoor, Oxfordshire

Location: SP 443057 – SP 444059
Lat. 51.44.52 N – 51.44.36 N; Long. 01.21.30 W – 00.37.57 W

Excavator: G Lambrick (Oxford Archaeological Unit), 1974 – 6

Site: Iron Age settlement.

References: Lambrick and Robinson 1979; 38, 143 – 4 (¹⁴C)

Objectives: to provide dating to support and refine the ceramic dating evidence.

Comments:
G Lambrick: there are problems with the above dates in that two samples were by no means of ideal size but there was insufficient bone from most of the phase 1 pits to produce reliable dates.

HAR-1374 2410 ± 100 BP

δ¹³C: –26.0 ‰

Sample: FAR1007, submitted by M Robinson on 20 October 1976

Material: charcoal.

Initial comment: from a well stratified deposit in an Iron Age hut circle ditch – a typical Middle Iron Age penannular house gully.

Calibrated date: 1σ : cal BC 770 – 390
2σ : cal BC 800 – 251

Final comments:
G Lambrick: surprisingly early for the type of feature and pottery, but the later end of the two standard deviation range is acceptable; the charcoal was not identified and could represent old wood or come from the centre of a large tree.

Harwell: a small sample accounts for the larger than normal error term.

HAR-1910 2070 ± 70 BP

δ¹³C: –21.3 ‰

Sample: FAR1053, submitted by M Robinson on 20 October 1976

Material: antler: red deer (*Cervus elaphus*).

Initial comment: from an Iron Age pit.

Calibrated date: 1σ : cal BC 190 – 0 cal AD
2σ : cal BC 360 – 70 cal AD

Final comments:
G Lambrick: surprisingly late for an apparently early pit, although the earlier end of the two standard deviation range is acceptable; there was very little associated pottery so the ceramic dating evidence might be misleading, although there is no reason to expect serious redeposition.

HAR-1925 2130 ± 80 BP

δ¹³C: –23.1 ‰

Sample: FAR1103, submitted by M Robinson on 20 October 1976

Material: bone.

Initial comment: from a Middle Iron Age penannular enclosure with a good group of Middle Iron Age pottery.

Calibrated date: 1σ : cal BC 360 – 90
2σ : cal BC 390 – 20 cal AD

Final comments:
G Lambrick: the date is in agreement with the pottery and is equally imprecise.

HAR-1926 2060 ± 70 BP

δ¹³C: –22.6 ‰

Sample: FAR1159, submitted by M Robinson on 20 October 1976

Material: bone.

Initial comment: from a waterlogged Iron Age enclosure with a small but useful group of pottery.

Calibrated date: 1σ : cal BC 180 – 10 cal AD
2σ : cal BC 355 – 80 cal AD

Final comments:
G Lambrick: this date is in agreement with the pottery.

Farningham, Kent

Location: TQ 550672
Lat. 51.22.56 N; Long. 00.13.39 E

Excavator: B Philp (Kent Archaeological Rescue Unit), 1974

Site: a pond in the river Darent near the Franks Roman villa.

Objectives: rescue work ahead of the M20 motorway.

HAR-2265   590 ± 70 BP

$\delta^{13}C$: −25.7 ‰

Sample: FARN1, submitted by R Morgan on 1 June 1977

Material: wood: *Quercus* sp., possibly the innermost 20 heartwood rings of a large waterlogged timber with 103 rings; no sapwood was present.

Initial comment: from a cut timber probably intended as a brace in a building but never used – not a pile.

Calibrated date: 1σ : cal AD 1290 – 1415
2σ : cal AD 1270 – 1440

Final comments:
B Philp: the mud and silt from which the timbers came was provisionally dated to AD 1200-1400; this date fits very well.

Fencott: Ivy Farm, Oxfordshire

Location: SP 57201688
Lat. 51.50.50 N; Long. 01.10.10 W

Excavator: R A Chambers (Oxford Archaeological Unit), 1979

Site: Roman bridge constructed soon after 5 AD.

References: Chambers 1986, 35 (^{14}C)

Objectives: to confirm the dendrochronological dates for the bridge.

HAR-4203   1810 ± 70 BP

$\delta^{13}C$: −25.1 ‰

Sample: IFFM80C1, submitted on 9 December 1980

Material: wood.

Initial comment: from a pile of the bridge.

Calibrated date: 1σ : cal AD 120 – 260
2σ : cal AD 60 – 390

Final comments:
R A Chambers: this result supports a dendrochronological date of *c* AD 95 for the construction of the bridge.

Harwell: the result was originally calibrated after Stuiver to AD 70 – 340 at the 68% confidence level; if the ^{14}C date is to conform with the dendrochronological date it would appear that old timbers were used.

Fingringhoe: Frog Hall Farm, Essex

Location: TM 034196
Lat. 51.50.15 N; Long. 00.57.10 E

Excavator: H Brooks (Colchester Archaeological Trust), 1975 – 6

Site: a post-built oval structure within a ditched enclosure in a complex of cropmarks; flint-gritted pottery from stratified contexts could indicate occupation within the Late Bronze Age – Early Iron Age.

Objectives: this sample is the only means of giving even an approximate date for the site and the pottery types represented.

HAR-2502   2760 ± 80 BP

$\delta^{13}C$: −21.5 ‰

Sample: FINGRING, submitted on 22 December 1977

Material: vegetable: burnt seeds of *Vicia faba* L. var minor.

Initial comment: from a stratified position in F11, found with several examples of local pottery which appear to be Iron Age in date.

Calibrated date: 1σ : cal BC 1005 – 830
2σ : cal BC 1125 – 800

Final comments:
H Brooks: this small occupation site is now firmly dated to the Late Bronze Age.

Fisherwick, Staffordshire

Location: SK 189081
Lat. 52.40.12 N; Long. 01.43.14 W

Excavator: C Smith, 1974

Site: part of a cropmark site with a subrectangular enclosure and three Iron Age round houses.

References: Smith 1979, 91 (^{14}C)

HAR-2469   1930 ± 80 BP

$\delta^{13}C$: −27.7 ‰

Sample: FWL93011, submitted on 22 December 1977

Material: wood: twigs: dried out and too distorted for identification.

Initial comment: from the waterlogged silts of an Iron Age enclosure ditch.

Calibrated date: 1σ : cal BC 18 – 135 cal AD
2σ : cal BC 110 – 240 cal AD

Final comments:
C Smith: 50 – 100 years later than expected from the archaeological evidence.

HAR-2470   2070 ± 80 BP

$\delta^{13}C$: −28.1 ‰

Sample: FWF8305d, submitted on 22 December 1977

Material: wood.

Initial comment: from the waterlogged silts of an Iron Age enclosure ditch.

Calibrated date: 1σ : cal BC 190 – 10 cal AD
2σ : cal BC 365 – 80 cal AD

Final comments:
C Smith: in close agreement with the archaeological evidence and BIRM-614.

References: Wheeler 1979, 170

HAR-2471 2100 ± 80 BP

$\delta^{13}C$: –27.9 ‰

Sample: FWE8305f, submitted on 22 December 1977

Material: wood.

Initial comment: from the waterlogged silts of an Iron Age enclosure ditch.

Calibrated date: 1σ : cal BC 340 – 35
2σ : cal BC 380 – 70 cal AD

Final comments:
C Smith: as for HAR-2470.

Foulness: Old Wall, north-west Shelford, Essex

Location: TQ 976908
Lat. 51.34.51 N; Long. 00.51.08 E

Excavator: R Crump (Atomic Weapons Research Establishment Archaeological Society), 1975

Site: an embankment containing box-like wooden structures made up of numerous posts and horizontal beams, laid across a tidal creek.

References: Crump 1981, 70 (^{14}C)
Radiocarbon **27**, 82 (^{14}C)

HAR-1689 500 ± 70 BP

$\delta^{13}C$: –26.2 ‰

Sample: FBM011, submitted by E Hyde on 1 July 1976

Material: wood: *Quercus* sp..

Initial comment: from a wooden structure *c* 1.12m below the surface in an ancient earth wall, embedded in blue – grey clay and sealed by brown-grey clay up to the topsoil.

Calibrated date: 1σ : cal AD 1400 – 1445
2σ : cal AD 1290 – 1490

Final comments:
R Crump: this compares very well with the dendrochronological felling date of AD 1490.

Harwell: replicate of HAR-1798.

HAR-1690 360 ± 80 BP

$\delta^{13}C$: –27.1 ‰

Sample: FBM021, submitted by E Hyde on 1 July 1976

Material: wood: *Quercus* sp..

Initial comment: from the same context as HAR-1689.

Calibrated date: 1σ : cal AD 1445 – 1645
2σ : cal AD 1410 – 1950

Final comments:
Harwell: the two dates are published as a combined mean of 1490 ± 75 (after Damon *et al* 1972).

Gallows Hill: Thetford, Norfolk

Location: TL 86438463
Lat. 52.25.39 N; Long. 00.44.32 E

Excavator: A J Lawson (Norfolk Archaeological Unit), 1978 – 9

Site: Roman mound on a chalk ridge, capped with glacial sands, to the north-west of Thetford; two hoards of Late Roman coins have have been found in the vicinity. In the post-medieval period the mound served as a stance for a gallows.

References: Lawson and Le Hegarat 1986; 65, 67 (^{14}C)

Objectives: to date the mound.

HAR-2905 1600 ± 70 BP

$\delta^{13}C$: –26.1 ‰

Sample: GHILL8, submitted by P Murphy on 27 October 1978

Material: soil and charcoal: very little identifiable charcoal (C A Keepax).

Initial comment: from charcoal spread on the old ground surface below the sand capping of an, apparently Bronze Age, barrow.

Comment on uncalibrated date: the expected date was Bronze Age, but the presence of charred spelt wheat in the same deposit supports this result, being characteristic of Iron Age and Roman sites and not known on Bronze Age sites in southern England; despite this and the evidence for Roman activity nearby, however, no Roman artefacts were found on the site.

Calibrated date: 1σ : cal AD 390 – 545
2σ : cal AD 255 – 610

Final comments:
A J Lawson: the dates are explicable, if unexpected.

Garton Slack, Humberside

Location: SE 6095
Lat. 54.20.49 N; Long. 01.04.37 W

Excavator: T C M Brewster (East Riding Archaeological Research Committee), 1965 – 75

Site: an extensive multiperiod palimpsest occupation dating from the Neolithic to Roman periods, with a cemetery and domestic sites excavated in advance of quarrying.

Objectives: to provide dating evidence.

Comments:
T C M Brewster: on the whole the ¹⁴C dates are well matched by the archaeological evidence.

Harwell: one sample, HAR-2487 (GS3FGP10), was withdrawn in May 1985.

HAR-1227   3200 ± 70 BP

$\delta^{13}C$: −25.4 ‰

Sample: GS149LG1, submitted on 12 July 1975

Material: wood: hawthorn type (*Crataegus/Malus/Pyrus/Sorbus* sp.); charcoal from fairly large timbers (C A Keepax).

Initial comment: from a layer of black soil at the bottom of a large Iron Age grave, *c* 1.87m below the bulldozed gravel surface and associated with an extended inhumation; neither this nor any other sample have been contaminated at any time.

Calibrated date: 1σ : cal BC 1525 – 1420
                    2σ : cal BC 1670 – 1320

HAR-1228   2130 ± 70 BP

$\delta^{13}C$: −25.8 ‰

Sample: GS93ZGS1, submitted on 12 July 1975

Material: wood: *Quercus* sp. from fairly large timbers; *c* 25% identified (C A Keepax).

Initial comment: from a deposit containing wood, charcoal, and carbonised grain at the base of Iron Age silo 1; *c* 1.0m below the surface prior to July 1970.

Calibrated date: 1σ : cal BC 355 – 95
                    2σ : cal BC 380 – 10 cal AD

HAR-1235   2340 ± 80 BP

$\delta^{13}C$: −25.2 ‰

Sample: GS1810P1, submitted on 12 July 1975

Material: wood: *Quercus* sp. from fairly large timbers; *c* 25% identified (C A Keepax).

Initial comment: from pit 1, trench X, section S5, layer C (Iron Age grain silo?); *c* 0.66m below the scraped surface.

Calibrated date: 1σ : cal BC 485 – 380
                    2σ : cal BC 765 – 200

HAR-1236   3550 ± 70 BP

$\delta^{13}C$: −24.7 ‰

Sample: GS74BAB1, submitted on 12 July 1975

Material: wood: *Quercus* sp. from fairly large timbers; *c* 25% identified (C A Keepax).

Initial comment: from a secondary cremation burial, at the bottom of an oval grave, in a round barrow; 0.86m below the bulldozed surface prior to April 1970.

Calibrated date: 1σ : cal BC 2020 – 1775
                    2σ : cal BC 2130 – 1705

HAR-1274   1920 ± 90 BP

$\delta^{13}C$: −21.4 ‰

Sample: GS7BCY31, submitted on 12 July 1975

Material: human bone.

Initial comment: from a grave in the south-east corner of the ring ditch of barrow 2; 0.99m below the bulldozed gravel surface.

Calibrated date: 1σ : cal BC 15 – 195 cal AD
                    2σ : cal BC 150 – 320 cal AD

Final comments:
Harwell: smaller than the ideal size.

References: Dent 1982, 439

HAR-1275   1870 ± 70 BP

$\delta^{13}C$: −22.8 ‰

Sample: GS7BCQ41, submitted on 12 July 1975

Material: human bone.

Initial comment: from the central grave in barrow 3; 0.56m below the bulldozed surface (original depth *c* 1.22m).

Calibrated date: 1σ : cal AD 65 – 230
                    2σ : cal BC 30 – 330 cal AD

References: Dent 1982, 439

HAR-1282   3520 ± 70 BP

$\delta^{13}C$: −22.7 ‰

Sample: GS61BAB1, submitted on 12 July 1975

Material: human bone.

Initial comment: from a Bronze Age grave which also contained six sheet bronze beads, 13 jet buttons, a jet toggle, and a necklace of 180 jet beads; depth *c* 0.46m below the surface prior to April 1970; no rootlets were present in the grave.

Calibrated date: 1σ : cal BC 1950 – 1750
                    2σ : cal BC 2090 – 1680

HAR-1283   2350 ± 120 BP

$\delta^{13}C$: −21.5 ‰

Sample: GSBCK51, submitted on 12 July 1975

Material: human bone.

Initial comment: from a grave between barrows 3 and 4 (Tr 3K5); *c* 1.22mm below the surface prior to 1970.

Calibrated date: 1σ : cal BC 755 – 265
                    2σ : cal BC 800 – 125

Final comments:
Harwell: this sample was supplemented with HAR-1396, which was not counted independently, but a low carbon yield accounts for the larger than normal error term.

References: Dent 1982, 439

HAR-1284   3870 ± 110 BP

$\delta^{13}C$: −22.8 ‰

Sample: GS283RP1, submitted on 12 July 1975

Material: antler: red deer (*Cervus elaphus*).

Initial comment: from trench 1, section A, ?a sunken path in a ritual pit.

Calibrated date: 1σ : cal BC 2555 – 2145
2σ : cal BC 2855 – 2030

Final comments:
Harwell: due to processing difficulties which produced only a small sample, the error term may be more than shown but cannot be quantified.

HAR-1296   1320 ± 100 BP

$\delta^{13}C$: −21.0 ‰

Sample: GS7BCX31, submitted on 12 July 1975

Material: human bone: adult female, 30 – 40 years old.

Initial comment: from the central grave in barrow 2 (TR IV x3), associated with an iron La Tène mirror; *c* 1.52m below the surface prior to 1970.

Calibrated date: 1σ : cal AD 640 – 790
2σ : cal AD 550 – 940

Final comments:
Harwell: a low carbon yield accounts for the larger than normal error term; this sample was recounted as HAR-3620.

References: Dent 1982, 439

HAR-2486   2140 ± 80 BP

$\delta^{13}C$: −25.2 ‰

Sample: GS9EG1P2, submitted on 22 December 1977

Material: charcoal: hawthorn type (Rosaceae, sub-family Pomoideae) and *Quercus* sp. from fairly large timbers; *c* 50% identified (C A Keepax).

Initial comment: from pit 2, section E, Ex Grid 1; *c* 0.73m below the surface prior to October 1970.

Calibrated date: 1σ : cal BC 360 – 95
2σ : cal BC 390 – 20 cal AD

HAR-2488   1750 ± 60 BP

$\delta^{13}C$: −26.9 ‰

Sample: GS103G2P1, submitted on 22 December 1977

Material: charcoal: hawthorn type (Rosaceae, sub-family Pomoideae) from branch-sized and fairly large timbers; *c* 25% identified (C A Keepax).

Initial comment: from pit 1, section G2, in the centre of a rectangular enclosure; *c* 0.61m below the surface prior to October 1970.

Calibrated date: 1σ : cal AD 220 – 370
2σ : cal AD 120 – 420

HAR-2489   1530 ± 70 BP

$\delta^{13}C$: −24.5 ‰

Sample: GS818ECB, submitted on 22 December 1977

Material: charcoal: *Fraxinus* sp. and *Sambucus nigra* from fairly large timbers (C A Keepax).

Initial comment: from a cremation burial in an Iron Age ditch, section I8; *c* 0.73m below the surface prior to 1970.

Calibrated date: 1σ : cal AD 430 – 605
2σ : cal AD 390 – 650

HAR-2490   1920 ± 80 BP

$\delta^{13}C$: −25.2 ‰

Sample: GS5D2P14, submitted on 12 July 1975

Material: charcoal: mainly *Fraxinus excelsior* with some *Quercus* sp. from fairly large timbers (C A Keepax).

Initial comment: from the remains of a plank in the bottom of pit 14, section D2, 0.84m below the surface prior to January 1970; expected date Iron Age.

Calibrated date: 1σ : cal BC 2 – 140 cal AD
2σ : cal BC 110 – 250 cal AD

HAR-2491   3462 ± 70 BP

$\delta^{13}C$: −24.4 ‰

Sample: GS131203, submitted on 22 December 1977

Material: charcoal: *Quercus* sp., *Fraxinus* sp., and *Corylus avellana* or *Alnus glutinosa* from fairly large timbers; *c* 25% identified (C A Keepax).

Initial comment: from pit 1, section O3/P3.

Calibrated date: 1σ : cal BC 1885 – 1690
2σ : cal BC 1970 – 1620

HAR-2492   3370 ± 70 BP

$\delta^{13}C$: −25.6 ‰

Sample: GS27EPH243, submitted on 22 December 1977

Material: charcoal: *Quercus* sp. from fairly large timbers (C A Keepax).

Initial comment: from posthole 3, Ext Section V2, *c* 0.76m below the surface prior to August 1973.

Calibrated date: 1σ : cal BC 1745 – 1540
2σ : cal BC 1880 – 1520

HAR-2493   3350 ± 80 BP

$\delta^{13}C$: −25.3 ‰

Sample: GS1814M7C1, submitted on 22 December 1977

Material: charcoal: *Quercus* sp. from fairly large timbers (C A Keepax).

Initial comment: from a cremation burial, *c* 0.29m below the surface prior to October 1972.

Calibrated date: 1σ : cal BC 1745 – 1525
2σ : cal BC 1880 – 1450

HAR-3620   2030 ± 70 BP

$\delta^{13}C$: −22.8 ‰

Sample: GARTONS7, submitted on 17 January 1980

Material: human bone: adult female burial.

Initial comment: as HAR-1296.

Calibrated date: 1σ : cal BC 150 – 50 cal AD
  2σ : cal BC 330 – 110 cal AD

Glastonbury: Silver Street, Somerset

Location: ST 501389
  Lat. 51.08.48 N; Long. 02.42.48 W

Excavator: P Ellis (Committee for Rescue Archaeology in Avon, Gloucestershire, and Somerset), 1978

Site: two ditches and banks to the north of Glastonbury Abbey precinct, perhaps forming a corner of the original *vallum monasterii* of the earliest monastery.

References: Ellis 1981 – 2, 17 (^{14}C)

Objectives: the aim of the excavation was to further locate a ditch originally found beneath the Abbey in 1956/7; a ditch was found, although not on the expected alignment, from which dating evidence was sought. Later machine excavation to the west located a deep excavated feature, perhaps a pond, for which dating was also required.

Comments:
J Hillam: dendrochronology suggests that HAR-2812 and HAR-2813 are contemporary, but too few rings are present to be certain.

HAR-2812 1340 ± 70 BP

$δ^{13}C$: −25.2 ‰

Sample: GL263, submitted by J Hillam on 4 September 1978

Material: wood: *c* 20 rings from a wood sample (*Quercus* sp.), containing 38 rings, obtained from near the outside of the tree; possibly contemporary with HAR-2814, but too few rings were present to be certain.

Initial comment: from stake F263, found in the primary silt of ditch F223; possibly derived from a palisade on the adjacent bank, which was apparently deliberately backfilled into the ditch.

Calibrated date: 1σ : cal AD 640 – 760
  2σ : cal AD 590 – 855

Final comments:
P Ellis: see HAR-2813.

References: *Radiocarbon* **29**, 93

HAR-2813 1450 ± 80 BP

$δ^{13}C$: −26.7 ‰

Sample: GL239, submitted by J Hillam on 4 September 1978

Material: wood: *Quercus* sp., rings 15 – 34 from a 79-year-old sample; probably from near the outside of the tree although no was sapwood present.

Initial comment: from stake F239, found together with HAR-2812.

Calibrated date: 1σ : cal AD 545 – 660
  2σ : cal AD 420 – 690

Final comments:
P Ellis: at the 95% confidence level HAR-2812 and HAR-2813 present a wide range of interpretation options, from silting and infilling of a Romano-British ditch to a Late Saxon feature. However, despite this wide range, and the difficulites of linking the evidence from the 1956/7 and 1978 excavations, the most likely interpretation for the ditch is as the seventh- or eighth-century boundary of the early monastery.

References: *Radiocarbon* **29**, 84

HAR-2814 1470 ± 80 BP

$δ^{13}C$: −27.5 ‰

Sample: GL249B, submitted by J Hillam on 4 September 1978

Material: wood: *Quercus* sp., *c* 20 rings. There is no way of knowing whether these are inner or outer rings.

Initial comment: from branches in layer 249, in the bottom of F222, a large feature of unknown function (?pond).

Calibrated date: 1σ : cal AD 535 – 650
  2σ : cal AD 410 – 680

Final comments:
P Ellis: a number of interpretations were offered in the report, among which the suggestion that the feature predated the monastic boundary seems preferable. Although the date range is wide, it may be that even at 95% confidence the ^{14}C date provides a *terminus post quem* for the northern abbey boundary; it is still the case, however, that neither the excavations nor the ^{14}C dates provide decisive data to clarify the origins of the abbey.

References: *Radiocarbon* **29**, 93

Gloucester: 1 Westgate Street, Gloucestershire

Location: SO 83141856
  Lat. 51.51.54 N; Long. 02.14.42 W

Excavator: C Heighway (Gloucester Excavation Unit), 1975

Site: post-Roman town.

References: Heighway *et al* 1979

Objectives: dates from five contexts are required to provide a chronological framework for a complete sequence of layers from the third to the tenth centuries, many of which are aceramic, and to complement the dendrochronological analyses.

HAR-1652 1540 ± 70 BP

$δ^{13}C$: −25.3 ‰

Sample: 49751, submitted on 29 February 1976

Material: wood, upper surface only burnt: *Quercus* sp. from fairly large timbers (C A Keepax).

Initial comment: from the charred sill beams of a Late Roman building which postdates the destruction of the major buildings in the town centre; the building was dated by coins to the late fourth or fifth centuries AD, but may have been considerably later.

Calibrated date: 1σ : cal AD 425 – 600
2σ : cal AD 380 – 650

Final comments:
C Heighway: useful confirmation of a sub-Roman date for timber-silled building in the centre of Gloucester (discussed in Heighway *et al* 1979).

References: Heighway *et al* 1979, 183
Radiocarbon **27**, 81

HAR-1655 1190 ± 70 BP

$\delta^{13}C$: –27.9 ‰

Sample: 497530, submitted on 27 February 1976

Material: wood: *Corylus avellana*, some bark remaining (C A Keepax).

Initial comment: from a stake in a well-preserved wattle fence in aceramic Saxon levels, as HAR-1778 (see also HAR-1658 and HAR-1787); its date could be ninth century or earlier as there seems to be no break between sub-Roman activity and the construction of the Anglo-Saxon buildings, but it should be earlier than HAR-1657.

Calibrated date: 1σ : cal AD 725 – 895
2σ : cal AD 670 – 990

Final comments:
C Heighway: this suggests a date for the preserved organic levels in the town centre (see Heighway *et al* 1979, 183). The presence of bark implies the wood was not reused; suggestions of possible contamination would favour this result rather than HAR-1788.

Harwell: replicated with HAR-1788.

References: Heighway *et al* 1979, 183
Radiocarbon **27**, 81

HAR-1656 1260 ± 80 BP

$\delta^{13}C$: –28.3 ‰

Sample: 49753, submitted on 27 February 1976

Material: wood, complete post: *Quercus* sp. (C A Keepax).

Initial comment: from the possible Saxo-Norman undercroft at the frontage of the site; the pottery dates to the early eleventh century or earlier.

Calibrated date: 1σ : cal AD 665 – 880
2σ : cal AD 640 – 960

Final comments:
C Heighway: this date seems too early; a more correct result was provided by the replicate HAR-3140.

References: *Radiocarbon* **27**, 81

HAR-1657 910 ± 60 BP

$\delta^{13}C$: –29.4 ‰

Sample: 49759, submitted on 27 February 1976

Material: wood: hawthorn type (Rosaceae, sub-family Pomoideae) (C A Keepax).

Initial comment: from a pit, containing late eleventh-century pottery and wooden artefacts, which postdates the Anglo-Saxon buildings, dated by HAR-1655, HAR-1658, HAR-1787, and HAR-1788; the sample has been dated dendrochronologically to after AD 1100.

Calibrated date: 1σ : cal AD 1025 – 1210
2σ : cal AD 1010 – 1250

Final comments:
C Heighway: this accords well with the artefactual and dendrochronological evidence.

References: *Radiocarbon* **27**, 81

HAR-1658 1040 ± 60 BP

$\delta^{13}C$: –28.4 ‰

Sample: 497527, submitted on 27 June 1979

Material: wood.

Initial comment: as HAR-1787, a different stake from the same fence as HAR-1655 and HAR-1778.

Calibrated date: 1σ : cal AD 960 – 1025
2σ : cal AD 890 – 1155

Final comments:
C Heighway: HAR-1655 and HAR-1788 give an earlier and more acceptable date.

References: *Radiocarbon* **27**, 81

HAR-1787 1000 ± 70 BP

$\delta^{13}C$: –28.7 ‰

Sample: 497527, submitted on 27 February 1976

Material: wood: hawthorn type (Rosaceae, sub-family Pomoideae) (C A Keepax).

Initial comment: as HAR-1658.

Calibrated date: 1σ : cal AD 980 – 1150
2σ : cal AD 890 – 1180

Final comments:
Harwell: replicate of HAR-1658.

References: *Radiocarbon* **27**, 81

HAR-1788 1170 ± 80 BP

$\delta^{13}C$: –25.0 ‰

Sample: 497530, submitted on 27 February 1978

Material: wood.

Initial comment: as HAR-1655, from the same wattle fence as HAR-1658 and HAR-1787.

Comment on uncalibrated date: as HAR-1658; this sample has been taken to date these aceramic levels.

Calibrated date: 1σ : cal AD 770 – 970
2σ : cal AD 670 – 1020

Final comments:
Harwell: replicate of HAR-1655.

References: *Radiocarbon* **27**, 81

HAR-3140   970 ± 70 BP

$\delta^{13}C$: −25.9 ‰

Sample: 49753, submitted by L Biek on 23 March 1979

Material: wood, a section from a complete post: *Quercus* sp. (C A Keepax).

Initial comment: as HAR-1656, from the undercroft, associated with tenth-century pottery.

Calibrated date: 1σ : cal AD 1000 – 1160
2σ : cal AD 900 – 1220

Final comments:
C Heighway: this accords with the date of the undercroft as indicated by the pottery, although HAR-1656, from the same post, gave an earlier date.

Harwell: replicate of HAR-1656.

Gloucester: 10 Lower Quay Street, Gloucestershire

Location: SO 8318 approx
Lat. 51.51.36 N; Long. 02.14.49 W

Excavator: C Heighway (Gloucester Excavation Unit), 1979

Site: Roman waterfront.

References: Garrod and Heighway 1984, 48 – 51

HAR-4044   unknown

$\delta^{13}C$: unknown

Sample: 287951, submitted on 23 August 1980

Material: wood, the sample was kept for some months in a tank containing a small amount of fungicide.

Initial comment: from timber stakes forming part of a second-century waterfront.

Final comments:
Harwell: this date was abandoned since the sample had been stored in a tank containing fungicide.

Gloucester: 11 – 17 Southgate Street, Bell Hotel, Gloucestershire

Location: SO 1832135
Lat. 51.49.00 N; Long. 02.12.20 W

Excavator: H Hurst, 1968

Site: the Roman forum.

References: Hurst 1972
Radiocarbon **21**, 375 – 6 (^{14}C)

Objectives: to date the post-Roman occupation levels.

Comments:
H Hurst: this is the earliest dating evidence for post-Roman occupation in the centre of Gloucester.

AML: one sample, HAR-1445 (85/68IIV), failed.

HAR-1443   1240 ± 70 BP

$\delta^{13}C$: −27.1 ‰

Sample: 85/68II, submitted on 28 November 1975

Material: wood: alder (*Alnus* sp.) stump.

Initial comment: from the earliest post-Roman occupation levels on the site of the forum (periods 6/7); cut down at the start of, or very early in, the occupation sequence.

Calibrated date: 1σ : cal AD 675 – 885
2σ : cal AD 650 – 960

Final comments:
Harwell: replicated with HAR-1636.

HAR-1444   1160 ± 80 BP

$\delta^{13}C$: −27.1 ‰

Sample: 85/68IIA, submitted on 19 December 1975

Material: wood.

Initial comment: from wall M1, timber A in the earliest post-Roman building (period 7).

Calibrated date: 1σ : cal AD 775 – 975
2σ : cal AD 670 – 1020

HAR-1446   1300 ± 70 BP

$\delta^{13}C$: −26.4 ‰

Sample: 85/68XXI, submitted on 19 December 1975

Material: wood.

Initial comment: from timber A, west section, from the earliest occupation level.

Calibrated date: 1σ : cal AD 655 – 780
2σ : cal AD 620 – 890

Final comments:
H Hurst: this date is too old; the timber may have been lying around for some time before deposition.

HAR-1636   1160 ± 70 BP

$\delta^{13}C$: −29.7 ‰

Sample: 85/68II, submitted on 19 December 1975

Material: wood.

Initial comment: as HAR-1443.

Calibrated date: 1σ : cal AD 780 – 970
2σ : cal AD 680 – 1010

Final comments:
Harwell: replicate check on HAR-1443; the results are sufficiently close to take a mean value of AD 750 ± 60.

Gloucester: 19 Berkeley Street, Gloucestershire

Location: SO 8318 approx
Lat. 51.51.36 N; Long. 02.14.49 W

Excavator: C Heighway (Gloucester Excavation Unit), 1980

Site: one of a series of excavations in the medieval town (site 19/79); complete section through medieval streets.

References: Garrod and Heighway 1984, 48 (^{14}C)

HAR-4187   1210 ± 80 BP

$δ^{13}C:$ −29.5 ‰

Sample: 197951, submitted on 23 August 1980

Material: wood, stored in a tank containing fungicide.

Initial comment: from under street 6.

Calibrated date: 1σ : cal AD 685 – 895
            2σ : cal AD 660 – 990

Final comments:
C Heighway: too early; the pottery suggests a late tenth- or eleventh-century date, possibly the latter end of the two standard deviation range.

Harwell: repeat of HAR-4045.

Gloucester: 34 – 8 Eastgate Street, Gloucestershire

Location: SO 835183
     Lat. 51.51.40 N; Long. 02.12.30 W

Excavator: C Heighway (Gloucester Excavation Unit), 1974

Site: Roman city wall and ditch (site 46/74).

References: Heighway 1983, 250 (^{14}C)
       Radiocarbon **21**, 374 (^{14}C)

HAR-1339   1600 ± 80 BP

$δ^{13}C:$ −27.7 ‰

Sample: W103/4, submitted on 29 October 1975

Material: wood, treated with fungicide: *Quercus* sp., 25 sapwood rings from rings 60 – 85 of an 85 year tree-ring sequence, cut from two wooden piles which came from the same tree.

Initial comment: from wooden piles under the fourth-century Roman city wall (period 5).

Calibrated date: 1σ : cal AD 380 – 550
            2σ : cal AD 250 – 620

Final comments:
C Heighway: general confirmation of the Late Roman date of the city wall; dendrochronological sequences may, in time, give a closer date (see Heighway 1983, 249-51).

Harwell: repeat of HAR-1239.

Gloucester: Gloucester Cathedral, Church House, Gloucestershire

Location: SO 83071883
     Lat. 51.52.02 N; Long. 02.14.45 W

Excavator: C Heighway (Gloucester Excavation Unit), 1980

Site: cemetery with some two generations of east – west burials, cutting through third- or fourth-century AD Roman tips, and sealed by the late eleventh- to twelfth-century Norman cloister (site 11/80).

References: Garrod and Heighway 1984, 53 (^{14}C)

HAR-3971   980 ± 60 BP

$δ^{13}C:$ −20.1 ‰

Sample: 1180BQ, submitted on 23 August 1980

Material: human bone, not washed.

Initial comment: from the cemetery beneath the Norman cloister; the estimated date is Late Saxon.

Calibrated date: 1σ : cal AD 1000 – 1155
            2σ : cal AD 960 – 1180

Final comments:
C Heighway: useful confirmation of the date range of these skeletons, which are a possible indicator of the position of the pre-1089 church.

Godmanchester: Park Lane, Cambridgeshire

Location: TL 245708
     Lat. 52.19.15 N; Long. 00.10.23 W

Excavator: H J M Green

Site: Iron Age occupation and possible third-century Roman kilns.

Objectives: to date an important group of Iron Age, West Harling style pottery.

HAR-1931   2880 ± 80 BP

$δ^{13}C:$ −24.7 ‰

Sample: F039:44, submitted on 16 November 1976

Material: carbonised grain: *Hordeum vulgare* L. (6-row hulled barley).

Initial comment: from the earliest Iron Age storage pit with a West Harling style pottery assemblage.

Calibrated date: 1σ : cal BC 1225 – 930
            2σ : cal BC 1370 – 845

Final comments:
H J M Green: the pottery has affinities with both the West Harling/Staple Howe and the Ivinghoe/Sandy groups; the mean result seems at least 100 years too old, but a true age within the younger half of the range would be satisfactory.

Gorhambury, Hertfordshire

Location: TL 116079
     Lat. 51.45.30 N; Long. 00.22.58 W

Excavator: D Neal (Department of the Environment), 1979

Site: Roman villa.

References: Neal *et al* 1990; 9, 175, 219 (^{14}C)

HAR-3484   4810 ± 80 BP

$\delta^{13}C$: −25.6 ‰

Sample: GORH1715, submitted by N Balaam on 12 October 1979

Material: charcoal: *Quercus* sp. from mature wood (N Balaam).

Initial comment: from a pre-Roman context, possibly Iron Age.

Calibrated date: 1σ : cal BC 3695 – 3390
     2σ : cal BC 3780 – 3370

Great Linford, Buckinghamshire

Location: SP 85544208
     Lat. 52.04.12 N; Long. 00.45.07 W

Excavator: R J Zeepvat (Milton Keynes Archaeology Unit), 1977

Site: medieval post-mill (site 3709).

References: Mynard and Zeepvat 1978

Objectives: to date the structure: no archaeological dating evidence was found in the bedding trench for the support timbers.

HAR-3121   750 ± 70 BP

$\delta^{13}C$: −25.5 ‰

Sample: M1098W1B, submitted on 9 February 1979

Material: wood: *Quercus* sp. from mature timbers, sample taken from near the centre of the beam (C A Keepax).

Initial comment: from one of the buried support timbers packed with stone in a cross-shaped trench cut into the natural gravel and backfilled with gravel and blue – grey Oxford clay; from the position of the packing stones the beam appears to have measured 300mm × 300mm × 50mm.

Calibrated date: 1σ : cal AD 1225 – 1285
     2σ : cal AD 1160 – 1385

Final comments:
R J Zeepvat: ties in favourably with the documentary reference of AD 1303 of a deed relating to a mill at Linford (*VCH Bucks IV*, 389).

HAR-3122   730 ± 80 BP

$\delta^{13}C$: −25.0 ‰

Sample: M1098W1A, submitted on 9 February 1979

Material: wood: *Quercus* sp. from mature timbers, sample taken from near the centre of the beam (C A Keepax).

Initial comment: from one of the buried support timbers (as HAR-3121).

Calibrated date: 1σ : cal AD 1230 – 1290
     2σ : cal AD 1160 – 1400

Final comments:
R J Zeepvat: as HAR-3121.

Great Yarmouth: Broads Barrage Bores, Norfolk

Location: TG 515080 approx
     Lat. 52.33.06 N; Long. 01.42.54 E

Excavator: P Murphy (Centre for East Anglian Studies, University of East Anglia), 1977

Site: borehole 1, part of investigations in advance of a proposed barrage.

References: Coles and Funnell 1981, 125 (^{14}C)

Objectives: to date the deep Holocene sequence in this area.

HAR-2535   7580 ± 90 BP

$\delta^{13}C$: −27.5 ‰

Sample: 25BH1, submitted on 21 February 1978

Material: peat and organic silt, both contained shell.

Initial comment: from a deep bore into the Broadland lower peat (depth 19.4m OD).

Calibrated date: 1σ : cal BC 6475 – 6260
     2σ : cal BC 6590 – 6185

Final comments:
P Murphy: this sample from an estuarine organic sediment dates the local Holocene transgression in the lower Yare.

Great Yarmouth: Fuller's Hill, Norfolk

Location: TG 52250796
     Lat. 52.35.30 N; Long. 01.42.45 E

Excavator: A Rogerson (Norfolk Archaeological Unit), 1974

Site: medieval coastal settlement buried below wind-blown sand.

References: Rogerson 1976; 161, 234 (^{14}C)
     Radiocarbon **21**, 369 (^{14}C)

Objectives: to date the site; apart from one coin the chronology is floating, for although the stratigraphy is very clear, pottery is the only other aid to dating.

HAR-1079   890 ± 70 BP

$\delta^{13}C$: −26.8 ‰

Sample: 1032197, submitted on 2 January 1975

Material: charcoal.

Initial comment: from a deposit of burnt wood and reed which lay over a clay floor and which may represent burnt collapsed wall and roofing (phase 9); it was sealed by a deposit of wind-blown sand.

Calibrated date: 1σ : cal AD 1030 – 1225
     2σ : cal AD 1010 – 1270

Final comments:
A Rogerson: on general archaeological grounds this date seems *c* 100 years too early. The calibrated dates do not further assist the site chronology.

HAR-1080 1010 ± 70 BP

$\delta^{13}C$: −25.1 ‰

Sample: 1032306, submitted on 2 January 1975

Material: charcoal.

Initial comment: from a deposit of charcoal, probably from burnt wattle walling; stratigraphically earlier than HAR-1079 and separated from it by two layers of wind-blown sand (phase 6); one coin of AD 1042 – 66 was found in this phase.

Calibrated date: 1σ : cal AD 975 – 1040
2σ : cal AD 890 – 1170

Final comments:
A Rogerson: as HAR-1079.

Grendon, Northamptonshire

Location: SP 873617
Lat. 52.14.16 N; Long. 00.43.21 W

Excavator: A G McCormick (Leicester University), 1974

Area G

Site: a single-ditched barrow, to the north of the barrow in Area B; the mound (if there was one) and any old land surface had been completely eroded; no burial was found and finds were sparse and undiagnostic; much of the circumference of the barrow was disturbed by later Iron Age ditches, but not the area sampled.

HAR-1145 3360 ± 80 BP

$\delta^{13}C$: −25.8 ‰

Sample: GSAMPL42, submitted on 30 April 1975

Material: charcoal: *Acer campestre* L. (G C Morgan).

Initial comment: from Area G, F4, within the primary silt of the barrow ditch, near to HAR-1147.

Calibrated date: 1σ : cal BC 1745 – 1530
2σ : cal BC 1880 – 1460

HAR-1147 3100 ± 130 BP

$\delta^{13}C$: −24.9 ‰

Sample: GSAMPL29, submitted on 30 May 1975

Material: charcoal: *Acer campestre* (G C Morgan).

Initial comment: from Area G, F4, near to HAR-1145.

Calibrated date: 1σ : cal BC 1520 – 1220
2σ : cal BC 1680 – 1000

Final comments:
Harwell: the sample needed topping up with dead carbon dioxide to enable benzene synthesis.

Area E

Site: a group of straight-sided pits, both round and square in plan, on the margins of the gravel lens on which the site is located.

Objectives: to establish the chronology of the pit types and their relationship to the ring ditches; the six square pits possibly predate the round ones, but finds were few and the stratigraphy only suggests that they are pre-Roman.

HAR-1148 3350 ± 60 BP

$\delta^{13}C$: −24.8 ‰

Sample: GSAMPLE5, submitted on 30 April 1975

Material: charcoal: mature *Quercus* sp. (G C Morgan).

Initial comment: from F41, a round pit, possibly deliberately backfilled; the charcoal was evenly distributed in the sandy fill.

Calibrated date: 1σ : cal BC 1735 – 1530
2σ : cal BC 1870 – 1520

HAR-1149 3400 ± 70 BP

$\delta^{13}C$: −24.9 ‰

Sample: GSAMPLE6, submitted on 30 April 1975

Material: charcoal: mature *Quercus* sp. (G C Morgan).

Initial comment: from F48, a square pit.

Calibrated date: 1σ : cal BC 1865 – 1625
2σ : cal BC 1890 – 1520

Area B

Site: a Bronze Age double-ditched barrow constructed on an alluvial gravel deposit of the River Nene, eroded by flood and plough damage.

HAR-1150 3090 ± 210 BP

$\delta^{13}C$: −26.0 ‰

Sample: GSAMPL47, submitted on 30 April 1975

Material: charcoal: mature *Quercus* sp. (G C Morgan).

Initial comment: from cremation 3, a patch of charcoal and bone near to the base of the ploughsoil, found during initial machine clearance.

Calibrated date: 1σ : cal BC 1605 – 1040
2σ : cal BC 1880 – 820

Final comments:
Harwell: a doubtful result due to a small sample.

HAR-1153 3330 ± 90 BP

$\delta^{13}C$: −24.2 ‰

Sample: GSAMPL48, submitted on 30 April 1975

Material: charcoal: *Acer campestre* (G C Morgan).

Initial comment: from F1, Section W, the upper fill of the outer ditch.

Calibrated date: 1σ : cal BC 1740 – 1520
2σ : cal BC 1880 – 1430

HAR-1154 2970 ± 150 BP

$\delta^{13}C$: −24.9 ‰

Sample: GSAMPL15, submitted on 30 April 1975

Material: charcoal: mature *Quercus* sp..

Initial comment: from F1, Section V, the upper fill of the outer ditch, a sandy soil with occasional tips of stone which suggest rapid ditch silting, possibly by flooding.

Calibrated date: 1σ : cal BC 1420 – 990
2σ : cal BC 1530 – 820

Final comments:
Harwell: the sample needed topping up with dead carbon dioxide to enable benzene synthesis.

HAR-1155   3590 ± 150 BP

$δ^{13}C$: –25.6 ‰

Sample: GSAMPLE2, submitted on 30 April 1975

Material: charcoal: mature *Quercus* sp. (G C Morgan).

Initial comment: from Feature F1, Section V, found in close proximity to HAR-1154.

Calibrated date: 1σ : cal BC 2180 – 1750
2σ : cal BC 2455 – 1530

Area C

Site: a Bronze Age double ditched ring with an unusually deep inner ditch; inside this was a Neolithic square enclosure with a deep ditch on three sides, and a palisade bedding trench on the fourth side.

Objectives: dates from Area C were required to assess the contemporaneity of the features, and to identify building sequences which were not apparent in the field.

HAR-1495   4280 ± 70 BP

$δ^{13}C$: –24.9 ‰

Sample: AREACF37, submitted on 30 April 1975

Material: charcoal: *Quercus* sp. (G C Morgan).

Initial comment: from the western half of palisade F37 (15W), which was interpreted as a substantial timber facade with a narrow central opening; post ghosts indicate posts *c* 0.20m in diameter.

Calibrated date: 1σ : cal BC 3015 – 2785
2σ : cal BC 3080 – 2665

HAR-1497   4700 ± 130 BP

$δ^{13}C$: –24.9 ‰

Sample: AREACF35, submitted on 30 April 1975

Material: charcoal: mixed *Prunus spinosa* L. and *Quercus* sp..

Initial comment: from the top of the primary silt of the wide deep ditch, F35, which formed three sides of the inner square enclosure.

Calibrated date: 1σ : cal BC 3640 – 3350
2σ : cal BC 3780 – 3045

Final comments:
Harwell: a very small sample accounts for the larger than normal error term.

HAR-1498   4950 ± 80 BP

$δ^{13}C$: –26.5 ‰

Sample: AREACF63, submitted on 30 April 1975

Material: charcoal: *Quercus* sp. (G C Morgan).

Initial comment: from one of five postholes within the square enclosure; these did not form a pattern, but the size of the timbers used suggests that they were contemporary with the palisade.

Calibrated date: 1σ : cal BC 3905 – 3690
2σ : cal BC 3970 – 3535

Gretton: Park Lodge Quarry, Northamptonshire

Location: SP 910946
Lat. 52.32.29 N; Long. 00.39.29 W

Excavator: D Jackson (for the Department of the Environment), 1972

Site: Iron Age ditches and a pit alignment; the ditches are Early Iron Age but may not be contemporary.

References: Jackson and Knight 1985, 81 (^{14}C)

Objectives: to date the ceramic assemblage.

Comments:
D Jackson: the four dates all agree with the stratigraphy and the ceramic types.

HAR-2760   2390 ± 60 BP

$δ^{13}C$: –25.8 ‰

Sample: SAMPLA24, submitted on 12 July 1980

Material: charcoal: *Quercus* sp., *Corylus/Alnus* sp., ?*Prunus* sp. (eg blackthorn), *Acer* sp., and Rosaceae, sub-family Pomoideae, all mainly from mature timbers; *c* 25% identified (C A Keepax).

Initial comment: from the fill of an Iron Age (?boundary) ditch.

Calibrated date: 1σ : cal BC 750 – 395
2σ : cal BC 770 – 380

Final comments:
D Jackson: as expected.

HAR-2761   2210 ± 70 BP

$δ^{13}C$: –25.9 ‰

Sample: SAMPLB30, submitted on 12 July 1978

Material: charcoal: *Quercus* sp., *Corylus/Alnus* sp., ?*Prunus* sp., *Salix/Populus* sp., *Acer* sp., and ?Rosaceae, sub-family Pomoideae, all from large timbers; *c* 25% identified (C A Keepax).

Initial comment: from the fill of an Iron Age ditch.

Calibrated date: 1σ : cal BC 390 – 185
2σ : cal BC 400 – 100

Final comments:
D Jackson: as expected.

HAR-3014   2240 ± 70 BP

$\delta^{13}C$: −25.3 ‰

Sample: BII, submitted on 29 November 1978

Material: charcoal: mainly *Quercus* sp. with *Corylus/Alnus* sp., hawthorn type (Rosaceae, sub-family Pomoideae), and ?*Prunus* sp. (eg blackthorn), all from mature timbers; *c* 25% identified (C A Keepax).

Initial comment: from ditch silts.

Calibrated date: 1σ : cal BC 395 – 200
2σ : cal BC 410 – 100

Final comments:
D Jackson: as expected.

Harwell: recheck of HAR-2671.

HAR-3015   2410 ± 80 BP

$\delta^{13}C$: −26.0 ‰

Sample: AISAMPLE1, submitted on 29 November 1978

Material: charcoal: mainly *Quercus* sp. with *Corylus/Alnus* sp., *Acer* sp., and hawthorn type (Rosaceae, sub-family Pomoideae), all from large timbers; *c* 25% identified (C A Keepax).

Initial comment: from ditch silts.

Calibrated date: 1σ : cal BC 760 – 395
2σ : cal BC 800 – 370

Final comments:
D Jackson: as expected.

Harwell: recheck of HAR-2670.

Grindale, Humberside

Location: TA 148704
Lat. 54.06.58 N; Long. 00.13.42 W

Excavator: T G Manby (Doncaster Museum and Art Gallery), 1973

Site: Barrow 1, one of three ploughed-out round barrows in Grindale parish, which adjoins Boynton parish (see above); a central pit feature was enclosed by two ditches, of which the inner, oval ditch, was 2.0m deep with vertical sides; this had silted up to within 0.40m of the top and a stable soil formed when in the second period a timber structure on the mound was burnt down and the remains (charred timbers, burnt earth, and chalk) collapsed into the silted-up ditch hollow.

References: Manby 1980, 27 (^{14}C)
Radiocarbon **19**, 402 – 3 (^{14}C)

Objectives: to confirm the two phases of construction suggested by the barrow ditches.

Comments:
T G Manby: HAR-269 compares well with a date from the Willoughby Wold long barrow (BM-188); the depth of the ditch silting indicates a considerable duration before the phase 2 event; HAR-266 and HAR-267 support each other, as they should, and place the monument within the Neolithic period.

HAR-266   4510 ± 90 BP

$\delta^{13}C$: −26.5 ‰

Sample: HAR1, submitted on 24 January 1973

Material: charcoal.

Initial comment: from a burnt and fallen timber in the upper fill of the inner ditch (phase 2).

Calibrated date: 1σ : cal BC 3360 – 3040
2σ : cal BC 3500 – 2920

HAR-267   4470 ± 120 BP

$\delta^{13}C$: −27.2 ‰

Sample: HAR2, submitted on 24 January 1973

Material: charcoal.

Initial comment: from same context as HAR-266.

Calibrated date: 1σ : cal BC 3360 – 2925
2σ : cal BC 3510 – 2790

HAR-269   4910 ± 120 BP

$\delta^{13}C$: −25.0 ‰

Sample: ANT3, submitted on 17 May 1973

Material: antler, coated in PVA while *in situ*: red deer (*Cervus elaphus*).

Initial comment: from the floor of the inner ditch, probably contemporary with the ditch construction.

Calibrated date: 1σ : cal BC 3905 – 3540
2σ : cal BC 3990 – 3430

Final comments:
Harwell: any PVA left on the bone may have biased the result to an older than true date; the larger than normal error term is due to an insufficient carbon yield.

Guiting Power, Gloucestershire

Location: SP 089250
Lat. 51.55.23 N; Long. 01.52.14 W

Excavator: A Saville (Cheltenham Art Gallery and Museum Service), 1974

Site: a previously unrecorded domestic Iron Age settlement in the North Cotswolds.

References: Saville 1979a, 153 (^{14}C)
Radiocarbon **21**, 374 (^{14}C)

Objectives: the samples are from the fills of storage pits which are regarded as broadly contemporary, or at least as belonging to a single cultural phase; there is no stratigraphic or artefactual means of isolating them.

Comments:
A Saville: both results are much too old for the cultural material with which they were associated; the survival of Mesolithic and Neolithic carbonised wood and its incorporation in first-millennium pits is remarkable and inexplicable; on ceramic evidence the settlement probably dates to 300 – 1 BC. This confirms the unreliability of using grouped samples of mixed and twiggy charcoal from pit contexts.

AML: also HAR-1324 (C112, submitted on 9 October 1975) which has not yet been dated.

HAR-1320 6780 ± 110 BP

$\delta^{13}C$: –24.5 ‰

Sample: C108ETC, submitted on 9 October 1975

Material: charcoal: mainly *Corylus avellana/Alnus glutinosa*, probable hawthorn type (*Crataegus/Pryus/Malus/Sorbus* sp.), and blackthorn type (*Prunus* sp.), with some *Fraxinus excelsior*, all twiggy; also some *Quercus* sp. (C A Keepax).

Initial comment: from the fills of pits F1, F6, F7, F10, F11, F14, F23: associated with Iron Age 'B' type pottery.

Calibrated date: 1σ : cal BC 5740 – 5560
2σ : cal BC 5840 – 5480

Final comments:
A Saville: this result cannot relate to the Iron Age cultural context of the sample.

Harwell: this seems very much earlier than the other samples but the records give no reason to doubt the result.

HAR-1323 3780 ± 100 BP

$\delta^{13}C$: –24.7 ‰

Sample: C110/114, submitted on 9 October 1975

Material: charcoal: *Corylus avellana/Alnus glutinosa* and hawthorn type (*Crataegus/Pyrus/Malus/Sorbus* sp.), some twiggy (C A Keepax).

Initial comment: from the fills of pits F3 and F5, associated with Iron Age 'B' type pottery.

Calibrated date: 1σ : cal BC 2455 – 2040
2σ : cal BC 2555 – 1940

Final comments:
A Saville: as HAR-1320.

Harwell: the small size of the sample accounts for the larger than normal error term.

Hadstock, Essex

Location: TL 55884474
Lat. 52.04.43 N; Long. 00.16.30 E

Excavator: W Rodwell (Essex Archaeological Society), 1974

Site: rescue excavation within an Anglo-Saxon church prior to the laying of new floors.

References: Rodwell 1976
Radiocarbon **29**, 85 – 6 (^{14}C)

Objectives: to date the construction of the church and the burials in it.

HAR-2559 880 ± 70 BP

$\delta^{13}C$: –26.1 ‰

Sample: HAD2, submitted on 3 March 1978

Material: charcoal: all *Quercus* sp. from large timbers (C A Keepax).

Initial comment: from the fill of a bell casting pit inside the church.

Calibrated date: 1σ : cal AD 1035 – 1230
2σ : cal AD 1010 – 1270

Final comments:
W Rodwell: the charcoal comes from the fuel used to produce a single bell, probably associated with the first masonry church in the early eleventh century.

HAR-2594 1080 ± 80 BP

$\delta^{13}C$: –22.0 ‰

Sample: HAD1, submitted on 3 March 1978

Material: animal bone, mixed large and small fragments.

Initial comment: from a Saxon domestic horizon in the buried soil below the church.

Calibrated date: 1σ : cal AD 885 – 1020
2σ : cal AD 780 – 1155

Final comments:
W Rodwell: the deposit is likely to date to the ninth or earlier tenth century on account of its being aceramic.

HAR-2595 860 ± 70 BP

$\delta^{13}C$: –17.7 ‰

Sample: HAD4, submitted on 3 March 1978

Material: human bone: lower long bones of an adult individual.

Initial comment: from human bones which had been placed in a reliquary in the south porticus of the Saxon church; stratigraphically earlier than HAR-2606, but the burial would seem to be Norman rather than contemporary with the Saxon church.

Calibrated date: 1σ : cal AD 1045 – 1255
2σ : cal AD 1020 – 1280

Final comments:
W Rodwell: the deposit seems likely to have been made in the mid eleventh century.

Harwell: replicated with HAR-2697.

HAR-2606 600 ± 80 BP

$\delta^{13}C$: –19.7 ‰

Sample: HAD3, submitted on 3 March 1978

Material: human bone: most of the skeleton of a child, probably aged 6 – 12 months.

Initial comment: from the burial of a child in the south porticus of the Anglo-Saxon church, which sealed the reliquary (HAR-2595 and HAR-2697).

Calibrated date: 1σ : cal AD 1285 – 1415
                    2σ : cal AD 1260 – 1440

Final comments:
W Rodwell: this date is archaeologically unacceptable.

HAR-2697   780 ± 70 BP

δ¹³C: −19.2 ‰

Sample: HAD4, submitted on 3 March 1978

Material: human bone: lower long bones of an adult individual.

Initial comment: as HAR-2595.

Calibrated date: 1σ : cal AD 1205 – 1275
                    2σ : cal AD 1045 – 1290

Final comments:
W Rodwell: this date is not significantly different from HAR-2595.
Harwell: replicate of HAR-2595.

Hambledon Hill, Dorset

Location: ST 852123
             Lat. 50.54.34 N; Long. 02.12.38 W

Excavator: R Mercer (University of Edinburgh and the Department of the Environment)

Site: a Neolithic causewayed enclosure.

References: Mercer 1980, 51 (¹⁴C)
               Mercer 1985

Comments:
AML: one small sample, HAR-1884, was withdrawn; one small sample, HAR-1883, failed; six small samples were submitted before, but dated after, April 1981: HAR-2369 (HH7631), HAR-2370 (HH7640), HAR-9166 (HH75/556), HAR-9167 (HH75/559), HAR-9168 (HH75/1535), and HAR-9169 (HH75/1498).

HAR-1882   4560 ± 90 BP

δ¹³C: −24.9 ‰

Sample: HH75/2134, submitted on 1 September 1976

Material: charcoal: hawthorn type (Rosaceae, sub-family Pomoideae), not twiggy; 50% identified (C A Keepax).

Initial comment: from site E, ditch segment II, layer 11, a problematic organic deposit which could be either a dump similar to that in site F, or a rich organic silt which incorporated cultural material in its formation.

Calibrated date: 1σ : cal BC 3490 – 3100
                    2σ : cal BC 3605 – 2930

References: Radiocarbon **27**, 85

HAR-1885   4480 ± 130 BP

δ¹³C: −25.0 ‰

Sample: HH741245, submitted on 1 September 1976

Material: charcoal: hawthorn type (Rosaceae, sub-family Pomoideae), *Corylus* sp., and *Prunus* cf *spinosa* from fairly large timbers; also one blackthorn (*Prunus spinosa*) twig; 50% identified (C A Keepax).

Initial comment: from site A, ditch area II, trench D20, F1; this was an oval feature cut into the ?middle/rubble fill of the ditch and filled with grey organic soil and charcoal flecks, with some burnt bone, pot, and burnt flint; the feature and ditch fill were overlain by secondary silt deposits.

Calibrated date: 1σ : cal BC 3360 – 2925
                    2σ : cal BC 3605 – 2785

Final comments:
Harwell: the δ¹³C measurement was assumed.

HAR-1886   4840 ± 150 BP

δ¹³C: −26.4 ‰

Sample: HH75/846, submitted on 1 September 1976

Material: charcoal: *Sorbus* sp. and *Corylus* sp. (not twiggy), 50% identified (C A Keepax).

Initial comment: from site D1, ditch segment B, layer 12: ashy, dark grey, silty soil with small chalk lumps and charcoal which abuts the causeway between segments A and B.

Calibrated date: 1σ : cal BC 3780 – 3380
                    2σ : cal BC 3980 – 3195

References: Radiocarbon **27**, 85

HAR-2041   4110 ± 80 BP

δ¹³C: −23.4 ‰

Sample: HH75/545, submitted on 1 September 1976

Material: burnt antler.

Initial comment: from site B, upper fill (layer 1) of pit F57: rich black loam with antler, one pot, bone, and fragments of a stone rubber.

Calibrated date: 1σ : cal BC 2880 – 2510
                    2σ : cal BC 2910 – 2470

Final comments:
R Mercer: a most important date.

References: Radiocarbon **27**, 85

HAR-2368   4520 ± 80 BP

δ¹³C: −25.2 ‰

Sample: HH7626, submitted on 7 September 1977

Material: charcoal: *Quercus* sp. from large timbers (C A Keepax).

Initial comment: from bank outwork ditch 2, fill of F8: dark brown-black soil with granular chalk and flint, grittier at edges, looser and more loamy at centre, browner and more compact at a depth of *c* 120mm; the feature contained charcoal and unabraded sherds.

Calibrated date: 1σ : cal BC 3360 – 3045
                    2σ : cal BC 3500 – 2925

References: Radiocarbon **27**, 85

HAR-2371   4680 ± 110 BP

$\delta^{13}C$: −27.5 ‰

Sample: HH7647, submitted on 7 September 1977

Material: charcoal and burnt matter: no identifiable charcoal (C A Keepax).

Initial comment: from site L, outwork ditch 1, layer 7: a deposit of large chalk lumps and flint nodules with bone, flint, human bone, and other burnt material, overlying the primary silt (layers 8 and 9); the burnt area seemed to have a definite edge where it came up against layer 9 (HAR-2375 and HAR-2377).

Comment on uncalibrated date: this date was expected to complement HAR-2372 and HAR-2378.

Calibrated date: 1σ : cal BC 3625 − 3350
2σ : cal BC 3700 − 3050

Final comments:
Harwell: a small sample accounts for the larger than normal error term; see also HAR-2379.

References: Radiocarbon **27**, 84

HAR-2372   4360 ± 80 BP

$\delta^{13}C$: −27.2 ‰

Sample: HH7646, submitted on 7 September 1977

Material: charcoal: *Quercus* sp. and *Corylus/Alnus* sp., not twiggy (C A Keepax).

Initial comment: from site L, outwork ditch, layer 7, as HAR-2371, which this result is expected to complement.

Calibrated date: 1σ : cal BC 3095 − 2910
2σ : cal BC 3330 − 2710

Final comments:
Harwell: see also HAR-2379.

References: Radiocarbon **27**, 86

HAR-2375   4670 ± 100 BP

$\delta^{13}C$: −25.8 ‰

Sample: HH7682, submitted on 7 September 1977

Material: charcoal: *Quercus* sp., *Corylus* sp., and ?hawthorn type (Rosaceae, sub-family Pomoideae), not twiggy (C A Keepax).

Initial comment: from site G, ditch segment 3, layer 9A: grey charcoal-stained silt, in a deep bowl-shaped pit which cut into layer 10, the vacuous rubble fill overlying the ditch floor; this date is expected to complement HAR-2377.

Calibrated date: 1σ : cal BC 3620 − 3350
2σ : cal BC 3690 − 3100

References: Radiocarbon **27**, 86

HAR-2377   4610 ± 90 BP

$\delta^{13}C$: −25.4 ‰

Sample: HH7679, submitted on 7 September 1977

Material: charcoal: *Quercus* sp. from fairly large timbers, 50% identified (C A Keepax).

Initial comment: from site G, ditch segment 3, layer 9A; as HAR-2375, which this result should complement.

Calibrated date: 1σ : cal BC 3505 − 3140
2σ : cal BC 3625 − 3040

References: Radiocarbon **27**, 84

HAR-2378   4820 ± 120 BP

$\delta^{13}C$: −26.4 ‰

Sample: HH7662, submitted on 7 September 1977

Material: charcoal: *Quercus* sp. and *Corylus/Alnus* sp., not twiggy, 50% identified (C A Keepax).

Initial comment: from site K, outwork ditch 1, layer 7: from a very ashy area, containing lumps of charcoal, within the vacuous chalk lumps and flint nodules which overlay the primary silts (layers 8 and 9); the ashy deposit was sieved and floated (no chemicals were used in the flotation process).

Calibrated date: 1σ : cal BC 3775 − 3385
2σ : cal BC 3940 − 3350

Final comments:
Harwell: a small sample accounts for the larger than normal error term.

References: Radiocarbon **27**, 84

HAR-2379   4350 ± 80 BP

$\delta^{13}C$: −26.3 ‰

Sample: HH7648: 7649: 7650, submitted on 7 September 1977

Material: charcoal, three combined samples: *Quercus* sp. (not twiggy) and *Corylus/Alnus* sp. (some twiggy) (C A Keepax).

Initial comment: from site L, outwork ditch 1, layer 7: large vacuous chalk lumps and flint nodules overlying the primary silt (layers 8 and 9); HH7648 and HH7649 were closely associated with human skeletal material (unburnt) in this deposit; HH7650 was from same area as HH7646 and HH7647 (HAR-2371 and HAR-2372).

Calibrated date: 1σ : cal BC 3090 − 2910
2σ : cal BC 3325 − 2705

Final comments:
Harwell: see HAR-2371 and HAR-2372.

References: Radiocarbon **27**, 86

HAR-3061   4680 ± 80 BP

$\delta^{13}C$: −25.4 ‰

Sample: HH7741, submitted on 9 February 1979

Material: charcoal: Rosaceae, sub-family Pomoideae (eg hawthorn), *Quercus* sp., and *Corylus* sp. from mature timbers (C A Keepax).

Initial comment: from site N (interior), upper fill (3) of pit F6: flint and chalk lumps in a dark soil matrix with a rich assemblage of antler, flints, bone, and pottery.

Calibrated date: 1σ : cal BC 3615 – 3360
2σ : cal BC 3640 – 3140

Hambledon Hill: Stepleton Enclosure, Dorset

Location: ST 856125
Lat. 50.54.40 N; Long. 02.12.17 W

Excavator: R Mercer (Edinburgh University)

Site: a Neolithic causewayed enclosure.

References: Mercer 1985
Radiocarbon **27**, 86 – 7 (^{14}C)

Comments:
AML: four samples were dated after 1981 (HAR-4433, HAR-4435, HAR-4437, and HAR-4438).

HAR-3058   4700 ± 90 BP

$\delta^{13}C$: –24.9 ‰

Sample: ST7883, submitted on 9 February 1979

Material: charcoal: *Quercus* sp., *Corylus* sp., and hawthorn type (Rosaceae, sub-family Pomoideae) from mature timbers (C A Keepax).

Initial comment: from ditch 1, segment A, quadrant 2, layer 5: an accumulation of silt, mixed with ash and charcoal, overlying natural chalk in the main enclosure ditch; under HAR-3062 and HAR-3060.

Calibrated date: 1σ : cal BC 3625 – 3365
2σ : cal BC 3690 – 3140

HAR-3060   4570 ± 90 BP

$\delta^{13}C$: –25.4 ‰

Sample: ST78121, submitted on 9 February 1979

Material: charcoal: *Quercus* sp. and *Corylus* sp. from mature timbers (C A Keepax).

Initial comment: from layer 4: under HAR-3062, over HAR-3058; a burnt area, associated with skeletal material, in the initial accumulation of rubble from the unstabilised bank.

Calibrated date: 1σ : cal BC 3495 – 3105
2σ : cal BC 3615 – 2935

HAR-3062   4700 ± 90 BP

$\delta^{13}C$: –25.6 ‰

Sample: ST78118, submitted on 9 February 1979

Material: charcoal: *Quercus* sp., *Corylus* sp., and hawthorn type (Rosaceae, sub-family Pomoideae) from mature timbers; *c* 10% identified (C A Keepax).

Initial comment: from layer 3a: over HAR-3060 and HAR-3058; chalk gravel in a matrix of chalk wash with little humic material, from the eroded bank; finds include a concentration of antler picks.

Calibrated date: 1σ : cal BC 3625 – 3365
2σ : cal BC 3690 – 3140

Harlow: Moor Hall Gravel Pit, Essex

Location: TL 495113
Lat. 51.46.48 N; Long. 00.10.03 E

Excavator: T Betts (M11 Excavation Committee), 1974

Site: rescue excavation on a motorway borrow pit.

Objectives: to date the site dug by rescue excavation.

HAR-1204   2880 ± 90 BP

$\delta^{13}C$: –25.0 ‰

Sample: SAMPLE3, submitted on 12 June 1975

Material: charcoal.

Initial comment: from cremation deposit F4.

Calibrated date: 1σ : cal BC 1255 – 925
2σ : cal BC 1385 – 840

Final comments:
T Betts: both sets of calibrated dates are too early for the Early pre-Roman Iron Age pottery found on the site. However, the unpotted cremation, from which the sample was taken, has no direct relationship with the pottery bearing features.

Harlyn Bay, Cornwall

Location: SW 87787529
Lat. 50.32.17 N; Long. 04.59.43 W

Excavator: R Whimster (Department of the Environment and Cornwall Archaeological Society), 1976

Site: Bronze Age settlement under an Iron Age cemetery, with a round house.

References: Whimster 1977, 68 (^{14}C)

Objectives: to date the construction of the house and establish its chronological relationship to the adjacent cemetery.

HAR-1922   3550 ± 90 BP

$\delta^{13}C$: –25.4 ‰

Sample: HA76AN, submitted on 9 November 1976

Material: charcoal: gorse/broom twig, *Quercus* sp. from large timbers, and cf blackthorn (*Prunus* sp.) and hawthorn type (Rosaceae, sub-family Pomoideae) mainly from large timbers (C A Keepax).

Initial comment: from the ancient land surface, which was sealed by accumulated brown sand immediately before the construction of the stone round house.

Comment on uncalibrated date: sample cannot be taken to represent a single undisturbed deposit, as the charcoal was widely dispersed, but the date provides a useful *terminus post quem* for the initial phase of dune formation.

Calibrated date: 1σ : cal BC 2030 – 1760
2σ : cal BC 2170 – 1680

HAR-1923   3460 ± 140 BP

$\delta^{13}C$: –26.7 ‰

Sample: HA76AV, submitted on 9 November 1976

Material: charcoal: mainly *Salix/Populus* sp. from large timbers, also blackthorn (*Prunus* sp.) and gorse/broom, both mainly twiggy, and one fragment of *Quercus* sp. from a large timber (C A Keepax).

Initial comment: from a deposit of burned material, including sand, on the bedrock floor of the circular building.

Calibrated date: 1σ : cal BC 1960 – 1620
 2σ : cal BC 2183 – 1440

Final comments:
R Whimster: the relationship of HAR-1922 (pre-construction) and HAR-1923 (immediately pre-destruction/abandonment) confirms the relatively short lifespan of the circular building already suspected from the notable lack of artefactual evidence.

References: Radiocarbon **30**, 298

Harpley, Norfolk

Location: TF 762279
 Lat. 52.49.30 N; Long. 00.36.10 E

Excavator: A J Lawson (Norfolk Archaeological Unit), 1973

Site: Early Bronze Age round barrow, much disturbed; one of a group of eight barrows, above the 200ft contour, on the chalk between the head waters of the rivers Wensum and Babingley.

References: Lawson 1976a, 45 and 62 (^{14}C)
 Lawson 1986b, 42 (^{14}C)
 Lawson *et al* 1981
 Radiocarbon **19**, 411 (^{14}C)

Objectives: to substantiate the *terminus post quem*, for the construction of the barrow, provided by the Collared Urn.

HAR-486 3720 ± 90 BP

$\delta^{13}C$: –26.2 ‰

Sample: Samples 1+2, submitted on 16 January 1974

Material: charcoal: a few small fragments of *Quercus* sp. are present (C A Keepax).

Initial comment: from the old ground surface beneath the mound, associated with sherds of Collared Urn.

Calibrated date: 1σ : cal BC 2285 – 1985
 2σ : cal BC 2460 – 1890

Final comments:
A J Lawson: this gives a *terminus post quem* for the construction of the barrow; the date for the associated sherds of Collared Urn is very early.

Harringworth, Northamptonshire

Location: SP 94159476
 Lat. 52.32.32 N; Long. 00.36.42 W

Excavator: D Jackson (for the Department of the Environment), 1978

Site: standing earthwork enclosure adjacent to a parish boundary.

References: Jackson 1980b, 158 (^{14}C)

Objectives: to confirm the presumed prehistoric date of the earthwork.

HAR-2959 970 ± 60 BP

$\delta^{13}C$: –25.1 ‰

Sample: HGWORTH, submitted on 29 November 1978

Material: charcoal: *Quercus* sp., hawthorn type (Rosaceae, sub-family Pomoideae), and *Corylus/Alnus* sp., all from mature and twig wood; also *Prunus* sp. (eg blackthorn) twig, and *Acer* sp. (eg maple) from mature wood; 25% identified (C A Keepax).

Initial comment: from the lower silts of the ditch adjacent to the earthwork; no other dating evidence was found.

Calibrated date: 1σ : cal AD 1005 – 1155
 2σ : cal AD 970 – 1210

Final comments:
D Jackson: this result is surprisingly late, but there is no reason to suggest it is wrong.

Harrow Weald: Grim's Dyke, Greater London

Location: TQ 14169288
 Lat. 51.37.22 N; Long. 00.21.03 W

Excavator: R Ellis (Inner London Archaeological Unit), 1979

Site: Linear earthwork of disputed date.

References: Ellis 1982, 176 (^{14}C)

Objectives: to establish whether the earthwork is prehistoric or Saxon.

HAR-3747 1900 ± 80 BP

$\delta^{13}C$: –27.6 ‰

Sample: GD79210, submitted on 30 January 1980

Material: charcoal: *Quercus* sp. from large timbers mixed with soil (A J Clark).

Initial comment: from hearth F209, within the bank.

Calibrated date: 1σ : cal AD 15 – 215
 2σ : cal BC 100 – 320 AD

Final comments:
R Ellis: not inconsistent with the findings of the 1957 excavations on the earthwork at Pinner Green, where Iron Age and Belgic pottery was found.

Hartfield: Garden Hill, East Sussex

Location: TQ 444319
 Lat. 51.04.04 N; Long. 00.03.40 E

Excavator: J H Money (Garden Hill Excavation Group), 1978

Site: Iron Age hillfort and Romano-British ironworking settlement on Ashdown Forest.

References: Money 1977

Objectives: dates were required to check the calibration of the archaeomagnetic dates for the site.

Comments:
J H Money: the archaeological evidence provides little to support the results of one technique rather the other, but the design of the hillfort defences favours the archaeomagnetic date.

AML: according to the archaeomagnetic measurements, this site provides the first direct evidence for Iron Age ironworking in the Wealden area. This result is at variance with the magnetic dates, none of which seems to be earlier than mid first century BC. The maturity of the timber and the imprecision of radiocarbon in this period may be significant.

HAR-2816   2220 ± 70 BP

$\delta^{13}C$: −24.9 ‰

Sample: C63/145, submitted by A J Clark on 1 September 1977

Material: charcoal: *Quercus* sp., *Ilex* sp., *Corylus/Alnus* sp., and *Betula* sp., all from mature timbers (C A Keepax).

Initial comment: from the slag pit of an iron smelting furnace.

Calibrated date: 1σ : cal BC 390 − 190
2σ : cal BC 400 − 100

HAR-2819   1970 ± 80 BP

$\delta^{13}C$: −24.9 ‰

Sample: C167/175, submitted by A J Clark on 1 September 1977

Material: charcoal: *Quercus* sp. from mature timber (C A Keepax).

Initial comment: from a dump of iron forging slag.

Calibrated date: 1σ : cal BC 90 − 115 cal AD
2σ : cal BC 180 − 220 cal AD

Harting Beacon, West Sussex

Location: SU 80671804
Lat. 50.57.20 N; Long. 00.51.05 W

Excavator: O Bedwin (Sussex Archaeological Field Unit), 1976

Site: barrow just inside the southern edge of a large, feebly defended univallate hillfort.

References: Bedwin 1978

Objectives: to date the burial; in the absence of grave goods, this depends on the ^{14}C result.

HAR-2207   1150 ± 70 BP

$\delta^{13}C$: −21.5 ‰

Sample: HBIII (101), submitted on 16 November 1976

Material: human bone.

Initial comment: from a disturbed skeleton, in a grave, in the barrow robber trench.

Calibrated date: 1σ : cal AD 785 − 975
2σ : cal AD 80 − 1020

Final comments:
O Bedwin: this confirms the suspicion that the barrow is of Saxon date.

Harting Beacon, West Sussex

Location: SU 80461835
Lat. 50.57.30 N; Long. 00.51.15 W

Excavator: O Bedwin (Sussex Archaeological Field Unit), 1977

Site: Area IV, the western entrance to the hillfort.

References: Bedwin 1979, 31 (^{14}C)

Objectives: to obtain a date for a useful assemblage of Early Iron Age pottery.

HAR-2411   22 ± 100 BP

$\delta^{13}C$: unknown

Sample: HBIV403

Material: human bone.

Initial comment: from a human skull in a shallow recut in the southern ditch terminal (layers 8 and 8A), associated with a considerable amount of bone and pottery, dating to the sixth − fifth centuries BC; pottery of similar date was also found in the primary ditch fill.

Comment on uncalibrated date: compatible with the accompanying pottery.

Calibrated date: 1σ : cal BC 400 − 170
2σ : cal BC 488 − 30

Final comments:
Harwell: no certificate has been found.

Hartlepool, Cleveland

Location: NZ 501305
Lat. 54.40.01 N; Long. 01.13.23 W

Excavator: M Brown (Cleveland County Council), 1976

Site: cemetery of graves mainly cut into the Magnesian Limestone bedrock, with most bodies buried in a crouched position; there was one prone burial. It appears that different areas of the cemetery were used for adults and for children; some graves were edged with pebbles at the original ground level.

Objectives: the cemetery was sealed by thirteenth-century material but itself produced no pottery or other dating evidence; dates may indicate whether there was continuous occupation of Hartlepool from the disappearance of the Saxon monastery until the early twelfth century, when it is known that there was a church, or whether there was also a secular community at the time of the monastery.

HAR-2466 1710 ± 60 BP

$\delta^{13}C$: −20.4 ‰

Sample: HCW72119, submitted by J Pinches on 22 December 1977

Material: human bone.

Initial comment: from skeleton F119 (a grave to the north of the site near the parish church), part of the earlier phase of the cemetery; there is some evidence to suggest that this phase represents the reinterrment of bone disturbed elsewhere.

Calibrated date: 1σ : cal AD 245 − 405
2σ : cal AD 145 − 440

Final comments:
M Brown: the result was expected to be earlier than HAR-2467, but not Roman.

HAR-2467 1160 ± 60 BP

$\delta^{13}C$: −20.8 ‰

Sample: HCW76134, submitted by J Pinches on 22 December 1977

Material: human bone.

Initial comment: from a skeleton in an east − west grave cut into the bedrock near the present churchyard, sealed by thirteenth-century material.

Calibrated date: 1σ : cal AD 785 − 960
2σ : cal AD 690 − 1000

Final comments:
M Brown: earlier than expected; but this result suggests that there was a substantial lay population at the time of the reported destruction of the monastery by the Vikings.

Hartlepool: Church Walk, Cleveland

Location: NZ 529338
Lat. 54.41.47 N; Long. 01.10.45 W

Excavator: J Hinchliffe (University of Durham), 1972

Site: an unusual medieval cemetery sealed by thirteenth-century deposits. The burials were aligned east − west, but did not follow the normal medieval practice of lying on their backs with the limbs tidily arranged. They either lay on either side with their legs flexed and arms up by the face, at one side, or in the lap. One even lay on its front with the head turned to one side. All the graves, with the exception of a few of the infants were hacked out of the rock with considerable labour.

Objectives: to confirm dates obtained from samples submitted after a previous excavation on the site (see above, HAR-2467 and HAR-2466).

HAR-3023 1200 ± 90 BP

$\delta^{13}C$: −20.4 ‰

Sample: HCW72127, submitted by M Brown on 11 January 1979

Material: human bone: adult left femur and right tibia (C A Keepax).

Initial comment: from the 'late' phase of the cemetery (a burial which disturbed the earlier group).

Calibrated date: 1σ : cal AD 685 − 955
2σ : cal AD 650 − 1010

Final comments:
J Hinchliffe: this is in accordance with the revised interpretation of the cemetery.

HAR-3041 1440 ± 90 BP

$\delta^{13}C$: −20.8 ‰

Sample: HCW72164, submitted by M Brown on 11 January 1979

Material: human bone: pair of adult tibiae (C A Keepax).

Initial comment: from a pebble-edged grave *c* 0.75m below the contemporary ground surface, sealed by a building probably dating to the thirteenth century AD.

Calibrated date: 1σ : cal AD 545 − 665
2σ : cal AD 420 − 765

Final comments:
J Hinchliffe: as above.

HAR-3056 1310 ± 70 BP

$\delta^{13}C$: −20.4 ‰

Sample: HCW72139, submitted by M Brown on 11 January 1979

Material: human bone: parts of a pair of femora and a right adult tibia.

Initial comment: from the 'early' phase of the cemetery where skeletal material had been disturbed by later burials (same group as HAR-2466).

Calibrated date: 1σ : cal AD 655 − 775
2σ : cal AD 610 − 880

Final comments:
J Hinchliffe: as above.

Hascombe: Hillfort, Surrey

Location: TQ 005386
Lat. 51.08.14 N; Long. 00.33.48 W

Excavator: F H Thompson (Society of Antiquaries), 1975 and 1977

Site: univallate, Iron Age, promontory hillfort, with a rock-cut ditch and earth rampart faced with stone.

References: Thompson 1979, 304 − 9 (^{14}C)

Objectives: the excavation was part of a research project including two other Surrey hillforts; the dating was a joint project between the AM Laboratory, the BM Research Laboratory, Harwell, and Birmingham, designed to compare archaeomagnetic dates with ^{14}C dates on different materials.

HAR-1289 1960 ± 70 BP

$\delta^{13}C$: −22.7 ‰

Sample: HA7555, submitted by A J Clark on 22 September 1975

Material: charred grain.

Initial comment: from the bottom of a fairly deep pit cut into the Lower Greensand bedrock.

Calibrated date: 1σ : cal BC 45 – 115 cal AD
2σ : cal BC 150 – 210 cal AD

HAR-1290 2100 ± 70 BP

$\delta^{13}C$: −22.8 ‰

Sample: HA7555, submitted by A J Clark on 22 September 1975

Material: charred grain.

Initial comment: from the base of a fairly deep pit cut into the Lower Greensand bedrock.

Calibrated date: 1σ : cal BC 350 – 40
2σ : cal BC 370 – 50 cal AD

Final comments:
Harwell: some rootlets present; complete check on HAR-1289 using the second part of the material provided.

HAR-1698 2240 ± 70 BP

$\delta^{13}C$: −25.2 ‰

Sample: HA75/119, submitted by A J Clark on 27 May 1976

Material: charcoal.

Initial comment: from the old ground surface beneath the rampart.

Calibrated date: 1σ : cal BC 395 – 200
2σ : cal BC 410 – 120

HAR-1699 2120 ± 70 BP

$\delta^{13}C$: −25.9 ‰

Sample: HA75/267, submitted by A J Clark on 27 May 1976

Material: charcoal.

Initial comment: from the core of the south entrance bank of the hillfort.

Calibrated date: 1σ : cal BC 350 – 90
2σ : cal BC 380 – 20 cal AD

HAR-1700 2060 ± 60 BP

$\delta^{13}C$: −25.4 ‰

Sample: HA75/5/5, submitted by A J Clark on 27 May 1976

Material: charcoal: mostly from sapling wood, found mixed with grain samples HAR-1289 and HAR-1290.

Initial comment: from the bottom of a fairly deep pit.

Calibrated date: 1σ : cal BC 180 – 10 cal AD
2σ : cal BC 355 – 80 cal AD

Final comments:
F H Thompson: this agrees very well with BM-1244.

Harwell: excess gas was burned as HAR-1783, (2100 ± 80 BP).

HAR-1701 1950 ± 100 BP

$\delta^{13}C$: −25.0 ‰

Sample: HA75/8/3, submitted by A J Clark on 27 May 1976

Material: charcoal.

Initial comment: from the filling of a small pit.

Calibrated date: 1σ : cal BC 90 – 130 cal AD
2σ : cal BC 190 – 315 cal AD

Final comments:
Harwell: a smaller than ideal sample accounts for the larger than normal error term; the $\delta^{13}C$ value is assumed.

HAR-2803 2020 ± 80 BP

$\delta^{13}C$: −26.2 ‰

Sample: HA7725CH, submitted by A J Clark on 30 August 1978

Material: charcoal: hawthorn type (Rosaceae, sub-family Pomoideae) of *c* 10 years growth, *Quercus* sp. (twig of three years growth and large timber), *Betula* sp. (twig of *c* three years growth and large timber), and *Corylus/Alnus* sp. of three years growth; this is the only charcoal found in 1977 with less than 10 years growth.

Initial comment: from a pit containing grain (HAR-2809 and HAR-2818).

Calibrated date: 1σ : cal BC 150 – 65 cal AD
2σ : cal BC 340 – 130 cal AD

HAR-2809 2120 ± 70 BP

$\delta^{13}C$: −22.7 ‰

Sample: HA7725GR, submitted by A J Clark on 30 August 1978

Material: grain, five small bags which were collected in 1977 and stored without deliberate drying, and one large bag which was collected in 1975; the charcoal was removed by A J Clark, some stones may be present.

Initial comment: from the grain pit.

Calibrated date: 1σ : cal BC 350 – 90
2σ : cal BC 380 – 20 cal AD

HAR-2817 2180 ± 80 BP

$\delta^{13}C$: −22.6 ‰

Sample: HA7725GR, submitted by A J Clark on 4 September 1978

Material: grain, as HAR-2809.

Initial comment: from the grain pit.

Calibrated date: 1σ : cal BC 380 – 115
2σ : cal BC 400 – 30

HAR-2818   2030 ± 70 BP

$\delta^{13}C$: −22.7 ‰

Sample: HA7725GR, submitted by A J Clark on 4 September 1978

Material: grain, as HAR-2809.

Initial comment: from the grain pit.

Calibrated date: 1σ : cal BC 150 – 50 cal AD
                     2σ : cal BC 330 – 110 cal AD

Heathfield: Turner's Green (also known as Warbleton), East Sussex

Location: TQ 64091954
              Lat. 50.57.05 N; Long. 00.20.11 E

Excavator: W R Beswick and O Bedwin, 1978

Site: iron smelting bloomery, centred on an area of 7 × 5m, comprising three domed furnaces in a line on one side of a shallow ditch, opposite and parallel to a stone sill where bloom refining and smithing had been carried out; three outlying furnaces were found not more than 150m from the main site.

References: Beswick 1978
               Beswick 1979, 10
               Radiocarbon **29**, 95 (^{14}C)

Objectives: to date a furnace type not previously known in the Wealden area; in July 1970 a date of 567 ± 45 AD (uncalibrated) was produced by the British Museum for a much more disturbed furnace 100m away; this site is also thought to be of sixth-century date, but produced no datable artefacts.

HAR-2930   1810 ± 70 BP

$\delta^{13}C$: −26.3 ‰

Sample: TG2, submitted on 29 November 1978

Material: charcoal: *Quercus* sp. from mature timbers (C A Keepax).

Initial comment: from an undisturbed level in the reaction zone of the furnace, which still contained some of its charge.

Calibrated date: 1σ : cal AD 120 – 320
                     2σ : cal AD 60 – 390

HAR-2932   1990 ± 70 BP

$\delta^{13}C$: −25.1 ‰

Sample: TG4, submitted on 29 November 1978

Material: charcoal: *Quercus* sp. from mature timbers (C A Keepax).

Initial comment: from the same deposit as HAR-2930, but lower down.

Calibrated date: 1σ : cal BC 95 – 75 cal AD
                     2σ : cal BC 180 – 130 cal AD

HAR-3017   1900 ± 70 BP

$\delta^{13}C$: −24.8 ‰

Sample: TG3, submitted on 29 November 1978

Material: slag and charcoal: *Quercus* sp. from large timbers.

Initial comment: from the level of a stone sill, 2m behind the anvil area of a smithy; 4.8m away from the furnace from which HAR-2930 and HAR-2932 were taken and 0.62m below the cultivation surface.

Calibrated date: 1σ : cal AD 20 – 195
                     2σ : cal BC 60 – 250 cal AD

Final comments:
W R Beswick and O Bedwin: this date lies between those provided for HAR-2930 and HAR-2932 and confirms that the smithy was contemporary with the furnace.

Helpringham Fen, Lincolnshire

Location: TF 155405
              Lat. 52.56.57 N; Long. 00.16.51 W

Excavator: P Chowne and B B Simmons (South Lincolnshire Archaeological Unit), 1972 – 3

Site: Iron Age saltern. The site consisted of a series of hearths, much rebuilt, on man-made mounds, each mound being composed of debris apparently from earlier saltmaking activity. Typical saltmaking briquetage was everywhere on the site.

References: Simmons 1975

Objectives: to date the period of use of the charcoal, assumed to be in waste from fires used to evaporate salt.

Comments:
P Chowne and B B Simmons: The excavation was not taken down to the earliest levels and there was much rodent disturbance which severely hindered the obtaining of well stratified material.

AML: one small sample not yet dated (HF75F186).

HAR-2280   2180 ± 80 BP

$\delta^{13}C$: −25.7 ‰

Sample: HF75L56, submitted by P Chowne on 1 June 1977

Material: charcoal: *Alnus* sp. from fairly large timbers.

Initial comment: from make-up material of mound C on which saltmaking hearths were sited. The make-up consisted of ash, fired clay fragments, and charcoal briquetage. It predates the latest use of the hearths.

Calibrated date: 1σ : cal BC 380 – 115
                     2σ : cal BC 400 – 30

Final comments:
H Healey: pottery from the site suggests a third- to fourth-century BC starting date, continuing to the first century BC.

HAR-3102   2330 ± 90 BP

$\delta^{13}C$: −26.9 ‰

Sample: HF7218, submitted by P Chowne on 1 June 1977

Material: charcoal: mainly *Alnus* sp. with some Rosaceae, sub-family Pomoideae, both from large timbers.

Initial comment: from charcoal and ash deposit in mound A, predating the latest use of the hearths.

Calibrated date: 1σ : cal BC 485 – 370
                     2σ : cal BC 770 – 190

Final comments:
H Healey: pottery from the site ranges from the third to first centuries BC.

Harwell: a small sample accounts for the larger than normal error term.

Hemp Knoll, Wiltshire

Location: SU 068674
              Lat. 51.24.18 N; Long. 01.54.08 W

Excavator: M E Robertson-Mackay (for the Department of the Environment), 1965

Site: Bronze Age round barrow (Wiltshire 563).

References: Robertson-Mackay 1980; 137, 147 (^{14}C)

HAR-2997   4580 ± 80 BP

$\delta^{13}C$: –22.6 ‰

Sample: HKNEOPT2, submitted on 4 January 1979

Material: animal bone: cattle (*Bos* sp.), sheep (*Ovis* sp.), and red deer (*Cervus elaphus*).

Initial comment: from one of two Neolithic pits below the barrow.

Comment on uncalibrated date: this result agrees well with the ^{14}C date for the early construction of Windmill Hill; the closeness in dating may suggest that Hemp Knoll was a small village associated with a probable tribal centre at Windmill Hill.

Calibrated date: 1σ : cal BC 3495 – 3110
                     2σ : cal BC 3610 – 3040

HAR-2998   3540 ± 70 BP

$\delta^{13}C$: –25.6 ‰

Sample: HKCGRAVE, submitted on 4 January 1979

Material: charcoal: *Quercus* sp. from mature timber; *c* 10% identified (C A Keepax).

Initial comment: from the north-west end of the coffin in the central grave; the adult inhumation was accompanied by a Beaker wristguard and bone toggle.

Comment on uncalibrated date: seemingly rather late for a Wessex/Middle Rhine Beaker, although this result agrees with a date for a Wessex/Middle Rhine burial at Barnack (NPL-139, 1795 ± 135 BC).

Calibrated date: 1σ : cal BC 2010 – 1770
                     2σ : cal BC 2125 – 1695

Hereford: 5 Cantilupe St, Hereford and Worcester

Location: SO 514397
              Lat. 52.3.11 N; Long. 02.42.32 W

Excavator: R Shoesmith (City of Hereford Archaeology Committee), 1972 and 1975

Site: slip and berm in front of the Saxon city wall and behind the medieval wall on the eastern line of the defences.

References: Shoesmith 1982, 70 – 1 (^{14}C)
               Radiocarbon **27**, 80 (^{14}C)

Objectives: to date the early city defences, thought to be Saxon; the bones could possibly come from ditch cleaning, but are probably Saxon, associated with the building or repair of the Saxon stone wall; the date should fall between the construction of the wall and the disuse of the defences.

HAR-1620   950 ± 70 BP

$\delta^{13}C$: –22.2 ‰

Sample: HE75B583, submitted on 6 February 1976

Material: animal bone.

Initial comment: from within the primary build-up on the berm of the period 2 defences, in front of the Saxon stone revetment wall (F560). The layer was deposited after the wall was built, and probably before it was disused; it contained much mortar (from the wall) and snails as well as animal bone.

Comment on uncalibrated date: although it is possible that the bones were deposited over a long period of time, contamination from earlier phases is unlikely. The most likely date for the construction of the wall is early in the tenth century. The indicated date is rather late for initial deposition and may relate to the repair works.

Calibrated date: 1σ : cal AD 1010 – 1165
                     2σ : cal AD 970 – 1230

Final comments:
R Shoesmith: the defences are thought to have fallen into disuse by the Norman Conquest and the bones should date before that event.

Harwell: a replacement for HAR-1624 which was too small for dating.

Hereford: Berrington Street, site 2, Hereford and Worcester

Location: SO 507398
              Lat. 52.03.15 N; Long. 02.43.05 W

Excavator: R Shoesmith (City of Hereford Archaeology Committee), 1973

Site: one of four sites examined in the area between the western defences and Berrington Street, which established details of the pre-Conquest development of the area, and later occupation on the site.

References: Shoesmith 1982, 70 and 72 (^{14}C)
Radiocarbon **21**, 373 (^{14}C)

Objectives: to establish the date of an extensive burnt layer, assumed to be of late eighth or ninth century date.

HAR-1375 970 ± 70 BP

$\delta^{13}C$: −26.4 ‰

Sample: He73.II.F129/F270, submitted on 18 September 1975

Material: charcoal: from twigs or small branches, possibly *Fraxinus* sp. with some contamination by modern rootlets.

Initial comment: from two different areas of burnt charcoal and daub (all layer 111), above period 1 timber buildings, which should predate the turf rampart.

Comment on uncalibrated date: contamination by rootlets would account for a date which is younger than the construction or destruction of period 1 buildings; it is probable that the branches were cut before the tenth century.

Calibrated date: 1σ : cal AD 1000 – 1160
2σ : cal AD 900 – 1220

Final comments:
R Shoesmith: contamination has provided an unreliable date (see Shoesmith 1982, 72).

Harwell: a replacement for HAR-955 which was too small for dating; two parts combined.

Hereford: Bewell House, Hereford and Worcester

Location: SO 507401
Lat. 52.03.30 N; Long. 02.43.10 W

Excavator: R Shoesmith (City of Hereford Archaeology Committee), 1975

Site: traces of Saxon extra-mural settlement; the north-west corner of the medieval walled city, including the tail of the extended northern defences.

References: Shoesmith 1982, 70 – 2 (^{14}C)
Radiocarbon **21**, 373 (^{14}C)

Objectives: to date the feature and overlying defences; a sample of the ditch silt was also taken for archaeomagnetic dating but was unsuccessful.

HAR-1260 870 ± 80 BP

$\delta^{13}C$: −22.3 ‰

Sample: HE74A380, submitted on 16 July 1975

Material: animal bone.

Initial comment: from the fill of a small, substantially silted, ditch (F380, period 1); apparently sealed by the period 2 gravel rampart, thought to date to *c* 1189 AD.

Comment on uncalibrated date: it is to be expected that some of the bone used came from the surrounding soils and could have been deposited prior to the cutting and silting of the ditch; the ^{14}C date is thus, likely to be older than the date of the silting. With this reservation, the date is probably reliable.

Calibrated date: 1σ : cal AD 1035 – 1250
2σ : cal AD 1010 – 1280

Final comments:
R Shoesmith: the corrected dates agree well with a construction date of AD 1189 for the rampart overlying the infilled ditch (see Shoesmith 1982, 72).

Harwell: one other sample, HAR-1317 (74A349), gave an unreliable result.

Hereford: Broad Street, City Arms, Hereford and Worcester

Location: SO 509400
Lat. 52.03.25 N; Long. 02.43.05 W

Excavator: R Shoesmith (City of Hereford Archaeology Committee), 1973

Site: a watching brief which showed that the ditch, associated with the pre-Conquest defences, was open until the thirteenth century and built upon by the the fifteenth century.

References: Shoesmith 1982, 70 – 2 (^{14}C)

Objectives: to date a timber structure built within the ditch.

Comments:
AML: one sample, HAR-5066, was submitted after 1981.

HAR-1735 750 ± 70 BP

$\delta^{13}C$: −27.6 ‰

Sample: He74.1.H, submitted on 9 October 1975

Material: wood: from the tip of a well-preserved wooden post (possibly *Quercus* sp.).

Initial comment: from a post associated with a timber structure built into the (presumably disused) defensive ditch (see Shoesmith 1982, M3 F12 – G6).

Calibrated date: 1σ : cal AD 1225 – 1285
2σ : cal AD 1160 – 1385

Final comments:
R Shoesmith: as the sample came from the tip of the post (ie from the inner rings) the ^{14}C date is likely to be older than the structure.

Hereford: Castle Green, Hereford and Worcester

Location: SO 513395
Lat. 52.03.05 N; Long. 02.42.35 W

Excavator: R Shoesmith (City of Hereford Archaeology Committee), 1973

Site: Saxon cemetery excavated in advance of rescarping the river bank of the castle bailey.

References: Shoesmith 1980, 39 (^{14}C)

Objectives: to establish the lifespan of the cemetery and its relationship with the castle, and to establish continuity of use of the charcoal burial type; no independent dating evidence was found for any of the burials, although they seemed to span a reasonable period of time.

Comments:
R Shoesmith: the charcoal (HAR-413 and HAR-414) came from fairly large timbers; the samples were not deliberately chosen to represent either the inside or the outside, and must be considered to be a mixture of the two. The ^{14}C dates are thus somewhere between the time when the earliest trees started to grow, and when they were cut down. There is no evidence to show that the trees were in use between felling and burning, and the presence of bark in HAR-413 suggests that they were not, but the possibility exists. The human bone should be more reliable, and the dates should be that of the individual concerned.

The sequence assumed from the stratigraphical evidence for the five burial groups is in agreement with the ^{14}C dating, although the general dating is slightly more modern than was anticipated; this suggests that the burial ground possibly continued in use throughout the eleventh and early twelfth centuries, at least until St Guthlac's monastery was transferred to a new site in *c* AD 1144.

HAR-413 960 ± 70 BP

$\delta^{13}C$: −25.6 ‰

Sample: He73I.S80.ch, submitted on 26 November 1974

Material: charcoal: from a large quantity of twigs and small branches with some bark and larger timbers.

Initial comment: from initial fill of the grave cut of burial S80 (group 4).

Comment on uncalibrated date: there is no evidence that the wood used to make the charcoal found in this grave was appreciably older than the time of use, but these dates may be a little earlier than the burials; the bone should be more reliable.

Calibrated date: 1σ : cal AD 1005 – 1165
                    2σ : cal AD 960 – 1230

Final comments:
R Shoesmith: the burial is assumed to be pre-Conquest and probably tenth-century on stratigraphical evidence.

References: Radiocarbon **19**, 406

HAR-414 1030 ± 80 BP

$\delta^{13}C$: −26.02 ‰

Sample: He73I.S74.ch, submitted on 26 November 1974

Material: charcoal: as HAR-413, from fairly large timbers.

Initial comment: two charcoal samples from the grave cut of burial S74 (group 2).

Calibrated date: 1σ : cal AD 900 – 1035
                    2σ : cal AD 830 – 1170

Final comments:
R Shoesmith: the burial is assumed to be of ninth- or early tenth-century date on stratigraphical evidence.

References: Radiocarbon **19**, 406

HAR-985 1250 ± 70 BP

$\delta^{13}C$: −20.1 ‰

Sample: He73I.S85, submitted on 26 November 1974

Material: human bone.

Initial comment: from burial S85 (group 1), one of two east – west inhumations, under burial S80 (HAR-413); possibly the earliest grave on the site.

Calibrated date: 1σ : cal AD 673 – 880
                    2σ : cal AD 650 – 950

Final comments:
R Shoesmith: this burial is assumed to be of seventh- or eighth-century date on stratigraphical evidence.

References: Radiocarbon **19**, 407

HAR-986 890 ± 80 BP

$\delta^{13}C$: −19.8 ‰

Sample: He73I.S46, submitted on 26 November 1974

Material: human bone.

Initial comment: from burial S46 (group 4), an east – west charcoal burial sealing the foundations of the building thought to be St Guthlac's church.

Calibrated date: 1σ : cal AD 1025 – 1230
                    2σ : cal AD 990 – 1270

Final comments:
R Shoesmith: this burial is assumed to be of pre-Conquest date, probably tenth-century.

References: Radiocarbon **19**, 407

HAR-988 820 ± 70 BP

$\delta^{13}C$: −19.5 ‰

Sample: He73I.S10, submitted on 26 November 1974

Material: human bone.

Initial comment: from burial S10 (group 6), an east – west burial in a stone cist; one of the latest adult graves on the site, although the cemetery may have continued in use within the castle.

Calibrated date: 1σ : cal AD 1160 – 1265
                    2σ : cal AD 1030 – 1280

Final comments:
R Shoesmith: does this suggest that burial continued in the castle bailey area into a post-Conquest period? The associated St Guthlac's monastery continued there until AD 1144.

References: Radiocarbon **19**, 407

HAR-1875 1020 ± 70 BP

$\delta^{13}C$: −19.8 ‰

Sample: He73I.S83, submitted on 25 January 1976

Material: human bone.

Initial comment: from burial S83 (group 3).

Calibrated date: 1σ : cal AD 970 – 1035
                    2σ : cal AD 890 – 1170

Final comments:
R Shoesmith: assumed to be of ninth- or early tenth-century date.

Harwell: a replacement for HAR-1625 (AML-757649, He73I.S82) which was too small for dating.

References: Radiocarbon **27**, 80

Heysham: St Patrick's Chapel, Lancashire

Location: SD 411618
Lat. 54.02.55 N; Long. 02.53.59 W

Excavator: T W Potter (University of Lancaster) and R D Andrews, 1977 – 8

Site: a medieval chapel.

Objectives: dates from the skeletons are of prime importance since there was a sparsity of datable finds; these samples were submitted to help establish a chronology for the cemetery.

HAR-2756   1010 ± 80 BP

$\delta^{13}C$: –23.1 ‰

Sample: H772A, submitted on 22 May 1978

Material: human bone.

Initial comment: from skeleton 46: a burial below the stone-lined graves, in the east bedrock gully.

Calibrated date: 1σ : cal AD 970 – 1150
                     2σ : cal AD 880 – 1210

Final comments:
T W Potter: perfectly consistent with the archaeological evidence.

HAR-2757   940 ± 80 BP

$\delta^{13}C$: –22.0 ‰

Sample: H771A, submitted on 22 May 1978

Material: human bone.

Initial comment: from skeleton 12, an undisturbed burial cutting the demolished east wall of the phase 1 stone chapel.

Calibrated date: 1σ : cal AD 1010 – 1185
                     2σ : cal AD 960 – 1260

Final comments:
T W Potter: a useful confirmation of the early date of the phase and the chapel.

HAR-2768   960 ± 70 BP

$\delta^{13}C$: –21.9 ‰

Sample: H773A, submitted on 22 May 1978

Material: human bone.

Initial comment: from skeleton 36, an undisturbed burial immediately outside the south door of the chapel and overlying the top step of a flight of four.

Calibrated date: 1σ : cal AD 1005 – 1165
                     2σ : cal AD 960 – 1230

Final comments:
T W Potter: a useful confirmation of the early date of the flight of stairs.

Hodcott Down, Berkshire

Location: SU 472815
Lat. 51.31.48 N; Long. 01.19.10 W

Excavator: J C Richards (Berkshire Archaeological Unit), 1979

Site: a round barrow.

HAR-3599   3340 ± 70 BP

$\delta^{13}C$: –25.4 ‰

Sample: HD79111A, submitted on 9 October 1979

Material: charcoal: *Fraxinus* sp. from mature timbers; *c* 50% identified (C A Keepax).

Initial comment: from the buried land surface beneath the barrow, associated with a cremation with an ogival bronze dagger.

Calibrated date: 1σ : cal BC 1735 – 1525
                     2σ : cal BC 1870 – 1460

HAR-3607   3490 ± 80 BP

$\delta^{13}C$: –26.8 ‰

Sample: HD79111B, submitted on 9 October 1979

Material: charcoal: mainly *Fraxinus* sp. with *Corylus/Alnus* sp., *Quercus* sp., and bark, all from mature timbers; *c* 50% identified (C A Keepax).

Initial comment: from the buried land surface, as HAR-3599.

Calibrated date: 1σ : cal BC 1925 – 1705
                     2σ : cal BC 2030 – 1630

HAR-3608   3370 ± 70 BP

$\delta^{13}C$: –26.2 ‰

Sample: HD79111D, submitted on 9 October 1979

Material: charcoal: mainly *Fraxinus* sp. from large timbers, with *Corylus/Alnus* sp. and *Quercus* sp. also from large timbers and bark; *c* 50% identified.

Initial comment: from the buried land surface, as HAR-3599.

Calibrated date: 1σ : cal BC 1745 – 1540
                     2σ : cal BC 1880 – 1520

Hog Cliff Hill, Dorset

Location: SY 625962
Lat. 50.46.02 N; Long. 02.31.55 W

Excavator: P Rahtz (for the Department of the Environment), 1960

Site: hillfort of 26 acres, much larger than Little Woodbury or Gussage All Saints, which might have served a specific pastoral function (cattle folding and leather working); the defences are slight and the occupation sparse – ten circular enclosures, with huts of posthole and wall slot construction, were investigated and an important ceramic assemblage was recovered.

References: Ellison and Rahtz 1987, M50 (^{14}C)
Radiocarbon **19**, 401 (^{14}C)

Objectives: the site is one of the earliest Iron Age settlements in Dorset and unique in form; the ceramic collection and house plans are extensive. A ^{14}C date was requested in order to suggest the position of the site in the Late Bronze Age – Early Iron Age sequence in Dorset.

HAR-234   2490 ± 70 BP

$\delta^{13}C$: −25.0 ‰

Sample: E105/121, submitted by A Ellison on 28 December 1972

Material: wood: *Corylus avellana* of *c* 15mm diameter and *Quercus robor* L. *c* 50mm+ diameter (AML-600471); *Corylus avellana c* 275mm diameter (AML-600472) (G C Morgan).

Initial comment: from pit E105 (*c* 450mm deep), and the base of posthole E121 (*c* 300mm deep), below soil and flints; the estimated result is *c* 2400 BP.

Calibrated date: 1σ : cal BC 795 – 420
  2σ : cal BC 810 – 400

Final comments:
P Rahtz: the result confirms the relationship of the site to others in Dorset such as Maiden Castle, and supports the generally 'early' date assigned to the pottery, which includes classic haematite wares.

Harwell: two samples were combined to increase the sample quantity.

Hogsthorpe, Lincolnshire

Location: TF 533718
  Lat. 53.13.12 N; Long. 00.17.47 E

Excavator: B Kirkham (Trust for Lincolnshire Archaeology), 1978

Site: Iron Age saltmaking hearth sealed by a thick layer of marine clay which shows signs of ?Roman ploughing.

References: Kirkham 1981, 9 (^{14}C)
  Fawn *et al* 1990, 43 (^{14}C)

Objectives: the site is stratigraphically important for the study of the relationships of marine transgression and regression in the area.

HAR-3092   2490 ± 80 BP

$\delta^{13}C$: −27.6 ‰

Sample: TF533718, submitted by B B Simmons on 29 November 1978

Material: burnt soil: no identifiable charcoal (C A Keepax).

Initial comment: from a well stratified deposit in the hearth, with salt making material and Iron Age pottery.

Calibrated date: 1σ : cal BC 795 – 410
  2σ : cal BC 810 – 400

Final comments:
B Kirkham: the ^{14}C dating is particularly valuable in determining the date of the marine transgression which put many Lincolnshire coastal sites out of operation.

Horbling Fen, Lincolnshire

Location: TF 143355
  Lat. 52.54.16 N; Long. 00.18.01 W

Excavator: B B Simmons (Trust for Lincolnshire Archaeology), 1976

Site: a drainage dyke section.

References: Chowne 1980, 295 (^{14}C)

Comments:
AML: three small samples (HAR-1747, HAR-1748, and HAR-1753) were abandoned as unsuitable and withdrawn.

HAR-1749   3010 ± 80 BP

$\delta^{13}C$: −27.2 ‰

Sample: 1LAYER4, submitted on 7 May 1976

Material: soil.

Initial comment: from a bulk peat sample.

Calibrated date: 1σ : cal BC 1400 – 1130
  2σ : cal BC 1440 – 1010

Final comments:
B B Simmons: this compares favourably with a date from Billingborough obtained from charcoal in an enclosure ditch abandoned as a result of freshwater flooding.

Harwell: the sample was full of rootlets.

HAR-1750   3750 ± 70 BP

$\delta^{13}C$: −25.5 ‰

Sample: FEATUREA, submitted on 7 May 1976

Material: soil.

Initial comment: from a palaeosol containing pockets of charcoal.

Calibrated date: 1σ : cal BC 2290 – 2040
  2σ : cal BC 2455 – 1970

Final comments:
B B Simmons: invaluable result when considered with the excavated evidence from Billingborough.

Houghton: Bury Hill, West Sussex

Location: TQ 003126
  Lat. 50.54.13 N; Long. 00.34.24 W

Excavator: O Bedwin (Sussex Archaeological Field Unit), 1979

Site: an Early Neolithic enclosure of *c* 1 hectare with a single continuous ditch and one entrance on the west side.

References: Bedwin 1981, 86 (^{14}C)

Objectives: the site was formerly thought to be of Iron Age date, but the 1979 excavations produced a quantity of Neolithic finds; precise dating is required, as part of a research project to date all the enclosures of the period *c* 4300 – 1000 BC in West Sussex.

HAR-3595   4570 ± 80 BP

$\delta^{13}C$: −21.2 ‰

Sample: BH791001, submitted on 9 October 1979

Material: antler.

Initial comment: from the floor of ditch 1 (layer 4).

Calibrated date: 1σ : cal BC 3490 – 3110
                    2σ : cal BC 3600 – 3040

Final comments:
O Bedwin: the date is consistent with the pottery and flintwork; the enclosure date is consistent with that of similar sites in southern England.

HAR-3596   4680 ± 80 BP

$\delta^{13}C$: −23.0 ‰

Sample: BH795002, submitted on 9 October 1979

Material: animal bone.

Initial comment: from the floor of ditch 1 (layer 4).

Calibrated date: 1σ : cal BC 3615 – 3360
                    2σ : cal BC 3640 – 3140

Final comments:
O Bedwin: as HAR-3595.

Hovingham: Church, North Yorkshire

Location: SE 666757
              Lat. 51.52.02 N; Long. 00.58.47 W

Excavator: A Pacitto (for the Department of the Environment)

HAR-3090   1460 ± 80 BP

$\delta^{13}C$: −25.2 ‰

Sample: HOV01, submitted by H Kenward on 9 February 1979

Material: charcoal: *Quercus* sp. (A R Hall).

Initial comment: from below Saxon building spread; EAU 29.

Calibrated date: 1σ : cal AD 540 – 655
                    2σ : cal AD 420 – 680

HAR-3091   1300 ± 70 BP

$\delta^{13}C$: −25.0 ‰

Sample: HOV20, submitted by H Kenward on 9 February 1979

Material: charcoal: *Quercus* sp. (A R Hall).

Initial comment: from the foundation trench of the Saxon church; EAU 28.

Calibrated date: 1σ : cal AD 655 – 780
                    2σ : cal AD 620 – 890

Ipswich, Suffolk

Location: TM 165445
              Lat. 52.03.22 N; Long. 01.09.29 E

Excavator: K Wade (Suffolk County Council)

Site: Middle Saxon and later town.

References: Wade 1988

Comments:
AML: two further samples (HAR-4627 and HAR-4628) were submitted in 1981.

HAR-2763   1230 ± 70 BP

$\delta^{13}C$: −28.1 ‰

Sample: 43020039, submitted by P Murphy on 12 July 1980

Material: wood: *Quercus* sp. from a large timber (C A Keepax).

Initial comment: from the hollowed-out tree-trunk lining of a well.

Calibrated date: 1σ : cal AD 680 – 885
                    2σ : cal AD 660 – 970

Final comments:
K Wade: this confirms the suspected Middle Saxon date of the well.

HAR-2764   1120 ± 70 BP

$\delta^{13}C$: −26.4 ‰

Sample: 55020280, submitted by P Murphy on 12 July 1980

Material: wood: *Quercus* sp. from a large timber (C A Keepax).

Initial comment: from a barrel reused to line a well which, on the pottery evidence, was abandoned in the late ninth century.

Calibrated date: 1σ : cal AD 830 – 990
                    2σ : cal AD 725 – 1020

Final comments:
K Wade: dendrochronological analysis has since shown that two trees were used, one felled after AD 871, the other undated.

HAR-2778   940 ± 80 BP

$\delta^{13}C$: −20 ‰

Sample: 55020524, submitted by P Murphy on 12 July 1978

Material: human bone, marked with ink.

Initial comment: disarticulated human bone of unknown date from a pit underlying a medieval cemetery.

Calibrated date: 1σ : cal AD 1010 – 1160
2σ : cal AD 900 – 1260

Final comments:
K Wade: this dating implies the reburial of eleventh-century skeletons presumably disturbed elsewhere in the town during the medieval period.

HAR-2781   1240 ± 70 BP

$\delta^{13}C$: –20.7 ‰

Sample: 3902BONE, submitted by P Murphy on 12 July 1978

Material: human bone.

Initial comment: disarticulated bone from different layers in the tenth-century town ditch.

Calibrated date: 1σ : cal AD 675 – 885
2σ : cal AD 650 – 960

Final comments:
K Wade: the dating confirms that the bone is derived from an earlier (Middle Saxon) cemetery disturbed by the construction of the town ditch.

Jarrow: St Paul's, County Durham

Location: NZ 339652
Lat. 54.58.49 N; Long. 01.28.13 W

Excavator: R Cramp (University of Durham), 1966

Site: Saxon and medieval monastery.

References: Cramp 1969
Cramp 1976

Objectives: to confirm the dating of a major Saxon building – building A, from the burnt timbers, which were thought to be structural.

HAR-960   2040 ± 80 BP

$\delta^{13}C$: –24.4 ‰

Sample: JA66ZP1, submitted on 26 November 1974

Material: charcoal.

Initial comment: from a hollow in the *opus signinum* floor of the building.

Comment on uncalibrated date: this sample was kept for a long time before submission and could have been contaminated.

Calibrated date: 1σ : cal BC 170 – 50 cal AD
2σ : cal BC 355 – 120 cal AD

Final comments:
R Cramp: this would imply the reuse of Roman wood as well as stone and tile in this building.

HAR-961   1540 ± 70 BP

$\delta^{13}C$: –24.8 ‰

Sample: JA66ZP2, submitted on 26 November 1974

Material: charcoal.

Initial comment: from a hollow in the *opus signinum* floor of building A.

Calibrated date: 1σ : cal AD 425 – 600
2σ : cal AD 380 – 650

Final comments:
R Cramp: the building was probably constructed c 685 – 700. This date confirms the use of seasoned timber and is within the expected range.

Jarrow: St Paul's, County Durham

Location: NZ 339652
Lat. 54.58.49 N; Long. 01.28.13 W

Excavator: R Cramp (University of Durham), 1978

Site: Saxon and medieval monastery.

References: Cramp 1969
Cramp 1976

Objectives: to confirm the dating of the hearth; this was expected, on archaeological grounds, to be of eighth- or early ninth-century date, but archaeomagnetic dating gave a result of 1200 ± 10 BP.

HAR-2910   1100 ± 80 BP

$\delta^{13}C$: –26.0 ‰

Sample: GP, submitted on 27 October 1978

Material: charcoal: *Quercus* sp. from mature timbers (C A Keepax).

Initial comment: from fill of hearth F50.

Calibrated date: 1σ : cal AD 880 – 1010
2σ : cal AD 725 – 1040

Final comments:
R Cramp: this is a date within the acceptable range, although it was crucial to know rather more precisely whether the hearth was in use during the monastic occupation of the site.

Kenchester, Herefordshire

Location: SO 448424
Lat. 52.04.36 N; Long. 02.48.20 W

Excavator: P Rahtz, T Wilmott, and S P Q Rahtz, 1977 – 9

Site: a Roman town.

References: Wilmott and Rahtz 1985

Objectives: to confirm the dating of ditch silts which were expected to be Late Roman on numismatic grounds, but which could have been as late as the fifth century.

Comments:
AML: one small sample, HAR-2526 (ORG2U89C), was withdrawn.

HAR-2531   1850 ± 80 BP

$\delta^{13}C$: –26.7 ‰

Sample: ORG37:9:7754C, submitted on 21 February 1978

Material: charcoal: *Quercus* sp., *Corylus* sp., and *Acer* sp., all mainly from fairly large timbers (C A Keepax).

Initial comment: from the middle layer of the latest ditch on the site, which cuts Late Roman features; sealed by the upper silt and ploughsoils. The expected date is late fourth century or later.

Calibrated date: 1σ : cal AD 70 – 245
2σ : cal BC 30 – 375 cal AD

Final comments:
P Rahtz, T Wilmott, and S P Q Rahtz: the charcoal seems to have been residual in the ditch fill, this result adds nothing to existing numismatic evidence.

Kimpton: Kalis Corner, Hampshire

Location: SU 288480
Lat. 51.13.48 N; Long. 01.35.15 W

Excavator: M Dacre (Andover Excavation Committee), 1966 – 9

Site: a Bronze Age cremation cemetery.

References: Dacre and Ellison 1981, 200 – 1 (^{14}C)

Objectives: the charcoal is associated with vessels which can only be be dated typologically within the date range 1400 – 1000 BC; ^{14}C dates may provide a better chronology.

Comments:
M Dacre: the dates are earlier than expected, although this may in part be due to the very small size of the samples.

Harwell: the samples were taken some ten years before, without ^{14}C dating in mind, and were all below the optimum size requirement for the standard measurement process; this deficiency is reflected in the larger than average error terms; HAR-4316, HAR-4317, and HAR-4320 especially may be less reliable than the larger samples; a combined mean of HAR-4316 and HAR-4320, 3490 ± 90, taken for the published report, calibrates as follows:

Calibrated date 1 σ : cal BC 1937 – 1696
2 σ cal BC 2115 – 1610

AML: one sample was dated after 1981, HAR-4572 (XVI).

HAR-4316   3560 ± 180 BP

$δ^{13}C:$ –25.0 ‰

Sample: SQXVII = C16, submitted on 12 January 1981

Material: charcoal.

Initial comment: from inside a burial urn of late Early Bronze Age or early Middle Bronze Age date, associated with a cremation; the expected date is late Early Bronze Age.

Comment on uncalibrated date: an early date relative to those of the Middle Bronze Age, which confirms the internal chronology of the site and highlights the importance of the phase C Barrel Urns.

Calibrated date: 1σ : cal BC 2180 – 1680
2σ : cal BC 2460 – 1465

HAR-4317   2970 ± 100 BP

$δ^{13}C:$ –26.3 ‰

Sample: XVA = C13, submitted on 12 January 1981

Material: charcoal.

Initial comment: from an urned burial of late Early Bronze Age or early Middle Bronze Age date; the expected date is 1200 – 1000 BC.

Calibrated date: 1σ : cal BC 1390 – 1030
2σ : cal BC 1440 – 910

Final comments:
M Dacre: anomalous; this may result from contamination of the deposit by Middle Bronze Age charcoal.

HAR-4319   3200 ± 70 BP

$δ^{13}C:$ –25.8 ‰

Sample: VIIE = F6/7, submitted on 12 January 1981

Material: charcoal.

Initial comment: from a context associated with a human cremation and a late Middle Bronze Age urn; the expected date is 1200 – 1000 BC.

Calibrated date: 1σ : cal BC 1525 – 1420
2σ : cal BC 1670 – 1320

HAR-4320   3470 ± 110 BP

$δ^{13}C:$ –26.5 ‰

Sample: VIIIA = G2, submitted on 12 January 1981

Material: charcoal.

Initial comment: from inside a Late Bronze Age jar containing a cremation; the expected date is 1000 – 800 BC.

Comment on uncalibrated date: as HAR-4316.

Calibrated date: 1σ : cal BC 1940 – 1680
2σ : cal BC 2130 – 1520

Kings Lynn: Queen Street, Norfolk

Location: TF 616199
Lat. 52.45.08 N; Long. 00.23.41 E

Excavator: P Wade-Martins (Norfolk Archaeological Unit), 1977

Site: medieval waterfront occupation underlying three stone houses dating, probably, from the later twelfth and early thirteenth centuries, which were much modified in the Middle Ages and later.

References: Richmond *et al* 1982, 110 (^{14}C)

Objectives: to date the medieval waterfront occupation.

HAR-2539   940 ± 70 BP

$δ^{13}C:$ –26.7 ‰

Sample: 999, submitted by P Murphy on 2 February 1978

Material: wood: *Quercus* sp..

Initial comment: from the pointed end of a stake recovered from mixed layers of peat and silt, at a depth of 2.5m below pavement level, in a mechanically-dug inspection pit roughly under the hearth within house 28.

Calibrated date: 1σ : cal AD 1015 – 1170
2σ : cal AD 970 – 1250

Final comments:
P Wade-Martins: this gives a date to the earliest phase of waterfront occupation.

Kingston-upon-Hull: Queen Street, Humberside

Location: TA 10022844
Lat. 53.20.30 N; Long. 01.02.30 W

Excavator: M Eddy and J Barnard (Hull Archaeological Unit), 1976

Site: an urban site (QU76).

Objectives: the sample was originally submitted for wood identification only.

HAR-2262   270 ± 70 BP

$\delta^{13}C$: –25.2 ‰

Sample: 124-47, submitted by R Morgan on 19 August 1976

Material: wood: *Pinus* sp. (C A Keepax).

Initial comment: a plank from the rebuilding of the Mytongate street frontage between AD 1668 and 1727 (context 47); the expected date is seventeenth century.

Calibrated date: 1σ : cal AD 1514 – 1952
2σ : cal AD 1450 – 1955

Final comments:
M Eddy and J Barnard: agrees well with the archaeological evidence.

References: Radiocarbon **27**, 90

HAR-2266   200 ± 90 BP

$\delta^{13}C$: –25.0 ‰

Sample: 104-33 (or 143-134?), submitted by R Morgan on 19 August 1976

Material: wood: conifer (?*Pinus* sp.).

Initial comment: from context 33 (or 134?).

Calibrated date: 1σ : cal AD 1640 – 1955
2σ : cal AD 1470 – 1950

Final comments:
D Evans: the sample was tentatively matched on a dendrochronological curve between AD 1568 and 1790. Context 33 was a modern cellar wall bonded into the seventeenth-century gaol garderobe wall, presumably postdating the demolition of the latter in *c* AD 1791. The excavator suggested a date of AD 1792 – 1806 for this context.

Kingston-upon-Thames: Eden Walk, Surrey

Location: TQ 180691
Lat. 51.24.29 N; Long. 00.18.12 W

Excavator: L Gillibrand (Kingston-upon Thames Museum), 1975 – 6

Site: waterlain deposits cut by Late Saxon or early medieval ditches, medieval rubbish pits, and a possible tannery adjacent to a pond.

HAR-2468   2330 ± 60 BP

$\delta^{13}C$: –22.5 ‰

Sample: A1A8, submitted by D Hinton on 22 December 1977

Material: bone.

Initial comment: from a surface sealing wood in a former prehistoric watercourse.

Calibrated date: 1σ : cal BC 405 – 385
2σ : cal BC 755 – 250

HAR-2497   3470 ± 80 BP

$\delta^{13}C$: –28.3 ‰

Sample: A1BI22, submitted by D Hinton on 22 December 1977

Material: wood: entirely bark (C A Keepax).

Initial comment: from the lower layers of wood in the prehistoric watercourse.

Calibrated date: 1σ : cal BC 1896 – 1690
2σ : cal BC 2030 – 1610

HAR-2498   3560 ± 90 BP

$\delta^{13}C$: –27.9 ‰

Sample: A1BIV27, submitted by D Hinton on 22 December 1977

Material: wood: *Alnus glutinosa* (C A Keepax).

Initial comment: from a layer of organic peat in a former river channel, sealing a deposit of Late Neolithic refuse comprising Mortlake pottery, worked antler, and flint, including a Petit-tranchet derivative; also associated with a brushwood feature of unknown function, possibly a natural accumulation of flotsam.

Calibrated date: 1σ : cal BC 2035 – 1770
2σ : cal BC 2185 – 1680

References: Field and Cotton 1987, 76 and 89

Kirkham: Priory, North Yorkshire

Location: SE 735658
Lat. 54.04.58 N; Long. 00.52.35 W

Excavator: R Williams (for the Department of the Environment), 1978

Site: Augustinian priory established *c* 1120 on the site of an earlier settlement.

Objectives: to establish the probable date of a cemetery below, and adjacent to, the monastic gatehouse.

HAR-3065   900 ± 80 BP

$\delta^{13}C$: −21.1 ‰

Sample: KP78/75, submitted on 4 January 1979

Material: human bone: 1 femur, 1 humerus, and 2 tibiae from an adult – small female in appearance (C A Keepax).

Initial comment: from a shallow grave sealed by a fifteenth- to sixteenth-century layer; no associated finds.

Calibrated date: 1σ : cal AD 1025 – 1225
                    2σ : cal AD 980 – 1270

Final comments:
R Williams: this establishes a pre-monastic date for the cemetery.

HAR-3066   920 ± 70 BP

$\delta^{13}C$: −20.5 ‰

Sample: KP78/71, submitted on 4 January 1979

Material: human bone.

Initial comment: from a deep grave sealed by a fifteenth- to sixteenth-century layer; no associated finds.

Calibrated date: 1σ : cal AD 1020 – 1210
                    2σ : cal AD 980 – 1260

Final comments:
R Williams: this establishes a pre-monastic date for the cemetery.

Lambourn: Barrow 19, Berkshire

Location: SU 330826
              Lat. 51.32.27 N; Long. 01.31.27 W

Excavator: J C Richards (Wessex Archaeological Unit)

Site: a Bronze Age barrow.

HAR-3818   3440 ± 90 BP

$\delta^{13}C$: −26.4 ‰

Sample: LB78F3, submitted on 5 March 1980

Material: charcoal: mainly hawthorn type (Rosaceae, subfamily Pomoideae) with occasional fragments of *Prunus* sp. (eg blackthorn) and *Corylus/Alnus* sp..

Initial comment: from charcoal associated with a cremation, in a bell-shaped pit, beneath the primary barrow mound.

Calibrated date: 1σ : cal BC 1885 – 1675
                    2σ : cal BC 2020 – 1520

Lamyatt Beacon, Somerset

Location: ST 669362
              Lat. 51.07.25 N; Long. 02.28.23 W

Excavator: R Leech (Committee for Rescue Archaeology in Avon, Gloucerstershire, and Somerset), 1973

Site: Romano-British temple and ?Dark Age cemetery.

References: Leech 1986; 270, 272 (^{14}C)

Objectives: to determine the relationship of the east – west burials to the temple.

HAR-2593   1180 ± 70 BP

$\delta^{13}C$: −23.2 ‰

Sample: LBF165, submitted on 3 March 1978

Material: human bone: skull and long bone fragments of a mature adult male (C A Keepax).

Initial comment: from east – west burial F165.

Calibrated date: 1σ : cal AD 770 – 955
                    2σ : cal AD 670 – 1000

HAR-2670   1430 ± 70 BP

$\delta^{13}C$: −22.0 ‰

Sample: LBF159, submitted on 3 March 1978

Material: human bone: long bone fragments.

Initial comment: from east – west burial F159.

Calibrated date: 1σ : cal AD 560 – 660
                    2σ : cal AD 450 – 690

Final comments:
R Leech: these results suggest that the east – west burials postdate the abandonment of the temple by 200 years or more.

Harwell: was such a difference between the dates expected? The experimental notes give no reason for doubt.

Launceston: Castle, Cornwall

Location: SX 331847
              Lat. 50.38.15 N; Long. 04.21.38 W

Excavator: A D Saunders (for the Department of the Environment), 1974 – 8

Site: the castle.

Objectives: dates are required to help resolve historical arguments.

Comments:
AML: two samples, HAR-982 (3319) and HAR-1651 (LAU7GNGW), were abandonned.

HAR-978   810 ± 70 BP

$\delta^{13}C$: −26.3 ‰

Sample: ZR333106, submitted on 26 November 1978

Material: charcoal: all oak (*Quercus* sp.); *c* 50% identified (C A Keepax).

Initial comment: from a midden deposit *c* 1.0m below the surface.

Calibrated date: 1σ : cal AD 1165 – 1270
                    2σ : cal AD 1030 – 1290

HAR-979   910 ± 70 BP

$\delta^{13}C$: −26.0 ‰

Sample: ZR333134, submitted on 26 November 1978

Material: charcoal: all *Quercus* sp.; *c* 50% identified (C A Keepax).

Initial comment: from *c* 1.5m below the surface, in the same layer as HAR-978.

Calibrated date: 1σ : cal AD 1025 – 1215
2σ : cal AD 990 – 1260

HAR-980   930 ± 100 BP

$\delta^{13}C$: −24.7 ‰

Sample: 3234, submitted on 26 November 1974

Material: charcoal.

Initial comment: from a context associated with an early structure, below the eleventh-century rampart.

Calibrated date: 1σ : cal AD 1010 – 1220
2σ : cal AD 890 – 1270

Final comments:
Harwell: a small sample, diluted to make up the deficiency, accounts for the larger than normal error term.

HAR-981   1120 ± 90 BP

$\delta^{13}C$: −26.35 ‰

Sample: 3318, submitted on 26 November 1974

Material: charcoal.

Initial comment: from below the eleventh-century rampart.

Calibrated date: 1σ : cal AD 790 – 1010
2σ : cal AD 680 – 1040

HAR-983   890 ± 80 BP

$\delta^{13}C$: −25.5 ‰

Sample: 3354, submitted on 26 November 1974

Material: charcoal.

Initial comment: from a context associated with an early structure, below the eleventh-century rampart.

Calibrated date: 1σ : cal AD 1025 – 1230
2σ : cal AD 990 – 1270

HAR-984   1490 ± 80 BP

$\delta^{13}C$: −26.6 ‰

Sample: 3320, submitted on 26 November 1974

Material: charcoal: mainly *Quercus* sp. with one fragment of *Corylus avellana* and one of ?*Acer campestre*; *c* 50% identified (C A Keepax).

Initial comment: The expected date is *c* AD 1250.

Calibrated date: 1σ : cal AD 445 – 645
2σ : cal AD 400 – 670

Layton, County Durham

Location: NZ 378269
Lat. 54.38.08 N; Long. 01.24.52 W

Excavator: J Clipson (Central Excavation Unit), 1978

Site: believed to be the site of a deserted medieval village but no evidence of occupation was found during excavations in advance of a road widening scheme.

Objectives: excavation of a deserted medieval village – it turned out not to be a village, but a series of medieval enclosures over ridge and furrow.

HAR-2917   11290 ± 90 BP

$\delta^{13}C$: −28.8 ‰

Sample: 27-306, submitted on 27 October 1978

Material: peat.

Initial comment: from presumed early post-glacial lake deposits, c1.5m beneath what was assumed to be the natural clay.

Final comments:
J Clipson: as expected.

Harwell: this result is too old to calibrate.

Ledston, West Yorkshire

Location: SE 433295
Lat. 53.45.35 N; Long. 01.20.35 W

Excavator: J Keighley and I Hodder (West Yorkshire County Council), 1976

Site: an Iron Age site on the Magnesian Limestone; one of very few cropmark sites in the area which have been excavated.

References: Radiocarbon **29**, 93 (^{14}C)

Objectives: to obtain dating evidence for the site.

Comments:
J Keighley and I Hodder: these are the first ^{14}C dates for a pre-Roman site in this area; they confirm that Ledston was occupied in the Iron Age and, together with cropmark evidence, suggest extensive prehistoric settlement in the area.

HAR-2805   2080 ± 100 BP

$\delta^{13}C$: −22.0 ‰

Sample: LEDSF363, submitted by R Yarwood on 14 August 1978

Material: human bone.

Initial comment: from a burial sealed in the bottom of a storage pit (F704).

Calibrated date: 1σ : cal BC 340 – 20 cal AD
2σ : cal BC 390 – 120 cal AD

Final comments:
J Keighley and I Hodder: this confirms the approximate dating suggested by the material remains.

HAR-2825 2270 ± 70 BP

$\delta^{13}C$: −24.6 ‰

Sample: LEDSSF418, submitted by R Yarwood on 14 August 1978

Material: charcoal.

Initial comment: from a sealed context in the fill of a posthole (F539).

Calibrated date: 1σ : cal BC 400 – 235
2σ : cal BC 410 – 180

Final comments:
J Keighley and I Hodder: as HAR-2805.

Leicester: Austin Friars, Leicestershire

Location: SK 580044
Lat. 52.38.02 N; Long. 01.08.34 W

Excavator: J E Mellor and T Pearce, 1973 – 8

Site: a shallow pond or lake in a low-lying area between two branches of the River Soar; in the fourteenth-century this was the site of the Austin Friary.

References: Shackley and Hunt 1984 – 5, 1 (^{14}C)

Objectives: to provide a chronological context for the palaeoenvironmental evidence.

HAR-4260 9920 ± 100 BP

$\delta^{13}C$: unknown

Sample: RCIIV75, submitted by P Clay on June 1981

Material: peat.

Initial comment: from a peat bed, beneath blue alluvial clay, representing a possible change in the pre-Roman river course.

Comment on uncalibrated date: this result places the deposit at the beginning of the pre-Boreal stage.

Final comments:
Harwell: this result is too old to calibrate.

Levington: Site LVT023, Suffolk

Location: TM 23664083
Lat. 52.01.13 N; Long. 01.15.36 E

Excavator: L Elmhirst (Suffolk Archaeological Unit), 1978

Site: one of three Bronze Age ring ditches excavated in advance of the construction of the Ipswich Southern Bypass; these formed part of the largest linear barrow cemetery in Suffolk.

References: Lawson *et al* 1981
Lawson 1986a; 2, fig 1 (^{14}C)
Martin 1980

Objectives: to date the ring ditches.

HAR-3706 1950 ± 70 BP

$\delta^{13}C$: −25.9 ‰

Sample: LVTO23-45, submitted by P Murphy on 5 March 1980

Material: charcoal: mostly or entirely from one timber *c* 150mm in diameter (A J Clark).

Initial comment: from a patch of burning in the upper fill of a Bronze Age ring ditch.

Comment on uncalibrated date: (E Martin) charcoal was associated with Iron Age pottery which could be contemporary with the ^{14}C date; sherds of Early Bronze Age pottery were found in the interior of the ring ditch, so the Iron Age pottery and date indicate later reuse of the site, whilst the ditch, and presumably the barrow mound, were still visible. Iron Age pottery was also found at site LVTO25 (see below).

Calibrated date: 1σ : cal BC 35 – 120 cal AD
2σ : cal BC 110 – 220 cal AD

Levington: Site LVT024, Suffolk

Location: TM 23824080
Lat. 52.01.12 N; Long. 01.15.44 E

Excavator: L Elmhirst (Suffolk Archaeological Unit), 1978

Site: as Levington site LVTO23.

References: Lawson *et al* 1981
Lawson 1986a; 2, fig 1 (^{14}C)
Martin 1980

Objectives: as Levington site LVTO23.

HAR-3741 3340 ± 80 BP

$\delta^{13}C$: −26.0 ‰

Sample: LVTO24-22, submitted by P Murphy on 5 March 1980

Material: charcoal: mostly from large timbers, contaminated by many rootlets (A J Clark).

Initial comment: from a small patch of cremated bone (containing ten human long bone fragments) found just inside, or on the edge of, the ring ditch (faint outline unverified at this point). Thought to be a Bronze Age cremation.

Calibrated date: 1σ : cal BC 1740 – 1525
2σ : cal BC 1880 – 1440

Final comments:
E Martin: this date is confirmed by the presence of Early Bronze Age pottery within the interior of the ring ditch.

Levington: Site LVT025, Suffolk

Location: TM 23864073
Lat. 52.01.09 N; Long. 01.15.46 W

Excavator: L Elmhirst (Suffolk Archaeological Unit), 1978

Site: as Levington site LVTO23. This site had an outer ring 35m in diameter and 2m deep, and a concentric inner depression 17m in diameter and 0.5m deep; at the centre of the ring ditch was a cremation under an Early Bronze Age Collared Urn.

References: Lawson *et al* 1981
Lawson 1986a; 2, fig 1 (^{14}C)
Martin 1980

Objectives: as Levington site LVTO23.

HAR-3742   1070 ± 70 BP

$\delta^{13}C$: −27.0 ‰

Sample: LVTO25-19, submitted by P Murphy on 5 March 1980

Material: charcoal: clean charcoal but contaminated by many rootlets (A J Clark).

Initial comment: (E Martin) from a small patch of charcoal, on the surface of the depression, within the interior of the Bronze Age ring ditch.

Calibrated date: 1σ : cal AD 890 – 1020
2σ : cal AD 790 – 1150

Final comments:
L Elmhirst: this date does not fit with the Early Bronze Age Collared Urn found at the centre of the ring ditch.

Lewes: St Pancras Priory, Southover, East Sussex

Location: TQ 41460961
Lat. 50.52.05 N; Long. 00.00.38 E

Excavator: D Freke (Sussex Archaeological Field Unit)

Site: massive earthwork enclosure.

Objectives: to establish whether the earthwork is part of the Saxon burgh, or part of an Iron Age hillfort.

Comments:
AML: two small samples, LEW2 and LEW4, were withdrawn.

HAR-1024   1130 ± 60 BP

$\delta^{13}C$: −25.9 ‰

Sample: LEW1, submitted on 26 November 1974

Material: charcoal.

Initial comment: from a pit beneath the bank (LLS 83).

Calibrated date: 1σ : cal AD 830 – 980
2σ : cal AD 770 – 1020

Final comments:
D Freke: within the acceptable range for the Saxon burgh.

HAR-1025   1600 ± 100 BP

$\delta^{13}C$: −25.65 ‰

Sample: LEW3, submitted on 26 November 1974

Material: charcoal.

Initial comment: from the secondary fill of a large pit near the edge of the bank (LLS 81).

Calibrated date: 1σ : cal AD 340 – 560
2σ : cal AD 230 – 650

Final comments:
D Freke: clearly predates the bank of the Saxon burgh and must be part of unknown Late Roman or Early Saxon activity.

Lincoln: Flaxengate, Lincolnshire

Location: SK 976714
Lat. 53.13.49 N; Long. 00.32.16 W

Excavator: C Colyer (Lincoln Archaeological Trust)

Site: medieval town.

References: Radiocarbon **27**, 84 (^{14}C)

Objectives: the pre-tenth-century levels produced no means of absolute dating; the aim is to determine whether the industrial activity on the site represents economic revival in the Danish period, or is earlier than this. The date of these levels also has an important bearing on the ceramic tradition, for they contain Stamford ware in what is so far its earliest context.

HAR-1837   1590 ± 80 BP

$\delta^{13}C$: −22.6 ‰

Sample: SMAF75BK, submitted on 9 September 1976

Material: animal bone.

Initial comment: from a rubbish deposit.

Comment on uncalibrated date: this date confirms the Late Roman origin of the material, which was in a secondary context of later date.

Calibrated date: 1σ : cal AD 390 – 555
2σ : cal AD 255 – 630

Lincoln: St Mark's, Lincolnshire

Location: SK 974708
Lat. 53.13.43 N; Long. 00.32.27 W

Excavator: B Gilmour (Lincoln Archaeological Trust), 1976

Site: a medieval church.

References: Gilmour and Stocker 1986, 17 (^{14}C)
Radiocarbon **27**, 88 (^{14}C)

Objectives: to establish a chronology for the cemetery and thus to obtain a *terminus post quem* for the earliest church. HAR-1961, HAR-2010, and HAR-2012 are from the southern part of the cemetery; HAR-2011 is from the northern part.

Comments:
AML: one sample, HAR-2023, failed.

HAR-1961   870 ± 70 BP

$\delta^{13}C$: −19.9 ‰

Sample: SMASS1, submitted by C Colyer on 24 February 1977

Material: human bone.

Initial comment: from a post-Roman burial which predates the earliest medieval church; later than two other graves (HAR-2010 and HAR-2012).

Calibrated date: 1σ : cal AD 1040 – 1245
2σ : cal AD 1010 – 1270

Final comments:
B Gilmour: a likely date.

HAR-2010   1040 ± 60 BP

$\delta^{13}C$: –21.0 ‰

Sample: 411AUJ, submitted by C Colyer on 9 September 1976

Material: human bone.

Initial comment: from a complete skeleton, a primary burial which predates the earliest medieval stone church.

Calibrated date: 1σ : cal AD 960 – 1025
2σ : cal AD 890 – 1155

Final comments:
B Gilmour: a likely date.

HAR-2011   980 ± 70 BP

$\delta^{13}C$: –20.4 ‰

Material: human bone.

Initial comment: from the deepest burial to the north of, and predating, the earliest medieval church.

Calibrated date: 1σ : cal AD 990 – 1155
2σ : cal AD 900 – 1220

Final comments:
B Gilmour: a likely date.

HAR-2012   1110 ± 70 BP

$\delta^{13}C$: –20.1 ‰

Sample: 401ATP, submitted by C Colyer on 9 September 1976

Material: bone.

Initial comment: from a post-Roman burial predating the first stone medieval church; the earliest but one of a sequence of burials, this was sealed by two more graves and cut away above the waist by the foundations of the porch.

Calibrated date: 1σ : cal AD 880 – 1000
2σ : cal AD 770 – 1030

Final comments:
B Gilmour: a likely date.

Lincoln: St Paul-in-the-Bail, Lincolnshire

Location: SK 976719
Lat. 53.14.06 N; Long. 00.32.15 W

Excavator: B Gilmour (Lincoln Archaeological Trust), 1979

Site: a medieval church, overlying a single-celled building on the site of the Roman forum.

References: Hunter and Foley 1987
Steane 1991

Objectives: to date the first use of the site; the samples were taken from stratigraphically the earliest graves in the first phase of the cemetery on the site, which was dated by related finds to the ninth – eleventh centuries.

Comments:
AML: also 20 samples dated or submitted after April 1981.

HAR-4116   1410 ± 80 BP

$\delta^{13}C$: –20.6 ‰

Sample: 29BNS517, submitted on 14 October 1980

Material: human bone.

Initial comment: from what is probably a plain burial, the head of which was truncated by the north-east corner of the single-celled church. In turn the skeleton lay over the north-west part of the robber trench of the apse of the early church.

Calibrated date: 1σ : cal AD 565 – 670
2σ : cal AD 450 – 770

Final comments:
B Gilmour: this provides ^{14}C dating evidence for the apsidal church: this inhumation cuts the apsidal church – so is the church Late Roman?

HAR-4120   2030 ± 110 BP

$\delta^{13}C$: –22.2 ‰

Sample: 32BPH532, submitted on 14 October 1980

Material: human bone.

Initial comment: from a north – south articulated burial against what is probably the west side of the robber trench of the division of the early church between the north – south arcade and the nave/apse.

Calibrated date: 1σ : cal BC 190 – 80 cal AD
2σ : cal BC 370 – 220 cal AD

Final comments:
B Gilmour: this date was not expected, as the burials must have been post-Roman at the earliest. A similar date to HAR-4177 was expected.

HAR-4121   1330 ± 90 BP

$\delta^{13}C$: –22.3 ‰

Sample: 38DCZ735, submitted on 14 October 1980

Material: human bone.

Initial comment: from the earliest grave to the east of wall YZ. Probably a plain burial cut by the construction pit for the Late Saxon sunken-featured building.

Calibrated date: 1σ : cal AD 635 – 775
2σ : cal AD 550 – 890

Final comments:
B Gilmour: C14 dating is the only dating evidence available. It is a possible date.

HAR-4131   1450 ± 80 BP

$\delta^{13}C$: −21.0 ‰

Sample: 30BOC519, submitted on 14 October 1980

Material: human bone.

Initial comment: from what is probably a plain burial, which was partially truncated by the north side of the north wall of the single-celled church. In turn it lay over the robber trench of the juction of the north walls of the apse and nave of the early church, possibly directly over one of the post sockets.

Calibrated date: 1σ : cal AD 545 – 660
                     2σ : cal AD 420 – 690

Final comments:
B Gilmour: C14 dating is the only evidence to date the apsidal church. The inhumation cuts the church – so is the church Late Roman?

HAR-4143   1500 ± 80 BP

$\delta^{13}C$: −21.2 ‰

Sample: 16BHL449, submitted on 14 October 1980

Material: human bone.

Initial comment: from an early grave to the east of the church.

Calibrated date: 1σ : cal AD 440 – 635
                     2σ : cal AD 400 – 670

Final comments:
B Gilmour: C14 dates are the only dates available. It is a possible date.

HAR-4177   1580 ± 90 BP

$\delta^{13}C$: −22.3 ‰

Sample: 34BQP534, submitted on 14 October 1980

Material: human bone.

Initial comment: from a north – south articulated burial against the west side of the probable robber trench of the north – south division of the early church between the arcade and the nave/apse. Radiocarbon dating is the only evidence to date the apsidal church – this inhumation cut the church, so it may be Late Roman.

Calibrated date: 1σ : cal AD 390 – 590
                     2σ : cal AD 250 – 650

HAR-4281   1350 ± 80 BP

$\delta^{13}C$: −22.4 ‰

Sample: 21BLP493, submitted on 14 October 1980

Material: bone.

Initial comment: from a probable plain burial, partially truncated by the north side of the north wall of the single-celled church.

Calibrated date: 1σ : cal AD 630 – 760
                     2σ : cal AD 550 – 860

Final comments:
B Gilmour: C14 dates are the only dating available. It is a possible date.

Lincoln: Saltergate, Lincolnshire

Location: SK 4976137126
              Lat. 52.55.44 N; Long. 01.15.35 W

Excavator: J Wacher and N M Reynolds (Department of the Environment), 1973

Site: part of the medieval and Roman lower town, immediately north of the River Witham waterfront. The three trenches were coded LIN73 D, E, F. The waterfront city wall was exposed, with Roman/post-Roman occupation to the rear. A substantial Late Roman house with hypocaust was found, with four burials postdating the destruction of this building. Stratigraphy suggests that the burials were Early or Middle Saxon.

References: Reynolds 1979, 88 (^{14}C)

Objectives: to date the burial.

Comments:
AML: one small sample was dated after 1981.

HAR-863   1170 ± 90 BP

$\delta^{13}C$: −21.2 ‰

Sample: Find No 4882, submitted on 5 September 1976

Material: animal and human bone.

Initial comment: from skeleton 4, context LIN73 E1193.

Calibrated date: 1σ : cal AD 725 – 975
                     2σ : cal AD 660 – 1020

Final comments:
P Miles: this sample was wrongly believed to be uncontaminated human bone. Were the samples taken from an agregation of all the human and animal bone in the sample or not? The date itself is however consistent with the stratigraphic evidence, which suggested that the burials were definitely post-Roman, and probably pre-tenth century.

Lincoln: Silver Street, Lincolnshire

Location: SK 97757137
              Lat. 53.13.48 N; Long. 00.32.08 W

Excavator: J Wacher and N M Reynolds (Department of the Environment), 1973

Site: three trenches coded LIN73 A, B, C, revealed part of the Roman and medieval lower town, including the eastern city wall and rampart; a Roman road sequence and occupation; a large rectangular early medieval pottery kiln with associated and later pits; medieval and/or post-medieval buildings and burials, some of which were probably associated with the Franciscan friary.

References: Miles *et al* 1989
                Miles forthcoming

Objectives: to date the kiln.

HAR-447   1470 ± 80 BP

$\delta^{13}C$: −27.2 ‰

Sample: Find Nos 636-641 and 738, submitted on September 1973

Material: charcoal, seven aggregated samples.

Initial comment: samples from contexts B103, B104, B106, B107, and B108 in the kiln.

Calibrated date: 1σ : cal AD 490 – 650
2σ : cal AD 410 – 680

Final comments:
P Miles: this date must surely be too early; the pottery being produced was in all probability of mid tenth-century date, and cannot be seen as earlier than the mid ninth century. But there is no particular reason to suspect contamination – the layers are from the middle of the sequence of kiln fills. Presumably one of the samples was contaminated by a piece of older material?

Litlington: The Mile Ditches, Cambridgeshire

Location: TL 3142 approx
Lat. 53.03.38 N; Long. 00.05.20 W

Excavator: G R Burleigh (Letchworth Museum), 1978

HAR-3485 2040 ± 80 BP

$\delta^{13}C$: –24.8 ‰

Sample: FIJJKKL6, submitted on 9 October 1979

Material: bone.

Initial comment: from the primary silt of the western ditch.

Calibrated date: 1σ : cal BC 170 – 50 cal AD
2σ : cal BC 355 – 120 cal AD

Little Cressingham, Norfolk

Location: TL 863988
Lat. 52.33.17 N; Long. 00.44.54 E

Excavator: A J Lawson (Norfolk Archaeological Unit), 1977

Site: remnant of a double-ditched round barrow (Norfolk 5053; AM 260b), one of a group of seven on the Cretaceous Upper Chalk above the River Blackwater; the inner ditch was partly silted up before the outer was cut; chalk from the second ditch filled the first and presumably enlarged the mound which had been ploughed away by the time of excavation; there was no trace of a burial.

References: Lawson *et al* 1981
Lawson 1986a; 2, fig 1 (^{14}C)
Lawson 1986b; 5, 10, 18 (^{14}C)

Objectives: to date the barrow: worked flint and Early Bronze Age and Iron Age pottery were stratified in the ditch fills but artefacts were sparse.

HAR-2541 3540 ± 110 BP

$\delta^{13}C$: –25.3 ‰

Sample: 54, submitted by P Murphy on 21 February 1978

Material: charcoal: *Quercus* sp. and *Corylus/Alnus* sp. from fairly large timbers; also *Prunus* sp., twigs; *c* 50% identified. (C A Keepax).

Initial comment: from a soil above the primary fill of the inner ditch; finds from below this comprise only flint flakes and animal bone; there is no ceramic evidence to complement the ^{14}C determination.

Comment on uncalibrated date: together with the pottery, this result suggests a date in the Early Bronze Age for the construction of the barrow; this agrees well with the Wessex style burials in an adjacent barrow excavated in 1849.

Calibrated date: 1σ : cal BC 2030 – 1740
2σ : cal BC 2195 – 1620

Final comments:
A J Lawson: this date provides a *terminus ante quem* for the primary barrow and a *terminus post quem* for its subsequent enlargement.

Little Hallingbury: Mid Field, Essex

Location: TL 507165
Lat. 51.49.35 N; Long. 00.11.13 E

Excavator: T Betts (M11 Excavation Committee), 1974

Site: the removal of top soil by the contractors for an M11 borrow pit exposed a rectangular area of some 60m × 40m which was defined on two sides by lines of shallow discontinuous trenches and pits interpreted as the possible remains of a palisade trench. Very fragmented pottery sherds were of a heavily flint tempered fabric. There were isolated cremations of which the ^{14}C sample was one.

Objectives: to date the site dug by rescue excavation.

HAR-865 2900 ± 90 BP

$\delta^{13}C$: –26.7 ‰

Sample: LHF8, submitted on 26 November 1974

Material: charcoal and small fragments of calcined bone.

Initial comment: from the fill of the cremation deposit in feature 8.

Calibrated date: 1σ : cal BC 1260 – 945
2σ : cal BC 1395 – 845

Final comments:
T Betts: the dating is very compatible with the nature of the site.

Little Somborne, Hampshire

Location: SU 389328
Lat. 51.05.34 N; Long. 01.26.40 W

Excavator: D Neal (Central Excavation Unit), 1977

Site: an oval Iron Age enclosure with two round houses and numerous two-post structures, dating from the fifth to the second centuries BC.

References: Neal 1979, 98 (^{14}C)

HAR-2222   2480 ± 90 BP

$\delta^{13}C$: −25.0 ‰

Sample: 502, submitted by N Balaam on 1 June 1977

Material: charcoal: *Quercus* sp. (N Balaam).

Initial comment: amalgamated samples from the postholes of an Iron Age round house.

Calibrated date: 1σ : cal BC 795 – 405
2σ : cal BC 820 – 390

Little Waltham, Essex

Location: TL 736129
Lat. 51.47.14 N; Long. 00.31.02 E

Excavator: P Drury (Chelmsford Excavation Committee), 1970 – 1

Site: Iron Age and Roman settlement, and a former watercourse.

References: Drury 1978; 118, 126 – 7 (^{14}C)
Radiocarbon **21**, 368 – 9 (^{14}C)

Objectives: to establish when the water channel began to silt rapidly and thus whether the channel in its early form was contemporary with the nearby Iron Age settlement.

HAR-1047   3360 ± 80 BP

$\delta^{13}C$: −28.2 ‰

Sample: LWALTHAM, submitted on 26 November 1974

Material: soil.

Initial comment: from lowest level of silt (layer 4) in a former channel of the River Chelmer; the estimated date is after the elm decline, ie post 3000 BC, and probably Iron Age.

Calibrated date: 1σ : cal BC 1745 – 1530
2σ : cal BC 1880 – 1460

Final comments:
P Drury: this seems acceptable; other evidence is scanty.

HAR-1081   2560 ± 80 BP

$\delta^{13}C$: −26.1 ‰

Sample: LW71C2-2, submitted on 22 January 1975

Material: soil, organic matter mixed with silt.

Initial comment: from burnt debris in the wall trench of hut CII.

Calibrated date: 1σ : cal BC 810 – 550
2σ : cal BC 895 – 410

Final comments:
P Drury: rather early possibly due to the presence of residual Neolithic charcoal.

HAR-1082   3340 ± 90 BP

$\delta^{13}C$: −25.6 ‰

Sample: LW71C2-1, submitted on 22 January 1975

Material: soil and charcoal.

Initial comment: from burnt debris in the wall trench of hut CII-1.

Calibrated date: 1σ : cal BC 1743 – 1521
2σ : cal BC 1880 – 1430

Final comments:
P Drury: as for HAR-1081.

HAR-1087   5120 ± 130 BP

$\delta^{13}C$: −25.4 ‰

Sample: LW71251-1, submitted on 22 January 1975

Material: soil and charcoal.

Initial comment: from a hearth, associated with plain Neolithic pottery.

Calibrated date: 1σ : cal BC 4040 – 3780
2σ : cal BC 4240 – 3650

Final comments:
P Drury: there is no reason why this should not be accepted – it fits with the pottery and other sites in the area at Broome Heath, Eaton Heath, and Shippea Hill.

Harwell: a small sample accounts for the larger than normal error term.

HAR-1088   2160 ± 80 BP

$\delta^{13}C$: −25.1 ‰

Sample: LW71C2-3, submitted on 22 January 1975

Material: charcoal.

Initial comment: from the fill of the wall trench in hut CII-3, which was probably destroyed by fire.

Calibrated date: 1σ : cal BC 370 – 105
2σ : cal BC 400 – 0 cal AD

HAR-1120   2100 ± 70 BP

$\delta^{13}C$: −25.1 ‰

Sample: LW71C2-34E, submitted on 22 January 1975

Material: charcoal.

Initial comment: from fill of the wall trench of hut CII-4.

Calibrated date: 1σ : cal BC 330 – 40
2σ : cal BC 370 – 50 cal AD

Final comments:
P Drury: with HAR-1088, this suggests a mid third-century date for the Iron Age occupation; this accords well with the archaeological evidence from the site.

Harwell: replicate of HAR-989; the result is a combined mean.

London: Baynard's Castle, City of London

Location: TQ 31948091
Lat. 51.30.40 N; Long. 00.05.55 W

Excavator: C Hill (Department of Urban Archaeology), 1975

Site: a Roman and medieval waterfront.

References: Hill *et al* 1980
Radiocarbon **21**, 372 (^{14}C)

HAR-1201   780 ± 70 BP

$δ^{13}C$: −26.2 ‰

Sample: BC75/3, submitted by B Hobley on 30 April 1975

Material: wood: *Quercus* sp..

Initial comment: from a base plate of a possible medieval waterfront.

Calibrated date: 1σ : cal AD 1210 – 1280
2σ : cal AD 1050 – 1290

London: Baynard's Castle, City of London

Location: TQ 31948091
Lat. 51.30.40 N; Long. 00.05.55 W

Excavator: C Hill (Department of Urban Archaeology), 1975

Site: the Roman riverside wall.

References: Hill 1975
Morgan 1980b (^{14}C)

Objectives: as the dendrochronological results could only be used to form a floating curve, radiocarbon dating offered the only means of fixing the date of the timbers with any accuracy.

Comments:
C Hill: the archaeological evidence points to a mid fourth-century date for the construction of the wall. HAR-1456 and HAR-1464 agree well with this date when the necessary growth allowances are added; HAR-1457 is, however, earlier than expected. The piles were probably felled *c* AD 300 – 50 in radiocarbon terms, which calibrates to *c* AD 400.

HAR-1456   1700 ± 70 BP

$δ^{13}C$: −26.4 ‰

Sample: BCI, submitted by R Morgan on 23 January 1976

Material: wood: *Quercus* sp., rings 30 – 50 of a 116-year floating tree-ring sequence based on nine piles in the Roman waterfront; consists of very hard inner wood near the pith, unlikely to be contaminated.

Initial comment: from pile 40 (growth allowance 80 years), one of many piles supporting the Roman stone riverside wall; expected date third – fourth century AD.

Calibrated date: 1σ : cal AD 245 – 415
2σ : cal AD 140 – 530

Final comments:
C Hill: this result is very consistent with those of HAR-1464 and HAR-1724 and with HAR-1083, indicating a felling date in the second quarter of the fourth century.

References: *Radiocarbon* **27**, 76

HAR-1457   1740 ± 60 BP

$δ^{13}C$: −26.1 ‰

Sample: BCII, submitted by R Morgan on 23 January 1976

Material: wood: *Quercus* sp., rings 55 – 75 of a 116-year floating tree-ring sequence; consists partly of wood softened by waterlogging and partly of hard, solid wood.

Initial comment: from pile 65 (growth allowance 50 years); context as HAR-1456.

Calibrated date: 1σ : cal AD 225 – 380
2σ : cal AD 130 – 420

Final comments:
C Hill: slightly older than HAR-1456, but consistent within one standard deviation.

References: *Radiocarbon* **27**, 76

HAR-1464   1640 ± 70 BP

$δ^{13}C$: −26.7 ‰

Sample: BCIII, submitted by R Morgan on 23 January 1976

Material: wood: *Quercus* sp., rings 80 – 100 (latest) of a 116-year floating tree-ring sequence; sample consists of the outer area of the piles and some sapwood, softened by waterlogging and perhaps liable to contamination.

Initial comment: from pile 90 (growth allowance 30 years); context as HAR-1456.

Calibrated date: 1σ : cal AD 270 – 450
2σ : cal AD 240 – 560

Final comments:
C Hill: see HAR-1456.

References: *Radiocarbon* **27**, 76

HAR-1590   1770 ± 80 BP

$δ^{13}C$: −26.4 ‰

Sample: BCIV, submitted by R Morgan on 23 January 1976

Material: wood: *Quercus* sp., the final 20 annual rings from a 109 – 29 year series, no sapwood was present.

Initial comment: from a timber 12; 119, part of a wooden revetment on the south side of the Roman wall, predating oak piles footing the wall; the date will be at least 25 years earlier than the felling date.

Comment on uncalibrated date: this result confirms a suspected dendrochronological date in the late second century.

Calibrated date: 1σ : cal AD 135 – 370
2σ : cal AD 70 – 430

Final comments:
C Hill: this result confirms a suspected dendrochronological date of *c* AD 200.

References: *Radiocarbon* **27**, 77

HAR-1724   1710 ± 70 BP

$δ^{13}C$: −26.7 ‰

Sample: BCIII, submitted by R Morgan on 23 January 1976

Material: wood: as HAR-1464.

Initial comment: replicate of HAR-1464.

Calibrated date: 1σ : cal AD 240 – 410
2σ : cal AD 130 – 450

Final comments:
Harwell: the combined mean with HAR-1654 is 1675 ± 70 BP, $\delta^{13}C$: –26.7 ‰.

London: Baynard's Castle, City of London

Location: TQ 31948091
Lat. 51.30.40 N; Long. 00.05.55 W

Excavator: J Willcox (Guildhall Museum), 1975?

Site: the Roman city wall.

References: Morgan 1980b; 88, fig 43 (^{14}C)

HAR-1083 1710 ± 80 BP

$\delta^{13}C$: –26.3 ‰

Sample: BC75PILE, submitted by R Morgan on 22 January 1975

Material: wood.

Initial comment: from timbers 4 and 5 (growth allowance 80 years), driven into the gravel beneath the southern Roman wall.

Calibrated date: 1σ : cal AD 235 – 415
2σ : cal AD 120 – 540

London: Custom House, City of London

Location: TQ 33308056
Lat. 51.30.28 N; Long. 00.04.44 W

Excavator: T Tatton-Brown (Guildhall Museum), 1973

Site: timber quay of the Roman waterfront.

References: Hillam and Morgan 1986; 81 – 3, fig 65 (^{14}C)
Tatton-Brown 1974
Radiocarbon **29**, 85 (^{14}C)

Objectives: to provide a date for the quay; at the time the timbers could not be dated by dendrochronology, although this was done successfuly a few years later.

Comments:
T Tatton-Brown: with the growth allowances shown, these samples were correlated with further Roman waterfront structures at New Fresh Wharf and Seal House (see HAR-1864, HAR-1865, HAR-1867, and HAR-1868 (Radiocarbon 27, 84)). Dendrochronology indicated that the Custom House timbers were felled after AD 122.

HAR-2530 1820 ± 70 BP

$\delta^{13}C$: –26.5 ‰

Sample: CUS2, submitted by J Hillam on 21 February 1978

Material: wood: *Quercus* sp.; years 124 – 33 (rings 70 – 90) from a 315-year sequence.

Initial comment: from beams forming the quay; growth allowance 190 years.

Calibrated date: 1σ : cal AD 110 – 315
2σ : cal AD 30 – 380

Final comments:
T Tatton-Brown: the actual (dendrochronological) dates are 17 – 8 BC.

HAR-2532 1970 ± 70 BP

$\delta^{13}C$: –26.6 ‰

Sample: CUS1, submitted by J Hillam on 21 February 1978

Material: wood: *Quercus* sp., years 91 – 110 (rings 40 – 60) from a 315-year sequence.

Initial comment: from beams forming the quay; growth allowance 220 years.

Calibrated date: 1σ : cal BC 55 – 90 cal AD
2σ : cal BC 160 – 200 cal AD

Final comments:
T Tatton-Brown: the actual (dendrochronological) dates are 40 – 31 BC.

HAR-2534 1900 ± 70 BP

$\delta^{13}C$: –25.6 ‰

Sample: CUS3, submitted by J Hillam on 21 February 1978

Material: wood: *Quercus* sp., years 167 – 86 (rings 115 – 35) from a 315-year sequence.

Initial comment: from beams forming the quay; growth allowance 150 years.

Calibrated date: 1σ : cal AD 20 – 195
2σ : cal BC 60 – 250 cal AD

Final comments:
T Tatton-Brown: the actual (dendrochronological) dates are AD 36 – 55.

London: Hampstead, West Heath Spa, Greater London

Location: TQ 25668676
Lat. 51.33.55 N; Long. 00.11.13 W

Excavator: D Collins (Hendon and District Archaeological Society), 1976

Site: a Mesolithic site.

Objectives: to date a sealed mesolithic hearth.

HAR-4115 930 ± 70 BP

$\delta^{13}C$: –26.3 ‰

Sample: WHSH1, submitted by M Girling on 14 October 1980

Material: charcoal.

Initial comment: the charcoal has produced two Saxon dates previously from Cambridge and Dr Collins therefore requested an independent date.

Calibrated date: 1σ : cal AD 1020 – 1185
2σ : cal AD 980 – 1250

London: Ludgate Hill, City of London

Location: TQ 31788117
Lat. 50.50.38 N; Long. 00.06.44 W

Excavator: C Hill (Department of Urban Archaeology), 1974

Site: 44 – 6 Ludgate Hill, 1 – 5 Old Bailey.

Objectives: to compare with the ceramic dating.

HAR-1717   920 ± 80 BP

$\delta^{13}C$: –26.4 ‰

Sample: LH74133, submitted by G H Willcox on 30 March 1976

Material: wood: *Quercus* sp..

Initial comment: from the infill of a defensive ditch just outside the city wall.

Calibrated date: 1σ : cal AD 1020 – 1220
2σ : cal AD 970 – 1270

Final comments:
C Maloney: thw excavator's initial comment still stands: no further work has been done.

London: New Fresh Wharf, City of London

Location: TQ 32958066
Lat. 51.30.31 N; Long. 00.05.02 W

Excavator: L Miller (Department of Urban Archaeology), 1978?

Site: a Roman and medieval waterfront.

References: Hillam and Morgan 1986; 79 – 80,fig 64 (^{14}C)

Objectives: three samples were submitted from an undated 161-year tree-ring chronology to help the relative and absolute dating of the Roman waterfront.

Comments:
L Miller: the radiocarbon results were of no help in tying down the tree-ring sequence. This was subsequently dated when more Roman tree-ring chronologies became available.

HAR-3103   2000 ± 110 BP

$\delta^{13}C$: –25.1 ‰

Sample: FRE3, submitted by J Hillam on 9 February 1979

Material: wood: rings 87 – 106 from a 161-year mean curve.

Initial comment: from the period 1, phase 4 waterfront (sample 5013).

Calibrated date: 1σ : cal BC 160 – 110 cal AD
2σ : cal BC 360 – 240 cal AD

Final comments:
L Miller: rings 87 – 106 are dated by dendrochronology to AD 132 – 51.

HAR-3104   1680 ± 80 BP

$\delta^{13}C$: –25.5 ‰

Sample: FRE1, submitted by J Hillam on 9 February 1979

Material: wood: rings 27 – 46 from a 161-year mean curve.

Initial comment: as above.

Calibrated date: 1σ : cal AD 250 – 430
2σ : cal AD 140 – 550

Final comments:
L Miller: these rings are dated by dendrochronology to AD 72 – 91.

HAR-3105   1930 ± 90 BP

$\delta^{13}C$: –25.4 ‰

Sample: FRE2, submitted by J Hillam on 9 February 1979

Material: wood: rings 57 – 76 from a 161-year mean curve.

Initial comment: as above.

Calibrated date: 1σ : cal BC 35 – 140 cal AD
2σ : cal BC 160 – 315 cal AD

Final comments:
L Miller: these rings were dated by dendrochronology to AD 102 – 21.

London: New Fresh Wharf, City of London

Location: TQ 32958066
Lat. 51.30.31 N; Long. 00.05.02 W

Excavator: L Miller (Department of Urban Archaeology)

Site: a Roman waterfront.

Comments:
L Miller: With the allowances quoted, HAR-1865 and HAR-1867 fit well into the series but HAR-1864 is slightly later than expected and HAR-1865 rather earlier. The general variability of the individual ^{14}C results suggests that this form of dating should only be used to obtain a rough indication of the date of a sample, not as a means of establishing an exact date.

HAR-1864   1660 ± 60 BP

$\delta^{13}C$: –26.2 ‰

Sample: NFW3, submitted by R Morgan on 19 August 1976

Material: wood: *Quercus* sp., rings 170 – 91 in a floating sequence of 270 years; from three timbers.

Initial comment: from the period 1, phase 3 waterfront, samples 311, 321, and 378 (growth allowance c 90 years).

Calibrated date: 1σ : cal AD 265 – 430
2σ : cal AD 240 – 540

References: Hillam and Morgan 1986; 81, fig 65
Morgan and Schofield 1978, 228
Radiocarbon **27**, 84

HAR-1865   1800 ± 60 BP

$\delta^{13}C$: −26.3 ‰

Sample: NFW2, submitted by R Morgan on 19 August 1976

Material: wood: *Quercus* sp., rings 120 – 40 in a floating sequence of 270 years; from two timbers.

Initial comment: as above, samples 311 and 378 (growth allowance *c* 140 years).

Calibrated date: 1σ : cal AD 130 – 320
2σ : cal AD 80 – 380

References: Hillam and Morgan 1986; 81, fig 65
Morgan and Schofield 1978, 228
Radiocarbon **27**, 84

HAR-1867   1840 ± 60 BP

$\delta^{13}C$: −26.8 ‰

Sample: NFW1, submitted by R Morgan on 19 August 1976

Material: wood: *Quercus* sp., rings 70 – 90 in a floating sequence of 270 years; from two timbers.

Initial comment: as above; growth allowance 190 years.

Calibrated date: 1σ : cal AD 90 – 240
2σ : cal AD 30 – 335

References: Hillam and Morgan 1986; 81, fig 65
Morgan and Schofield 1978, 228
Radiocarbon **27**, 84

HAR-1868   1760 ± 60 BP

$\delta^{13}C$: −26.1 ‰

Sample: NFW4, submitted by R Morgan on 19 August 1976

Material: wood: *Quercus* sp., rings 220 – 40 in a floating sequence of 270 years; from two timbers.

Initial comment: as above, samples 321 and 378; growth allowance *c* 40 years.

Calibrated date: 1σ : cal AD 215 – 345
2σ : cal AD 120 – 410

References: Hillam and Morgan 1986; 81, fig 65
Morgan and Schofield 1978, 228
Radiocarbon **27**, 84

HAR-1913   1930 ± 90 BP

$\delta^{13}C$: −26.1 ‰

Sample: NFW4, submitted by R Morgan on 19 August 1976

Material: wood.

Calibrated date: 1σ : cal BC 35 – 140 cal AD
2σ : cal BC 160 – 315 cal AD

HAR-1917   1820 ± 80 BP

$\delta^{13}C$: −26.8 ‰

Sample: NFW1, submitted by R Morgan on 19 August 1976

Material: wood.

Calibrated date: 1σ : cal AD 90 – 320
2σ : cal AD 10 – 400

HAR-1918   unknown

$\delta^{13}C$: unknown

Sample: NFW1, submitted by R Morgan on 19 August 1976

Material: wood.

London: New Fresh Wharf, St Magnus House, City of London

Location: TQ 32948067
Lat. 51.30.32 N; Long. 00.05.03 W

Excavator: J Schofield (Department of Urban Archaeology), 1974

Site: samples from different dated waterfronts at St Magnus, part of the New Fresh Wharf site, Billingsgate, London.

Comments:
AML: one sample was submitted after April 1981, HAR-5481 (FRE78138).

HAR-2542   1000 ± 60 BP

$\delta^{13}C$: −26.9 ‰

Sample: NFW74494, submitted by M Rhodes on 21 February 1978

Material: wood, the sample was not originally taken for ^{14}C dating and may have been handled less carefully than is usually desirable: too dry and distorted for identification (C A Keepax).

Initial comment: from part of a brushwood hard, used as a base for a possibly Saxon clay bank forming part of the River Thames dyke.

Calibrated date: 1σ : cal AD 985 – 1040
2σ : cal AD 900 – 1170

HAR-2548   1590 ± 90 BP

$\delta^{13}C$: unknown

Sample: SM75288, submitted by M Rhodes on 21 February 1978

Material: wattle, the sample was not originally taken for ^{14}C dating and may have been handled less carefully than is desirable: to dry and distorted for identification (C A Keepax).

Initial comment: from a revetment associated with the early medieval waterfront near St Magnus church.

Calibrated date: 1σ : cal AD 380 – 560
2σ : cal AD 240 – 640

References: Hobley and Schofield 1977
Miller and Schofield 1986
Morgan and Schofield 1978; 227, 229 (^{14}C)
Radiocarbon **21**, 375 (^{14}C)

HAR-1421   1630 ± 70 BP

$\delta^{13}C$: −27.0 ‰

Sample: SM75213, submitted by J Willcox on 28 November 1975

Material: wood: *Quercus* sp. (C A Keepax).

Initial comment: from a Roman pile (213) associated with the period 1, phase III waterfront structure.

Comment on uncalibrated date: pottery and parallels for the structure suggest an earlier date.

Calibrated date: 1σ : cal AD 340 – 530
    2σ : cal AD 240 – 590

References: Hillam and Morgan 1986, 79 – 80
    Morgan 1977, 42

HAR-1422   1080 ± 80 BP

$\delta^{13}C$: −28.2 ‰

Sample: SM751711, submitted by J Willcox on 28 November 1975

Material: wood, two samples combined: *Quercus* sp. (C A Keepax).

Initial comment: from a Late Saxon vertical stake associated with a Middle – Late Saxon waterfront.

Comment on uncalibrated date: fits well with the pottery and stratigraphic sequence.

Calibrated date: 1σ : cal AD 885 – 1020
    2σ : cal AD 780 – 1155

References: Hobley and Schofield 1977, 37

London: Southwark, 124 Borough High Street, Greater London

Location: TQ 32517993
    Lat. 51.30.08 N; Long. 00.05.26 W

Excavator: M Hammerson (Southwark and Lambeth Excavation Committee), 1977

Site: possible early prehistoric occupation with an Iron Age burial and grid of post pits sealed by a Roman road. One medieval and several post-medieval pits.

References: Dean and Hammerson 1980, 17 (^{14}C)

HAR-2524   850 ± 80 BP

$\delta^{13}C$: −21.6 ‰

Sample: 124BHS, submitted on 21 February 1978

Material: human bone.

Initial comment: from an inhumation below layers sealed by Roman road. The construction date of this road is at present thought to be *c* AD 50 – 5; the burial should therefore not be dated later than *c* AD 40 – 50 and may be earlier.

Calibrated date: 1σ : cal AD 1045 – 1260
    2σ : cal AD 1010 – 1280

Final comments:
M Hammerson: the date is conflicting and must be anomalous.

London: Southwark, 213 Borough High Street, Greater London

Location: TQ 32497981
    Lat. 51.30.04 N; Long. 00.05.27 W

Excavator: H Sheldon (Southwark and Lambeth Excavation Committee), 1977

Site: rescue excavation on, and adjacent to, the line of a Roman road revealed prehistoric, Romano-British, medieval, and later features.

References: Richardson 1978, 168

Objectives: to date the various contexts from which samples were taken.

HAR-2499   2010 ± 80 BP

$\delta^{13}C$: −29.6 ‰

Sample: 213XII102, submitted on 22 December 1977

Material: wood.

Initial comment: from what may have been a road timber; thought to be Roman or possibly prehistoric.

Calibrated date: 1σ : cal BC 110 – 70 cal AD
    2σ : cal BC 330 – 130 cal AD

Final comments:
H Sheldon: as above.

HAR-2501   1620 ± 80 BP

$\delta^{13}C$: −30.5 ‰

Sample: 213B666, submitted on 22 December 1977

Material: wood: *Alnus* sp. from large timbers (C A Keepax).

Initial comment: from road timbers in a marshy area overlain by a sandy deposit containing prehistoric pottery.

Calibrated date: 1σ : cal AD 340 – 540
    2σ : cal AD 240 – 610

Final comments:
H Sheldon: this date seems much too late for the context.

HAR-2698   2010 ± 80 BP

$\delta^{13}C$: unknown

Sample: 213BHS66, submitted on 22 May 1978

Material: wood: *Alnus* sp. from large timbers (C A Keepax).

Initial comment: from a context beneath the metalled Roman road; possibly part of the road or an earlier timber causeway.

Calibrated date: 1σ : cal BC 110 – 70 cal AD
    2σ : cal BC 330 – 130 cal AD

Final comments:
H Sheldon: the calibrated dates fit either interpretation.

HAR-2733 unknown

$\delta^{13}C:$ unknown

Sample: 213D666, submitted on 22 December 1977

Material: wood.

Initial comment: a repeat of HAR-2501.

London: Southwark, Elephant and Castle Leisure Centre, Greater London

Location: TQ 31907890
Lat. 51.29.35 N; Long. 00.05.59 W

Excavator: H Sheldon (Southwark and Lambeth Excavation Committee), 1977

Site: a watching brief revealed topographical evidence including Tilbury IV peat deposits.

References: Tyers 1988; 7, table 1 (^{14}C)

Objectives: to provide a date for pollen analyses.

HAR-2346 2180 ± 80 BP

$\delta^{13}C:$ −27.9 ‰

Sample: SLC4, submitted on 1 June 1977

Material: wood: probably *Corylus/Alnus* sp. and *Betula* sp.; *c* 50% identified (C A Keepax).

Initial comment: from a peat deposit overlying blue – grey clay, sealed by grey waterlaid clay containing Roman material. The peat was cut by a channel containing a second layer of peat; the pollen analyses suggest that this peat was redeposited, and that it was therefore formed before the Tilbury IV regression.

Calibrated date: 1σ : cal BC 380 – 115
2σ : cal BC 400 – 30

Final comments:
H Sheldon: the Iron Age date suggests that the deposit, although possibly formed in the Late Bronze Age (as the so-called Tilbury IV horizon), had been disturbed, if not redeposited.

London: Southwark, Hays Lane Junction Box, Greater London

Location: TQ 33018023
Lat. 51.30.17 N; Long. 00.05.00 W

Excavator: H Sheldon (Southwark and Lambeth Excavation Committee), 1975

Site: a silt deposit in the River Thames.

References: Graham 1978, 512 (^{14}C)
Radiocarbon **21**, 373 (^{14}C)

Objectives: to date the river silt.

Comments:
AML: one sample, HAR-1328 (HS755TH1), was abandoned.

HAR-1318 1540 ± 90 BP

$\delta^{13}C:$ −28.1 ‰

Sample: HS75HLJB, submitted on 9 October 1975

Material: wood.

Initial comment: from a silt deposit in the River Thames.

Comment on uncalibrated date: the date shows that the River Thames was depositing clay, at OD (Newlyn) height in the low area along the south bank, in the Late Roman or immediate post-Roman period.

Calibrated date: 1σ : cal AD 415 – 610
2σ : cal AD 265 – 660

Final comments:
H Sheldon: the calibrated dates seem to confirm a Late Roman date for the silting up of one of the many river channels crossing the north Southwark floodplain.

London: Southwark, Hibernia Wharf, Greater London

Location: TQ 32758035
Lat. 51.30.22 N; Long. 00.05.13 W

Excavator: G Dennis (Southwark and Lambeth Excavation Committee), 1979 – 80

Site: prehistoric peat deposits, a Roman gravel quarry, Late Saxon or early medieval pits, and a sixteenth-century cellar.

References: Tyers 1988; 10, table 1 (^{14}C)

Objectives: to date a possible prehistoric feature which produced no finds.

HAR-3931 2630 ± 80 BP

$\delta^{13}C:$ −28.6 ‰

Sample: HIB110, submitted by A Slack on 1 July 1980

Material: peat.

Initial comment: from a large, naturally-formed feature containing a very organic silty clay with some wood fragments and lenses of sand and gravel, overlying natural gravels; it was overlain by redeposited gravels.

Calibrated date: 1σ : cal BC 845 – 790
2σ : cal BC 930 – 540

Final comments:
G Dennis: this result, which is the only available dating evidence, tends to support the excavator's interpretation of this possibly prehistoric feature.

London: Southwark, Mark Brown's Wharf, Greater London

Location: TQ 33478018
Lat. 51.30.15 N; Long. 00.04.36 W

Excavator: B Yule (Southwark and Lambeth Excavation Committee), 1973

Site: later prehistoric peat deposits beneath seventeenth- and eighteenth-century building debris and waste dumping from nearby delftware kilns.

References: Hinton *et al* 1988, 133 (^{14}C)
Tyers 1988; 10, table 1 (^{14}C)

Objectives: to date the peat deposit.

HAR-333   2810 ± 80 BP

$\delta^{13}C$: −24.2 ‰

Sample: MB73-D, submitted by H Keeley on 30 May 1973

Material: peat.

Initial comment: from the lower peat, at −0.25m OD; this peat is comparable to the peat bed at Westminster; these peats are generally thought to span the Roman period.

Calibrated date: 1σ : cal BC 1060 – 895
2σ : cal BC 1255 – 810

Final comments:
B Yule: like HAR-2506, this date confirms that the peat deposit can be correlated with the Tilbury IV horizon (Devoy 1979).

London: Southwark, Pilgrimage Street, Chaucer House, Greater London

Location: TQ 32667961
Lat. 51.29.58 N; Long. 00.05.19 W

Excavator: B Yule (Southwark and Lambeth Excavation Committee), 1975 – 6

Site: prehistoric peat deposits, Roman occupation and ditches, a fourteenth- to fifteenth-century chalk-walled building, and post-medieval pits and dumped deposits.

References: Yule 1976

Objectives: to date the inhumation burial.

HAR-1653   1640 ± 70 BP

$\delta^{13}C$: −21.7 ‰

Sample: CH753129, submitted on 10 June 1976

Material: human bone.

Initial comment: from a female, inhumation, burial in a shallow grave.

Calibrated date: 1σ : cal AD 268 – 448
2σ : cal AD 240 – 560

Final comments:
B Yule: this result points to a Late Roman date for the inhumation, which was made outside a cemetery on waste or cultivated land.

London: Southwark, Tabard Street, Chaucer House, Greater London

Location: TQ 32637960
Lat. 51.29.57 N; Long. 00.05.21 W

Excavator: H Sheldon (Southwark and Lambeth Excavation Committee), 1975 – 6

Site: Roman features indicating possible agricultural activity, twelfth- to thirteenth-century pits and ditches, and fifteenth-century and later buildings.

Objectives: this is one of a series of samples taken to date Tilbury IV peat deposits in Southwark.

HAR-2504   2010 ± 80 BP

$\delta^{13}C$: −26.5 ‰

Sample: CH88889, submitted on 22 December 1977

Material: wood: *Quercus* sp. from large timbers (C A Keepax).

Initial comment: from vertical timbers of unknown function driven into waterlain clays; stratigraphically later than HAR-2506, thought to be Roman.

Calibrated date: 1σ : cal BC 110 – 70 cal AD
2σ : cal BC 330 – 130 cal AD

Final comments:
H Sheldon: the timbers, which belonged to a structure of unknown function, are assumed to be of Early Roman date. At that period this area of the site was waterlogged ground.

HAR-2506   2700 ± 60 BP

$\delta^{13}C$: −28.7 ‰

Sample: CH8BIRCH, submitted on 22 December 1977

Material: wood: *Betula* sp., strips of bark, function unknown (C A Keepax).

Initial comment: from peaty deposits containing a few sherds of prehistoric pottery with wood, roots, and birch strips; the peat overlay a grey clay and was sealed by a deposit of blue – grey clay which was cut by Roman timber posts; stratigraphically earlier than HAR-2504.

Calibrated date: 1σ : cal BC 910 – 810
2σ : cal BC 990 – 800

Final comments:
H Sheldon: this date confirms that the peaty deposit can be correlated with the Tilbury IV horizon (Devoy 1979), which formed during a period of relatively low sea/river level in the Late Bronze Age.

References: Tyers 1988; 10, table 1

London: Southwark, Willson's Wharf, Greater London

Location: TQ 33198028
Lat. 51.30.19 N; Long. 00.04.51 W

Excavator: B Yule (Southwark and Lambeth Excavation Committee), 1978

Site: Late Bronze Age – Early Iron Age fen edge with Tilbury IV peat deposit, recorded during a watching brief.

References: Tyers 1988; 9 – 10, table 1, fig 2 (^{14}C)

Objectives: to provide dates for a pollen diagram.

Comments:
B Yule: the results place the initiation of peat accumulation in the later Bronze Age period (probably as a result of the lowered sea level), extending through to the earlier Iron Age.

HAR-3925 3010 ± 70 BP

$\delta^{13}C$: −31.1 ‰

Sample: WW16, submitted by A Slack on 5 May 1980

Material: peaty soil.

Initial comment: from the lower section of the peat deposit, depth 0.10m OD.

Calibrated date: 1σ : cal BC 1395 − 1135
2σ : cal BC 1430 − 1030

HAR-3926 2770 ± 80 BP

$\delta^{13}C$: −30.8 ‰

Sample: WW17, submitted by A Slack on 5 March 1980

Material: wood: root-like nodules, originally *c* 30mm in diameter (A J Clark).

Initial comment: from the middle of the peat deposit, depth 0.18m OD.

Calibrated date: 1σ : cal BC 1010 − 835
2σ : cal BC 1155 − 800

HAR-3927 2570 ± 80 BP

$\delta^{13}C$: −30.5 ‰

Sample: WW21, submitted by A Slack on 5 May 1980

Material: peat.

Initial comment: from the upper section of the peat deposit, depth 0.38m OD.

Calibrated date: 1σ : cal BC 815 − 600
2σ : cal BC 900 − 410

London: Tower of London, Greater London

Location: TQ 336804
Lat. 51.30.22 N; Long. 00.04.29 W

Excavator: G Parnell (Department of the Environment), 1979?

HAR-3353 1710 ± 70 BP

$\delta^{13}C$: −26.4 ‰

Sample: TOWER1, submitted by J Hillam on 11 May 1979

Material: wood: years 56 − 75 of tree 199, which was felled in its 86 − 87th year; this sample contains some sapwood.

Initial comment: from a Roman waterfront.

Calibrated date: 1σ : cal AD 240 − 410
2σ : cal AD 130 − 450

HAR-3363 1840 ± 70 BP

$\delta^{13}C$: −25.8 ‰

Sample: TOWER2, submitted by J Hillam on 11 May 1979

Material: wood: *Quercus* sp., years 36 − 55 of tree 199, as HAR-3353.

Initial comment: from a Roman waterfront.

Calibrated date: 1σ : cal AD 80 − 245
2σ : cal AD 10 − 340

London: Tower of London, Greater London

Location: TQ 336804
Lat. 51.30.22 N; Long. 00.04.29 W

Excavator: G Parnell (Department of the Environment)

References: Parnell 1977, 97 − 9
Dean and Hammerson 1980, 19 (^{14}C)

HAR-2239 1880 ± 70 BP

$\delta^{13}C$: −20.7 ‰

Sample: TL109, submitted on 1 June 1977

Material: bone.

Initial comment: from a shallow grave on the river foreshore, sealed by waterlain organic material deposited during extreme conditions of flooding and by Early Roman dumping of sand and gravel.

Calibrated date: 1σ : cal AD 55 − 220
2σ : cal BC 40 − 320 cal AD

London: Trig Lane, City of London

Location: TQ 320808
Lat. 51.30.37 N; Long. 00.05.52 W

Excavator: G Milne (Department of Urban Archaeology), 1976

Site: a series of medieval timber and stone waterfronts.

References: Milne and Milne 1982

HAR-2416 670 ± 80 BP

$\delta^{13}C$: −24.9 ‰

Sample: TAML-74408B, submitted by D W Brett on 7 September 1977

Material: wood: *Quercus* sp., rings 38 − 48 of a timber with 88 rings; the date suggested by dendrochronolgy is AD 1303 − 13.

Initial comment: from a medieval waterfront.

Calibrated date: 1σ : cal AD 1270 − 1390
2σ : cal AD 1220 − 1420

HAR-2417 730 ± 60 BP

$\delta^{13}C$: −24.9 ‰

Sample: TAML-74408A, submitted by D W Brett on 7 September 1977

Material: wood: *Quercus* sp., rings 18 – 27 of a timber with 88 rings; the date suggested by dendrochronology is AD 1283 – 92.

Initial comment: from a medieval waterfront.

Calibrated date: 1σ : cal AD 1250 – 1285
2σ : cal AD 1210 – 1385

HAR-2418 620 ± 70 BP

$\delta^{13}C$: −26.7 ‰

Sample: TAML-741764, submitted by D W Brett on 7 September 1977

Material: wood: *Quercus* sp., rings 8 – 28 from a sample with 85 rings; the date suggested by dendrochronology is AD 1321 – 41.

Initial comment: from a medieval and stone waterfront.

Calibrated date: 1σ : cal AD 1280 – 1405
2σ : cal AD 1260 – 1430

HAR-2419 750 ± 70 BP

$\delta^{13}C$: −25.3 ‰

Sample: TAML-74425, submitted by D W Brett on 7 September 1977

Material: wood: *Quercus* sp., rings 41 – 60 from a timber with 95 rings; the date suggested by dendrochronology is AD 1300 – 20.

Initial comment: from a medieval waterfront.

Calibrated date: 1σ : cal AD 1225 – 1285
2σ : cal AD 1160 – 1385

HAR-2425 910 ± 70 BP

$\delta^{13}C$: −26.1 ‰

Sample: TAML-742271, submitted by D W Brett on 7 September 1977

Material: wood: *Quercus* sp., rings 9 – 28 from a timber with 180 rings; the date suggested by dendrochronology is AD 1122 – 41, but possibly earlier.

Initial comment: from a medieval waterfront.

Calibrated date: 1σ : cal AD 1025 – 1220
2σ : cal AD 990 – 1260

HAR-2426 530 ± 70 BP

$\delta^{13}C$: −26.3 ‰

Sample: TAML-741613, submitted by D W Brett on 7 September 1977

Material: wood: *Quercus* sp., rings 60 – 84 from a timber with 99 rings; dated by dendrochronology to AD 1364 – 88.

Initial comment: from a medieval waterfront.

Calibrated date: 1σ : cal AD 1320 – 1440
2σ : cal AD 1280 – 1470

London: Westminster, Cromwell Green, Greater London

Location: TQ 3019079550
Lat. 51.29.58 N; Long. 00.07.27 W

Excavator: P Mills (Inner London Archaeological Unit), 1978

HAR-2692 1350 ± 70 BP

$\delta^{13}C$: −28.8 ‰

Sample: WCG7810, submitted on 22 May 1978

Material: wood.

Calibrated date: 1σ : cal AD 635 – 690
2σ : cal AD 565 – 790

HAR-2696 1230 ± 70 BP

$\delta^{13}C$: −24.9 ‰

Sample: WCG789, submitted on 22 May 1978

Material: wood.

Calibrated date: 1σ : cal AD 680 – 885
2σ : cal AD 660 – 970

HAR-3423 1220 ± 80 BP

$\delta^{13}C$: −26.1 ‰

Sample: WCG5120, submitted on 1 May 1979

Material: wood: *Quercus* sp..

Initial comment: from the top of a watercourse.

Calibrated date: 1σ : cal AD 680 – 890
2σ : cal AD 650 – 990

London: Westminster, Jewel Tower, Greater London

Location: TQ 303795 approx
Lat. 51.29.56 N; Long. 00.07.21 W

Excavator: D W Brett, 1978

Objectives: HAR-2765 and HAR-2766 were submitted to check the Saxon date produced by HAR-1433, which suggests reuse of timber; if confirmed this date will be of great interest since timber of this age is rarely encountered.

HAR-1432 630 ± 80 BP

$\delta^{13}C$: unknown

Sample: JTX0, submitted on 5 December 1975

Material: wood.

Calibrated date: 1σ : cal AD 1280 – 1405
2σ : cal AD 1250 – 1430

HAR-1433 1310 ± 70 BP

$\delta^{13}C$: unknown

Sample: JT102, submitted on 5 December 1975

Material: wood.

Calibrated date: 1σ : cal AD 655 – 780
2σ : cal AD 610 – 880

HAR-2765 1630 ± 60 BP

$\delta^{13}C$: –26.1 ‰

Sample: JT7703, submitted on 12 July 1978

Material: wood: *Quercus* sp..

Initial comment: from a roof beam probably used in AD 1365.

Calibrated date: 1σ : cal AD 350 – 450
2σ : cal AD 250 – 560

HAR-2766 1540 ± 70 BP

$\delta^{13}C$: –25.7 ‰

Sample: JT7704, submitted on 12 July 1978

Material: wood: *Quercus* sp., 20 rings adjacent to those in HAR-2765.

Initial comment: from a roof beam probably used in AD 1365.

Calibrated date: 1σ : cal AD 425 – 600
2σ : cal AD 380 – 650

London: Westminster, New Palace Yard, Greater London

Location: TQ 30227962
Lat. 51.30.00 N; Long. 00.07.25 W

Excavator: B Davison (Department of the Environment), 1972 – 5

HAR-329 2190 ± 60 BP

$\delta^{13}C$: –27.1 ‰

Sample: S11, submitted by H Keeley on 25 May 1973

Material: wood.

Initial comment: from the base of the lowest peat deposits.

Calibrated date: 1σ : cal BC 375 – 175
2σ : cal BC 390 – 100

HAR-330 960 ± 70 BP

$\delta^{13}C$: –26.9 ‰

Sample: S13, submitted by H Keeley on 25 May 1973

Material: charcoal.

Initial comment: from a layer associated with chalk rubble, sunk into marsh clay.

Calibrated date: 1σ : cal AD 1005 – 1165
2σ : cal AD 960 – 1230

HAR-331 1520 ± 70 BP

$\delta^{13}C$: –26.2 ‰

Sample: S14, submitted by H Keeley on 25 May 1973

Material: wood.

Initial comment: from sandy clay at the base of the marsh deposits, in a zone of iron panning; the wood is thought to have sunk through the marsh clay, not to have been deposited there; the expected date is eleventh century AD.

Calibrated date: 1σ : cal AD 435 – 610
2σ : cal AD 400 – 660

HAR-332 2810 ± 80 BP

$\delta^{13}C$: –24.2 ‰

Sample: S27, submitted by H Keeley on 25 May 1973

Material: wood.

Initial comment: from the upper fill of a channel cutting through the main peat deposits.

Calibrated date: 1σ : cal BC 1060 – 895
2σ : cal BC 1255 – 810

Marc 3: Bridget's Farm, R5, Hampshire

Location: SU 51373453
Lat. 51.06.26 N; Long. 01.15.58 W

Excavator: P Fasham (M3 Archaeological Rescue Committee), 1974

Site: a linear feature, also excavated at Burnt Wood Farm.

References: Fasham 1979, 80 (^{14}C)
Fasham and Whinney 1991, 143 – 7 (^{14}C)
Radiocarbon **29**, 79 (^{14}C)

Objectives: to better understand the woodland clearance evidenced by the land molluscan data and to date a series of otherwise undatable pits; HAR-2745 was later submitted to give a check on the first date.

Comments:
P Fasham: the discrepancy in these dates means that the vegetational history deduced from the land snails is tentative; either there was dense woodland for 1000 years, or both determinations are invalid. They do, however, indicate a broadly Bronze Age horizon for the pits.

HAR-1695 3790 ± 70 BP

$\delta^{13}C$: –24.5 ‰

Sample: R5-816, submitted on 27 May 1976

Material: charcoal and hazelnut shells.

Initial comment: from pit 10, one of a series of otherwise undated pits.

Calibrated date: 1σ : cal BC 2345 – 2135
2σ : cal BC 2460 – 2030

Final comments:
P Fasham: this is unacceptable.

HAR-2745 2800 ± 80 BP

$\delta^{13}C$: −24.2 ‰

Sample: R5-817, submitted on 22 April 1978

Material: animal bone: cattle (*Bos* sp.) skull.

Initial comment: from F27, one of a series of undated pits.

Calibrated date: 1σ : cal BC 1045 – 845
   2σ : cal BC 1255 – 810

Final comments:
P Fasham: this is unacceptable.

Marc 3: Burntwood Farm, R6, Hampshire

Location: SU 51133411
   Lat. 51.06.13 N; Long. 01.16.11 W

Excavator: P Fasham (M3 Archaeological Rescue Committee), 1974

Site: Early Bronze Age pits, a negative 'Celtic' lynchet, a Roman hollow-way flanked by eight inhumations, and sub-Roman postholes, presumably fences, which respected the road but not the burials.

References: Fasham 1979
   Radiocarbon **29**, 79 (^{14}C)

Objectives: three samples were submitted in an attempt to obtain closer dating for Iron Age and Romano-British pottery in the area.

Comments:
AML: three small samples (HAR-1014, HAR-1022, and HAR-1046) were withdrawn.

HAR-1021 1980 ± 110 BP

$\delta^{13}C$: −19.6 ‰

Sample: R6-801, submitted on 26 November 1974

Material: human bone: leg bones.

Initial comment: from grave 55 (with grave goods).

Calibrated date: 1σ : cal BC 110 – 120 cal AD
   2σ : cal BC 355 – 250 cal AD

Final comments:
P Fasham: this confirms the broad dating from the excavation sequence.

Harwell: a poor experimental yield may produce additional uncertainty in result quoted.

Marc 3: Easton Down, R7, Hampshire

Location: SU 495313
   Lat. 51.04.42 N; Long. 01.17.36 W

Excavator: P Fasham (M3 Archaeological Rescue Committee), 1974

Site: a probable bell barrow; represented by a ring ditch containing a primary central cremation, associated with a knife dagger of Early Bronze Age type and three amber beads; six later inhumations and four cremations are of possible Beaker date. Many Iron Age pits with domestic debris were also found.

References: Fasham 1982
   Fasham and Whinney 1991, 143 – 7 (^{14}C)

Objectives: to date the barrow and burials; HAR-1039 is the only sample which will give an approximation to the primary date of the site.

Comments:
AML: one sample, HAR-1694 (R7-110), was withdrawn in 1985.

HAR-1023 3130 ± 70 BP

$\delta^{13}C$: −21.2 ‰

Sample: R7-159, submitted on 26 November 1974

Material: human bone.

Initial comment: from one of four presumed secondary inhumations buried with no grave goods.

Calibrated date: 1σ : cal BC 1505 – 1320
   2σ : cal BC 1530 – 1230

Final comments:
P Fasham: the three dates from HAR-1023, HAR-3344, and HAR-3417 are contemporary in radiocarbon terms and also contemporary with the filling of the ditch.

References: Fasham 1982, 29

HAR-1039 32460 ± 1100 BP

$\delta^{13}C$: −19.9 ‰

Sample: R7-158, submitted on 26 November 1974

Material: charcoal with soil.

Initial comment: from organic matter in the top of the primary silt of ditch.

Final comments:
Harwell: this result is too old to calibrate; it must have been obtained from derived material and is not associated with the archaeological contexts. The result cannot be treated as a realistic date.

HAR-1040 3070 ± 120 BP

$\delta^{13}C$: −26.3 ‰

Sample: R7-157, submitted on 26 November 1974

Material: charcoal with soil.

Initial comment: from the top of the primary ditch silt.

Calibrated date: 1σ : cal BC 1490 – 1165
   2σ : cal BC 1620 – 1000

Final comments:
P Fasham: this sample most likely represents the filling of the ditch.

Harwell: a small sample accounts for the larger than normal error term.

HAR-3344 3160 ± 70 BP

$\delta^{13}C$: –22.2 ‰

Sample: R7-F43, submitted on 11 May 1979

Material: human bone.

Initial comment: from the ring ditch.

Calibrated date: 1σ : cal BC 1515 – 1400
2σ : cal BC 1610 – 1270

Final comments:
P Fasham: see HAR-1023.

References: Fasham 1982, 29

HAR-3417 3080 ± 80 BP

$\delta^{13}C$: –22.7 ‰

Sample: F26, submitted on 11 May 1979

Material: ?human bone.

Initial comment: from the ring ditch.

Calibrated date: 1σ : cal BC 1435 – 1265
2σ : cal BC 1520 – 1105

Final comments:
P Fasham: see HAR-1023.

References: Fasham 1982, 29

Marc 3: Micheldever Wood, R4, Hampshire

Location: SU 52553653
Lat. 51.07.30 N; Long. 01.14.56 W

Excavator: P Fasham (M3 Archaeological Rescue Committee), 1974

Site: an oval barrow comprising three axially aligned mounds, two of earth and flint delimited by chalk blocks, with a flint cairn between them. These sealed three cremation pits, two covered with inverted Collared Urns; there was one secondary cremation, also in a Collared Urn.

References: Fasham 1978
Fasham 1979, 37 – 8 (^{14}C)
Fasham and Ross 1978; 49, 51 (^{14}C)
Fasham and Whinney 1991, 143 – 7 (^{14}C)
Radiocarbon **27**, 75 – 6 (^{14}C)

Objectives: samples HAR-1041 and HAR-1044 were probably submitted to give dates for a layer of fine, probably wind-blown soil and to check archaeomagnetic samples taken from detritus.

HAR-1041 3100 ± 90 BP

$\delta^{13}C$: –25.4 ‰

Sample: R4-3, submitted on 26 November 1974

Material: charcoal.

Initial comment: from a layer of fine, wind-blown sand in the barrow ditch, overlying flint debris.

Calibrated date: 1σ : cal BC 1495 – 1265
2σ : cal BC 1590 – 1105

Final comments:
P Fasham: this provides a *terminus post quem* for the construction of the barrow.

Harwell: a small sample accounts for the larger than normal error term (NB it appears that this sample was published as 1050 ± 90 BC).

HAR-1042 3670 ± 80 BP

$\delta^{13}C$: –23.7 ‰

Sample: R4-144, submitted on 26 November 1974

Material: charcoal.

Initial comment: from the flint core of the western barrow mound.

Calibrated date: 1σ : cal BC 2190 – 1945
2σ : cal BC 2300 – 1830

Final comments:
P Fasham: this date was regarded as being too early for the Collared Urns of the primary cremations and was interpreted as being derived from earlier charcoal incorporated into the mound. This may not be correct and this may well date the construction of the mound.

HAR-1043 6900 ± 170 BP

$\delta^{13}C$: –16.9 ‰

Sample: R4-167, submitted on 26 November 1974

Material: soil with charcoal.

Initial comment: from a pit beneath the barrow.

Calibrated date: 1σ : cal BC 5970 – 5630
2σ : cal BC 6090 – 5480

Final comments:
P Fasham: this date presented interpretational problems. The sample was from a feature sealed beneath the mound of the barrow in Micheldever Wood where there was virtually no evidence for mesolithic remains. The determination, however, seems to be valid and presumably is an indication of pre-barrow activity.

Harwell: this very small sample was topped up (× 2) with ^{14}C dead carbon dioxide before benzene synthesis; the $\delta^{13}C$ value is unlikely for charcoal and suggests contamination with ground carbonate which could result in a date older than the true one.

References: Fasham 1983, 7

HAR-1044 3370 ± 90 BP

$\delta^{13}C$: –24.7 ‰

Sample: R4-5, submitted on 26 November 1974

Material: charcoal with soil.

Initial comment: from a layer in the ditch sealing the possible wind-blown soil (see HAR-1041).

Calibrated date: 1σ : cal BC 1855 – 1530
2σ : cal BC 1900 – 1450

Final comments:
P Fasham: this provides a good *terminus ante quem* for the construction of the barrow.

Marc 3: Micheldever Wood, R27, Hampshire

Location: SU 527370
Lat. 51.07.46 N; Long. 01.14.48 W

Excavator: P Fasham (M3 Archaeological Rescue Committee)

Site: a banjo enclosure.

References: Fasham and Whinney 1991, 143 – 7 (^{14}C)

Objectives: to provide a close dating sequence for the ceramics.

Comments:
P Fasham: HAR-2604, HAR-2693, HAR-2770, HAR-2780, and HAR-2799 were submitted to provide a close dating sequence for the ceramics, but this was not particularly successful in a situation lacking the depth of stratigraphy which was so useful at Danebury (Cunliffe 1984). They do come from two discrete pits with pooled dates of 2290 ± 59 BP and 2047 ± 43 BP. These two dates may indicate, in general terms, the main period of activity on the site.

AML: one small sample, HAR-2822 (R27-3654), was withdrawn.

HAR-2604 2290 ± 110 BP

$\delta^{13}C$: –25.8 ‰

Sample: R27-3271, submitted on 22 May 1978

Material: charcoal.

Initial comment: from Iron Age pit 415 (see also HAR-2799).

Calibrated date: 1σ : cal BC 410 – 200
2σ : cal BC 770 – 100

Final comments:
Harwell: repeated with HAR-2704, but HAR-2604 was found to be the correct result.

HAR-2693 1930 ± 70 BP

$\delta^{13}C$: –25.6 ‰

Sample: R27-1999, submitted on 22 May 1978

Material: soil and charcoal.

Initial comment: from an Iron Age pit (as HAR-2270 and HAR-2780).

HAR-2770 2150 ± 70 BP

$\delta^{13}C$: –25.75 ‰

Sample: R27-3607, submitted on 22 May 1978

Material: soil and charcoal: no identifiable charcoal (C A Keepax).

Initial comment: from the same pit as HAR-2693 and HAR-2780.

Calibrated date: 1σ : cal BC 360 – 105
2σ : cal BC 390 – 10

HAR-2780 2070 ± 90 BP

$\delta^{13}C$: –25.8 ‰

Sample: R27-1938, submitted on 22 May 1978

Material: soil and charcoal: no identifiable charcoal (C A Keepax).

Initial comment: from the same pit as HAR-2693 and HAR-2770.

Calibrated date: 1σ : cal BC 195 – 15 cal AD
2σ : cal BC 370 – 110 cal AD

HAR-2795 830 ± 90 BP

$\delta^{13}C$: –26.1 ‰

Sample: R27-1654, submitted on 15 February 1977

Material: charcoal.

Initial comment: from the same pit as HAR-2880, expected date 2300 – 2100 BP.

Calibrated date: 1σ : cal AD 1045 – 1270
2σ : cal AD 1010 – 1290

Final comments:
P Fasham: the expected date was 300 – 150 BC; there is no archaeological reason for this discrepancy. This date and the one for HAR-2800 cannot be explained satisfactorily but they are too consistent with each other to be ignored. The pit must have been dug into during the medieval period, although there was no obvious stratigraphical evidence for such disturbance.

Harwell: the experimental notes give no technical reason to doubt this result.

HAR-2799 2290 ± 70 BP

$\delta^{13}C$: –24.6 ‰

Sample: R27-1916, submitted on 22 May 1978

Material: charcoal.

Initial comment: from the same pit as HAR-2604 and HAR-2704.

Calibrated date: 1σ : cal BC 400 – 255
2σ : cal BC 520 – 190

Final comments:
Harwell: HAR-2704 was submitted privately.

HAR-2800 750 ± 80 BP

$\delta^{13}C$: –24.9 ‰

Sample: R27-1769, submitted on 9 September 1978

Material: charcoal.

Initial comment: from the same pit as HAR-2795.

Calibrated date: 1σ : cal AD 1220 – 1285
2σ : cal AD 1055 – 1390

Final comments:
P Fasham: as for HAR-2795.

Harwell: as for HAR-2795.

Marc 3: Stratton Park, R1, Hampshire

Location: SU 547423
Lat. 51.10.36 N; Long. 01.13.03 W

Excavator: P Fasham (M3 Archaeological Rescue Committee), 1974

Site: the Roman road from Winchester to Silchester, and possible Saxon occupation.

References: Fasham and Whinney 1991, 143 – 7 (^{14}C)
Fasham 1981; 171, 173, 186 (^{14}C)

Objectives: to assist in the resolution of archaeological problems.

Comments:
P Fasham: these three dates present problems of interpretation. All could be perfectly valid measurements and be accounted for by the fact that the charcoal originated from the heartwood from a mature tree or alternatively buried soils, especially if ploughed, often contain charcoal of different ages. HAR-2769 is probably the best estimate of when the soil was buried.

HAR-1703   1550 ± 80 BP

$\delta^{13}C$: –25.3 ‰

Sample: R1-TR4, submitted on 27 May 1976

Material: charcoal.

Initial comment: from the period 3 occupation deposit, layer 57 (?associated with sherds of Middle Saxon pottery).

Calibrated date: 1σ : cal AD 415 – 600
2σ : cal AD 270 – 650

HAR-2027   1790 ± 80 BP

$\delta^{13}C$: –25.6 ‰

Sample: R1-15, submitted on 15 February 1977

Material: charcoal: hawthorn type (Rosaceae, sub-family Pomoideae), *Corylus* sp., and ?blackthorn type (*Prunus* sp.); 50% identified (C A Keepax).

Initial comment: from a buried soil beneath the bank beside the Roman road.

Comment on uncalibrated date: these dates do not agree with the Saxon period and perhaps indicate activity in the Roman period associated with the road.

Calibrated date: 1σ : cal AD 125 – 340
2σ : cal AD 60 – 420

HAR-2769   1220 ± 70 BP

$\delta^{13}C$: –22.8 ‰

Sample: R1-16, submitted on 22 May 1978

Material: animal bone and teeth.

Initial comment: from a partially developed soil which lies under, and immediately predates, the Roman road; this sample was submitted to complement HAR-2027.

Calibrated date: 1σ : cal AD 685 – 890
2σ : cal AD 660 – 980

Final comments:
P Fasham: unlike the other samples this agrees with the dating of the pottery.

Harwell: are we talking about a Saxon road here?

Marc 3: Winnall Down, R17, Hampshire

Location: SU 49853035
Lat. 51.04.11 N; Long. 01.17.18 W

Excavator: P Fasham (M3 Archaeological Rescue Committee), 1976 – 7

Site: multiperiod, but predominantly Iron Age.

References: Fasham 1982
Fasham 1985
Fasham and Whinney 1991, 143 – 7 (^{14}C)

Objectives: C14 dates were required:

1. to confirm the theory that the subrectangular pits are contemporary with the main Early Iron Age enclosure, and that they are earlier than the circular pits (HAR-2194)

2. to establish Roman activity on this multiperiod site (HAR-2195)

3. to establish the relationship of a circular series of scoops with the rest of site (HAR-2196, HAR-2201, and HAR-2202)

4. to date the filling of the ditch (HAR-2251)

5. to establish the relationship of the pit to the main and later enclosures (HAR-2252)

6. to establish a dating sequence for the pottery (HAR-2591).

Comments:
AML: two samples were withdrawn in 1982, (R17-1475) and HAR-2598 (R17-1498). 2650 and 2651 were dated in 1985 – 6 as small samples.

HAR-2194   2160 ± 80 BP

$\delta^{13}C$: –23.6 ‰

Sample: R17-1396, submitted on 15 February 1977

Material: animal bone.

Initial comment: from the primary fill (layer 3113) of subrectangular pit F3111; the associated pottery is typical of the Early Iron Age.

Calibrated date: 1σ : cal BC 370 – 105
2σ : cal BC 400 – 0 cal AD

Final comments:
P Fasham: this is significantly later than the other phase 3 dates (HAR-2651 and HAR-2653) and suggests that this phase continued into the third century BC.

References: Fasham 1985, 18

HAR-2195   2070 ± 80 BP

$\delta^{13}C$: –21.0 ‰

Sample: R17-35, submitted on 15 February 1977

Material: human bone.

Initial comment: from a possible Roman grave.

Calibrated date: 1σ : cal BC 190 – 10 cal AD
2σ : cal BC 365 – 80 cal AD

Final comments:
P Fasham: an acceptable result.

References: Fasham 1985, 30

HAR-2196   4800 ± 80 BP

$\delta^{13}C$: −23.4 ‰

Sample: R17-1146, submitted on 15 February 1977

Material: antler.

Initial comment: from one of an anomalous series of circular scoops.

Calibrated date: 1σ : cal BC 3695 – 3385
2σ : cal BC 3780 – 3370

Final comments:
P Fasham: this date, with HAR-2201 and HAR-2202, provides a compact group, all from antler, for establishing a date in the middle of the fourth millennium BC for a rather enigmatic 'ring ditch'.

References: Fasham 1982, 21

HAR-2201   4650 ± 80 BP

$\delta^{13}C$: −22.3 ‰

Sample: R17-1211, submitted on 15 February 1977

Material: antler.

Initial comment: from one of an anomalous series of circular scoops.

Calibrated date: 1σ : cal BC 3595 – 3345
2σ : cal BC 3630 – 3105

Final comments:
P Fasham: see HAR-2196.

References: Fasham 1982, 21

HAR-2202   4680 ± 90 BP

$\delta^{13}C$: −22.0 ‰

Sample: R17-1379, submitted on 15 February 1977

Material: antler.

Initial comment: from one of an anomalous series of circular scoops.

Calibrated date: 1σ : cal BC 3620 – 3355
2σ : cal BC 3690 – 3110

Final comments:
P Fasham: see HAR-2196.

References: Fasham 1982, 21

HAR-2251   2540 ± 90 BP

$\delta^{13}C$: −25.7 ‰

Sample: R17-828, submitted on 1 June 1977

Material: charcoal: some *Acer* sp. (twiggy); 1 bag of 5 identified (C A Keepax).

Initial comment: from hearth F574, layer 575, in segment 5A of the main, D-shaped, Early Iron Age enclosure ditch, which is roughly datable to the fifth century BC; the hearth (associated with a tripartite jar) is immediately above the primary silt and below a deposit containing a sherd from a haematite-coated bowl.

Comment on uncalibrated date: see HAR-2194; HAR-2251, HAR-2651, and HAR-2653 indicate that the enclosure ditch had probably been dug no later than the sixth century BC. The range of the dates, while broad, is acceptable. This is one of the more variable parts of the calibration curve.

Calibrated date: 1σ : cal BC 805 – 530
2σ : cal BC 895 – 400

References: Fasham 1985, 18

HAR-2252   2140 ± 80 BP

$\delta^{13}C$: −24.6 ‰

Sample: R17-1388, submitted on 1 June 1977

Material: charcoal: mainly *Quercus* sp., with some *Fraxinus* sp., all from fairly large timbers (C A Keepax).

Initial comment: from the top layer of a slightly bell-shaped storage pit (3738) in phase 4, associated with a wide-mouthed jar.

Calibrated date: 1σ : cal BC 360 – 95
2σ : cal BC 390 – 20 cal AD

Final comments:
P Fasham: an acceptable date.

References: Fasham 1985, 26

HAR-2591   2190 ± 60 BP

$\delta^{13}C$: −25.0 ‰

Sample: R17-1467, submitted on 3 March 1978

Material: charcoal: mainly oak (*Quercus* sp.) from large timbers and some hazel/alder (*Corylus/Alnus* sp.).

Initial comment: from layer 5828, in the bottom of a circular storage pit F5789; this contained a mixed ceramic assemblage: bowls, jars, saucepan style pottery with St Catherine's Hill type decoration, and some residual pottery.

Calibrated date: 1σ : cal BC 375 – 175
2σ : cal BC 390 – 100

Final comments:
P Fasham: an acceptable result.

References: Fasham 1985, 30

HAR-2592   2100 ± 80 BP

$\delta^{13}C$: −24.8 ‰

Sample: R17-1495, submitted on 3 March 1978

Material: charcoal: mainly *Corylus* sp. from small twigs and branches.

Initial comment: from pit 7399 (phase 4), which was filled with material derived from an Early Iron Age midden and cut by a Late Iron Age ditch.

Calibrated date: 1σ : cal BC 340 – 35
2σ : cal BC 380 – 70 cal AD

Final comments:
P Fasham: an acceptable result.

References: Fasham 1985, 30

HAR-2652 1830 ± 70 BP

$\delta^{13}C$: −22.2 ‰

Sample: R17-1489, submitted on 3 March 1978

Material: animal bone.

Initial comment: from the base of an Early Iron Age storage pit.

Calibrated date: 1σ : cal AD 85 – 250
2σ : cal AD 20 – 375

Final comments:
P Fasham: this date seems to be at variance with dates reached by other methods. The Roman determination from an apparent Early Iron Age pit may well be a consequence of Roman activity that was not stratigraphically observed during excavation. This is plausible with the lengthy sequence of superimposed activities.

Harwell: not published in Fasham 1985.

HAR-2653 2560 ± 80 BP

$\delta^{13}C$: −22.3 ‰

Sample: R17-1470, submitted on 3 March 1978

Material: animal bone.

Initial comment: from about a third way up in the fill (layer 4749) of the Early Iron Age enclosure ditch F5FF (phase 3), directly associated with a shouldered jar and sealing sherds of haematite-coated pottery.

Calibrated date: 1σ : cal BC 810 – 550
2σ : cal BC 895 – 410

Final comments:
P Fasham: see HAR-2251.

References: Fasham 1985, 18

HAR-2937 2250 ± 90 BP

$\delta^{13}C$: −20.2 ‰

Sample: 1507, submitted on 29 November 1978

Material: human bone.

Initial comment: from burial 629 (grave 10312, layer 10278) cut into a series of quarry pits.

Calibrated date: 1σ : cal BC 400 – 195
2σ : cal BC 520 – 100

Final comments:
P Fasham: an acceptable result.

References: Fasham 1985, 30

HAR-2938 1990 ± 70 BP

$\delta^{13}C$: −20.6 ‰

Sample: 1501, submitted on 29 November 1978

Material: human bone.

Initial comment: from skeleton 500 in the mid silt of a circular storage pit (F8564, layer 8597); this sealed deposits containing saucepan pottery and a round-bodied bowl.

Calibrated date: 1σ : cal BC 95 – 75 cal AD
2σ : cal BC 180 – 130 cal AD

Final comments:
P Fasham: an acceptable result.

References: Fasham 1985, 30

HAR-2980 2150 ± 80 BP

$\delta^{13}C$: −24.7 ‰

Sample: 1528, submitted on 29 November 1978

Material: human bone.

Initial comment: from skeleton 574 at the base of a circular storage pit (F8630), layer 8690, associated with a saucepan pot.

Calibrated date: 1σ : cal BC 365 – 100
2σ : cal BC 390 – 10 cal AD

Final comments:
P Fasham: an acceptable date.

References: Fasham 1985, 30

Marton Pool, Shropshire

Location: SJ 295027
Lat. 52.37.02 N; Long. 03.02.29 W

Excavator: S M Colledge (University of Birmingham), 1978

HAR-2762 8730 ± 80 BP

$\delta^{13}C$: −28.5 ‰

Sample: MP200, submitted on 12 July 1978

Material: peat.

Initial comment: from a peat monolith collected for pollen analysis, probably from zone VI.

Final comments:
S M Colledge: we were hoping for more recent vegetational history than this!

Harwell: this result is too old to calibrate.

Middleborough: Multi-storey Car Park, Essex

Location: TL 99332554
Lat. 51.53.32 N; Long. 00.53.50 E

Excavator: P Crummy and H Brooks (Colchester Archaeological Trust), 1978

Site: trial trenches, on the bank of the River Colne, revealed a mass of broken branches and twigs in a waterlogged gravelly deposit, which overlay natural clay at about 2.0m below modern ground level. Amongst the wood was the base of a large wooden post *in situ*.

References: Crummy 1984, 209 (^{14}C)

Objectives: to date the post and associated debris/structural remains.

HAR-3264   530 ± 70 BP

$\delta^{13}C$: −26.0 ‰

Sample: MID3251, submitted by J Hillam on 14 May 1979

Material: wood: *Quercus* sp., years 27 – 46 from a 109-year-old trunk.

Initial comment: from the base of a large post *c* 0.3m in diameter found *in situ*.

Calibrated date: 1σ : cal AD 1315 – 1435
    2σ : cal AD 1280 – 1470

Final comments:
P Crummy and H Brooks: this result suggests the presence of a medieval riverside structure.

Middleborough: New Market Tavern, Essex

Location: TL 99332554
    Lat. 51.53.32 N;   Long. 00.53.50 E

Excavator: P Crummy and H Brooks (Colchester Archaeological Trust), 1978

Site: building 76, originally a fourteenth-century structure, rebuilt in the fifteenth century, demolished and rebuilt in the late fifteenth or sixteenth century, and converted into a tavern in 1862.

References: Crummy 1984, 208 – 9 (^{14}C)

Objectives: to provide supplementary evidence for dendrochronology.

Comments:
P Crummy and H Brooks: the date ranges are too wide to be useful; it would have been helpful to have had more samples from the cross-wing.

HAR-3391   240 ± 70 BP

$\delta^{13}C$: −25.4 ‰

Sample: MID1658, submitted by J Hillam on 14 May 1979

Material: wood: years 33 – 42 from a 72-year-old timber (growth allowance 40 years).

Initial comment: from the 'rebuilt hall-block' (phase 5) of the fifteenth- to seventeenth-century timber-framed tavern; the expected date is seventeenth century.

Calibrated date: 1σ : cal AD 1530 – 1955
    2σ : cal AD 1470 – 1955

Final comments:
P Crummy and H Brooks: the corrected felling dates for this timber are 1488 – 1848 (one standard deviation) and 1510 – 1900+ (two standard deviations).

HAR-3393   300 ± 70 BP

$\delta^{13}C$: −25.6 ‰

Sample: MID1656, submitted by J Hillam on 14 May 1979

Material: wood: years 11 – 30 from a 60-year-old beam (growth allowance 48 years); the sample contained nails which have been avoided as far as possible.

Initial comment: from the cross-wing (phase 3); the timber-framing is thought to be of late fifteenth-century date.

Calibrated date: 1σ : cal AD 1480 – 1655
    2σ : cal AD 1440 – 1955

Final comments:
P Crummy and H Brooks: the corrected felling date for this timber is 1528 – 1708 (one standard deviation), and 1570 – 1710 (two standard deviations). This date seems to indicate that it is unlikely that the tree was felled before *c* 1490. If correct, this would place the construction of the phase 3 cross-wing at the very end of the fifteenth century at the earliest, thus making too early the date range of 1450 – 1500 assumed for this event in the publication report. This ^{14}C date combined with the presence in the cross-wing of the simple central tenon suggests the wing was built 1490 – 1500.

Mildenhall: West Row Fen, Gravel Drove, MNL-124, Suffolk

Location: TL 65767555
    Lat. 52.21.09 N;   Long. 00.26.03 E

Excavator: E A Martin (Suffolk Archaeological Unit), 1976

Site: one of a number of patches of burnt flint, sometimes quite large in extent, which are a feature of the area, where much Bronze Age pottery and metalwork has been found.

References: Martin 1988, 358 (^{14}C)

Objectives: the sample was submitted to confirm the supposed Bronze Age date of these sites, none of which had been previously dated.

HAR-1876   3720 ± 70 BP

$\delta^{13}C$: −25.8 ‰

Sample: MNL-124, submitted on 1 September 1976

Material: charcoal: *Quercus* sp. and *Corylus* sp. all from fairly large timbers; *c* 50% identified (C A Keepax).

Initial comment: from a patch of burnt and crackled flints in a field on the fen edge.

Calibrated date: 1σ : cal BC 2275 – 2035
    2σ : cal BC 2350 – 1930

Final comments:
E A Martin: this date confirms the assumed Early Bronze Age date for this potboiler site. It can now be seen as one of a number of similarly dated sites in the West Row Fen area – see also HAR-2690 and HAR-9271 (from site MNL-165,

dated after 1981). These seem to be specialised cooking places, though some have argued for a sauna or bathing function for similar sites elsewhere.

Mildenhall: West Row Fen, MNL-130, Suffolk

Location: TL 65967762
Lat. 52.22.16 N; Long. 00.26.17 E

Excavator: E A Martin (Suffolk Archaeological Unit), 1977

Site: Early Bronze Age site on the south-eastern fen edge. One of a number of settlement sites in the West Row Fen area.

References: Longworth 1984, 270 (^{14}C)

Objectives: to date a settlement site with Collared Urn pottery.

HAR-2510   3670 ± 80 BP

$\delta^{13}C$: −25.9 ‰

Sample: MNL130-0481, submitted by P Murphy on 24 January 1978

Material: wood: *Quercus* sp. from a large timber.

Initial comment: from a Bronze Age occupation surface spreading into the fen edge; the sample was exposed to the air during excavation, so there is a slight possibility of contamination of the outer surface.

Calibrated date: 1σ : cal BC 2190 – 1945
2σ : cal BC 2300 – 1830

Final comments:
E A Martin: this date confirms the Early Bronze Age date of the site. The date comes from a large oak timber, which probably accounts for it being slightly earlier than HAR-2517.

HAR-2516   3510 ± 80 BP

$\delta^{13}C$: −26.9 ‰

Sample: MNL130-0486, submitted by P Murphy on 24 January 1978

Material: wood: *Fraxinus* sp. from a large timber.

Initial comment: as HAR-2510.

Calibrated date: 1σ : cal BC 1950 – 1745
2σ : cal BC 2115 – 1670

HAR-2517   3390 ± 80 BP

$\delta^{13}C$: −28.5 ‰

Sample: MNL130-0482, submitted by P Murphy on 24 January 1978

Material: wood: *Salix* sp. (twigs), *Alnus* sp. and *Quercus* sp. (large timbers), and bark; *c* 25% of wood fragments identified.

Initial comment: from a Bronze Age occupation layer (0418) spreading into the peat.

Calibrated date: 1σ : cal BC 1865 – 1615
2σ : cal BC 1900 – 1520

Final comments:
E A Martin: this date confirms the Early Bronze Age date for the site. As this date was obtained from small pieces of wood and twigs, it probably gives a more accurate date for the occupation than HAR-2510, which was taken from a large oak timber.

Mildenhall: West Row Fen, MNL-137, Suffolk

Location: TL 65547764
Lat. 52.22.17 N; Long. 00.25.55 E

Excavator: E A Martin (Suffolk Archaeological Unit), 1978

Site: a typical fen-edge potboiler deposit, sealing a fossil soil developed from a calcareous marl.

References: Martin 1988, 358 (^{14}C)

Objectives: to confirm whether the site is contemporary with others of a similar nature in the area; expected date 2000 – 1500 BC.

HAR-2690   3650 ± 70 BP

$\delta^{13}C$: −28.4 ‰

Sample: MNL-137, submitted by P Murphy on 24 January 1978

Material: charcoal: from large timbers, 10 rings were visible in one piece of the sample.

Initial comment: from a burnt flint potboiler deposit, sealing a fossil soil developed from a calcareous marl.

Calibrated date: 1σ : cal BC 2140 – 1935
2σ : cal BC 2275 – 1830

Final comments:
E A Martin: the date confirms the Early Bronze Age attribution. For similar sites in the area see HAR-1876 and HAR-9271.

Milton Keynes: Hartigan's Gravel Pit, MK-19, Buckinghamshire

Location: SP 882388
Lat. 52.02.25 N; Long. 00.42.50 W

Excavator: H S Green (Milton Keynes Archaeology Unit), 1973

Site: settlement with circular houses and enclosures.

Objectives: to date the construction of the main enclosure.

Comments:
AML: one sample HAR-343 (MK19) has been abandoned.

HAR-872   2310 ± 90 BP

$\delta^{13}C$: −22.5 ‰

Sample: MK1900JB, submitted on 4 December 1974

Material: bone, marked with ink.

Initial comment: from level 1158.

Calibrated date: 1σ : cal BC 410 – 260
 2σ : cal BC 765 – 180

HAR-873 2100 ± 80 BP

$\delta^{13}C$: –21.2 ‰

Sample: MK1900JA, submitted on 4 December 1974

Material: bone.

Initial comment: from level 1157.

Calibrated date: 1σ : cal BC 340 – 35
 2σ : cal BC 380 – 70 cal AD

Milton Keynes: Hartigan's Gravel Pit, MK-23, Buckinghamshire

Location: SP 88183864
 Lat. 52.02.19 N; Long. 00.42.51 W

Excavator: H S Green (Milton Keynes Archaeology Unit), 1972

Site: a Late Bronze Age pit near a ring ditch.

Objectives: to date an important assemblage of Late Bronze Age pottery.

Comments:
AML: two samples, HAR-848 (MK23RD5) and HAR-859 (MK23NW1B), have been abandoned.

HAR-339 2790 ± 70 BP

$\delta^{13}C$: –23.0 ‰

Sample: PIT1MK23, submitted in 1973

Initial comment: from the north-west quadrant of pit 1, associated with Late Bronze Age pottery.

Comment on uncalibrated date: this agrees with the pottery dates.

Calibrated date: 1σ : cal BC 1035 – 840
 2σ : cal BC 1250 – 810

References: Radiocarbon **19**, 403

HAR-860 2790 ± 80 BP

$\delta^{13}C$: –25.6 ‰

Sample: MK23NW1A, submitted on 19 September 1974

Material: charcoal.

Initial comment: from a pit, excavated in 1972, which produced pottery of Late Bronze Age date.

Calibrated date: 1σ : cal BC 1035 – 840
 2σ : cal BC 1250 – 810

Milton Keynes: Hartigan's Gravel Pit, MK-223, Buckinghamshire

Location: SP 882387
 Lat. 52.02.21 N; Long. 00.42.50 W

Excavator: H S Green (Milton Keynes Archaeology Unit)

Site: an Iron Age occupation site.

Objectives: to closely date a group of ceramics which will be of key importance in the dating of Iron Age pottery traditions; the estimated date is probably second or first century BC.

Comments:
AML: one small sample, HAR-854 (MK223K-1), was dated after 1981.

HAR-855 2590 ± 90 BP

$\delta^{13}C$: –28.6 ‰

Sample: MK223K2, submitted on 19 September 1974

Material: charcoal and wood.

Initial comment: from a large Iron Age pit which produced both organic remains and a large extremely important group of Iron Age pottery.

Calibrated date: 1σ : cal BC 830 – 610
 2σ : cal BC 920 – 410

HAR-856 2320 ± 90 BP

$\delta^{13}C$: –28.0 ‰

Sample: MK223K2B, submitted on 19 September 1974

Material: charcoal and wood.

Initial comment: as HAR-855.

Calibrated date: 1σ : cal BC 510 – 264
 2σ : cal BC 765 – 180

HAR-857 2200 ± 110 BP

$\delta^{13}C$: –24.8 ‰

Sample: MK223K-3, submitted on 19 September 1974

Material: charcoal and wood.

Initial comment: as HAR-855.

Calibrated date: 1σ : cal BC 390 – 110
 2σ : cal BC 487 – 20 cal AD

Milton Keynes: Stacey Bushes, MK-228, Buckinghamshire

Location: SP 82053992
 Lat. 52.03.04 N; Long. 00.48.12 W

Excavator: H S Green (Milton Keynes Archaeology Unit), 1974

Site: Neolithic occupation.

References: Green and Sofranoff 1985, 17 (^{14}C)

HAR-858   3780 ± 150 BP

$\delta^{13}C$: −25.9 ‰

Sample: MK228-8B, submitted on 19 September 1974

Material: charcoal.

Initial comment: from a layer of hearth sweepings in the fill of a ditch, associated with sherds of plain Neolithic carinated bowls and pottery with Rinyo-Clacton affinities.

Calibrated date: 1σ : cal BC 2460 – 1985
2σ : cal BC 2850 – 1775

Final comments:
Harwell: a small sample, diluted before conversion to benzene, accounts for the large error term.

Moel y Gaer, Clwyd

Location: SJ 211690
Lat. 53.12.00 N; Long. 53.12.00 W

Excavator: G Guilbert, 1972

Site: a hillfort with numerous post-built round houses and an anomalous structure, comprising an irregular ring of seven posts around a large subrectangular pit of unknown function.

References: Guilbert 1975a
Guilbert 1975b
Guilbert 1976, 317

HAR-603   2190 ± 80 BP

$\delta^{13}C$: −27.2 ‰

Sample: MO476, submitted on 16 April 1975

Material: charcoal: *Corylus avellana*, *c* 5 years growth.

Initial comment: from brown silt with charcoal, beneath the tail of the second rampart; this is a crucial horizon in the site sequence, interpreted as vegetational clearance being between two phases of settlement.

Calibrated date: 1σ : cal BC 385 – 125
2σ : cal BC 400 – 40

Final comments:
G Guilbert: later than expected, but nearer the end of the stratigraphic sequence; this provides an acceptable *terminus ante quem* for the construction of the second rampart.

Harwell: replicated with HAR-1562 (2110 ± 70 BP).

References: Guilbert 1975b, 115
Guilbert 1976, 317
Radiocarbon **19**, 414

HAR-604   2530 ± 90 BP

$\delta^{13}C$: −26.3 ‰

Sample: MO3, submitted on 16 April 1975

Material: charcoal.

Initial comment: from packing material in the foundation trench for the front revetment timbers of the first timber-framed rampart.

Comment on uncalibrated date: this provides a *terminus ante quem* for the construction of the rampart, and hence the settlement, which is broadly in accordance with the structural affinities of the rampart with others of Iron Age date.

Calibrated date: 1σ : cal BC 805 – 520
2σ : cal BC 840 – 400

References: Guilbert 1975a, 203
Guilbert 1975b, 115
Guilbert 1976, 317
Radiocarbon **19**, 414

HAR-605   3590 ± 80 BP

$\delta^{13}C$: −25.6 ‰

Sample: MO467, submitted on 16 April 1975

Material: charcoal.

Initial comment: from a dark grey rectilinear area; an occupation layer beneath the rampart.

Comment on uncalibrated date: this is not surprising since there is a scatter of Late Neolithic and Early Bronze Age artefacts across the whole area, notably flint arrowheads.

Calibrated date: 1σ : cal BC 2114 – 1829
2σ : cal BC 2192 – 1740

References: *Radiocarbon* **19**, 414

HAR-606   2570 ± 70 BP

$\delta^{13}C$: −26.0 ‰

Sample: MO468, submitted on 16 April 1975

Material: charcoal.

Initial comment: from dark grey clay, probably an occupation layer in a post-built round house sealed by the first rampart.

Comment on uncalibrated date: stratigraphically consistent with, although statistically indistinguishable from, HAR-604; this suggests that the early occupation was at the interface of the Late Bronze Age/Early Iron Age; see also HAR-1126.

Calibrated date: 1σ : cal BC 810 – 610
2σ : cal BC 840 – 510

References: Guilbert 1975a, 205
Guilbert 1975b, 115
Guilbert 1976, 317
Radiocarbon **19**, 414

HAR-1122   2210 ± 70 BP

$\delta^{13}C$: −25.8 ‰

Sample: MO470, submitted on 16 April 1975

Material: charcoal: *Corylus avellana* and *Crataegus* sp., both *c* 10 years old.

Initial comment: from an isolated patch of charcoal in the core of what was probably the first timber-framed rampart.

Calibrated date: 1σ : cal BC 390 – 185
2σ : cal BC 400 – 100

Final comments:
G Guilbert: at worst, this provides a *terminus post quem* for the construction of the rampart, not the timber *in situ*.

References: Radiocarbon **21**, 369

HAR-1123   2540 ± 100 BP

$\delta^{13}C$: −25.7 ‰

Sample: MO1167, submitted on 16 April 1975

Material: charcoal: over 40-year-old *Quercus* sp. and 10-year-old *Corylus avellana*.

Initial comment: from a posthole of a large four-post rectangular structure in the phase 2 settlement.

Calibrated date: 1σ : cal BC 810 – 520
   2σ : cal BC 900 – 400

Final comments:
Harwell: a small sample due to poor laboratory yield in the benzene synthesis.

HAR-1125   2430 ± 100 BP

$\delta^{13}C$: −25.9 ‰

Sample: MO1838, submitted on 16 April 1975

Material: charcoal: over 10-year-old *Quercus* sp. and *c* 10-year-old *Corylus avellana*.

Initial comment: non-structural timber from a postpipe *c* 0.20m diameter, which held one side of the doorframe of a stake-walled round house in the phase 2 settlement.

Calibrated date: 1σ : cal BC 780 – 400
   2σ : cal BC 810 – 265

References: Radiocarbon **21**, 369

HAR-1126   2510 ± 100 BP

$\delta^{13}C$: −25.6 ‰

Sample: MO316, submitted on 16 April 1975

Material: charcoal: *c* 10-year-old *Corylus avellana*.

Initial comment: from dark grey clay filling in a posthole forming part of the porch of a post-ring round house.

Calibrated date: 1σ : cal BC 800 – 410
   2σ : cal BC 840 – 390

Final comments:
G Guilbert: this result is compatible with HAR-606, which was derived from another round house, thought on archaeological grounds to be broadly contemporary with this one.

Harwell: a small sample accounts for the larger than normal error term.

References: Radiocarbon **21**, 370

HAR-1127   2660 ± 70 BP

$\delta^{13}C$: −24.8 ‰

Sample: MO1071, submitted on 16 April 1975

Material: charcoal: over 50-year-old *Quercus* sp. with heavy rootlet contamination.

Initial comment: from one of a ring of twelve small pits comprising an anomalous structure 6.4m in diameter.

Calibrated date: 1σ : cal BC 895 – 800
   2σ : cal BC 980 – 770

References: Radiocarbon **21**, 370

HAR-1195   3570 ± 100 BP

$\delta^{13}C$: −26.7 ‰

Sample: M1362, submitted on 26 May 1975

Material: charcoal: *c* 7-year-old *Corylus avellana*.

Initial comment: from clay packing of one of the posts surrounding a large subrectangular pit.

Calibrated date: 1σ : cal BC 2115 – 1770
   2σ : cal BC 2200 – 1680

Final comments:
G Guilbert: quite acceptable archaeologically and although not directly related, this is highly compatible with HAR-605.

HAR-1196   2420 ± 80 BP

$\delta^{13}C$: −26.4 ‰

Sample: M1628-36, submitted on 26 May 1975

Material: charcoal: *c* 7-year-old *Corylus avellana*, which was washed into postholes after the collapse or demolition of the building.

Initial comment: from the silt fills of seven postholes forming the ring and entrance of a roundhouse (composite sample).

Calibrated date: 1σ : cal BC 765 – 400
   2σ : cal BC 800 – 380

HAR-1197   2560 ± 90 BP

$\delta^{13}C$: −26.3 ‰

Sample: M1603-04, submitted on 26 May 1975

Material: charcoal: *Corylus avellana c* 10 years age, with fragments of *Quercus* sp. and *Crataegus* sp..

Initial comment: from the silt fills of two adjacent postholes of a post-ring round house, the plan of which overlaps with that dated by HAR-1196.

Calibrated date: 1σ : cal BC 815 – 545
   2σ : cal BC 900 – 400

Montgomery: Breiddin, Powys

Location: SJ 292144
   Lat. 52.43.20 N; Long. 03.02.54 W

Excavator: C Musson (Clwyd-Powys Archaeological Trust)

Site: Iron Age hillfort.

References: Musson 1970
   Musson 1972
   Musson 1976, 302 (^{14}C)
   Musson 1991; 22, 62, 39, 130, 174, 179, 181, 195, M2: 187 – 92 (^{14}C)

HAR-467   2410 ± 100 BP

δ¹³C: −24.4 ‰

Sample: H1, submitted on 13 November 1973

Material: charcoal.

Initial comment: from collapsed packing and postpipes in the postholes of the porch of round house B37.

Comment on uncalibrated date: much as expected.

Calibrated date: 1σ : cal BC 770 – 390
                     2σ : cal BC 800 – 250

References: Radiocarbon **19**, 409

HAR-468   2190 ± 80 BP

δ¹³C: −25.1 ‰

Sample: H2, submitted on 13 November 1973

Material: charcoal.

Initial comment: combined small samples from collapsed packing and postpipes in thirteen postholes of four four-post structures (B31, B36, B37, B50); should be contemporary with HAR-469.

Comment on uncalibrated date: as HAR-467.

Calibrated date: 1σ : cal BC 385 – 125
                     2σ : cal BC 400 – 40

References: Radiocarbon **19**, 409

HAR-469   2120 ± 70 BP

δ¹³C: −26.0 ‰

Sample: H3, submitted on 13 November 1973

Material: charcoal.

Initial comment: from the postpipe of one of a pair of posts in B36 in the interior.

Comment on uncalibrated date: as HAR-467

Calibrated date: 1σ : cal BC 350 – 90
                     2σ : cal BC 380 – 20 cal AD

References: Radiocarbon **19**, 409

HAR-470   2500 ± 100 BP

δ¹³C: −24.8 ‰

Sample: H4, submitted on 13 November 1973

Material: charcoal.

Initial comment: from a round house, expected date fifth – fourth century BC.

Calibrated date: 1σ : cal BC 800 – 410
                     2σ : cal BC 840 – 390

Final comments:
C Musson: considerably earlier than expected.

Harwell: a recount failed; there is nothing in the records to doubt the first result.

HAR-842   2270 ± 90 BP

δ¹³C: −25.0 ‰

Sample: H5, submitted on 24 October 1974

Material: charcoal.

Initial comment: five combined samples from a round house; expected date fifth – fourth century BC.

Comment on uncalibrated date: in reasonable agreement with HAR-468 and HAR-469.

Calibrated date: 1σ : cal BC 400 – 205
                     2σ : cal BC 750 – 110

HAR-843   100 ± 70 BP

δ¹³C: −24.4 ‰

Sample: H6, submitted on 24 October 1974

Material: charcoal.

Initial comment: three combined samples from a round house; expected date fifth – fourth century BC, but there may have been modern disturbance.

Comment on uncalibrated date: acceptable; this clarifies the problem of the interpretation.

Calibrated date: 1σ : cal AD 1675 – 1955
                     2σ : cal AD 1650 – 1955

Mucking, Essex

Location: TQ 673803
              Lat. 51.29.47 N; Long. 00.24.38 E

Excavator: M U Jones (Mucking Excavation Committee), 1965 – 78

Site: multiperiod settlements and cemeteries, of prehistoric to Anglo-Saxon date, on the 30m Boyne terrace overlooking the Thames estuary.

References: Clarke 1993
                Hamerow 1993
                Jones and Bond 1980

Objectives: most samples were submitted in order to obtain closer dating for prehistoric pottery assemblages (HAR-2338, HAR-2340, and HAR-2342), or to date some of the Iron Age structures (HAR-1632 and HAR-1633); good charcoal from Anglo-Saxon features was sparse and the samples submitted are of importance in view of the large number of sunken huts at Mucking (HAR-2341 and HAR-2344).

HAR-450   3580 ± 90 BP

δ¹³C: −23.4 ‰

Sample: CHAROL, submitted on 10 October 1973

Material: charcoal: combined sample of partially humified oak (*Quercus* sp.).

Initial comment: from a planked coffin in grave 786; site coordinate 1152N 193E.

Calibrated date: 1σ : cal BC 2115 – 1780
                     2σ : cal BC 2195 – 1695

HAR-451   1390 ± 80 BP

$\delta^{13}C$: −25.0 ‰

Sample: WOODB, submitted on 10 October 1973

Material: wood.

Initial comment: from grave 871 in Anglo-Saxon cemetery II; site coordinate 830N 584E.

Calibrated date: 1σ : cal AD 600 – 675
      2σ : cal AD 530 – 780

HAR-1632   2020 ± 70 BP

$\delta^{13}C$: −24.5 ‰

Sample: 13095145, submitted on 27 May 1976

Material: charcoal: large timbers and branches of *Quercus* sp. (C A Keepax).

Initial comment: from a charred post butt of a rectangular structure with nine posts; site coordinate 1309N 514ft 5in E (pit 4112).

Calibrated date: 1σ : cal BC 110 – 60 cal AD
      2σ : cal BC 200 – 120 cal AD

HAR-1633   2090 ± 70 BP

$\delta^{13}C$: −23.6 ‰

Sample: 1749587, submitted on 27 May 1976

Material: charcoal: large timbers and branches of *Quercus* sp. (C A Keepax).

Initial comment: from a charred post butt of a rectangular structure with six posts; site coordinate 1749N 587E (pit 10,226).

Calibrated date: 1σ : cal BC 195 – 35
      2σ : cal BC 365 – 60 cal AD

HAR-2337   2929 ± 130 BP

$\delta^{13}C$: −25.6 ‰

Material: charcoal: carbonised twig.

Initial comment: from pit 25487, which produced a good group of pottery; site coordinate 2295N 899ft 6in E.

Calibrated date: 1σ : cal BC 1375 – 930
      2σ : cal BC 1450 – 820

Final comments:
Harwell: this result was produced after 1981, but is included for completeness.

References: Radiocarbon **30**, 298

HAR-2338   2360 ± 70 BP

$\delta^{13}C$: −21.4 ‰

Sample: 22431008, submitted on 1 June 1977

Material: carbonised grain and other seeds.

Initial comment: from storage pit 25,564, site coordinate 2243N 1008E; this contained a late group of pottery which may range from Middle Bronze Age to earliest Iron Age in date.

Calibrated date: 1σ : cal BC 515 – 390
      2σ : cal BC 765 – 255

HAR-2339   3100 ± 90 BP

$\delta^{13}C$: −24.8 ‰

Sample: 19621075, submitted on 1 June 1977

Material: charcoal.

Initial comment: from barrow 3 ditch fill, which yielded no archaeologically datable material; site coordinate 1962N 1075E.

Calibrated date: 1σ : cal BC 1495 – 1265
      2σ : cal BC 1590 – 1105

HAR-2340   3210 ± 80 BP

$\delta^{13}C$: −23.3 ‰

Sample: 22691030, submitted on 1 June 1977

Material: charcoal.

Initial comment: from the primary ditch fill of barrow 5, probably associated with Ardleigh type pottery (see also HAR-2342); site coordinate 2269N 1030E.

Calibrated date: 1σ : cal BC 1600 – 1420
      2σ : cal BC 1680 – 1315

HAR-2341   1480 ± 70 BP

$\delta^{13}C$: −25.2 ‰

Sample: 13306600, submitted on 1 June 1977

Material: charcoal.

Initial comment: from charred timbers in the fill of Saxon hut 115; site coordinate 1330N 660E.

Comment on uncalibrated date: (H Hamerow) this feature produced no closely datable finds. The date range indicated here is quite plausible given the position of the hut in the settlement (Hamerow 1993).

Calibrated date: 1σ : cal AD 555 – 643
      2σ : cal AD 420 – 670

HAR-2342   3290 ± 80 BP

$\delta^{13}C$: −24.4 ‰

Sample: 22671034, submitted on 1 June 1977

Material: charcoal.

Initial comment: as HAR-2340; site coordinate 2267N 1034E.

Calibrated date: 1σ : cal BC 1680 – 1510
      2σ : cal BC 1750 – 1420

HAR-2343   2980 ± 100 BP

$\delta^{13}C$: −25.0 ‰

Sample: 21901180, submitted on 1 June 1977

Material: charcoal dust.

Initial comment: from pit 25131, also containing calcined flint, dug through the silted ditch of barrow 4, which yielded no archaeologically datable material; site coordinate 2172N 1175E.

Calibrated date: 1σ : cal BC 1395 – 1040
2σ : cal BC 1450 – 920

HAR-2344   1400 ± 80 BP

$δ^{13}C$: –25.7 ‰

Sample: 17517680, submitted on 1 June 1977

Material: charcoal and charcoal dust.

Initial comment: from the ash layer of Saxon hearth 11640; site coordinate 1651N 768E. This was cut into the Roman turf-line of a 2m deep ditch, which has been silt-dated to c100 BC.

Calibrated date: 1σ : cal AD 595 – 675
2σ : cal AD 460 – 780

Final comments:
H Hamerow: this feature cannot be so precisely dated; it is more likley to date to the sixth or seventh century AD.

Mucking: North Ring, Essex

Location: TQ 67558112
Lat. 51.30.13 N; Long. 00.24.52 E

Excavator: D Bond (Central Excavation Unit), 1978

Site: circular, single-ditched enclosure *c* 0.5m in diameter with opposed entrances to the north-west and south-east.

References: Bond 1988; 8, 37, 55 (^{14}C)
Jones and Bond 1980, 475 (^{14}C)
Wainwright and Smith 1980, 117 (^{14}C)
Radiocarbon **29**, 94 (^{14}C)

Objectives: to provide confirmation of the dating of the major phases of the site.

Comments:
AML: one sample, HAR-2933 (23-33) from the primary fill of the original ditch, failed.

HAR-2893   2630 ± 110 BP

$δ^{13}C$: –24.2 ‰

Sample: 23-1658, submitted by N Balaam on 26 October 1978

Material: charcoal: *Acer* sp. from mature timbers and some *Corylus/Alnus* sp. and *Prunus* sp. (C A Keepax).

Initial comment: from immediately above the primary fill of the recut, cutting feature 1541 (phase 5 ditch silts).

Calibrated date: 1σ : cal BC 900 – 770
2σ : cal BC 1010 – 410

Final comments:
D Bond: this accords with the later Bronze Age cultural material.

Harwell: a small sample (one third of the optimum size) accounts for the larger than normal error term.

HAR-2911   2700 ± 80 BP

$δ^{13}C$: –24.6 ‰

Sample: 23-34, submitted by N Balaam on 26 November 1978

Material: charcoal: *Acer* sp., *Quercus* sp., and *Corylus/Alnus* sp. from mature timbers (C A Keepax).

Initial comment: from the primary fill of the recut Bronze Age/Iron Age ditch, cutting F51 (phase 5 ditch silts).

Calibrated date: 1σ : cal BC 920 – 805
2σ : cal BC 1020 – 780

Final comments:
D Bond: this accords with the later Bronze Age cultural material.

Mucking: South Ring, Essex

Location: TQ 673803
Lat. 51.29.47 N; Long. 00.24.38 E

Excavator: M U Jones and T Jones (Mucking Excavation Committee), 1966 – 8

Site: double-ditched, Late Bronze Age – Early Iron Age 'Springfield' type enclosure, on the Thames gravel terrace, with opposed entrances to the north-west and south-east; total diameter *c* 74.4m.

References: Bond 1988; 37, 55 (^{14}C)
Jones and Bond 1980; 471, 475 (^{14}C)

Objectives: to provide closer dating for a key assemblage of pottery which can otherwise only be ordered on typological grounds.

Comments:
M U Jones and T Jones: these three dates are quite close and the results are satisfactory.

HAR-1630   2790 ± 90 BP

$δ^{13}C$: –25.3 ‰

Sample: 144293S1, submitted on 27 May 1976

Material: charcoal: mainly *Quercus* sp. and *Alnus* sp. (C A Keepax).

Initial comment: from secondary silts in the inner ditch (303); site coordinate 144N 293E.

Calibrated date: 1σ : cal BC 1045 – 840
2σ : cal BC 1256 – 800

Final comments:
Harwell: this result agrees nicely with HAR-1634.

HAR-1634   2770 ± 110 BP

$δ^{13}C$: –25.7 ‰

Sample: 16534512, submitted on 27 May 1976

Material: charcoal: *Quercus* sp. and *Salix* sp. (C A Keepax).

Initial comment: from primary silts in the outer ditch (310); site coordinate 165N 345E.

Calibrated date: 1σ : cal BC 1040 – 820
2σ : cal BC 1260 – 790

HAR-1708   2810 ± 70 BP

$δ^{13}C$: –25.1 ‰

Sample: 1403409, submitted on 27 May 1976

Material: charcoal: twiggy *Quercus* sp. and *Populus* sp. from large timbers; also a few twigs, possibly of *Prunus* sp. (eg blackthorn).

Initial comment: from primary silts in the outer ditch (310); site coordinate 140N 340ft 9in E.

Calibrated date: 1σ : cal BC 1045 – 900
2σ : cal BC 1250 – 820

Nantwich: Crown Car Park, Cheshire

Location: SJ 6552 approx
Lat. 53.03.50 N; Long. 02.31.20 W

Excavator: R McNeil-Sale, 1978

Site: a medieval castle.

HAR-3313   1090 ± 70 BP

$δ^{13}C$: –26.1 ‰

Sample: C1, submitted on 11 May 1979

Material: soil and charcoal: *Corylus/Alnus* sp., *Fraxinus* sp., and *Salix/Populus* sp., mainly from mature timbers (C A Keepax).

Initial comment: from the second phase of terracing for the castle; pottery from the ditch associated with the first phase of terracing is of thirteenth-century date.

Calibrated date: 1σ : cal AD 885 – 1010
2σ : cal AD 780 – 1030

HAR-3347   980 ± 80 BP

$δ^{13}C$: –26.1 ‰

Sample: P78C13, submitted on 11 May 1979

Material: charcoal and burnt soil: *Quercus* sp., Rosaceae, sub-family Pomoideae, *Corylus/Alnus* sp., and *Salix/Populus* sp., mainly from mature timbers (C A Keepax).

Initial comment: from an industrial horizon which predates a thirteenth-century defensive ditch and is stratigraphically over an earlier ditch.

Calibrated date: 1σ : cal AD 985 – 1160
2σ : cal AD 890 – 1230

HAR-3368   660 ± 70 BP

$δ^{13}C$: –27.0 ‰

Sample: P78C10, submitted on 11 May 1979

Material: wood: *Quercus* sp. from partially burnt branches (C A Keepax).

Initial comment: from an early defensive ditch, which is pre-thirteenth century in date.

Calibrated date: 1σ : cal AD 1270 – 1390
2σ : cal AD 1240 – 1410

HAR-3432   790 ± 70 BP

$δ^{13}C$: –29.1 ‰

Sample: P78C5:P78C6, submitted on 11 May 1979

Material: twigs, uncharred; two combined samples: C5: ?*Prunus* sp. of c 10 years growth; C6: *Corylus/Alnus* sp. of c 11 years growth (C A Keepax).

Initial comment: from the very bottom, of the primary silt, of the large medieval ditch.

Calibrated date: 1σ : cal AD 1180 – 1275
2σ : cal AD 1045 – 1290

Nazeingbury: Nursery Road, Essex

Location: TL 386066
Lat. 51.44.26 N; Long. 00.00.27 E

Excavator: P J Huggins (Waltham Abbey Historical Society), 1976

Site: two Anglo-Saxon timber churches and an inhumation cemetery thought to belong to a hospice run by nuns; 180 graves were found oriented east – west and without grave goods, some overlying Belgic and first- or second-century Roman occupation; there was no medieval or later occupation until the 1930s.

References: Huggins 1978, 54 (^{14}C)
Radiocarbon **27**, 82 (^{14}C)

Objectives: to date the cemetery, thought to be Saxon and pre-1200.

Comments:
P J Huggins: these two results were very helpful at the time. However, in the light of the discovery of the charter evidence, they appear less so. The lack of shell-tempered pottery in the area of the cemetery led to the suggestion that the nunnery did not survive the Danish invasions of c AD 870. The ^{14}C dates allow this terminus to apply. The date of sample HAR-1666 certainly lies within the one standard deviation range, and that of HAR-1681 quite possibly does too if the 122 burials all preceded the 53 secondary ones.

HAR-1666   1280 ± 80 BP

$δ^{13}C$: –22.4 ‰

Sample: NZ75GR54, submitted on 27 May 1976

Material: human bone, no suggestion of contamination: female aged 50+.

Initial comment: the sample is from one of two female burials in the east end of church 1. The sample is from one of 122 primary burials on the site.

Calibrated date: 1σ : cal AD 660 – 850
2σ : cal AD 620 – 940

Final comments:
P J Huggins: since the excavation, two sixteenth-century copies of charters of c AD 700 have been found (Bascombe 1987), which record the grant of land at Nazeing by King

Suebred to 'you ffyme' to share in erecting a house of God. It is suggested that the sample is from one of the two founders of the house. The lady in question is likely to have died within a few years of c AD 700, so the calibrated date, even at one standard deviation level of confidence, seems entirely appropriate.

HAR-1681 1120 ± 80 BP

$\delta^{13}C$: −22.7 ‰

Sample: NZ75GR26, submitted on 27 May 1976

Material: human bone, no suggestion of contamination: female aged 40.

Initial comment: this sample is one of 53 secondary burials, at a high level in the ground, when the cemetery was being used for a second time. Another sample, HAR-1666 is expected to be several generations earlier.

Calibrated date: 1σ : cal AD 810 – 1000
2σ : cal AD 690 – 1030

Final comments:
P J Huggins: the calibrated date in this case only confirms that the burial is of pre-Conquest date.

North Elmham Park, Norfolk

Location: TF 987214
Lat. 52.45.12 N; Long. 00.56.41 E

Excavator: P Wade-Martins (Norfolk Archaeological Unit), 1968 – 72

Site: an Anglo-Saxon settlement.

References: Wade-Martins 1980

Objectives: to confirm the phasing of the site; the date of ditches 950 and 1018 is uncertain but thought to be Middle Saxon; pit 44a is thought to be of tenth-century date.

HAR-759 1310 ± 70 BP

$\delta^{13}C$: −24.0 ‰

Sample: NO878966, submitted on 11 July 1974

Material: animal bone.

Initial comment: from the Middle Saxon ditch F950, layer 4.

Calibrated date: 1σ : cal AD 655 – 775
2σ : cal AD 610 – 880

Final comments:
P Wade-Martins: the period I/2 ditch A is now believed to date to the eighth century.

References: Wade-Martins 1980; 31 – 2, 124

HAR-760 1080 ± 90 BP

$\delta^{13}C$: −22.7 ‰

Sample: 44A216, submitted on 11 July 1974

Material: animal bone.

Initial comment: from F44a, layer 2, a ?Late Saxon cess pit.

Calibrated date: 1σ : cal AD 885 – 1020
2σ : cal AD 725 – 1160

Final comments:
P Wade-Martins: the period II/1 building X is now believed to date to the late ninth century.

References: Wade-Martins 1980; 31 – 2, 124

HAR-763 1210 ± 80 BP

$\delta^{13}C$: −23.4 ‰

Sample: 1018220, submitted on 11 July 1974

Material: animal bone.

Initial comment: from F1018, layer 2; possibly a Middle Saxon ditch.

Calibrated date: 1σ : cal AD 685 – 895
2σ : cal AD 660 – 990

Final comments:
P Wade-Martins: the period I/2 ditch D is now believed to date to the eighth century.

References: Wade-Martins 1980, 31 – 2 and 124
Radiocarbon **19**, 418

North Elmham: Spong Hill, Norfolk

Location: TF 983195
Lat. 52.44.11 N; Long. 00.56.15 E

Excavator: C Hills (Department of the Environment), 1972 – 81 and 1984

Site: an Anglo-Saxon cemetery (late sixth- to early seventh-century) over Roman and Iron Age occupation.

Objectives: to secure more precise dating for 'prehistoric' features and to help disentangle the complex history of a major Roman enclosure ditch.

HAR-2398 1620 ± 70 BP

$\delta^{13}C$: −26.3 ‰

Sample: 823, submitted by P Murphy on 7 September 1977

Material: charcoal: *Quercus* sp., large timbers; *Prunus* cf *spinosa*, *Corylus/Alnus* sp., and *Sarothamnus* sp. (or possibly *Ulex* sp.), all twig; also hawthorn type (Rosaceae, sub-family Pomoideae).

Initial comment: from a ditch cut in the second century, in use thereafter through the Roman period, still partly in the open in the Anglo-Saxon period.

Calibrated date: 1σ : cal AD 345 – 535
2σ : cal AD 250 – 600

Final comments:
C Hills: context 823 is a layer forming part of dump layers in the ditch; these layers are of fourth-century date, probably late fourth-century AD.

HAR-2901 3440 ± 90 BP

$\delta^{13}C$: −25.0 ‰

Sample: SPON1584, submitted by P Murphy on 27 October 1978

Material: charcoal: *Quercus* sp. and *Corylus/Alnus* sp. from mature timbers (C A Keepax).

Initial comment: from charcoal from pit 1584, associated with Collared Urn sherds.

Calibrated date: 1σ : cal BC 1885 – 1675
                     2σ : cal BC 2040 – 1510

Final comments:
C Hills: see Healey 1988, 20.

References: Healy 1988, 104

HAR-2903   8150 ± 100 BP

$\delta^{13}C$: −24.9 ‰

Sample: SPON1334, submitted by P Murphy on 27 October 1978

Material: charcoal: all conifer, probably *Pinus* sp., from mature timbers; this is unusual in an archaeological context and may mean that the feature is earlier or later than supposed (C A Keepax).

Initial comment: from a pit, identification and date indicate Mesolithic origin but from a feature cutting the fill continuous with the spread, which contained almost exclusively Neolithic ?residual charcoal (?fossil fuel).

Final comments:
C Hills: see Healey 1988, 18.

Harwell: too old to calibrate.

References: Healy 1988, 104

North Molton: Shallowmead, Devon

Location: SS 738364
             Lat. 51.06.45 N; Long. 03.48.11 W

Excavator: H Miles (Exeter University Department of Extra-Mural Studies), 1977

Site: Bronze Age ring cairn *c* 10m across incorporating white quartz in the stones of the revetment ring, excavated in advance of agricultural improvement; the site is on the edge of a very substantial Exmoor barrow cemetery and would relate to the five-barrow and two-barrow groups on the top of the ridge above the site; the cairn itself contained no burial.

Objectives: the site is the first in the area to be excavated with modern techniques; a ^{14}C date would provide one fixed point in the chronology of the prehistoric use of Exmoor and may perhaps indicate until what date structures of this type were built in the West Country.

HAR-2829   3060 ± 80 BP

$\delta^{13}C$: −24.9 ‰

Sample: A2431, submitted on 30 August 1978

Material: charcoal: *Quercus* sp. from mature timbers (C A Keepax).

Initial comment: from soil sealed immediately by the wall of the ring cairn; the finds, although few, and the method of construction point to a date in the Early Bronze Age (2000 – 1500 BC).

Calibrated date: 1σ : cal BC 1425 – 1225
                     2σ : cal BC 1510 – 1070

Final comments:
H Miles: the calibrated date at both standard deviation levels of confidence is rather later than expected. However, little is still known about the duration of ritual monument construction of this type in Devon.

Northampton: Briar Hill, Northamptonshire

Location: SF 740593
             Lat. 53.01.50 N; Long. 06.51.44 W

Excavator: H Bamford (Northampton Development Corporation), 1974 – 8

Site: the first Neolithic causewayed enclosure in the Midlands to be examined extensively, and the only site in the area to have any ^{14}C dates.

References: Bamford 1985, 126 – 9 (^{14}C)

Objectives: to establish the longevity of the site, for which all other means are too imprecise, and to compare the dates with those from enclosures in the Thames Valley and south-western groups.

Comments:
AML: one sample failed, HAR-2317 (P76A7-36); four samples, HAR-4110 (P76C3275), HAR-5216-I (C15), HAR-5217 (P76A3021), and HAR-5271 (P76C8330) were dated after April 1981.

HAR-2282   5440 ± 110 BP

$\delta^{13}C$: −24.4 ‰

Sample: P76E8-77, submitted by J Williams on 1 June 1977

Material: charcoal.

Initial comment: from F77, layers 76 and 77: outer causewayed ditch segment, halfway down in a tip against the south-east corner.

Calibrated date: 1σ : cal BC 4370 – 4160
                     2σ : cal BC 4510 – 4000

Final comments:
H Bamford: this sample is probably, but not certainly, contemporary with the original construction of the outer ditch circuit.

HAR-2283   1700 ± 60 BP

$\delta^{13}C$: −24.5 ‰

Sample: P76C9-25, submitted by J Williams on 1 June 1977

Material: charcoal.

Initial comment: from F29, layer 25 (125 and 127), the fill of a probable Early Saxon sunken-featured building.

Calibrated date: 1σ : cal AD 250 – 410
                     2σ : cal AD 210 – 440

HAR-2389 3540 ± 90 BP

$\delta^{13}C$: −25.5 ‰

Sample: P76E7-41, submitted by J Williams on 1 June 1977

Material: charcoal.

Initial comment: from F41, layers 41 and 42 (68): fill of a pit, or third recut, in an inner causewayed ditch segment; the expected date is Late Neolithic or Early Bronze Age.

Comment on uncalibrated date: the result is consistent with the pottery evidence.

Calibrated date: 1σ : cal BC 2025 – 1750
2σ : cal BC 2140 – 1680

Final comments:
Harwell: repeat of HAR-2284 which failed.

HAR-2607 4010 ± 90 BP

$\delta^{13}C$: −25.2 ‰

Sample: PC76B6-60, submitted by J Williams on 21 March 1978

Material: charcoal: *Quercus* sp., *Corylus/Alnus* sp., cf blackthorn (*Prunus* sp.), and *Salix/Populus* sp., mainly from branch-sized and larger timber.

Initial comment: from timber slots, forming the base of a rectangular structure, associated with later Neolithic Grooved Ware; possibly Late Neolithic.

Calibrated date: 1σ : cal BC 2855 – 2460
2σ : cal BC 2880 – 2300

References: *Radiocarbon* **19**, 417

HAR-2625 4290 ± 80 BP

$\delta^{13}C$: −30.4 ‰

Sample: PC76B7390, submitted by J Williams on 21 March 1978

Material: charcoal: *Quercus* sp. from large timbers.

Initial comment: from a large postpit; possibly Neolithic.

Calibrated date: 1σ : cal BC 3025 – 2785
2σ : cal BC 3095 – 2630

HAR-3208 4600 ± 90 BP

$\delta^{13}C$: −24.5 ‰

Sample: PC76D7-83, submitted by J Williams on 11 May 1979

Material: soil and charcoal.

Initial comment: from F52, a flat-bottomed scoop with a cremation deposit cut into the fill of a recut inner causewayed ditch segment; possibly Early Bronze Age.

Calibrated date: 1σ : cal BC 3500 – 3140
2σ : cal BC 3625 – 3040

HAR-4057 4250 ± 70 BP

$\delta^{13}C$: −27.7 ‰

Sample: P76B6116, submitted by J Williams on 29 September 1980

Material: charcoal: *Quercus* sp. from mature timber (C A Keepax).

Initial comment: from F218, a large postpit inside the enclosure, with a central depression or slot containing charcoal and burnt material; the expected date is Neolithic.

Calibrated date: 1σ : cal BC 2920 – 2705
2σ : cal BC 3030 – 2620

HAR-4058 3700 ± 150 BP

$\delta^{13}C$: −26.0 ‰

Sample: P76B3001, submitted by J Williams on 29 September 1980

Material: charcoal.

Initial comment: from F240, the fill of a cremation burial, accompanied by a burnt barbed-and-tanged flint arrowhead; probably Early Bronze Age.

Calibrated date: 1σ : cal BC 2330 – 1890
2σ : cal BC 2565 – 1695

Final comments:
H Bamford: an acceptable result.

HAR-4065 3180 ± 70 BP

$\delta^{13}C$: −27.1 ‰

Sample: P76B3168, submitted by J Williams on 29 September 1980

Material: charcoal.

Initial comment: from F275, the fill around the remains of a Bucket Urn, containing cremated bone, in the interior of the enclosure; probably Early Bronze Age.

Calibrated date: 1σ : cal BC 1520 – 1410
2σ : cal BC 1620 – 1310

Final comments:
H Bamford: this result is acceptable.

HAR-4066 4080 ± 70 BP

$\delta^{13}C$: −26.95 ‰

Sample: P76A3020, submitted by J Williams on 29 September 1980

Material: charcoal: *Prunus* sp., Rosaceae, sub-family Pomoideae, *Quercus* sp., and *Corylus/Alnus* sp., all from mature timbers (C A Keepax).

Initial comment: from F248, a segment of the inner ditch of the outer enclosure; the middle fill of the second of three phases.

Calibrated date: 1σ : cal BC 2865 – 2500
2σ : cal BC 2885 – 2470

HAR-4067 3730 ± 70 BP

$\delta^{13}C$: −27.0 ‰

Sample: P76C3251, submitted by J Williams on 29 September 1980

Material: charcoal: *Quercus* sp. from mature timber (C A Keepax).

Initial comment: from F228A, pit (possibly part of a structure) cut into the upper fill of inner ditch segment F192C; the expected date is Neolithic.

Calibrated date: 1σ : cal BC 2280 – 2035
2σ : cal BC 2450 – 1940

HAR-4071   4610 ± 90 BP

$δ^{13}C$: −26.1 ‰

Sample: P76C3116, submitted by J Williams on 29 September 1980

Material: charcoal: *Prunus* sp. from mature timber (C A Keepax).

Initial comment: from F199, a segment of the inner ditch of the outer enclosure; the middle fill of the final phase (of four).

Calibrated date: 1σ : cal BC 3505 – 3140
2σ : cal BC 3625 – 3040

HAR-4072   5680 ± 70 BP

$δ^{13}C$: −26.5 ‰

Sample: P76C2011, submitted by J Williams on 29 September 1980

Material: charcoal: *Quercus* sp. from mature timbers (C A Keepax).

Initial comment: from F219, a pit cut by the weathered outer edge of an outer ditch segment, possibly part of an entrance structure; this sample is probably, but not certainly, contemporary with the original construction of the outer ditch circuit.

Calibrated date: 1σ : cal BC 4665 – 4460
2σ : cal BC 4720 – 4360

HAR-4073   3790 ± 100 BP

$δ^{13}C$: −27.8 ‰

Sample: P76C3503, submitted by J Williams on 29 September 1980

Material: charcoal: *Quercus* sp. from mature timber (C A Keepax).

Initial comment: from F192C, the inner ditch of the outer enclosure; the middle fill of the third phase cut (of four).

Calibrated date: 1σ : cal BC 2455 – 2045
2σ : cal BC 2560 – 1950

Final comments:
H Bamford: this result is consistent with the ceramic evidence.

HAR-4074   4370 ± 80 BP

$δ^{13}C$: −25.2 ‰

Sample: P76B6047, submitted by J Williams on 29 September 1980

Material: charcoal: *Prunus* sp., *Quercus* sp., and *Corylus/Alnus* sp., mainly from mature timbers (C A Keepax).

Initial comment: from F137, a pit inside the enclosure containing a large number of worked flints; probably Neolithic.

Calibrated date: 1σ : cal BC 3095 – 2915
2σ : cal BC 3340 – 2785

HAR-4075   4660 ± 70 BP

$δ^{13}C$: −25.2 ‰

Sample: P76A7185, submitted by J Williams on 29 September 1980

Material: charcoal: *Prunus* sp. from mature timber (C A Keepax).

Initial comment: from F124, a segment of the inner ditch of the outer enclosure, lower fill of the final phase; the expected date is Neolithic.

Calibrated date: 1σ : cal BC 3595 – 3355
2σ : cal BC 3630 – 3140

HAR-4089   3620 ± 90 BP

$δ^{13}C$: −25.7 ‰

Sample: P76C3335, submitted by J Williams on 29 September 1980

Material: charcoal: *Quercus* sp. (C A Keepax).

Initial comment: from F258, a possible pit in the upper fill of the inner ditch segment F192B (possibly connected with F228); the expected date is Neolithic.

Calibrated date: 1σ : cal BC 2135 – 1885
2σ : cal BC 2280 – 1750

HAR-4092   5540 ± 140 BP

$δ^{13}C$: −24.2 ‰

Sample: P76A6051, submitted by J Williams on 29 September 1980

Material: charcoal, a combined sample: *Quercus* sp., *Prunus* sp., Rosaceae, sub-family Pomoideae, and *Fraxinus* sp., all from mature timbers (C A Keepax).

Initial comment: from F128, a segment of the inner ditch circuit (inner spiral), middle fill of the final phase (of four); the expected date is Neolithic.

Calibrated date: 1σ : cal BC 4520 – 4245
2σ : cal BC 4720 – 4040

Northampton: Chalk Lane, Northamptonshire

Location: SF 749605
Lat. 53.02.31 N; Long. 06.51.00 W

Excavator: J Williams (Northampton Development Corporation), 1975 – 8

Site: prehistoric and Saxon occupation below the bank of the outer bailey of the medieval castle.

References: Williams and Shaw 1981, 95 (^{14}C)
Williams *et al* 1985, 65 – 6 (^{14}C)

Comments:
1985: as expected the dates from the two bone samples agree closely; the third sample comes from another building.

HAR-3688   1510 ± 80 BP

$\delta^{13}C$: −23.5 ‰

Sample: M139D86, submitted on 30 January 1980

Material: animal bone.

Initial comment: from D86, the fill of an Early or Middle Saxon sunken-featured building (as HAR-3689).

Calibrated date: 1σ : cal AD 435 – 630
                    2σ : cal AD 390 – 660

HAR-3689   1450 ± 70 BP

$\delta^{13}C$: −23.8 ‰

Sample: M139D86, submitted on 30 January 1980

Material: animal bone.

Initial comment: from D86, the fill of an Early or Middle Saxon sunken-featured building (as HAR-3688).

Calibrated date: 1σ : cal AD 550 – 655
                    2σ : cal AD 430 – 680

HAR-3935   1320 ± 70 BP

$\delta^{13}C$: −27.5 ‰

Sample: M139A141

Material: charcoal: *Quercus* sp. from mature timber (C A Keepax).

Initial comment: from a single half-sawn timber in the fill of posthole A171 in A141, an Early or Middle Saxon sunken-featured building.

Comment on uncalibrated date: I would have been happier if the date were closer to HAR-3689, but nothing in the stratigraphy necessitates this.

Calibrated date: 1σ : cal AD 650 – 775
                    2σ : cal AD 600 – 880

Northampton: St Peter's Street, Northamptonshire

Location: SP 750603
             Lat. 52.13.55 N; Long. 00.54.55 W

Excavator: J Williams (Northampton Development Corporation), 1973 – 6

Site: a medieval street frontage over Saxon structures and mortar mixers.

References: Williams 1979, 247 (^{14}C)
               Williams *et al* 1985, 65 – 6 (^{14}C)

Comments:
1985: the archaeological evidence suggests that all these results should relate quite closely to one another, but attempts to combine the results show that they fall into a number of groups.

HAR-1225   1190 ± 70 BP

$\delta^{13}C$: −26.2 ‰

Sample: M1152854, submitted on 30 April 1975

Material: charcoal with soil.

Initial comment: from a heavy charcoal layer, possibly a burnt floor, within fill of K172: house 10, sunken-featured building 2B, phase 4 (rebuilt, possibly with a wooden floor, since burnt, with a clay hearth on top); possibly Late Saxon, stratigraphically later than HAR-1437.

Calibrated date: 1σ : cal AD 725 – 895
                    2σ : cal AD 670 – 990

Final comments:
J Williams: this is 100 – 150 years earlier than expected.

References: Radiocarbon **21**, 373

HAR-1244   1110 ± 80 BP

$\delta^{13}C$: −22.3 ‰

Sample: M1153302 (759/J14), submitted on 4 June 1975

Material: animal bone.

Initial comment: from the sandy fill of A759, house 2 gully, probably phase 3A (*c* 1m wide and 0.6m deep), same as HAR-1454; possibly Middle Saxon.

Calibrated date: 1σ : cal AD 830 – 1010
                    2σ : cal AD 715 – 1040

References: Radiocarbon **21**, 373

HAR-1245   1300 ± 60 BP

$\delta^{13}C$: −22.3 ‰

Sample: M1153303 (F56 and equivalents), submitted on 4 June 1975

Material: animal bone.

Initial comment: from house 8, phase 3; sand and mortar spreads (F56, F272, F274, F276, F284, and F291) varying from a few centimetres to *c* 0.5m in depth, overlying destroyed mortar mixers. Phase 3 is at the same level as F282 (H1246); possibly Late Saxon.

Calibrated date: 1σ : cal AD 660 – 775
                    2σ : cal AD 640 – 880

References: Radiocarbon **21**, 373

HAR-1246   1310 ± 90 BP

$\delta^{13}C$: −22.3 ‰

Sample: M1153304, submitted on 4 June 1975

Material: animal bone.

Initial comment: from F282, house 8, phase 3; destruction of mortar mixers, same level as F56 (HAR-1245).

Calibrated date: 1σ : cal AD 645 – 785
                    2σ : cal AD 565 – 890

References: Radiocarbon **21**, 373

HAR-1431 700 ± 70 BP

$\delta^{13}C$: −22.0 ‰

Sample: M1153338 (K171), submitted on 29 July 1976

Material: animal bone.

Initial comment: from K171, house 10, the lower fill of sunken-featured building 3 (cut 0.50m into the natural ironstone bedrock), associated with local and imported Saxo-Norman pottery.

Calibrated date: 1σ : cal AD 1260 – 1375
 2σ : cal AD 1220 – 1400

HAR-1437 880 ± 70 BP

$\delta^{13}C$: −22.2 ‰

Sample: M1153339 (K177), submitted on 29 July 1976

Material: animal bone.

Initial comment: from a dark organic layer in K177, house 10, the primary fill over what was probably the floor of sunken-featured building 2B, associated with local and imported Saxo-Norman pottery; stratigraphically earlier than HAR-1225.

Calibrated date: 1σ : cal AD 1035 – 1230
 2σ : cal AD 1010 – 1270

HAR-1452 1080 ± 60 BP

$\delta^{13}C$: −22.5 ‰

Sample: M1153336 (F293), submitted on 29 July 1976

Material: animal bone.

Initial comment: from F293, house 8, the fill of mortar mixer 2, phase 3; associated with Early/Middle Saxon pottery and fragments of probably Roman brick.

Calibrated date: 1σ : cal AD 890 – 1010
 2σ : cal AD 810 – 1030

HAR-1454 1030 ± 80 BP

$\delta^{13}C$: −22.1 ‰

Sample: M1153337 (J14), submitted on 29 July 1976

Material: animal bone.

Initial comment: from A759, house 2, probably phase 3A, the fill of a gully to the south of the gas and waterpipe trenches; same as HAR-1244.

Calibrated date: 1σ : cal AD 900 – 1035
 2σ : cal AD 830 – 1170

HAR-1720 1240 ± 80 BP

$\delta^{13}C$: −22.4 ‰

Sample: M1153482, submitted on 29 July 1976

Material: animal bone.

Initial comment: from N133, a robber trench of the possible church, associated with faced mortar fragments and possibly with reused Roman tile; possibly Saxon.

Comment on uncalibrated date: this date fits fairly well with HAR-1245 and HAR-1246 which were also associated with the construction of the Anglo-Saxon church.

Calibrated date: 1σ : cal AD 675 – 885
 2σ : cal AD 650 – 970

Northchurch, Hertfordshire

Location: SP 973092
 Lat. 51.46.21 N; Long. 00.35.23 W

Excavator: D Neal (Department of the Environment), 1973

Site: a Roman villa.

References: Neal 1977, 17 (^{14}C)

Objectives: a ^{14}C date was required to determine whether the context is Roman or modern.

HAR-448 1800 ± 60 BP

$\delta^{13}C$: −25.4 ‰

Sample: CHAROL

Material: charcoal.

Initial comment: from a water leet with 'modern' watercress beds, so that there was doubt as to whether the feature was in fact Roman.

Calibrated date: 1σ : cal AD 130 – 320
 2σ : cal AD 80 – 380

Final comments:
Harwell: this confirms the Roman date of the feature.

Norwich: 3 – 5 Lobster Lane, 336N, Norfolk

Location: TG 2208 approx
 Lat. 52.37.26 N; Long. 01.16.49 E

Excavator: the late A Carter (Norwich Castle Museum), 1977

Site: a Thetford type ware kiln (site 336N).

References: Atkin and Sutermeister 1980
 Atkin *et al* 1983, 92 and 97 (^{14}C)

Objectives: to date the kiln and thus the manufacture of Thetford type ware.

HAR-2560 770 ± 80 BP

$\delta^{13}C$: −25.9 ‰

Sample: 16, submitted by P Murphy on 21 February 1978

Material: charcoal with soil: *Quercus* sp. (twig and large timbers), *Corylus/Alnus* sp., and *Salix/Populus* sp. (C A Keepax).

Initial comment: from the kiln.

Calibrated date: 1σ : cal AD 1205 – 1280
 2σ : cal AD 1045 – 1385

Norwich: 49 – 63 Botolph Street, Norfolk

Location: TG 23000942 – TG 22970944
Lat. 52.38.10 N – 52.38.11 N; Long. 01.17.45 E – 01.17.44 E

Excavator: J P Roberts (Norwich Castle Museum), 1975

Site: a Late Saxon defensive ditch.

References: Davison and Evans 1985, 116 (^{14}C)

Objectives: the archaeological dating of the Late Saxon defensive ditch north of Norwich is weak (AD 850 – 1100); a more accurate determination would be of value not only to the chronology of Norwich but also to that of the other East Anglian towns, none of the early defences of which is accurately dated.

Comments:
J P Roberts: the real value of these dates is that they confirm the pre-Conquest date of the northern defences, which otherwise rested solely on a handful of pottery sherds. The next question to be resolved is whether these defences are Danish in origin (ie late ninth century), or were they erected after Edward's reconquest of East Anglia in c 917. No material was obtained from the silting of the first ditch; thereafter, the sequence of dates from the successive layers of deposition and recutting should read HAR-2071, HAR-2710, and HAR-2700. Sadly, these offer little help in resolving the archaeological problem without further corroborating evidence. Although they could be made to fit into a coherent pattern at a two standard deviation level of confidence, it would be a brave man indeed who would be prepared to argue on these alone for a set of Danish defences which were twice refurbished in the tenth century, for the second time at least presumably by the Saxons.

HAR-2700   1190 ± 70 BP

$\delta^{13}C$: –21.6 ‰

Sample: 281N641/642, submitted on 21 March 1978

Material: bone, all samples are contaminated with fossil fuels.

Initial comment: from the lower filling of the second recut ditch, which seals the contexts from which HAR-2701 and HAR-2702 derived and could be up to 100 years later than them.

Calibrated date: 1σ : cal AD 725 – 895
2σ : cal AD 670 – 990

HAR-2701   1090 ± 60 BP

$\delta^{13}C$: –22.0 ‰

Sample: 281N643, submitted on 21 March 1978

Material: bone, see HAR-2700.

Initial comment: from the lower filling of the first recut ditch, sealed beneath HAR-2702.

Calibrated date: 1σ : cal AD 890 – 1010
2σ : cal AD 790 – 1030

HAR-2702   1260 ± 90 BP

$\delta^{13}C$: –22.8 ‰

Sample: 281N640, submitted on 21 March 1978

Material: bone, see HAR-2700.

Initial comment: from the upper filling of the first recut ditch, this seals HAR-2701.

Calibrated date: 1σ : cal AD 665 – 885
2σ : cal AD 620 – 970

Norwich: Anglia TV, Norfolk

Location: TG 2308 approx
Lat. 52.37.24 N; Long. 01.17.42 W

Excavator: B S Ayers (Norfolk Archaeological Unit), 1979

Site: Anglian Television Extension Site, Norwich.

References: Clark 1985, 62 (^{14}C)

Objectives: samples were taken to obtain a date for an early medieval building, which was subsequently identified as a timber church.

Comments:
AML: one sample, HAR-3650 (4I6N2139), produced insufficient material for dating.

HAR-3585   1200 ± 70 BP

$\delta^{13}C$: –26.9 ‰

Sample: 416N1465, submitted on 9 October 1979

Material: charcoal.

Initial comment: as HAR 3722.

Calibrated date: 1σ : cal AD 715 – 895
2σ : cal AD 670 – 990

Final comments:
B S Ayers: as HAR-3722.

HAR-3656   1230 ± 70 BP

$\delta^{13}C$: –27.0 ‰

Sample: 416N1115, submitted on 9 October 1979

Material: charcoal.

Initial comment: from an early medieval posthole.

Comment on uncalibrated date: the posthole is now interpreted as part of a timber building, the second in a sequence of three buildings.

Calibrated date: 1σ : cal AD 680 – 885
2σ : cal AD 660 – 970

Final comments:
B S Ayers: the result is consistent with the stratigraphic interpretation, that the sampled feature was part of a pre-Conquest structure. The relatively early dating might suggest reused timber as the structure is unlikely to predate AD 1000.

HAR-3707   1300 ± 90 BP

$\delta^{13}C$: –25.0 ‰

Sample: 416N1409, submitted on 12 October 1979

Material: charcoal.

Initial comment: from a fill of a construction slot or trench which lay within the same interpreted structure as HAR-3656.

Calibrated date: 1σ : cal AD 650 – 790
2σ : cal AD 590 – 940

Final comments:
B S Ayers: as HAR-3656.

HAR-3722 1170 ± 70 BP

$\delta^{13}C$: –27.6 ‰

Sample: 416N1465, submitted on 9 October 1979

Material: charcoal.

Initial comment: from a pit fill (same context as HAR-3585).

Calibrated date: 1σ : cal AD 775 – 960
2σ : cal AD 680 – 1010

Final comments:
B S Ayers: the result is consistent with a pre-Conquest interpretation. This, and sample HAR-3585 above, predate the above samples, as far as could be established from poor stratigraphic relationships.

Norwich: Bowthorpe, Norfolk

Location: TG 17230989
Lat. 52.38.34 N; Long. 01.12.40 E

Excavator: A J Lawson (Norfolk Archaeological Unit), 1979

Site: site 11,431, a Bronze Age round barrow with two concentric ring ditches, with a central crouched inhumation in a coffin, ten satellite burials (one with an inverted Collared Urn), and one grave beneath the outer ditch. Earlier activity is attested by Beaker pottery and a small number of early features; Iron Age and Roman pottery was found in the upper fill of the outer ditch.

References: Lawson 1986a, 2 (^{14}C)
Lawson 1986c; 20, 29 – 31, 40, 47, figs 27, 29, 34 (^{14}C)

Objectives: to provide a series of dates to corroborate, or clarify, the sequence of burials and to provide dating for a class of monument seldom dated by ^{14}C in Norfolk.

Comments:
A J Lawson: these results show that the barrow may have been in use from 2100 – 1500 BC.

HAR-3611 3610 ± 80 BP

$\delta^{13}C$: –25.4 ‰

Sample: BOW74, submitted by P Murphy on 9 October 1979

Material: charcoal.

Initial comment: from a discontinous deposit of charcoal (possibly the remains of a coffin) within grave 74, which cut an earlier grave and which was itself inserted into the infilled inner ditch.

Calibrated date: 1σ : cal BC 2130 – 1885
2σ : cal BC 2200 – 1750

Final comments:
A J Lawson: the result offers a *terminus ante quem* for the digging of the ditch and the first burials.

HAR-3630 3530 ± 70 BP

$\delta^{13}C$: –28.1 ‰

Sample: BOW92, submitted by P Murphy on 9 October 1979

Material: charcoal.

Initial comment: from a grave marker or shoring to the west of a plank-built coffin in grave 92, which contained an incomplete Beaker; the grave lay 7m outside the inner ditch, and 3m beneath the fill of the outer ditch.

Calibrated date: 1σ : cal BC 1960 – 1760
2σ : cal BC 2115 – 1690

Final comments:
Harwell: this grave is probably broadly contemporary with the others but its isolation cannot be explained.

HAR-3687 3370 ± 80 BP

$\delta^{13}C$: –25.8 ‰

Sample: BOW66, submitted by P Murphy on 9 October 1979

Material: charcoal: *Quercus* sp..

Initial comment: from a charcoal deposit 10mm thick representing a single timber in the base of grave 66, which lay just outside the inner ditch circuit.

Calibrated date: 1σ : cal BC 1750 – 1530
2σ : cal BC 1890 – 1510

Final comments:
A J Lawson: this is the latest date; it is tempting to see this peripheral grave as one of the latest dug.

Norwich: Whitefriars, Norfolk

Location: TG 23430912
Lat. 52.38.00 N; Long. 01.18.07 E

Excavator: B S Ayers (Norfolk Archaeological Unit), 1979

Site: possibly Late Saxon and early medieval waterfront on the River Wensum.

References: Atkin and Sutermeister 1980
Ayers and Murphy 1983; 1, 51 (^{14}C)

Objectives: to obtain a date for the waterfront; three samples were submitted from one stake (99E).

HAR-3852 1070 ± 70 BP

$\delta^{13}C$: –27.8 ‰

Sample: 42IN99EA, submitted by P Murphy on 5 May 1980

Material: wood: *Quercus* sp. of about 0.10m radius, rings not visible (A J Clark).

Initial comment: a stake from the early phase of the tenth- or eleventh-century waterfront.

Calibrated date: 1σ : cal AD 890 – 1020
                      2σ : cal AD 790 – 1150

Final comments:
B S Ayers: a late tenth- or early eleventh-century date is the most probable.

HAR-3877   1080 ± 80 BP

$\delta^{13}C$: –29.3 ‰

Sample: 42IN99EC, submitted by P Murphy on 5 May 1980

Material: wood: *Quercus* sp. of about 0.10m radius, no rings visible (A J Clark).

Initial comment: as HAR-3852.

Calibrated date: 1σ : cal AD 885 – 1020
                      2σ : cal AD 780 – 1155

Final comments:
B S Ayers: as HAR-3852.

HAR-3878   970 ± 70 BP

$\delta^{13}C$: –28.2 ‰

Sample: 42IN99EB, submitted by P Murphy on 5 May 1980

Material: wood: *Quercus* sp. of about 0.10m radius (A J Clark).

Initial comment: as HAR-3852.

Calibrated date: 1σ : cal AD 1000 – 1160
                      2σ : cal AD 900 – 1220

Final comments:
B S Ayers: as HAR-3852.

Oakley, Northamptonshire

Location: SP 887869
              Lat. 52.28.21 N; Long. 00.41.38 W

Excavator: D Jackson (for the Department of the Environment), 1971

Site: Early Iron Age occupation.

References: Jackson 1982, 5 (^{14}C)

Objectives: to date the occupation of an Early Iron Age site. An ironworking furnace was nearby and there was some slag on the site.

Comments:
D Jackson: there was iron slag in some of the features but the dates are very early for ironworking.

HAR-4064   2500 ± 80 BP

$\delta^{13}C$: –25.9 ‰

Sample: OAKF28/9, submitted on 26 September 1980

Material: charcoal.

Initial comment: from pits 28 and 29. Both contained Early Iron Age pottery. There was a piece of iron slag from a pit in the same area.

Calibrated date: 1σ : cal BC 795 – 420
                      2σ : cal BC 820 – 400

Final comments:
D Jackson: the date is compatible with the ceramic material.

HAR-4494   2630 ± 90 BP

$\delta^{13}C$: –26.2 ‰

Sample: OAKF9, submitted on 26 September 1980

Material: charcoal.

Initial comment: from pit F9. Pottery from the pit and nearby structures was of Early Iron Age date. There was no direct relationship with HAR-4064.

Calibrated date: 1σ : cal BC 890 – 785
                      2σ : cal BC 985 – 530

Final comments:
D Jackson: this is a very early date if the ironworking is associated.

Harwell: repeat of HAR-4059, which was abandoned.

Octon Wold: Barrow 1, Humberside

Location: TA 043691
              Lat. 54.6.25 N; Long. 00.24.16 W

Excavator: T C M Brewster (East Riding Archaeological Research Committee), 1966

Site: a chalk barrow mound sealing two shaft graves and other burials cut into the old ground surface; shaft 1 was reopened once and most of the burial removed; shaft 2 was reused three times before a large high mound of stone-free soil was erected over the chalk in the final phase of the Beaker period, crushing the greater part of an uneroded long-necked Beaker.

Objectives: to provide a date for the long-necked Beaker culture and the use of shaft graves on the Wolds and in north-east England; estimated date 3600 BP.

HAR-4250   3780 ± 80 BP

$\delta^{13}C$: –21.5 ‰

Sample: OWSG2A, submitted on 14 February 1981

Material: human bone, handled and joined with glue.

Initial comment: from the bottom of shaft grave 2, 5.25ft from the 1966 ground surface, 3.5ft below the top of the grave.

Calibrated date: 1σ : cal BC 2345 – 2045
                      2σ : cal BC 2470 – 1980

HAR-4251   3820 ± 80 BP

$\delta^{13}C$: –21.8 ‰

Sample: OWSG2B, submitted on 14 February 1981

Material: human bone.

Initial comment: from the bottom of shaft grave 2, as HAR-4250.

Calibrated date: 1σ : cal BC 2460 – 2140
2σ : cal BC 2555 – 2040

Odell, Bedfordshire

Location: SP 956568
Lat. 52.12.03 N; Long. 00.36.04 W

Excavator: B Dix (Bedfordshire County Council), 1974 – 8

Site: a cropmark site comprising a Late Iron Age – Early Roman farmstead with stock enclosures, associated wells, and a cremation cemetery, and Saxon occupation with wells; excavated in advance of gravel extraction.

References: Dix 1980

Objectives: the pottery suggests a Middle – Late Saxon date; ^{14}C dates will provide a better chronology for similar pottery from sites in the Northamptonshire/Bedfordshire area. HAR-3629 was submitted to check against dendrochronology.

Comments:
AML: one small sample HAR-3082 (77F837) has been withdrawn.

HAR-1038   1230 ± 70 BP

$\delta^{13}C$: −27.5 ‰

Sample: T19, submitted on 26 November 1974

Material: wood.

Initial comment: from one of four piles, at the base of a Saxon well, driven into the natural gravel to form a box frame, around which the well lining was constructed.

Calibrated date: 1σ : cal AD 720 – 870
2σ : cal AD 660 – 980

Final comments:
B Dix: this is consistent with archaeological expectations, but in the light of HAR-1096, an earlier rather than a later date may be true.

References: Dix 1980, 18
Radiocarbon **21**, 367

HAR-1096   1410 ± 70 BP

$\delta^{13}C$: −27.25 ‰

Sample: ODLSWT19, submitted on 15 January 1975

Material: wood.

Initial comment: from one of four piles, as HAR-1038.

Calibrated date: 1σ : cal AD 595 – 665
2σ : cal AD 530 – 760

Final comments:
B Dix: see HAR-1038.

HAR-1427   1240 ± 80 BP

$\delta^{13}C$: −28.7 ‰

Sample: 74F123S7, submitted on 15 January 1975

Material: wood: probably *Corylus/Alnus* sp. (C A Keepax).

Initial comment: from the outer lining of the well, originally driven into the natural at the side of the well pit.

Calibrated date: 1σ : cal AD 675 – 885
2σ : cal AD 650 – 970

Final comments:
B Dix: this slightly later date may indicate that this stake was replaced. In the light of HAR-1428 and HAR-1838, an earlier rather than later date may be true. Dendrochronology suggests that the feature of which this sample formed part was constructed after AD 607.

References: Dix 1980, 18
Radiocarbon **21**, 367

HAR-1428   1390 ± 70 BP

$\delta^{13}C$: −28.3 ‰

Sample: 74F123WB, submitted on 15 January 1975

Material: wood: all *Salix* sp. twigs of *c* 1 years growth with bark still on; vivianite deposits present in some (C A Keepax).

Initial comment: from part of a wicker basket forming an integral part of a Saxon well; well silt had accumulated around the basket.

Calibrated date: 1σ : cal AD 605 – 675
2σ : cal AD 540 – 770

Final comments:
B Dix: this is consistent with the archaeological expectations; the timber was probably reused. The basket was clearly reused to act as a filter within the well; prior to this its base had been cut and torn off. See also comments at HAR-1427.

References: Dix 1980, 18
Radiocarbon **21**, 368

HAR-1838   1350 ± 70 BP

$\delta^{13}C$: −26.4 ‰

Sample: 74F123TA, submitted on 19 December 1975

Material: wood: *Quercus* sp..

Initial comment: from a timber, probably a reused plank which, together with others, formed a sort of platform for access to the Saxon well.

Calibrated date: 1σ : cal AD 635 – 690
2σ : cal AD 565 – 790

Final comments:
B Dix: as for HAR-1428.

Harwell: a repeat of HAR-1455 whihch failed due to experimental difficulties.

References: Dix 1980, 18
Radiocarbon **21**, 368

HAR-2802   1330 ± 70 BP

$\delta^{13}C$: −27.3 ‰

Sample: 77F868, submitted on September 1978

Material: wood: *Salix/Populus* sp. from large timbers and hawthhorn type (Rosaceae, sub-family Pomoideae) twig.

Initial comment: from part of basketry used in the refurbishment of the well.

Calibrated date: 1σ : cal AD 645 – 765
2σ : cal AD 600 – 860

Final comments:
B Dix: dendrochronology indicates that the well within which this sample was taken was constructed after AD 634.

HAR-2851   2020 ± 80 BP

$\delta^{13}C$: –27.9 ‰

Sample: 77F824, submitted on 1 September 1978

Material: wood: probably hawthorn type (Rosaceae, sub-family Pomoideae) twig.

Initial comment: from an integral part of the well structure.

Calibrated date: 1σ : cal BC 150 – 65 cal AD
2σ : cal BC 340 – 130 cal AD

Final comments:
B Dix: pottery evidence suggests a date in the first century BC is most likely.

HAR-2853   2050 ± 80 BP

$\delta^{13}C$: –28.3 ‰

Sample: 77F855, submitted on 1 September 1978

Material: wood: probably hawthorn type (Rosaceae, subfamily, Pomoideae) twig and *Corylus/Alnus* sp. (C A Keepax).

Initial comment: from the horizontals of the well framework. There were no associated datable artefacts.

Calibrated date: 1σ : cal BC 180 – 20 cal AD
2σ : cal BC 360 – 110 cal AD

Final comments:
B Dix: if belonging in the earliest phases of site occupation, then most likely first century BC.

HAR-2913   1930 ± 90 BP

$\delta^{13}C$: –28.1 ‰

Sample: 77F836, submitted on 26 October 1978

Material: wood: possibly *Salix/Populus* sp. from large timber (it was difficult to section) (C A Keepax).

Initial comment: from the horizontals forming the well framework.

Calibrated date: 1σ : cal BC 50 – 170 cal AD
2σ : cal BC 170 – 330 cal AD

Final comments:
B Dix: pottery evidence suggests a date around the turn of the first century BC into the early first century AD.

Harwell: a replacement for HAR-2852 which failed.

HAR-3083   1370 ± 80 BP

$\delta^{13}C$: –30.4 ‰

Sample: 75F283, submitted on 9 February 1979

Material: wood: *Fraxinus* sp. of *c* 10 years growth.

Initial comment: from an upright in the well-lining.

Calibrated date: 1σ : cal AD 610 – 685
2σ : cal AD 540 – 790

Final comments:
B Dix: dendrochronology shows that the feature of which this sample formed a part was in use after AD 524.

HAR-3629   1500 ± 80 BP

$\delta^{13}C$: –26.8 ‰

Sample: ODL50, submitted by J Hillam on 12 October 1979

Material: wood: *Quercus* sp., taken from years 24 – 43 of a timber containing 69 years growth.

Initial comment: from inside the well (F861).

Calibrated date: 1σ : cal AD 440 – 635
2σ : cal AD 400 – 670

Final comments:
B Dix: dendrochronology of the same sample is calculated as AD 573.

Okehampton: Meldon Quarry, Devon

Location: SX 573928
Lat. 50.43.00 N; Long. 04.01.18 W

Excavator: D Austin (Lampeter University), 1978

Site: a 1m section of peat deposits, located *c* 100m to the north of a group of medieval long houses and within a medieval field system fossilised by the creation of a deer park *c* 1300 AD; this is part of a wider review of the clearance of the north Dartmoor upland fringe for arable cultivation in the post-Roman period.

HAR-3343 and HAR-3344 suggest local woodland *c* AD 800 and open grassland *c* 1800: between the two there is woodland clearance and some arable farming.

References: Austin 1978
Austin *et al* 1980; 48, 51 – 2 (^{14}C)

Objectives: to provide a chronology for the data on changing land use in the medieval period, obtained from the pollen analysis of samples from the peat; HAR-3906 was submitted as a check on HAR-3443 in the hope of finding the critical twelfth- to thirteenth-century horizon.

Comments:
D Austin: these calibrations do not materially affect the interpretations and their inherent problems.

HAR-3443   230 ± 60 BP

$\delta^{13}C$: –30.2 ‰

Sample: M40, submitted on 11 May 1979

Material: peat: grass and sedge.

Initial comment: from *c* 0.40m above the base of the peat section.

Calibrated date: 1σ : cal AD 1640 – 1955
2σ : cal AD 1500 – 1955

Final comments:
D Austin: unexpectedly late; falling after AD 1450 this is a little suspect, but it agrees with a period of well-documented pasture.

Harwell: there are problems in the interpretation of dates after 1450 caused by oscillations in the initial ^{14}C level induced by cosmic ray variations since that time.

HAR-3444   1160 ± 70 BP

$δ^{13}C$: −29.0 ‰

Sample: M80, submitted on 11 May 1979

Material: peat: grass and sedge.

Initial comment: probably from 0.80m above the base of the peat section.

Calibrated date: 1σ : cal AD 780 – 970
                     2σ : cal AD 680 – 1010

Final comments:
D Austin: HAR-3444 is, and should be, earlier than HAR-3443; it dates a period of hazel and alder woodland.

HAR-3906   710 ± 70 BP

$δ^{13}C$: −30.7 ‰

Sample: M-60, submitted on 11 May 1979

Material: peat.

Initial comment: from 0.60m below the top of the peat section (possibly the same level as HAR-3443).

Calibrated date: 1σ : cal AD 1260   1295
                     2σ : cal AD 1200 – 1400

Final comments:
D Austin: the results as a whole are most interesting.

Old Windsor: Mill, Berkshire

Location: SU 9974 approx
              Lat. 51.27.21 N; Long. 00.34.30 W

Excavator: B Hope-Taylor (Department of the Environment)

Site: a Saxon settlement and mill.

References: Fletcher 1981

Objectives: to date the structure. The samples all come from the same slice of timber; this had 225 rings, but other timbers from the same tree show that there was a sequence of 252 rings in addition to the sapwood; HAR-1648 and HAR-1649 only come *c* 25years apart when growth allowance is applied and suggest a Middle rather than a Late Saxon date.

Comments:
J Fletcher: all the archaeological and other evidence suggests a date within the period AD 650 – 700. Accordingly, I have accepted the earliest date possible within the dendrochronological dating of AD 690+ (Fletcher 1981). AD 690 itself is certainly not unduly early.

HAR-1648 and HAR-1649 clearly fall well within the predicted range. HAR-1670 also readily allows a date of AD 690 or earlier, but I am somewhat puzzled that its upper extreme strays so far into a later period, compared with the others.

Apart from this minor query, all the results seem consistent and satisfactory. All in all, a date *c* AD 690 seems consonant with all the indications.

HAR-1648   1480 ± 70 BP

$δ^{13}C$: −25.9 ‰

Sample: WINDSOR1, submitted by J Fletcher on 7 February 1976

Material: wood: *Quercus* sp..

Initial comment: from the horizontal foundation beams of the Saxon water mill. These, about 3.4m long, were sealed under approximately 3m of successively stratified deposits in the huge mill leat. In *c* AD 900, when the bed of the leat was already covered by silted and other deposits to a depth of 2m, an extremely narrow channel was dug along its western edge. This new channel, triangular in section, reached, and partially exposed, the original timbers at right-angles (approximately 1/2m exposure), but left them quite intact.

The stratigraphy is agreed to be impeccable. All the infilling deposits are abundant in artefactual and environmental material. Each layer is coherent and is free from later inclusions. Thus, there is an extraordinarily vast and elegant zoning of metalwork, pottery, etc, securely sealing down the timbers in question.

Calibrated date: 1σ : cal AD 555 – 643
                     2σ : cal AD 420 – 670

HAR-1649   1350 ± 70 BP

$δ^{13}C$: −25.6 ‰

Sample: WINDSOR2, submitted by J Fletcher on 7 February 1976

Material: wood: *Quercus* sp..

Initial comment: as HAR-1648.

Calibrated date: 1σ : cal AD 635 – 690
                     2σ : cal AD 565 – 790

HAR-1676   1240 ± 70 BP

$δ^{13}C$: −25.7 ‰

Sample: WINDSOR3, submitted by J Fletcher on 7 February 1976

Material: wood: *Quercus* sp..

Initial comment: as HAR-1648.

Calibrated date: 1σ : cal AD 675 – 885
                     2σ : cal AD 650 – 960

Oving, West Sussex

Location: SU 895054
              Lat. 50.50.26 N; Long. 00.43.43 W

Excavator: O Bedwin (Sussex Archaeological Field Unit), 1980

Site: a Late Iron Age farmstead followed by an Early Romano-British farmstead.

References: Bedwin and Holgate 1985, 219 (^{14}C)

Objectives: F61 contained a large amount of metalworking debris and an interesting terret ring; confirmation of a suggested Late Iron Age date is sought.

HAR-4252   2180 ± 70 BP

$\delta^{13}C$: −25.1 ‰

Sample: 5000B61, submitted on 12 December 1980

Material: charcoal, originally one plank.

Initial comment: from the base of pit F60, associated with saucepan pottery and daub; the upper fill contained pottery dating to the late first century BC and a terret ring (copper alloy).

Calibrated date: 1σ : cal BC 375 – 125
2σ : cal BC 400 – 50

Final comments:
O Bedwin: this is a good match for the associated saucepan pottery.

Oxford: 79 – 80 St Aldate's, Oxfordshire

Location: SP 514058
Lat. 51.44.53 N; Long. 01.15.19 W

Excavator: T Hassall and B Durham (Oxford Archaeological Unit)

References: Durham 1977; 174 – 8, table 9 (^{14}C)

Objectives: HAR-717 was submitted as the only means of obtaining a date for the intermediate levels of the site, which is independent of the pottery evidence.

Comments:
T Hassall and B Durham: these dates give a good agreement for a mid ninth-century date for phase 2, but reverse the order of the stratigraphy; this gives an estimate for the accumulation of the river silt.

H79/85   1120 ± 110 BP

$\delta^{13}C$: −27.9 ‰

Sample: WATTLE-434

Material: wood.

Initial comment: from vertical stake of hazel wood, 25mm in diameter with bark, supporting a wattle fence set on the clay bank. The surface of the bank was unweathered; the clay had either been dumped, or radically reshaped shortly before the erection of the fence. Both were apparently rapidly sealed by layers of alluvium.

Calibrated date: 1σ : cal AD 780 – 1020
2σ : cal AD 670 – 790

Final comments:
T Hassall and B Durham: the result agrees well with the ceramic and stratigraphic evidence. Pottery from the clay surface was dated by thermoluminescence to AD 745 ± 62 (OX TL-141C).

References: Radiocarbon **16**, 179

HAR-125   1140 ± 110 BP

$\delta^{13}C$: −28.6 ‰

Sample: WAT-472

Material: wood: hazel (*Corylus* sp.).

Initial comment: from a stake (30mm diam) that supported a low wattle fence but was set in alluvium on the side of a clay bank.

Calibrated date: 1σ : cal AD 770 – 1010
2σ : cal AD 660 – 1155

Final comments:
T Hassall and B Durham: stratigraphically the date should be later than HAR-79/85 but the result is generally satisfactory. The thermoluminescence date was also earlier than that relative to HAR-70/85, ie, AD 700 ± 74 (OX TL-141D).

References: Radiocarbon **16**, 180

HAR-209   2600 ± 120 BP

$\delta^{13}C$: −28.4 ‰

Sample: LINCOLL-46

Material: seed and vegetable deposits.

Initial comment: from gritty silt overlying floodplain gravel and sealed by thick blue clay, assumed to be part of the bank, at 79 – 80, St Aldates on the opposite side of the road.

Comment on uncalibrated date: if the date is accurate for the deposition of the clay bank, then the clay must be alluvial because a man-made structure of that date is almost inconceivable. If the clay was laid down by people, an earlier date than HAR-79/85 is expected, ie, late eighth century AD.

Calibrated date: 1σ : cal BC 890 – 550
2σ : cal BC 1000 – 400

References: Radiocarbon **16**, 180

HAR-717   870 ± 70 BP

$\delta^{13}C$: −25.7 ‰

Sample: SPL319, submitted on 25 July 1974

Material: charcoal: twigs (15mm in diameter) with bark.

Initial comment: from a midden layer (123/2) associated with features of structural phase 8; sealed by another midden and then a layer of medieval garden soil.

Calibrated date: 1σ : cal AD 1040 – 1245
2σ : cal AD 1010 – 1270

HAR-718   1150 ± 90 BP

$\delta^{13}C$: −25.4 ‰

Sample: SPL406, submitted on 25 July 1974

Material: charcoal, preserved wattle stake (30mm in diameter) charred by subsequent burning.

Initial comment: from a stake driven into the base of a hearth or ash pit (structural phase 2), associated with the earliest major event on the bank; this was sealed by a succession of layers relating to a further twelve structural phases.

Calibrated date: 1σ : cal AD 775 – 985
2σ : cal AD 650 – 1030

Oxford: All Saints Church, Oxfordshire

Location: SP 51500625
Lat. 51.45.08 N; Long. 01.15.14 W

Excavator: T Hassall and B Durham (Oxford Archaeological Unit)

References: Hassall *et al* 1974

HAR-418 920 ± 70 BP

$\delta^{13}C$: −19.5 ‰

Sample: SPL196

Material: human bone.

Initial comment: from skeleton F55 which was laid on a bed of charcoal in a stone-lined grave, thought to be stratigraphically later than a coin of Edward I; part of the grave overlay the footings of an early church wall, but the legs had subsided into the backfill of cess pit F75.

Comment on uncalibrated date: rather earlier than was expected from the pottery and numismatic evidence.

Calibrated date: 1σ : cal AD 1020 – 1210
2σ : cal AD 980 – 1260

References: *Radiocarbon* **19**, 407

HAR-419 980 ± 70 BP

$\delta^{13}C$: −27.2 ‰

Sample: SPL184

Material: charcoal.

Initial comment: from a charred wattle fence, F118, set into a yard surface; the layer was sealed by several others and all were cut by a cellar pit tentatively dated to the early eleventh century.

Calibrated date: 1σ : cal AD 990 – 1155
2σ : cal AD 900 – 1220

Final comments:
T Hassall and B Durham: this agrees well with the provisional dating of the site.

References: Hassall *et al* 1974, 55
Radiocarbon **19**, 407

HAR-466-I 1060 ± 70 BP

$\delta^{13}C$: −21.9 ‰

Sample: SPL205, submitted on 1 January 1973

Material: carbonised grain: largely wheat (*Triticum aestivum* L.) and loam.

Initial comment: from a large heap of charred grain scattered through the earliest stratified layer (113/9) above the topsoil; sealed by a number of deposits including that from which HAR-419 was taken.

Calibrated date: 1σ : cal AD 895 – 1020
2σ : cal AD 810 – 1155

Final comments:
T Hassall and B Durham: this agrees well with the provisional dating of the site.

References: Hassall *et al* 1974, 55
Radiocarbon **19**, 407

HAR-466-II 1070 ± 80 BP

$\delta^{13}C$: −22.1 ‰

Sample: SPL205, submitted on 1 January 1973

Material: carbonised grain.

Initial comment: the grain was mixed with loam overlying the original topsoil. It was sealed by Saxon domestic layers and the medieval church.

Calibrated date: 1σ : cal AD 890 – 1020
2σ : cal AD 780 – 1155

Final comments:
T Hassall and B Durham: the results agree well with the provisional date of the site.

Harwell: measured as a completely separate sample for an independent check on the benzene synthesis process of HAR-466-I.

References: Hassall *et al* 1974, 55
Radiocarbon **19**, 407

HAR-729 870 ± 60 BP

$\delta^{13}C$: −19.4 ‰

Sample: SPL273, submitted on 25 July 1974

Material: human bone.

Initial comment: from a context adjacent to that from which HAR-418 was taken, submitted as a check on HAR-418.

Calibrated date: 1σ : cal AD 1045 – 1230
2σ : cal AD 1020 – 1270

HAR-730 650 ± 70 BP

$\delta^{13}C$: −19.3 ‰

Sample: SPL274, submitted on 25 July 1974

Material: human bone.

Initial comment: from a burial overlying an unrobbed section of the east wall of the north aisle; this will help date the removal of this wall in the construction of the north chancel.

Calibrated date: 1σ : cal AD 1275 – 1395
2σ : cal AD 1250 – 1420

Oxford: Blackfriars, Oxfordshire

Location: SP 5106 approx
Lat. 51.45.00 N; Long. 01.15.40 W

Excavator: T Hassall

References: Hassall *et al* 1974, 57 – 9
Radiocarbon **16**, 179 (^{14}C)

HAR-191 730 ± 100 BP

$\delta^{13}C$: –28.4 ‰

Sample: Wattle 80

Material: wood: 30mm in diameter with bark.

Initial comment: from a wattle fence in a silted-up ditch, dug into alluvium on which the priory of Blackfriars, Oxford was built. The ditch was sealed by the floor levels of the priory.

Comment on uncalibrated date: the result agrees well with the documentary evidence of the friars' arrival in Oxford in 1221. They began building the priory in *c* 1236 and finished in 1245. Alluvium possibly accumulated as a result of Late Saxon bridge building; the ditch was used for agriculture or land drainage shortly before the friars occupied the site.

Calibrated date: 1σ : cal AD 1220 – 1275
2σ : cal AD 1045 – 1410

Oxford: Christchurch Cathedral, Oxfordshire

Location: SP 105060 approx
Lat. 51.45.08 N; Long. 01.50.52 W

Excavator: T Hassall, 1973

HAR-190(S) 1110 ± 100 BP

$\delta^{13}C$: –28.4 ‰

Sample: GRAVE2

Material: charcoal: probably oak (*Quercus* sp.).

Initial comment: from a charcoal burial, ie an extended inhumation on a bed of cold charcoal, outside the west end of Christchurch cathedral, Oxford; the presumed site of St Frideswide's minster, founded in the eighth century.

Comment on uncalibrated date: this date confirms the existence of religious activity on the site in the ninth century and supports the theory of a religious foundation in the eighth century. It predates the earliest certain documentary reference to St Frideswide's minster by 150 years and shows that this form of burial was Saxon and not Danish as supposed.

Calibrated date: 1σ : cal AD 790 – 1020
2σ : cal AD 680 – 1160

Oxford: The Hamel, Oxfordshire

Location: SP 507061
Lat. 51.45.00 N; Long. 01.15.40 W

Excavator: N Palmer (Oxford Archaeological Unit)

Site: prehistoric occupation and a crouched inhumation burial backfilled with material containing domestic rubbish, on the alluvium over the floodplain gravel; medieval settlement.

References: Hall forthcoming
Palmer 1980, 128 (^{14}C)

HAR-3409+HAR-3410 3470 ± 80 BP

$\delta^{13}C$: –20.0 ‰

Sample: 2AB:1HB, submitted on 24 January 1979

Material: animal and human bone, marked with Indian ink. Some of the skull fragments were joined with HMG glue: cattle and sheep bone, and a human skull.

Initial comment: from a crouched burial of a child of *c* 2 – 4 years old, buried on the right side, head to the south-east, in a pit cutting a layer of orange/brown alluvium which overlay natural gravel and sealed by a layer of darker brown alluvium; associated with Late Beaker pottery and flints. The animal bone is presumed to be discarded domestic rubbish.

Calibrated date: 1σ : cal BC 1895 – 1690
2σ : cal BC 2030 – 1610

Final comments:
N Palmer: this result falls well within the range of Late Beaker dates, although towards the end.

Harwell: combined samples.

Pagham, West Sussex

Location: SZ 885974
Lat. 50.46.08 N; Long. 00.44.41 W

Excavator: V L Gregory (Sussex Archaeological Field Unit), 1974

Site: Roman and Anglo-Saxon occupation.

References: Gregory 1976, 117 (^{14}C)

Objectives: the ^{14}C date was intended to determine the period of Anglo-Saxon activity.

HAR-1085 1130 ± 60 BP

$\delta^{13}C$: –24.0 ‰

Sample: PAG893A, submitted on 22 January 1975

Material: charcoal.

Initial comment: from a small gully, sealed by a wall, overlying Roman and Saxon features, possibly ninth- to twelfth-century.

Calibrated date: 1σ : cal AD 830 – 980
2σ : cal AD 770 – 1020

Final comments:
V L Gregory: the calibrated date is broadly in line with the most recent work from Medmerry Farm (Selsey) and Steyming.

Peldon: Red Hill, Site 117, Essex

Location: TM 0100551560
Lat. 52.07.31 N; Long. 00.56.12 E

Excavator: K de Brisay (Colchester Archaeological Group), 1973 – 6

Site: pre-Roman Iron Age or Romano-British saltworks flooded at every high tide, near the Strood causeway to Mersea island (Essex site 117).

References: De Brisay 1979, 58 (^{14}C)

Objectives: dates were required for confirmation of the archaeomagnetic dates from the same feature.

Comments:
A Fawn: at the time the characteristics of the associated artefacts suggested to the excavator that these dates were too early. A reappraisal of the finds indicates that the dating may be considerd quite satisfactory as to range, since it comes within the expected period, but more precise dates are needed which could be related to changes in the site during the many years it was in use. In both publications HAR-1832 was quoted as the average ^{14}C age for the site.

Harwell: the mean of these three results was originally calculated as 20 ± 70, or 60 BC – AD 130 (Ralph *et al* 1973); the possible date of 46 BC – AD 94 agrees well with the archaeomagnetic dates.

HAR-1832   2000 ± 70 BP

$\delta^{13}C$: –24.4 ‰

Sample: PRH1, submitted by A J Clark on 26 November 1976

Material: charcoal, saturated with brine: *Quercus* sp. from large timbers; some bark also present (C A Keepax).

Initial comment: from the base of an evaporating hearth. Other samples for archaeomagnetic dating were taken from the upper levels.

Calibrated date: 1σ : cal BC 100 – 70 cal AD
2σ : cal BC 190 – 130 cal AD

References: Fawn *et al* 1990, 38

HAR-2073   1790 ± 70 BP

$\delta^{13}C$: –24.4 ‰

Sample: PRH1, submitted by A J Clark on 26 November 1976

Material: charcoal: as HAR-1832.

Initial comment: from the base of an evaporating furnace.

Calibrated date: 1σ : cal AD 130 – 335
2σ : cal AD 70 – 410

Final comments:
Harwell: replicate of HAR-1832.

HAR-2390   2000 ± 80 BP

$\delta^{13}C$: –25.1 ‰

Sample: PRH1, submitted by A J Clark on 26 November 1976

Material: charcoal: as HAR-1832.

Initial comment: from the base of an evaporating furnace, as HAR-1832.

Calibrated date: 1σ : cal BC 105 – 75 cal AD
2σ : cal BC 200 – 140 cal AD

Final comments:
Harwell: replicate of HAR-1832.

Peterborough, Cambridgeshire

Location: TL 1998 approx
Lat. 52.33.59 N; Long. 00.14.39 W

Excavator: A Challands

HAR-1089   3790 ± 80 BP

$\delta^{13}C$: –24.9 ‰

Sample: LFL41192, submitted on 6 February 1975

Material: bone.

Calibrated date: 1σ : cal BC 2450 – 2050
2σ : cal BC 2470 – 1985

HAR-1090   3770 ± 170 BP

$\delta^{13}C$: –26.0 ‰

Sample: LFL41192, submitted on 6 February 1975

Material: charcoal.

Calibrated date: 1σ : cal BC 2470 – 1960
2σ : cal BC 2860 – 1740

HAR-1091   2100 ± 80 BP

$\delta^{13}C$: –25.8 ‰

Sample: LFIL43C, submitted on 6 February 1975

Material: charcoal.

Calibrated date: 1σ : cal BC 340 – 35
2σ : cal BC 380 – 70 cal AD

HAR-1092   3790 ± 80 BP

$\delta^{13}C$: –25.0 ‰

Sample: LFL41194, submitted on 6 February 1975

Material: charcoal.

Calibrated date: 1σ : cal BC 2450 – 2050
2σ : cal BC 2470 – 1985

Peterborough: Bridge Street West, Cambridgeshire

Location: TL 1998 approx
Lat. 52.33.59 N; Long. 00.14.39 W

Excavator: D Mackreth (Nene Valley Research Committee), 1974 – 6

Site: medieval town, apparently laid out on the flood plain of peat/silt during the reign of Abbot Martin (AD 1133 – 1155); until then the flood plain was not occupied but covered with water-loving vegetation (many of the lowest deposits were waterlogged); thereafter the site was occupied continuously until c 1930.

Objectives: the archaeological dating depends entirely on the pottery; this supports a twelfth-century date, but (in 1978) the assessment of all the pottery from Peterborough is entirely impressionistic; ^{14}C dates will establish a better chronology for the pottery and confirm whether there was occupation on the site prior to the documentary date.

HAR-2545   870 ± 60 BP

$\delta^{13}C:$ −25.0 ‰

Sample: 2705, submitted on 3 March 1978

Material: wood: *Alnus glutinosa*, twigs and small branches (C A Keepax).

Initial comment: from a stake/wattle fence F542 covered with silt/clay and gravel acting as east – west boundary to a town ditch/drainage channel; thought to be broadly contemporary with the structure to the east of the bank and ditch.

Calibrated date: 1σ : cal AD 1045 – 1230
                     2σ : cal AD 1020 – 1270

Final comments:
D Mackreth: the archaeological date is AD 1150 – 1200, period 2.

HAR-2549   760 ± 70 BP

$\delta^{13}C:$ −27.0 ‰

Sample: 2626, submitted on 3 March 1978

Material: wood: *Quercus* sp. from a large timber (C A Keepax).

Initial comment: from a timber upright, F527; forming part of an internal partition in a wattle/daub, timber framed building constructed on a naturally developed bank of peat/silt; this is the earliest domestic building on the site.

Calibrated date: 1σ : cal AD 1220 – 1280
                     2σ : cal AD 1160 – 1380

Final comments:
D Mackreth: the archaeological date is AD 1150 – 1200, period 2. The stratigraphic relationships will not allow the feature to be later, and the pottery supports the archaeological date.

Pewsey: Blacknall Field, Wiltshire

Location: SU 15555806
              Lat. 51.19.15 N; Long. 01.46.37 W

Excavator: F K Annable (Wiltshire Archaeological and Natural History Society) and P H Robinson (Department of the Environment), 1969 – 76

Site: an Iron Age settlement and Anglo-Saxon cemetery.

References: anon 1970, 206
                anon 1971, 189 – 90
                anon 1972, 175
                anon 1973, 135 – 6

Objectives: to locate and completely excavate the pagan Saxon cemetery within Blacknall field, and to determine the character of the material finds and the period of use of the site. The Iron Age features were excavated and recorded as far as they turned up on the site, but no attempt was made to fully excavate the Iron Age settlement. Soil samples were submitted from the Iron Age pit F193 and Neolithic pit F162, in the hope that indications of absolute dates for both features would be forthcoming. The dates suggested so far for both pits have been based on the typological assessment of the pit finds.

HAR-1121   2220 ± 70 BP

$\delta^{13}C:$ −24.8 ‰

Sample: BPPEWSEY, submitted on 22 January 1975

Material: charcoal.

Initial comment: from an Iron Age storage pit (feature 103); cutting DD (1974).

Calibrated date: 1σ : cal BC 390 – 190
                     2σ : cal BC 400 – 100

Final comments:
F K Annable: the calibrated dates, as indicated, do not at first sight accord with the archaeological dating of the ceramic types found throughout its layers. The pottery is entirely characteristic (the types are constant within all the pits and postholes excavated) in form and fabric of the situlate jars and haematite coated bowl forms of the initial Iron Age phase, beginning c 700 BC. The upper limit of 400BC might be seen to suggest a continuity of use of these types down to the beginning of the Middle Iron Age (probably c 400 BC), but the Iron Age features have yielded no other pottery representative of the middle phase. This one would have expected to be present.

Harwell: repeat of HAR-990.

HAR-1954   4150 ± 130 BP

$\delta^{13}C:$ −26.6 ‰

Sample: 760340, submitted on 9 November 1976

Material: soil.

Initial comment: from feature 162, a possible storage pit of the Late Neolithic/Beaker phase (excavated in 1976). The initial fill was a dark, humus-like soil with occupation debris, animal bone, wood traces, sherds of Late Neolithic and Beaker type, and flint tools. The secondary fill was of creamy soil with chalk fragments and traces of charcoal.

Calibrated date: 1σ : cal BC 2910 – 2505
                     2σ : cal BC 3050 – 2405

Final comments:
F K Annable: the calibrated date for this pit accords reasonably well with the dating of archaeological finds.

Pitchbury Ramparts, Essex

Location: TL 96632904
Lat. 51.55.29 N; Long. 00.51.36 E

Excavator: P Crummy (Colchester Excavation Committee), 1973

Site: a hillfort, first excavated in 1933 and thought to be Belgic; no buildings of any date were found in 1973 and only a few sherds of Belgic and Iron Age pottery (c third- to second-century BC).

References: Crummy 1974, 8

Objectives: to date the hillfort.

HAR-452 1960 ± 80 BP

$\delta^{13}C$: −25.2 ‰

Sample: MIS111F34, submitted on 10 October 1973

Material: charcoal.

Initial comment: from the fill of the main ditch.

Calibrated date: 1σ : cal BC 55 – 120 cal AD
    2σ : cal BC 170 – 230 cal AD

Final comments:
P Crummy: an earlier date would have been more useful; this is rather inconclusive – the implied date depends on how quickly the ditch silted up, so that, with the inevitable error term in ^{14}C dating, no positive date for the hillfort can be deduced.

Harwell: this is the mean of two counts.

HAR-453 2400 ± 90 BP

$\delta^{13}C$: −24.4 ‰

Sample: MIS46F37, submitted on 10 October 1973

Material: charcoal.

Initial comment: from an Iron Age or inter-periglacial feature.

Calibrated date: 1σ : cal BC 760 – 395
    2σ : cal BC 800 – 255

Poldowrian, Cornwall

Location: SW 74901707
Lat. 50.00.38 N; Long. 05.08.32 W

Excavator: D Harris (Cornwall Archaeological Society), 1978

Site: a low mound made up of layers of stone, which produced c 100 sherds of Beaker pottery; outside the mound was a pit filled with dark grey clay, which contained an almost complete, coarse, gritty, pot, which was smashed down on a stone.

References: Harris 1979, 30 (^{14}C)

Objectives: to date the only 'burnt mound' known in Cornwall and the Beaker settlement here.

HAR-2892 3490 ± 90 BP

$\delta^{13}C$: −25.3 ‰

Sample: PDN101, submitted on 27 October 1978

Material: charcoal: *Quercus* sp., *Betula* sp., and *Corylus/Alnus* sp. from large timbers; also Papilionaceae (eg *Ulex* sp.) from twig-sized and large timber; c 25% identified.

Initial comment: from among the stones forming the bottom layer of the mound, which lay directly on the natural gabbroic clay; sealed by the upper layers, although some fine roots reached down to this layer.

Calibrated date: 1σ : cal BC 1935 – 1695
    2σ : cal BC 2115 – 1610

Final comments:
D Harris: the date is later than expected, but consistent with HAR-3107.

References: Christie 1985, 108

HAR-3107 3360 ± 70 BP

$\delta^{13}C$: −26.5 ‰

Sample: PDN99, submitted on 9 February 1979

Material: charcoal: *Quercus* sp., *Prunus* sp. (eg blackthorn), *Corylus/Alnus* sp., *Betula* sp., and Rosaceae, sub-family Pomoideae, (eg hawthorn) all from mature timbers (C A Keepax).

Initial comment: from the bottom layer of the mound, c 1m away from HAR-2982.

Calibrated date: 1σ : cal BC 1745 – 1530
    2σ : cal BC 1880 – 1510

Final comments:
D Harris: the date is later than expected, but is consistent with HAR-2892.

References: Christie 1985, 108

HAR-3108 4000 ± 150 BP

$\delta^{13}C$: −27.2 ‰

Sample: PDN169, submitted on 9 February 1979

Material: charcoal: *Quercus* sp. and *Prunus* sp. (eg blackthorn) from mature timbers (C A Keepax).

Initial comment: from a pit, containing a coarse pot, adjacent to, but not stratigraphically connected with the mound.

Calibrated date: 1σ : cal BC 2865 – 2330
    2σ : cal BC 2920 – 2045

Final comments:
D Harris: this date shows that there was occupation on the site from the beginning of the second millennium BC. It proves that the pit was earlier and not contemporary with the mound. Other pits with Neolithic pottery have since been found nearby.

Poldowrian, Cornwall

Location: SW 74851690
Lat. 50.00.34 N; Long. 05.08.28 W

Excavator: G Smith (Central Excavation Unit), 1980

Site: area of later Mesolithic, Early Neolithic, and Early Bronze Age settlement.

References: Smith and Harris 1982, 49 (^{14}C)

Objectives: to date the different phases of occupation.

Comments:
AML: three samples, HAR-4323 (33-110), HAR-4567 (33-369A), and HAR-4568 (33-369B) were submitted after April 1981.

HAR-4033   3880 ± 60 BP

$\delta^{13}C$: −25.5 ‰

Sample: 33-152, submitted by N Balaam on 10 August 1980

Material: charcoal: mostly *Quercus* sp., with some *Corylus/Alnus* sp. and *Crataegus* type (N Balaam).

Initial comment: from a presumed mesolithic feature.

Comment on uncalibrated date: this suggests a Late Neolithic date.

Calibrated date: 1σ : cal BC 2465 – 2290
2σ : cal BC 2565 – 2145

Final comments:
G Smith: unfortunately this does not help to date any of the three phases of activity recognised on the site, although previous excavations have shown Late Neolithic material nearby.

HAR-4052   4870 ± 130 BP

$\delta^{13}C$: −25.6 ‰

Sample: 33-130, submitted by N Balaam on 16 September 1980

Material: charcoal: *Quercus* sp..

Initial comment: from a posthole of later Mesolithic or Neolithic date.

Comment on uncalibrated date: this shows that the structure was part of the Early Neolithic phase of activity recognised by excavation and artefacts.

Calibrated date: 1σ : cal BC 3790 – 3520
2σ : cal BC 3980 – 3360

Final comments:
G Smith: this accords well with the accompanying artefactual evidence (pot and flint) and with ^{14}C dates from a similar site in the general area (Carn Brea).

Pontardulais: Pentre Barrow, West Glamorgan

Location: SN 592025
Lat. 51.42.11 N; Long. 04.02.16 W

Excavator: A Ward (Ancient Monuments Welsh Office and Carmarthen Museum), 1974

Site: a composite barrow of presumed Bronze Age date.

References: Ward 1978, 59 and 63 (^{14}C)
Radiocarbon **21**, 364 (^{14}C)

Objectives: to determine the period(s) to which activity, on or around the barrow, belonged.

HAR-958   3470 ± 70 BP

$\delta^{13}C$: −24.6 ‰

Sample: P1:4, submitted on 1 November 1974

Material: charcoal: numerous fragments of oak (*Quercus* sp.) from fairly large timbers (C A Keepax).

Initial comment: associated with cremated bone in a small pit cut into the earth mound, which was sealed by the stones of the cairn cap covering the mound.

Comment on uncalibrated date: this result corresponds well with the structural style of the monument, which was interpreted as an Early Bronze Age ritual site.

Calibrated date: 1σ : cal BC 1890 – 1695
2σ : cal BC 2010 – 1630

Final comments:
A Ward: the calibrated range does not affect the initial interpretation.

HAR-959   1500 ± 70 BP

$\delta^{13}C$: −26.7 ‰

Sample: P1:13, submitted on 1 November 1974

Material: charcoal: mainly *Quercus* sp. from large timbers and *Alnus glutinosa*; also several fragments of hawthorn type twig (*Crataegus/Pyrus/Malus/Sorbus* sp.) and *Corylus avellana* (C A Keepax).

Initial comment: from a large pit outside the edge of the mound; the sample was taken from the uppermost of three successive layers of burning in the pit.

Comment on uncalibrated date: at first thought to be a 'ritual' pit associated with the barrow, but now shown to be a post-Roman cooking hearth; temporary hearths such as this with Roman or later pottery seem to be frequently situated in the lee of prehistoric mounds.

Calibrated date: 1σ : cal AD 445 – 630
2σ : cal AD 410 – 660

Final comments:
A Ward: the calibrated range does not affect the initial interpretation.

Poole: Canford Heath, Dorset

Location: SZ 01889586
Lat. 50.45.42 N; Long. 01.58.24 W

Excavator: I P Horsey (Poole Museums Service), 1980

Site: Bronze Age barrow Poole 24; a 'Dorset' type of disc barrow with a bank and ditch, but no burials, either primary or secondary; one of more than forty barrows known on the heath to the north of Poole.

References: Horsey and Shackley 1980, 34 (^{14}C)

Objectives: to confirm the dating of this type of barrow, which has been classed as probably late in the Wessex culture.

HAR-2278   3060 ± 110 BP

$\delta^{13}C$: −27.0 ‰

Sample: PM16F26, submitted on 1 June 1977

Material: charcoal, perhaps incompletely charred: *Quercus* sp. from fairly large timbers; *c* 25% of one bottle out of two identified.

Initial comment: from a primary pit (0.60m diameter × 0.55m maximum depth; fill 10YR 2/2; pH value 3.1); this was the only primary feature: there is as no evidence for a cremation or inhumation.

Calibrated date: 1σ : cal BC 1440 – 1165
                     2σ : cal BC 1590 – 1000

Final comments:
Harwell: a small sample accounts for the larger than normal error term.

Poole: Pex Marine, Dorset

Location: SZ 010905
              Lat. 50.42.49 N; Long. 01.59.09 W

Excavator: I P Horsey (Poole Museum Archaeological Unit), 1976

Site: samples from very substantial oyster deposits around the waterfront in Poole.

References: Horscy 1981, 145 (^{14}C)
                Horsey and Winder 1991, 104 (^{14}C)

Objectives: to date the establishment of the oyster processing industry.

Comments:
I P Horsey: a correction factor (Harkness formula) of 400 radiocarbon years has to be added to these dates, as the ^{14}C in oyster shells is derived from marine reservoirs rather than directly from the atmosphere. The dates then fall mainly in the Late Saxon to early post-Conquest period suggesting an oyster processing industry before the medieval town developed.

HAR-3462   970 ± 70 BP

$\delta^{13}C$: −1.6 ‰

Sample: PM24/12, submitted on July 1979

Material: shell: oyster (*Ostrea* sp.).

Initial comment: from a context dated to pre-1300.

Calibrated date: 1σ : cal AD 1000 – 1160
                     2σ : cal AD 900 – 1220

HAR-3463   1360 ± 70 BP

$\delta^{13}C$: −0.5 ‰

Sample: PM9/16, submitted on July 79

Material: shell: oyster (*Ostrea* sp.).

Initial comment: from an oyster midden.

Calibrated date: 1σ : cal AD 630 – 685
                     2σ : cal AD 560 – 790

Poole: The Town Cellars, Dorset

Location: SZ 010905
              Lat. 50.42.49 N; Long. 01.59.09 W

Excavator: I P Horsey (Poole Museum Archaeological Unit), 1976

Site: a shell midden sealed beneath the medieval woolhouse.

References: Horsey and Winder 1991, 104 (^{14}C)

Objectives: to ascertain whether the shell midden is medieval or earlier and derived by natural or human action; the archaeological context suggests a date of pre-1320.

Comments:

HAR-2774   1260 ± 100 BP

$\delta^{13}C$: −0.32 ‰

Sample: PM11142, submitted on 22 May 1978

Material: shell: oyster (*Ostrea* sp.).

Initial comment: from a substantial oyster deposit, sealing the natural, beneath the town cellars; sealed by layers dated to *c* 1300 by French polychrome pottery, upon which the town cellars were constructed.

Calibrated date: 1σ : cal AD 660 – 890
                     2σ : cal AD 600 – 990

HAR-2775   1260 ± 100 BP

$\delta^{13}C$: −0.32 ‰

Sample: PM2158, submitted on 22 May 1978

Material: shell: oyster (*Ostrea* sp.).

Initial comment: from the waterfront in front of the town cellars.

Calibrated date: 1σ : cal AD 660 – 890
                     2σ : cal AD 600 – 990

Poundbury, Dorset

Location: SY 68559116
              Lat. 50.43.07 N; Long. 02.26.29 W

Excavator: C J S Green (Dorchester Excavation Committee), 1966 – 80

Site: Late Neolithic or Early Bronze Age pits, Middle Bronze Age enclosure with farmstead, Iron Age settlement, Late Iron Age hillfort, Roman aqueduct, Roman settlement, Late Roman cemeteries, early post-Roman settlement.

References: Green 1971
                Green 1973
                Green 1976
                Green 1982
                Green 1987

Objectives: the samples were submitted for the following reasons:

HAR-993 and HAR-994: to give a date for one of the few Deverel-Rimbury settlements to have produced buildings both rectangular and circular in plan.

HAR-995 and HAR-996: to give date for one of few the sunken-featured buildings discerned in the south and west of Britain.

HAR-995, HAR-996, HAR-2281, HAR-3079, HAR-3080, and HAR-3081: to place in a historical context the settlement postdating the fourth-century cemetery, which displays both sub-Roman and Anglo-Saxon characteristics; this date is crucial as it may show Early Saxon influence in an area where it would not be expected on any scale until the seventh century, and may indicate continuity of occupation on the site.

Comments:
C J S Green: HAR-2281, HAR-3079, HAR-3080, and HAR-3081 form a very satisfactory group which derives from features which, on archaeological grounds, should date within a close period after the disuse of the Late Roman cemetery. The dating also coincides with the archaeological interpretation, that the character of the settlement is consistent with a sub-Roman rather than a Saxon context; a date in the fifth or sixth century, in this region, would be earlier than the recorded Saxon invasion.

HAR-993   3380 ± 70 BP

$\delta^{13}C:$ −25.3 ‰

Sample: PC71C B6, 17, 208, submitted on 22 January 1975

Material: charcoal.

Initial comment: from the fill of a posthole, of a timber structure, associated with Deverel-Rimbury pottery; the expected date is twelfth or eleventh century BC.

Comment on uncalibrated date: the result is earlier than expected, but the feature from which the sample came was not closely associated with the Deverel-Rimbury structure, and could be part of an earlier phase; this reinforces the continuity of occupation from the second to the late first millennia.

Calibrated date: 1σ : cal BC 1750 – 1615
                     2σ : cal BC 1880 – 1520

Final comments:
C J S Green: the charcoal may either be residual from earlier occupation present on the site or may be derived from old heartwood.

References: Green 1987, 31
                Radiocarbon **21**, 365

HAR-994   3030 ± 90 BP

$\delta^{13}C:$ −27.2 ‰

Sample: PC71C BS, 31, 136, submitted on 22 January 1975

Material: charcoal.

Initial comment: from the basal fill of a V-shaped ditch demarcating the southern side of the Middle Bronze Age settlement.

Comment on uncalibrated date: the result fits very well with the expected date.

Calibrated date: 1σ : cal BC 1415 – 1135
                     2σ : cal BC 1510 – 1010

Final comments:
C J S Green: the result fits very well with the expected date: possibly charcoal from old timber, on the dating of associated pottery.

References: Green 1987, 994
                Radiocarbon **21**, 365

HAR-995   1880 ± 70 BP

$\delta^{13}C:$ −24.7 ‰

Sample: PC73E147CH-2, submitted on 22 January 1975

Material: charcoal.

Initial comment: from the destruction level in the base of a post-Roman sunken-featured building.

Calibrated date: 1σ : cal AD 55 – 220
                     2σ : cal BC 40 – 322 cal AD

Final comments:
C J S Green: acceptable only if derived fom old timber or heartwood.

References: *Radiocarbon* **21**, 365

HAR-996   2400 ± 70 BP

$\delta^{13}C:$ −22.9 ‰

Sample: PC73E147CH, submitted on 22 January 1975

Material: charcoal.

Initial comment: from the destruction level in the base of a post-Roman sunken-featured building (as HAR-995).

Comment on uncalibrated date: unacceptable, almost 1000 years too old.

Calibrated date: 1σ : cal BC 755 – 395
                     2σ : cal BC 790 – 380

Final comments:
C J S Green: unacceptable, almost 1000 years too old: possibly derived from old timber or heartwood but this would have had to have been 800 years old.

References: *Radiocarbon* **21**, 365

HAR-2281   1590 ± 80 BP

$\delta^{13}C:$ −27.5 ‰

Sample: PC76E276, submitted on 1 June 1977

Material: charcoal: *Quercus* sp. from large timber.

Initial comment: from a deposit of dark brown soil with flecks of chalk, in the base of a pit of unknown function in the post-Roman settlement; associated with animal bones and occupation debris.

Calibrated date: 1σ : cal AD 390 – 555
                     2σ : cal AD 255 – 630

Final comments:
C J S Green: entirely consistent with a context in a settlement of early post-Roman character.

References: Green 1987, 87

HAR-3079 1450 ± 100 BP

$\delta^{13}C$: −26.1 ‰

Sample: E115SS53, submitted on 9 February 1979

Material: grain.

Initial comment: from charred debris in the chamber of corn-drying oven F115.

Calibrated date: 1σ : cal AD 530 – 660
　　　　　　　　2σ : cal AD 400 – 770

Final comments:
C J S Green: consistent with a context in a settlement of early post-Roman character.

References: Green 1987, 87

HAR-3080 1490 ± 80 BP

$\delta^{13}C$: −24.1 ‰

Sample: E1150B12, submitted on 9 February 1979

Material: grain.

Initial comment: from corn-drying oven F115 (as HAR-3079).

Calibrated date: 1σ : cal AD 445 – 600
　　　　　　　　2σ : cal AD 400 – 670

Final comments:
C J S Green: consistent with a context in a settlement of early post-Roman character.

References: Green 1987, 87

HAR-3081 1530 ± 60 BP

$\delta^{13}C$: −24.1 ‰

Sample: E53OB21, submitted on 9 February 1979

Material: grain.

Initial comment: from corn-drying oven E53.

Calibrated date: 1σ : cal AD 435 – 600
　　　　　　　　2σ : cal AD 400 – 640

Final comments:
C J S Green: consistent with a context in a settlement of early post-Roman date.

References: Green 1987, 87

Poundisford Park, Somerset

Location: ST 21562074
　　　　　Lat. 50.58.49 N; Long. 03.07.03 W

Excavator: S Adams and M Newson

Site: possibly Bronze Age.

HAR-2412 1020 ± 80 BP

$\delta^{13}C$: −25.3 ‰

Sample: 21562074, submitted on 7 December 1977

Material: charcoal and ash: *Quercus* sp., *Corylus/Alnus* sp., and possibly blackthorn (*Prunus spinosa*), not twiggy (C A Keepax).

Initial comment: from a charcoal layer (2) running through two adjoining pits (A and B); layer 1 contained a sherd of Bronze Age pottery.

Calibrated date: 1σ : cal AD 960 – 1040
　　　　　　　　2σ : cal AD 880 – 1180

Praa Sands: Breage, Cornwall

Location: SW 270578
　　　　　Lat. 55.42.09 N; Long. 03.12.15 E

Excavator: H L Douch (a chance find), 1974

Site: a black compact paleosol *c* 100mm in thickness with fairly large branches compacted into it, interpreted as a 'forest level', was exposed when winter storms displaced the overlying sand dunes. At the interface of this 'forest level' and the underlying dark brown soil four tin 'ingots' were found. Beneath the dark brown soil was a grey clay deposit which merged into the natural sand.

References: Penhallurick 1986, 233 – 4 (^{14}C)

Objectives: to date the tin ingots.

Comments:
R D Penhallurick: whether the ingots belong to this period, or are much older than the date of the forest's inundation by the dunes, is not known, but it is tempting to regard the ingots as evidence of smelting in the post-Roman period.

HAR-962 1290 ± 70 BP

$\delta^{13}C$: −28.2 ‰

Sample: PRASANDS, submitted by H Keeley on 26 November 1974

Material: wood.

Initial comment: from the peat deposit.

Calibrated date: 1σ : cal AD 660 – 785
　　　　　　　　2σ : cal AD 630 – 890

Final comments:
H L Douch: the find was first thought to be Late Bronze Age, but is now shown to be Saxon.

Prudhoe: Castle, Northumbria

Location: NZ 091634
　　　　　Lat. 54.57.54 N; Long. 01.51.28 W

Excavator: L Keen and D Thackray, 1974 – 81

Site: excavations carried out within the inner ward of the medieval castle, to investigate the nature of the surviving structures in advance of possible consolidation for display.

References: Keen 1982, 175 – 84

HAR-3937 720 ± 70 BP

$\delta^{13}C$: −27.9 ‰

Sample: PC1023, submitted on 7 July 1980

Material: charcoal: large and medium sized timbers and many fragments.

Initial comment: from an occupation deposit on the phase 4 mortared floor of building F, against the southern part of the circuit of the curtain wall. The artefactual evidence suggests a general thirteenth-century date for this phase.

Calibrated date: 1σ : cal AD 1250 – 1290
                        2σ : cal AD 1180 – 1395

Final comments:
L Keen and D Thackray: this confirms the date suggested by the artefactual evidence.

HAR-3938   840 ± 70 BP

$δ^{13}C$: –27.6 ‰

Sample: PC1305, submitted on 7 July 1980

Material: charcoal: mostly from large timbers (A J Clark).

Initial comment: from an extensive burnt deposit (context 1305) which covers the remains of the buildings ranged along the southern side of the phase 1 palisade. This context may represent the destruction of the wooden palisade. The pottery evidence suggests a date in the mid eleventh or early twelfth century AD.

Calibrated date: 1σ : cal AD 1055 – 1260
                        2σ : cal AD 1020 – 1280

Final comments:
L Keen and D Thackray: the date covers the expected time span but has too wide a date range to be of much use.

HAR-3939   670 ± 70 BP

$δ^{13}C$: –26.5 ‰

Sample: PC1113, submitted on 7 July 1980

Material: charcoal: from large timbers (A J Clark).

Initial comment: from an extensive burnt layer (context 1113), one of several excavated along the southern edge of the phase 2 ringwork. This context overlay the tail of the earthen rampart and may relate to the destruction of the postulated wooden superstructure on these defences. The pottery suggests a mid eleventh- or early twelfth-century AD date. A *terminus ante quem* in the mid to late twelfth century is suggested from the details of the surviving architecture erected during the subsequent phase.

Calibrated date: 1σ : cal AD 1270 – 1390
                        2σ : cal AD 1230 – 1410

Final comments:
L Keen and D Thackray: if the architectural dating is correct then the ^{14}C date would appear to be rather too late.

Radwell, Bedfordshire

Location: TL 01065887
            Lat. 52.13.06 N; Long. 00.31.14 W

Excavator: P J Woodward (Bedfordshire County Council), 1976

Site: an Early Bronze Age ring ditch, probably a shallow mounded bell barrow; reuse in the Middle Bronze Age as indicated by the cleaning out of the ditch for use as a habitation enclosure.

References: Hall and Woodward 1977; 8, 13, 15 (^{14}C)
                Woodward 1978, 55 (^{14}C)
                Radiocarbon **21**, 375 (^{14}C)

Objectives: to date the cutting of the ditch and the associated, assumed, Middle Bronze Age material.

HAR-1420   3000 ± 90 BP

$δ^{13}C$: –26.2 ‰

Sample: RAD75233, submitted on 28 November 1975

Material: charcoal: mostly twiggy, very small fragments; *Prunus* sp. (blackthorn type) and hawthorn type (Rosaceae, sub-family Pomoideae) were tentatively identified (C A Keepax).

Initial comment: from a silty layer (33) just above the primary fill of the ditch (19), associated with occupation debris of Middle Bronze Age date. The charcoal deposit was not well defined, but may represent a clearance horizon.

Calibrated date: 1σ : cal BC 1400 – 1100
                        2σ : cal BC 1450 – 990

Final comments:
P J Woodward: this deposit also contained a jet toggle and an amber bead. This 'Wessex' material is considered to be derived from a disturbed burial of earlier date, although a late date for this cultural material maybe the case.

Rainham: Scotts Barn, Kent

Location: TQ 827656
            Lat. 51.21.17 N; Long. 00.35.59 E

Excavator: M C Bridge (Portsmouth Polytechnic)

HAR-3957   230 ± 80 BP

$δ^{13}C$: –26.1 ‰

Sample: SCB01, submitted on 7 July 1980

Material: wood: *Quercus* sp..

Initial comment: possibly dating to the second half of the eighteenth century: the sample could be later by *c* 50 to 60 years, or even re-used timber from even earlier.

Calibrated date: 1σ : cal AD 1530 – 1955
                        2σ : cal AD 1470 – 1950

Ramsbury: High Street, Wiltshire

Location: SU 272715
            Lat. 51.26.29 N; Long. 01.36.31 W

Excavator: J Haslam (Devizes Museum), 1974

Site: a complex of three bowl-shaped iron smelting furnaces and one later shaft furnace with associated working areas under a wooden shelter, sealed by early ninth-century and later occupation and further working areas. The site had a comparatively short working life. This is the first complete Middle Saxon ironworking site to be excavated in England.

References: Haslam 1980, 54 – 5 (^{14}C)

Objectives: to provide further dating evidence for the site.

Comments:
J Haslam: the ^{14}C results fit well with the expected eighth- to ninth-century date range of the few diagnostic artefacts. This fits with the wider context of an economic revival in England at that time, which can be inferred from other sources.

Harwell: at the time of publication Harwell suggested that the results should be taken as a single group with a weighted mean of 1160 ± 35 AD.

HAR-1606   1170 ± 70 BP

$δ^{13}C$: –25.4 ‰

Sample: RA7454, submitted on 27 June 1976

Material: charcoal: *Quercus* sp. and *Corylus* sp., large timbers and branches (C A Keepax).

Initial comment: from layer (50) associated with the second phase of the furnace.

Calibrated date: 1σ : cal AD 775 – 960
　　　　　　　　　2σ : cal AD 680 – 1010

Final comments:
J Haslam: very close to the date expected on the basis of the metal artefacts.

HAR-1607   1320 ± 70 BP

$δ^{13}C$: –26.1 ‰

Sample: RA7458, submitted on 27 June 1976

Material: charcoal: *Quercus* sp., *Salix* sp., and possibly *Acer* sp., large timbers and branches (C A Keepax).

Initial comment: from the lowest fill of the stokehole of a second phase furnace.

Comment on uncalibrated date: statistically this cannot be rejected out of hand; it must be an outlier of the +70 year standard deviation.

Calibrated date: 1σ : cal AD 650 – 775
　　　　　　　　　2σ : cal AD 600 – 880

HAR-1608   1090 ± 80 BP

$δ^{13}C$: –26.1 ‰

Sample: RA7453, submitted on 27 June 1976

Material: charcoal.

Initial comment: from layer (41), equivalent to the layer sealing the furnaces.

Calibrated date: 1σ : cal AD 885 – 1015
　　　　　　　　　2σ : cal AD 770 – 1150

HAR-1609   1180 ± 70 BP

$δ^{13}C$: –24.8 ‰

Sample: RA74/510, submitted on 27 June 1976

Material: charcoal: *Quercus* sp. and *Corylus* sp., large timbers and branches (C A Keepax).

Initial comment: from the interior of furnace 83 (last phase of operations).

Comment on uncalibrated date: as HAR-1606.

Calibrated date: 1σ : cal AD 770 – 955
　　　　　　　　　2σ : cal AD 670 – 1000

HAR-1626   1130 ± 70 BP

$δ^{13}C$: –29.5 ‰

Sample: RA7455, submitted on 27 June 1976

Material: charcoal.

Initial comment: from the filling of a smithing hearth 117.

Calibrated date: 1σ : cal AD 810 – 985
　　　　　　　　　2σ : cal AD 715 – 1020

HAR-1704   1070 ± 70 BP

$δ^{13}C$: –25.5 ‰

Sample: RA7455, submitted on 27 June 1976

Material: charcoal.

Initial comment: from layer (51), associated with the first phase of furnaces.

Calibrated date: 1σ : cal AD 890 – 1020
　　　　　　　　　2σ : cal AD 790 – 1150

Ravenstone: Ring Ditch II, Buckinghamshire

Location: SP 85354895
　　　　　　Lat. 52.07.55 N; Long. 00.45.11 W

Excavator: D Allen (County Museum, Aylesbury), 1978

Site: the second ring ditch to be excavated in the parish, an isolated site; two graves were found, both of the Beaker period, with one inhumation (crouched, female), in the later grave; finds from the site suggest leatherworking. The primary grave contained an empty coffin.

References: Allen 1981, 82 (^{14}C)
　　　　　　　Taylor and Woodward 1985, 112 (^{14}C)

Objectives: to date the secondary burial.

HAR-3000   3760 ± 90 BP

$δ^{13}C$: –26.3 ‰

Sample: RAV10B, submitted on 4 January 1979

Material: charcoal: *Quercus* sp. from mature timbers (C A Keepax).

Initial comment: from an intermittent spread of charcoal (0.6m × 0.2m × 0.03m) interpreted as a charred board, in the secondary grave at the centre of the ring ditch; the charcoal sealed a bronze awl and was immediately adjacent to a shale button and flint implements; the grave also contained a long-necked Beaker.

Calibrated date: 1σ : cal BC 2335 – 2040
2σ : cal BC 2470 – 1930

Final comments:
D Allen: exactly as expected.

Ringmer, East Sussex

Location: TQ 452128
Lat. 50.53.45 N; Long. 00.03.54 E

Excavator: J Hadfield (Sussex Archaeological Field Unit), 1979

Site: medieval kiln (late twelfth- to early thirteenth-century) of Musty type 2a, with a semi-permanent upper dome of wattle and daub, located on the Gault clay just to the north of the South Downs.

References: Hadfield 1981, 105 (^{14}C)

Objectives: the pottery spans the twelfth to fifteenth centuries and gives little indication as to the peak period of production; an early or a late cluster of ^{14}C measurements may help to elucidate the use of the kiln more accurately.

Comments:
J Hadfield: the mean date is earlier than expected, but is not unacceptable. It seems that the expected dating of the kiln may have simply been too late.

AML: (A J Clark) the mean calibrated date is AD 1193.

HAR-3616 860 ± 60 BP

$\delta^{13}C$: −27.0 ‰

Sample: 1980ID48, submitted on 9 October 1979

Material: charcoal.

Initial comment: from the area of the kiln and stokehole.

Calibrated date: 1σ : cal AD 1045 – 1245
2σ : cal AD 1020 – 1270

HAR-3617 880 ± 70 BP

$\delta^{13}C$: −27.6 ‰

Sample: 1980ID23, submitted on 9 October 1979

Material: charcoal.

Initial comment: from the area of the kiln and stokehole.

Calibrated date: 1σ : cal AD 1035 – 1230
2σ : cal AD 1010 – 1270

HAR-3618 740 ± 70 BP

$\delta^{13}C$: −26.8 ‰

Sample: 1980ID17, submitted on 9 October 1979

Material: charcoal.

Initial comment: from the area of the kiln and stokehole.

Comment on uncalibrated date: this date is notably later than the other two.

Calibrated date: 1σ : cal AD 1230 – 1285
2σ : cal AD 1170 – 1390

Ringstead, Northamptonshire

Location: SP 977748
Lat. 52.21.44 N; Long. 00.33.54 W

Excavator: D Jackson (for the Department of the Environment), 1974

Site: a Neolithic or Iron Age settlement site.

References: Jackson 1980a, 14 (^{14}C)

Objectives: to determine whether the prehistoric features are Neolithic or Iron Age since the pottery is not diagnostic.

HAR-1664 2180 ± 80 BP

$\delta^{13}C$: −22.7 ‰

Sample: RGSD75, submitted on 27 May 1976

Material: bone.

Calibrated date: 1σ : cal BC 380 – 115
2σ : cal BC 400 – 30

Final comments:
D Jackson: the date is compatible with the Middle Iron Age pit group.

Rivenhall, Essex

Location: TL 828178
Lat. 51.49.42 N; Long. 00.39.11 E

Excavator: W Rodwell (Chelmsford Archaeological Trust), 1972 – 3

Site: rescue excavations around the Anglo-Saxon church and in the north-east corner of the churchyard in advance of development and restoration works.

References: Rodwell and Rodwell 1985 – 6

Objectives: the dates are intended to ellucidate the relative and absolute chronology of the churchyard and its relation to the first stone-built church.

Comments:
W Rodwell: on the whole the Rivenhall dates have come out slightly later than was expected on archaeological and architectural grounds. In all cases the earliest possible date (especially in the two standard deviation range) does cover the expected period; the latter ends of the date brackets are in several instances clearly far too late.

HAR-2015 980 ± 60 BP

$\delta^{13}C$: −19.1 ‰

Sample: GR135, submitted on 9 November 1976

Material: human bone.

Initial comment: from the earliest of a stratified series of graves at the east end of the church (cemetery area 2); the only burial with associated grave goods: two bone pins, one with a gold head.

Calibrated date: 1σ : cal AD 1000 – 1155
2σ : cal AD 960 – 1180

Final comments:
W Rodwell: surprisingly this is slightly later than expected; it should not be later than the tenth century.

HAR-2016   970 ± 80 BP

$\delta^{13}C$: −19.7 ‰

Sample: GR89, submitted on 9 November 1976

Material: human bone.

Initial comment: from one of a small number of tile-lined graves (cemetery area 2); associated with the Saxon church and sealed by the fourteenth-century chancel extension.

Calibrated date: 1σ : cal AD 990 – 1165
                     2σ : cal AD 890 – 1230

Final comments:
W Rodwell: this should be tenth or early eleventh century.

HAR-2017   980 ± 70 BP

$\delta^{13}C$: −19.8 ‰

Sample: GR165, submitted on 9 November 1976

Material: human bone.

Initial comment: from a grave which should be early in the sequence, being outside the Saxon timber church and predating the Saxon stone church (cemetery area 2).

Calibrated date: 1σ : cal AD 990 – 1155
                     2σ : cal AD 900 – 1220

Final comments:
W Rodwell: a tenth-century date would be most likely here.

HAR-2018   860 ± 80 BP

$\delta^{13}C$: −19.1 ‰

Sample: GR257, submitted on 9 November 1976

Material: human bone.

Initial comment: from one of a small number of graves, not aligned east – west but set around the curvature of the apse of the second period stone church (presumably Norman in date).

Calibrated date: 1σ : cal AD 1040 – 1260
                     2σ : cal AD 1010 – 1280

Final comments:
W Rodwell: this date accords well with the architectural and archaeological evidence.

HAR-2019   1000 ± 70 BP

$\delta^{13}C$: −20.2 ‰

Sample: GR284, submitted on 9 November 1976

Material: human bone.

Initial comment: from a burial with the skull encased in a tile cist; situated at the eastern extremity of the possibly Middle Saxon cemetery (cemetery area 1) and stratigraphically earlier than the boundary ditch of the medieval churchyard.

Calibrated date: 1σ : cal AD 980 – 1150
                     2σ : cal AD 890 – 1180

Final comments:
W Rodwell: this, and HAR-2021, have turned out to be later than expected (Rodwell and Rodwell 1985-6, 83); a date in the late ninth or early tenth century was expected on stratigraphic grounds.

HAR-2021   970 ± 70 BP

$\delta^{13}C$: −20.1 ‰

Sample: GR316, submitted on 9 November 1976

Material: human bone.

Initial comment: from a stratigraphically early burial in the regularly planned Saxon cemetery (cemetery area 1), sealed by a later burial with a stone and tile lining; the skeleton was partly cut away and the bone survival not good due to acid soil conditions.

Calibrated date: 1σ : cal AD 1000 – 1160
                     2σ : cal AD 900 – 1220

Final comments:
W Rodwell: see HAR-2019.

HAR-2326   820 ± 60 BP

$\delta^{13}C$: −20.1 ‰

Sample: GR298, submitted on 9 November 1976

Material: human bone.

Initial comment: from one of a series of graves forming part of the regularly laid out Saxon cemetery (cemetery area 1); stratigraphically earlier than a Saxon or medieval building (function unknown), but later than grave 326 (HAR-2404).

Calibrated date: 1σ : cal AD 1165 – 1265
                     2σ : cal AD 1040 – 1280

Final comments:
W Rodwell: reassessment of the site evidence suggests that this grave belongs to the early medieval cemetery and therefore the ^{14}C date is not errant.

Harwell: repeat of HAR-2020 (940 ± 90 BP).

HAR-2404   1140 ± 70 BP

$\delta^{13}C$: −19.6 ‰

Sample: GR326, submitted on 9 November 1976

Material: human bone.

Initial comment: from a deep and early grave (cemetery area 1 in the regularly planned cemetery), stratigraphically earlier than grave 298 (HAR-2326).

Calibrated date: 1σ : cal AD 790 – 980
                     2σ : cal AD 690 – 1020

Final comments:
W Rodwell: the earliest date from the site, appropriately from one of the earliest graves. Archaeological assessment suggests a broadly ninth-century date for this phase.

HAR-2427   950 ± 60 BP

$\delta^{13}C$: −26.2 ‰

Sample: R9, submitted on 9 July 1977

Material: wood: *Quercus* sp. from large timbers.

Initial comment: from part of an oak sill inserted in the eleventh century, in one of the chancel windows of the tenth-century church (site period 5c). The window was blocked in the fourteenth century, sealing in the old sill.

Calibrated date: 1σ : cal AD 1015 – 1165
2σ : cal AD 980 – 1220

Romsey: Abbey, Hampshire

Location: SU 35102120
Lat. 50.59.19 N; Long. 01.29.59 W

Excavator: K Stubbs (Romsey Archaeological Research Committee), 1975 – 6 and 1979

Site: the Saxon church was traditionally founded in AD 907, although archaeological and architectural evidence suggest an earlier date; the Norman church was constructed *c* 1120.

Objectives: the foundations of the Anglo-Saxon church could not be dated archaeologically and a ^{14}C date is the only hope of establishing the chronology of the site, for which there is no reliable evidence before AD 970.

Comments:
K Stubbs: the dates from HAR-3760 and HAR-3765 are important because they indicate that burials took place on the site prior to the recorded foundation of the abbey by Edward the Elder in the early tenth century.

HAR-2527   1000 ± 70 BP

$δ^{13}C$: –26.0 ‰

Sample: RRA75CB1, submitted on 22 February 1978

Material: charcoal: *Quercus* sp. from fairly large timbers, mainly with no curvature visible in the growth rings (C A Keepax).

Initial comment: from a charcoal burial immediately to the west of the Anglo-Saxon north porticus and cut by the foundation trench of the Norman church.

Calibrated date: 1σ : cal AD 980 – 1150
2σ : cal AD 890 – 1180

HAR-3760   1100 ± 70 BP

$δ^{13}C$: –27.0 ‰

Sample: RA79E5CB, submitted on 5 March 1980

Material: charcoal: *Quercus* sp., probably mature timber (C A Keepax).

Initial comment: from charcoal burial 1.

Calibrated date: 1σ : cal AD 885 – 1010
2σ : cal AD 780 – 1030

HAR-3765   1170 ± 70 BP

$δ^{13}C$: –27.3 ‰

Sample: RA79E6CB, submitted on 5 March 1980

Material: charcoal.

Initial comment: from charcoal burial 2.

Calibrated date: 1σ : cal AD 775 – 960
2σ : cal AD 680 – 1010

Rose Ash: Lower Ashmore Farm, Devon

Location: SS 798200
Lat. 50.57.59 N; Long. 03.42.43 W

Excavator: G J Wainwright (for the Department of the Environment)

Site: a cremation burial in an urn, buried in a pit with a stone cap of local marlstone, revealed by chance during ploughing.

References: Wainwright 1980, 13 (^{14}C)

HAR-2992   2980 ± 70 BP

$δ^{13}C$: –25.0 ‰

Sample: 28-000, submitted by N Balaam on 11 December 1978

Material: charcoal: *Quercus* sp. (N Balaam).

Initial comment: from the fill of the cremation pit.

Calibrated date: 1σ : cal BC 1375 – 1100
2σ : cal BC 1420 – 1000

Final comments:
G J Wainwright: this result shows that the burial belongs to the same time range as the Middle Bronze Age settlements at Trevisker and Gwithian.

Roxton, Bedfordshire

Location: TL 157535
Lat. 52.10.02 N; Long. 00.18.29 W

Excavator: P J Woodward and A F Taylor, 1973

Site: one ring ditch (D) in a group of five.

References: Taylor and Woodward 1983; 13, 26 (^{14}C)
Taylor and Woodward 1985
Radiocarbon **21**, 358 (^{14}C)

Objectives: to date the hearth cut into the silt of the ditch.

HAR-711   1420 ± 70 BP

$δ^{13}C$: –26.3 ‰

Sample: ROXD73, submitted on 21 June 1975

Material: charcoal.

Initial comment: from a hearth cut into the silt of the ring ditch, which contained third-century AD Roman pottery; the expected date is Roman or later.

Comment on uncalibrated date: the difference in the dates from HAR-711 and HAR-1004 is rather surprising as the hearths were nearly identical and both were covered with hawthorn charcoal and burnt flints.

Calibrated date: 1σ : cal AD 565 – 665
2σ : cal AD 460 – 690

Final comments:
P J Woodward and A F Taylor: the date in the Late Roman/early medieval period is consistent with the ditch silting history (Taylor and Woodward 1983).

Roxton, Bedfordshire

Location: TL 157535
Lat. 52.10.02 N; Long. 00.18.29 W

Excavator: P J Woodward and A F Taylor, 1974

Site: one ring ditch (B) in a group of five, which surrounded a central cremation burial contained in two Early or Middle Bronze Age Collared Urns in a small pit; part of the ditch was backfilled after its construction, sealing charcoal (HAR-998).

References: Hall and Woodward 1977
Taylor and Woodward 1983
Taylor and Woodward 1985
Radiocarbon **21**, 359 (^{14}C)

Objectives: to date the ditch; HAR-997 and HAR-998 should give a date of a few years after the construction of this feature.

HAR-997   3620 ± 80 BP

$\delta^{13}C$: −25.2 ‰

Sample: ROXBQ2/338, submitted on 21 June 1975

Material: charcoal: numerous fragments of *Quercus* sp. from fairly large timbers (C A Keepax).

Initial comment: from the central cremation, at the base of a pit containing a Collared Urn cremation; the date should be similar to HAR-998, probably Early or Middle Bronze Age.

Calibrated date: 1σ : cal BC 2135 – 1890
2σ : cal BC 2200 – 1760

Final comments:
P J Woodward and A F Taylor: this date is satisfactory; it should be considered as a *terminus post quem* for the Collared Urn burial (ApSimon 1985; Taylor and Woodward 1985).

References: ApSimon 1985
Hall and Woodward 1977, 15
Longworth 1984, 140
Woodward 1978, 55

HAR-998   7700 ± 170 BP

$\delta^{13}C$: −25.5 ‰

Sample: ROXBQIV23, submitted on 21 June 1975

Material: charcoal.

Initial comment: from charcoal found around the fill of a posthole and in the primary fill of the ring ditch; the date should be similar to HAR-997.

Calibrated date: 1σ : cal BC 6690 – 6410
2σ : cal BC 7050 – 6170

Final comments:
P J Woodward and A F Taylor: this result is older than anticipated; the expected date was slightly later than HAR-997; the charcoal can perhaps be considered to derive from a very early clearance, but does not provide a date for the ring ditch construction (Taylor and Woodward 1985).

Harwell: the small size of the sample accounts for the larger than normal error term.

Roxton, Bedfordshire

Location: TL 158535
Lat. 52.10.02 N; Long. 00.18.24 W

Excavator: P J Woodward and A F Taylor, 1974

Site: ring ditch (C) in a group of five; the primary burial in a Collared Urn was disturbed by the digging of two pits for the second burial; a third burial was inserted into the ditch silt, while a hearth, possibly Roman was found in the upper fill of the ditch.

References: ApSimon 1985
Taylor and Woodward 1985
Radiocarbon **21**, 359 – 60 (^{14}C)

Objectives: the ^{14}C samples were taken:

1. to date the construction of the monument and the primary burial, and to give a date for the final phase of pit construction: this should be later than HAR-999 and HAR-1000 (perhaps *c* 150 years or more), but within the Bronze Age, although a later date is possible

2. to compare HAR-1004 with results of magnetic dating carried out on the hearth and the date from HAR-711; the date is expected to be Roman or Saxon

3. to date the silt which occurs in all five ring ditches; the urn is probably Middle Bronze Age in date; the result should be slightly later than HAR-999

4. to establish the association of the cremated bone.

Comments:
AML: one small sample, HAR-1005 (ROX74CQ3), was abandoned.

HAR-999   3800 ± 130 BP

$\delta^{13}C$: −25.3 ‰

Sample: ROXCQ2/330, submitted on 21 June 1975

Material: charcoal.

Initial comment: from the scattered pottery and cremation of the robbed primary burial, which was thrown back into the fill of the secondary pits.

Calibrated date: 1σ : cal BC 2460 – 2040
2σ : cal BC 2590 – 1890

Final comments:
P J Woodward and A F Taylor: this date agrees with the probable date of the burial (Taylor and Woodward 1985). It should be considered as a *terminus post quem* for the Collared Urn burial (ApSimon 1985).

References: Hall and Woodward 1977, 15
Woodward 1978, 55

HAR-1000   3660 ± 80 BP

$\delta^{13}C$: −25.0 ‰

Sample: ROXCQ2/339, submitted on 21 June 1975

Material: charcoal.

Initial comment: from a concentration of cremated bone at the base of the smaller secondary pit, below the scattered pottery and bone from the first burial (HAR-1001).

Comment on uncalibrated date: this result is satisfactory since the intermediate date between HAR-999 and HAR-1001 indicates that this charcoal is not entirely associated with either the primary or the secondary burials.

Calibrated date: 1σ : cal BC 2185 – 1935
2σ : cal BC 2290 – 1785

Final comments:
P J Woodward and A F Taylor: the charcoal probably derives from the redeposited remains of the Collared Urn primary burial (HAR-1002, HAR-1000, and HAR-999); see Taylor and Woodward 1985.

HAR-1001   3130 ± 60 BP

$\delta^{13}C$: –25.5 ‰

Sample: ROXCQ3XI21, submitted on 21 June 1975

Material: charcoal.

Initial comment: from the assumed main secondary burial; represented by a compact mass of cremated bones and two bone toggles, probably contained in a leather bag, beneath HAR-999 and HAR-1000; the date should still be within the Bronze Age.

Calibrated date: 1σ : cal BC 1495 – 1325
2σ : cal BC 1520 – 1270

Final comments:
P J Woodward and A F Taylor: this date for a central cremation burial provides a *terminus ante quem* for the primary Collared Urn burial that it replaces (HAR-999), (ApSimon 1985; Taylor and Woodward 1985).

References: Hall and Woodward 1977, 15
Woodward 1978, 55

HAR-1002   3620 ± 80 BP

$\delta^{13}C$: –24.6 ‰

Sample: ROXCQ3XI11, submitted on 21 June 1975

Material: charcoal.

Initial comment: from a small but intense fire burnt, *in situ*, in the larger pit near the secondary burial.

Calibrated date: 1σ : cal BC 2135 – 1890
2σ : cal BC 2200 – 1760

Final comments:
P J Woodward and A F Taylor: the charcoal probably derives, primarily, from the redeposited remains of the disturbed Collared Urn (HAR-999, HAR-1000, and HAR-1001); see Taylor and Woodward 1985.

HAR-1003   3200 ± 50 BP

$\delta^{13}C$: –26.0 ‰

Sample: ROXCQIV39/10, submitted on 21 June 1975

Material: charcoal.

Initial comment: from a cremation in part of an inverted Middle Bronze Age urn, set into the primary fill of the ring ditch; the date should be slightly later than HAR-999.

Calibrated date: 1σ : cal BC 1520 – 1425
2σ : cal BC 1610 – 1400

Final comments:
P J Woodward and A F Taylor: the calibrated date is entirely consistent with other Bucket and biconical urns of the Early or Middle Bronze Age (ApSimon 1985; Taylor and Woodward 1985).

References: Hall and Woodward 1977, 15
Taylor and Woodward 1983; 13, 26
Woodward 1978, 55

HAR-1004   1640 ± 80 BP

$\delta^{13}C$: –26.0 ‰

Sample: ROXCQ2VII, submitted on 21 June 1975

Material: charcoal: mainly blackthorn (*Prunus* cf *spinosa*), some hawthorn type (*Crataegus/Pryus/Malus/Sorbus* sp.), and a small amount of buckthorn (*Rhamnus catharticus*); three bags submitted, *c* 25% of one bag examined (C A Keepax).

Initial comment: from a hearth in the top silting of the ring ditch, identical to one found in the same position in ring ditch D (HAR-711); the expected date is Roman or Saxon.

Calibrated date: 1σ : cal AD 265 – 530
2σ : cal AD 230 – 600

Final comments:
P J Woodward and A F Taylor: as HAR-711; this date is consistent with the silting history of the ring ditch (Taylor and Woodward 1983).

Runcorn: Norton Priory, Cheshire

Location: SJ 548831
Lat. 53.20.33 N; Long. 02.40.44 W

Excavator: P Greene, 1971 – 8

Site: twelfth-century Augustinian foundation with a medieval tile kiln, ironworking, and two bell pits; after the Dissolution the priory was partly demolished and partly incorporated in a Tudor and then a Georgian country house.

Objectives: the bell pit produced pottery of thirteenth- to fourteenth-century date but this is a period of change in bellmaking techniques; HAR-2279 was submitted to obtain a more precise date.

HAR-2279   730 ± 70 BP

$\delta^{13}C$: –26.2 ‰

Sample: 108140, submitted on 1 June 1977

Material: charcoal: *Quercus* sp., *Alnus* sp., and *Corylus* sp. from fairly large timbers; *c* 50% identified (C A Keepax).

Initial comment: from a bell founding pit; the charcoal was in a primary position and undoubtedly connected with the manufacture of the bell; it was buried 1.5m below the ground surface and sealed by a substantial deposit of clay.

Calibrated date: 1σ : cal AD 1245 – 1290
2σ : cal AD 1170 – 1390

HAR-3885 870 ± 60 BP

$\delta^{13}C$: –26.4 ‰

Sample: NP78112, submitted on 5 March 1980

Material: charcoal.

Initial comment: from the lowest layer in a bell casting pit, found to the north of the church, which may have been used for casting the original bell.

Calibrated date: 1σ : cal AD 1045 – 1230
2σ : cal AD 1020 – 1270

Runnymede Bridge, Surrey

Location: TQ 019718
Lat. 54.38.39 N; Long. 02.10.25 W

Excavator: D Longley (Surrey Archaeological Society), 1975 – 6

Site: a Late Bronze Age settlement on the south bank of the Thames.

References: Longley 1976
Longley 1980, 71 – 5 (^{14}C)

Objectives: to date the occupation of the site.

HAR-1833 2620 ± 70 BP

$\delta^{13}C$: –24.7 ‰

Sample: 76F312, submitted on 21 June 1975

Material: wood.

Initial comment: from the collapsed remains of a building which appears to have been burnt down; stratigraphically contemporary with HAR-1834.

Calibrated date: 1σ : cal BC 835 – 790
2σ : cal BC 910 – 550

HAR-1834 2750 ± 70 BP

$\delta^{13}C$: –23.8 ‰

Sample: 76F311, submitted on 1 September 1976

Material: wood.

Initial comment: from stratigraphically the same context as HAR-1833.

Calibrated date: 1σ : cal BC 995 – 830
2σ : cal BC 1060 – 800

Final comments:
D Longley: although, after calibration, the dates are somewhat earlier than anticipated, they are nonetheless compatible with the evidence from the pottery and metalwork.

Runnymede Bridge, Surrey

Location: TQ 019718
Lat. 51.26.08 N; Long. 00.32.02 W

Excavator: S Needham (British Museum), 1978 – 89

Site: a Late Bronze Age settlement on the south bank of the Thames.

Objectives: to date different stages of the deep rivers edge and adjacent bank sequence, containing *in situ* structures, dense occupation refuse and rich environmental data.

Comments:
S Needham: C14 determinations were run on 30 Late Bronze Age samples, 28 of which belong to five stratigraphically interlinked contexts. Each of these contexts is considered to represent a short-lived event and to have a very small likelihood of containing residual material or old growth rings. Each set of determinations for a given event were tested for internal compatibility (Needham 1991, 347-53). With the exception of three results, compatibility was good and mean dates were calculated. Calibration of these correlated well with the site sequence and suggested a span in the order of one century, *c* 900 – 800 cal BC.

The three aberrant results (HAR-3752, HAR-3116, and HAR-4273) all gave significantly earlier dates than others in the respective contexts. Indeed all three were on split samples for which the siblings gave results within the date clusters. The early dates are probably not therefore due to residuality.

AML: twelve samples were submitted after April 1981.

HAR-3112 2700 ± 70 BP

$\delta^{13}C$: –24.8 ‰

Sample: A6L6L10b, submitted on 9 February 1979

Material: charcoal.

Initial comment: from a concentrated and discrete layer of charcoal, stratified midway in the fill of a large Late Bronze Age pit, which cut the 'midden' sequence on the ancient river bank, and was sealed by a concentrated layer of daub.

Calibrated date: 1σ : cal BC 915 – 805
2σ : cal BC 1000 – 790

References: Needham 1991, 346 – 53

HAR-3113 2670 ± 80 BP

$\delta^{13}C$: –25.4 ‰

Sample: A6F6L10a, submitted on 9 February 1979

Material: charcoal.

Initial comment: from a large Late Bronze Age pit, as HAR-3112.

Calibrated date: 1σ : cal BC 905 – 800
2σ : cal BC 1000 – 770

References: Needham 1991, 346 – 53

HAR-3114 2690 ± 80 BP

$\delta^{13}C$: –25.8 ‰

Sample: A6L44, submitted on 9 February 1979

Material: charcoal.

Initial comment: from a mass of burnt debris lying on the slope of the ancient river bank, possibly representing a clearance horizon at the commencement of the Late Bronze Age occupation.

Calibrated date: 1σ : cal BC 915 – 805
2σ : cal BC 1010 – 780

References: Needham 1991, 346 – 53

HAR-3115 2720 ± 80 BP

$\delta^{13}C$: –25.5 ‰

Sample: A6L65/1, submitted on 9 February 1979

Material: charcoal.

Initial comment: from a mass of burnt debris, as HAR-3114.

Calibrated date: 1σ : cal BC 975 – 810
2σ : cal BC 1050 – 790

References: Needham 1991, 346 – 53

HAR-3116 3090 ± 120 BP

$\delta^{13}C$: –26.1 ‰

Sample: A6F195a, submitted on 9 February 1979

Material: wood.

Initial comment: from one of a series of branches collapsed on the ancient river bank, from the same context as HAR-3114.

Calibrated date: 1σ : cal BC 1510 – 1220
2σ : cal BC 1630 – 1010

References: Needham 1991, 346 – 53

HAR-3117 2700 ± 70 BP

$\delta^{13}C$: –26.5 ‰

Sample: A6F195b, submitted on 9 February 1979

Material: wood.

Initial comment: from branches, as HAR-3116.

Calibrated date: 1σ : cal BC 915 – 805
2σ : cal BC 1000 – 790

References: Needham 1991, 346 – 53

HAR-3118 2720 ± 90 BP

$\delta^{13}C$: unknown

Sample: A6F11L2a, submitted on 9 February 1979

Material: charcoal: *Quercus* sp. from branch-sized timber, c 20 years growth (C A Keepax).

Initial comment: as HAR-3119.

Calibrated date: 1σ : cal BC 985 – 805
2σ : cal BC 1090 – 780

References: Needham 1991, 346 – 53

HAR-3119 2710 ± 130 BP

$\delta^{13}C$: –26.1 ‰

Sample: A6F11L2b, submitted on 9 February 1979

Material: charcoal: *Quercus* sp. from branch-sized and large timbers (C A Keepax).

Initial comment: from a concentration of charcoal stratified midway in a large Late Bronze Age pit (F11, layer 2), possibly early in the sequence of occupation.

Calibrated date: 1σ : cal BC 1000 – 800
2σ : cal BC 1255 – 530

Final comments:
Harwell: a small sample accounts for the larger than normal error term.

References: Needham 1991, 346 – 53

HAR-3120 2690 ± 80 BP

$\delta^{13}C$: –25.3 ‰

Sample: A6L65/2, submitted on 9 February 1979

Material: charcoal.

Initial comment: from a mass of burnt debris, as HAR-3114.

Calibrated date: 1σ : cal BC 915 – 805
2σ : cal BC 1010 – 780

References: Needham 1991, 346 – 53

HAR-3750 2690 ± 80 BP

$\delta^{13}C$: –27.5 ‰

Sample: A6F164/1b, submitted on 5 March 1980

Material: wood.

Initial comment: from a branch lying over a bundle of withies; part of a laid structure on top of excavated context L35, immediately outside the river frontage.

Calibrated date: 1σ : cal BC 915 – 805
2σ : cal BC 1010 – 780

References: Needham 1991, 346 – 53

HAR-3751 2800 ± 60 BP

$\delta^{13}C$: –30.0 ‰

Sample: A6F163/1b, submitted on 5 March 1980

Material: wood.

Initial comment: from a branch lying on the ancient river bank behind pile rows and under excavated contexts 33, 45, 53, 55, 56, and 63; possibly representing vegetation clearance. Context as HAR-3114.

Calibrated date: 1σ : cal BC 1025 – 900
2σ : cal BC 1125 – 830

References: Needham 1991, 346 – 53

HAR-3752 2970 ± 70 BP

$\delta^{13}C$: –30.3 ‰

Sample: A6F163/1a, submitted on 5 March 1980

Material: wood.

Initial comment: from possible vegetation clearance, as HAR-3751.

Calibrated date: 1σ : cal BC 1370 – 1090
2σ : cal BC 1410 – 1000

References: Needham 1991, 346 – 53

HAR-3759 2540 ± 70 BP

$\delta^{13}C$: −27.4 ‰

Sample: A6F155/3b, submitted on 5 March 1980

Material: wood.

Initial comment: from a small horizontal log between excavated contexts 35 and 18 in the river channel, just in front of the Late Bronze Age river frontage; probably part of a laid structure.

Calibrated date: 1σ : cal BC 805 – 545
2σ : cal BC 830 – 410

References: Needham 1991, 346 – 53

HAR-3761 2530 ± 70 BP

$\delta^{13}C$: −28.8 ‰

Sample: A6F164/1a, submitted on 5 March 1980

Material: wood.

Initial comment: from part of a laid structure, as HAR-3750.

Calibrated date: 1σ : cal BC 800 – 535
2σ : cal BC 820 – 410

References: Needham 1991, 346 – 53

HAR-3762 2580 ± 60 BP

$\delta^{13}C$: −27.2 ‰

Sample: A6F155/3a, submitted on 5 March 1980

Material: wood.

Initial comment: from a small log, as HAR-3759.

Calibrated date: 1σ : cal BC 810 – 770
2σ : cal BC 840 – 540

References: Needham 1991, 346 – 53

HAR-4257 2650 ± 70 BP

$\delta^{13}C$: −26.1 ‰

Sample: A6F276a, submitted on 14 February 1981

Material: wood.

Initial comment: from a pile in the inner row, trench 2.

Calibrated date: 1σ : cal BC 895 – 597
2σ : cal BC 930 – 770

References: Needham 1991, 346 – 53

HAR-4264 2640 ± 70 BP

$\delta^{13}C$: −28.6 ‰

Sample: A6F215a, submitted on 20 February 1981

Material: wood.

Initial comment: from a pile in the outer row, trench 2.

Calibrated date: 1σ : cal BC 845 – 795
2σ : cal BC 920 – 605

References: Needham 1991, 346 – 53

HAR-4265 2630 ± 60 BP

$\delta^{13}C$: −27.1 ‰

Sample: A6F144a, submitted on 20 February 1981

Material: wood.

Initial comment: from a pile in the outer row, trench 2.

Calibrated date: 1σ : cal BC 835 – 795
2σ : cal BC 910 – 770

References: Needham 1991, 346 – 53

HAR-4266 unknown

$\delta^{13}C$: unknown

Sample: A6F187a, submitted on February 1982

Material: wood.

HAR-4267 2640 ± 70 BP

$\delta^{13}C$: −28.6 ‰

Sample: A6F210a, submitted on 20 February 1981

Material: wood.

Initial comment: from a pile in the outer row, trench 1.

Calibrated date: 1σ : cal BC 845 – 795
2σ : cal BC 920 – 605

References: Needham 1991, 346 – 53

HAR-4268 2750 ± 70 BP

$\delta^{13}C$: −26.7 ‰

Sample: A6F236a, submitted on 14 February 1981

Material: wood.

Initial comment: from a pile in the inner row, trench 1.

Calibrated date: 1σ : cal BC 995 – 830
2σ : cal BC 1060 – 800

References: Needham 1991, 346 – 53

HAR-4269 2690 ± 70 BP

$\delta^{13}C$: −28.0 ‰

Sample: A6F117a, submitted on 14 February 1981

Material: wood.

Initial comment: from a pile in the inner row, trench 1.

Calibrated date: 1σ : cal BC 910 – 805
2σ : cal BC 1000 – 790

References: Needham 1991, 346 – 53

HAR-4270 2580 ± 80 BP

$\delta^{13}C$: −29.0 ‰

Sample: A6F215b, submitted on 20 February 1981

Material: wood.

Initial comment: from a pile in the outer row, trench 2.

Calibrated date: 1σ : cal BC 820 – 610
2σ : cal BC 900 – 420

References: Needham 1991, 346 – 53

HAR-4272 2690 ± 80 BP

$\delta^{13}C$: −28.9 ‰

Sample: A6F187b, submitted on February 1982

Material: wood.

Initial comment: from a pile in the outer row, trench 2.

Calibrated date: 1σ : cal BC 915 – 805
2σ : cal BC 1010 – 780

Final comments:
Harwell: this sample combined with A6F187a (HAR-4276: 2790 ± 90 BP).

References: Needham 1991, 346 – 53

HAR-4273 2920 ± 90 BP

$\delta^{13}C$: −27.3 ‰

Sample: A6F210b, submitted on February 1982

Material: wood.

Initial comment: from a pile in the outer row, trench 1.

Calibrated date: 1σ : cal BC 1265 – 995
2σ : cal BC 1410 – 900

References: Needham 1991, 346 – 53

HAR-4274 2770 ± 90 BP

$\delta^{13}C$: −27.2 ‰

Sample: A6F285b, submitted on 20 February 1981

Material: wood.

Initial comment: from a pile in the inner row, trench 2.

Calibrated date: 1σ : cal BC 1020 – 830
2σ : cal BC 1250 – 800

References: Needham 1991, 346 – 53

HAR-4275 2820 ± 70 BP

$\delta^{13}C$: −26.1 ‰

Sample: A6F276b, submitted on 20 February 1981

Material: wood.

Initial comment: from a pile in the inner row, trench 2.

Calibrated date: 1σ : cal BC 1060 – 905
2σ : cal BC 1255 – 830

References: Needham 1991, 346 – 53

HAR-4277 2730 ± 70 BP

$\delta^{13}C$: −27.1 ‰

Sample: A6F117b, submitted on 20 February 1981

Material: wood.

Initial comment: from a pile in the inner row of trench 1.

Calibrated date: 1σ : cal BC 975 – 820
2σ : cal BC 1040 – 800

References: Needham 1991, 346 – 53

HAR-4340 2810 ± 90 BP

$\delta^{13}C$: −27.2 ‰

Sample: A6F144b, submitted on 20 February 1981

Material: wood.

Initial comment: from a pile in the outer row, trench 2.

Calibrated date: 1σ : cal BC 1095 – 845
2σ : cal BC 1260 – 810

Final comments:
Harwell: repeat of HAR-4271.

References: Needham 1991, 346 – 53

HAR-4341 2780 ± 80 BP

$\delta^{13}C$: −27.5 ‰

Sample: A6F285a, submitted on 20 February 1981

Material: wood.

Initial comment: from a pile in the inner row, trench 2.

Calibrated date: 1σ : cal BC 1025 – 840
2σ : cal BC 1160 – 800

Final comments:
Harwell: repeat of HAR-4258.

References: Needham 1991, 346 – 53

HAR-4413 2790 ± 90 BP

$\delta^{13}C$: −30.1 ‰

Sample: A6F236b, submitted on 20 February 1981

Material: wood.

Initial comment: from a pile in the main row, trench 1.

Calibrated date: 1σ : cal BC 1045 – 840
2σ : cal BC 1255 – 800

References: Needham 1991, 346 – 53

St Buryan: Tregiffian, Cornwall

Location: SW 430244
Lat. 50.03.48 N; Long. 05.35.29 W

Excavator: A ApSimon (Department of the Environment), 1972

Site: a stone-built chambered tomb of entrance grave type, so far not dated; the presence of identical soil horizons in the old ground surface and in the turves forming the mound shows that the ground surface was permanent grassland at the time of construction.

References: ApSimon 1973

Objectives: to provide an earlier date limit for the construction of the tomb (a later limit is given by a ^{14}C date for a secondary burial in the floor of the chamber and to date the clearance phase and activity focus indicated by the charcoal and artefacts recovered; the only other dates from Cornwall are from from Carn Brae.

HAR-1702   11080 ± 30 BP

$\delta^{13}C$: −24.1 ‰

Sample: TRE972, submitted on 27 May 1976

Material: charcoal: mainly *Quercus* sp. from fairly large timbers, with a few fragments of hawthorn type (*Crataegus/Malus/Pyrus/Sorbus* sp.); also some coal (C A Keepax).

Initial comment: from the old ground surface below the turf mound of the tomb; the soil contained fragmented sherds of pottery and flint artefacts, probably of Early or Middle Neolithic date.

Final comments:
A ApSimon: the result is not according to expectation; oak would not have been growing in the late Glacial period suggested by this result; if the presence of coal is the cause, why was this not removed during identification or pretreatment?

Harwell: this result is too old to calibrate.

St Kew: Tregilders, Cornwall

Location: SX 01837410
Lat. 50.31.57 N; Long. 04.47.48 W

Excavator: P Trudgian (Cornwall Committee for Rescue Archaeology and the Department of the Environment), 1976

Site: an Iron Age enclosure with distinctive pottery, possibly related to the late phase of the Iron Age hillfort at Killibury.

References: Trudgian 1977; 126, 128 (^{14}C)
Radiocarbon **27**, 90 (^{14}C)

Objectives: to place site chronologically in relation to the nearby hillfort of Killibury.

Comments:
AML: one sample was submitted after April 1981, HAR-4927 (1340-8095).

HAR-2227   1980 ± 70 BP

$\delta^{13}C$: −25.0 ‰

Sample: TRG105, submitted on 3 March 1977

Material: charcoal.

Initial comment: from concentrations of charcoal just outside the remains of a circular oven or hearth, probably Iron Age.

Comment on uncalibrated date: (H Quinnell (née Miles)) this suggests that the site might be contemporary with the later stages of Killibury hillfort, where similar Cordonned ware was found, although it seems that Tregilders started later, as no Glastonbury ware was found.

Calibrated date: 1σ : cal BC 90 – 85
2σ : cal BC 170 – 140

Final comments:
P Trudgian: the calibrated dates, at both the one and two standard deviation levels of confidence, are earlier than current dates for the pottery; the dated context is however not closely linked to the pottery and it would be unwise to place too much reliance on this single date.

St Neot: Colliford Reservoir, site II, Cornwall

Location: SX 17927132
Lat. 50.30.46 N; Long. 04.34.06 W

Excavator: F Griffith, 1977 – 8

Site: the valley is to be flooded (centred on SX178713); the ^{14}C samples are from three, of a series of four, round barrows excavated as part of a multiperiod rescue project.

References: Griffith 1984; 59, 64 – 5 (^{14}C)
Maltby and Caseldine 1982

Objectives: to date the barrows.

Comments:
F Griffith: the three dates are internally compatible and fit well with the limited range of ^{14}C dates available for southwestern barrows as a whole (although cf Shaugh Moor); see also below.

HAR-2617   3500 ± 80 BP

$\delta^{13}C$: −25.1 ‰

Sample: CRII86, submitted on 23 March 1978

Material: charcoal: mainly *Quercus* sp. (with curvature of growth rings), and some *Betula* sp. (C A Keepax).

Initial comment: from a probable ceremonial pit believed to predate the cairn, possibly contemporary with HAR-2622, stratigraphically earlier than HAR-2624.

Calibrated date: 1σ : cal BC 1940 – 1740
2σ : cal BC 2040 – 1640

HAR-2622   3490 ± 90 BP

$\delta^{13}C$: −25.0 ‰

Sample: CRII85, submitted on 23 March 1980

Material: charcoal: *Quercus* sp. from large timbers (C A Keepax).

Initial comment: see HAR-2617.

Calibrated date: 1σ : cal BC 1940 – 1695
2σ : cal BC 2115 – 1610

HAR-2624 3610 ± 70 BP

$\delta^{13}C$: −24.2 ‰

Sample: CRII70, submitted on 23 March 1978

Material: charcoal: *Quercus* sp. from large timbers.

Initial comment: from the lowest level of the fill of the inner of two rings forming the cairn; overlying a pit, and sealed by layers of mixed stone, clay, and burnt material which were interpreted as contemporary fills of the inner ring.

Calibrated date: 1σ : cal BC 2125 – 1890
2σ : cal BC 2190 – 1770

St Neot: Colliford Reservoir, site IV, Cornwall

Location: SX 17717108
Lat. 50.30.38 N; Long. 04.34.17 W

Excavator: F Griffith, 1977 – 8

Site: as above.

References: Griffith 1984; 69, 76 (^{14}C)
Maltby and Caseldine 1982

Objectives: as above.

Comments:
AML: also two samples submitted in November 1981, and three in 1983.

HAR-2991 3580 ± 80 BP

$\delta^{13}C$: −24.7 ‰

Sample: CRIVC213, submitted on 29 November 1978

Material: charcoal: *Quercus* sp. from mature timbers; c 25% of the four largest bags were identified (C A Keepax).

Initial comment: from a pit containing some burnt bone, sealed by the turf barrow.

Calibrated date: 1σ : cal BC 2040 – 1790
2σ : cal BC 2185 – 1740

HAR-2994 3510 ± 100 BP

$\delta^{13}C$: −25.4 ‰

Sample: CRIVA99, submitted on 29 November 1978

Material: charcoal: *Quercus* sp. from large timbers; c 25% of each box identified.

Calibrated date: 1σ : cal BC 2010 – 1705
2σ : cal BC 2140 – 1610

St Stephen-in-Brannel: Watch Hill, Cornwall

Location: SW 974544
Lat. 50.22.48 N; Long. 03.26.35 W

Excavator: H Miles (for the Department of the Environment), 1973

Site: a barrow with a cairn ring of granite inside a single ditch; the ditch was later backfilled and a mound constructed over a central pit containing a wooden coffin.

References: Christie 1985, 108 (^{14}C)
Miles 1975a, 15 (^{14}C)
Wainwright and Smith 1980, 117 (^{14}C)

Objectives: to confirm the dating of the barrow, which on palynological grounds has been placed second in the series of barrows recently excavated on the St Austell granite.

HAR-654 3470 ± 70 BP

$\delta^{13}C$: −26.5 ‰

Sample: 162-29, submitted on 4 June 1974

Material: charcoal.

Initial comment: from a pit in the bottom of the barrow ditch, sealed by sherds from a Food Vessel Urn; should be contemporary with HAR-655; the similarity of this barrow to others in Cornwall suggests an Early Bronze Age date.

Comment on uncalibrated date: the result agrees well with the expected date.

Calibrated date: 1σ : cal BC 1890 – 1695
2σ : cal BC 2010 – 1630

Final comments:
H Miles: the date fits well with the emerging pattern of dates from barrows from Devon and Cornwall.

References: Radiocarbon **19**, 416

HAR-655 3420 ± 80 BP

$\delta^{13}C$: −27.1 ‰

Sample: 149-60, submitted on 23 August 1973

Material: charcoal.

Initial comment: from ?primary ditch fill, should be contemporary with HAR-654.

Calibrated date: 1σ : cal BC 1880 – 1640
2σ : cal BC 1940 – 1520

Final comments:
H Miles: as HAR-654.

Sandwich: Town Walls, Kent

Location: TR 33505810
Lat. 51.16.25 N; Long. 01.20.53 E

Excavator: V Fenwick (National Maritime Museum), 1973

Site: the town ditch.

References: Trussler 1974

Objectives: a date within 100 years was required to establish whether or not rescue work should be undertaken when a sewer trench was extended.

HAR-969 590 ± 70 BP

$\delta^{13}C$: −27.4 ‰

Sample: SANDWICH, submitted by D Sherlock on 26 November 1974

Material: wood: probably *Quercus robor*.

Initial comment: from a ship found in the fill of the town ditch *c* 3.0 – 3.5m below the surface; the estimated date is fourteenth – sixteenth century AD.

Calibrated date: 1σ : cal AD 1285 – 1415
                       2σ : cal AD 1270 – 1440

Final comments:
V Fenwick: the date range is entirely consonent with the 33m+ long clinker-built ship, which was scuttled or abandoned in the medieval town defences.

Scilly Isles: Nornour, Cornwall

Location: SV 944148
           Lat. 49.57.15 N; Long. 06.15.40 W

Excavator: S Butcher (Department of the Environment), 1969 – 73

Site: Bronze Age – Early Iron Age settlement, with some Roman occupation.

References: Butcher 1978; 33, 46, 49, 66 (^{14}C)

Objectives: to date the material rescued from a sea-damaged site.

Comments:
Harwell: three overlapping dates suggest continuous activity across the site from about 1950 – 1130 BC; the occupation of building 5 may have followed after about 160 years, but this need not imply discontinuity, because the ^{14}C samples do not represent every phase.

HAR-457   2990 ± 100 BP

$δ^{13}C$: –25.8 ‰

Sample: SAMPLE1, submitted on 10 October 1973

Material: charcoal, six small samples combined.

Initial comment: from a well-sealed midden in the lower fill of building 9, period 5, from the same context as HAR-460.

Calibrated date: 1σ : cal BC 1400 – 1060
                      2σ : cal BC 1495 – 930

Final comments:
Harwell: the result agrees well with HAR-460.

HAR-459   1840 ± 70 BP

$δ^{13}C$: –24.7 ‰

Sample: SAMPLE3, submitted on 10 October 1973

Material: charcoal, two combined samples.

Initial comment: from a box hearth in building 7, period 6, sealed by the loosely constructed east wall when the house was rebuilt.

Calibrated date: 1σ : cal AD 80 – 245
                      2σ : cal AD 10 – 340

Final comments:
S Butcher: it is difficult to accept so late a date (see Butcher 1978, 63 for discussion).

HAR-460   3020 ± 70 BP

$δ^{13}C$: –1.80 ‰

Sample: S22, submitted on 10 October 1973

Material: shell.

Initial comment: from site E1, layer 4a, a midden sealed by the stone fill of house 9, period 5.

Calibrated date: 1σ : cal BC 1400 – 1165
                      2σ : cal BC 1430 – 1040

Scilly Isles: St Martin's, Little Bay, Cornwall

Location: SV 924166
           Lat. 49.58.09 N; Long. 06.17.26 W

Excavator: S Butcher and D Neal (for the Department of the Environment), 1974

Site: a stone-built round house and walls of other stuctures in a Bronze Age settlement, exposed by winter storms; the house had a central hearth, replaced five times, and radial partitions, sealed by occupation debris.

References: Neal 1983, 48 – 9 (^{14}C)
                 Radiocarbon **27**, 83 (^{14}C)

Comments:
AML: one sample, HAR-4324 (34-060), was submitted after April 1981.

HAR-1715   3190 ± 110 BP

$δ^{13}C$: –25.3 ‰

Sample: 1792E16, submitted by H Keeley on 1 May 1976

Material: charcoal: *Quercus* sp. from fairly large timbers with some *Corylus* sp.; *c* 25% identified (C A Keepax).

Calibrated date: 1σ : cal BC 1605 – 1330
                      2σ : cal BC 1735 – 1220

HAR-1726   2780 ± 80 BP

$δ^{13}C$: –25.9 ‰

Sample: 4314E/F, submitted by H Keeley on 1 May 1976

Material: charcoal: *Quercus* sp. from fairly large timbers with some gorse (*Ulex* sp.) or broom (*Sarothamnus* sp.) twig, *c* 25% identified (C A Keepax).

Initial comment: from the upper fill of building 2.

Calibrated date: 1σ : cal BC 1025 – 840
                      2σ : cal BC 1160 – 800

Final comments:
S Butcher and D Neal: these dates indicate that occupation may have spanned the latter half of the second millennium BC.

Scilly Isles: St Mary's, Bar Point, Cornwall

Location: SW 915130
Lat. 49.58.48 N; Long. 04.54.31 W

Excavator: J G Evans (Central Excavation Unit)

Site: a prehistoric field system buried beneath blown sand.

References: Evans 1984; 7, 22, 26 (^{14}C)

Objectives: to establish a *terminus post quem* for the ploughsoil.

HAR-3483   2140 ± 70 BP

$\delta^{13}C$: −26.8 ‰

Sample: 31-032, submitted by N Balaam on 15 October 1979

Material: charcoal: twigs or young wood, mostly Leguminosae with some *Quercus* sp..

Initial comment: from a ditch fill, sealed by a ploughsoil thought to be of Bronze Age date.

Calibrated date: 1σ : cal BC 360 – 100
2σ : cal BC 390 – 0 cal AD

Scilly Isles: St Mary's, Porthellick, Cornwall

Location: SW 929105
Lat. 49.57.29 N; Long. 04.53.16 W

Excavator: R G Scaife

Objectives: to provide dates for the calculation of a peat accumulation/time curve.

HAR-3694   3100 ± 70 BP

$\delta^{13}C$: −29.0 ‰

Sample: PH65cm, submitted on 9 October 1979

Material: peat.

Initial comment: from an initial phase of forest clearance.

Calibrated date: 1σ : cal BC 1440 – 1310
2σ : cal BC 1520 – 1170

HAR-3695   6260 ± 90 BP

$\delta^{13}C$: −29.4 ‰

Sample: PH75cm, submitted on 9 October 1979

Material: peat.

Initial comment: from the basal deposits of the bog (0.75m) showing forested environment.

Calibrated date: 1σ : cal BC 5320 – 5145
2σ : cal BC 5410 – 4945

HAR-3723   2360 ± 70 BP

$\delta^{13}C$: −29.0 ‰

Sample: PH50cm, submitted on 9 October 1979

Material: peat.

Initial comment: from a phase of final deforestation (0.5m).

Calibrated date: 1σ : cal BC 515 – 390
2σ : cal BC 765 – 255

HAR-3724   2540 ± 80 BP

$\delta^{13}C$: −28.9 ‰

Sample: PH35cm, submitted on 9 October 1979

Material: peat.

Initial comment: from open verbaceous vegetation (0.35m).

Calibrated date: 1σ : cal BC 805 – 535
2σ : cal BC 840 – 400

Scorton, North Yorkshire

Location: NZ 232003
Lat. 54.23.51 N; Long. 01.38.33 W

Excavator: T Schadla-Hall, 1977

Site: ring ditch/pit alignment excavated in advance of gravel extraction; close to a cursus, henge, and ring ditches excavated in 1976.

HAR-2482   3890 ± 120 BP

$\delta^{13}C$: −24.2 ‰

Sample: SCOR1, submitted on 22 December 1977

Material: charcoal: *Quercus* sp. fairly large timbers (C A Keepax).

Initial comment: from a grave lined with stones (right side of the body near the feet).

Calibrated date: 1σ : cal BC 2570 – 2150
2σ : cal BC 2865 – 2030

Final comments:
Harwell: a small sample accounts for the larger than normal error term.

Sea Palling, Norfolk

Location: TG 434273
Lat. 51.01.36 N; Long. 00.02.42 E

Excavator: P Murphy (Centre for East Anglian Studies, University of East Anglia), 1978

Site: peat deposits buried beneath the present beach, exposed after winter storms.

Objectives: dates are required to complement pollen/soil analyses.

Comments:
P Murphy: the two dates establish that this is an outcrop of the Broadland 'Middle Peat', which Coles and Funnell (1981) estimated to date between *c* 5000 and 2000 BP.

HAR-2602 2220 ± 70 BP

$\delta^{13}C$: −28.3 ‰

Sample: SPTOP, submitted on 21 August 1978

Material: peat.

Initial comment: from the top of the peat deposit, assumed to be related to the peaty clay on the Horsey foreshore, which contained sherds of Romano-British pottery.

Calibrated date: 1σ : cal BC 390 – 190
2σ : cal BC 400 – 100

HAR-2612 5040 ± 70 BP

$\delta^{13}C$: −28.2 ‰

Sample: SPBOTTOM, submitted on 21 August 1978

Material: peat.

Initial comment: from the base of the peat deposit.

Calibrated date: 1σ : cal BC 3965 – 3725
2σ : cal BC 3990 – 3700

Seamer Carr, North Yorkshire

Location: TA 033820
Lat. 54.13.23 N; Long. 00.24.55 W

Excavator: T Schadla-Hall

Site: a Late Neolithic/Early Bronze Age settlement.

Comments:
AMI.: further samples were submitted after April 1981.

HAR-2823 2250 ± 80 BP

$\delta^{13}C$: −26.3 ‰

Sample: A155, submitted on 1 September 1978

Material: charcoal: *Quercus* sp. from fairly large timbers; *c* 25% identified (C A Keepax).

Initial comment: from a shallow feature containing no cultural material; thought to be associated with possibly Bronze Age ditches etc, on boulder clay, separated from the plough soil by a layer 50 – 70mm thick.

Calibrated date: 1σ : cal BC 395 – 200
2σ : cal BC 410 – 110

Shaugh Moor, Devon

Location: SX 553635
Lat. 50.27.10 N; Long. 04.02.18 W

Excavator: G J Wainwright and K Smith (Central Excavation Unit), 1976 – 80

Site: a programme of survey, excavation, and environmental studies related to the prehistoric settlements, land boundaries, burial mounds, and ceremonial structures in this part of Dartmoor.

References: Balaam *et al* 1982
Smith *et al* 1981
Wainwright and Smith 1980
Wainwright *et al* 1979, 8 (^{14}C)

Objectives: to establish a chronological framework for early human activity in the area.

HAR-1830 320 ± 70 BP

$\delta^{13}C$: −26.9 ‰

Sample: SPHFLUSH, submitted on 9 November 1976

Material: wood: probably hawthorn type (Rosaceae, sub-family Pomoideae); perhaps rather modern in appearance (C A Keepax).

Initial comment: from the base of a peat-filled depression near the top of Saddlesborough.

Calibrated date: 1σ : cal AD 1470 – 1650
2σ : cal AD 1440 – 1955

Shaugh Moor: Blacka Brook, Devon

Location: SX 573634
Lat. 50.27.09 N; Long. 04.00.37 W

Excavator: G J Wainwright and K Smith (Central Excavation Unit), 1976 – 80

Site: from a peat monolith.

Comments:
S Beckett: it seems most logical to reject HAR-3377 since it is older than HAR-3359 and HAR-3593, both of which were obtained from lower down the profile.

HAR-2671 6770 ± 80 BP

$\delta^{13}C$: −28.7 ‰

Sample: 15/100, submitted on 9 May 1978

Material: peat.

Initial comment: from the base of the peat.

Calibrated date: 1σ : cal BC 5720 – 5575
2σ : cal BC 5760 – 5500

HAR-3359 740 ± 80 BP

$\delta^{13}C$: −28.3 ‰

Sample: 210-003, submitted on 14 May 1979

Material: peat, moderately humified detritus.

Initial comment: from a peat monolith, 0.24 – 0.26m below the ground surface.

Calibrated date: 1σ : cal AD 1225 – 1290
2σ : cal AD 1160 – 1395

References: Smith *et al* 1981; 214 – 36, 245 – 71

HAR-3360 8520 ± 120 BP

$\delta^{13}C$: −29.4 ‰

Sample: 201-002, submitted on 14 May 1979

Material: peat.

Initial comment: from a peat monolith – 1.17 – 1.19m.

Final comments:
S Beckett: the date (for the top of this pollen assemblage zone) seems rather young in comparison with dated profiles from Bodmin Moor. A radiocarbon date of before 9000 BP would be more appropriate.

Harwell: too old to calibrate.

References: Smith *et al* 1981; 214 – 36, 245 – 71

HAR-3377   2530 ± 70 BP

$\delta^{13}C$: −27.9 ‰

Sample: 210-004, submitted on 14 May 1979

Material: peat, slight danger of modern rootlet contamination.

Initial comment: from a peat monolith, 0.13 – 0.15m below the ground surface.

Calibrated date: 1σ : cal BC 800 – 535
                     2σ : cal BC 820 – 410

References: Smith *et al* 1981; 214 – 36, 245 – 71

HAR-3379   4070 ± 70 BP

$\delta^{13}C$: −29.0 ‰

Sample: 210-001, submitted on 14 May 1979

Material: peat, possibly from elm decline.

Initial comment: from a peat monolith, 0.49 – 0.51m below the ground surface.

Calibrated date: 1σ : cal BC 2865 – 2500
                     2σ : cal BC 2885 – 2460

Final comments:
S Beckett: a somewhat equivocal date. With much younger dates higher in the profile it seems likely that at least the top part of this zone represents the Bronze Age.

References: Smith *et al* 1981; 214 – 36, 245 – 71

HAR-3380   8250 ± 80 BP

$\delta^{13}C$: −22.3 ‰

Sample: 210-005, submitted on 14 May 1979

Material: peat.

Initial comment: from a peat monolith, 0.89 – 0.91m below the ground surface.

Comment on uncalibrated date: this dates the middle of the pollen zone.

Final comments:
Harwell: too old to calibrate.

References: Smith *et al* 1981; 214 – 36, 245 – 71

HAR-3593   1130 ± 70 BP

$\delta^{13}C$: −26.9 ‰

Sample: 210-006, submitted on 21 December 1979

Material: peat.

Initial comment: from a peat monolith, depth 0.26 – 0.28m; previous dates from this peat deposit were incompatible with the results of the pollen analysis.

Calibrated date: 1σ : cal AD 810 – 985
                     2σ : cal AD 715 – 1020

References: Smith *et al* 1981; 214 – 36, 245 – 71

HAR-3594   5690 ± 80 BP

$\delta^{13}C$: −28.0 ‰

Sample: 210-007, submitted on 21 December 1979

Material: peat.

Initial comment: from a peat monolith, 0.51 – 0.53m below the surface; pollen anlysis indicates that this sample should date to *c* 5500 BP, as the sample from 0.49 – 0.51m was dated to *c* 3500 BP.

Calibrated date: 1σ : cal BC 4675 – 4465
                     2σ : cal BC 4780 – 4360

References: Smith *et al* 1981; 214 – 36, 245 – 71

Shaugh Moor: Cholwich Town, site 203, Devon

Location: SX 5962 approx
              Lat. 50.26.25 N; Long. 03.59.09 W

Excavator: G J Wainwright and K Smith (Central Excavation Unit), 1976 – 80

Comments:
AML: another sample (211-000; HAR-3811) was abandonned.

HAR-2676   6200 ± 100 BP

$\delta^{13}C$: −29.2 ‰

Sample: 203/1, submitted on 9 May 1978

Material: peat.

Initial comment: from the base of peat deposits exposed in the quarry face.

Calibrated date: 1σ : cal BC 5240 – 5005
                     2σ : cal BC 5340 – 4900

HAR-2694   2650 ± 70 BP

$\delta^{13}C$: −26.5 ‰

Sample: 10/BAH, submitted on 9 May 1978

Material: soil.

Calibrated date: 1σ : cal BC 895 – 795
                     2σ : cal BC 930 – 770

HAR-3046   2920 ± 80 BP

$\delta^{13}C$: −25.9 ‰

Sample: 209-001, submitted on 11 January 1979

Material: charcoal: *Quercus* sp., from mature timbers, *Corylus avellana, Alnus glutinosa, Crataegus/Sorbus/Pyrus/Malus* type, twigs and mature timber (C A Keepax).

Initial comment: from charcoal obtained in earlier excavations by Plymouth Museum in a possible hearth at the centre of hut 1.

Calibrated date: 1σ : cal BC 1265 – 1005
2σ : cal BC 1395 – 910

Final comments:
G J Wainwright and K Smith: partly contemporary with enclosure 15 but their general relationships are uncertain.

References: Balaam *et al* 1982, 231 – 40

HAR-3590   5560 ± 90 BP

$\delta^{13}C$: −27.6 ‰

Sample: 208-385, submitted on 21 December 1979

Material: charcoal: *Alnus glutinosa* from mature wood.

Initial comment: from peat underlying a Bronze Age land boundary.

Calibrated date: 1σ : cal BC 4495 – 4345
2σ : cal BC 4660 – 4240

References: Balaam *et al* 1982, 231 – 40

HAR-4008   2730 ± 100 BP

$\delta^{13}C$: −29.9 ‰

Sample: 208-1015, submitted on 14 August 1980

Material: peat.

Calibrated date: 1σ : cal BC 1000 – 810
2σ : cal BC 1155 – 780

HAR-4240   2950 ± 70 BP

$\delta^{13}C$: −28.4 ‰

Sample: 216-004, submitted on 11 February 1981

Material: peat.

Calibrated date: 1σ : cal BC 1300 – 1045
2σ : cal BC 1400 – 940

References: Balaam *et al* 1982, 231 – 40

HAR-4248   3940 ± 60 BP

$\delta^{13}C$: −28.4 ‰

Sample: 208-1020, submitted on 1 February 1981

Material: peat.

Calibrated date: 1σ : cal BC 2565 – 2400
2σ : cal BC 2590 – 2290

Final comments:
G J Wainwright and K Smith: this date is surprisingly early and may be due to truncation of the surface of the peat.

References: Balaam *et al* 1982, 231 – 40

Shaugh Moor: Enclosure 15, site 15, Devon

Location: SX 565638
Lat. 50.27.21 N; Long. 04.01.18 W

Excavator: G J Wainwright and K Smith (Central Excavation Unit), 1976 – 80

Site: a complex of houses and enclosures.

References: Balaam *et al* 1982; 211, 214, 231 – 40, 256, 268 – 71 (^{14}C)

Comments:
G J Wainwright and K Smith: there is a substantial difference between HAR-2983 and HAR-2960, both of which date house 66. We are obliged to favour the younger date. The dating of this house is particularly important because the course of the house drain demonstrates that the enclosure wall must either postdate the house, or be contemporary with it. This date lies within one standard deviation of HAR-2475 from context 91 which should relate to a period shortly after the enclosure wall was built. The combined evidence of these two dates could favour a date for the construction of the enclosure wall around 3100 BP. The date of HAR-3358 for the phase 2 cobbles is 100 radiocarbon years older than that of HAR-2979 for the phase 1 drain which it supersedes. This discrepancy lies well within the overlap on one standard deviation of the two dates and is an acceptable error.

It will be apparent from HAR-2474 that the settlement may have been founded by 3450 BP. By 3150 BP the settlement was probably enclosed by a stone wall (HAR-2475) and occupation during this period is represented by spreads of debris (HAR-2986), pits (eg HAR 2989), and the first stone-walled building, house 15 (HAR-2474). The dates imply that houses 18, 66, and 67 may in their earliest phase also predate the building of the enclosure wall (HAR-2987, HAR-2983, and HAR-3358). The dates from house 19 suggest that it was built around 2950 BC (HAR-2978) and that it continued to be occupied until the middle of the first millennium bc (HAR-2978). On the basis of radiocarbon dates alone, house 15 was occupied for a maximum of 600 years, house 18 for 500 years, house 66 for 400 years, and house 67 for between 300 and 400 years.

The radiocarbon evidence from the stone-walled houses therefore confirms that derived from the structures themselves, that they were occupied, either permanently or intermittently, for long periods and that in some cases they pre-date the enclosure of the settlement. After the building of the enclosure wall, occupation continued throughout the period 3000 – BP and a date from house 19 (HAR-2978) indicates some settlement of unknown intensity until *c* 1550 BP.

Otlet and Walker (in Balaam *et al* 1981):

1. the general distribution lying between 2800 BP and 4000 BP represents a true continuous occupation period, the range being far too large to be due to measurement imprecision alone.

2. a peak activity period was possible in the earlier years (3600-3800 BP).

HAR-2472   3020 ± 70 BP

$\delta^{13}C$: −25.4 ‰

Sample: 15/265 (house 18), submitted on 22 December 1977

Material: charcoal.

Initial comment: from a sandy clay matrix between flagstones.

Calibrated date: 1σ : cal BC 1400 – 1165
   2σ : cal BC 1430 – 1040

Final comments:
G J Wainwright and K Smith: the determination should relate to the phase 2 occupation of the building.

HAR-2473   2880 ± 70 BP

$\delta^{13}C$: −25.5 ‰

Sample: 15/228 (house 19), submitted on 22 December 1977

Material: charcoal.

Initial comment: from a sandy loam, beneath the floor of a house, resting on a worn and weathered subsoil surface; presumed to be of Bronze Age date.

Comment on uncalibrated date: this date suggests that the house may be the last in the sequence, however the date need not necessarily approximate to its construction.

Calibrated date: 1σ : cal BC 1210 – 945
   2σ : cal BC 1300 – 900

HAR-2474   3430 ± 90 BP

$\delta^{13}C$: −25.6 ‰

Sample: 15/176 (area 540), submitted on 22 December 1977

Material: charcoal.

Initial comment: from a posthole which is part of the phase 1 post-ring for house 15.

Calibrated date: 1σ : cal BC 1885 – 1640
   2σ : cal BC 2010 – 1520

Final comments:
G J Wainwright and K Smith: this date is by far the earliest on the site and, if accepted, it could place the first building 100 years before the next dated evidence for occupation. This may indicate the reuse of old timber.

HAR-2475   3160 ± 70 BP

$\delta^{13}C$: −25.3 ‰

Sample: 15/91 (enclosure wall), submitted on 22 December 1977

Material: charcoal.

Initial comment: from a primary occupation deposit against the Bronze Age enclosure wall.

Calibrated date: 1σ : cal BC 1515 – 1400
   2σ : cal BC 1610 – 1270

Final comments:
G J Wainwright and K Smith: this date relates to a time when the settlement was surrounded by the enclosure wall and should approximate to the construction of the latter as it occurs under tumbled stone from it.

It is stratigraphically later than HAR-2986, HAR-3418, and HAR-2989 suggesting that enclosure took place some time between 1300 – 1100 BP.

HAR-2960   3060 ± 80 BP

$\delta^{13}C$: −26.7 ‰

Sample: 15-1149 (house 66), submitted on 30 November 1978

Material: charcoal: *Alnus glutinosa* (alder) from fairly large timbers; *c* 25% identified (C A Keepax).

Initial comment: from a hollow securely stratified beneath the wall of house 66; presumed to be of Bronze Age date.

Calibrated date: 1σ : cal BC 1425 – 1225
   2σ : cal BC 1510 – 1070

Final comments:
G J Wainwright and K Smith: this relates to the second phase in the development of the settlement. The sample from beneath the walls provides a *terminus post quem* for the structures.

HAR-2968   3070 ± 70 BP

$\delta^{13}C$: −25.4 ‰

Sample: 15-486 (house 15), submitted on 30 November 1978

Material: charcoal: hawthorn type (Rosaceae, sub-family Pomoideae) from mature timbers, oak (*Quercus* sp.) from mature and twig wood, Leguminosae (cf *Ulex* sp.) from twig- and branch-sized wood, and *Corylus/Alnus* sp. from large timbers; *c* 25% identified (C A Keepax).

Initial comment: from the fill of a drain in a Bronze Age hut.

Calibrated date: 1σ : cal BC 1425 – 1265
   2σ : cal BC 1510 – 1130

Final comments:
G J Wainwright and K Smith: this relates to a house in its earliest form and may predate the building of the enclosure wall.

HAR-2976   2940 ± 90 BP

$\delta^{13}C$: −25.0 ‰

Sample: 15-1188 (structure 804), submitted on 30 November 1978

Material: charcoal: *Quercus* sp. and Rosaceae, sub-family Pomoideae, from mature timbers; Leguminosae (cf *Ulex* sp.) and *Calluna* sp. from twig-sized wood; *c* 25% of two bags identified (C A Keepax).

Initial comment: from the filling of a posthole; part of a circular timber structure in the centre of the enclosure.

Calibrated date: 1σ : cal BC 1310 – 1010
   2σ : cal BC 1420 – 910

HAR-2978   2640 ± 70 BP

$\delta^{13}C$: −25.7 ‰

Sample: 15-276 (house 19), submitted on 30 November 1978

Material: charcoal: *Quercus* sp. and Rosaceae, sub-family Pomoideae, from large timbers, *Salix/Populus* sp., *Corylus/Alnus* sp. from mature and twig-sized wood, Leguminosae (cf *Ulex* sp.) from twig- and branch-sized wood, and cf *Calluna* sp. from twig-sized wood; all identified (C A Keepax).

Initial comment: from the fill of a drain in a Bronze Age hut.

Calibrated date: 1σ : cal BC 845 – 795
                     2σ : cal BC 920 – 605

HAR-2979   3220 ± 80 BP

$\delta^{13}C$: −25.6 ‰

Sample: 15-1169 (house 67), submitted on 30 November 1978

Material: charcoal: *Corylus/Alnus* sp. and *Betula* sp. from mature timbers, *Quercus* sp. from mature and twig-sized wood, and cf *Calluna* sp. from twig-sized wood; c 25% identified (C A Keepax).

Initial comment: from a silty clay drain fill; the sample was taken from beneath the house wall where it was sealed by a dark, humificd layer.

Calibrated date: 1σ : cal BC 1610 – 1425
                     2σ : cal BC 1690 – 1320

HAR-2983   3260 ± 80 BP

$\delta^{13}C$: −25.5 ‰

Sample: 15-1146 (house 66), submitted on 30 November 1978

Material: charcoal: *Quercus* sp., *Corylus/Alnus* sp., and Rosaceae, sub-family Pomoideae, from fairly large (mature) timbers; Leguminosae (cf *Ulex* sp.) from twig-sized material (C A Keepax).

Initial comment: from a greyish brown loam that filled an irregular gully that flanked the east wall of hut 66.

Calibrated date: 1σ : cal BC 1670 – 1445
                     2σ : cal BC 1740 – 1400

Final comments:
G J Wainwright and K Smith: since this appears to be the only single phase structure, the early date from the gulley hints at the former presence of a structure which may have been totally demolished in the rebuilding.

HAR-2986   3270 ± 80 BP

$\delta^{13}C$: −25.4 ‰

Sample: 15-631 (area 45), submitted on 30 November 1978

Material: charcoal: *Quercus* sp. and *Corylus/Alnus* sp. from large (mature) timbers; c 25% identified (C A Keepax).

Initial comment: from the surface of a dark greyish brown sandy loam which has been interpreted as the original Bronze Age turf or Ah horizon.

Calibrated date: 1σ : cal BC 1675 – 1450
                     2σ : cal BC 1740 – 1410

HAR-2987   3260 ± 120 BP

$\delta^{13}C$: −25.7 ‰

Sample: 15-786 (house 18), submitted on 30 November 1978

Material: charcoal: *Alnus* sp., *Quercus* sp., and Rosaceae, sub-family Pomoideae, from mature timbers; Leguminosae (cf *Ulex* sp.) from twig-sized and larger wood and cf *Calluna* sp. from twig-sized wood; c 25% of one bag of two identified (C A Keepax).

Initial comment: from a fine silt loam: the fill of a drain in house 18.

Calibrated date: 1σ : cal BC 1690 – 1420
                     2σ : cal BC 1880 – 1270

Final comments:
Harwell: this sample was only a quarter of the optimum size, therefore it carries a larger than average error term.

HAR-2989   3280 ± 90 BP

$\delta^{13}C$: −25.6 ‰

Sample: 15-634 (area 45), submitted on 30 November 1978

Material: charcoal: *Corylus/Alnus* sp. and *Betula* sp. from mature timbers, also *Quercus* sp. from mature and twig-sized wood; 25% identified (C A Keepax).

Initial comment: from the fill of an isolated pit: a soft, friable, sandy loam containing charcoal and a quantity of stone together with a complete (fragmented) pottery vessel.

Calibrated date: 1σ : cal BC 1680 – 1450
                     2σ : cal BC 1855 – 1400

References: Christie 1985, 108

HAR-3358   3320 ± 80 BP

$\delta^{13}C$: −26.6 ‰

Sample: 15/579 (house 67), submitted on 19 July 1979

Material: charcoal: *Quercus* sp. and *Alnus* sp. from large timbers (C A Keepax).

Initial comment: from a silty loam matrix between cobbles in the entrance passage to the phase 2 building.

Calibrated date: 1σ : cal BC 1735 – 1520
                     2σ : cal BC 1870 – 1430

HAR-3418   3210 ± 70 BP

$\delta^{13}C$: −26.8 ‰

Sample: 15/794, submitted on 19 July 1979

Material: charcoal: *Quercus* sp., *Fraxinus* sp., *Corylus/Alnus* sp., and cf *Prunus* sp., all from mature timbers; c 20% identified (C A Keepax).

Initial comment: from a charcoal spread below an enclosure wall.

Calibrated date: 1σ : cal BC 1590 – 1425
2σ : cal BC 1670 – 1325

HAR-3419   2930 ± 90 BP

$\delta^{13}C$: −27.6 ‰

Sample: 15/175, submitted on 19 July 1979

Material: charcoal: *Corylus/Alnus* sp., *Quercus* sp., *Betula* sp., and ?Papilionaceae from mature timbers; also *Salix* sp. from twig-sized wood; *c* 25% identified (C A Keepax).

Initial comment: from the latest Bronze Age occupation layer within the hut circle.

Calibrated date: 1σ : cal BC 1300 – 1005
2σ : cal BC 1410 – 900

Shaugh Moor: Saddlesborough Main Reave, site 208, Devon

Location: SX 564627
Lat. 50.26.45 N; Long. 04.01.22 W

Excavator: G J Wainwright and K Smith (Central Excavation Unit), 1976 – 80

References: Balaam *et al* 1982; 211, 214, 231 – 40, 256, 268 – 71 (^{14}C)
Smith *et al* 1981; 214 – 36, 245 – 71 (^{14}C)

HAR-3592   4250 ± 70 BP

$\delta^{13}C$: −27.6 ‰

Sample: 208-000, submitted on 21 December 1979

Material: peat.

Initial comment: from a peat monolith, 0.02 – 0.04m below a presumed Bronze Age reave.

Calibrated date: 1σ : cal BC 2920 – 2705
2σ : cal BC 3030 – 2620

HAR-4003   3340 ± 90 BP

$\delta^{13}C$: −29.2 ‰

Sample: 208-552, submitted on 14 August 1980

Material: wood: oak (*Quercus* sp.).

Initial comment: from a pointed stake, which may have been part of hurdle fencing, found in the waterlogged base of the boundary ditch.

Calibrated date: 1σ : cal BC 1745 – 1520
2σ : cal BC 1880 – 1430

Final comments:
G J Wainwright and K Smith: if the timbers are the remains of the phase 1 fence, the date is likely to approximate to the laying out of the first major land boundary.

HAR-4005   3180 ± 80 BP

$\delta^{13}C$: −29.4 ‰

Sample: 208-1007, submitted on 14 August 1980

Material: peat.

Initial comment: from the old land surface below Saddlesborough Reave.

Calibrated date: 1σ : cal BC 1525 – 1405
2σ : cal BC 1670 – 1270

HAR-4013   3540 ± 80 BP

$\delta^{13}C$: −27.7 ‰

Sample: 208-1024, submitted on 14 August 1980

Material: peat.

Initial comment: from a turf-line in the base of the southern boundary ditch.

Calibrated date: 1σ : cal BC 2020 – 1760
2σ : cal BC 2135 – 1680

Shaugh Moor: The Cairn field, site 10, Devon

Location: SX 5662 approx
Lat. 50.26.22 N; Long. 04.01.41 W

Excavator: G J Wainwright and K Smith (Central Excavation Unit), 1976 – 80

Site: a group of six ceremonial structures including 2 ring cairns.

References: Balaam *et al* 1982; 211, 214, 231 – 40, 256, 268 – 71 (^{14}C)
Wainwright *et al* 1979, 14 – 26 (^{14}C)
Radiocarbon **27**, 89 – 90 (^{14}C)

Comments:
A D Hewson (in Wainwright *et al* 1979): assuming that sampling variation, due for instance to the timber samples being old at the time of use or possible short term ^{14}C variations, has a negligible effect and that the 'wiggles' in the true radiocarbon calibration curve do not introduce any sizeable distortion in the relationship between the dates, then the calibrated weighted mean age calculated using Clark (1975) is 3723 ± 67 BP.

HAR-2213   3430 ± 80 BP

$\delta^{13}C$: −25.9 ‰

Sample: 10/94 (cairn 71), submitted on 11 July 1977

Material: charcoal.

Initial comment: from a small charcoal pit discovered close against a large boulder when soil pits were being dug; presumed to be of Bronze Age date.

Calibrated date: 1σ : cal BC 1880 – 1675
2σ : cal BC 1950 – 1530

HAR-2214   3240 ± 80 BP

$\delta^{13}C$: −25.7 ‰

Sample: 10/150 (ring cairn 2), submitted on 4 July 1977

Material: charcoal.

Initial comment: from a pit, cut through the old land surface; presumed to be of Bronze Age date.

Calibrated date: 1σ : cal BC 1620 – 1430
                 2σ : cal BC 1735 – 1330

HAR-2216   3520 ± 70 BP

$\delta^{13}C$: –25.6 ‰

Sample: 10/175 (ring cairn 1), submitted on 4 July 1977

Material: charcoal.

Initial comment: from a pit fill, sandy loam with 20 – 30% charcoal; presumed to be of Bronze Age date.

Calibrated date: 1σ : cal BC 1950 – 1750
                 2σ : cal BC 2090 – 1680

HAR-2219   3430 ± 80 BP

$\delta^{13}C$: –25.3 ‰

Sample: 10/153 (cairn 70), submitted on 4 July 1977

Material: charcoal.

Initial comment: from the fill of a pit consisting almost entirely of charcoal.

Calibrated date: 1σ : cal BC 1880 – 1675
                 2σ : cal BC 1950 – 1530

HAR-2220   3430 ± 90 BP

$\delta^{13}C$: –25.5 ‰

Sample: 10/145 (ring cairn 2), submitted on 4 July 1977

Material: charcoal.

Initial comment: from the fill of a pit which contained a pot base and segmented faience beads; presumed to be of Bronze Age date.

Comment on uncalibrated date: chronology compares closely with that obtained for settlement with Deverel-Rimbury tendencies in the thirteenth and twelfth centuries BC. Barrett (1976) has indicated that the terminal date for rich Wessex graves may lie in the early twelfth century and that some overlap is apparent with post-Deverel-Rimbury groups of the first half of the first millennium BC (Barrett 1980). This date and the associated beads attest to this connection.

Calibrated date: 1σ : cal BC 1885 – 1640
                 2σ : cal BC 2010 – 1520

HAR-2221   3350 ± 70 BP

$\delta^{13}C$: –25.0 ‰

Sample: 10/168 (cairn 126), submitted on 4 July 1977

Material: charcoal.

Initial comment: from a shallow scoop containing loose peaty loam and charcoal. This feature, cut through the body of the monument, was directly above feature 183, a charcoal pit.

Calibrated date: 1σ : cal BC 1740 – 1530
                 2σ : cal BC 1875 – 1510

Final comments:
Harwell: the $\delta^{13}C$ value has been assumed.

HAR-2285   3400 ± 90 BP

$\delta^{13}C$: –25.2 ‰

Sample: 10/193 (cairn 126), submitted on 4 July 1977

Material: charcoal.

Initial comment: from a pit containing a shallow, grey fibrous soil which overlay a fine black loam containing lumps of charcoal; see HAR-2221.

Calibrated date: 1σ : cal BC 1875 – 1615
                 2σ : cal BC 1940 – 1510

Final comments:
G J Wainwright and K Smith: because of the contemporaniety of the ^{14}C dates, the cairn group probably relates to a particular phase of the development of the settlements.

Shaugh Moor: Trowlesworthy Cross Dyke, site 202, Devon

Location: SX 583642
            Lat. 50.27.36 N; Long. 03.59.48 W

Excavator: G J Wainwright and K Smith (Central Excavation Unit), 1976 – 80

References: Smith *et al* 1981, 214 – 36 and 245 – 71 (^{14}C)

HAR-4017   810 ± 110 BP

$\delta^{13}C$: unknown

Material: peat.

Initial comment: from a peat monolith – 1.18 – 1.20m.

Calibrated date: 1σ : cal AD 1045 – 1280
                 2σ : cal AD 1010 – 1390

Shaugh Moor: Trowlesworthy Warren, site 204, Devon

Location: SX 5764 approx
            Lat. 53.57.50 N; Long. 01.04.51 W

Excavator: G J Wainwright and K Smith (Central Excavation Unit), 1976 – 80

HAR-2673   7150 ± 80 BP

$\delta^{13}C$: –28.5 ‰

Sample: 204/2, submitted on 9 May 1978

Material: peat.

Initial comment: from the base of peat deposits in the Plym valley.

Calibrated date: 1σ : cal BC 6085 – 5965
                 2σ : cal BC 6130 – 5830

Shaugh Moor: Wotter Common, site 69, Devon

Location: SX 557627
Lat. 50.26.45 N; Long. 04.01.57 W

Excavator: G J Wainwright and K Smith (Central Excavation Unit), 1976 – 80

HAR-3591   2120 ± 80 BP

$\delta^{13}C$: −26.5 ‰

Sample: 208-432, submitted on 21 December 1979

Material: charcoal: oak (*Quercus* sp.).

Initial comment: from the mineral soil of a possible Neolithic platform terraced into the slope of Wotter Common.

Calibrated date: 1σ : cal BC 355 – 50
2σ : cal BC 390 – 50 cal AD

Final comments:
G J Wainwright and K Smith: it is probable that these platforms were cultivation terraces and the charcoal represents an initial clearance and burning horizon. The date, therefore, suggests that clearance took place late in the Iron Age.

Harwell: two bags combined.

References: Balaam *et al* 1982; 211, 214, 231 – 40, 268 – 71

HAR-3812   3400 ± 80 BP

$\delta^{13}C$: −31.3 ‰

Sample: A208-550, submitted on 24 April 1980

Material: peat.

Initial comment: from a peat monolith – 0.83 – 0.85m.

Calibrated date: 1σ : cal BC 1870 – 1620
2σ : cal BC 1910 – 1520

References: Balaam *et al* 1982; 211, 214, 231 – 40, 268 – 71

HAR-3816   2520 ± 80 BP

$\delta^{13}C$: −29.6 ‰

Sample: B208-550, submitted on 24 April 1980

Material: peat.

Initial comment: from a peat monolith – 0.68 – 0.70m.

Calibrated date: 1σ : cal BC 800 – 520
2σ : cal BC 830 – 400

HAR-4181   3510 ± 80 BP

$\delta^{13}C$: −28.7 ‰

Sample: 208-1015, submitted on 14 August 1980

Material: peat.

Initial comment: from the old land surface beneath a bank.

Calibrated date: 1σ : cal BC 1950 – 1745
2σ : cal BC 2115 – 1670

References: Balaam *et al* 1982; 211, 214, 231 – 40, 268 – 71

Shaugh Moor: Wotter Playground, site 201, Devon

Location: SX 555618
Lat. 50.26.15 N; Long. 04.02.06 W

Excavator: G J Wainwright and K Smith (Central Excavation Unit), 1976 – 80

References: Balaam *et al* 1982; 211, 214, 231 – 40, 256, 268 – 71 (^{14}C)
Smith *et al* 1981; 214 – 36, 245 – 71 (^{14}C)

HAR-2669   3680 ± 70 BP

$\delta^{13}C$: −25.3 ‰

Sample: 201/33, submitted on 9 May 1978

Material: charcoal.

Initial comment: from a shallow, puddle-like, charcoal-filled depression beneath a lynchet that had formed against a stone-walled reave.

Calibrated date: 1σ : cal BC 2190 – 1970
2σ : cal BC 2290 – 1890

Final comments:
G J Wainwright and K Smith: the date may indicate a land clearance phase, but the charcoal could have been produced by natural causes. If the date is accepted it predates the beginning of the Shaugh Moor complex.

Shortlanesend, Cornwall

Location: SW 80504756
Lat. 50.17.11 N; Long. 05.04.54 W

Excavator: D Harris (Cornwall Archaeological Society), 1979

Site: a Romano-British round, surrounded by a bank and ditch cut into the clay subsoil, excavated in advance of housing development. Inside the ploughed out bank, which survived to 0.30m below the present topsoil, occupation comprised drains and pits, apparently all of one period; the pits were filled almost entirely with charcoal.

References: Harris 1980, 73 (^{14}C)

Objectives: to establish that this was a Roman period round, not pre-Roman Iron Age.

Comments:
D Harris: these samples should be roughly contemporary. The overlap shows that the site was probably occupied between 125 – 245 cal AD.

HAR-3424   1840 ± 70 BP

$\delta^{13}C$: −26.5 ‰

Sample: SLEC4, submitted on 19 July 1979

Material: charcoal: *Quercus* sp. mainly from mature timbers but with some twig, with *Corylus/Alnus* sp. twig; *c* 50% identified (C A Keepax).

Initial comment: from a pit filled and lined with charcoal, which was cut into the natural clay subsoil from the occupation level inside the round; all the samples were collected by trowel and as far as possible were untouched by hand; they were placed in polythene bags.

Calibrated date: 1σ : cal AD 80 – 245
   2σ : cal AD 10 – 340

HAR-3427   1800 ± 70 BP

$\delta^{13}C$: –25.7 ‰

Sample: SLEC3, submitted on 19 July 1979

Material: charcoal: *Quercus* sp. from mature timber and Leguminosae (eg *Ulex* sp.) and *Betula* sp., twigs; *c* 50% identified (C A Keepax).

Initial comment: from a pit, as HAR-3424.

Calibrated date: 1σ : cal AD 125 – 330
   2σ : cal AD 60 – 400

HAR-3428   1830 ± 80 BP

$\delta^{13}C$: –25.0 ‰

Sample: SLEC1, submitted on 19 July 1979

Material: charcoal: *Quercus* sp. mainly from mature wood, but with some twig-sized fragments; also *Betula* sp. from mature timber and Leguminosae, twig; *c* 50% identified (C A Keepax).

Initial comment: from a pit, as HAR-3424.

Calibrated date: 1σ : cal AD 80 – 315
   2σ : cal AD 10 – 390

HAR-3429   1780 ± 90 BP

$\delta^{13}C$: –26.3 ‰

Sample: SLEC2, submitted on 19 July 1979

Material: charcoal: *Quercus* sp. and *Betula* sp. from mature timbers with Leguminosae (eg *Ulex* sp.) twig; *c* 50% identified (C A Keepax).

Initial comment: from a pit, as HAR-3424.

Calibrated date: 1σ : cal AD 125 – 370
   2σ : cal AD 30 – 430

HAR-3430   1780 ± 70 BP

$\delta^{13}C$: –25.9 ‰

Sample: SLEC5, submitted on 19 July 1979

Material: charcoal: *Quercus* sp. from twigs (less than 15-years-old) and mature wood, Leguminosae (eg *Ulex* sp.) from twigs, and ?*Salix* sp. from twigs (less than 15-years-old); *c* 50% identified (C A Keepax).

Initial comment: from a pit, as HAR-3424.

Calibrated date: 1σ : cal AD 135 – 340
   2σ : cal AD 80 – 410

Silchester, Berkshire

Location: SU 64166285
   Lat. 51.21.46 N;   Long. 01.24.06 W

Excavator: M Fulford (Reading University), 1978

Site: linear earthwork to the north-east of the Roman town.

References: Fulford 1984, 81 – 2 (^{14}C)

Objectives: the earthwork produced no archaeologically datable material; ^{14}C is the only means of establishing its relationship to the Roman town.

HAR-3422   930 ± 80 BP

$\delta^{13}C$: –27.1 ‰

Sample: SIL78001, submitted on 19 July 1979

Material: charcoal: mainly *Quercus* sp. with some *Corylus/Alnus* sp., all from mature timbers; *c* 25% identified (C A Keepax).

Initial comment: from the primary fill of the earthwork ditch; the date is most probably Late Iron Age or Early Roman, but could be medieval.

Comment on uncalibrated date: there is a long-standing preconception of an Early Roman outer earthwork on the eastern side of Roman Silchester; however there are serious topographic difficulties with this interpretation; the medieval date is acceptable.

Calibrated date: 1σ : cal AD 1015 – 1210
   2σ : cal AD 970 – 1260

Skendleby, Lincolnshire

Location: TF 428711 – TF 429710
   Lat. 53.13.03 N – 53.12.59 N;   Long. 00.08.20 E – 00.08.25 E

Excavator: J Evans and D Simpson (University of Leicester), 1975 – 6

Site: a Neolithic long barrow excavated in advance of ploughing.

References: Evans and Simpson 1986, 129 (^{14}C)
   Evans and Simpson 1991, 40 (^{14}C)

Objectives: to determine the date of construction of the long barrow.

Comments:
J Evans and D Simpson: the two dates are different at the two standard deviation level of confidence. HAR-1850 is preferred because it is the same as the date of the skulls OXA-639, 640 is the primary bone deposit and two other samples CAR-820 and CAR-819 for the ditch and mound respectively. HAR-1869 was small and according to the laboratory caused experimental difficulties; it may also have been from curated antler.

HAR-1850   4700 ± 80 BP

$\delta^{13}C$: –23.6 ‰

Sample: B139/751, submitted on 6 February 1976

Material: antler.

Initial comment: from the bottom of the barrow ditch.

Calibrated date: 1σ : cal BC 3625 – 3365
  2σ : cal BC 3690 – 3195

HAR-1869 5090 ± 80 BP

δ*¹³C:* –25.4 ‰

Sample: B139/752, submitted on 6 February 1976

Material: antler.

Initial comment: from the bottom of the barrow ditch.

Calibrated date: 1σ : cal BC 3990 – 3785
  2σ : cal BC 4040 – 3705

References: Evans and Simpson 1986, 126

Smallburgh: Wayford Bridge, Norfolk

Location: TG 34792481
  Lat. 52.46.09 N; Long. 01.28.51 E

Excavator: E Rose (Norfolk Archaeological Unit), 1976

Site: timber structure/boat discovered *c* 2m deep during construction of a new bridge, at least 10.75m long and 2m wide, containing silt, unlike the surrounding peat; some timbers resembled planks, others were thick and heavy; no nails were observed. The structure lay beside the base of a causeway, of white peaty material capped by large cobbles, which ran from north-west to south-east towards the bridge; alongside, at intervals, were wooden posts which appeared to be joined by cross-bars beneath the cobbles.

References: Rose 1978, 26 (¹⁴C)

Objectives: to date the timber structure.

HAR-1719 1740 ± 80 BP

δ*¹³C:* –26.9 ‰

Sample: SMBORO1, submitted on 27 June 1976

Material: wood.

Initial comment: from a pointed timber found with the possible boat; the causeway appears to lead towards the ford which existed before the bridge was constructed *c* 1797; the result should be earlier than this.

Calibrated date: 1σ : cal AD 215 – 400
  2σ : cal AD 90 – 440

Final comments:
E Rose: the calibrated dates make no real difference to the original date, which supports the theory that the causeway is of Roman origin.

Somerset Levels, Somerset

Location: ST 3542 – ST 4539 approx
  Lat. 51.10.23 N – 51.08.51 N; Long. 02.55.48 W – 02.47.11 W

Excavator: J Coles (Department of the Environment)

Site: a series of prehistoric wooden trackways crossing the wetlands in the area of Glastonbury. They were gradually engulfed, and thereby preserved, through the build up of peat in the Levels.

References: Coles and Dobson 1989
  Coles and Orme 1976b
  Coles and Orme 1979
  Coles and Orme 1981
  Coles and Orme 1984
  Morgan 1979, 98 (¹⁴C)
  Orme 1982

Somerset Levels: Ashcott Heath, Somerset

Location: ST 450390
  Lat. 51.08.48 N; Long. 02.47.12 W

Excavator: J Coles (Department of the Environment)

References: Coles 1979
  Coles and Dobson 1989, 67 (¹⁴C)
  Orme 1982

Objectives: to assess the chronological position of the peat-clay interface in the northern part of the Levels.

HAR-1831 5650 ± 70 BP

δ*¹³C:* –27.9 ‰

Sample: SLP768, submitted by M Girling on 15 February 1976

Material: peat.

Initial comment: from the interface between lower marine clay and freshwater peat.

Calibrated date: 1σ : cal BC 4655 – 4400
  2σ : cal BC 4720 – 4350

Final comments:
J Coles: this dates the transition to freshwater conditions and agrees with HAR-1856 and HAR-1857.

Somerset Levels: Ashcott Heath, Rowlands Track, Somerset

Location: ST 44983896
  Lat. 51.08.48 N; Long. 02.47.12 W

Excavator: J Coles (Department of the Environment)

Site: a wooden hurdle trackway in a previously unknown area of the Levels.

References: Coles and Dobson 1989
  Coles and Fordham 1977
  Coles and Orme 1977a, 11 (¹⁴C)
  Orme 1982, 17 (¹⁴C)
  Radiocarbon **21**, 362 (¹⁴C)

Objectives: to assess the chronological position of the hurdle track in relation to the Walton Heath structures.

HAR-1383 4210 ± 90 BP

$\delta^{13}C$: −28.65 ‰

Sample: SLP756, submitted on 8 July 1975

Material: wood.

Initial comment: from a structure low in the peat.

Calibrated date: 1σ : cal BC 2915 – 2625
2σ : cal BC 3030 – 2510

Final comments:
J Coles: this result corresponds well with the Walton Heath series and helps reinforce the archaeological suggestion of the exact contemporaneity of the Rowlands and Walton Heath tracks.

Somerset Levels: Ashcott Heath, Signal Pole Ground, Somerset

Location: ST 425410
Lat. 51.09.53 N; Long. 02.49.21 W

Excavator: J Coles (Department of the Environment)

Site: a platform of brushwood in raised peat bogs; the most northerly exposure of the complex.

References: Coles and Dobson 1989
Coles and Orme 1985
Orme *et al* 1985a, 64 (^{14}C)
Radiocarbon **29**, 89 (^{14}C)

Objectives: to assess the relationships of the Walton Heath series.

HAR-4739 4580 ± 70 BP

$\delta^{13}C$: −29.1 ‰

Sample: SLP-8108, submitted on 1 December 1981

Material: wood.

Initial comment: from a newly discovered structure in the peat.

Calibrated date: 1σ : cal BC 3490 – 3135
2σ : cal BC 3510 – 3045

Final comments:
J Coles: this shows a close relationship with Jones' track (HAR-3078).

Somerset Levels: East Moors, Ashcott Heath, Somerset

Location: ST 440394
Lat. 51.09.02 N; Long. 02.48.03 W

Excavator: J Coles (Department of the Environment)

Site: a hurdle trackway in raised peat bogs.

References: Coles and Dobson 1989
Coles *et al* 1980
Orme 1982, 17 (^{14}C)

Objectives: to assess the chronological position of the Eclipse hurdle track to the north.

Comments:
J Coles: these dates suggest that the East Moors hurdle track, some 1000m south of the Eclipse track, is a separate structure, which marks an early attempt to provide access onto the raised bogs of Meare Heath. The Eclipse hurdle track may have been built soon after, continuing or consolidating the same route from the Polden Hills to Meare Island.

HAR-3447 3870 ± 80 BP

$\delta^{13}C$: −29.0 ‰

Sample: SLP7907, submitted on 14 August 1979

Material: wood.

Initial comment: from area 6; the hurdles were severely damaged by old peat cutting and were thus exposed.

Calibrated date: 1σ : cal BC 2470 – 2205
2σ : cal BC 2575 – 2050

Final comments:
J Coles: rather older than the Eclipse hurdle.

HAR-3448 3770 ± 70 BP

$\delta^{13}C$: −30.8 ‰

Sample: SLP7906, submitted on 14 August 1979

Material: wood.

Initial comment: from area 3.

Calibrated date: 1σ : cal BC 2315 – 2045
2σ : cal BC 2460 – 1985

Final comments:
J Coles: this date, and HAR-3449, overlap with the Eclipse hurdle track HAR-3838 at the one standard deviation range, but HAR-680 lies outside the East Moors range. The two tracks are likely to have been built as separate structures, but within the same time frame, *c* 2100 BC.

References: Orme *et al* 1980, 59

HAR-3449 3750 ± 70 BP

$\delta^{13}C$: −29.3 ‰

Sample: SLP7908, submitted on 14 August 1979

Material: wood.

Initial comment: from area 10.

Calibrated date: 1σ : cal BC 2290 – 2040
2σ : cal BC 2455 – 1970

Final comments:
J Coles: as for HAR-3448.

References: Orme *et al* 1980, 59

Somerset Levels: Edington Burtle, Chilton Moor, Somerset

Location: ST 387428
Lat. 51.10.50 N; Long. 02.52.38 W

Excavator: J Coles (Department of the Environment)

Site: a series of brushwood trackways leading off the Burtle Island.

References: Coles and Coles 1975
Coles and Dobson 1989
Coles and Orme 1977b
Orme 1982
Radiocarbon **19**, 415 (^{14}C)

Objectives: to assess the chronological position of the site within the Brue Valley series.

HAR-649   4760 ± 80 BP

$\delta^{13}C$: −28.2 ‰

Sample: SLP744 (Chilton 1-2), submitted on 4 June 1974

Material: wood: *Betula* sp..

Initial comment: from horizontal timbers of a double trackway under 0.5m of peat; this sample was collected in 1969.

Comment on uncalibrated date: a sample from an adjacent trackway (Chilton 4) was dated to 4760 ± 65 BP (Lu-327).

Calibrated date: 1σ : cal BC 3645 – 3380
2σ : cal BC 3775 – 3360

Final comments:
J Coles: this suggests that the structures south of the island are contemporary with the series if wooden trackways east of Burtle (see HAR-651).

Somerset Levels: Meare Heath, Somerset

Location: ST 4582405
Lat. 51.09.40 N; Long. 02.46.30 W

Excavator: J Coles (Department of the Environment)

Site: peatbog wih occasional stray finds.

References: Coles 1979
Coles and Orme 1979, 55 (^{14}C)
Orme 1982
Radiocarbon **27**, 78 (^{14}C)

Objectives: to establish the chronology of various finds.

HAR-2224   4560 ± 80 BP

$\delta^{13}C$: −28.6 ‰

Sample: SLP771, submitted on 8 March 1977

Material: peat.

Initial comment: associated with a flint axe of Neolithic type, closely comparable to an axe from the Early Neolithic Sweet track 3km distant.

Comment on uncalibrated date: this date is outside the range of the Sweet track (3807/3806 BC). The peat was exactly contemporary with the axe or slightly older. This suggests some anomaly in dates on peat, if the typological similarities of the Meare Heath and Sweet track axes are accepted. Otherwise the date agrees with activity on Walton Heath (HAR-3078 and HAR-4078) only a few hundred metres away.

Calibrated date: 1σ : cal BC 3375 – 3105
2σ : cal BC 3510 – 2945

Final comments:
J Coles: the axes are remarkably alike, hence the peat date may be erroneous.

Somerset Levels: Meare Heath Field, site 4, Somerset

Location: ST 446410
Lat. 51.09.54 N; Long. 02.47.33 W

Excavator: J Coles (Department of the Environment)

Site: base of the Meare island slope, probable terminal area.

References: Coles and Dobson 1989
Morgan 1982a, 45 (^{14}C)
Morgan 1988
Orme 1982
Radiocarbon **29**, 87 (^{14}C)

Objectives: to assess the chronology of bog oak.

HAR-3195   5180 ± 70 BP

$\delta^{13}C$: −26.8 ‰

Sample: SLP7902, submitted on 12 March 1976

Material: wood: bog oak (*Quercus* sp.), outermost 30 rings.

Initial comment: from the northern limit of this site.

Comment on uncalibrated date: the date of the wood was completely unknown but is very satisfactory as it is roughly contemporary with floating Neolithic tree-ring chronology. It falls within the range of dates from the Sweet track, suggesting a slightly earlier felling date but every possibility of an overlap with the 410 year Sweet chronology.

Calibrated date: 1σ : cal BC 4040 – 3830
2σ : cal BC 4225 – 3815

Final comments:
J Coles: slightly older than the Sweet track construction date; calibrates to a period from which little wood has yet been found in England to provide a tree-ring record.

Somerset Levels: Meare Heath, Diffords Site 1, Somerset

Location: ST 44954073
Lat. 51.09.46 N; Long. 02.47.15 W

Excavator: J Coles (Department of the Environment)

Site: a natural pool in a raised bog, edged with roundwood (possibly a fishing station or retting pool).

References: Coles 1979
Coles and Dobson 1989
Coles and Orme 1978c, 97 (^{14}C)
Orme 1982
Radiocarbon **27**, 77 (^{14}C)

Objectives: to assess the chronological position of an unusual feature.

HAR-1842 1710 ± 80 BP

$\delta^{13}C$: −28.2 ‰

Sample: SLP7610, submitted on 25 November 1976

Material: wood.

Initial comment: from young brushwood from the lowest deposit of a structure in the pool peat; the wood was worked with iron blades.

Comment on uncalibrated date: agrees well with HAR-1854 and with the series of dates for the highest levels of peat in which the structure lay.

Calibrated date: 1σ : cal AD 235 – 415
                    2σ : cal AD 120 – 540

Final comments:
J Coles: possibly contemporary with the final activity at Meare Village East, but likely to be later, and unusual in that widespread flooding is considered to have submerged areas of the Levels at this time. Pewter and coin hoards were buried in the uppermost peats in the area *c* 350 AD.

HAR-1854 1730 ± 70 BP

$\delta^{13}C$: −29.4 ‰

Sample: SLP769, submitted on 25 November 1976

Material: wood.

Initial comment: from young brushwood from a structure in the pool peat.

Calibrated date: 1σ : cal AD 225 – 400
                    2σ : cal AD 120 – 440

Final comments:
J Coles: agrees well with HAR-1842.

Somerset Levels: Meare Heath, Eclipse Track, Somerset

Location: ST 449406
             Lat. 51.09.41 N; Long. 02.47.17 W

Excavator: J Coles (Department of the Environment)

Site: hurdle trackway across the heath.

References: Coles and Dobson 1989
              Coles, Orme, and Hibbert 1975
              Coles *et al* 1982; 26, 36 (^{14}C)
              Orme 1982, 17 (^{14}C)

Objectives: to assess the chronological position of the hurdles in the upper raised peat bogs.

HAR-680 3460 ± 60 BP

$\delta^{13}C$: −29.0 ‰

Sample: SLP747 (Eclipse 1), submitted on 21 June 1974

Material: wood: *Corylus* sp..

Initial comment: from a newly discovered trackway of young wood very near the exposed surface of *Eriophorum-Calluna* peat (depth 0.4m).

Calibrated date: 1σ : cal BC 1885 – 1695
                    2σ : cal BC 1940 – 1640

Final comments:
J Coles: this result should relate closely to HAR-3838, but does not; the date is earlier than expected.

References: Coles and Coles 1975
              Coles and Orme 1978c
              Radiocarbon **19**, 416

HAR-3838 3600 ± 70 BP

$\delta^{13}C$: −29.8 ‰

Sample: SLP8009, submitted on 7 May 1980

Material: wood: *Corylus* sp..

Initial comment: from an Early Bronze Age hurdle structure.

Comment on uncalibrated date: this date lies between the first Eclipse date (HAR-680) and the dates for the East Moors track (HAR-3447, HAR-3448, and HAR-3449). The question of whether or not these two tracks are contemporary, therefore, remains unresolved (see HAR-3448).

Calibrated date: 1σ : cal BC 2115 – 1885
                    2σ : cal BC 2185 – 1760

Final comments:
J Coles: as for HAR-680. At the two standard deviation level of confidence, this date extends into the East Moors range, but HAR-680 lies outside this range.

References: Coles *et al* 1982
              Radiocarbon **30**, 332

Somerset Levels: Meare Heath, Eclipse Track (peat sequence), Somerset

Location: ST 449406
             Lat. 51.09.41 N; Long. 02.47.17 W

Excavator: J Coles (Department of the Environment)

Site: trackways in a peat bog.

References: Coles and Dobson 1989
              Coles and Orme 1985
              Radiocarbon **29**, 90 – 1 (^{14}C)

HAR-4542 3990 ± 100 BP

$\delta^{13}C$: −26.7 ‰

Sample: SLP8107, submitted on 1 July 1981

Material: peat.

Initial comment: Sphagnum-Calluna peat from 0.42 – 0.43m below the present ground surface.

Comment on uncalibrated date: this provides an essential date for the pollen zone boundary E4/E5 and marks the beginning of increased clearance activity in area. The Eclipse track was constructed during this phase.

Calibrated date: 1σ : cal BC 2855 – 2405
                    2σ : cal BC 2880 – 2205

Final comments:
J Coles: earlier than the dates obtained for the assumed equivalent regional zone boundary E/F at Meare Heath (SRR-915) and Abbot's Way (SRR-534), and earlier than the peat date HAR-4867 (which stratigraphically occurs below), but consistent with dates from the track itself.

HAR-4543   4230 ± 80 BP

$\delta^{13}C$: −28.1 ‰

Sample: SLP8105, submitted on 1 August 1980

Material: peat.

Initial comment: Sphagnum/Calluna/Eriophorum peat from 0.70 – 0.71m below the present ground surface.

Comment on uncalibrated date: this dates the E3/E4 boundary, regional assemblage zone boundary C/D, an the end of the forest regeneration phase.

Calibrated date: 1σ : cal BC 2915 – 2670
                     2σ : cal BC 3030 – 2590

Final comments:
J Coles: in close agreement with the C/D boundary dates from Sweet track west (HAR-5294) and Meare Village East (HAR-7065), but possibly earlier than dates from Abbot's Way (SRR-536), Sweet Factory (SRR-879), and Meare Heath (SRR-917).

HAR-4544   4640 ± 70 BP

$\delta^{13}C$: −27.6 ‰

Sample: SLP8106, submitted on 1 August 1981

Material: peat.

Initial comment: Eriophorum-Calluna peat from 0.94 – 0.95m below the present ground surface.

Comment on uncalibrated date: this dates the E2/E3 boundary, regional assemblage zone boundary B/C, and the end of the first major clearance in the area.

Calibrated date: 1σ : cal BC 3510 – 3345
                     2σ : cal BC 3625 – 3110

Final comments:
J Coles: this is the earliest date obtained from B/C boundary, with close agreement with Sweet track west (HAR-5295). Other dates for the boundary from Abbot's Way (SRR-539) and Sweet Factory (SRR-890) are slightly later.

Somerset Levels: Meare Heath, Meare Heath Track, Somerset

Location: ST 444406
            Lat. 51.09.41 N; Long. 02.47.43 W

Excavator: J Coles (Department of the Environment)

Site: a substantial timber trackway.

References: Coles and Dobson 1989
                Coles *et al* 1988
                Morgan 1982a, 43 (^{14}C)
                Orme 1982, 18 (^{14}C)

Objectives: to assess the chronological position of the timber track in an area of raised peat bog. HAR-1489, HAR-1494, and HAR-1627 were submitted for dating with the aim of attempting to wiggle-match the 152-year floating chronology against the calibration curve and fixing the exact time span of the chronology (see below).

Comments:
R Morgan (1991): calibration suggests a very approximate date span of 1400 – 1250 BC for the chronology.

Recently discovered tree-ring links with the Tinney's track complex chronology by J Hillam add to the complexity of the dating of this structure, which shows little archaeological or tree-ring evidence of reuse to account for the wide range of dates. It is however a period in the calibration curve during which a wide span of BC dates can be read from a single ^{14}C date.

R Morgan: in all cases the wood was quite decayed due to the peat drying out; with the necessary growth allowances added, HAR-1489 and HAR-1494 are consistent with the Meare Heath series, but HAR-1627 is rather later.

HAR-683, HAR-943, Q-52 (2840 ± 110 BP), and Q-53 (3230 ± 110 BP) are not internally consistent, unless we assume that the oak plank (HAR-683) was in fact a reused piece from an older structure; its position in the track suggests a small area where timber was dumped to fill a pool or boggy patch. The sample was taken from the peat section as seen in January 1974 and the plank is likely to have come from a tree at least 50 and possibly 100 years old when felled. The most accurate sample for dating the track is HAR-943; the brushwood was only a very few years old.

HAR-683, HAR-943, HAR-1489, HAR-1627, and HAR-1494 are not internally consistent, the most reliable should be those for the younger wood used in the construction shortly after felling (ie the brushwood and the outermost rings of the sequence). These place the trackway at the end of the second millennium BC. HAR-943 and HAR-1494 date the track.

HAR-683   3290 ± 70 BP

$\delta^{13}C$: −27.0 ‰

Sample: SLP746 (Meare Lake track 1-3), submitted on 21 June 1974

Material: wood: *Quercus* sp..

Initial comment: from a newly discovered trackway in an area hitherto without traces of human activity, beneath 1.0m peat; part of the Meare Heath track (Meare Lake segment).

Calibrated date: 1σ : cal BC 1680 – 1515
                     2σ : cal BC 1740 – 1430

Final comments:
J Coles: the timber dated was probably a reused foundation piece (see HAR-1489).

References: Coles and Coles 1975
                Coles and Orme 1976a
                Coles and Orme 1976c, 300
                Coles and Orme 1978a, 32
                Radiocarbon **19**, 415

HAR-943 2980 ± 70 BP

$\delta^{13}C$: −29.8 ‰

Sample: SLP7411, submitted on 26 November 1974

Material: wood: *Alnus* sp. and *Corylus* sp..

Initial comment: from the brushwood platform, below HAR-683.

Comment on uncalibrated date: this result suggests that the heavy planking (HAR-683) used for the upper layer was already old when put into use; the date also helps to relate this structure to others in the area.

Calibrated date: 1σ : cal BC 1375 – 1100
                     2σ : cal BC 1420 – 1000

Final comments:
J Coles: this date should be close to the time of construction; it agrees well with HAR-1494.

References: Coles and Fordham 1977
               Coles and Orme 1976a
               Coles and Orme 1976c, 300
               Coles and Orme 1978a, 32
               Radiocarbon **21**, 360

HAR-1489 3200 ± 80 BP

$\delta^{13}C$: −26.8 ‰

Sample: SLP761, submitted by R Morgan on 27 January 1976

Material: wood.

Initial comment: from rings 44 – 64 of a 152-year floating tree-ring sequence, taken from two timbers of the Meare Heath track. This sample, HAR-1494, and HAR-1627 each cover 20 annual rings and come from 30-year intervals of a floating 152-year chronology (see objective); each thus requires known adjustment to reach the felling year of the tree and the likely construction year of the trackway (since the survival of sapwood was good).

Comment on uncalibrated date: a growth allowance of about 100 years should be added to give a date of 3300 ± 80 BP.

Calibrated date: 1σ : cal BC 1590 – 1415
                     2σ : cal BC 1680 – 1310

Final comments:
J Coles: with the growth allowance this calibrates to *c* 1330 BC; this is internally consistent with the series.

References: Clark and Morgan 1983
               Coles 1979
               Morgan 1978a, 41
               Morgan 1979
               Radiocarbon **27**, 79

HAR-1494 3060 ± 80 BP

$\delta^{13}C$: −27.2 ‰

Sample: SLP763, submitted by R Morgan on 27 January 1976

Material: wood.

Initial comment: from rings 104 – 24 of a 152-year floating sequence; includes sections from two timbers.

Comment on uncalibrated date: a growth allowance of about 40 years should be added to give a date of 3100 ± 80 BP.

Calibrated date: 1σ : cal BC 1425 – 1225
                     2σ : cal BC 1510 – 1070

Final comments:
J Coles: with the growth allowance this calibrates to *c* 1270 BC, which is internally consistent with the series.

References: Clark and Morgan 1983
               Coles 1979
               Morgan 1978a, 41
               Morgan 1979
               Radiocarbon **27**, 79

HAR-1627 3000 ± 80 BP

$\delta^{13}C$: −26.8 ‰

Sample: SLP762, submitted by R Morgan on 27 January 1976

Material: wood.

Initial comment: from rings 74 – 94 of a 152-year floating sequence, taken from four timbers.

Comment on uncalibrated date: a growth allowance of about 70 years should be added to give a date of 3070 ± 80 BP.

Calibrated date: 1σ : cal BC 1395 – 1105
                     2σ : cal BC 1430 – 1000

Final comments:
J Coles: with the growth allowance this calibrates to *c* 1140 BC; this is internally inconsistent with the series, but agrees with HAR-2538 (Tinney's Ground timber series).

References: Clark and Morgan 1983
               Coles 1979
               Morgan 1978a, 41
               Morgan 1979
               Radiocarbon **27**, 79

HAR-2619 2900 ± 80 BP

$\delta^{13}C$: −27.0 ‰

Sample: SLP7807, submitted on 7 April 1978

Material: peat.

Initial comment: from a horizon of burned peat immediately overlying the Meare Heath track.

Comment on uncalibrated date: this fits the stratigraphy in placing the burned horizon slightly later than the trackway.

Calibrated date: 1σ : cal BC 1260 – 990
                     2σ : cal BC 1380 – 900

Final comments:
J Coles: this helps assess the relative merits of HAR-683 and HAR-943. HAR-2619 must be slightly younger than HAR-943 on stratigraphical grounds. The result agrees with the pollen zone dates SRR-914 and SRR-915 and with Q-53 (peat below the track).

References: Coles 1979
               Radiocarbon **27**, 78 – 9

Somerset Levels: Meare Lake Village West, Somerset

Location: ST 445422
Lat. 51.10.33 N; Long. 02.47.38 W

Excavator: J Coles (Department of the Environment)

Site: Iron Age occupation on the surface of a raised bog north of Meare Island.

References: Coles *et al* 1986
Orme *et al* 1981, 38 (^{14}C)
Orme *et al* 1979, 16 – 17 (^{14}C)

Objectives: to assess the chronological position of the occupation.

Comments:
J Coles: four samples provide dating for the surfaces of the raised bog shortly or immediately before the occupation (HAR-3546, HAR-2620, HAR-3864, and HAR-3891). The major occupation seems to lie between 350 and 100 BC (eleven dates), with some indication of later activity extending down to *c* 1 AD. This occupation at Meare Village West probably precedes part of the activity at Meare Village East (HAR-5000, HAR-5001, and HAR-5002) and may predate the occupation at the Glastonbury Lake Village, although ^{14}C and/or dendrochronological dating is urgently needed for the latter site.

AML: one sample (HAR-3522, SLP7916) was inadequate and abandoned.

HAR-2620   2340 ± 80 BP

$\delta^{13}C$: -26.4 ‰

Sample: SLP7804 (MVW W5), submitted by S Beckett on 7 April 1978

Material: peat.

Initial comment: from a raised bog peat underlying the settlement.

Comment on uncalibrated date: the stratigraphic relationship between the establishment of settlement and environmental conditions in the Levels seems secure on basis of this date and HAR-2654.

Calibrated date: 1σ : cal BC 485 – 380
2σ : cal BC 765 – 200

Final comments:
J Coles: this date marks a late phase of raised bog prior to Iron Age occupation; it agrees well with HAR-3864 from peat below the north mound.

References: Beckett 1979, 19
Coles 1979
Coles and Dobson 1989
Orme *et al* 1979, 16
Radiocarbon **27**, 80

HAR-2654   2200 ± 70 BP

$\delta^{13}C$: -27.6 ‰

Sample: SLP7806 (MVW W6), submitted on 7 April 1978

Material: brushwood.

Initial comment: from the lowest level of settlement.

Calibrated date: 1σ : cal BC 385 – 175
2σ : cal BC 400 – 100

Final comments:
J Coles: this dates the lowest horizon of the lake village; it is in general agreement with the archaeological dating, which suggests that occupation began in the later third century BC or shortly thereafter.

References: Coles 1979
Coles and Dobson 1989
Orme *et al* 1979, 16
Radiocarbon **27**, 80

HAR-2668   2130 ± 90 BP

$\delta^{13}C$: -27.7 ‰

Sample: SLP7805 (MVW W3), submitted on 7 April 1978

Material: wood: *Quercus* sp..

Initial comment: from a stake in a construction (wind break or tent setting).

Calibrated date: 1σ : cal BC 360 – 50
2σ : cal BC 390 – 60 cal AD

Final comments:
J Coles: this dates a major constructional phase of the settlement.

References: Coles and Dobson 1989
Orme *et al* 1979, 16
Radiocarbon **27**, 80

HAR-3489   2200 ± 70 BP

$\delta^{13}C$: -29.7 ‰

Sample: SLP7918, submitted on 26 September 1979

Material: wood: *Alnus* sp..

Initial comment: from planking in a gully between mounds, part of a series of stratified horizons of occupation debris marking several phases of activity; associated with bone, wood, bronze, iron, lead, pottery, and glass.

Calibrated date: 1σ : cal BC 385 – 175
2σ : cal BC 400 – 100

Final comments:
J Coles: as for HAR-2668, but the planking of HAR-3489 was possibly old when dumped, or the sample was taken from an aged segment; alder is not likely to be more than 100 years old when felled.

References: Coles 1979
Coles and Dobson 1989
Orme *et al* 1981, 38
Radiocarbon **30**, 332

HAR-3492   2130 ± 60 BP

$\delta^{13}C$: -25.6 ‰

Sample: SLP7910 (MVW79.3800), submitted on 26 September 1979

Material: wood: *Ulmus* sp..

Initial comment: plank associated with a hearth; part of a series of stratified horizons of peat, wood, and occupation debris marking several phases of activity, associated with bone, wood, bronze, iron, lead, pottery, glass etc.

Calibrated date: 1σ : cal BC 350 – 100
2σ : cal BC 380 – 10

Final comments:
J Coles: this dates an episode of intense activity on a seasonal site; it agrees well with the archaeological dating.

HAR-3521 2830 ± 100 BP

$\delta^{13}C$: –25.0 ‰

Sample: SLP7917 (MVW79.4611), submitted on 26 September 1979

Material: charred wood.

Initial comment: from a plank under a slab on the central hearth on the northern mound; rather a poor sample.

Calibrated date: 1σ : cal BC 1155 – 900
2σ : cal BC 1310 – 810

Final comments:
J Coles: this date is too early for the occupation.

Harwell: an inadequate sample.

HAR-3535 2250 ± 70 BP

$\delta^{13}C$: –26.8 ‰

Sample: SLP7915 (MVW79.3254), submitted on 26 September 1979

Material: peat (blackearth) with charcoal.

Initial comment: from beneath central floor, associated with large storage vessel, occupation deposit, peat, and charcoal.

Calibrated date: 1σ : cal BC 395 – 205
2σ : cal BC 410 – 125

Final comments:
J Coles: the date of this major episode of activity is likely to be in the later section of the two standard deviation range.

References: Coles and Dobson 1989
Orme *et al* 1981, 38
Radiocarbon **30**, 332

HAR-3546 2410 ± 80 BP

$\delta^{13}C$: –28.8 ‰

Sample: SLP7911 (MVW79.3356), submitted on 26 September 1979

Material: peat.

Initial comment: from the peat surface (fissured) which mostly underlies the major occupation.

Calibrated date: 1σ : cal BC 760 – 395
2σ : cal BC 800 – 370

Final comments:
J Coles: this predates the occupation (cf HAR-2620); it agrees with the dating of the upper raised bog.

References: Coles and Dobson 1989
Orme *et al* 1981, 38
Radiocarbon **30**, 333

HAR-3633 2700 ± 70 BP

$\delta^{13}C$: –29.2 ‰

Sample: SLP7913 (MVW79.3358), submitted on 26 September 1979

Material: peat.

Initial comment: from the top of the peat surface underlying the occupation.

Calibrated date: 1σ : cal BC 915 – 805
2σ : cal BC 1000 – 790

Final comments:
J Coles: a little earlier than expected; this suggests that the peat surface was skimmed prior to occupation.

References: Coles and Dobson 1989
Orme *et al* 1981, 38
Radiocarbon **30**, 333

HAR-3634 2230 ± 60 BP

$\delta^{13}C$: –27.6 ‰

Sample: SLP7912, submitted on 26 September 1979

Material: peat with charcoal.

Initial comment: from a black earth occupation deposit.

Calibrated date: 1σ : cal BC 390 – 200
2σ : cal BC 400 – 125

Final comments:
J Coles: this dates the early occupation on the site; it agrees with HAR-2654.

References: Coles and Dobson 1989
Orme *et al* 1981, 38
Radiocarbon **30**, 333

HAR-3693 2170 ± 80 BP

$\delta^{13}C$: –23.3 ‰

Sample: SLP8004 (MVW79.3855), submitted on 3 March 1980

Material: wood: *Ulmus* sp..

Initial comment: from near a hearth on the occupation floor.

Calibrated date: 1σ : cal BC 375 – 110
2σ : cal BC 400 – 10

Final comments:
J Coles: this agrees closely with the archaeological dating of the deposit.

References: Coles and Dobson 1989
Orme *et al* 1981, 38
Radiocarbon **30**, 333

HAR-3719 2190 ± 70 BP

$\delta^{13}C$: –28.0 ‰

Sample: SLP7914 (MVW79.2810), submitted on 26 September 1979

Material: wood.

Initial comment: from the remains of wood under the central floor of the occupation site.

Calibrated date: 1σ : cal BC 380 – 170
                       2σ : cal BC 400 – 90

Final comments:
J Coles: this agrees with the archaeological dating of the occupation.

References: Coles and Dobson 1989
              Orme *et al* 1981, 38
              Radiocarbon **30**, 333

HAR-3740   2810 ± 70 BP

$\delta^{13}C$: –29.6 ‰

Sample: SLP8002 (MVW79.3856), submitted on 3 March 1980

Material: wood.

Initial comment: from the peat surface, to the north-west of the main occupation floor.

Calibrated date: 1σ : cal BC 1045 – 900
                       2σ : cal BC 1250 – 820

Final comments:
J Coles: this predates the occupation surface (see HAR-3633).

References: Coles and Dobson 1989
              Orme *et al* 1981, 38
              Radiocarbon **30**, 333

HAR-3744   2280 ± 80 BP

$\delta^{13}C$: –27.3 ‰

Sample: SLP8003 (MVW79.3273), submitted on 3 March 1980

Material: wood and peat.

Initial comment: from an occupation surface.

Calibrated date: 1σ : cal BC 400 – 235
                       2σ : cal BC 520 – 170

Final comments:
J Coles: this agrees with the archaeological dating of the occupation.

References: Coles and Dobson 1989
            Orme *et al* 1981, 38
            Radiocarbon **30**, 333

HAR-3745   2080 ± 60 BP

$\delta^{13}C$: –28.5 ‰

Sample: SLP8001 (MVW79.3241), submitted on 3 March 1980

Material: charcoal in clay soil.

Initial comment: from the central occupation floor.

Calibrated date: 1σ : cal BC 185 – 35
                     2σ : cal BC 355 – 50 cal AD

Final comments:
J Coles: this agrees with the archaeological dating.

References: Coles and Dobson 1989
            Orme *et al* 1981, 38

HAR-3864   2370 ± 70 BP

$\delta^{13}C$: –28.6 ‰

Sample: SLP8005 (MVW79.4583A), submitted on 7 May 1980

Material: peat, with a few very fine rootlets in the samples.

Initial comment: from a peat monolith base 2.98 – 3.00m OD, below occupation on the northern mound.

Calibrated date: 1σ : cal BC 525 – 390
                     2σ : cal BC 770 – 265

Final comments:
J Coles: this predates the occupation; it agrees with peat date HAR-2620.

References: Coles and Dobson 1989
            Orme *et al* 1981, 38

HAR-3891   2210 ± 70 BP

$\delta^{13}C$: –28.0 ‰

Sample: SLP8006 (MVW79.4583B), submitted on 7 May 1980

Material: peat.

Initial comment: from a peat monolith, 3.04 – 3.06m OD, just below and prior to occupation on the northmound.

Calibrated date: 1σ : cal BC 390 – 185
                     2σ : cal BC 400 – 100

Final comments:
J Coles: this dates an increase in agricultural activity. The result agrees broadly with the F/G pollen zone boundary from Meare Heath (SRR-912) and an estimated date from the Abbot's Way sequence.

References: Coles and Dobson 1989
            Orme *et al* 1981, 38
            Radiocarbon **30**, 334

HAR-3892   1870 ± 70 BP

$\delta^{13}C$: –28.3 ‰

Sample: SLP8007 (MVW79.4583C), submitted on 7 May 1980

Material: peat with charcoal.

Initial comment: from a peat monolith 3.10 – 3.12m OD; lower occupation deposit on the northern mound.

Comment on uncalibrated date: rather recent, cf other occupation dates such as HAR-3492.

Calibrated date: 1σ : cal AD 65 – 230
                   2σ : cal BC 30 – 330 cal AD

Final comments:
J Coles: this should date earlier occupation; it does not agree with HAR-3896 above.

References: Coles and Dobson 1989
            Orme *et al* 1981, 38
            Radiocarbon **30**, 334

HAR-3896 2220 ± 90 BP

$\delta^{13}C$: −27.8 ‰

Sample: SLP8008 (MVW79.4583D), submitted on 7 May 1980

Material: peat.

Initial comment: from a peat monolith 3.14 – 3.16m OD; upper occupation deposit.

Calibrated date: 1σ : cal BC 395 – 175
2σ : cal BC 410 – 50

Final comments:
J Coles: somewhat older than expected; it should date occupation of the first century AD. This does not agree with HAR-3892 below; if these two dates were reversed they would make more sense stratigraphically.

References: Coles and Dobson 1989
Orme *et al* 1981, 38
Radiocarbon **30**, 334

Somerset Levels: Meare Village, West Meare, Somerset

Location: ST 445422
Lat. 51.10.33 N; Long. 02.47.38 W

Excavator: J Coles (Department of the Environment)

References: Coles 1979
Coles and Dobson 1989, 67 (^{14}C)
Orme 1982
Radiocarbon **27**, 80 (^{14}C)

Objectives: to assess the chronological position of the peat-clay interface in the northern part of the Levels.

HAR-2616 5210 ± 80 BP

$\delta^{13}C$: −29.5 ‰

Sample: SLP7803 (MVW W10), submitted by S Beckett on 7 April 1978

Material: peat.

Initial comment: from the peat – clay interface beneath fen peat.

Comment on uncalibrated date: this date is comparable with, but slightly younger than, those dates (HAR-1831 and HAR-1856) from the equivalent marine clay – upper peat interface further south in the Somerset Levels.

Calibrated date: 1σ : cal BC 4220 – 3975
2σ : cal BC 4240 – 3815

Final comments:
J Coles: this agrees with HAR-7064 (Meare Village East) which dates the stratigraphically later A/B pollen zone boundary; see also HAR-1857.

Somerset Levels: Meare, Meare Heath Field 12.3, Somerset

Location: ST 44654115
Lat. 51.09.59 N; Long. 02.47.30 W

Excavator: J Coles (Department of the Environment)

Site: a Bronze Age track.

References: Coles 1979
Coles and Dobson 1989, 68 (^{14}C)
Orme 1982
Radiocarbon **27**, 78 (^{14}C)

Objectives: to assess the chronological position of wood at the terminal of Meare Heath track.

HAR-2428 4580 ± 60 BP

$\delta^{13}C$: −27.9 ‰

Sample: SLP773, submitted on 29 September 1977

Material: wood, collected by S Beckett.

Initial comment: a small piece of wood from the terminal area of the Meare Heath Bronze Age track (not part of the actual construction).

Comment on uncalibrated date: this date is older than the series from track timbers to the south including HAR-943 (Coles and Orme 1978a) area, but was not part of construction.

Calibrated date: 1σ : cal BC 3375 – 3140
2σ : cal BC 3510 – 3050

Final comments:
J Coles: this is unconnected to Meare Heath track, but possibly marks an earlier episode of activity at the base of Meare Island.

Somerset Levels: Meare, Stileway, Somerset

Location: ST 546408
Lat. 51.09.51 N; Long. 02.38.58 W

Excavator: J Coles (Department of the Environment)

References: Coles 1979
Coles and Dobson 1989, 67 (^{14}C)
Orme 1982

Objectives: to assess the chronological position of the peat-clay interface in the northern part of the Levels.

HAR-1465 4470 ± 70 BP

$\delta^{13}C$: −26.7 ‰

Sample: SLP7515, submitted by M Girling on 3 September 1975

Material: peat.

Initial comment: twigs from peat *c* 0.15m above the Jurassic clay.

Comment on uncalibrated date: this dates an episode of peat formation shortly after the onset of freshwater flooding in the eastern part of the Brue Valley.

Calibrated date: 1σ : cal BC 3340 – 2950
2σ : cal BC 3370 – 2920

Final comments:
J Coles: this dates the transition to freshwater conditions and agrees with HAR-1856 and HAR-1857; this date confirms the Neolithic and Bronze Age date of the beetle fauna from the peat sequence.

Somerset Levels: Meare, Stileway, Somerset

Location: ST 546408
Lat. 51.09.51 N; Long. 02.38.58 W

Excavator: J Coles (Department of the Environment)

Site: remnants of wooden trackways and platforms.

References: Coles 1979
Coles and Dobson 1989
Girling 1985
Orme *et al* 1985b, 79 (^{14}C)

Objectives: to assess the chronological position of a series of structures.

HAR-1221 3050 ± 70 BP

$δ^{13}C:$ −29.0 ‰

Sample: SLP753, submitted on 8 July 1975

Material: wood.

Initial comment: from wooden structure running towards Glastonbury.

Comment on uncalibrated date: this dates a feature in a new archaeological area and adds to the growing number of structures of the later second millennium.

Calibrated date: 1σ : cal BC 1415 – 1225
2σ : cal BC 1495 – 1100

Final comments:
J Coles: one of a series of unconnected platforms (possibly for hunting) just off the edge of Meare Island.

References: Coles and Fordham 1977
Coles and Orme 1978c, 92
Radiocarbon **21**, 362

HAR-4477 2810 ± 90 BP

$δ^{13}C:$ −25.0 ‰

Sample: SLP8103, submitted on 12 June 1981

Material: wood.

Initial comment: from a structure at a complex Bronze Age site in raised bog peat; same area as HAR-1221, but a younger structure.

Calibrated date: 1σ : cal BC 1095 – 845
2σ : cal BC 1260 – 810

Final comments:
J Coles: same period of activity as seen elsewhere in structures to the south of Meare Island.

References: Coles and Orme 1985
Orme 1982
Radiocarbon **29**, 88

Somerset Levels: Sedgemoor, Chedzoy Tracks, Somerset

Location: ST 356371
Lat. 51.07.44 N; Long. 02.55.14 W

Excavator: J Coles (Department of the Environment)

Site: from a prehistoric structure of wood, observed in a field drain.

References: Coles and Dobson 1989
Coles and Orme 1985
Norman and Clements 1979
Radiocarbon **30**, 335 (^{14}C)

Objectives: to assess the chronological position of the wooden structure.

HAR-4374 4510 ± 80 BP

$δ^{13}C:$ −28.6 ‰

Sample: SLP8101, submitted on 1 July 1981

Material: wood.

Initial comment: from site 81.6A.

Comment on uncalibrated date: this suggests an episode of activity on Sedgemoor which matches that in the Brue Valley to the north.

Calibrated date: 1σ : cal BC 3355 – 3040
2σ : cal BC 3495 – 2925

Final comments:
J Coles: this extends the range of brushwood structures over both Sedgemoor and the Brue Valley in the late fourth millennium BC; cf Garvin's tracks and the Honeygore complex.

HAR-4375 4690 ± 90 BP

$δ^{13}C:$ −28.3 ‰

Sample: SLP8102, submitted on 1 April 1981

Material: wood.

Initial comment: from site 81.6B.

Comment on uncalibrated date: as for HAR-4374; the dates should be very closely related.

Calibrated date: 1σ : cal BC 3625 – 3360
2σ : cal BC 3690 – 3135

Final comments:
J Coles: as for HAR-4374; the date range falls within the Baker platform series.

Somerset Levels: Shapwick Heath, Decoy Pool Wood, Somerset

Location: ST 42284010
Lat. 51.09.24 N; Long. 02.49.32 W

Excavator: J Coles (Department of the Environment)

Site: a peat bog with occasional stray finds.

References: Coles and Dobson 1989
Orme 1982
Radiocarbon **30**, 332 (^{14}C)

Objectives: to date a stone axe of local character.

HAR-4130   4280 ± 70 BP

$\delta^{13}C$: −28.0 ‰

Sample: SLP8011, submitted on 1 November 1980

Material: peat.

Initial comment: peat in direct association with a Neolithic stone axe (SF 80.37).

Calibrated date: 1σ : cal BC 3015 − 2785
2σ : cal BC 3080 − 2665

Final comments:
J Coles: this is contemporary with wooden structures in adjacent areas (HAR-682, HAR-1383, and HAR-1470).

Somerset Levels: Shapwick Heath, Skinners Wood, Somerset

Location: ST 416404
Lat. 51.09.34 N; Long. 02.50.07 W

Excavator: J Coles (Department of the Environment)

Site: a series of trackways built during flooding and associated with wooden objects.

References: Coles and Dobson 1989
Coles and Orme 1978d; 114, 118 (^{14}C)
Orme 1982

Objectives: to provide dates for the associated objects.

HAR-650   2360 ± 70 BP

$\delta^{13}C$: −25.9 ‰

Sample: Skinner's Wood, submitted on 4 June 1974

Material: wood: *Fraxinus* sp..

Initial comment: from a vertical peg under *c* 1.0m of peat; this represents the sole surviving element of a brushwood trackway.

Calibrated date: 1σ : cal BC 515 − 390
2σ : cal BC 765 − 255

Final comments:
J Coles: this provides a time frame for a complex of wooden structures observed during their complete destruction in 1974 − 5 and 1990.

References: Coles and Coles 1975
Radiocarbon **19**, 415

HAR-1159   3330 ± 70 BP

$\delta^{13}C$: −28.1 ‰

Sample: SLP751, submitted on 30 April 1975

Material: peat.

Initial comment: taken from beside a Bronze Age wooden pitchfork, sealed beneath 0.5m of peat, the stratigraphy of which follows the standard sequence.

Calibrated date: 1σ : cal BC 1735 − 1525
2σ : cal BC 1870 − 1450

Final comments:
J Coles: this result dates a unique implement.

References: Coles and Fordham 1977
Radiocarbon **21**, 361

HAR-1843   3770 ± 80 BP

$\delta^{13}C$: −27.7 ‰

Sample: SLP764, submitted on 14 June 1976

Material: peat.

Initial comment: adjacent to a hoard of flint flakes preserved with grass or moss packing.

Calibrated date: 1σ : cal BC 2335 − 2045
2σ : cal BC 2460 − 1970

Final comments:
J Coles: this provides a date for an unusual lithic assembly.

References: *Radiocarbon* **27**, 77

Somerset Levels: Shapwick Heath, Sweet Track, Somerset

Location: ST 425410
Lat. 51.09.54 N; Long. 02.49.19 W

Excavator: J Coles (Department of the Environment)

References: Coles 1979
Coles and Dobson 1989, 67 (^{14}C)
Coles and Orme 1976b
Coles and Orme 1979
Orme 1982
Radiocarbon **27**, 78 (^{14}C)

Objectives: to assess the chronological position of the peat − clay interface in the northern part of the Levels.

HAR-1857   5290 ± 80 BP

$\delta^{13}C$: −27.6 ‰

Sample: SLP765, submitted on 26 July 1976

Material: peat.

Initial comment: from interface between lower marine clay and peat formation.

Comment on uncalibrated date: this dates the transition to freshwater conditions in Levels.

Calibrated date: 1σ : cal BC 4240 − 4000
2σ : cal BC 4340 − 3970

Final comments:
J Coles: agrees with HAR-2616, HAR-1831, and HAR-1856 in marking the gradual transition from brackish conditions to freshwater reed swamp in the northern part of the Levels.

Somerset Levels: Shapwick Heath, Withy Bed Copse, Somerset

Location: ST 435394
Lat. 51.09.02 N; Long. 02.48.28 W

Excavator: J Coles (Department of the Environment)

Site: a dismantled structure at the edge of the fen, originally beneath 1 – 2m of peat (0.2m in 1974).

References: Coles and Dobson 1989
Coles *et al* 1975a
Orme 1982, 12 – 13 (^{14}C)

Objectives: to assess the chronological position of timbers at the base of Polden Hills.

HAR-944   2740 ± 70 BP

$\delta^{13}C$: –28.6 ‰

Sample: SLP7412, submitted on 26 November 1974

Material: wood: *Quercus* sp..

Initial comment: from the timbers of the dismantled structure.

Comment on uncalibrated date: this date provides a useful reference for relating this material to other known structures to the north and east of this site.

Calibrated date: 1σ : cal BC 985 – 825
2σ : cal BC 1050 – 800

Final comments:
J Coles: agrees well with Westhay track (Q-308) and Vipers track (Q-312), but somewhat earlier than the adjacent Shapwich Heath track (Q-39).

References: Coles and Fordham 1977
Radiocarbon **21**, 361

HAR-3446   2630 ± 80 BP

$\delta^{13}C$: –27.7 ‰

Sample: SLP7909, submitted on 5 September 1979

Material: brushwood.

Initial comment: associated with a pottery vessel and wooden platform.

Comment on uncalibrated date: appears to be contemporary with the timbers (HAR-944).

Calibrated date: 1σ : cal BC 845 – 790
2σ : cal BC 930 – 540

Somerset Levels: Shapwick Terminal Site 1, Shapwick Heath, Somerset

Location: ST 42653962
Lat. 51.09.09 N; Long. 02.49.12 W

Excavator: J Coles (Department of the Environment)

Site: a reported massive timber platform at the base of the Polden Hills.

References: Coles and Dobson 1989
Coles and Orme 1979
Orme 1982

Objectives: to assess the chronological position of the platform.

HAR-2772   3270 ± 70 BP

$\delta^{13}C$: –30.7 ‰

Sample: SLP7809, submitted on 27 September 1978

Material: wood.

Initial comment: from the terminal of the Bronze Age trackways.

Comment on uncalibrated date: this date is rather too early for close connections with the first-millennium trackways to the north (Q-311, Q-313, and Q-312).

Calibrated date: 1σ : cal BC 1670 – 1465
2σ : cal BC 1735 – 1420

Final comments:
J Coles: this probably reflects earlier activity at the edge of the raised bog, perhaps related to Meare Heath (HAR-683).

Somerset Levels: Shapwick, Sweet Track Heath, Somerset

Location: ST 42534103
Lat. 51.09.54 N; Long. 02.49.19 W

Excavator: J Coles (Department of the Environment)

Site: a Neolithic trackway running north – south across the Levels, probably from the Polden hills to Meare – Westhay I. All the samples in this series are from the Sweet Track Railway site.

References: Beckett 1979
Clark and Morgan 1983
Coles 1972
Coles 1979
Coles 1989
Coles and Coles 1975
Coles and Coles 1988
Coles and Dobson 1989
Coles and Fordham 1977
Coles and Hibbert 1975
Coles and Orme 1976a
Coles and Orme 1976b
Coles and Orme 1976c
Coles and Orme 1977a
Coles and Orme 1977b
Coles and Orme 1978a
Coles and Orme 1978b
Coles and Orme 1978c
Coles and Orme 1978d
Coles and Orme 1979
Coles and Orme 1980
Coles and Orme 1981

Coles and Orme 1984
Coles and Orme 1985
Coles, Caseldine, and Morgan 1988
Coles, Orme, and Hibbert 1975
Coles *et al* 1970
Coles *et al* 1975a
Coles *et al* 1975b
Coles *et al* 1980
Coles *et al* 1982
Coles *et al* 1985a
Coles *et al* 1985b
Coles *et al* 1986
Coles *et al* 1988
Girling 1985
Godwin 1960
Morgan 1978a
Morgan 1978b
Morgan 1979
Morgan 1980a
Morgan 1982a
Morgan 1988
Norman and Clements 1979
Orme 1982
Orme *et al* 1979
Orme *et al* 1980
Orme *et al* 1981
Orme *et al* 1982
Orme *et al* 1985a
Orme *et al* 1985b

Objectives: as part of the dendrochronological studies included in the Somerset Levels project, a number of samples taken from this track were submitted in order to attempt the wiggle-matching of a series of ^{14}C dates from a floating oak tree-ring chronology against the bristle-cone pine calibration curve. Each sample, covering fifteen annual rings, was selected from 40-year intervals of a 314-year floating chronology established on 129 oak timbers from the track. This chronology was later extended by the correlation of further tree-ring patterns to 410 years, the last ring being the year of felling of at least some of the trees. Subsequently a revised chronology was dated to 4202 – 3807/3806 BC (Hillam *et al* 1990).

Comments:
R Morgan: a survey of the results shows two anomalies – the very late date of the earliest sample (HAR-1379) and the large gap between HAR-1477 and HAR-1478 of almost 1000 years, although these came from the same wood sample.

The remaining dates show a fairly consistent trend in direction, though suggesting some variation in ^{14}C level. For example pairs HAR-1475/6 and HAR-1364/1469 give almost identical results and yet are 80 years apart in calendar years. The rather younger date between (HAR-1478) may suggest the presence of a 'wiggle'.

(1991) the dendrochronological dating shows three of the paired dates (HAR-1472/3, HAR-1475/6, and HAR-1384/1469) to be quite consistent, but all these dates are too young by 100 – 900 years. With the growth allowance added to the ^{14}C dates, and the results calibrated, the six final values should be approximately contemporary; with the much too recent HAR-1379, the results span some 400 years.

HAR-1379   4550 ± 70 BP

$\delta^{13}C$: −27.2 ‰

Sample: SLP759, submitted on 22 October 1975

Material: wood.

Initial comment: from annual rings 58-73 (earliest) of the tree-ring sequence; includes sections cut from nine timbers.

Comment on uncalibrated date: younger than expected; this should antedate the construction of the track by some 300 years. Without growth allowance this calibrates to *c* 3210 BC; with growth allowance this calibrates to *c* 2890 BC.

Calibrated date: 1σ : cal BC 3370 – 3105
                     2σ : cal BC 3500 – 3040

Final comments:
J Coles: inconsistent with the series. A dendrochronological date of 4120 BC shows that this is 900 years too young.

References: Radiocarbon **21**, 363

HAR-1384   5030 ± 90 BP

$\delta^{13}C$: −27.1 ‰

Sample: SLP7513 (1), submitted on 22 October 1975

Material: wood.

Initial comment: from rings 218 – 33; includes sections from twelve timbers (see HAR-1469).

Comment on uncalibrated date: both this result and that from HAR-1469 agree with the site date and tree-ring series; averaged with HAR-1469, without growth allowance added, this calibrates to *c* 3850 BC; with growth allowance it calibrates to *c* 3770 BC.

Calibrated date: 1σ : cal BC 3970 – 3705
                     2σ : cal BC 4030 – 3640

Final comments:
J Coles: averaged with HAR-1469, this date is within 100 years of the dendrochronological date of 3960 BC and is consistent with the series.

References: Radiocarbon **21**, 364

HAR-1469   5110 ± 90 BP

$\delta^{13}C$: −27.0 ‰

Sample: SLP7513 (2), submitted on 22 October 1975

Material: wood.

Initial comment: as HAR-1384.

Calibrated date: 1σ : cal BC 4030 – 3790
                     2σ : cal BC 4220 – 3705

Final comments:
J Coles: as for HAR-1384.

References: Radiocarbon **21**, 364

HAR-1472   5070 ± 80 BP

$\delta^{13}C$: −26.2 ‰

Sample: SLP7510 (1), submitted on 28 November 1975

Material: wood.

Initial comment: from rings 98 – 113; includes sections cut from sixteen timbers (see also HAR-1473).

Comment on uncalibrated date: this corresponds well with the site and date expected from the tree-ring evidence. Averaged with HAR-1473, without growth allowance added, this calibrates to *c* 3850 BC; with growth allowance it calibrates to *c* 3590 BC.

Calibrated date: 1σ : cal BC 3985 – 3785
   2σ : cal BC 4035 – 3700

Final comments:
J Coles: averaged with HAR-1473, this date is 200 years earlier than the dendrochronological date of 4080 BC and consistent with the series.

Harwell: rootlets and insect infestation were present in the original material.

References: *Radiocarbon* **21**, 363

HAR-1473   4940 ± 150 BP

$\delta^{13}C$: –27.2 ‰

Sample: SLP7510 (2), submitted on 28 November 1975

Material: wood.

Initial comment: as HAR-1472.

Calibrated date: 1σ : cal BC 3950 – 3540
   2σ : cal BC 4040 – 3370

Final comments:
J Coles: as for HAR-1472.

Harwell: unreliable result determined from residue reburn after zero result in acetylene preparation.

References: *Radiocarbon* **21**, 363

HAR-1475   5020 ± 100 BP

$\delta^{13}C$: –27.3 ‰

Sample: SLP7511 (1), submitted on 22 October 1975

Material: wood.

Initial comment: from rings 138 – 53; includes sections from eleven timbers (see also HAR-1476).

Comment on uncalibrated date: this result and HAR-1476 are consistent with the site dating and tree ring series. Averaged with HAR-1476, without growth allowance added, calibrates to *c* 3850 BC; with growth allowance added it calibrates to *c* 3670 BC.

Calibrated date: 1σ : cal BC 3970 – 3700
   2σ : cal BC 4035 – 3630

Final comments:
J Coles: averaged with HAR-1476, this date is 200 years earlier than the dendrochronological date of 4040 BC and is consistent with the series.

References: *Radiocarbon* **21**, 363

HAR-1476   5110 ± 90 BP

$\delta^{13}C$: –26.6 ‰

Sample: SLP7511 (2), submitted on 22 October 1975

Material: wood.

Initial comment: see HAR-1475.

Calibrated date: 1σ : cal BC 4030 – 3790
   2σ : cal BC 4220 – 3705

Final comments:
J Coles: as for HAR-1475.

Harwell: there were rootlets and insect infestation in the original material.

References: *Radiocarbon* **21**, 363

HAR-1477   3940 ± 90 BP

$\delta^{13}C$: –27.0 ‰

Sample: SLP7512 (1), submitted on 22 October 1975

Material: wood.

Initial comment: from rings 178 – 93; includes sections cut from twelve timbers (see also HAR-1478).

Calibrated date: 1σ : cal BC 2575 – 2335
   2σ : cal BC 2860 – 2145

Final comments:
J Coles: this date is rejected.

Harwell: there were rootlets and insect contamination in the original material.

References: *Radiocarbon* **21**, 364

HAR-1478   4800 ± 90 BP

$\delta^{13}C$: –26.4 ‰

Sample: SLP7512 (2), submitted on 22 October 1975

Material: wood.

Initial comment: as HAR-1477.

Comment on uncalibrated date: slightly younger than expected. Without growth allowance this calibrates to *c* 3630 BC; with growth allowance added it calibrates to *c* 3370 BC.

Calibrated date: 1σ : cal BC 3695 – 3385
   2σ : cal BC 3780 – 3370

Final comments:
J Coles: having rejected the duplicate sample HAR-1477, this date alone is 400 years too young compared to the dendrochronological date of 4000 BC; it is not very consistent with the series.

References: *Radiocarbon* **21**, 364

HAR-1479   4710 ± 100 BP

$\delta^{13}C$: –27.2 ‰

Sample: SLP7514 (1), submitted on 22 October 1975

Material: wood.

Initial comment: from rings 258 – 73; includes sections from nine timbers (see also HAR-1480).

Comment on uncalibrated date: slightly younger than expected. Averaged with HAR-1480, without growth allowance added, this calibrates to *c* 3570 BC; with growth allowance added it calibrates to *c* 3470 BC.

Calibrated date: 1σ : cal BC 3635 – 3360
2σ : cal BC 3770 – 3135

Final comments:
J Coles: averaged with HAR-1480, this date is about 350 years too young compared with the dendrochronolgical date of 3290 BC.

Harwell: there were rootlets and insect contamination in the original material.

References: Radiocarbon **21**, 364

HAR-1480 4870 ± 80 BP

$\delta^{13}C$: –26.6 ‰

Sample: SLP7514 (2), submitted on 22 October 1975

Material: wood.

Initial comment: as HAR-1479.

Calibrated date: 1σ : cal BC 3775 – 3540
2σ : cal BC 3905 – 3385

Final comments:
J Coles: as for HAR-1479.

Harwell: as HAR-1479.

References: Radiocarbon **21**, 361

Somerset Levels: Shapwick, Sweet Track Terminal Site, Somerset

Location: ST 42954180
Lat. 51.10.19 N; Long. 02.48.58 W

Excavator: J Coles (Department of the Environment)

Site: Westhay, field SWX/SWY.

References: Coles and Dobson 1989
Coles and Orme 1979
Coles and Orme 1985

Objectives: to date wood from the terminal area to the north.

HAR-4541 5780 ± 100 BP

$\delta^{13}C$: –26.2 ‰

Sample: SLP8104, submitted on 14 July 1981

Material: wood: *Quercus* sp..

Initial comment: from field SWX/SWY, terminal area of the Sweet Track.

Calibrated date: 1σ : cal BC 4780 – 4520
2σ : cal BC 4900 – 4401

Final comments:
J Coles: this wood does not appear to relate to the Sweet Track.

Somerset Levels: Sharpham, Durston's Works, Somerset

Location: ST 45873846
Lat. 51.08.32 N; Long. 02.46.26 W

Excavator: J Coles (Department of the Environment)

Site: a peat quarry extended down into the underlying clays.

References: Coles 1979
Coles and Dobson 1989, 67 (^{14}C)
Orme 1982
Radiocarbon **27**, 77 (^{14}C)

Objectives: to provide a date for the lower peat horizon buried in marine clays.

HAR-1855 6520 ± 90 BP

$\delta^{13}C$: –29.8 ‰

Sample: SLP767, submitted on 26 July 1976

Material: peat.

Initial comment: from lower peat deposit beneath clay 2.0m thick, an early peat formation in a trough of the Levels prior to marine inundation.

Comment on uncalibrated date: agrees with Q-134 at Burnham-on-Sea (6262 ± 130 BP).

Calibrated date: 1σ : cal BC 5500 – 5355
2σ : cal BC 5620 – 5245

Final comments:
J Coles: This provides an indicator of the time range of the marine inundation bracketed by this date, HAR-1831, HAR-1856, and HAR-1857.

Somerset Levels: Sharpham, Tinney's Ground, Somerset

Location: ST 470382
Lat. 51.08.24 N; Long. 02.45.28 W

Excavator: J Coles (Department of the Environment)

Site: an area where multiple tracks were built leading from the promontory settlement towards Glastonbury Tor.

References: Coles and Dobson 1989
Coles and Orme 1978b
Coles and Orme 1980
Coles *et al* 1975b
Morgan 1978b
Morgan 1980a, 72 (^{14}C)
Orme 1982

Objectives: to assess the chronological positions of a series of brushwood tracks in raised peat bogs.

HAR-2538 and HAR-2544 (two wood samples spanning 20 years each from a 100-year interval) were submitted for dating from a 246-year floating oak tree-ring chronology. It was hoped that the dates would help indicate the exact times pan of the chronology, which was based on planks reused beneath several brushwood bundle trackways. No sapwood survived on the planks, so the felling year of the trees cannot be estimated with any real precision.

Comments:
R Morgan: when growth allowances of 170+ years and 70+ years (approximate in the absence of sapwood on the planks) are added to these two results, they provide very consistent felling dates for the tree of around 950 – 900 BC. When

calibrated (Pearson *et al* 1986), these dates move back to a range of 1150 – 1050 BC. The planks were reused under a series of brushwood tracks, but probably within a relatively short time (too short to be detectable from ^{14}C dating); the dating exercise was done to assist in fixing the floating tree-ring chronology, not to date the trackways, for which dates on brushwood are more precise.

Links between the tree-ring curve for Tinney's and the Meare Heath tracks (made by J Hillam in 1978) show the latter to be at least 70 – 80 years earlier in date. The ^{14}C results can also be related; HAR-1627 is now known to cover the same time span in calendar years as HAR-2538 and the ^{14}C determinations are close.

HAR-681   3040 ± 70 BP

$\delta^{13}C$: –27.7 ‰

Sample: SLP749 (Tinney's track A), submitted on 21 June 1974

Material: wood.

Initial comment: from newly discovered track A (head 18.7) beneath 0.75m of *Eriophorum-Sphagnum* peat.

Comment on uncalibrated date: agrees with the stratigraphic position on the peat; young wood.

Calibrated date: 1σ : cal BC 1410 – 1220
        2σ : cal BC 1450 – 1070

Final comments:
J Coles: agrees with HAR-684 and HAR-945 (same structure) and HAR-946, HAR-947, and HAR-948 (adjacent structures).

References: Coles and Coles 1975
      Coles and Orme 1978b, 73
      Radiocarbon **19**, 415

HAR-684   3020 ± 70 BP

$\delta^{13}C$: –28.9 ‰

Sample: SLP7410 (Tinney's track A), submitted on 21 June 1974

Material: wood.

Initial comment: from newly discovered track A (head 17.7) in complex of multiple structures beneath 0.75m *Eriophorum-Sphagnum* peat.

Comment on uncalibrated date: as for HAR-681.

Calibrated date: 1σ : cal BC 1400 – 1165
        2σ : cal BC 1430 – 1040

Final comments:
J Coles: as for HAR-681.

References: Coles and Coles 1975
      Radiocarbon **19**, 415

HAR-945   3040 ± 70 BP

$\delta^{13}C$: –29.3 ‰

Sample: SLP7413 (Tinney's track A), submitted on 26 November 1974

Material: wood.

Initial comment: from the brushwood (head 1-2) of the wooden track A.

Comment on uncalibrated date: this confirms the projected uninterrupted trackway (see HAR-681 and HAR-684) across the peatfield.

Calibrated date: 1σ : cal BC 1410 – 1220
        2σ : cal BC 1450 – 1070

Final comments:
J Coles: as above. This sample comes from ST 469382 (Lat. 51.08.24 N; Long. 02.45.33 W).

References: Coles and Fordham 1977
      Coles and Orme 1978b, 73
      Radiocarbon **21**, 361

HAR-946   2950 ± 80 BP

$\delta^{13}C$: –30.0 ‰

Sample: SLP7414 (Tinney's track), submitted on 26 November 1974

Material: wood.

Initial comment: from the brushwood (head 1-2) of a trackway adjacent to track A.

Comment on uncalibrated date: this result indicates the general contemporaneity of the trackways close to one another (see HAR-945).

Calibrated date: 1σ : cal BC 1310 – 1035
        2σ : cal BC 1410 – 930

Final comments:
J Coles: as above. This sample came from ST 469382 (Lat. 51.08.24 N; Long. 02.45.33 W).

References: Coles and Fordham 1977
      Radiocarbon **21**, 361

HAR-947   2960 ± 70 BP

$\delta^{13}C$: –29.4 ‰

Sample: SLP7415 (Tinney's track B), submitted on 26 November 1974

Material: wood.

Initial comment: from brushwood of the wooden track B (head 1-2).

Comment on uncalibrated date: as HAR-946, contemporary with track A.

Calibrated date: 1σ : cal BC 1310 – 1055
        2σ : cal BC 1410 – 990

Final comments:
J Coles: as above.

References: Coles and Fordham 1977
      Radiocarbon **21**, 361

HAR-948   3020 ± 70 BP

$\delta^{13}C$: –28.0 ‰

Sample: SLP7416 (Tinney's track B), submitted on 26 November 1974

Material: wood.

Initial comment: from the brushwood of wooden track B (head 9-10); structure continuing across the peat bog.

Comment on uncalibrated date: as HAR-947.

Calibrated date: 1σ : cal BC 1400 – 1165
2σ : cal BC 1430 – 1040

Final comments:
J Coles: as above.

References: Coles and Fordham 1977
Coles and Orme 1978b, 73
Radiocarbon **21**, 361

HAR-2243 3480 ± 90 BP

$\delta^{13}C$: –29.1 ‰

Sample: SLP772, submitted on 10 August 1977

Material: peat, collected by S Coleman.

Initial comment: found immediately below the lowest wooden structure, track A.

Comment on uncalibrated date: this date is at variance with the other Tinney's track A dates (HAR-945, HAR-948, and HAR-681), and conflicts with the observed stratigraphy of the track and with the tree-ring evidence.

Calibrated date: 1σ : cal BC 1925 – 1690
2σ : cal BC 2040 – 1540

Final comments:
J Coles: as above. Variation from the expected result could be due to exposure of more ancient peats if the surface was scraped flat prior to the construction of the track.

References: Coles 1979
Coles and Orme 1978b, 73
Radiocarbon **27**, 78

HAR-2429 2920 ± 60 BP

$\delta^{13}C$: –29.6 ‰

Sample: SLP774 (Tinney's track B), submitted on 29 September 1977

Material: wood, collected by S M Fordham.

Initial comment: from the lowest roundwood of a major Bronze Age track, track B.

Comment on uncalibrated date: HAR-947 and HAR-948 relate to other exposures of the same track.

Calibrated date: 1σ : cal BC 1260 – 1020
2σ : cal BC 1370 – 930

Final comments:
J Coles: contemporary with track A and presumably the whole series of structures in the same raised bog.

References: Coles 1979
Radiocarbon **27**, 78

HAR-2538 3050 ± 70 BP

$\delta^{13}C$: –25.4 ‰

Sample: SLP7801, submitted by R Morgan on 1 February 1978

Material: wood.

Initial comment: waterlogged oak, rings 120 – 40, from the planking of the track A, Tinney's Ground.

Comment on uncalibrated date: with growth allowance, this gives a felling date of after 930 ± 70 BC.

Calibrated date: 1σ : cal BC 1415 – 1225
2σ : cal BC 1495 – 1100

Final comments:
J Coles: calibrates to 1050/1090 BC, the expected date range for the structure, and consistent with the related sample HAR-2544.

References: Clark and Morgan 1983
Coles 1979
Morgan 1979
Morgan 1980a
Radiocarbon **27**, 79

HAR-2544 2990 ± 60 BP

$\delta^{13}C$: –26.3 ‰

Sample: SLP7802, submitted by R Morgan on 1 March 1978

Material: wood.

Initial comment: waterlogged oak, rings 220 – 40, from the planking of the track A, Tinney's Ground.

Comment on uncalibrated date: with growth allowance this gives a felling date of after 970 ± 60 BC.

Calibrated date: 1σ : cal BC 1375 – 1130
2σ : cal BC 1410 – 1030

Final comments:
J Coles: calibrates to 1070/1140 BC, the expected date range for the structure, and consistent with the related sample HAR-2538.

References: Clark and Morgan 1983
Coles 1979
Morgan 1979
Morgan 1980a
Radiocarbon **27**, 79

HAR-2773 2960 ± 70 BP

$\delta^{13}C$: –29.7 ‰

Sample: SLP7808 (Tinney's track D), submitted on 27 September 1978

Material: wood.

Initial comment: from brushwood trackway intersection with oak planking and wooden artefacts.

Comment on uncalibrated date: agrees well with dates for a group of Bronze Age structures in the same area.

Calibrated date: 1σ : cal BC 1310 – 1055
2σ : cal BC 1410 – 990

Final comments:
J Coles: contemporary with track A and presumably the whole series of structures in the same raised bog; part of a complex constructed over a very short period of time. This

sample came from ST 470382 (Lat. 51.08.24 N; Long. 02.45.28 W.

References: *Radiocarbon* **29**, 89

HAR-3388   3800 ± 80 BP

δ¹³C: −28.7 ‰

Sample: SLP7903, submitted on 4 July 1979

Material: wood.

Initial comment: from a wooden structure well below the main series of tracks.

Comment on uncalibrated date: indication of structures earlier than main bulk of trackways in same field, now totally destroyed (head F2).

Calibrated date: 1σ : cal BC 2455 – 2135
                    2σ : cal BC 2470 – 2030

Final comments:
J Coles: very sparse wooden remains may mark the earliest human activity on the developing raised bog just off Sharpham Peninsula.

References: Coles and Orme 1980, 68
               Radiocarbon **29**, 89

Somerset Levels: Walton Heath, Somerset

Location: ST 45853845
             Lat. 51.08.32 N; Long. 02.46.27 W

Excavator: J Coles (Department of the Environment)

References: Coles 1979
               Coles and Dobson 1989, 67 (¹⁴C)
               Orme 1982
               Radiocarbon **27**, 77 – 8 (¹⁴C)

Objectives: to assess the chronological position of the peat – clay interface in the northern part of the Levels.

HAR-1856   5600 ± 70 BP

δ¹³C: −27.3 ‰

Sample: SLP766, submitted on 26 July 1976

Material: peat.

Initial comment: from the interface between lower marine clay and peat formation.

Comment on uncalibrated date: this date dates the transition to freshwater conditions in the Levels.

Calibrated date: 1σ : cal BC 4515 – 4360
                    2σ : cal BC 4665 – 4340

Final comments:
J Coles: as for HAR-1857 and HAR-1831.

Somerset Levels: Walton Heath, Bisgrove, Somerset

Location: ST 45473880
             Lat. 51.08.43 N; Long. 02.46.47 W

Excavator: J Coles (Department of the Environment)

Site: a wooden platform or damaged track, part of the complex on Walton Heath.

References: Coles and Dobson 1989
               Coles, Caseldine, and Morgan 1988, 38 (¹⁴C)
               Orme 1982, 17 (¹⁴C)
               Orme *et al* 1982, 56 (¹⁴C)
               Radiocarbon **30**, 332 (¹⁴C)

Objectives: an assessment of the chronology for the platform.

HAR-4078   4880 ± 100 BP

δ¹³C: −27.4 ‰

Sample: SLP8010, submitted on 1 October 1980

Material: wood.

Initial comment: from a newly discovered wooden structure in the peat.

Comment on uncalibrated date: this date is considerably earlier than those from Garvin's track (HAR-682, HAR-1219, and HAR-1222) with which it was thought the structure was contemporary.

Calibrated date: 1σ : cal BC 3780 – 3535
                    2σ : cal BC 3950 – 3380

Final comments:
J Coles: this structure may have been the earliest known attempt to penetrate onto the raised peat bog of Walton Heath, prior to the extensive series of trackways of Garvin's and Jones' complex. The western track complex of Chilton Moor (HAR-649) seems to be contemporary with Bisgrove.

Somerset Levels: Walton Heath, Garvin's Tracks, Somerset

Location: ST 453385
             Lat. 51.08.33 N; Long. 02.46.55 W

Excavator: J Coles (Department of the Environment)

Site: a series of birch brushwood trackways and platforms in raised peat bogs.

References: Coles and Dobson 1989
               Coles and Orme 1977b, 79 (¹⁴C)
               Orme 1982, 15 (¹⁴C)
               Orme *et al* 1982 (¹⁴C)

Objectives: to assess the chronological positions of structures near the southern edge of Walton Heath.

Comments:
J Coles: tree-ring studies of the brushwood revealed similar and sometimes virtually identical patterns of growth for samples from the two diverging roots, confirming their contemporaneity. The three dates (HAR-682, HAR-1219, and HAR-1222) are, therefore, from wood that grew over a period

of about 30 years, and the trackway was built immediately after the wood was felled.

HAR-682   4380 ± 70 BP

$\delta^{13}C$: −28.3 ‰

Sample: SLP74.8, submitted on 21 June 1974

Material: wood: *Betula* sp..

Initial comment: from a newly discovered trackway (site 1) in terminal position under 0.4m *Sphagnum* peat.

Comment on uncalibrated date: this date exactly fits the peat stratigraphy. It confirms the Late Neolithic date suggested by the nature of the surrounding peat and by the level of the trackway.

Calibrated date: 1σ : cal BC 3095 − 2915
                      2σ : cal BC 3330 − 2790

Final comments:
J Coles: this agrees with HAR-1219, HAR-1222, and HAR-3387.

References: Coles and Coles 1975
                 Coles and Orme 1977b
                 Radiocarbon **19**, 416

HAR-1219   4460 ± 90 BP

$\delta^{13}C$: −27.8 ‰

Sample: SLP755, submitted on 8 July 1975

Material: wood.

Initial comment: this track (Garvin West) and another (see HAR-1222) join to form one track (see HAR-682).

Calibrated date: 1σ : cal BC 3340 − 2930
                      2σ : cal BC 3370 − 2910

Final comments:
J Coles: as HAR-1222.

References: Coles and Fordham 1977
                 Coles and Orme 1977a
                 Coles and Orme 1977b
                 Radiocarbon **21**, 361 − 2

HAR-1222   4280 ± 70 BP

$\delta^{13}C$: −28.5 ‰

Sample: SLP754, submitted on 8 July 1975

Material: wood.

Initial comment: from a brushwood track (Garvin's East) running north of the Polden Hills.

Calibrated date: 1σ : cal BC 3015 − 2785
                      2σ : cal BC 3080 − 2665

Final comments:
J Coles: this date also agrees with those of HAR-682 and HAR-1219, and also with the peat stratigraphy. It suggests a broad contemporaneity of the Walton Heath and the Garvin's tracks and the same can be said for Rowland's track on Ashcott Heath.

References: Coles and Fordham 1977
                 Coles and Orme 1977a
                 Coles and Orme 1977b
                 Radiocarbon **21**, 362

HAR-3387   4340 ± 80 BP

$\delta^{13}C$: −28.8 ‰

Sample: SLP7905, submitted on 4 July 1979

Material: wood.

Initial comment: from branches that were part of a trackway or similar structure near the Garvin's tracks, part of a large complex of Late Neolithic structures on Walton Heath forming a network of raised bogs.

Comment on uncalibrated date: closely related to Garvin's track (HAR-1222, HAR-1219, and HAR-682).

Calibrated date: 1σ : cal BC 3070 − 2900
                      2σ : cal BC 3310 − 2705

References: *Radiocarbon* **29**, 88

Somerset Levels: Walton Heath, Jones' Track, Somerset

Location: ST 455387
             Lat. 51.08.40 N; Long. 02.46.45 W

Excavator: J Coles (Department of the Environment)

Site: one of several Neolithic structures discovered on Walton Heath.

References: Coles and Dobson 1989
                 Orme 1982
                 Orme *et al* 1982; 58, 62 (^{14}C)
                 Radiocarbon **29**, 87 − 8 (^{14}C)

Objectives: to establish the general chronology of a complex of wooden structures in an area of raised peat bog just north of the Polden Hills.

Comments:

HAR-3078   4590 ± 70 BP

$\delta^{13}C$: −28.0 ‰

Sample: SLP7901, submitted on 21 February 1979

Material: wood.

Initial comment: from a substantial wooden trackway (part of the Walton Heath complex), associated with HAR-3386.

Calibrated date: 1σ : cal BC 3495 − 3140
                      2σ : cal BC 3600 − 3045

HAR-3386   4220 ± 80 BP

$\delta^{13}C$: −30.9 ‰

Sample: SLP7904, submitted on 4 July 1979

Material: wood.

Initial comment: an associated part of HAR-3078.

Calibrated date: 1σ : cal BC 3308 − 2922
                      2σ : cal BC 3350 − 2900

Somerset Levels: Walton Heath, Walton Meare, Somerset

Location: ST 454393
Lat. 51.08.59 N; Long. 02.46.51 W

Excavator: J Coles (Department of the Environment)

Site: a wooden structure in low level peat, comprising multiple hurdles of coppiced hazel, alder, and willow.

References: Coles and Dobson 1989
Coles and Fordham 1977
Coles and Orme 1977a, 10 (^{14}C)
Orme 1982, 17 (^{14}C)
Orme *et al* 1982
Radiocarbon **21**, 362 (^{14}C)

Objectives: to assess the chronolgical position of the hurdle tracks.

HAR-1220   4160 ± 100 BP

$\delta^{13}C$: −28.8 ‰

Sample: SLP752, submitted on 30 April 1975

Material: wood.

Initial comment: from the upper level of the hurdle complex.

Comment on uncalibrated date: this date agrees with the peat stratigraphy and with the absolute level OD.

Calibrated date: 1σ : cal BC 2900 – 2590
2σ : cal BC 3020 – 2470

HAR-1467   4330 ± 90 BP

$\delta^{13}C$: −29.3 ‰

Sample: SLP757 (A), submitted on 8 July 1975

Material: wood: coppiced hazel (*Corylus* sp.), alder (*Alnus* sp.), and willow (*Salix* sp.).

Initial comment: from stray wooden hurdles off the line of Walton Heath track.

Comment on uncalibrated date: this sample and HAR-1468 date the oldest surviving hurdles known from Britain (older than those at Walton Heath, HAR-1220) other than those from Frank's Ground (HAR-6265).

Calibrated date: 1σ : cal BC 3070 – 2890
2σ : cal BC 3325 – 2670

Final comments:
J Coles: this sample came from ST 454393 (Lat. 51.08.59 N; Long. 02.46.48 W).

HAR-1468   4250 ± 90 BP

$\delta^{13}C$: −26.7 ‰

Sample: SLP757 (B), submitted on 22 October 1975

Material: wood.

Initial comment: from wooden hurdles (duplicate of HAR-1467).

Calibrated date: 1σ : cal BC 2925 – 2700
2σ : cal BC 3090 – 2590

Final comments:
J Coles: as HAR-1467.

HAR-1470   4250 ± 80 BP

$\delta^{13}C$: −29.8 ‰

Sample: SLP758 (1), submitted on 8 July 1975

Material: wood: 4-8 years growth.

Initial comment: from the lowest level wood below the trackway.

Calibrated date: 1σ : cal BC 2925 – 2705
2σ : cal BC 3040 – 2615

Final comments:
J Coles: this result and HAR-1471 date the commencement of the wooden structure on Walton Heath and agree well with HAR-1220. It also agrees with the Rowland's hurdle track (HAR-1383).

HAR-1471   4420 ± 90 BP

$\delta^{13}C$: −26.2 ‰

Sample: SLP758 (2), submitted on 22 October 1975

Material: wood.

Initial comment: as HAR-1470.

Calibrated date: 1σ : cal BC 3320 – 2920
2σ : cal BC 3360 – 2890

Final comments:
J Coles: rather older than expected; cf HAR-1470 (duplicate) and HAR-1220.

Somerset Levels: Westhay Level, Baker Platform, Somerset

Location: ST 42854230
Lat. 51.10.36 N; Long. 02.49.04 W

Excavator: J Coles (Department of the Environment)

Site: structure at the western edge of the island of Westhay.

References: Coles and Dobson 1989
Coles *et al* 1980, 20 (^{14}C)
Orme 1982, 12 (^{14}C)
Radiocarbon **29**, 90 (^{14}C)

Objectives: to assess the chronological position of a complex of structures, including the Honeygore tracks and Abbot's Way.

HAR-2843   4720 ± 80 BP

$\delta^{13}C$: −28.5 ‰

Sample: SLP7810, submitted on 27 September 1978

Material: wood: *Alnus* sp..

Initial comment: from lowest platform of a large wooden structure of brushwood and roundwood.

Comment on uncalibrated date: this dates the basal foundation.

Calibrated date: 1σ : cal BC 3630 – 3370
2σ : cal BC 3690 – 3340

Final comments:
J Coles: the platform appears to be wholly of the later fourth millennium BC and predates the Abbot's Way, a heavy road that terminates near the platform.

HAR-2844 4520 ± 90 BP

$\delta^{13}C$: –29.1 ‰

Sample: SLP7811, submitted on 27 September 1978

Material: wood.

Initial comment: from the brushwood edging of the platform.

Calibrated date: 1σ : cal BC 3365 – 3040
2σ : cal BC 3510 – 2920

Final comments:
J Coles: as HAR-2843.

HAR-2845 4950 ± 80 BP

$\delta^{13}C$: –28.5 ‰

Sample: SLP7812, submitted on 27 September 1978

Material: wood: *Alnus* sp..

Initial comment: from a slipway at the western edge of a wide platform.

Calibrated date: 1σ : cal BC 3905 – 3690
2σ : cal BC 3970 – 3535

Final comments:
J Coles: earlier than other dates from this structure; the slipway could have been the earliest formation at the island edge. The peat stratigraphy did not allow separation to be observed.

HAR-2846 4450 ± 100 BP

$\delta^{13}C$: –28.4 ‰

Sample: SLP7813, submitted on 27 September 1978

Material: wood.

Initial comment: from upper brushwood of the platform.

Calibrated date: 1σ : cal BC 3340 – 2925
2σ : cal BC 3490 – 2900

Final comments:
J Coles: as HAR-2843; this dates the final building phase.

Somerset Levels: Westhay Level, Baker Track, Somerset

Location: ST 42854230
Lat. 51.10.36 N; Long. 02.49.04 W

Excavator: J Coles (Department of the Environment)

Site: structure associated with the platform at the edge of Westhay Island (see above).

References: Coles and Dobson 1989
Coles *et al* 1980, 20 (^{14}C)
Orme 1982, 12 (^{14}C)

Objectives: to assess the chronological position relative to the platform and other adjacent structures.

Comments:
J Coles: (on the platform and track): all dates except HAR-2845 agree with the stratigraphy of the site and with BM-386 (4450 ± 110 BP), Lu-328 (4280 ± 65 BP), and Q-987 (4230 ± 60 BP) which date the uppermost structures. The Baker series may relate to the Honeygore complex which lies to the west of the platform, the Honeygore track itself being the earliest of the complex (HAR-5721).

HAR-2919 4540 ± 80 BP

$\delta^{13}C$: –30.2 ‰

Sample: SLP7814, submitted on 13 November 1978

Material: wood: *Alnus* sp..

Initial comment: track extension from the lower timbers of the Baker platform edge.

Calibrated date: 1σ : cal BC 3370 – 3100
2σ : cal BC 3510 – 2930

Final comments:
J Coles: this dates the basal structure of the Neolithic track at the junction with the platform; the result is contemporary with the upper platform phase.

HAR-2920 4520 ± 70 BP

$\delta^{13}C$: –30.2 ‰

Sample: SLP7815, submitted on 13 November 1978

Material: wood: *Alnus* sp. and *Corylus* sp..

Initial comment: from a platform track extension.

Calibrated date: 1σ : cal BC 3355 – 3050
2σ : cal BC 3495 – 2930

Final comments:
J Coles: as HAR-2919.

Somerset Levels: Westhay Level, Honeygore Complex, Somerset

Location: ST 416428
Lat. 51.10.51 N; Long. 02.50.08 W

Excavator: J Coles (Department of the Environment)

Site: a complex of five trackways under *c* 1.0 – 2.0m of peat on Westhay Level. All are of the mid to late fourth millennium BC, with Honeydew and Honeycat the youngest, Honeygore and Honeypot the oldest.

References: Coles and Coles 1975
Coles and Dobson 1989, 65 (^{14}C)
Coles and Hibbert 1975
Coles, Caseldine, and Morgan 1988
Coles *et al* 1985a, 58 (^{14}C)
Orme 1982
Radiocarbon **19**, 415 (^{14}C)

Objectives: to assess the chronological position of a series of wooden trackways.

HAR-651 4460 ± 90 BP

$\delta^{13}C$: −28.5 ‰

Sample: SLP742 (Honeydew GVII.1), submitted on 4 June 1974

Material: wood: *Betula* sp..

Initial comment: from one of the trackways.

Calibrated date: 1σ : cal BC 3340 – 2930
2σ : cal BC 3370 – 2910

Final comments:
J Coles: this result exactly fits the peat stratigraphy; HAR-6699 dates a trackway similar to Honeydew, but is older on the basis of one date for each structure.

HAR-652 4370 ± 80 BP

$\delta^{13}C$: −28.5 ‰

Sample: SLP743 (Honeycat GVI.5), submitted on 4 June 1974

Material: wood: *Corylus* sp..

Initial comment: from horizontal timbers under *c* 2.0m of peat.

Calibrated date: 1σ : cal BC 3095 – 2915
2σ : cal BC 3340 – 2785

Final comments:
J Coles: see HAR-651; this date is suitable for the stratigraphic location and matches HAR-653.

HAR-653 4440 ± 70 BP

$\delta^{13}C$: −29.1 ‰

Sample: SLP741 (Honeycat GV.I), submitted on 4 June 1974

Material: wood: *Betula* sp..

Initial comment: from a trackway under 1.5m of peat.

Calibrated date: 1σ : cal BC 3320 – 2930
2σ : cal BC 3350 – 2910

Final comments:
J Coles: this date helps resolve some of the horizontal and vertical stratigraphic problems of multiple trackways in the area; HAR-5724 is in agreement with this and HAR-652. See HAR-651.

Southampton: 24 Hamwih Six Dials, Hampshire

Location: SU 424122
Lat. 50.54.26 N; Long. 01.23.49 W

Excavator: P Holdsworth and P E Andrews (Southampton Archaeological Research Committee) and A D Morton (Southampton City Council Archaeology Section), 1979

Site: the Middle Saxon town.

Comments:
A D Morton: the value of a high precision curve to calibrate normal precision samples is doubtful.

HAR-3291 1060 ± 60 BP

$\delta^{13}C$: −26.1 ‰

Sample: 13604 SOU24, submitted on 11 May 1979

Material: burnt thatch.

Initial comment: from a layer in a Middle Saxon pit, sandwiched with redeposited natural.

Calibrated date: 1σ : cal AD 895 – 1020
2σ : cal AD 880 – 1040

HAR-3390 1180 ± 70 BP

$\delta^{13}C$: −26.8 ‰

Sample: 8337 SOU24, submitted on 11 May 1979

Material: wood: one large piece of bark (C A Keepax).

Initial comment: from a waterlogged deposit at the bottom of a Middle Saxon pit.

Calibrated date: 1σ : cal AD 770 – 955
2σ : cal AD 670 – 1000

Southampton: Hamwih, Hampshire

Location: SU 425120
Lat. 50.54.19 N; Long. 01.23.44 W

Excavator: P Holdsworth (Southampton Archaeological Research Committee) and A D Morton (Southampton Archaeology and Heritage Management Section), 1981 – present

Site: the Middle Saxon town.

Comments:
Post-Excavator: the value of a high precision curve to calibrate standard precision samples such as these is doubtful.

AML: one sample, HAR-566 (SS80) was abandoned. Also one small sample, HAR-1487 (XX114SS3) failed.

HAR-328 1140 ± 60 BP

$\delta^{13}C$: unknown

Sample: F16 SOU5, submitted on 17 April 1974

Material: wood.

Initial comment: from F16.

Calibrated date: 1σ : cal AD 785 – 985
2σ : cal AD 680 – 1020

HAR-569 1240 ± 70 BP

$\delta^{13}C$: −28.9 ‰

Sample: F46 SOU11, submitted on 17 April 1974

Material: wood.

Initial comment: from F46.

Calibrated date: 1σ : cal AD 675 – 885
                    2σ : cal AD 650 – 960

Final comments:
Harwell: possibly a replicate of HAR-573.

HAR-570   1100 ± 80 BP

δ¹³C: –28.9 ‰

Sample: F47 SOU11, submitted on 17 April 1974

Material: wood.

Initial comment: from F47.

Calibrated date: 1σ : cal AD 880 – 1010
                    2σ : cal AD 725 – 1040

HAR-572   1170 ± 80 BP

δ¹³C: –27.2 ‰

Sample: F90 SOU11, submitted on 17 April 1974

Material: wood.

Initial comment: from F90.

Calibrated date: 1σ : cal AD 770 – 970
                    2σ : cal AD 670 – 1020

HAR-573   1060 ± 90 BP

δ¹³C: –26.9 ‰

Sample: F46 SOU11, submitted on 17 April 1974

Material: wood.

Initial comment: from F46.

Calibrated date: 1σ : cal AD 890 – 1030
                    2σ : cal AD 780 – 1170

Final comments:
Harwell: possibly a replicate of HAR-569.

HAR-728   1120 ± 80 BP

δ¹³C: –27.4 ‰

Sample: F62 SOU11, submitted on 17 April 1974

Material: wood.

Initial comment: from F62.

Calibrated date: 1σ : cal AD 810 – 1000
                    2σ : cal AD 690 – 1030

Final comments:
Harwell: a repeat of HAR-571, which failed.

HAR-1164   1270 ± 60 BP

δ¹³C: –25.7 ‰

Sample: SOU15 F75-2, submitted on 16 April 1975

Material: charcoal.

Calibrated date: 1σ : cal AD 670 – 790
                    2σ : cal AD 650 – 890

HAR-1165   1020 ± 70 BP

δ¹³C: –25.7 ‰

Sample: SOU16 F55-2, submitted on 16 April 1975

Material: charcoal.

Calibrated date: 1σ : cal AD 970 – 1035
                    2σ : cal AD 890 – 1170

HAR-1166   1440 ± 70 BP

δ¹³C: –25.6 ‰

Sample: SOU15 F81-3, submitted on 16 April 1975

Material: charcoal.

Comment on uncalibrated date: (P Holdsworth) rather early for the expected date range of AD 630 – 950.

Calibrated date: 1σ : cal AD 555 – 660
                    2σ : cal AD 440 – 680

Final comments:
Harwell: replicate measurement: 1290 ± 60 BP, δ¹³C: –25.6 ‰.

HAR-1167   1510 ± 70 BP

δ¹³C: –26.2 ‰

Sample: SOU6, submitted on 16 April 1975

Material: charcoal.

Comment on uncalibrated date: (P Holdsworth) as HAR-1166.

Calibrated date: 1σ : cal AD 440 – 625
                    2σ : cal AD 400 – 660

Final comments:
Harwell: a crystalline precipitate formed in the vial during counting.

HAR-1191   1770 ± 160 BP

δ¹³C: –25.6 ‰

Sample: SARXV3, submitted on 16 April 1975

Material: soil.

Initial comment: from F10, layer 3.

Calibrated date: 1σ : cal AD 70 – 420
                    2σ : cal BC 110 – 610 cal AD

Final comments:
A D Morton: see laboratory comment.

Harwell: an unsatisfactory yield due to too small a carbon yield; the sample needed topping up with inactive carbon dioxide, after pretreatment and combustion, to get any yield at all.

HAR-1486   1260 ± 80 BP

δ¹³C: –27.1 ‰

Sample: SOU20 F131SS4, submitted on 28 January 1976

Material: impregnated soil.

Initial comment: from a context which produced two eighth-century coins.

Calibrated date: 1σ : cal AD 665 – 880
2σ : cal AD 640 – 960

HAR-1673   1370 ± 70 BP

δ¹³C: −26.1 ‰

Sample: SOU22 F114-4, submitted on 29 March 1976

Material: soil.

Initial comment: from a layer of burnt material (bone, clay, and charcoal) in a pit; Saxon, but the pottery cannot be more accurately dated than *c* AD 700 – 900.

Calibrated date: 1σ : cal AD 620 – 680
2σ : cal AD 550 – 780

Final comments:
Harwell: replicated by HAR-1853.

HAR-1853   1370 ± 80 BP

δ¹³C: −26.5 ‰

Sample: SOU22 F114-4, submitted on 13 August 1976

Material: soil and charcoal.

Initial comment: from a layer in a pit.

Calibrated date: 1σ : cal AD 610 – 685
2σ : cal AD 540 – 790

Final comments:
Harwell: a replicate of HAR-1673.

Southampton: Quilter's Vaults, Hampshire

Location: SU 410110
Lat. 50.53.47 N; Long. 01.25.01 W

Excavator: P Holdsworth (Southampton Archaeological Research Committee), 1976

Site: five medieval tenements dating from the eleventh century onwards.

References: Walker 1978, 194 (¹⁴C)

HAR-2185   910 ± 80 BP

δ¹³C: −24.0 ‰

Sample: QV3119, submitted on 20 January 1977

Material: animal bone.

Initial comment: from the fill of the earliest feature on the site, a U-shaped ditch; the expected date is Saxon.

Calibrated date: 1σ : cal AD 1020 – 1220
2σ : cal AD 980 – 1270

Southampton: Upper Bugle Street, Hampshire

Location: SU 410110
Lat. 50.53.47 N; Long. 01.25.01 W

Excavator: P Holdsworth (Southampton Archaeological Research Committee), 1976

Site: medieval tenements and castle.

HAR-2090   1290 ± 70 BP

δ¹³C: −26.1 ‰

Sample: UBS723, submitted on 8 February 1977

Material: charcoal.

Initial comment: from a ditch; the expected date is Saxon.

Calibrated date: 1σ : cal AD 660 – 785
2σ : cal AD 630 – 890

Southampton: Westgate Street, Hampshire

Location: SU 419111
Lat. 50.53.50 N; Long. 01.24.15 W

Excavator: R G Thompson (Southampton City Council Archaeology Section), 1972

Site: the Late Saxon town.

Objectives: to determine the age and growth of the Saxon settlement, and to help work out the pottery sequence, which at the time of submission had no fixed points at all.

HAR-568   1020 ± 80 BP

δ¹³C: −27.8 ‰

Sample: SOU111 WOODWG, submitted by L Keen on 17 April 1974

Material: wood.

Initial comment: from a Late Saxon well.

Calibrated date: 1σ : cal AD 960 – 1040
2σ : cal AD 880 – 1180

Sproughton: Devil's Wood, site 2, Suffolk

Location: TM 13364447
Lat. 52.03.25 N; Long. 01.06.45 E

Excavator: E A Martin (Suffolk Archaeological Unit), 1974

Site: a Late Neolithic and Early Bronze Age settlement situated within a bow of the River Gipping, which has produced Mortlake type pottery and some possible Beaker material; the site, which was sealed by a build up of marsh clay, was excavated in advance of gravel extraction.

References: Rose 1976
Wymer 1975
Wymer 1976
Radiocarbon **21**, 371 (¹⁴C)

Objectives: it is likely that the cremation pit and settlement are contemporary; a date for the pit would help in dating the settlement and also provide a *terminus post quem* for the build up of marsh clay.

HAR-1163 3290 ± 130 BP

$\delta^{13}C$: −26.5 ‰

Sample: SP74F3, submitted on 30 April 1975

Material: charcoal, containing a large proportion of soil: some fragments of *Alnus glutinosa* from branch-sized timbers (C A Keepax).

Initial comment: from a small pit (0.55m in diameter × 0.23m deep) at the centre of the settlement, which was cut into the natural gravel; this contained a human cremation, but no pottery or artefacts.

Calibrated date: 1σ : cal BC 1740 – 1430
   2σ : cal BC 1900 – 1310

Final comments:
E A Martin: the date, even at the two standard deviation level of confidence, seems rather young for the material recovered.

Harwell: a repeat of the original sample HAR-1163, which gave an anomalous result; this small sample needed topping up with inactive carbon dioxide to enable measurement.

Sproxton: Barrow, Leicestershire

Location: SK 867278
   Lat. 52.50.25 N; Long. 00.42.46 W

Excavator: P Clay (Leicestershire Museums Arts and Records Service), 1978

Site: a composite Bronze Age barrow; the primary burial was surrounded by a series of four stake circles, with a number of satellite burials; the barrow was capped with limestone derived from the ring ditch.

References: Clay 1981b, 23 (^{14}C)

Objectives: to establish the date and sequence of burials on the barrow in advance of plough damage.

HAR-3129 3500 ± 80 BP

$\delta^{13}C$: −24.8 ‰

Sample: RC2, submitted on 9 February 1979

Material: charcoal: *Fraxinus* sp. and *Quercus* sp. from large timbers; *c* 25% identified (C A Keepax).

Initial comment: from charcoal surrounding the primary cremation in the central burial pit, possibly derived from a carbonised wooden container; should be contemporary with HAR-3130.

Calibrated date: 1σ : cal BC 1935 – 1740
   2σ : cal BC 2040 – 1640

Final comments:
P Clay: the multiphase aspect of this site supports an earlier date for HAR-3129 than HAR-3130 (*pace* initial comment).

HAR-3130 3330 ± 90 BP

$\delta^{13}C$: −24.3 ‰

Sample: RC3, submitted on 9 February 1979

Material: charcoal: *Quercus* sp. and a few fragments of *Corylus/Alnus* sp.; *c* 25% identified (C A Keepax).

Initial comment: from a pit to the south of the barrow containing a satellite cremation which was only partly calcined; the charcoal was possibly derived from a carbonised wooden container and should be contemporary with HAR-3129.

Calibrated date: 1σ : cal BC 1740 – 1520
   2σ : cal BC 1880 – 1430

Final comments:
P Clay: as above.

HAR-3131 3440 ± 70 BP

$\delta^{13}C$: −24.9 ‰

Sample: RC4, submitted on 9 February 1979

Material: charcoal: *Quercus* sp.; *c* 25% identified (C A Keepax).

Initial comment: from a cremation in a shallow hearth, on the south side of the barrow, possibly a secondary burial; should be contemporary with HAR-3132.

Calibrated date: 1σ : cal BC 1880 – 1680
   2σ : cal BC 1940 – 1540

HAR-3132 3350 ± 90 BP

$\delta^{13}C$: −25.0 ‰

Sample: RC6, submitted on 9 February 1979

Material: charcoal: *Quercus* sp. and *Fraxinus* sp. from large timbers; *c* 50% identified (C A Keepax).

Initial comment: from large timbers overlying a hearth feature cut into the south side of the mound, possibly a secondary insertion, which contained charcoal and a very little burnt bone; should be contemporary with HAR-3131.

Calibrated date: 1σ : cal BC 1745 – 1525
   2σ : cal BC 1890 – 1440

HAR-3133 5170 ± 90 BP

$\delta^{13}C$: −25.7 ‰

Sample: RC8, submitted on 9 February 1979

Material: charcoal: *Quercus* sp.; *c* 50% identified (C A Keepax).

Initial comment: from the earliest feature on the site, a small pit containing charcoal and possibly some burnt bone, sealed by the old ground surface and cut by the ring ditch.

Calibrated date: 1σ : cal BC 4210 – 3820
   2σ : cal BC 4235 – 3780

Final comments:
P Clay: possibly evidence of fire setting a tree stump and initial forest clearance?

Stafford: King's Pool, Staffordshire

Location: SJ 925234
   Lat. 52.48.28 N; Long. 02.06.41 W

Excavator: S M Colledge and J Greig (University of Birmingham), 1977

Site: Stafford town.

References: Colledge 1978
Radiocarbon **29**, 86 (^{14}C)

Objectives: to date a pollen diagram; the peat is the most recent deposit in a deep depression formed by glacial action.

HAR-2577   960 ± 80 BP

$\delta^{13}C$: −29.6 ‰

Sample: KP100, submitted on 22 December 1978

Material: peat.

Initial comment: from 1.0m depth within the deposit.

Calibrated date: 1σ : cal AD 1000 – 1165
   2σ : cal AD 900 – 1250

HAR-2578   920 ± 60 BP

$\delta^{13}C$: −29.0 ‰

Sample: KP140, submitted on 22 December 1978

Material: peat.

Initial comment: from 1.4m depth within the deposit.

Calibrated date: 1σ : cal AD 1025 – 1185
   2σ : cal AD 1000 – 1250

Final comments:
S M Colledge and J Greig: this a shows slight date reversal with HAR-2577.

HAR-2582   1620 ± 60 BP

$\delta^{13}C$: −28.8 ‰

Sample: KP230, submitted on 22 December 1978

Material: peat.

Initial comment: from 2.3m depth within the deposit.

Calibrated date: 1σ : cal AD 380 – 530
   2σ : cal AD 255 – 560

Stafford: Tipping Street, Staffordshire

Location: SJ 920230
   Lat. 52.48.15 N; Long. 02.07.07 W

Excavator: M Carver (University of Birmingham), 1977

Site: a Late Saxon kiln.

Objectives: to date the production of 'Stafford ware'.

HAR-3039   1160 ± 90 BP

$\delta^{13}C$: −26.1 ‰

Sample: STS778d, submitted on 29 November 1978

Material: charcoal.

Initial comment: from a layer of charcoal associated with a late tenth-century pottery kiln, sealing a layer of charcoal and ash and two postholes.

Calibrated date: 1σ : cal AD 770 – 980
   2σ : cal AD 670 – 1020

Final comments:
M Carver: the date confirms that Stafford ware (= Chester type ware) was produced in Stafford in the Late Saxon period.

Staines: Friends Burial Ground, Surrey

Location: TQ 03857152
   Lat. 51.25.58 N; Long. 00.30.21 W

Excavator: K R Crouch (London and Middlesex Archaeological Society), 1975 – 6

Site: excavations on the edges of the Roman town (first- to fourth-century AD); Bronze Age and Early Iron Age pottery and other finds also indicate prehistoric activity in the area.

References: Chapman 1984, 119 (^{14}C)

Objectives: to aid the dating of prehistoric features and the land surface sealed beneath a flood deposit.

HAR-3235   2820 ± 100 BP

$\delta^{13}C$: −24.1 ‰

Sample: QK578, submitted on 11 May 1979

Material: animal bone: cow ribs (*Bos* sp.).

Initial comment: from a complete cow skelton in a pit sealed by a clay flood deposit; date uncertain but pre-Roman.

Calibrated date: 1σ : cal BC 1125 – 845
   2σ : cal BC 1300 – 800

Final comments:
K R Crouch: this confirms the date suggested by sherds of residual Bronze Age pottery and other features associated with the cow burial.

Stainmore, Cumbria

Location: NY 871130
   Lat. 54.30.43 N; Long. 02.11.57 W

Excavator: A Donaldson (probably Durham University)

Site: a pollen diagram from *c* 0.70m of peat showing extensive clearance of post-elm decline woodland at this level.

HAR-2689   2480 ± 70 BP

$\delta^{13}C$: −26.7 ‰

Sample: ST50-51, submitted on 22 May 1978

Material: peat.

Calibrated date: 1σ : cal BC 790 – 410
   2σ : cal BC 810 – 400

Stamford: Castle, Lincolnshire

Location: TF 028071
   Lat. 52.39.05 N; Long. 00.28.49 W

Excavator: believed to be C Mahany

Site: an early Stamford ware kiln.

Objectives: a ¹⁴C date is important both for dating the production of early Stamford ware and to provide calibration for the samples taken from the kiln for archaeomagnetic dating.

HAR-2274   1300 ± 80 BP

$\delta^{13}C$: −25.8 ‰

Sample: STA76409, submitted by A J Clark on 21 June 1977

Material: charcoal: all *Quercus* sp. from large timbers (C A Keepax).

Initial comment: from the kiln.

Calibrated date: 1σ : cal AD 555 – 786
                      2σ : cal AD 600 – 890

HAR-2275   1140 ± 70 BP

$\delta^{13}C$: −25.3 ‰

Sample: STA76409, submitted by A J Clark on 21 June 1977

Material: charcoal.

Initial comment: from the kiln.

Calibrated date: 1σ : cal AD 780 – 980
                      2σ : cal AD 690 – 1020

Stonehenge: Avenue, Wiltshire

Location: SU 123423
              Lat. 51.10.45 N; Long. 01.49.26 W

Excavator: F J Vatcher (for the Department of the Environment), 1968

Site: Avenue ditch east of Heelstone, primary silt.

References: Atkinson *et al* 1976
                 Pitts 1982, 128 (¹⁴C)

Objectives: to date the construction of the Avenue.

HAR-2013   3720 ± 70 BP

$\delta^{13}C$: −23.6 ‰

Sample: STAVI968, submitted on 9 November 1976

Material: antler.

Initial comment: from near the base of the ditch.

Calibrated date: 1σ : cal BC 2275 – 2035
                      2σ : cal BC 2350 – 1930

Final comments:
F J Vatcher: the date is comparable with that (BM-1164 3678 ± 68 BP) derived from the west ditch; both indicate the date of construction of the initial, straight section of the avenue.

Stonehenge: Car Park, Wiltshire

Location: SU 121424
              Lat. 51.10.49 N; Long. 01.49.37 W

Excavator: H L Vatcher and F J Vatcher (for the Department of the Environment), 1966

Site: postholes discovered during the construction of the carpark; the presence of pine charcoal is of interest since this was not thought to have been growing on the chalk-lands at that time, although it has been found on other monumental sites in the area.

References: *Radiocarbon* **29**, 79 (¹⁴C)

Objectives: these postholes are included in various interpretations of Stonehenge as an observatory and their dating is therefore important.

Comments:
H L Vatcher and F J Vatcher: these dates are unexpectedly early; we do not know why HAR-456 is *c* 1000 years younger than HAR-455, when both posts should be contemporary. Possibly the samples were of poor quality and mixed with material other than the posts.

HAR-455   9130 ± 180 BP

$\delta^{13}C$: −24.2 ‰

Sample: CHAR1, submitted by H Keeley in 1966

Material: charcoal: pine (*Pinus* sp.) (S Limbrey).

Initial comment: from hole A (depth 0.76m), half way between the top (natural chalk) and the base, at the edge of the hole.

Calibrated date: 1σ : cal BC 7210 – 6810
                      2σ : cal BC 7210 – 6620

Final comments:
Harwell: this result is too old to calibrate usefully.

HAR-456   8090 ± 140 BP

$\delta^{13}C$: −25.4 ‰

Sample: CHAR2, submitted by H Keeley on 1966

Material: charcoal: pine (*Pinus* sp.).

Initial comment: from hole B, depth 0.91m from the surface of the natural chalk.

Calibrated date: 1σ : cal BC 7210 – 6810
                      2σ : cal BC 7210 – 6620

Final comments:
Harwell: this result is too old to calibrate usefully.

Swell: Cow Common, Gloucestershire

Location: SP 13502625
              Lat. 51.56.03 N; Long. 01.48.13 W

Excavator: A Saville (Cheltenham City Museum and Art Gallery), 1974 – 5

Site: barrow 8, part of a barrow cemetery on Cow Common comprising one long barrow and ten possible round barrows. At the centre of this barrow was a burial pit containing fragments of cremated bone, but no datable artefacts; this was sealed by a number of carbonised timbers, which probably represent the deposition/collapse of smouldering timbers rather than an *in situ* pyre type cremation.

References: Saville 1979b; 88, 113 – 4 (¹⁴C)
                 Radiocarbon **21**, 374 (¹⁴C)

Objectives: to date the construction of barrow F3 (F8A).

Comments:
A Saville: the two (uncalibrated) dates are in good agreement and correlate with the expected age range for primary cremations beneath the round barrows. The date from these mature wood samples could in fact be considerably older than the burial; this suggests that the barrow is not earlier than the 1450 BC, and possibly considerably later. As the first Cotswold round barrow to be dated there is no absolute chronology for Bronze Age burials in the area to which it can be related.

HAR-1325 3430 ± 80 BP

$\delta^{13}C$: −25.0 ‰

Sample: C19A, submitted on 9 October 1975

Material: charcoal: *Quercus* sp., not twiggy (C A Keepax).

Initial comment: from burnt timber at the centre of F3 (F8A).

Calibrated date: 1σ : cal BC 1880 – 1675
                    2σ : cal BC 1950 – 1530

HAR-1326 3390 ± 80 BP

$\delta^{13}C$: −24.6 ‰

Sample: C28A, submitted on 9 October 1975

Material: charcoal: *Quercus* sp., not twiggy (C A Keepax).

Initial comment: as HAR-1325; from a different area of the burnt deposit, but possibly from the same timber.

Calibrated date: 1σ : cal BC 1865 – 1615
                    2σ : cal BC 1900 – 1520

Swindon: Old Town, Wiltshire

Location: SU 158836
Lat. 51.33.02 N; Long. 01.46.20 W

Excavator: R Canham (Wiltshire County Council), 1975 – 9

Site: crude Roman stone buildings were succeeded by a Saxon settlement, possibly established *c* AD 500, with a number of sunken-featured buildings, one rendered with plaster on a wattle wall and one containing the remains of a loom.

Objectives: to date the sequence of the Saxon structures.

HAR-2336   700 ± 80 BP

$\delta^{13}C$: −26.7 ‰

Sample: 770600W, submitted by M Corfield on 1 June 1977

Material: charcoal: all *Quercus* sp. from fairly large timbers; c 25% identified (C A Keepax).

Initial comment: from a sunken-featured building.

Calibrated date: 1σ : cal AD 1260 – 1380
                    2σ : cal AD 1180 – 1410

Final comments:
R Canham: result too recent. The context was stratified and undoubtedly Early or Middle Saxon.

HAR-2734   1440 ± 70 BP

$\delta^{13}C$: −26.2 ‰

Sample: 760719, submitted by M Corfield on 1 June 1977

Material: charcoal: *Quercus* sp. from fairly large timbers; c 25% identified.

Initial comment: from the main fill of a Saxon sunken-featured building.

Calibrated date: 1σ : cal AD 555 – 660
                    2σ : cal AD 440 – 680

Final comments:
R Canham: this result accords well with the pottery and evidence from analagous sites.

Tadcaster: Bypass, North Yorkshire

Location: SE 4943 approx
Lat. 53.52.50 N; Long. 01.15.16 W

Excavator: H Kenward (York Archaeological Trust), 1976

Objectives: a date is required to establish the chronology of the biological history of the rural surroundings of York.

HAR-2590 7810 ± 90 BP

$\delta^{13}C$: −27.4 ‰

Sample: TAD1, submitted on 3 March 1978

Material: wood, stored moist, double bagged in polythene, in a cool dark place; washed in tap water, soaked in distilled water (with changes) for one week, then air dried and bagged; mineral encrustation developed after bagging dry: *Betula* sp..

Initial comment: from within a sequence of organic deposits in a presumed post-glacial lake.

Calibrated date: 1σ : cal BC 6705 – 6495
                    2σ : cal BC 7030 – 6450

Tamworth: Bolebridge Street, Staffordshire

Location: SK 209039
Lat. 52.37.56 N; Long. 01.41.28 W

Excavator: R Meeson and P Rahtz (Department of the Environment), 1978

Site: excavation of the Saxon and medieval defences, at the south-west corner of the town, revealed an eighth-century horizontal-wheeled water mill and mill pool of two phases, possibly spanned by a timber bridge.

References: Rahtz and Meeson 1992; 14, 31, 122 – 4, 5A13 – B7 (^{14}C)

Objectives: C14 dates were primarily required to corroborate the artefactual dating of the phases. A wider objective was to be served by comparing the ^{14}C dates with those obtained by dendrochronology.

HAR-2858   1180 ± 70 BP

$\delta^{13}C$: −25.6 ‰

Sample: A142, submitted by R Meeson on 1 September 1978

Material: wood, all samples were cut by a mechanical saw and could have traces of deisel fuel on them: *Quercus* sp., from the latter part of the growth cycle (C A Keepax).

Initial comment: from a large sloping post projecting through the silt, over the bed of the second phase leat, sealed by the medieval rampart. This timber has been interpreted as part of a bridge across the Anglo-Saxon mill pool, carrying a road which entered Tamworth by way of a putative gateway through the south-east rampart.

Calibrated date: 1σ : cal AD 770 – 955
2σ : cal AD 670 – 1000

Final comments:
R Meeson and P Rhatz: the dendrochronological date for this sample was 855 ± 9; this almost exactly coincides with the centre of the one standard deviation ^{14}C range.

HAR-2860   1130 ± 90 BP

$\delta^{13}C$: −26.3 ‰

Sample: A114, submitted by R Meeson on 1 September 1978

Material: wood: *Sambucus* sp., *Corylus* sp., and *Fraxinus* sp., branches and twigs; 50% identified (C A Keepax).

Initial comment: from young driftwood in the soft grey silt (A114) on the bed of the second phase leat; this seals the first phase leat and is sealed by the medieval rampart.

Calibrated date: 1σ : cal AD 785 – 1000
2σ : cal AD 680 – 1040

HAR-2861   1440 ± 70 BP

$\delta^{13}C$: −28.3 ‰

Sample: A153, submitted by R Meeson on 1 September 1978

Material: wood: *Quercus* sp. from large timber (C A Keepax).

Initial comment: from a long inclined stake pile-driven into the bed of the second phase leat, sealed by the medieval rampart, possibly part of a bridge (see HAR-2851).

Calibrated date: 1σ : cal AD 555 – 660
2σ : cal AD 440 – 680

Final comments:
R Meeson and P Rhatz: this date is anomalous in comparison with the other dates from this site.

Harwell: the dendrochronological date for this sample was calculated at 855 ± 9, rather later than the ^{14}C date ranges; this could be because the ^{14}C sample was taken from heartwood while the dendrochronological samples were taken from outer rings.

Tarraby, Cumbria

Location: NY 40495735 – NY 40535755
Lat. 54.54.26 N – 54.54.33 N; Long. 02.55.42 W – 02.55.40 W

Excavator: G Smith (Central Excavation Unit), 1976

Site: an area of *c* 21ha, mainly between Hadrian's wall and close to the fort of Petriana at Stanwix, Carlisle.

References: Smith 1978

Objectives: to allow dating of strata and features lacking good artefactual evidence of date.

Comments:
G Smith: as the history of Roman activity is so well evidenced we can only really make use of these dates if we use the calibrated date, ignore the ranges, and argue from that point.

HAR-1908   1630 ± 60 BP

$\delta^{13}C$: −29.4 ‰

Sample: 341, submitted by N Balaam on 15 November 1976

Material: peat.

Initial comment: from a cutting through Hadrian's wall's fighting ditch. The sample was submitted to show by what date the ditch had become silted up.

Comment on uncalibrated date: this date appears to be too early.

Calibrated date: 1σ : cal AD 345 – 450
2σ : cal AD 250 – 560

Final comments:
G Smith: the date range could include the true date of peat developed, *in situ*, above the silted-in ditch. Hadrian's wall was abandoned in the late fourth century.

HAR-1909   2270 ± 80 BP

$\delta^{13}C$: −30.3 ‰

Sample: 343, submitted by N Balaam on 15 November 1976

Material: organic silt.

Initial comment: from a cutting through Hadrian's wall's fighting ditch (see HAR-1908), possibly medieval.

Comment on uncalibrated date: much earlier than the well documented construction of the ditch. Presumed to be contaminated by earlier organic remains preserved in the subsoil (late glacial features).

Calibrated date: 1σ : cal BC 400 – 205
2σ : cal BC 520 – 125

Final comments:
Harwell: this date was abandoned as contaminated.

HAR-2024   1780 ± 70 BP

$\delta^{13}C$: −26.7 ‰

Sample: 4/298, submitted by N Balaam on 15 February 1977

Material: wood.

Initial comment: from a post butt found 0.48m below the base of the ploughsoil; one of a north – south alignment of very large posts.

Comment on uncalibrated date: the date agrees with the artefactual evidence for a Roman date.

Calibrated date: 1σ : cal AD 135 – 340
2σ : cal AD 80 – 410

Final comments:
G Smith: this may suggest a late third-century date, but as the sample is from oak, presumably heartwood, it may be up to 100 years earlier. It cannot, therefore, put it into a particular phase of documented activity on the wall.

References: Smith 1978, 31

HAR-2025   2080 ± 90 BP

$\delta^{13}C$: –27.5 ‰

Sample: 4/393:4/573, submitted by N Balaam on 15 February 1977

Material: charcoal.

Initial comment: from the primary silt of ditch 78/320, in field 4; contextually later than HAR-2158, possibly Roman.

Comment on uncalibrated date: this suggests that the ditch is part of a pre-Hadrian's wall, Iron Age field system.

Calibrated date: 1σ : cal BC 330 – 10 cal AD
2σ : cal BC 380 – 90 cal AD

Final comments:
G Smith: this suggests that the sample is residual material.

References: Smith 1978, 26

HAR-2158   1880 ± 90 BP

$\delta^{13}C$: –28.2 ‰

Sample: 4/714, submitted by N Balaam on 15 February 1977

Material: charcoal.

Initial comment: from a stratigraphically earlier level than HAR-2025.

Comment on uncalibrated date: this would agree with an immediately pre-Hadrian's wall date for the field system and its drainage ditches.

Calibrated date: 1σ : cal AD 20 – 235
2σ : cal BC 100 – 340 cal AD

Final comments:
G Smith: calibration suggests that the ditch may be more likely to be Roman, perhaps Hadrianic but the range does not rule out a pre-Hadrianic or even Late Iron Age date.

Taunton, Somerset

Location: ST 229249
Lat. 51.01.04 N; Long. 03.05.57 W

Excavator: P Leach (Committee for Rescue Archaeology in Avon, Gloucestershire, and Somerset), 1978

Site: the Augustinian priory.

References: Radiocarbon **29**, 92 – 3 (^{14}C)

HAR-2804   840 ± 90 BP

$\delta^{13}C$: –26.4 ‰

Sample: TAUN40A, submitted by J Hillam on 4 September 1978

Material: wood: *Fraxinus* sp., seven-year-old twig.

Initial comment: part of a bulk wood sample from layer 40.

Calibrated date: 1σ : cal AD 1045 – 1265
2σ : cal AD 1010 – 1290

HAR-2806   1090 ± 80 BP

$\delta^{13}C$: –28.3 ‰

Sample: TAUN96, submitted by J Hillam on 4 September 1978

Material: wood: *Quercus* sp., with at least 20 growth rings (growth allowance not known).

Initial comment: from layer 96.

Calibrated date: 1σ : cal AD 885 – 1015
2σ : cal AD 770 – 1150

HAR-2815   870 ± 70 BP

$\delta^{13}C$: –27.4 ‰

Sample: TAUN40B, submitted by J Hillam on 4 September 1978

Material: wood: *Salix/Populus* sp., a *c* 17-year-old branch or twig; the outer rings appear to be present.

Initial comment: part of a bulk, wood sample from layer 40.

Calibrated date: 1σ : cal AD 1040 – 1245
2σ : cal AD 1010 – 1270

Taunton: Castle, Somerset

Location: ST 225247
Lat. 51.00.57 N; Long. 03.06.18 W

Excavator: P Leach (Committee for Rescue Archaeology in Avon, Gloucestershire, and Somerset), 1972 and 1977

Site: excavation in 1972 within the former coin room, in the inner ward of the castle, revealed three burials beneath the original curtain wall, which are possibly part of an extensive cemetery predating the castle and moat; the bones were retrieved in 1977 for dating purposes.

References: Leach 1983, 28 (^{14}C)

Objectives: to ascertain whether the cemetery is Saxon or early medieval; the curtain wall of the castle was built in 1245.

HAR-2674   1090 ± 70 BP

$\delta^{13}C$: –20.1 ‰

Sample: TC1, submitted on 21 March 1978

Material: human bone.

Initial comment: from a skeleton in a grave cut by the castle wall.

Comment on uncalibrated date: while a single date should be treated with caution, this fits the supporting evidence that the graves are pre- AD 1200; they probably represent burials which were disturbed and reinterred when the curtain wall was constructed.

Calibrated date: 1σ : cal AD 885 – 1010
2σ : cal AD 780 – 1030

Tewkesbury: Holm Castle, Windmill Hill, Gloucestershire

Location: SO 887321
Lat. 51.59.13 N; Long. 02.09.52 W

Excavator: A Hannan (Tewkesbury Borough Council), 1975

Site: during a watching brief on the development of the site of a medieval manor house a possible Late Neolithic pit was observed together with a linear feature, a circular feature, and other possible pits; no medieval material was found in this area.

References: Radiocarbon **21**, 372 (^{14}C)

Objectives: to confirm the supposed Late Neolithic – Mid Bronze Age date of the early features and pottery.

HAR-1192   2310 ± 70 BP

$\delta^{13}C$: –26.1 ‰

Sample: HC75F312, submitted on 5 May 1975

Material: charcoal.

Initial comment: from an oval pit *c* 1.50m × 1.0m containing a large number of heavily burned river pebbles and pottery of possibly later Neolithic date, in a dark ashy soil, *c* 0.75m below present ground level and sealed by 0.20m of clay.

Calibrated date: 1σ : cal BC 405 – 270
2σ : cal BC 755 – 200

Final comments:
A Hannan: this result permits a broader approach to the material.

Thirlings: Ewart, Northumberia

Location: NT 956322
Lat. 55.35.00 N; Long. 02.04.11 W

Excavator: R Miket

Site: Neolithic and Anglo-Saxon settlements.

Comments:
AML: one sample, HAR-1450 (F71), was dated after 1981; six samples were submitted after April 1981, HAR-6636 (L1684), HAR-6637 (C1634), HAR-6638 (P1861), HAR-6639 (N1666), HAR-6640, and HAR-6658 (F72); one small sample (F25) was withdrawn.

HAR-844   7200 ± 390 BP

$\delta^{13}C$: –26.0 ‰

Sample: SMPL.F1, submitted on 5 September 1974

Material: charcoal: one fragment of *Quercus* sp., one fragment of *Corylus* sp., both not twiggy (C A Keepax).

Initial comment: from the dark/medium fill of F1, trench 2.

Calibrated date: 1σ : cal BC 6440 – 5650
2σ : cal BC 7025 – 5350

HAR-845   1380 ± 80 BP

$\delta^{13}C$: –24.5 ‰

Sample: 748263, submitted on 5 September 1974

Material: charcoal.

Initial comment: from the northern door post of the doorway at the eastern end of structure B.

Calibrated date: 1σ : cal AD 605 – 680
2σ : cal AD 540 – 790

HAR-1118   5230 ± 110 BP

$\delta^{13}C$: –26.15 ‰

Sample: 748261, submitted on 5 September 1974

Material: charcoal: one fragment of slow-grown *Quercus* sp., not twiggy, and *Corylus* sp. from a fairly small branch (C A Keepax).

Initial comment: from the doorpost at the western side of the southern entrance.

Calibrated date: 1σ : cal BC 4230 – 3830
2σ : cal BC 4340 – 3790

Final comments:
Harwell: a small size of sample accounts for a larger than normal error term.

HAR-1119   1460 ± 80 BP

$\delta^{13}C$: –25.9 ‰

Sample: 748262, submitted on 5 September 1974

Material: charcoal: one fragment, probably *Betula* sp. (C A Keepax).

Initial comment: from F4, trench 2.

Calibrated date: 1σ : cal AD 540 – 655
2σ : cal AD 420 – 680

Final comments:
Harwell: a small sample.

HAR-1451   4080 ± 130 BP

$\delta^{13}C$: –25.9 ‰

Sample: F77, submitted on 19 December 1977

Material: charcoal: *Quercus* sp., *Corylus* sp., and possibly *Populus* sp.; *c* 20% identified (C A Keepax).

Initial comment: from a Late Neolithic, clay-lined pit containing pottery.

Calibrated date: 1σ : cal BC 2885 – 2470
2σ : cal BC 2920 – 2290

Final comments:
Harwell: not a very reliable result due to an initial inadequate sample quantity and experimental difficulties in the benzene synthesis process.

Thwing: Paddock Hill, Humberside

Location: TA 03057070
Lat. 54.07.18 N; Long. 00.25.23 W

Excavator: T G Manby (Yorkshire Archaeological Society), 1974 – 87

Site: a small Bronze Age hillfort with a box rampart constructed over earlier occupation.

Objectives: dates are required for the chronology of the features, as the site is relevant to the whole question of the development of hillfort fortification and the Middle – Late Bronze Age transition.

HAR-1398   2900 ± 70 BP

$\delta^{13}C$: –26.0 ‰

Sample: T74I3BN/T7SAMP1, submitted on 16 July 1975

Material: soil and charcoal: *Quercus* sp., *Fraxinus excelsior*, *Corylus avellana*, and hawthorn type (*Crataegus/Pyrus/Malus/Sorbus* sp.); c 10% of one bag identified (C A Keepax).

Initial comment: from a pre-rampart occupation layer (the sample, in a plastic bag, includes mineral material, it was not air dried).

Comment on uncalibrated date: this result should predate the Late Bronze Age; expected date c 1000 BC.

Calibrated date: 1σ : cal BC 1255 – 1000
2σ : cal BC 1310 – 910

Final comments:
T G Manby: this date falls within Middle Bronze Age 3.

Harwell: a replicate check of HAR-1251; a poor quality sample with much sand.

HAR-4282   3120 ± 80 BP

$\delta^{13}C$: –22.7 ‰

Sample: T79F13AT, submitted on 4 February 1981

Material: antler.

Initial comment: from the primary layers of the outer ditch, selected from broken antler picks.

Comment on uncalibrated date: this should be contemporary with HAR-1398, from pre-rampart or later occupation.

Calibrated date: 1σ : cal BC 1505 – 1315
2σ : cal BC 1590 – 1215

Final comments:
T G Manby: this is too old in comparison with the expected sequence.

HAR-4283   3110 ± 80 BP

$\delta^{13}C$: –23.85 ‰

Sample: T78G8G, submitted on 4 February 1981

Material: antler.

Initial comment: from a layer of primary silt in the inner ditch.

Comment on uncalibrated date: an Early Bronze Age date was expected for this deposit.

Calibrated date: 1σ : cal BC 1495 – 1310
2σ : cal BC 1530 – 1165

Final comments:
T G Manby: this date is later than expected for S-Beaker pottery in this deposit.

HAR-4284   3010 ± 100 BP

$\delta^{13}C$: –21.5 ‰

Sample: T79H10GP, submitted on 4 February 1981

Material: antler.

Initial comment: from a layer of occupation debris filling the upper part of the inner ditch.

Comment on uncalibrated date: a Middle Bronze Age date was expected.

Calibrated date: 1σ : cal BC 1410 – 1100
2σ : cal BC 1510 – 940

Final comments:
T G Manby: satisfactory for the post Deverel-Rimbury pottery associations.

HAR-4285+HAR-4530   3400 ± 130 BP

$\delta^{13}C$: –25.0+3.0 ‰

Sample: HIIGU, submitted on 4 February 1981

Material: charcoal: *Corylus/Alnus* sp., *Fraxinus excelsior*, hawthorn type (Rosaceae, sub-family Pomoideae), and *Quercus* sp., all from mature timbers (C A Keepax).

Initial comment: from a layer of occupation debris filling the upper part of the inner ditch.

Comment on uncalibrated date: a Middle Bronze Age date was expected, contemporary with HAR-4284.

Calibrated date: 1σ : cal BC 1890 – 1530
2σ : cal BC 2040 – 1420

Final comments:
T G Manby: this earlier date reflects the use of mature timber for firewood.

Harwell: the $\delta^{13}C$ value is assumed.

Trowse: Barrow, Norfolk

Location: TG 24200627
Lat. 52.36.27 N; Long. 01.18.41 E

Excavator: R Clark (Norwich Castle Museum), 1958

Site: a double-ditched barrow with at least four grave pits, in the upper fills of two of which (pits I and II) fires had apparently been lit. The barrow forms part of the ritual/funerary complex focussed on the Arminghall henge, which lies some 200m to the south-west.

References: Clarke 1970
Healy 1982, 12, 14, and 25 – 6 (^{14}C)
Lawson 1986a, 2 and fig 1 (^{14}C)
Lawson *et al* 1981

Objectives: to obtain an estimate for the length of time over which burials were made on the barrow.

Comments:
F Healy: the determinations indicate that burials were made in the barrow over an extended period. This is consistent with the cutting of grave pit III by grave pit I. Stratigraphically, the determinations give *termini post quos* for the use of the grave pits, but the timbers may have been of some age when burnt, especially in the case of the apparently squared ones over pit II, which may have formed part of a structure.

HAR-3265 3550 ± 70 BP

$\delta^{13}C$: –26.5 ‰

Sample: TBPIT568, submitted by P Murphy on 11 May 1979

Material: charcoal: *Quercus* sp. from mature timbers (C A Keepax).

Initial comment: from just above and to the west of grave pit V.

Calibrated date: 1σ : cal BC 2020 – 1775
2σ : cal BC 2130 – 1705

HAR-3268 3790 ± 80 BP

$\delta^{13}C$: –25.2 ‰

Sample: TBPIT2, submitted by P Murphy on 11 May 1979

Material: charcoal: *Quercus* sp. from mature timbers (C A Keepax).

Initial comment: from the upper fill of grave pit II, in which a fire had apparently been lit. The charcoal, from which the sample was taken, was recorded as three roughly squared branches.

Calibrated date: 1σ : cal BC 2450 – 2050
2σ : cal BC 2470 – 1985

HAR-3269 3810 ± 80 BP

$\delta^{13}C$: –25.6 ‰

Sample: TBPIT1, submitted by P Murphy on 11 May 1979

Material: charcoal: *Quercus* sp. and some hawthorn type (Rosaceae, sub-family Pomoideae) from mature timbers (C A Keepax).

Initial comment: from upper fill of grave pit I in which a fire had apparently been lit. A complete Beaker of Clarke's (1970) developed southern group one was found on the base of the grave, while further Beaker sherds were associated with the sample. Pit I cut an earlier grave, pit III, which contained a European Bell Beaker and perhaps two rusticated vessels.

Calibrated date: 1σ : cal BC 2455 – 2140
2σ : cal BC 2470 – 2040

Uley Bury, Gloucestershire

Location: ST 784989
Lat. 51.41.17 N; Long. 00.37.17 W

Excavator: A Saville and A Ellison (Committee for Rescue Archaeology in Avon, Gloucestershire, and Somerset), 1976

Site: multivallate Iron Age hillfort on the scarp edge of the Cotswolds; 32 acres, with three entrances.

References: Saville and Ellison 1983; 7, MC5 (^{14}C)

Objectives: to obtain dating evidence for the early phase of the hillfort defences and the associated pottery assemblage.

HAR-2289 2250 ± 80 BP

$\delta^{13}C$: –25.5 ‰

Sample: UB76/C1, submitted on 1 June 1977

Material: charcoal: *Quercus* sp., *Corylus/Alnus* sp., *Salix/Populus* sp., and hawthorn type (Rosaceae, sub-family Pomoideae); also cf blackthorn (*Prunus* sp.), cf *Acer* sp., and cf *Sambucus* sp.; all from twig and larger timbers; *c* 25% identified (C A Keepax).

Initial comment: from cutting 1, layer 11, a lense containing occupation debris at the base of the terrace make-up; the date is expected to relate to a late phase of the local Iron Age B sequence.

Calibrated date: 1σ : cal BC 395 – 200
2σ : cal BC 410 – 110

Final comments:
A Saville and A Ellison: this date is entirely consistent with the anticipated age of the early phase of hillfort construction at Uley Bury, both on grounds of the hillfort typology and the associated finds. However, it must be said that, the broad spread of the calibrated age of this one date is of little help in gauging the start and duration of occupation at Uley Bury, or in any wider assessment of the Cotswold Iron Age.

Unstone, Derbyshire

Location: SK 373769
Lat. 53.17.15 N; Long. 01.26.26 W

Excavator: T Courtney (North Derbyshire Archaeological Trust), 1977

Site: a hearth in close proximity to a Mesolithic posthole and stakehole structures, from which carbonised grain was recovered.

Objectives: to establish whether the charcoal is Mesolithic or intrusive and to assess the importance of the site.

HAR-2589 2740 ± 170 BP

$\delta^{13}C$: –29.1 ‰

Sample: U77C2F49, submitted on 21 March 1978

Material: charcoal: *Corylus/Alnus* sp. from branch-sized timber (C A Keepax).

Initial comment: from a layer of burnt sand in a hearth hollow, sealed by an upper layer of sand and then ploughsoil.

Calibrated date: 1σ : cal BC 1100 – 790
2σ : cal BC 1395 – 410

Final comments:
T Courtney: this date confirms a late reoccupation of site. This hollow is not stratigraphically linked to the main Mesolithic part of the site.

Harwell: a small sample accounts for the larger than normal error term.

HAR-2657 unknown

$\delta^{13}C$: unknown

Sample: U77C2F48, submitted on 21 April 1978

Material: charcoal or wood: one fragment of oak (*Quercus* sp.) from a large timber, the remainder was unidentified because of its poor condition.

Final Comments:
AML: no result has been found; presumed abandoned.

Upper Lambourn: Park Farm, Berkshire

Location: SU 3081 approx
Lat. 51.31.36 N; Long. 01.34.03 W

Excavator: J C Richards (Wessex Archaeological Unit), 1979

Site: a denuded round barrow on the Berkshire chalk with a primary group of three crouched inhumations: an adult male and female (aged *c* 40 and 35 years respectively) buried in one part of the circular trench grave, and an adolescent male (*c* 16 yrs); the bodies were covered with a loose cairn of sarsens.

Objectives: the barrow contained no grave goods and all the overlying stratigraphy had been removed by ploughing; dates were required to establish whether the monument is Bronze Age or Saxon.

HAR-3883 4870 ± 70 BP

$\delta^{13}C$: –23.4 ‰

Sample: PF7927, submitted on 31 March 1980

Material: human bone, very fragmentary due to the weight of the sarsen cairn which crushed them. The bones were washed in tapwater and reassembled using HMG glue, after examination they were disassembled by sawing *c* 50mm to either side of the glued joints and any visible glue was scraped off.

Initial comment: from a crouched inhumation (grave III); part of the primary burial group.

Calibrated date: 1σ : cal BC 3775 – 3545
2σ : cal BC 3890 – 3390

HAR-3884 4780 ± 70 BP

$\delta^{13}C$: –23.0 ‰

Sample: PF7926, submitted on 31 March 1980

Material: human bone.

Initial comment: from a crouched inhumation (grave II); part of the primary burial group.

Calibrated date: 1σ : cal BC 3645 – 3385
2σ : cal BC 3775 – 3370

HAR-3898 4800 ± 90 BP

$\delta^{13}C$: –22.2 ‰

Sample: PF7925, submitted on 31 March 1980

Material: human bone.

Initial comment: from a crouched inhumation (grave I); part of the primary burial group.

Calibrated date: 1σ : cal BC 3695 – 3385
2σ : cal BC 3780 – 3370

Upper Teesdale: Simy Folds Bog, County Durham

Location: NY 888277
Lat. 54.38.39 N; Long. 02.10.25 W

Excavator: A Donaldson (University of Durham), 1980

Site: a peat bog near a Viking settlement.

References: Coggins *et al* 1983, 24 (^{14}C)

Objectives: ^{14}C dates would provide a fixed context for a pollen diagram and would be of great interest in terms of the archaeology and local history of the whole dale, which has clearly undergone major environmental changes.

Comments:
AML: three samples, HAR-5068 (300-10mm), HAR-5069 (320-50mm), and HAR-5070 (600-40mm) were submitted after April 1981.

HAR-3791 2440 ± 80 BP

$\delta^{13}C$: –30.6 ‰

Sample: SF40-60W, submitted on 1 May 1980

Material: wood.

Initial comment: from an extensive layer of alder (*Alnus glutinosa*) wood and roots within the peat, 0.4 – 0.6m.

Calibrated date: 1σ : cal BC 770 – 400
2σ : cal BC 800 – 390

HAR-4076 5920 ± 80 BP

$\delta^{13}C$: –28.3 ‰

Sample: SF100, submitted on 29 July 1980

Material: wood and peat.

Initial comment: from the lowest level of the peat (1.02m) from which sufficient material can be collected for dating.

Calibrated date: 1σ : cal BC 4935 – 4725
2σ : cal BC 5040 – 4605

Walcott Commons, Lincolnshire

Location: TF 35565123
Lat. 53.02.27 N; Long. 00.01.20 E

Excavator: V Ancliffe and R Siddaway (South Lincolnshire Archaeological Unit), 1978

Site: a rescue excavation on a dyke section within a barrow group. The barrows appeared through later peat deposit; between Sleaford and Lincoln.

References: Chowne 1980, 303 (^{14}C)
Healey and Hurcombe 1989

Objectives: to approximately date the post-barrow vegetation.

HAR-3362 2550 ± 100 BP

$\delta^{13}C$: –29.6 ‰

Sample: WS19, submitted by R Siddaway on 11 May 1979

Material: wood: probably *Corylus/Alnus* sp. (C A Keepax).

Initial comment: from peat overlying the barrow that was cut by the dyke.

Calibrated date: 1σ : cal BC 815 – 530
2σ : cal BC 910 – 400

Final comments:
H Healey: later rescue excavation of a further barrow in the cemetery produced a crouched adult male inhumation. Artefacts included an almost complete food vessel, possibly belonging to the main burial, but removed by a JCB prior to the archaeological excavation. Sherds of Early Bronze Age and Beaker vessels in grave fill which predates burial (pottery information in archive note by P Chowne).

Waltham Abbey, Essex

Location: TL 382006
Lat. 51.41.12 N; Long. 00.00.02 W

Excavator: P J Huggins (Waltham Abbey Historical Society), 1977

Site: rescue excavation within the precinct of an Augustinian monastery, which was founded in 1177.

References: Huggins 1988, 151 (^{14}C)
Radiocarbon **27**, 89 (^{14}C)

Objectives: to date this part of the cemetery, at the time of the excavation this was expected, on pottery evidence, to be *c* AD 660 – 870.

HAR-2209 1140 ± 70 BP

$\delta^{13}C$: –23.7 ‰

Sample: WAGR876, submitted on 1 June 1977

Material: human bone, no suggestion of contamination: female aged 35 – 45 years.

Initial comment: this burial was one of 30 individuals, the graves of which were cut by a ditch with twelfth-century pottery.

Calibrated date: 1σ : cal AD 790 – 980
2σ : cal AD 690 – 1020

Final comments:
P J Huggins: the result supported the suggestion that this was a Saxon cemetery.

Ware: Allen and Hanbury's, Hertfordshire

Location: TL 352145
Lat. 51.48.44 N; Long. 00.02.19 W

Excavator: C Partridge (Hertfordshire Archaeological Unit), 1978

Site: Roman well, late fourth-century (a silver siligua of Theodosius I (379-395) was found in the lining fill of the well); all the archaeological material from the well was diagnostically Roman, but it may have continued in use after this period, since it was associated with a gravel-floored posthole building and a single posthole, sunken-floored building, probably of late fourth- or early fifth-century date.

Objectives: to ascertain whether the well was of single construction. All the samples were from the lower part of the framework, and therefore should be datable to the well's period of use – but are they contemporary?

Comments:
C Partridge: the overall suite of dates fits well with the artefactual dating. Only WARE 15 falls outside the considered dating range. This variation may indicate a longer period of use than that indicated by the datable artefacts and will need to be taken into account when the full site chronology is assessed.

HAR-3657 1640 ± 70 BP

$\delta^{13}C$: –24.9 ‰

Sample: WARE7, submitted by J Hillam on 9 October 1979

Material: wood: *Quercus* sp.; *c* 20 annual rings taken from a sample with 24 measurable rings (there are more rings to the outside but these are obscured by a large root).

Initial comment: from one of the uppermost vertical supporting timbers.

Calibrated date: 1σ : cal AD 270 – 450
2σ : cal AD 240 – 560

Final comments:
C Partridge: both the calibrated dates would fall within the supposed period of use of the well.

HAR-3658 1650 ± 60 BP

$\delta^{13}C$: –28.5 ‰

Sample: WARE13, submitted by J Hillam on 9 October 1979

Material: wood: *Betula* sp.; the timber was 20 – 30 years old when felled.

Initial comment: from a stake driven into the chalk bottom of the well as support for the lower timbers.

Calibrated date: 1σ : cal AD 270 – 435
2σ : cal AD 240 – 540

Final comments:
C Partridge: as HAR-3657.

HAR-3686   1520 ± 70 BP

$\delta^{13}C$: −28.1 ‰

Sample: WARE15, submitted by J Hillam on 9 October 1979

Material: wood: *Quercus* sp.; 8 – 9 sapwood rings from a *c* 22-year-old tree.

Initial comment: from one of the three large lower cross supports (also examined dendrochronologically).

Calibrated date: 1σ : cal AD 435 – 610
2σ : cal AD 400 – 660

Final comments:
C Partridge: it is possible that the large frame supports found were replacements for earlier, rotted ones. This calibrated date range is somewhat later than that from the other samples – it could reflect the continuing use of the well into the second half of the fourth century, at least.

Weekley, Northamptonshire

Location: SP 888818
Lat. 52.25.36 N; Long. 00.41.38 W

Excavator: D Jackson (for the Department of the Environment), 1976

Site: a boundary ditch.

References: Radiocarbon **27**, 87 (^{14}C)

Objectives: to date the ditch, which is mentioned in Anglo-Saxon literature, but which may be of Iron Age date (Ditch section on line of the above – no earthwork visible at this point).

Comments:
AML: a second sample, HAR-2014 (BD2), failed.

HAR-1899   3420 ± 100 BP

$\delta^{13}C$: −25.9 ‰

Sample: BD1, submitted on 9 November 1976

Material: charcoal: hawthorn type (Rosaceae, sub-family Pomoideae), *Quercus* sp., and cf blackthorn (*Prunus* sp.), all from fairly large timbers (C A Keepax).

Initial comment: from the silts of the first phase ditch.

Comment on uncalibrated date: the result is surprisingly early.

Calibrated date: 1σ : cal BC 1880 – 1620
2σ : cal BC 2020 – 1510

Final comments:
D Jackson: unreliable for dating the ditch referred to above.

Weekley, Northamptonshire

Location: SP 884818
Lat. 52.25.36 N; Long. 00.14.59 W

Excavator: D Jackson (for the Department of the Environment), 1970 – 8

Site: Roman villa and kilns, Late Iron Age occupation with a ditch containing a good group of curvilinear decorated pottery.

References: Jackson and Dix 1986 – 7, 49 (^{14}C)

Objectives: it is possible that the Iron Age pottery was also made on site; in order to obtain a really close date for the decorated pottery, which is of a type characteristic of and important to the whole region, five samples from the same ditch were submitted for measurement.

Comments:
D Jackson: a date in the first century BC would fit the archaeological evidence. Some recutting or cleaning out phases may account for the wide variation but no 'Belgic' or Roman pottery was found on this part of the site.

Harwell: the results show a larger scatter than expected, but each measurement appears valid; the straight mean of these results is 2048 BP; the recommended result to be quoted is 2050 ± 45 BP.

HAR-1725   2050 ± 70 BP

$\delta^{13}C$: −25.2 ‰

Sample: WKLY-K1, submitted on 27 May 1976

Material: charcoal.

Initial comment: from a ditch deposit which has produced curvilinear, decorated pottery.

Calibrated date: 1σ : cal BC 170 – 15 cal AD
2σ : cal BC 350 – 80 cal AD

HAR-1779   1910 ± 80 BP

$\delta^{13}C$: −25.0 ‰

Sample: WKLY-K1, submitted on 27 May 1976

Material: charcoal.

Initial comment: as HAR-1725.

Calibrated date: 1σ : cal AD 5 – 195
2σ : cal BC 100 – 315 cal AD

Final comments:
Harwell: the $\delta^{13}C$ value is assumed.

HAR-1844   2120 ± 90 BP

$\delta^{13}C$: −25.2 ‰

Sample: WKLY-K1, submitted on 27 May 1976

Material: charcoal.

Initial comment: as HAR-1725.

Calibrated date: 1σ : cal BC 360 – 40
2σ : cal BC 390 – 70 cal AD

HAR-2007   2160 ± 70 BP

$\delta^{13}C$: −25.5 ‰

Sample: WKLY-K1, submitted on 27 May 1976

Material: charcoal.

Initial comment: as HAR-1725.

Calibrated date: 1σ : cal BC 365 – 110
2σ : cal BC 390 – 30

HAR-2008   2000 ± 70 BP

$\delta^{13}C$: −24.9 ‰

Sample: WKLY-K1, submitted on 27 May 1976

Material: charcoal.

Initial comment: as HAR-1725.

Calibrated date: 1σ : cal BC 101 – 70 cal AD
2σ : cal BC 190 – 130 cal AD

Final comments:
D Jackson: a date of 100 BC or slightly later fits well with the archaeological evidence.

Wells Cathedral: The Camery, Somerset

Location: ST 552458
Lat. 51.12.33 N; Long. 02.38.29 W

Excavator: W Rodwell (Western Archaeological Trust), 1978 – 9

Site: excavations in the angle between the south transept and the east cloister revealed evidence for prehistoric and unsuspected Roman occupation, a Saxon cemetery, and the medieval lady chapel by the cloister.

Objectives: to date the early burial sequences and, by association, structures relating to the Saxon minster of Wells.

HAR-3374   980 ± 80 BP

$\delta^{13}C$: −24.1 ‰

Sample: WC7901, submitted on 25 July 1979

Material: animal bone.

Initial comment: from a domestic midden on the floor of a secular building (part of the domestic range) on the south side of the later Saxon lady chapel (layer 720).

Calibrated date: 1σ : cal AD 985 – 1160
2σ : cal AD 890 – 1230

Final comments:
W Rodwell: the site of the domestic range on the south side of the later Saxon cathedral, probably associated with the first half of the eleventh century. An agreeable result.

HAR-3375   910 ± 80 BP

$\delta^{13}C$: −20.9 ‰

Sample: WC7902, submitted on 25 July 1979

Material: human bone.

Initial comment: from part of a skeleton sealed below the west wall of the later Saxon lady chapel (grave 61).

Calibrated date: 1σ : cal AD 1020 – 1220
2σ : cal AD 980 – 1270

Final comments:
W Rodwell: a date before the mid eleventh century is implied structurally, and I would not have expected the burial to be later than the tenth century. It could just fall within the calibrated range.

HAR-3376   970 ± 80 BP

$\delta^{13}C$: −21.2 ‰

Sample: WC7905, submitted on 25 July 1979

Material: human bone.

Initial comment: from fragments of human bone built into the foundation (layer 1100) of the north – south rubble wall, sealed beneath the later Saxon cemetery to the north of the lady chapel.

Calibrated date: 1σ : cal AD 990 – 1165
2σ : cal AD 890 – 1230

Final comments:
W Rodwell: the wall ought not to be later than the late eleventh century (and certainly not after *c* AD 1140). A date for the bone in the tenth century, or earlier, is to be expected on the cemetery evidence generally.

HAR-3397   1220 ± 70 BP

$\delta^{13}C$: −21.3 ‰

Sample: WC7903, submitted on 25 July 1979

Material: human bone.

Initial comment: from part of a skeleton sealed beneath the east wall of the later Saxon lady chapel (grave 115).

Calibrated date: 1σ : cal AD 685 – 890
2σ : cal AD 660 – 980

Final comments:
W Rodwell: this result is an excellent fit. The burial is one of a group assigned to the late eighth or early ninth century.

HAR-3398   870 ± 70 BP

$\delta^{13}C$: −21.1 ‰

Sample: WC7904, submitted on 25 July 1979

Material: human bone.

Initial comment: from part of a skeleton cut through the pink mortar floor outside the lady chapel to the north, also cut by the late Saxon cloister wall (grave 69).

Calibrated date: 1σ : cal AD 1040 – 1245
2σ : cal AD 1010 – 1270

Final comments:
W Rodwell: this is another case where a date at the early end of the calibrated date range would just fit. On structural evidence the burial can hardly be later than *c* AD 1050.

Wensleydale: Old Gayle Lane, North Yorkshire

Location: SD 876894
Lat. 54.18.00 N; Long. 02.11.26 W

Excavator: P Turnbull (North Yorkshire County Council), 1979

Site: a defended earthwork.

References: Turnbull 1986, 208 (^{14}C)

Objectives: the site appears to be typical of an area, in which little modern excavation has taken place; no datable artefacts were recovered and a ^{14}C date was requested to establish whether the earthwork is of prehistoric or Dark Age date.

HAR-3748   1100 ± 70 BP

$\delta^{13}C$: −29.6 ‰

Sample: OGL1, submitted on 5 March 1980

Material: wood.

Initial comment: from a primary ditch fill.

Calibrated date: 1σ : cal AD 885 – 1010
2σ : cal AD 780 – 1030

Final comments:
P Turnbull: it is unfortunate that a suite of dates was not available: this single date however reinforces the possibility of many upland sites of 'prehistoric' appearance actually being of Dark Age date.

West Ashby, Lincolnshire

Location: TF 250728
Lat. 53.14.14 N; Long. 00.07.37 W

Excavator: N Field (North Lincolnshire Archaeological Unit), 1977

Site: an Early Bronze Age multiphase barrow, with three successive mounds and three ditches; the earliest monument on the site was possibly a class one henge.

References: Field 1985, 106 (^{14}C)

HAR-3270   3480 ± 70 BP

$\delta^{13}C$: −24.9 ‰

Sample: WA78B, submitted on 11 May 1979

Material: charcoal: *Corylus* sp.; c 25% identified (C A Keepax).

Initial comment: from a small deposit of charcoal (F2) in the inner ditch (F3), the earliest of three ditches.

Calibrated date: 1σ : cal BC 1895 – 1705
2σ : cal BC 2020 – 1640

HAR-3290   3670 ± 80 BP

$\delta^{13}C$: −26.9 ‰

Sample: WA78A, submitted on 11 May 1979

Material: charcoal: mainly *Quercus* sp. with some *Prunus* sp. from mature timbers (C A Keepax).

Initial comment: from a charcoal layer (F72) under the barrow, which also runs into the inner ditch; the earliest context on the site.

Calibrated date: 1σ : cal BC 2190 – 1945
2σ : cal BC 2300 – 1830

West Heath Common, West Sussex

Location: SU 786226
Lat. 50.59.49 N; Long. 00.52.47 W

Excavator: P Drewett (Sussex Archaeological Field Unit), 1973 – 5 and 1980

Site: a Bronze Age barrow cemetery.

Objectives: to date the barrow cemetery.

Comments:
AML: eleven samples were subsequently dated: HAR-5282 (4988VIY), HAR-5281 (4988VIZ), HAR-5283 (4988VIX), HAR-5284 (49888W), HAR-5285 (4988VIV), HAR-5320 (4988735), HAR-5321 (4988VI21), HAR-5322 (4988VI17), HAR-5323 (4988VI20), and HAR-5284 (49888W).

HAR-645   8100 ± 70 BP

$\delta^{13}C$: −23.9 ‰

Sample: WHC1, submitted on 4 June 1974

Material: charcoal.

Initial comment: from layer 13, pit F1, sealed beneath barrow I.

Calibrated date: 1σ : cal BC 7145 – 7040
2σ : cal BC 7210 – 6820

Final comments:
P Drewett: this date fits well with the suspected Mesolithic date of the pit.

References: Drewett 1976, 150

HAR-646   3110 ± 160 BP

$\delta^{13}C$: −26.0 ‰

Sample: WHC2, submitted on 4 June 1974

Material: charcoal.

Initial comment: from a lens of charcoal just above the old land surface under the barrow (layer 4).

Calibrated date: 1σ : cal BC 1530 – 1165
2σ : cal BC 1740 – 930

Final comments:
Harwell: a small sample accounts for the larger than normal error term.

References: Drewett 1976, 150

HAR-647   3630 ± 100 BP

$\delta^{13}C$: −25.8 ‰

Sample: WHC3, submitted on 4 June 1974

Material: charcoal, recovered by flotation.

Initial comment: from the old land surface beneath barrow I (layer 4).

Calibrated date: 1σ : cal BC 2140 – 1890
2σ : cal BC 2300 – 1740

Final comments:
P Drewett: the result is fine for the construction of the barrow.

References: Drewett 1976, 150

HAR-648   3220 ± 180 BP

$\delta^{13}C$: unknown

Sample: WHC4, submitted on 4 June 1974

Material: charcoal.

Initial comment: from a lens of charcoal in the phase 1 ditch, sealed beneath the upcast from the phase 2 ditch of barrow III.

Calibrated date: 1σ : cal BC 1735 – 1310
2σ : cal BC 1940 – 1020

Final comments:
P Drewett: this result is rather later than expected, but it is not yet known how long-lived the barrow cemeteries were.

References: Drewett 1976, 150

HAR-1646   6900 ± 110 BP

$\delta^{13}C$: –25.6 ‰

Sample: WHIVF7, submitted on 27 May 1976

Material: charcoal: mainly oak (*Quercus* sp.) from fairly large timbers with a few fragments of pine (*Pinus* sp.) and birch (*Betula* sp.) (C A Keepax).

Initial comment: from barrow IV, layer 7.

Calibrated date: 1σ : cal BC 5950 – 5640
2σ : cal BC 5980 – 5565

Final comments:
P Drewett: this must relate to Mesolithic occupation under the barrow.

West Mersea: The Strood, Essex

Location: TM 01401502
Lat. 51.47.49 N; Long. 00.55.16 E

Excavator: P Crummy (Colchester Archaeological Excavation Committee), 1978

Site: a watching brief at a causeway approximately half a mile long across to Mersea island, constructed of some 15 – 20 rows of timber piles, each 400 – 500m long, making a total of 3000 – 5000 piles in all; such a major undertaking suggests the presence of an important structure on the island to warrant such expense.

References: Crummy *et al* 1982, 82 – 3 (^{14}C)

Objectives: to supplement dendrochronological dating from five timbers which together produced a sequence of 217 years, and to date the causeway. The presence of extensive Roman remains on the island suggests that the samples may be of Roman date, but there is documentary evidence that timbers were ordered for West Mersea church and the Strood in *c* 1868.

Comments:
P Crummy: the (uncalibrated) dates were unexpected since it was thought that the causeway was of Roman origin.

HAR-3369   1420 ± 70 BP

$\delta^{13}C$: –26.5 ‰

Sample: MS4, submitted by J Hillam on 11 May 1979

Material: wood: *Quercus* sp.; sample taken from years 103 – 22.

Initial comment: from one of five piles from the causeway.

Calibrated date: 1σ : cal AD 565 – 665
2σ : cal AD 460 – 690

Final comments:
P Crummy: a Roman rather than a Saxon date was expected.

HAR-3808   1260 ± 60 BP

$\delta^{13}C$: –28.9 ‰

Sample: MS5, submitted by J Hillam

Material: wood: years 13 – 22 from a timber with 46 annual rings; this sample is undated dendrochronologically due to its short ring pattern.

Initial comment: from same context as HAR-3369; submitted to check the Saxon date produced.

Calibrated date: 1σ : cal AD 675 – 850
2σ : cal AD 650 – 890

West Stow, Suffolk

Location: TL 797714
Lat. 52.18.39 N; Long. 00.38.11 E

Excavator: S E West (Suffolk Archaeological Unit), 1965 – 72

Site: Iron Age and Anglo-Saxon settlement in the Lark valley beside the River Lark, near to Lackford Bridge.

References: West 1985

HAR-3381   1630 ± 80 BP

$\delta^{13}C$: –27.1 ‰

Sample: WSW083, submitted on 11 May 1979

Material: charcoal with soil: mainly *Quercus* sp., with some *Fraxinus* sp. and diffuse porous species, from mature timbers (C A Keepax).

Initial comment: from a hearth, probably Iron Age.

Calibrated date: 1σ : cal AD 270 – 535
2σ : cal AD 230 – 600

HAR-3382   1280 ± 70 BP

$\delta^{13}C$: –25.6 ‰

Sample: WSW026, submitted on 11 May 1979

Material: charcoal with soil: *Quercus* sp. and *Prunus* sp. from mature timbers (C A Keepax).

Initial comment: from a fire pit containing abundant charred cereals, Iron Age or Anglo-Saxon.

Calibrated date: 1σ : cal AD 663 – 790
2σ : cal AD 640 – 890

HAR-4054   1610 ± 70 BP

$\delta^{13}C$: −25.6 ‰

Sample: SFB2, submitted on 26 September 1980

Material: animal bone.

Initial comment: from the latest period of the Saxon site.

Calibrated date: 1σ : cal AD 380 – 540
2σ : cal AD 250 – 600

HAR-4055   1600 ± 70 BP

$\delta^{13}C$: −21.9 ‰

Sample: SFB44, submitted on 26 September 1980

Material: animal bone.

Initial comment: from the middle period of the Saxon site.

Calibrated date: 1σ : cal AD 390 – 545
2σ : cal AD 255 – 610

HAR-4093   1670 ± 70 BP

$\delta^{13}C$: −22.6 ‰

Sample: SFB52, submitted on 26 September 1980

Material: animal bone.

Initial comment: from the earliest period of the Saxon site.

Calibrated date: 1σ : cal AD 255 – 430
2σ : cal AD 220 – 540

HAR-4111   1460 ± 70 BP

$\delta^{13}C$: −21.5 ‰

Sample: SFB50, submitted on 26 September 1980

Material: animal bone.

Initial comment: from the middle period of the Saxon site.

Calibrated date: 1σ : cal AD 545 – 650
2σ : cal AD 430 – 670

HAR-4145   1830 ± 70 BP

$\delta^{13}C$: −22.1 ‰

Sample: SFB49, submitted on 26 September 1980

Material: animal bone.

Initial comment: from the middle period of the Saxon site.

Calibrated date: 1σ : cal AD 85 – 250
2σ : cal AD 20 – 375

HAR-4146   1600 ± 90 BP

$\delta^{13}C$: −22.6 ‰

Sample: SFB15, submitted on 26 September 1980

Material: animal bone.

Initial comment: from the middle period of the Saxon site.

Calibrated date: 1σ : cal AD 345 – 555
2σ : cal AD 240 – 640

HAR-4147   2080 ± 90 BP

$\delta^{13}C$: −22.4 ‰

Sample: SFB61, submitted on 26 September 1980

Material: animal bone.

Initial comment: from the earliest period of the Saxon site.

Calibrated date: 1σ : cal BC 330 – 10 cal AD
2σ : cal BC 380 – 90 cal AD

HAR-4191   2030 ± 90 BP

$\delta^{13}C$: −22.2 ‰

Sample: SFB45, submitted on 26 September 1980

Material: animal bone.

Initial comment: from the middle period of the Saxon site.

Calibrated date: 1σ : cal BC 170 – 65 cal AD
2σ : cal BC 360 – 130 cal AD

HAR-4194   1490 ± 80 BP

$\delta^{13}C$: −25.4 ‰

Sample: SFB36, submitted on 26 September 1980

Material: animal bone.

Initial comment: from the earliest period of the Saxon site.

Calibrated date: 1σ : cal AD 445 – 645
2σ : cal AD 400 – 670

HAR-4255   1500 ± 70 BP

$\delta^{13}C$: −23.2 ‰

Sample: SFB48, submitted on 26 September 1980

Material: bone.

Initial comment: from the middle period of the Saxon site.

Calibrated date: 1σ : cal AD 445 – 630
2σ : cal AD 410 – 660

Final comments:
Harwell: repeat of HAR-4056.

West Stow: Lackford Bridge, Suffolk

Location: TL 792712
Lat. 52.18.33 N; Long. 00.37.44 E

Excavator: P Murphy and R Darrah (Suffolk Archaeological Unit), 1977

Site: prehistoric 'burnt flint' sealed by a peat deposit discovered during quarrying.

Objectives: dates are required to supplement the analysis of pollen and plant remains.

HAR-2484   3940 ± 70 BP

$\delta^{13}C$: −26.7 ‰

Sample: WSW027, submitted by P Murphy on 22 December 1977

Material: charcoal: *Quercus* sp. and *Alnus* sp. present (not twiggy), but mostly too small for identification; *c* 10% of a very large sample identified (C A Keepax).

Initial comment: from a layer of charcoal and burnt flint 0.2m deep, sealed within the peats of the Lark Valley.

Comment on uncalibrated date: this is an early example of a common, but still enigmatic, type of prehistoric valley floor site.

Calibrated date: 1σ : cal BC 2570 − 2355
                      2σ : cal BC 2850 − 2210

Final comments:
E Martin: similar areas of burnt flint are known from nearby Swales and West Row Fens in Mildenhall, Suffolk, associated in at least one case with a pit or trough (perhaps for cooking). Radiocarbon dates from these are broadly similar to the above, but slightly younger.

Wetwang Slack, Humberside

Location: SE 946601 (centre)
              Lat. 54.01.41 N; Long. 00.33.20 W

Excavator: J Dent (Humberside Excavation Committee), 1975 − 80

Site: Beaker/Bronze Age cemetery, Iron Age settlement and cemetery, a continuation of the Garton Slack complex.

References: Dent 1978
                Dent 1979
                Dent 1983

Objectives: to relate the cultural evidence to a fixed chronological scale.

Comments:
J Dent: (on HAR-1665, HAR-2771, HAR-2776, and HAR-2777) the one standard deviation ranges are acceptable for 3 of the 4, but are still rather broad to be of value in refining the chronology of the cemetery beyond the range suggested by the artefacts.

HAR-1665   2110 ± 80 BP

$\delta^{13}C$: −22.0 ‰

Sample: WEAF, submitted on 27 May 1976

Material: human bone, packed damp .

Initial comment: from grave 155 (female), found together with two bronze bracelets, a bronze and coral brooch, a bronze earring, and a necklace of blue glass beads. From its position this grave seems to be one of the earliest; the brooch and one of the bracelets are paralleled by finds at the Arras cemetery and seem to fix the early part of the Wetwang site at a stage late in La Tène 1.

Comment on uncalibrated date: this grave is now judged to belong to phase 2 (of 4) in the group.

Calibrated date: 1σ : cal BC 350 − 40
                      2σ : cal BC 380 − 60 cal AD

Final comments:
J Dent: a date in the fourth or third century BC seems possible on artefactual grounds.

References: Dent 1978, 49
                Dent 1982, 439

HAR-1878   3450 ± 90 BP

$\delta^{13}C$: −25.0 ‰

Sample: WSVIAK, submitted on 1 September 1976

Material: charcoal: *Quercus* sp. and hawthorn type (Rosaceae, sub-family Pomoideae), not twiggy; *c* 50% identified (C A Keepax).

Initial comment: from probable coffin remains in grave 3, one of three graves not enclosed by barrow ditches, which contained an inhumation with what was possibly a deer scapula; thought to be Bronze Age, although among a number of Iron Age square barrows. This grave clearly cut through a cremation, also thought to be of Bronze Age date.

Comment on uncalibrated date: further unenclosed burials were later found, some with evidence of Beaker or Bronze Age date.

Calibrated date: 1σ : cal BC 1890 − 1675
                      2σ : cal BC 2030 − 1530

Final comments:
J Dent: this result confirms misgivings of Iron Age date based upon cultural differences.

References: Dent 1979, 32
                Dent 1983, 10

HAR-1879   3160 ± 90 BP

$\delta^{13}C$: −26.0 ‰

Sample: WSVINS, submitted on 1 September 1976

Material: charcoal: no identifiable charcoal (C A Keepax).

Initial comment: from a postpipe in a circle of nine posts (9m in diameter), probably a funerary or ritual monument.

Calibrated date: 1σ : cal BC 1520 − 1325
                      2σ : cal BC 1670 − 1225

Final comments:
J Dent: comparison with Bronze Age funerary/ritual monuments is justified.

HAR-2771   2140 ± 80 BP

$\delta^{13}C$: −21.6 ‰

Sample: WTCR, submitted on 12 July 1978

Material: human bone, packed dry.

Initial comment: from burial 236, associated with a bronze bracelet, iron brooch, and a necklace of glass beads, Iron Age.

Comment on uncalibrated date: grouped in phase 2 (of 4) in the cemetery seriation.

Calibrated date: 1σ : cal BC 360 – 95
　　　　　　　　　　2σ : cal BC 390 – 20 cal AD

Final comments:
J Dent: a fourth- or third-century date is suggested on artefactual grounds. This is the earliest context for a brooch of the type.

References: Dent 1982, 439

HAR-2776   1790 ± 70 BP

$\delta^{13}C$: –23.1 ‰

Sample: WSIVMD, submitted on 12 July 1978

Material: human bone, packed dry.

Initial comment: from burial 117, associated with an iron brooch and pig bones.

Comment on uncalibrated date: grouped in phase 4 (of 4) in the cemetery seriation.

Calibrated date: 1σ : cal AD 130 – 335
　　　　　　　　　　2σ : cal AD 70 – 410

Final comments:
J Dent: a date in the second or first century BC seems more likely on artefactual grounds for this type of La Tène 3 brooch.

References: Dent 1982, 439

HAR-2777   2080 ± 80 BP

$\delta^{13}C$: –21.6 ‰

Sample: WSIVJU, submitted on 12 July 1978

Material: human bone, packed dry.

Initial comment: from burial 98, accompanied by a sword and shield.

Comment on uncalibrated date: grouped in phase 4 (of 4) in the cemetery seriation.

Calibrated date: 1σ : cal BC 195 – 0 cal AD
　　　　　　　　　　2σ : cal BC 370 – 80 cal AD

Final comments:
J Dent: this is the date range which would be expected for this phase, at a one standard deviation level of confidence.

References: Dent 1982, 439

HAR-4425   2270 ± 100 BP

$\delta^{13}C$: –26.0 ‰

Sample: WG218EC, submitted on 14 February 1981

Material: charcoal: *Quercus* sp., *Prunus* sp. from mature timbers, *Corylus/Alnus* sp., twig or branch, and Rosaceae, sub-family Pomoideae, twig (C A Keepax).

Initial comment: from a posthole inside an Early Iron Age round house, one of a line of four.

Comment on uncalibrated date: these buildings appear to be contemporary with the earlier stages of the Iron Age cemetery.

Calibrated date: 1σ : cal BC 405 – 200
　　　　　　　　　　2σ : cal BC 755 – 100

Final comments:
J Dent: about right at the one standard deviation level of confidence.

HAR-4426   3900 ± 100 BP

$\delta^{13}C$: unknown

Sample: WT55BF, submitted on 14 February 1981

Material: charcoal: *Quercus* sp. from mature timbers (C A Keepax).

Initial comment: from a possible timber coffin or cist in an early grave (Beaker period) containing a long-necked, decorated Beaker.

Comment on uncalibrated date: the Beaker is southern British S2 (W) type.

Calibrated date: 1σ : cal BC 2565 – 2210
　　　　　　　　　　2σ : cal BC 2855 – 2045

References: Dent 1983, 10

HAR-4427   3780 ± 70 BP

$\delta^{13}C$: –25.4 ‰

Sample: WG7AX, submitted on 14 February 1981

Material: charcoal: *Quercus* sp. from mature timbers (C A Keepax).

Initial comment: from the timber lining of a burial cist in an Early Bronze Age grave containing a crouched inhumation with pig bones and a fine battle axe; this is most important as the first such grave to be found in Yorkshire since the advent of ^{14}C dating.

Calibrated date: 1σ : cal BC 2335 – 2050
　　　　　　　　　　2σ : cal BC 2460 – 2030

References: Dent 1983, 10

HAR-4428   4260 ± 80 BP

$\delta^{13}C$: –25.6 ‰

Sample: WE47IUW, submitted on 14 February 1981

Material: charcoal: *Quercus* sp. from mature timbers (C A Keepax).

Initial comment: from a pit at the centre of an interrupted ditch enclosure in close proximity to both Bronze Age and Iron Age funerary monuments. The sample was submitted to establish to which period the pit relates; although no bone was found in the pit, it seems likely that this was a ritual, and possibly a funerary, monument (cf Ravenstone, Buckinghamshire above).

Comment on uncalibrated date: the pit may have contained a large upright post, the charred base of which provided the sample. This stengthens a ritual interpretation.

Calibrated date: 1σ : cal BC 2925 – 2705
　　　　　　　　　　2σ : cal BC 3075 – 2620

Final comments:
J Dent: broadly in the period of large ritual monuments.

Wharram Percy, North Yorkshire

Location: SE 858642
Lat. 54.03.59 N; Long. 00.41.20 W

Excavator: J G Hurst (Deserted Medieval Village Research Group), 1972 – 81

Site: dam and pond at the southern end of the deserted medieval village.

References: Beresford 1977
Hurst 1986, 102 (^{14}C)
Treen and Atkin forthcoming

Objectives: to investigate the sequence of dams, the millpond, and any other utilisation of water from the springs and stream.

HAR-1329   1300 ± 80 BP

$\delta^{13}C$: –25.0 ‰

Sample: D25/29, submitted on 9 October 1975

Material: grain.

Initial comment: from a dump of charred grain on the edge of the mill pond on a chalk pebble platform above the natural clay of the valley bottom.

Calibrated date: 1σ : cal AD 655 – 785
2σ : cal AD 600 – 890

Final comments:
J G Hurst: this is much earlier than expected and is to be repeated as the possibility of contamination by the chalk stream has been raised.

HAR-1337   1200 ± 80 BP

$\delta^{13}C$: –26.1 ‰

Sample: D20/21, submitted on 9 October 1975

Material: grain.

Initial comment: as HAR-1329.

Comment on uncalibrated date: much earlier than expected, but in the right relationship to HAR-1329 (ie later).

Calibrated date: 1σ : cal AD 690 – 895
2σ : cal AD 660 – 1000

Final comments:
J G Hurst: this sample and HAR-1329 may have been contaminated by the chalk stream and have subsequently been resubmitted.

Wharram Percy, North Yorkshire

Location: SE 858642
Lat. 54.03.59 N; Long. 00.41.20 W

Excavator: J G Hurst (Deserted Medieval Village Research Group), 1962 – 79

Site: St Martin's church and cemetery in the deserted medieval village; some prehistoric activity, including a crouched burial.

References: Bell *et al* 1986, 53 – 8 and 178 – 80 (^{14}C)
Treen and Atkin forthcoming

Objectives: to date the construction of the church.

Comments:
AML: three samples, HAR-1438 (C2352 small), HAR-2461 (C2051), and HAR-991 (C2235:C2236) failed; one sample, HAR-3692 (56/66), was not dated. There were also a number of samples submitted after April 1981.

HAR-2208   2030 ± 60 BP

$\delta^{13}C$: –21.4 ‰

Sample: GTA16746, submitted on 1 June 1977

Material: human bone: female aged 25 – 35 years.

Initial comment: from possible Iron Age crouched burial (334) in medieval graveyard, adjacent to the Late Saxon church, no grave goods.

Comment on uncalibrated date: this is just about right as the burial was respected by a Roman ditch.

Calibrated date: 1σ : cal BC 110 – 20 cal AD
2σ : cal BC 190 – 80 cal AD

HAR-2460   910 ± 70 BP

$\delta^{13}C$: –20.2 ‰

Sample: C2027, submitted on 22 December 1977

Material: human bone, marked with Indian ink.

Initial comment: from burial LXXXII, one of a group of burials under Saxon grave slabs outside the church, south of the phase II chancel.

Calibrated date: 1σ : cal AD 1025 – 1215
2σ : cal AD 990 – 1260

Final comments:
J G Hurst: this date fits with the stylistic dating of the grave slabs to the tenth or eleventh century.

HAR-2462   980 ± 70 BP

$\delta^{13}C$: –21.1 ‰

Sample: C2042, submitted on 22 December 1977

Material: human bone, marked with Indian ink.

Initial comment: from burial LXXXIII, as HAR-2460.

Calibrated date: 1σ : cal AD 990 – 1155
2σ : cal AD 900 – 1220

Final comments:
J G Hurst: as HAR-2460.

HAR-2631   890 ± 70 BP

$\delta^{13}C$: –20.8 ‰

Sample: C2051, submitted on 22 December 1977

Material: human bone.

Initial comment: from burial LXXXVII, associated with, and probably under, a group of Saxon burials outside the church.

Calibrated date: 1σ : cal AD 1030 – 1225
2σ : cal AD 1010 – 1270

Final comments:
J G Hurst: as HAR-2460.

HAR-2672   910 ± 80 BP

δ¹³C: unknown

Sample: C2066, submitted on 21 March 1978

Material: human bone.

Initial comment: from burial LXXXI, one of a group of burials under Saxon grave slabs outside the church, south of the phase II chancel.

Calibrated date: 1σ : cal AD 1020 – 1220
2σ : cal AD 980 – 1270

Final comments:
J G Hurst: as HAR-2460.
AML: (A J Clark) the wide date bracket for the calibrated result is caused by a flat spot on the curve between *c* AD 1040 and AD 1160, but this result fits with the others in indicating that if they are Saxon they are quite close to the Conquest.

HAR-3575   980 ± 70 BP

δ¹³C: −21.6 ‰

Sample: C237, submitted on 9 October 1979

Material: human bone: articulated leg bones, probably cut by the phase II chancel revetment.

Initial comment: from a burial which predates the small two-celled Saxon church, for which a starting date has yet to be established.

Calibrated date: 1σ : cal AD 990 – 1155
2σ : cal AD 900 – 1220

Final comments:
J G Hurst: this adds to the probability of an eleventh-century date for the two-celled church.

HAR-3584   1240 ± 90 BP

δ¹³C: −22.7 ‰

Sample: C238, submitted on 9 October 1979

Material: animal and human bone.

Initial comment: from the pre-Saxon ground surface at the east end of the church (layer 215); sealed by the mortar foundation layer (217) for the phase II chancel of the stone church.

Calibrated date: 1σ : cal AD 670 – 890
2σ : cal AD 640 – 990

Final comments:
J G Hurst: this is a satisfactory date for the pre-church Saxon activity on the terrace.

Wicken Bonhunt, Essex

Location: TL 511335
Lat. 51.58.55 N; Long. 00.12.00 W

Excavator: R Carr and S Dunmore (Suffolk Archaeological Unit), 1972

Site: a well containing Middle Saxon pottery in an Anglo-Saxon settlement.

References: Wade 1974
Wade 1980, 96 (¹⁴C)
Radiocarbon **19**, 412 (¹⁴C)

Objectives: to date the well; the timbers had been cut 'through and through' so that they were unsuitable for dendrochronology.

Comments:
R Carr and S Dunmore: these two results place the construction of the well within the Middle Saxon period.

HAR-512   1195 ± 63 BP

δ¹³C: −25.8 ‰

Sample: SPL1, submitted by J Fletcher on 19 June 197

Material: wood: *Quercus* sp., wet heartwood covering 15 annual rings, growth allowance 65 ± 10 years.

Initial comment: from the shaft of well 2, phase 1, plank east 1.

Calibrated date: 1σ : cal AD 725 – 895
2σ : cal AD 670 – 980

Final comments:
R Carr and S Dunmore: this corresponds well with HAR-513 and the expected Middle Saxon date for the well.

HAR-513   1200 ± 70 BP

δ¹³C: −26.7 ‰

Sample: SPL2WD, submitted by J Fletcher on 19 June 1974

Material: wood: *Quercus* sp., heartwood (dried before submission), covering 15 annual rings, growth allowance 40 ± 10 years.

Initial comment: from the shaft of well 2, phase 1 plank east 2.

Calibrated date: 1σ : cal AD 715 – 895
2σ : cal AD 670 – 990

Final comments:
R Carr and S Dunmore: corresponds well with HAR-512 and the expected Anglo-Saxon date for the well.

Wighton, Norfolk

Location: TF 944348
Lat. 52.52.30 N; Long. 00.53.20 E

Excavator: A J Lawson (Norfolk Archaeological Unit), 1974

Site: five skeletons were found in graves sealed by the old ground surface beneath the bank of a late or sub-Roman D-shaped enclosure (County no 1113 WGT).

References: Lawson 1976b; 65, 72 (¹⁴C)
Radiocarbon **21**, 370 – 1 (¹⁴C)

Objectives: to date the previously unknown cemetery and superimposed defensive earthwork.

HAR-1142 1710 ± 70 BP

$\delta^{13}C$: −20.0 ‰

Sample: 1113WGTA, submitted on 30 April 1975

Material: human bone: long bones.

Initial comment: from skeleton 19; date unknown, probably second century AD.

Comment on uncalibrated date: this result agrees with the very meagre archaeological evidence.

Calibrated date: 1σ : cal AD 240 – 410
 2σ : cal AD 130 – 450

Final comments:
A J Lawson: the date implies a Late Roman date for the cemetery, as anticipated.

Harwell: this should be the more reliable of the two results.

HAR-1143 1900 ± 120 BP

$\delta^{13}C$: −22.1 ‰

Sample: 1113WGTB, submitted on 30 April 1975

Material: animal bone: *Bos* sp..

Initial comment: from the middle silt of a small ditch sealed by the enclosure bank associated with Roman coarse pottery and one iron nail; the pottery could be late first century AD.

Comment on uncalibrated date: the ditch appears to be broadly contemporary, or slightly earlier, than the associated cemetery.

Calibrated date: 1σ : cal BC 40 – 240 cal AD
 2σ : cal BC 190 – 400 cal AD

Final comments:
Harwell: a small sample accounts for the larger than normal error term.

Willington, Derbyshire

Location: SK 285278
 Lat. 52.50.48 N; Long. 01.34.36 W

Excavator: H Wheeler (Trent Valley Archaeological Research Unit), 1970 – 2

Site: multiperiod site including two Late Neolithic settlements, Iron Age occupation, two Romano-British farms, and a small Saxon settlement.

References: Wheeler 1979

Objectives: to date the Late Bronze Age/Iron Age occupation.

HAR-956 6110 ± 130 BP

$\delta^{13}C$: −25.1 ‰

Sample: W170EE55, submitted on 26 November 1974

Material: charcoal.

Initial comment: from hearth F55 in the top of a partially silted pit associated with Late Bronze Age – Early Iron Age pottery; adjacent to a similar hearth, F56.

Comment on uncalibrated date: this result is misleading as the associated artefacts are not earlier than *c* 800 BC, and belong to the Early Iron Age.

Calibrated date: 1σ : cal BC 5230 – 4865
 2σ : cal BC 5330 – 4730

Final comments:
Harwell: a small sample, diluted before conversion to benzene, accounts for the larger than normal error term.

References: Wheeler 1979, 84

HAR-957 4130 ± 100 BP

$\delta^{13}C$: −25.6 ‰

Sample: W170KA56, submitted on 26 November 1974

Material: charcoal.

Initial comment: from a hearth, as HAR-956.

Calibrated date: 1σ : cal BC 2890 – 2510
 2σ : cal BC 2920 – 2460

Wilmington: Gravel Pit, Kent

Location: TQ 5371 approx
 Lat. 51.25.01 N; Long. 00.12.02 E

Excavator: B Philp (Kent Archaeological Rescue Unit)

Site: a possibly Iron Age settlement.

Comments:
B Philp: HAR-1234, HAR-1226, and HAR-1261 form a tight group and fall in the correct order.

HAR-1226 4620 ± 80 BP

$\delta^{13}C$: −29.2 ‰

Sample: WGPBJP14, submitted on 16 July 1975

Material: wood.

Initial comment: from the central peat zone in a natural lake.

Calibrated date: 1σ : cal BC 3505 – 3200
 2σ : cal BC 3625 – 3050

HAR-1234 4230 ± 110 BP

$\delta^{13}C$: −27.6 ‰

Sample: WGPBJP11, submitted on 16 July 1975

Material: wood.

Initial comment: from domestic rubbish in the upper peat zone in a natural lake.

Calibrated date: 1σ : cal BC 2925 – 2526
 2σ : cal BC 3095 – 2505

Final comments:
Harwell: the larger than usual error term is due to a poor laboratory yield in the conversion of carbon dioxide to acetylene.

HAR-1261 5100 ± 80 BP

$\delta^{13}C$: −25.3 ‰

Sample: WGPBJP31, submitted on 16 July 1975

Material: animal bone.

Initial comment: from domestic rubbish in the lower peat zone in a natural lake.

Calibrated date: 1σ : cal BC 3995 – 3790
2σ : cal BC 4210 – 3705

HAR-1685   6440 ± 100 BP

$\delta^{13}C$: −25.8 ‰

Sample: BJP51/38, submitted on 27 May 1976

Material: bone.

Initial comment: from domestic rubbish in the central peat zone, submitted as a replacement for HAR-1262 which was too small.

Comment on uncalibrated date: c 1300 years earlier than expected; this should be the same date as HAR-1261 (combined samples from the same peat zone).

Calibrated date: 1σ : cal BC 5480 – 5245
2σ : cal BC 5540 – 5230

Final comments:
Harwell: this result is unusual but not impossible; nothing in the experimental notes gives cause for doubt.

HAR-2399   4880 ± 80 BP

$\delta^{13}C$: −28.9 ‰

Sample: BJP15, submitted on 7 September 1977

Material: peat.

Calibrated date: 1σ : cal BC 3780 – 3545
2σ : cal BC 3930 – 3385

Final comments:
Harwell: this sample was also labelled WGP-12.

HAR-2407   7110 ± 90 BP

$\delta^{13}C$: −27.5 ‰

Sample: BJP58, submitted on 7 September 1977

Material: peat.

Calibrated date: 1σ : cal BC 6080 – 5848
2σ : cal BC 6120 – 5740

HAR-2408   4570 ± 80 BP

$\delta^{13}C$: −24.3 ‰

Sample: BJP4, submitted on 7 September 1977

Material: wood: yew (*Taxus baccata*) (C A Keepax).

Calibrated date: 1σ : cal BC 3490 – 3105
2σ : cal BC 3600 – 3040

HAR-2409   4900 ± 70 BP

$\delta^{13}C$: −28.6 ‰

Sample: BJP5, submitted on 7 September 1977

Material: wood: alder (*Alnus glutinosa*) (C A Keepax).

Calibrated date: 1σ : cal BC 3780 – 3640
2σ : cal BC 3930 – 3525

HAR-2410   4750 ± 70 BP

$\delta^{13}C$: −28.0 ‰

Sample: BJP16, submitted on 7 September 1977

Material: compressed organic matter: no identifiable wood (C A Keepax).

Calibrated date: 1σ : cal BC 3635 – 3380
2σ : cal BC 3700 – 3360

Winchcombe: Co-Op, Gloucestershire

Location: SP 025284
Lat. 52.26.21 N; Long. 01.57.48 W

Excavator: A Saville (Cheltenham City Museum and Art Gallery), 1977

Site: multiperiod site with two graves which ostensibly belong to a Late Roman cemetery.

References: Saville 1985, 135 – 6 (^{14}C)

Objectives: to date the graves, which could be Roman or Late Saxon, and to date the limestone-tempered pottery, which at the time of submission is unparalled in Gloucester.

Comments:
A Saville: the results from HAR-4263 and HAR-4352 are acceptable in themselves, as there is no other dating evidence, but they are problematic in terms of their wide divergence, since it appeared archaeologically that the two burials were part of the same phase of cemetery activity.

Harwell: the repeat measurements were made to clarify the divergence of HAR-4263 and HAR-4352; the differences between the first and second dates are still considerable, as are those obtained from the mean dates. Burial F1 probably dates from the mid sixth to the mid seventh century, burial F17 probably dates from the late eighth to the tenth century; the cemetery was probably used from the sixth to the tenth centuries.

HAR-4262   930 ± 80 BP

$\delta^{13}C$: −22.6 ‰

Sample: WN77F34, submitted on 4 February 1981

Material: animal bone.

Initial comment: from the basal fill of a pit (F34) containing limestone-tempered pottery (?tenth- or eleventh-century).

Comment on uncalibrated date: entirely acceptable: a Late Saxon or early medieval date was anticipated for the pottery.

Calibrated date: 1σ : cal AD 1015 – 1210
2σ : cal AD 970 – 1260

HAR-4263   1280 ± 90 BP

$\delta^{13}C$: −20.5 ‰

Sample: WN77F17, submitted on 4 February 1981

Material: human bone: left and right femur, tibia, and right humerus; from an adult female age 30 – 35 years (skeleton 4).

Initial comment: from grave 17, which contained one sherd of Roman pottery, possibly residual.

Calibrated date: 1σ : cal AD 655 – 860
2σ : cal AD 600 – 960

HAR-4352   1530 ± 70 BP

$\delta^{13}C$: −22.3 ‰

Sample: WN77F1S1, submitted on 4 February 1981

Material: human bone: femurs, tibiae, left radius, left humerus, and right ulna from a female aged *c* 35 years (skeleton 1).

Initial comment: from grave 1, which contained one rim sherd of Late Saxon or early medieval limestone-tempered ware, possibly an admixture into an earlier grave.

Calibrated date: 1σ : cal AD 430 – 605
2σ : cal AD 390 – 650

HAR-5921   1100 ± 70 BP

$\delta^{13}C$: −22.7 ‰

Sample: WN77F17, submitted on 4 February 1981

Material: human bone.

Initial comment: from grave F17, as HAR-4263.

Calibrated date: 1σ : cal AD 885 – 1010
2σ : cal AD 780 – 1030

Final comments:
Harwell: repeat of HAR-4263.

HAR-5922   1330 ± 80 BP

$\delta^{13}C$: −29.2 ‰

Sample: WN77F1S1, submitted on 4 February 1981

Material: animal bone.

Initial comment: from same context as HAR-4352.

Calibrated date: 1σ : cal AD 640 – 775
2σ : cal AD 565 – 880

Final comments:
Harwell: repeat of HAR-4352.

HAR-5921+HAR-4352   1445 ± 55 BP

$\delta^{13}C$: unknown

Sample: WN77F17+WN77F34, submitted on 4 February 1981

Material: animal and human bone.

Initial comment: see above.

Calibrated date: 1σ : cal AD 560 – 650
2σ : cal AD 465 – 670

Final comments:
Harwell: a mean date.

HAR-5922+HAR-4263   1170 ± 55 BP

$\delta^{13}C$: unknown

Sample: WN77F1S1+WN77F17, submitted on 4 February 1981

Material: bone.

Initial comment: see above.

Calibrated date: 1σ : cal AD 780 – 945
2σ : cal AD 690 – 990

Final comments:
Harwell: a mean date.

Winchester: Lower Brook Street, Hampshire

Location: SU 484295
Lat. 51.03.44 N; Long. 01.18.33 W

Excavator: M Biddle, 1965 – 71

Site: a large area excavation (1200 m²) on the west side of Lower Brook Street. The first occupation is of a large early Roman ditched enclosure followed by a temple, several houses, and a minor street belonging to the Roman town. Following extensive demolition in the early fourth century, a new stone building, later used as a workshop, was constructed in the western part of the area. The Roman period was followed by the development of a Middle Saxon residence. This complex evolved into the church of St Mary which, following the layout of the late Saxon street plan, stood on the street frontage flanked by houses to the south (House IX/X) and north (Houses XI and XII). A lane (St Pancras Lane) led west from the street to pass around St Pancras' church in the middle of the block between Lower and Middle Brook Streets. The last of the houses was abandoned by the late fifteenth century. The churches went out of use in the early sixteenth century. Thereafter the site lay open until it was reoccupied, following sparse eighteenth-century activity, in the mid-nineteenth century.

References: Biddle 1969
Biddle 1972

Objectives: samples for radiocarbon dating were taken from the Roman, post-Roman, and early and later medieval deposits. They come from 11 different groups, each with internal sequences, lettered from earliest to latest.

Group 1 (a) – (e) Trench I, House IX. On this tenement site a group of pits was succeeded by a timber-built house (House IX) of two main phases.

Group 2 (a) – (b) Trench I, Houses IX and X. Samples from a timber-lined water-channel running from north to south between the tenements and the medieval street.

Group 3 (a) – (h) A series of pits and wells in an area which had been open since the Late Roman period behind Houses IX and X. The stratigraphic relationships between the pits were difficult and a continuous sequence could not be established; the dates suggested are based partly upon the dating of the pottery.

Group 4 (a) – (b) Trench II, St Mary's church.

Group 5 (a) – (e) Trench III, House XI. Samples from a well and overlying timber houses.

Group 6 (a) – (b) Trench III, House XI. Samples from the smaller timber-lined water-channels at the street frontage of the tenement.

Group 7 Trench III, St Pancras Lane. Animal bone from successive lane surfaces.

Group 8 (a) – (e) Trench III, House XII. Samples from a succession of structures on the medieval frontage of the tenement.

Group 9 (a) – (d) Trench III, House XII. Samples from a succession of timber-lined water-channels running between House XII and the medieval street.

Group 10 (a)-(g) Trench III, House XII. Samples from an area in the rear of the tenement, occupied first with pits and later by a wing added behind the house along the north side of St Pancras Lane. Group 11 (a)-(j) Trench IV, St Pancras' Church.

The samples were chosen with the following purposes in mind:

1. to provide a series of absolute dates essential for the interpretation of the site

2. since nearly all the samples can be precisely related to long stratigraphic and structural sequences, their dates can be checked against these fixed relative sequences

3. the samples are in a wide variety of materials intended to provide a check on the comparability of dates derived from different materials

4. most of the timber samples are independently dated by dendrochronology. The calibration of the radiocarbon dates for the medieval period can thus be tested

5. independent dates could be provided by archaeomagnetic examination of pottery from layers associated with the radiocarbon samples.

This combination of scientific dating and stratigraphic evidence is important for the interpretation of the site, but also provides a means of evaluating the comparative reliability of each technique and its potential contribution to medieval archaeology as a whole.

Comments:
AML: no result has been found for HAR-756; this may have been a small sample which was not dated.

HAR-288   1240 ± 60 BP

$\delta^{13}C$: –26.0 ‰

Sample: OF 1199, submitted in 1973

Material: wood: *Quercus* sp. – a rectangular piece cut across the trunk but not quite including the centre; at least 59 rings were preserved but any number could have been lost from the outside. The sample included no more than 11 rings from the inside of the timber.

Initial comment: from BS, trench III, house XI, F778. Group 5 (a). HAR-878, HAR-1279, and HAR-1852 are also from F778 but from different timbers.

Calibrated date: 1σ : cal AD 680 – 880
                     2σ : cal AD 660 – 940

Final comments:
M Biddle: residence, stone building [G]; final phase 4 (P.ph. 163), ninth-century. Rephased as: residence, stone building, date group 4 – 6 (P.Ph. 163a), late eighth- to late ninth-century. The rings dated are from the inside of a timber with an unknown number of rings. The radiocarbon date could be in agreement with the phasing.

HAR-289   1260 ± 80 BP

$\delta^{13}C$: unknown

Sample: OF 1046, submitted in 1973

Material: wood: *Quercus* sp. – roughly squared half tree trunk; the total number of rings counted was 104, with no sapwood. The sample was of no more than 13 rings from the outside of the trunk, separated by 65 rings from HAR-290. HAR-289 and HAR-290 were from the same post, and are repeated by HAR-366 and HAR-367, subsequent samples from the same timber. .

Initial comment: from BS, trench I, house IX, posthole 2392, layer 871. Group 1 (d).

Calibrated date: 1σ : cal AD 665 – 880
                     2σ : cal AD 640 – 990

Final comments:
M Biddle: house IX/X, timber; final phase 76 (P.ph. 516), eleventh-century. The radiocarbon date is early in relation to the phasing.

Samples were taken for dendrochronology and measured, but not dated.

Harwell: no certificate has been found.

HAR-290   1210 ± 80 BP

$\delta^{13}C$: unknown

Sample: OF 1046, submitted in 1973

Material: wood: *Quercus* sp. – roughly squared half tree trunk; the total number of rings counted was 104, with no sapwood. The sample was no more than 16 rings from the inside of the trunk. This sample was separated by 65 rings from HAR-289. HAR-289 and HAR-290 were from the same post, to be compared with HAR-366 and HAR-367, subsequent samples from the same timber.

Initial comment: from BS, trench I, house IX, posthole 2392, layer 871. Group 1 (d).

Calibrated date: 1σ : cal AD 685 – 895
                     2σ : cal AD 660 – 990

Final comments:
M Biddle: house IX/X, timber; final phase 76 (P.ph. 516), eleventh-century. The radiocarbon date is early in relation to the phasing.

A sample was taken for dendrochronology and measured, but not dated.

Harwell: no certificate has been found.

HAR-291   1170 ± 70 BP

δ¹³C: unknown

Sample: OF 1181, submitted in 1973

Material: wood: *Quercus* sp. – split untrimmed tree trunk; the total number of rings counted was 116. 10 – 15 rings have possibly been lost from the outside. No sapwood was present. The sample consisted of no more than 18 rings from the inside of the trunk. This sample is separated by 75 rings from HAR-292. HAR-291 and HAR-292 are from the same timber and are repeated by HAR-368 and HAR-369.

Initial comment: from BS, trench III, house XII, posthole 2574. Group 8 (c).

Calibrated date: 1σ : cal AD 775 – 960
      2σ : cal AD 680 – 1010

Final comments:
M Biddle: the post probably belongs to house XII, timber; final phase 41 (P.ph. 711) late eleventh- to early twelfth-century. The radiocarbon date is in agreement with the phasing.

A sample was taken for dendrochronology and measured, but not dated.

Harwell: no certificate has been found.

HAR-292   940 ± 60 BP

δ¹³C: unknown

Sample: OF 1181, submitted in 1973

Material: wood: *Quercus* sp. – split untrimmed tree trunk; the total number of rings counted was 116. 10 – 15 rings have possibly been lost from the outside. No sapwood was present. The sample was of no more than 23 rings from the outside of the trunk. This sample was separated by 75 rings from HAR-291. HAR-291 and HAR-292 were from the same timber. They are repeated by HAR-368 and HAR-369.

Initial comment: from BS, trench III, house XII, posthole 2574. Group 8 (c).

Calibrated date: 1σ : cal AD 1020 – 1165
      2σ : cal AD 980 – 1230

Final comments:
M Biddle: the post probably belongs to house XII, timber; final phase 41 (P.ph. 711) late eleventh- to early twelfth-century. The radiocarbon date is in agreement with the phasing.

A sample was taken for dendrochronology and measured, but not dated.

HAR-354   1060 ± 60 BP

δ¹³C: –26.1 ‰

Sample: OF 746, submitted on 26 July 1974

Material: wood: *Quercus* sp..

Initial comment: from BS, trench III, house XII, F806, layer 1835.

Calibrated date: 1σ : cal AD 895 – 1020
      2σ : cal AD 880 – 1040

Final comments:
M Biddle: house XII, timber; final phase 37 (P.ph. 735) mid to late tenth-century. The radiocarbon date could be in agreement with the phasing.

A sample was taken for dendrochronology and measured, but not dated.

Harwell: no certificate or submission form has been found.

HAR-362   960 ± 60 BP

δ¹³C: –23.3 ‰

Sample: OF 345, submitted in 1973

Material: wood: *Quercus* sp. – post. The total number of rings counted was 116, with no sapwood. The sample consisted of no more than 25 rings taken 21 rings inside the outer edge of the trunk. This sample is separated by 65 rings from HAR-363.

Initial comment: fom BS, trench III, house XII, posthole 1194. It could be from the same construction as HAR-291, HAR-292, HAR-368, and HAR-369. Group 8 (c).

Calibrated date: 1σ : cal AD 1010 – 1160
      2σ : cal AD 970 – 1220

Final comments:
M Biddle: house XII, timber; final phase 40 (P.ph. 683), mid eleventh-century. The radiocarbon date is in agreement with the phasing and the dendrochronological dates.

Dendrochronological date: the last ring of the timber from posthole 1194 is placed at 1081, making the felling date *c* 1106 or later and placing the midpoint of the rings dated by HAR-362 at 1048. The centre of the calibrated one standard deviation range of the radiocarbon date is 1085, 37 years later than the dendrochronological centrepoint of the rings covered by the radiocarbon sample [cc/1085–dc/1048 = 37].

HAR-363   990 ± 70 BP

δ¹³C: –23.4 ‰

Sample: OF 345, submitted in 1973

Material: wood: *Quercus* sp. – post. The total number of rings counted was 116, with no sapwood present. The sample consisted of no more than 26 rings from the inside of the trunk. This sample is separated by 65 rings from HAR-362.

Initial comment: from BS, trench III, house XII. ii, posthole 1194. It could be from the same construction as HAR-291, HAR-292, HAR-368, and HAR-369. Group 8 (c).

Calibrated date: 1σ : cal AD 985 – 1155
      2σ : cal AD 890 – 1210

Final comments:
M Biddle: house XII, timber; final phase 40 (P.ph.683), mid eleventh-century. The radiocarbon date is late in relation to the phasing and dendrochronological dates.

Dendrochronological date: the last ring of the timber from posthole 1194 is placed at 1081, making the felling date *c* 1106 or later and placing the midpoint of the rings dated by HAR-363 at 956. The centre of the calibrated one standard deviation range of the radiocarbon date is 1070, 114 years later than the dendrochronological centrepoint of the rings covered by the radiocarbon sample [cc/1070–dc/956 = 114].

HAR-366   1280 ± 80 BP

$\delta^{13}C$: −27.0 ‰

Sample: OF 1046, submitted in 1973

Material: wood: *Quercus* sp. – roughly squared half tree trunk. The total number of rings counted was 95, with no sapwood present. The sample consisted of no more than 20 rings from the outside of the trunk. This sample was separated by 55 rings from HAR-367 .

Initial comment: from BS, trench I, house IX, posthole 2392, layer 871. HAR-366 and HAR-367 are from the same post, and repeat HAR-289 and HAR-290, previous samples from the same timber. Group 1 (d).

Calibrated date: 1σ : cal AD 660 – 850
                      2σ : cal AD 620 – 940

Final comments:
M Biddle: house IX/X, timber; final phase 77 (P.ph. 516), late eleventh- to twelfth-century. The radiocarbon date is good to slightly late. This timber is most likely reused. The radiocarbon date is in agreement with the dendrochronological dates.

Dendrochronological date: the last ring of the timber is placed at 734, making the felling date c 759 or later, and placing the midpoint of the rings dated by HAR-366 at 721. The centre of the calibrated one standard deviation range of the radiocarbon date is 755, 34 years later than the dendrochronological centrepoint of the rings covered by the radiocarbon sample [cc/735-dc 721 = 34].

HAR-367   1270 ± 80 BP

$\delta^{13}C$: −24.8 ‰

Sample: OF 1046, submitted in 1973

Material: wood: *Quercus* sp. – roughly squared half tree trunk. The total number of rings counted was 95, with no sapwood present. The sample consisted of no more than 25 rings from the inside of the trunk. This sample was separated by 55 rings from HAR-367 .

Initial comment: from BS, trench I, house IX, posthole 2392, later 871. HAR-366 and HAR-367 are from the same post, and repeat HAR-289 and HAR-290, previous samples from the same timber. Group I (d).

Calibrated date: 1σ : cal AD 665 – 860
                      2σ : cal AD 630 – 955

Final comments:
M Biddle: house IX/X, timber; final phase 77 (P.ph. 516), late eleventh- to twelfth-century. The radiocarbon date is late in relation to the phasing and dendrochronological dates.

Dendrochronological date: the last ring of the timber is placed at 734, making the felling date c 759 or later, and placing the midpoint of the rings dated by HAR-367 at 648. The centre of the calibrated one standard deviation range of the radiocarbon date is 763, 115 years later than the dendrochronological centrepoint of the rings covered by the radiocarbon sample [cc/763–dc/648 = 115].

HAR-368   1230 ± 70 BP

$\delta^{13}C$: −22.5 ‰

Sample: OF 1181, submitted in 1973

Material: wood: *Quercus* sp. – split untrimmed tree trunk. The total number of rings counted was 80. 10 – 15 rings possibly lost from the outside. No sapwood was present. The sample consisted of no more than 10 rings from the inside of the trunk. This sample is separated by 70 rings from HAR-369. HAR-368 and HAR-369 are from the same timber and repeat HAR-291 and HAR-292.

Initial comment: from BS, trench III, house XII, posthole 2574. Group 8 (c).

Calibrated date: 1σ : cal AD 680 – 885
                      2σ : cal AD 660 – 970

Final comments:
M Biddle: the post probably belongs to house XII, timber; final phase 41 (P.ph. 711), late eleventh- to early twelfth-century. The radiocarbon date is early in relation to the phasing.

A sample was taken for dendrochronology and measured, but not dated.

HAR-369   1170 ± 90 BP

$\delta^{13}C$: −21.4 ‰

Sample: OF 1181, submitted in 1973

Material: wood: *Quercus* sp. – split untrimmed tree trunk, possibly 10 – 15 years lost from the outside. The total number of rings counted was 80, with no sapwood present. The sample consisted of no more than 20 rings from the outside of the trunk. This sample is separated by 70 rings from HAR-368. HAR-368 and HAR-369 are from the same timber and repeat HAR-291 and HAR-292.

Initial comment: from BS, trench III, house XII, posthole 2574. Group 8 (c).

Calibrated date: 1σ : cal AD 725 – 975
                      2σ : cal AD 660 – 1020

Final comments:
M Biddle: the post probably belongs to house XII, timber; final phase 41 (P.ph. 711) late eleventh- to twelfth-century. The radiocarbon date is early in relation to the phasing.

A sample was taken for dendrochronology and measured, but not dated.

HAR-748   990 ± 70 BP

$\delta^{13}C$: −26.7 ‰

Sample: OF 1012, submitted on 26 July 1974

Material: wood: *Quercus* sp. – plank. The total number of rings counted was 131. There were in addition 20 sapwood rings. The sample consisted of 40 rings from the outside of the tree.

Initial comment: from BS, trench III, house XII, pit 283, posthole 2352. Group 10 (b).

Calibrated date: 1σ : cal AD 985 – 1155
                      2σ : cal AD 890 – 1210

Final comments:
M Biddle: house XII, timber; final phase 37 (P.ph. 735), mid to late tenth-century. The radiocarbon date is late in relation to the phasing and dendrochronological dates.

Dendrochronological date: the last ring of the timber is placed at 924, making the felling date c 949 and placing the midpoint of the rings dated by HAR-748 at 856. The centre of the calibrated one standard deviation range of the radiocarbon date is 1070, 214 years later than the dendrochronological centrepoint of the rings covered by the radiocarbon sample [cc/1070–dc/856 = 214].

HAR-749   1510 ± 100 BP

$\delta^{13}C$: –27.8 ‰

Sample: OF 39, submitted on 26 July 1974

Material: wood: *Quercus* sp. – plank. The total number of rings counted was 136, with no sapwood present. The sample consisted of about 136 rings from the outermost rings of the plank. It was necessary to include so many rings to make up the weight required.

Initial comment: from BS, trench III, house XII, F3128. Group 9 (b).

Calibrated date: 1σ : cal AD 420 – 640
                    2σ : cal AD 270 – 680

Final comments:
M Biddle: house XII, stone and timber; final phase 43 (P.ph. 712) mid to possibly late thirteenth century. The radiocarbon date is impossibly early.

Dendrochronological date: the last ring of the timber is placed at 1078, making the felling date c 1103 or later, and placing the midpoint of the rings dated by HAR-749 at 985. The centre of the calibrated one standard deviation range of the radiocarbon date is 530, 480 years earlier than the dendrochronological date of the rings covered by the radiocarbon sample [cc/530–dc/985 = –480].

Harwell: a small sample accounts for the larger than normal error term.

HAR-750   1230 ± 80 BP

$\delta^{13}C$: –28.0 ‰

Sample: OF 311, submitted on 27 July 1974

Material: wood: *Quercus* sp. – plank. The total number of rings counted was 70, plus about 4 rings on the outside edge. No sapwood. The sample consisted of approximately 74 outermost rings of the timber. It was necessary to include so many rings to make up the weight required.

Initial comment: from BS, trench I, house IX, F435. Group 2 (a).

Calibrated date: 1σ : cal AD 675 – 890
                    2σ : cal AD 650 – 980

Final comments:
M Biddle: house IX/X, timber; final phase 77 (P.ph. 511), late eleventh- to twelfth-century. The radiocarbon date is in agreement with the phasing and the dendrochronological dates.

Dendrochronological date: the last ring of the timber is placed at 894, making the felling date c 919 or later, and placing the midpoint of the rings dated by HAR-750 at 765. The centre of the calibrated one standard deviation range of the radiocarbon date is 783, 18 years later than the dendrochronological centrepoint of the rings covered by the radiocarbon sample [cc/783–dc/765 = 18].

HAR-751   unknown

$\delta^{13}C$: unknown

Sample: OF 261, submitted on 26 February 1974

Material: wood: *Quercus* sp. – plank. The total number of rings counted was 70. About 20 of the rings, of which the outermost is probably sapwood, are on the outside of the sample. The sample contained about 50 rings.

Initial comment: from BS, trench I, house IX, F424. Group 2 (a).

Final comments:
M Biddle: no certificate has been found. There is some suggestion that the sample was small.

A sample was taken for dendrochronology and measured, but not dated.

Harwell: the result is unknown.

HAR-752   930 ± 70 BP

$\delta^{13}C$: –27.6 ‰

Sample: OF 339, submitted on 26 July 1974

Material: wood: *Quercus* sp. – post. The total number of rings counted was about 32. No sapwood. The sample consisted of about 25 rings; there were at least 7 rings on the outside of the sample.

Initial comment: from BS, trench III, house XII, posthole 858. Group 8 (d).

Calibrated date: 1σ : cal AD 1020 – 1185
                    2σ : cal AD 980 – 1250

Final comments:
M Biddle: house XII, timber; final phase 40 (P.ph. 683), mid eleventh-century. The radiocarbon date is in agreement with the phasing.

A sample was taken for dendrochronology and measured, but not dated.

HAR-753   1430 ± 80 BP

$\delta^{13}C$: –21.13 ‰

Sample: Grave 21, submitted on 26 June 1974

Material: human bone: femur, ribs, vertebrae, and fragments of pelvis.

Initial comment: from BS, trench IV, grave 21. Group 11 (a). Primary count of sample.

Calibrated date: 1σ : cal AD 555 – 665
                    2σ : cal AD 430 – 760

Final comments:
M Biddle: pre-St Pancras church, cemetery; final phase 8A (P.ph. 874) possibly eighth- to ninth-century; rephased as St Pancras' church, cemetery; date group 44 – 8 (P.ph. 874a), mid tenth- to early eleventh-century.

Note in WRU file: repeat count ad 540 ± 70, calibrated date: 1 σ : cal AD 560 – 660, 2 σ : cal AD 450 – 690.

The first date here is the first count, and the only one for which there is a certificate. The radiocarbon date from both counts is too early in relation to the phasing.

HAR-754   1060 ± 60 BP

$\delta^{13}C$: −27.0 ‰

Sample: OF 346, submitted on 12 July 1974

Material: wood: *Quercus* sp. – post. The total number of rings counted was 30, with no sapwood present. The sample consisted of about 25 rings, plus about 5 more on the outside of the sample.

Initial comment: from BS, trench III, house XII, posthole 1626. Group 8 (d).

Calibrated date: 1σ : cal AD 895 – 1020
2σ : cal AD 880 – 1040

Final comments:
M Biddle: house XII, timber; final phase 40 (P.ph. 683), mid eleventh-century. The radiocarbon date is in agreement with the phasing.

A sample was taken for dendrochronology and measured, but not dated.

HAR-755   1180 ± 60 BP

$\delta^{13}C$: −27.2 ‰

Sample: OF 472, submitted on 26 July 1974

Material: wood: *Quercus* sp. – plank. The total number of rings counted was 75. The sample consisted of about 30 rings plus about 5 more rings on the outside of the sample.

Initial comment: from BS, trench III, house XII, F641. Group 8 (c).

Calibrated date: 1σ : cal AD 775 – 940
2σ : cal AD 680 – 990

Final comments:
M Biddle: house XII, timber; final phase 40 (P.ph. 683), mid eleventh-century. The radiocarbon date is too early in relation to the phasing, unless the timber was reused.

A sample was taken for dendrochronology and measured, but not dated.

HAR-757   1080 ± 80 BP

$\delta^{13}C$: −26.7 ‰

Sample: OF 576, submitted on 26 July 1974

Material: wood: *Quercus* sp. – beam. The total number of rings counted was 138, with no sapwood present. The sample consisted of not less than 30 rings from the inside.

Initial comment: from BS, trench III, house XII, pit 244, layer 1785. Group 10 (d).

Calibrated date: 1σ : cal AD 885 – 1020
2σ : cal AD 780 – 1155

Final comments:
M Biddle: house XII, timber; final phase 38 (P.ph. 726), early to possibly mid eleventh century. The radiocarbon date is in agreement with the phasing and position of the rings dated.

A sample was taken for dendrochronology and measured, but not dated.

HAR-758   1240 ± 80 BP

$\delta^{13}C$: −19.6 ‰

Sample: Grave 20, submitted on 26 July 1974

Material: human bone: femur, ribs, and fragments of pelvis.

Initial comment: from BS, trench IV, F899, grave 20. Group 11 (b).

Calibrated date: 1σ : cal AD 675 – 885
2σ : cal AD 650 – 970

Final comments:
M Biddle: St Pancras' church, period I; final phase 9 (P.ph. 177) (P.ph. 873), possibly ninth- to tenth-century; rephased as St Pancras' church, period I, date group 44 (P.ph. 873a) early to mid tenth-century. The radiocarbon date is early in relation to the rephasing.

Harwell: this date is the mean of two counts which gave 1280 BP (19 September 1975) and 1210 BP (15 October 1975).

HAR-876   1170 ± 120 BP

$\delta^{13}C$: −27.7 ‰

Sample: OF 995, submitted on 26 July 1974

Material: wood: *Quercus* sp. – post. The total number of rings counted was about 60, with about 10 of these outside the sample and no sapwood. The sample consisted of about 60 rings towards the outside of the post.

Initial comment: from BS, trench III, house XII, pit 283, posthole 2351. There are three samples from this pit; two from OF 995: HAR-876, covering 60 rings about 10 rings in from the outermost surviving ring and HAR-1278, covering the next 45 rings towards the inside; and HAR-1509, from another timber. Group 10 (b).

Calibrated date: 1σ : cal AD 680 – 990
2σ : cal AD 640 – 1150

Final comments:
M Biddle: house XII, timber; final phase 37 (P.ph. 735), mid to late tenth-century. The radiocarbon date seems early in relation to the phasing.

A sample was taken for dendrochronology and measured, but not dated.

Harwell: a small sample accounts for the larger than normal error term. There is a further sample from this timber, HAR-1278.

HAR-877   1130 ± 80 BP

$\delta^{13}C$: −26.5 ‰

Sample: OF 1284, submitted on 26 July 1974

Material: wood: *Quercus* sp. – plank. The total number of rings counted was 30, with about 10 rings of sapwood outside the sample. The sample consisted of about 30 rings towards the outside of the trunk.

Initial comment: from BS, trench I, house IX, pit 240, layer 907. Group 1 (b).

Calibrated date: 1σ : cal AD 790 – 990
2σ : cal AD 680 – 1030

Final comments:
M Biddle: house IX/X, timber; final phase 75 (P.ph. 170), early to mid tenth-century. The radiocarbon date seems early in relation to the dendrochronological dates, but is in agreement with the phasing.

Dendrochronological date: the last ring of the timber is placed at 1020, making the felling date *c* 1045 or later, and placing the midpoint of the rings dated by HAR-877 at 1005. The centre of the calibrated one standard deviation range of the radiocarbon date is 890, 115 years earlier than the dendrochronological centrepoint of the rings covered by the radiocarbon sample [cc/890–dc/1005 = –115].

HAR-878   1420 ± 80 BP

$\delta^{13}C$: –27.6 ‰

Sample: OF 1195, submitted on 26 July 1974

Material: wood: *Quercus* sp. – plank. The total number of rings counted was 130. There were about 16 sapwood rings outside this sample. The sample consisted of at least 30 rings on the outside of the timber.

Initial comment: from BS, trench III (house XI), F778. There are four samples from this pit; two from OF 1195: HAR-878 and HAR-1279, covering the inner 60 rings; and two from different timbers from F778, HAR-288 and HAR-1852. HAR-878 is repeated as HAR-1279. Group 5 (a).

Calibrated date: 1σ : cal AD 560 – 665
   2σ : cal AD 440 – 765

Final comments:
M Biddle: residence, stone building [G]; final phase 4 (Ph.p. 163), ninth-century; rephased as: residence, stone building; date group 4 – 6 (P.ph. 163a), late eighth- to late ninth-century. The radiocarbon date is early in relation to the phasing.

A sample was taken for dendrochronology and measured, but not dated.

Harwell: the final benzene appeared slightly coloured and smelled of ammonia.

HAR-879   940 ± 90 BP

$\delta^{13}C$: –25.3 ‰

Sample: OF 1120, submitted on 26 July 1974

Material: wood: *Quercus* sp. – plank. The total number of rings counted was at least 50, plus about 1 ring of sapwood. The sample consisted of at least 50 rings.

Initial comment: from BS, trench III, house XII, pit 295. The sample is repeated by HAR-1277. Group 8 (a).

Calibrated date: 1σ : cal AD 1005 – 1210
   2σ : cal AD 900 – 1260

Final comments:
M Biddle: house XII, timber; final phase 39 (P.ph. 721), early to possibly mid eleventh-century. The radiocarbon date is in agreement with the phasing.

A sample was taken for dendrochronology and measured, but not dated.

Harwell: a small sample.

HAR-880   1190 ± 70 BP

$\delta^{13}C$: –27.6 ‰

Sample: OF 1240, submitted on 26 July 1974

Material: wood: *Quercus* sp. – plank. The total number of rings counted was 90, plus 5 rings, and about 5 more of sapwood, on the outside of the sample. The sample consisted of at least 30 rings.

Initial comment: from BS, trench III, house XII, pit 383. Group 8 (b).

Calibrated date: 1σ : cal AD 725 – 895
   2σ : cal AD 670 – 990

Final comments:
M Biddle: pre-house XII, pits and occupation; final phase 36 (P.ph. 665), early to ?mid tenth-century. The radiocarbon date is in agreement with the phasing and the dendrochronological dates.

Dendrochronological date: the last ring of the timber is placed at 906, making the felling date *c* 931 or later, and placing the midpoint of the rings dated by HAR-880 at 796. The centre of the calibrated one standard deviation range of the radiocarbon date is 810, 14 years later than the dendrochronlogical centrepoint of the rings covered by the radiocarbon sample [cc/810–dc/796 = 14].

HAR-881   970 ± 70 BP

$\delta^{13}C$: –28.9 ‰

Sample: OF 1186, submitted on 26 July 1984

Material. wood: *Quercus* sp. – post. The total number of rings counted was 25 plus about 5 more on the outer edge of the sample. The sample consisted of 25 rings, the latest rings from the post.

Initial comment: from BS, trench I, house IX, posthole 2558, layer 877. Group 1 (e).

Calibrated date: 1σ : cal AD 1000 – 1160
   2σ : cal AD 900 – 1220

Final comments:
M Biddle: house IX/X, timber; final phase 76 (P.ph. 513), eleventh-century. The radiocarbon date is late in relation to the phasing and the dendrochronological dates.

Dendrochronological date: the last ring of the timber is placed at 1038, making the felling date c 1065 or later, and placing the midpoint of the rings dated by HAR-881 at 1023. The centre of the calibrated one standard deviation range of the radiocarbon date is 1080, 57 years later than the dendrochronological centrepoint [cc/1080–dc/1023 = 57].

HAR-882   1290 ± 70 BP

$\delta^{13}C$: –28.1 ‰

Sample: OF 1109, submitted on 26 July 1974

Material: wood: *Quercus* sp. – plank. The total number of rings counted was 170, plus about 5 more outside the sample, and about 5 sapwood rings. The sample consisted of at least 30 rings from the inside of the timber.

Initial comment: from BS, trench III, house XII, pit 295. Group 8 (a).

Calibrated date: 1σ : cal AD 660 – 785
2σ : cal AD 630 – 890

Final comments:
M Biddle: house XII, timber; final phase 39 (P.ph. 721), early to possibly mid eleventh-century. If the HAR sample is correctly identified on the dendrochronological chart, the radiocarbon date is too early.

Dendrochronological date: the last ring of the average of all the samples from pit 295 is placed at 1062, making the felling date *c* 1087 or later, and placing the midpoint of the rings dated by HAR-882 at 876. The centre of the calibrated one standard deviation range of the radiocarbon date is 723, 153 years earlier than the dendrochronological centrepoint of the rings covered by the radiocarbon sample [cc/723–dc/876 = –153].

HAR-883   1140 ± 60 BP

$\delta^{13}C$: –27.3 ‰

Sample: OF 1238, submitted on 26 July 1974

Material: wood: *Quercus* sp. – plank. The total number of rings counted was 36. There were about 5 rings of sapwood outside the sample. The sample consisted of at least 36 rings from the outside edge of the timber.

Initial comment: from BS, trench III, house XII, pit 383. Group 8 (b).

Calibrated date: 1σ : cal AD 810 – 975
2σ : cal AD 725 – 1010

Final comments:
M Biddle: pre-house XII, pits and occupation; final phase 36 (P.ph. 665), early to possibly mid tenth-century. The radiocarbon date is in agreement with the phasing and the dendrochronological date.

Dendrochronological date: the last ring of the timber is placed at 907, making the felling date *c* 925 or later, and placing the midpoint of the rings dated by HAR-883 at 889. The centre of the calibrated one standard deviation range of the radiocarbon date is 893, 4 years later than the dendrochronological centrepoint of the rings covered by the radiocarbon sample [cc/893–dc/889 = 4].

HAR-884   1030 ± 70 BP

$\delta^{13}C$: –26.6 ‰

Sample: OF 1017, submitted on 26 July 1974

Material: wood: *Quercus* sp. – post. The total number of rings counted was 37. There were about 4 rings of sapwood on the outside of the sample. The sample consisted of about 37 rings.

Initial comment: from BS, trench I, house IX/X, layer 871, posthole 2360. Group 1 (d).

Calibrated date: 1σ : cal AD 960 – 1030
2σ : cal AD 880 – 1160

Final comments:
M Biddle: house IX/X, timber; final phase 77 (P.ph. 516), late eleventh- to twelfth-century. The radiocarbon date is early in relation to the phasing.

A sample was taken for dendrochronology and measured, but not dated.

HAR-885   1210 ± 70 BP

$\delta^{13}C$: –1.8 ‰

Sample: S 238, submitted on 26 July 1974

Material: shell, 200g unwashed: oyster (*Ostrea* sp.).

Initial comment: from BS, trench III, house XII, layer 1666. Group 10 (e).

Calibrated date: 1σ : cal AD 690 – 890
2σ : cal AD 660 – 980

Final comments:
M Biddle: house XII, timber; final phase 41 (P.ph. 742), late eleventh- to early twelfth-century. Without $\delta^{13}C$ correction, the date would be 770 ± 70 BP; calibrated this is:

1 σ : cal AD 1215 – 1280

two sigma cal AD 1060 – 1375.

The date with $\delta^{13}C$ correction is much too early in relation to the phasing; the date without the $\delta^{13}C$ correction is too late.

Harwell: the result is AD 1180 if no $\delta^{13}C$ correction is applied.

HAR-886   1100 ± 70 BP

$\delta^{13}C$: –26.4 ‰

Sample: OF 1055, submitted on 26 July 1974

Material: wood: *Quercus* sp. – plank. The total number of rings counted was at least 142. There are at least 112 rings on the outside of this sample. The sample contained no less than 30 rings from the inside of the trunk.

Initial comment: from BS, trench III, house XII, pit 244. Group 10 (d).

Calibrated date: 1σ : cal AD 885 – 1010
2σ : cal AD 780 – 1030

Final comments:
M Biddle: house XII, timber; final phase 38 (P.ph. 726), early to possibly mid eleventh-century. The radiocarbon date is in agreement with the phasing and the dendrochronological dates.

Dendrochronological date: the last ring of the timber is placed at 1094, making the felling date *c* 1119 or later, and placing the midpoint of the rings dated by HAR-886 at 977. The centre of the calibrated one standard deviation range of the radiocarbon date is 948, 29 years earlier than the dendrochronological centrepoint of the rings covered by the radiocarbon sample [cc/948–dc/977 = –29].

Harwell: this date is the mean of two counts.

HAR-887   1070 ± 70 BP

$\delta^{13}C$: –26.1 ‰

Sample: OF 1183, submitted on 26 July 1974

Material: wood: *Quercus* sp. – plank. The total number of rings counted was about 124. There were at least 87 rings, plus about 7 rings and *c* 15 rings of sapwood outside the sample. The sample consisted of about 30 rings from the inside of the trunk.

Initial comment: from BS, trench III, house XII, F869, posthole 2574, layer 1183. Group 8 (c).

Calibrated date: 1σ : cal AD 890 – 1020
2σ : cal AD 790 – 1150

Final comments:
M Biddle: house XII, timber; final phase 42 (P.ph. 778), late twelfth- to early thirteenth-century. The radiocarbon date is in agreement with the phasing and the dendrochronological dates.

Dendrochronological date: the last ring of the timber is placed at 1042, making the felling date c 1067, and placing the midpoint of the rings dated by HAR-887 at 937. The centre of the calibrated one standard deviation range of the radiocarbon date is 955, 18 years later than the dendrochronological centrepoint of the rings covered by the radiocarbon sample [cc/955–dc/937 = 18].

Harwell: this date is the mean of two check counts which gave 1090 BP (25 January 1975) and 1050 BP (24 February 1975).

HAR-888   1060 ± 70 BP

$\delta^{13}C$: –26.7 ‰

Sample: OF 686, submitted on 26 July 1974

Material: wood: *Quercus* sp. – post. The total number of rings counted was 32. There were about 7 rings on the outside of the sample, with no sapwood. The sample consisted of 25 rings.

Initial comment: from BS, trench III, house XII, posthole 2184. Goup 10 (f).

Calibrated date: 1σ : cal AD 895 – 1020
2σ : cal AD 810 – 1155

Final comments:
M Biddle: house XII, timber; final phase 42 (P.ph. 760), late twelfth- to early thirteenth-century. The radiocarbon date is early in relation to the phasing.

No sample was submitted for dendrochronology.

HAR-889   1160 ± 70 BP

$\delta^{13}C$: –26.1 ‰

Sample: OF 359, submitted on 27 June 1974

Material: peat.

Initial comment: from BS, trench I, pit 298, layer 872 or 972. Repeated by HAR-1271. Group 1 (c).

Calibrated date: 1σ : cal AD 780 – 970
2σ : cal AD 680 – 1010

Final comments:
M Biddle: house IX/X, timber; final phase 76 (P.ph. 477), eleventh-century. The radiocarbon date is early in relation to the phasing.

Harwell: physical examination of the pretreated sample indicated the presence of residual carbonate (chalk), although this is not apparent in the $\delta^{13}C$ value.

HAR-1060   1080 ± 70 BP

$\delta^{13}C$: –26.1 ‰

Sample: OF 1329, submitted on 28 November 1974

Material: wood: *Quercus* sp. – a complete cross-section. The total number of rings counted was 37, with no sapwood. The sample consisted of 37 rings.

Initial comment: from BS, trench IV, pit 463, posthole 3165. Group 11 (d).

Calibrated date: 1σ : cal AD 890 – 1015
2σ : cal AD 780 – 1040

Final comments:
M Biddle: St Pancras' church, period III; final phase 12 (P.ph. 266), eleventh-century; rephased as date group 57 (P.ph. 266e), mid twelfth-century. The radiocarbon date is early in relation to the phasing.

No sample was submitted for dendrochronology.

HAR-1061   1060 ± 70 BP

$\delta^{13}C$: –27.0 ‰

Sample: OF 21, submitted on 28 November 1974

Material: wood: *Quercus* sp. – a section from a round stake with 12 rings plus nearly all the sapwood; the outer rings represent the greater proportion of the sample.

Initial comment: from BS, trench III, F312, posthole 756. Group 9 (c).

Calibrated date: 1σ : cal AD 895 – 1020
2σ : cal AD 810 – 1155

Final comments:
M Biddle: house XII, stone and timber; final phase 43 (P.ph.712), mid to possibly late thirteenth-century. The radiocarbon date is early in relation to the phasing.

No sample was submitted for dendrochronology.

HAR-1062   1100 ± 70 BP

$\delta^{13}C$: –28.7 ‰

Sample: OF 1279, submitted on 28 November 1974

Material: wood: *Corylus* sp. – a wedge-shaped section. The total number of rings counted was about 60, with sapwood present. The sample consisted of a complete cross-section of the timber, the outer rings forming the greater proportion of this.

Initial comment: from BS, trench I, pit 448. Group 1 (a).

Calibrated date: 1σ : cal AD 885 – 1010
2σ : cal AD 780 – 1030

Final comments:
M Biddle: house IX/X, timber; final phase 75 (P.ph. 502), early to mid tenth-century. The radiocarbon date is in agreement with the phasing.

HAR-1063   960 ± 90 BP

$\delta^{13}C$: –27.4 ‰

Sample: OF 749, submitted on 28 November 1974

Material: wood: *Quercus* sp.. The total number of rings counted was c 50, with no sapwood present. The sample consisted of the outermost 20 rings.

Initial comment: from BS, trench III, house XI, posthole 1403, layer 2506. Group 5 (d).

Calibrated date: 1σ : cal AD 990 – 1170
2σ : cal AD 890 – 1260

Final comments:
M Biddle: house XI, timber; final phase 58 (P.ph. 559), mid eleventh- to ?mid twelfth-century. The radiocarbon date is in agreement with the phasing.

A sample was taken for dendrochronology and measured, but not dated.

HAR-1064   1110 ± 60 BP

$\delta^{13}C$: −27.5 ‰

Sample: OF 268, submitted on 28 November 1974

Material: wood: *Fraxinus* sp., one piece with 6 rings and one piece with 9 rings and *Corylus* sp., one piece with 9 rings. The sample consisted of complete sections of three sticks from the hurdle lining pit 146. The *Fraxinus* sp. with 9 rings was the largest sample.

Initial comment: from BS, trench I, pit 146. Group 3 (c).

Calibrated date: 1σ : cal AD 885 – 990
2σ : cal AD 780 – 1020

Final comments:
M Biddle: house IX/X, timber; final phase 77 (P.ph. 441), late eleventh- to twelfth-century. The radiocarbon date is early in relation to the phasing.

No sample was submitted for dendrochronology.

HAR-1065   1020 ± 80 BP

$\delta^{13}C$: −27.4 ‰

Sample: OF 509, submitted on 28 November 1974

Material: wood: *Quercus* sp. – stake containing 25 rings (including the sapwood) representing the complete branch or trunk. The sample included a complete section of the stake.

Initial comment: from BS, trench I, house IX, posthole 1281. Group 2 (b).

Calibrated date: 1σ : cal AD 960 – 1040
2σ : cal AD 880 – 1180

Final comments:
M Biddle: house IX/X, timber; final phase 77 (P.ph. 511), late eleventh- to twelfth-century. The radiocarbon date is early in relation to the phasing.

No sample was submitted for dendrochronology.

HAR-1066   1570 ± 70 BP

$\delta^{13}C$: −27.2 ‰

Sample: OF 453, submitted on 28 November 1974

Material: wood: *Quercus* sp.. The total number of rings counted was 63, with no sapwood present. The sampled consisted of a complete section of the timber. .

Initial comment: from BS, trench V (house IX/X), F605, layer 1258. Group 3 (d).

Calibrated date: 1σ : cal AD 410 – 560
2σ : cal AD 270 – 630

Final comments:
M Biddle: house IX/X, timber; final phase 75 (P.ph. 437), mid to late tenth-century. Rephased as date group 1 (P.ph. 437b), early seventh- to early eighth-century. Residence, western timber buildings, *Grubenhaus*, and reuse of Roman building. The radiocarbon date is early in relation to the phasing and the dendrochronological dates.

No sample was taken for dendrochronology.

Harwell: cloudiness in the synthesised benzene apparently had no effect on the counting efficiency (70.2%).

HAR-1067   1110 ± 60 BP

$\delta^{13}C$: −26.5 ‰

Sample: OF 297, submitted on 28 November 1974

Material: wood: *Quercus* sp. – plank. The total number of rings counted was 105, with no sapwood. The sample consisted of the outermost 105 rings.

Initial comment: from BS, trench I, pit 177, layer 1097. Group 3 (b).

Calibrated date: 1σ : cal AD 885 – 990
2σ : cal AD 780 – 1020

Final comments:
M Biddle: house IX/X, timber; final phase 75 (P.ph. 433), mid to late tenth-century. The radiocarbon date is in agreement with the phasing.

A sample was taken for dendrochronology and measured, but not dated.

HAR-1068   660 ± 80 BP

$\delta^{13}C$: −28.5 ‰

Sample: OF 1171, submitted on 28 November 1974

Material: wood: *Quercus* sp. – a whole wedge-shaped section of a stake containing 10 – 20 rings, with sapwood nearly present. The sample contained 10 – 20 rings.

Initial comment: from BS, trench III, house XI, posthole 1087. Group 6 (b).

Calibrated date: 1σ : cal AD 1270 – 1395
2σ : cal AD 1220 – 1420

Final comments:
M Biddle: house XI, timber; final phase 59 (P.ph. 595), early thirteenth-century. The radiocarbon date is late in relation to the phasing.

No sample was submitted for dendrochronology.

HAR-1069   910 ± 80 BP

$\delta^{13}C$: −27.2 ‰

Sample: OF 756, submitted on 28 November 1974

Material: wood: *Quercus* sp. – post. The total number of rings counted was 80 – 90, with no sapwood. The sample consisted of the outermost 46 rings.

Initial comment: from BS, trench III, house XI, posthole 1344, layer 2506. Group 6 (a).

Calibrated date: 1σ : cal AD 1020 – 1220
 2σ : cal AD 980 – 1270

Final comments:
M Biddle: house XI, timber; final phase 59 (P.ph. 595), early thirteenth-century. The radiocarbon date is late in relation to the dendrochronological date.

Dendrochronological date: the last ring of the timber is placed at 872, making the felling date *c* 897 or later, and placing the midpoint of the rings dated by HAR-1069 at 849. The centre of the calibrated one standard deviation range of the radiocarbon date is 1120, 271 years later than the dendrochronological centrepoint of the rings covered by the radiocarbon sample [cc/1120–dc/849 = 271].

HAR-1070 1110 ± 80 BP

$\delta^{13}C$: –27.0 ‰

Sample: OF 1273, submitted on 28 November 1974

Material: wood: *Quercus* sp. – a complete cross-section of a post. The total number of rings counted was 58, with no sapwood. The sample consisted of 58 rings.

Initial comment: from BS, trench III, house XI, posthole 2939. Group 5 (b).

Calibrated date: 1σ : cal AD 830 – 1010
 2σ : cal AD 715 – 1040

Final comments:
M Biddle: house XI, timber; final phase 58 (P.ph. 559), eleventh- to possibly mid twelfth-century. The radiocarbon date is early in relation to the phasing.

No sample was submitted for dendrochronology.

HAR-1075 870 ± 70 BP

$\delta^{13}C$: –26.3 ‰

Sample: SA 236, submitted on 28 November 1974

Material: peat.

Initial comment: from BS, trench I, house IX/X, pit 197. A substitute for an unsuitable sample from pit 173. Group 3 (h).

Calibrated date: 1σ : cal AD 1040 – 1245
 2σ : cal AD 1010 – 1270

Final comments:
M Biddle: house IX/X, stone and timber; final phase 78 (P.ph. 419), thirteenth-century. The radiocarbon date is in agreement with the phasing.

HAR-1076 1920 ± 70 BP

$\delta^{13}C$: –23.1 ‰

Sample: SA 263, submitted on 28 November 1974

Material: peat with some soil.

Initial comment: from BS, trench I, pit 258, layer 1277. A substitute for a sample from pit 167. Group 3 (g).

Calibrated date: 1σ : cal AD 5 – 135
 2σ : cal BC 100 – 240 cal AD

Final comments:
M Biddle: house IX/X, stone and timber; final phase 78 (P.ph. 420), thirteenth-century. The radiocarbon date is impossibly early.

Harwell: the $\delta^{13}C$ is atypical (too positive), geological contamination may be suspected; see HAR-1257.

HAR-1077 1860 ± 90 BP

$\delta^{13}C$: –21.2 ‰

Sample: GR 14, submitted on 28 November 1974

Material: human bone, with some tape adhering: fragments of pelvis, femur, and vertebrae.

Initial comment: from BS, trench IV, grave 14, in St Pancras church. Repeated by HAR-1740. Group 11.

Calibrated date: 1σ : cal AD 60 – 245
 2σ : cal BC 60 – 380 cal AD

Final comments:
M Biddle: St Pancras' church, period VII; final phase 16 (P.ph. 233), fifteenth-century. Rephased as: date group 70 (P.ph. 233b), mid fifteenth-century. St Pancras' church, use of the third north aisle. Grave 14 is a charnel and/or a reburial. The radiocarbon date is impossibly early.

HAR-1078 600 ± 70 BP

$\delta^{13}C$: –19.3 ‰

Sample: G 24, submitted on 28 November 1974

Material: human bone: fragments of pelvis, femur, tibia, and fibula.

Initial comment: from BS, trench II, F751, grave 2. Repeated by HAR-1739. Group 4 (a).

Calibrated date: 1σ : cal AD 1285 – 1410
 2σ : cal AD 1270 – 1440

Final comments:
M Biddle: residence, cemetery; final phase 1 (P.ph. 141), mid seventh- to eighth-century. Rephased as date group 1 (P.ph. 141a), late seventh- to early eighth-century. Cemetery earlier than St Mary's church. The radiocarbon date is impossibly late.

Harwell: the same material is dated by HAR-1739.

HAR-1084 590 ± 70 BP

$\delta^{13}C$: –18.4 ‰

Sample: G 19, submitted on 28 November 1974

Material: human bone: fragments of femur, ribs, and pelvis.

Initial comment: from BS, trench IV, grave 19, in St Pancras' church. Group 11 (f).

Calibrated date: 1σ : cal AD 1285 – 1415
 2σ : cal AD 1270 – 1440

Final comments:
M Biddle: St Pancras' church, period VI; final phase 15 (P.ph. 231), fourteenth-century. Rephased as date group 68-9 (P.ph. 231b), late fourteenth- to mid fifteenth-century. St Pancras' church, use of the second north aisle floor. The radiocarbon date is in agreement with the phasing.

HAR-1101 980 ± 60 BP

$\delta^{13}C$: −21.9 ‰

Sample: L 475, submitted on 28 November 1974

Material: animal bone: includes some teeth.

Initial comment: from trench 3, layer 475, in the middle part of the St Pancras Lane sequence. Group 7.

Comment on uncalibrated date: this is *c* 300 years too early; the proper date should be *c* 1280 according to the results from group 7 – perhaps this is residual material?

Calibrated date: 1σ : cal AD 1000 – 1155
2σ : cal AD 960 – 1180

Final comments:
M Biddle: Tanner Street and lanes; final phase 68 (P.ph. 343), mid to late thirteenth-century. The radiocarbon date is early in relation to the phasing.

HAR-1102 1790 ± 90 BP

$\delta^{13}C$: −22.4 ‰

Sample: G 23, submitted on 28 November 1974

Material: human bone, with tape adhering: fragments of pelvis and femur.

Initial comment: from BS, trench II, F733, grave 23, layer 920. Repeated by HAR-1738. Group 4 (a).

Comment on uncalibrated date: archaeologically unacceptable.

Calibrated date: 1σ : cal AD 120 – 345
2σ : cal AD 20 – 430

Final comments:
M Biddle: residence, cemetery; final phase 1 (P.ph. 141), mid seventh- to eighth-century. Rephased as date group 1 (P.ph. 141a), late seventh- to early eighth-century. Cemetery earlier than St Mary's church. The radiocarbon date is impossibly early.

Harwell: a small sample, repeated by HAR-1738.

HAR-1103 770 ± 130 BP

$\delta^{13}C$: −21.9 ‰

Sample: L 71, submitted on 28 November 1974

Material: animal bone.

Initial comment: from BS, trench III, layer 71, in the later part of the St Pancras Lane sequence. Group 7.

Comment on uncalibrated date: a date in the fourteenth to fifteenth century was expected; this is too early, but the error term is large.

Calibrated date: 1σ : cal AD 1160 – 1290
2σ : cal AD 1010 – 1420

Final comments:
M Biddle: Tanner Street and lanes, final surfaces and use; final phase 70 (P.ph. 350), fifteenth- to possibly sixteenth-century. The radiocarbon date is early in relation to the phasing.

Harwell: a very small sample, which needed topping up with dead carbon dioxide to enable benzene synthesis.

HAR-1117 1020 ± 90 BP

$\delta^{13}C$: −22.1 ‰

Sample: L 1164, submitted on 28 November 1974

Material: animal bone.

Initial comment: from BS, trench III, layer 1164, near the bottom of the St Pancras Lane sequence. Group 7.

Calibrated date: 1σ : cal AD 900 – 1150
2σ : cal AD 810 – 1220

Final comments:
M Biddle: Tanner Street and lanes; final phase 67 (P.ph. 304), twelfth- to thirteenth-century. The radiocarbon date is early in relation to the phasing.

HAR-1257 1070 ± 70 BP

$\delta^{13}C$: −26.6 ‰

Sample: S 263, submitted on 3 February 1976

Material: peat.

Initial comment: from BS, trench I, yard, pit 258. Replicate of HAR-1076. Group 3 (g).

Comment on uncalibrated date: this is still too early; the context appears to be of twelfth-century date.

Calibrated date: 1σ : cal AD 890 – 1020
2σ : cal AD 790 – 1150

Final comments:
M Biddle: house IX/X, stone and timber; final phase 78 (P.ph. 420), thirteenth-century. The radiocarbon date is early in relation to the phasing.

Harwell: repeat of HAR-1076, which was suspected of being inadequately pretreated.

HAR-1259 910 ± 70 BP

$\delta^{13}C$: −27.1 ‰

Sample: S 236, submitted on 3 February 1976

Material: peat.

Initial comment: from BS, trench I, house IX/X, pit 197. Repeats HAR-1075. Group 3 (h).

Calibrated date: 1σ : cal AD 1025 – 1215
2σ : cal AD 990 – 1260

Final comments:
M Biddle: house IX/X, stone and timber; final phase 78 (P.ph. 419), thirteenth-century. The radiocarbon date is early in relation to the phasing.

Harwell: replicate of HAR-1075.

HAR-1271 1030 ± 80 BP

$\delta^{13}C$: −26.3 ‰

Sample: S 359, submitted on 3 February 1976

Material: peat-like material, over 500g.

Initial comment: from BS, trench I, house IX, pit 298, layer 872. Repeats HAR-889. Group 1 (c).

Calibrated date: 1σ : cal AD 900 – 1035
2σ : cal AD 830 – 1170

Final comments:
M Biddle: house IX/X, timber; final phase 76 (P.ph. 477), eleventh-century. The radiocarbon date is early in relation to the phasing, with a small overlap in the one standard deviation range.

Harwell: a check measurement on the same initial material as HAR-889; violent effervescence was observed on the addition of acid.

HAR-1277   1000 ± 90 BP

$\delta^{13}C$: –26.6 ‰

Sample: OF 1120, submitted on 3 February 1976

Material: wood: *Quercus* sp. – plank. The total number of rings counted was at least 50, plus about 1 ring of sapwood. The sample contained at least 50 rings.

Initial comment: from BS, trench III, house XII, pit 295. Repeat of HAR-879. Group 8 (a).

Calibrated date: 1σ : cal AD 970 – 1160
2σ : cal AD 880 – 1230

Final comments:
M Biddle: house XII, timber; final phase 39 (P.ph. 721), early to possibly mid eleventh-century. The radiocarbon date is in agreement with the phasing.

A sample was submitted for dendrochronology and measured, but not dated.

Harwell: replicate of HAR-879.

HAR-1278   1080 ± 70 BP

$\delta^{13}C$: –26.9 ‰

Sample: OF 995, submitted on 3 February 1976

Material: wood: *Quercus* sp.. The total number of rings counted was 115, with no sapwood. The sample consisted of 45 rings from the inside of the trunk.

Initial comment: from BS, trench III, house XII, pit 283. There are three samples from this pit; two from OF 995: HAR-876, covering 60 rings about 10 rings in from the outermost surviving ring, and HAR-1278, covering the next 45 rings towards the inside; and HAR-1509 from another timber. Group 10 (b).

Calibrated date: 1σ : cal AD 890 – 1015
2σ : cal AD 780 – 1040

Final comments:
M Biddle: house XII, timber; final phase 37 (P.ph. 735), mid to late tenth-century. The radiocarbon date is late in relation to the dendrochronological date.

Dendrochronological date: the last ring of the timber is placed at 975, making the felling date *c* 1000 or later, and placing the midpoint of the rings dated by HAR-1278 at 883. The centre of the calibrated one standard deviation range of the radiocarbon date is 953, 70 years later than the dendrochronological centrepoint of the rings covered by the radiocarbon sample [cc/953–dc/883 = 70].

Harwell: HAR-876 is from this timber.

HAR-1279   960 ± 70 BP

$\delta^{13}C$: –26.8 ‰

Sample: OF 1195, submitted on 3 February 1976

Material: wood: *Quercus* sp. – plank. The total number of rings counted was 130. There were in addition 16 rings of sapwood. HAR-878 covered the latest 30 rings before the sapwood and is separated from HAR-1279 by 40 rings. The sample consisted of 60 rings from the inside of the trunk.

Initial comment: from BS, trench III, F778. There are four samples from this pit; two from OF 1195: HAR-1279, covering the inner 60 rings and HAR-878, covering the outer 30 rings; and two, HAR-288 and HAR-1852, from different timbers. Group 5 (a).

Comment on uncalibrated date: the date of felling seems significantly late for the probable date of the context.

Calibrated date: 1σ : cal AD 1005 – 1165
2σ : cal AD 960 – 1230

Final comments:
M Biddle: residence, stone building [G]; final phase 4 (P.ph. 163), ninth-century. Rephased as date group 4 – 6 (P.ph. 163a), ninth-century. The radiocarbon date is late in relation to the phasing.

A sample was taken for dendrochronology and measured, but not dated.

Harwell: replacement for HAR-878 which was thought to have been affected by experimental difficulties.

HAR-1488   1090 ± 60 BP

$\delta^{13}C$: –21.1 ‰

Sample: G 21, submitted on 3 February 1976

Material: human bone: femur, part of scapula, and vertebrae.

Initial comment: from BS, trench IV, grave 21, in St Pancras' church. Repeats HAR-753, on different bones from the same body. Group 11 (a).

Calibrated date: 1σ : cal AD 890 – 1010
2σ : cal AD 790 – 1030

Final comments:
M Biddle: pre-St Pancras' church, cemetery; final phase 8A (P.ph. 874) possibly eighth- to ninth-century. Rephased as: St Pancras' church, cemetery; date group 44 – 8 (P.ph. 874a), mid tenth- to early eleventh-century. The radiocarbon date is in agreement with the phasing.

HAR-1491   unknown

$\delta^{13}C$: unknown

Sample: G 30, submitted on 3 February 1976

Material: human bone: femur, pelvic area, and vertebrae.

Initial comment: from BS, trench IV, grave 30, inside St Pancras' church. This was sent in as grave 11, but the bones are most probably from grave 30. HAR-1741 repeats this date, and is perhaps the only date.

Final comments:
M Biddle: St Pancras' church, period VIII; final phase 17 (P.ph. 196), fourteenth century. Rephased as St Pancras' church, secondary graves in the south chapel; date group 67 – 70 (P.ph. 196c), mid fourteenth to early fifteenth-century.

Harwell: no submission or certificate has been found. The result is unknown.

HAR-1508   1110 ± 70 BP

$\delta^{13}C$: –27.7 ‰

Sample: OF 546, submitted on 3 February 1976

Material: wood: *Quercus* sp.. The total number of rings counted was 95. There were 5 rings outside the sample and 60 inside, with no sapwood. The sample contained at least 30 rings towards the outside of the trunk.

Initial comment: from BS, trench III, house IX, F449. Group 9 (a).

Comment on uncalibrated date: other dates from this context (HAR-1511 and HAR-1515) and the probably contemporary group 8 (c) all agree with an eleventh-century date; however HAR-368 and HAR-369 from group 8 (c) have produced dates like this one and the reuse of timber is a strong possibility.

Calibrated date: 1σ : cal AD 880 – 1000
                     2σ : cal AD 770 – 1030

Final comments:
M Biddle: house XII, timber; final phase 41 (P.ph. 711), late eleventh- to early twelfth-century. The radiocarbon date is early in relation to the phasing. For other dates from this context, see: HAR-1511 and HAR-1515, and also the probably contemporary HAR-368, HAR-369, HAR-755, and HAR-887 (Group 8 (c)).

A sample was taken for dendrochronology and measured, but not dated.

HAR-1509   1220 ± 80 BP

$\delta^{13}C$: –27.6 ‰

Sample: OF 718, submitted on 3 February 1976

Material: wood: *Quercus* sp. – a full section of a plank. The total number of rings counted was about 70, with no sapwood. The sample consisted of about 70 rings.

Initial comment: from BS, trench III, house XII, pit 283, layer 1815. There are two other samples from this pit: HAR-876 and HAR-1278 from another timber. Group 10 (b).

Comment on uncalibrated date: this date is 300 years too early when compared with HAR-748 and HAR-1278, but this could be a reused timber.

Calibrated date: 1σ : cal AD 680 – 890
                     2σ : cal AD 650 – 990

Final comments:
M Biddle: house XII, timber; final phase 37 (P.ph. 735), mid to late tenth-century. The radiocarbon date is in agreement with the phasing and the dendrochronological dates.

Dendrochronological date: the last ring of the timber is placed at 940, making the felling date *c* 965 or later, and placing the midpoint of the rings dated by HAR-1509 at 817. The centre of the calibrated one standard deviation range of the radiocarbon date is 785, 32 years earlier than the dendrochronological centrepoint of the rings covered by the radiocarbon sample [cc/785–dc/817 = –32].

HAR-1510   840 ± 80 BP

$\delta^{13}C$: –26.4 ‰

Sample: OF 52, submitted on 3 February 1976

Material: wood: *Quercus* sp. – post. The total number of rings counted was about 90. There were about 20 rings outside the sample, and no sapwood. The sample consisted of 70 rings.

Initial comment: from BS, trench III, F312, posthole 784. Repeated by HAR-1639.

Calibrated date: 1σ : cal AD 1045 – 1265
                     2σ : cal AD 1020 – 1280

Final comments:
M Biddle: house XII, stone and timber; final phase 43 (P.ph. 712), mid to possibly late thirteenth-century. The radiocarbon date is in agreement with the phasing. A sample was taken for dendrochronology and measured, but not dated.

HAR-1511   1070 ± 80 BP

$\delta^{13}C$: –26.2 ‰

Sample: OF 259, submitted on 3 February 1976

Material: wood: *Quercus* sp. – plank. The total number of rings counted was 180 – 200, with no sapwood. The sample consisted of about the 100 outermost rings.

Initial comment: from BS, trench III, house XII, F449. Group 9 (a).

Calibrated date: 1σ : cal AD 890 – 1020
                     2σ : cal AD 780 – 1155

Final comments:
M Biddle: house XII, timber; final phase 41 (P.ph. 711), late eleventh- to early twelfth-century. The radiocarbon date is early in relation to the phasing.

A sample was taken for dendrochronology and measured, but not dated.

HAR-1512   680 ± 70 BP

$\delta^{13}C$: –27.6 ‰

Sample: OF 1138, submitted on 3 February 1976

Material: wood: the complete section of a small branch with *c* 12 rings.

Initial comment: from BS, trench III, house XII, pit 342. Group 10 (c).

Comment on uncalibrated date: 200 years too late; this should be earlier than Group 10 (d) which is well dated to the eleventh century by HAR-757 and HAR-886.

Calibrated date: 1σ : cal AD 1265 – 1385
                     2σ : cal AD 1220 – 1410

Final comments:
M Biddle: house XII, timber; final phase 37 (P.ph. 724), mid to late tenth-century. The radiocarbon date is late in relation to the phasing. Group 10 (c) should be earlier than Group 10 (d).

No sample was submitted for dendrochronology.

HAR-1513 950 ± 70 BP

$\delta^{13}C$: −26.6 ‰

Sample: OF 340, submitted on 3 February 1976

Material: wood: *Quercus* sp. – post. The total number of rings counted was 99, with no sapwood. The sample consisted of *c* 40 outermost rings.

Initial comment: from BS, trench III, house XII, posthole 1625. Group 8 (e).

Calibrated date: 1σ : cal AD 1010 – 1165
                    2σ : cal AD 970 – 1230

Final comments:
M Biddle: house XII, timber; final phase 40 (P.ph. 683), mid eleventh-century. The radiocarbon date is late in relation to the phasing and dendrochronological dates.

Dendrochronological date: the last ring of the timber is placed at 1010, making the felling date *c* 1035 or later, and placing the midpoint of the rings dated by HAR-1513 at 990. The centre of the calibrated one standard deviation range of the radiocarbon date is 1088, 98 years later than the dendrochronological centrepoint of the rings covered by the radiocarbon sample [cc/1088–dc/990 = 98].

HAR-1515 880 ± 70 BP

$\delta^{13}C$: −28.8 ‰

Sample: OF 236, submitted on 3 February 1976

Material: wood: beech (*Fagus sylvatica* L.) – from a cross-section of a branch with 15 or more rings.

Initial comment: from BS, trench III, F449, posthole 1562. Group 9 (a).

Calibrated date: 1σ : cal AD 1035 – 1230
                    2σ : cal AD 1010 – 1270

Final comments:
M Biddle: house XII, timber; final phase 41 (P.ph. 711), late eleventh- to early twelfth-century. The radiocarbon date is in agreement with the phasing.

HAR-1516 860 ± 70 BP

$\delta^{13}C$: −26.9 ‰

Sample: OF 491, submitted on 3 February 1976

Material: wood: *Quercus* sp.. The total number of rings counted was 40, with no sapwood. The sample consisted of the outermost 40 rings.

Initial comment: from BS, trench I, F435. Group 2 (a).

Calibrated date: 1σ : cal AD 1045 – 1255
                    2σ : cal AD 1020 – 1280

Final comments:
M Biddle: house IX/X, timber; final phase 77 (P.ph. 511), late eleventh- to twelfth-century. The radiocarbon date is in agreement with the phasing. HAR-882 is from the same context, and HAR-880 and HAR-883 are from group 8 (b), which should be, and is, earlier.

A sample was taken for dendrochronology and measured, but not dated.

HAR-1517 820 ± 80 BP

$\delta^{13}C$: −21.0 ‰

Sample: G 2, submitted on 3 February 1976

Material: human bone: femur, left arm, ribs, and fragments.

Initial comment: from BS, trench II, F428. Grave 2 in St Mary's church. Group 4 (b).

Comment on uncalibrated date: too early by 300 years; the expected date was *c* AD 1490.

Calibrated date: 1σ : cal AD 1160 – 1270
                    2σ : cal AD 1020 – 1290

Final comments:
M Biddle: Tanner Street and lanes, final surfaces and use; final phase 69 (P.ph. 325), fourteenth-century. Rephased as St Mary's church; date group 35 (P.ph. 325a), late fifteenth- to early sixteenth-century. The radiocarbon date is too early.

HAR-1518 920 ± 70 BP

$\delta^{13}C$: −26.9 ‰

Sample: OF 1026, submitted on 3 February 1976

Material: wood: *Quercus* sp. – post. The total number of rings counted was *c* 200. No sapwood was observed, but the curved outer edge of the post may indicate that it was near. The sample consisted of the outermost 60 rings.

Initial comment: from BS, trench III, house XII, pit 295, posthole 2362. Group 8 (a).

Calibrated date: 1σ : cal AD 1020 – 1210
                    2σ : cal AD 980 – 1260

Final comments:
M Biddle: house XII, timber; final phase 39 (P.ph. 721), early to ?mid eleventh-century. The radiocarbon date is late in relation to the phasing and dendrochronological dates.

Dendrochronological date: the last ring of the timber is placed at 1062, making the felling date *c* 1087 or later, and placing the midpoint of the rings dated by HAR-1518 at 963. The centre of the calibrated one standard deviation range of the radiocarbon date is 1115, 152 years later than the dendrochronological centrepoint of the rings covered by the radiocarbon sample [cc/1115–dc/963 = 152].

HAR-1519 1380 ± 70 BP

$\delta^{13}C$: −27.2 ‰

Sample: OF 883, submitted on 3 February 1976

Material: wood: *Quercus* sp. – a small branch. The sample consisted of a complete section of about 18 rings.

Initial comment: from BS, trench V, pit 278, the fill of a fourth-century well. Group 3 (a).

Calibrated date: 1σ : cal AD 610 – 675
                    2σ : cal AD 550 – 780

Final comments:
M Biddle: workshop and agriculture; final phase 56 (P.ph. 127), fifth-century. Rephased as date group 0 (P.ph. 127a), early to mid seventh-century. The last fill of a post-Roman pit. The radiocarbon date is in agreement with the phasing.

No sample was submitted for dendrochronology.

HAR-1520 560 ± 70 BP

$\delta^{13}C$: −19.5 ‰

Sample: G 15, submitted on 3 February 1976

Material: human bone: from femur and pelvic area.

Initial comment: from BS, trench IV, grave 15. Group 11 (e).

Calibrated date: 1σ : cal AD 1300 − 1425
2σ : cal AD 1280 − 1450

Final comments:
M Biddle: St Pancras' church, period VIII; final phase 17 (P.ph. 211), late fifteenth- to early sixteenth-century. Rephased as St Pancras' church, use of fourth nave floor; date group 66 − 9 (P.ph. 211e), fourteenth-century. The radiocarbon date is in agreement with the phasing.

HAR-1521 480 ± 60 BP

$\delta^{13}C$: −20.5 ‰

Sample: G 4, submitted on 3 February 1976

Material: human bone: femur, ribs, vertebrae, scapula, and from pelvic area.

Initial comment: from BS, trench IV, grave 4, inside St Pancras' church. Group 11 (i).

Calibrated date: 1σ : cal AD 1405 − 1450
2σ : cal AD 1315 − 1490

Final comments:
M Biddle: St Pancras' church, period VIII; final phase 17 (P.ph. 237), late fifteenth- to early sixteenth-century. Rephased as St Pancras' church, secondary graves in the fourth nave floor; date group 69 (P.ph. 237c), early to mid fifteenth-century. The radiocarbon date is in agreement with the phasing.

HAR-1531 570 ± 80 BP

$\delta^{13}C$: −19.2 ‰

Sample: G 1, submitted on 3 February 1976

Material: human bone: femur, parts of pelvic area, and scapula.

Initial comment: from BS, trench IV, grave 1, inside St Pancras' church. Group 11 (g).

Calibrated date: 1σ : cal AD 1290 − 1425
2σ : cal AD 1270 − 1450

Final comments:
M Biddle: St Pancras' church, period VII; final phase 16 (P.ph. 233), fifteenth-century. Rephased as St Pancras' church, use of third north aisle floor; date group 70 (P.ph. 233b), fifteenth-century. The radiocarbon date is in agreement with the phasing.

HAR-1534 440 ± 80 BP

$\delta^{13}C$: −20.0 ‰

Sample: G 3, submitted on 3 February 1976

Material: human bone: femur, ribs, scapula, and from pelvic area.

Initial comment: from BS, trench IV, grave 3, inside St Pancras' church. Group 11 (i).

Calibrated date: 1σ : cal AD 1415 − 1485
2σ : cal AD 1315 − 1640

Final comments:
M Biddle: St Pancras' church, period VIII; final phase 17 (P.ph. 237), late fifteenth- to early sixteenth-century. Rephased as St Pancras' church; date group 69 (P.ph. 237c), early to mid fifteenth-century. The radiocarbon date is in agreement with the phasing.

HAR-1537 850 ± 70 BP

$\delta^{13}C$: −26.8 ‰

Sample: OF 1248, submitted on 3 February 1976

Material: wood: *Quercus* sp.. The total number of rings counted was about 80. Sapwood may just be present. The sample consisted of the outermost 30 rings.

Initial comment: from BS, trench I, yard, pit 333. Group 3 (e).

Calibrated date: 1σ : cal AD 1045 − 1260
2σ : cal AD 1020 − 1280

Final comments:
M Biddle: house IX/X, timber; final phase 75 (P.ph. 446), early to mid tenth-century. The radiocarbon date is late in relation to the phasing and dendrochronological dates.

Dendrochronological date: the last ring of the timber is placed at 1032, making the felling date *c* 1057 or later, and placing the centrepoint of the rings dated by HAR-1537 at 1017. The centre of the calibrated one standard deviation range of the radiocarbon date is 1153, 136 years later than the dendrochronological centrepoint of the rings covered by the radiocarbon sample [cc/1153−dc/1017 = 136].

HAR-1551 450 ± 80 BP

$\delta^{13}C$: −19.2 ‰

Sample: G 10, submitted on 3 February 1976

Material: human bone: vertebrae, arm, pelvis, ribs, and hands.

Initial comment: from BS, trench IV, grave 10, layer 239; inside St Pancras' church. Group 11 (c).

Comment on uncalibrated date: a thirteenth-century date was expected.

Calibrated date: 1σ : cal AD 1410 − 1480
2σ : cal AD 1310 − 1640

Final comments:
M Biddle: St Pancras' church, period VIII; final phase 17 (P.ph. 196), late fifteenth- to early sixteenth-century. Rephased as: St Pancras' church, date group 71 − 2 (P.ph. 196d), mid to late fifteenth-century. The radiocarbon date is in agreement with the phasing.

HAR-1561 350 ± 80 BP

$\delta^{13}C$: −19.2 ‰

Sample: G 7, submitted on 3 February 1976

Material: human bone: femurs, parts of pelvic area, scapula, ribs, and vertebrae.

Initial comment: from BS, trench IV, grave 7, inside St Pancras' church. Group 11 (i).

Calibrated date: 1σ : cal AD 1445 – 1645
2σ : cal AD 1420 – 1955

Final comments:
M Biddle: St Pancras' church, period VIII; final phase 17 (P.ph. 214), late fifteenth- to early sixteenth-century. Rephased as: St Pancras' church, secondary graves in the fifth nave floor, date group 72 (P.ph. 214d), late fifteenth- to early sixteenth-century. The radiocarbon date is in agreement with the phasing.

HAR-1563 810 ± 70 BP

$\delta^{13}C$: –22.4 ‰

Sample: L 1210, submitted on 3 February 1976

Material: animal bone: cattle (*Bos* sp.).

Initial comment: from BS, trench 3, layer 1210. Also identified as sample 66, layer 94, St Pancras Lane. Group 7.

Calibrated date: 1σ : cal AD 1165 – 1270
2σ : cal AD 1030 – 1290

Final comments:
M Biddle: Tanner Street and lanes; final phase 67 (P.ph. 304), twelfth- to thirteenth-century. The radiocarbon date is in agreement with the phasing.

HAR-1564 1240 ± 70 BP

$\delta^{13}C$: –21.2 ‰

Sample: G 25, submitted on 3 February 1976

Material: human bone: femur, part of pelvis, vertebrae, and foot.

Initial comment: from BS, trench II, F720, grave 25. Group 4 (a).

Calibrated date: 1σ : cal AD 675 – 885
2σ : cal AD 650 – 960

Final comments:
M Biddle: residence, cemetery; final phase 1 (P.ph. 141), mid seventh- to early eighth-century. Rephased as date group 1 (P.ph. 141a), late seventh- to early eighth-century. Cemetery earlier than St Mary's church. The radiocarbon date is in agreement with the phasing.

HAR-1565 720 ± 80 BP

$\delta^{13}C$: –22.2 ‰

Sample: L 94, submitted on 3 February 1976

Material: animal bone: sheep (*Ovis* sp.) and bird.

Initial comment: from BS, trench III, layer 94, St Pancras Lane. Group 7.

Comment on uncalibrated date: the estimated date is fourteenth-century.

Calibrated date: 1σ : cal AD 1245 – 1295
2σ : cal AD 1170 – 1400

Final comments:
M Biddle: Tanner Street and lanes, final surfaces and use; final phase 70 (P.ph. 348), fifteenth- to ?sixteenth-century. The radiocarbon date is early in relation to the phasing.

HAR-1573 740 ± 70 BP

$\delta^{13}C$: –26.0 ‰

Sample: OF 741, submitted on 3 February 1976

Material: wood: branch. The total number of rings counted was 35, plus 15 sapwood rings. The sample consisted of 35 rings, a full cross-section of the branch, including 15 sapwood rings.

Initial comment: from BS, trench III, house XI, posthole 2178, probably layer 1506. Group 5 (e).

Calibrated date: 1σ : cal AD 1230 – 1285
2σ : cal AD 1170 – 1390

Final comments:
M Biddle: this posthole is difficult to phase. It may belong to house XI, timber; final phase 58 (P.ph. 559), eleventh- to possibly mid twelfth-century. The radiocarbon date could be in agreement with the phasing.

No sample was submitted for dendrochronology.

HAR-1574 640 ± 60 BP

$\delta^{13}C$: –21.7 ‰

Sample: L 278, submitted on 3 February 1976

Material: animal bone: cattle (*Bos* sp.).

Initial comment: from BS, trench III, layer 278, St Pancras Lane. Group 7.

Comment on uncalibrated date: the estimated date is fourteenth-century.

Calibrated date: 1σ : cal AD 1280 – 1395
2σ : cal AD 1260 – 1410

Final comments:
M Biddle: Tanner Street and lanes; final phase 69 (P.ph. 344), fourteenth-century. The radiocarbon date is in agreement with the phasing.

HAR-1580 850 ± 80 BP

$\delta^{13}C$: –28.5 ‰

Sample: OF 342, submitted on 3 February 1976

Material: wood: *Quercus* sp. – post. The total number of rings counted was 35, representing a complete section of the post. The sample consisted of approximately 35 rings, all but one of which appeared to be sapwood.

Initial comment: from BS, trench III, house XII, posthole 1624. Group 8 (e).

Calibrated date: 1σ : cal AD 1045 – 1260
2σ : cal AD 1010 – 1280

Final comments:
M Biddle: house XII, timber; final phase 40 (P.ph. 683), mid eleventh century. The radiocarbon date is in agreement with the phasing.

No sample was submitted for dendrochronology.

HAR-1582 940 ± 70 BP

$\delta^{13}C$: −27.7 ‰

Sample: OF 480, submitted on 3 February 1976

Material: wood: *Quercus* sp.. The total number of rings counted was 30. There were 18 sapwood rings outside the sample. The sample consisted of 30 rings.

Initial comment: from BS, trench I, F435. Group 2 (a) 2.

Calibrated date: 1σ : cal AD 1015 – 1170
　　　　　　　　　2σ : cal AD 970 – 1250

Final comments:
M Biddle: house IX/X, timber; final phase 77 (P.ph. 511), late eleventh- to twelfth-century. The radiocarbon date is in agreement with the phasing.

A sample was taken for dendrochronology and measured, but not dated.

HAR-1583 720 ± 80 BP

$\delta^{13}C$: −22.1 ‰

Sample: L 1017, submitted on 3 February 1976

Material: animal bone: cattle (*Bos* sp.).

Initial comment: from BS, trench III, layer 1017, St Pancras Lane. Group 7.

Comment on uncalibrated date: the estimated date is thirteenth-century.

Calibrated date: 1σ : cal AD 1245 – 1295
　　　　　　　　　2σ : cal AD 1170 – 1400

Final comments:
M Biddle: Tanner Street and lanes; final phase 67 (P.ph. 321), twelfth- to thirteenth-century. The radiocarbon date is in agreement with the phasing.

HAR-1584 790 ± 70 BP

$\delta^{13}C$: −22.2 ‰

Sample: L 1013, submitted on 3 February 1976

Material: animal bone: cattle (*Bos* sp.), pig (*Sus* sp.), and sheep or goat (*Ovis/Capra* sp.).

Initial comment: from BS, trench III, layer 1013, St Pancras Lane. Group 7.

Comment on uncalibrated date: the estimated date is thirteenth-century.

Calibrated date: 1σ : cal AD 1180 – 1275
　　　　　　　　　2σ : cal AD 1045 – 1290

Final comments:
M Biddle: Tanner Street and lanes; final phase 68 (P.ph. 342), mid to late thirteenth-century. The radiocarbon date is in agreement with the phasing.

HAR-1587 1020 ± 70 BP

$\delta^{13}C$: −28.7 ‰

Sample: OF 282, submitted on 3 February 1976

Material: wood: *Quercus* sp. with no sapwood. The sample consisted of the outermost 30 rings.

Initial comment: from BS, trench III, house XII, posthole 1738. Group 10 (g).

Calibrated date: 1σ : cal AD 960 – 1035
　　　　　　　　　2σ : cal AD 890 – 1170

Final comments:
M Biddle: house XII, timber; final phase 42 (P.ph. 760), late twelfth- to early thirteenth-century. The radiocarbon date is late in relation to the dendrochronological date.

Dendrochronological date: the last ring of the timber is placed at 933, making the felling date *c* 958 or later, and placing the midpoint of the rings dated by HAR-1587 at 918. The centre of the calibrated one standard deviation range of the radiocarbon date is 998, 80 years later than the dendrochronological centrepoint of the rings covered by the radiocarbon sample [cc/998–dc/918 = 80].

Harwell: a low benzene yield (67%).

HAR-1588 unknown

$\delta^{13}C$: unknown

Sample: OF 1025, submitted on 3 February 1976

Material: wood.

Final comments:
M Biddle: HAR-1677 is another date of the same timber. It is likely that HAR-1588 was never done. No second Harwell certificate covering OF 1025 exists.

Harwell: sample replaced by HAR-1677.

HAR-1603 740 ± 70 BP

$\delta^{13}C$: −22.5 ‰

Sample: L 1166, submitted on 3 February 1976

Material: animal bone: cattle (*Bos* sp.).

Initial comment: from BS, trench III, layer 1166, St Pancras Lane. Group 7.

Calibrated date: 1σ : cal AD 1230 – 1285
　　　　　　　　　2σ : cal AD 1170 – 1390

Final comments:
M Biddle: Tanner Street and lanes; final phase 67 (P.ph. 305), twelfth- to thirteenth-century. The radiocarbon date is in agreement with the phasing.

HAR-1604 900 ± 70 BP

$\delta^{13}C$: −23.8 ‰

Sample: L 1800, submitted on 3 February 1976

Material: animal bone: cattle (*Bos* sp.).

Initial comment: from BS, trench III, pit 244, layer 1800. Group 10 (d).

Calibrated date: 1σ : cal AD 1025 – 1220
　　　　　　　　　2σ : cal AD 1000 – 1270

Final comments:
M Biddle: house XII, timber; final phase 38 (P.ph. 726), early to mid eleventh-century. The radiocarbon date is late in relation to the phasing.

HAR-1610 850 ± 100 BP

$\delta^{13}C$: −22.4 ‰

Sample: L 1788, submitted on 3 February 1976

Material: animal bone: cattle (*Bos* sp.), horse (*Equus ferus*), goat (*Capra* sp.), and pig (*Sus* sp.).

Initial comment: from BS, trench III, house XII, layer 1788. Group 8 (b).

Calibrated date: 1σ : cal AD 1030 – 1270
                    2σ : cal AD 990 – 1290

Final comments:
M Biddle: house XII, timber; final phase 37 (P.ph. 670), mid to late tenth-century. The radiocarbon date is late in relation to the phasing.

HAR-1639 980 ± 60 BP

$\delta^{13}C$: −26.4 ‰

Sample: OF 52, submitted on 3 February 1976

Material: wood: *Quercus* sp. – post. The total number of rings counted was about 90, with no sapwood. There were about 20 rings outside the sample. The sample consisted of 70 rings.

Initial comment: from BS, trench III, F312, posthole 784. Group 9 (b).

Calibrated date: 1σ : cal AD 1000 – 1160
                    2σ : cal AD 960 – 1180

Final comments:
M Biddle: house XII, stone and timber; final phase 43 (P.ph. 712), mid to possibly late thirteenth-century. The radiocarbon date is in agreement with the dendrochronological date.

Dendrochronological date: the last ring of the timber is placed at 1078, making the felling date *c* 1103 or later, and placing the midpoint of the rings dated by HAR-1639 at 1034. The centre of the calibrated one standard deviation range of the radiocarbon date is 1080, 46 years later than the dendrochronological centrepoint of the rings covered by the radiocarbon sample [cc/1080–dc/1034 = 46].

Harwell: a repeat of HAR-1510.

HAR-1677 960 ± 60 BP

$\delta^{13}C$: −26.9 ‰

Sample: OF 1025, submitted on 2 July 1976

Material: wood: *Quercus* sp. – corner post. The total number of rings counted was 110, with 25 sapwood rings. The 30 rings immediately outside HAR-1677, before the sapwood, were to be dated by HAR-1588, but no certificate for HAR-1588 has been found. The sample consisted of the inner 80 rings.

Initial comment: from BS, trench III, house XII, pit 295, posthole 2361. Group 8 (b).

Calibrated date: 1σ : cal AD 1010 – 1160
                    2σ : cal AD 970 – 1220

Final comments:
M Biddle: house XII, timber; final phase 39 (P.ph. 721), early to possibly mid eleventh-century. The radiocarbon date is in agreement with the phasing.

A sample was taken for dendrochronology and measured, but not dated.

HAR-1678 990 ± 60 BP

$\delta^{13}C$: −26.6 ‰

Sample: OF 67, submitted on 25 March 1976

Material: wood: *Quercus* sp. – a complete section of a small oak post. The total number of rings counted was 100, with no sapwood present. The sample contained *c* 100 rings.

Initial comment: from BS, trench III, F312, posthole 799. Group 9 (d).

Comment on uncalibrated date: the expected date was twelfth century.

Calibrated date: 1σ : cal AD 990 – 1150
                    2σ : cal AD 900 – 1170

Final comments:
M Biddle: house XII, stone and timber; final phase 43 (P.ph. 712), mid to possibly late thirteenth-century. The radiocarbon date is early in relation to the phasing.

No sample was submitted for dendrochronology.

HAR-1680 930 ± 80 BP

$\delta^{13}C$: −26.3 ‰

Sample: OF 1048, submitted on 25 March 1976

Material: wood: *Quercus* sp. – post. The total number of rings counted was 34. The sapwood began immediately outside the sample. The sample contained 34 rings.

Initial comment: from BS, trench I, house IX, posthole 1394. Group 1 (e).

Calibrated date: 1σ : cal AD 1015 – 1210
                    2σ : cal AD 970 – 1260

Final comments:
M Biddle: house IX/X, timber; final phase 77 (P.ph. 516), late eleventh- to twelfth-century. The radiocarbon date is in agreement with the phasing.

A sample was taken for dendrochronology and measured, but not dated.

HAR-1686 860 ± 70 BP

$\delta^{13}C$: −27.6 ‰

Sample: OF 1044, submitted on 25 March 1976

Material: wood: *Quercus* sp. – branch. The total number of rings counted was 21. This was a complete section of an oak branch or sapling, with the sapwood beginning immediately outside the sample. The sample contained 21 rings.

Initial comment: from BS, trench I, house IX, posthole 2390. Group 1 (e).

Calibrated date: 1σ : cal AD 1045 – 1255
                    2σ : cal AD 1020 – 1280

Final comments:
M Biddle: house IX/X, timber; final phase 77 (P.ph. 239), late eleventh- to twelfth-century. The radiocarbon date is in agreement with the phasing.

A sample was taken for dendrochronology and measured, but not dated.

HAR-1687 990 ± 60 BP

$\delta^{13}C$: –27.5 ‰

Sample: OF 943, submitted on 25 March 1976

Material: wood: *Quercus* sp. – post. The total number of rings counted was 40, with no sapwood. The sample consisted of the 40 outermost rings.

Initial comment: from BS, pit 244, posthole 2324, layer 1689. Group 10 (d).

Calibrated date: 1σ : cal AD 990 – 1150
2σ : cal AD 900 – 1170

Final comments:
M Biddle: house XII, timber; final phase 38 (P.ph. 727), early to mid eleventh-century. The radiocarbon date is in agreement with the phasing.

A sample was taken for dendrochronology and measured, but not dated.

HAR-1688 1000 ± 70 BP

$\delta^{13}C$: –26.5 ‰

Sample: OF 361, submitted on 25 March 1976

Material: wood: *Quercus* sp. – plank. The total number of rings counted was 103, with no sapwood present. The sample consisted of 103 rings. A complete section was taken because of the size of the material available from sampling and the difficulty of determining the pith direction.

Initial comment: from BS, trench III, wall 269, F624. Group 8 (d).

Calibrated date: 1σ : cal AD 980 – 1150
2σ : cal AD 890 – 1180

Final comments:
M Biddle: house XII, stone and timber; final phase 44 (P.ph. 779), late thirteenth- to early fourteenth-century. The radiocarbon date is late in relation to the dendrochronological dates, but the plank must have been reused or residual in its much later context.

Dendrochronological date: the last ring of the timber is placed at 825, making the felling date *c* 850 or later, and placing the midpoint of the rings dated by HAR-1688 at 777. The centre of the calibrated one standard deviation range of the radiocarbon date is 1065, 288 years later than the dendrochronological centrepoint of the rings covered by the radiocarbon sample [cc/1065–dc/777 = 288].

HAR-1737 unknown

$\delta^{13}C$: unknown

Sample: OF 1195, submitted on 1 February 1976

Material: wood: *Quercus* sp..

Initial comment: from the same timber as HAR-878 and HAR-1279.

Final comments:
Harwell: no certificate or submission has been found. The result is unknown.

HAR-1738 1210 ± 80 BP

$\delta^{13}C$: –21.1 ‰

Sample: G 23, submitted on 3 February 1976

Material: human bone: femurs, leg bones, vertebrae, and scapula.

Initial comment: from BS, trench II, F733, grave 23, layer 920. Group 4 (a).

Calibrated date: 1σ : cal AD 685 – 895
2σ : cal AD 660 – 990

Final comments:
M Biddle: residence, cemetery; final phase 1 (P.ph. 141), mid seventh- to eighth-century. Rephased as date group 1 (P.ph. 141a), late seventh- to early eighth-century. Cemetery earlier than St Mary's church. The radiocarbon date is in agreement with the phasing.

Harwell: a repeat of HAR-1102.

HAR-1739 1790 ± 80 BP

$\delta^{13}C$: –22.1 ‰

Sample: G 24, submitted on 3 February 1976

Material: human bone: parts of pelvis and legs.

Initial comment: from BS, trench II, F751, grave 24, layer 966. Group 4 (a).

Calibrated date: 1σ : cal AD 125 – 340
2σ : cal AD 60 – 420

Final comments:
M Biddle: residence, cemetery; final phase 1 (P.ph. 141), mid seventh- to early eighth-century. Rephased as date group 1 (P.ph. 141a), late seventh- to early eighth-century. Cemetery earlier than St Mary's church. The radiocarbon date is impossibly early.

Harwell: a repeat of HAR-1078 on the same material.

HAR-1740 520 ± 80 BP

$\delta^{13}C$: –20.0 ‰

Sample: G 14, submitted on 3 February 1976

Material: human bone.

Initial comment: from BS, trench IV, grave 14, inside St Pancras' church.

Comment on uncalibrated date: this date is archaeologically acceptable.

Calibrated date: 1σ : cal AD 1315 – 1445
2σ : cal AD 1280 – 1490

Final comments:
M Biddle: St Pancras' church, period VII; final phase 16 (P.ph. 233), fifteenth-century. Rephased as St Pancras' church, use of third north aisle floor; date group 70 (P.ph.233b), fifteenth-century. The radiocarbon date seems in agreement with the phasing.

Harwell: repeats HAR-1077.

HAR-1741 590 ± 60 BP

$\delta^{13}C$: −19.1 ‰

Sample: G 30, submitted on 29 July 1976

Material: human bone.

Initial comment: from BS, trench IV, grave 11, layer 361, in St Pancras' church. Repeats HAR-1491, for which no submission or certificate has been found. The bones belong to G30 not G11. Group 11 (h).

Comment on uncalibrated date: a thirteenth-century date was expected.

Calibrated date: 1σ : cal AD 1290 – 1410
                     2σ : cal AD 1280 – 1430

Final comments:
M Biddle: St Pancras' church, period VIII; final phase 17 (P.ph. 196), late fifteenth- to early sixteenth-century. Rephased as St Pancras' church, secondary graves in the south chapel; date group 67 – 70 (P.ph. 196c), mid fourteenth- to early fifteenth-century. The radiocarbon date is in agreement with the phasing.

HAR-1823   unknown

$\delta^{13}C$: unknown

Sample: BSGR21, submitted on 1 September 1976

Material: bone.

Final comments:
M Biddle: no trace of this date has been found.

Harwell: no submission form or certificate has been found. The result of this date is unknown.

HAR-1851 920 ± 80 BP

$\delta^{13}C$: −28.5 ‰

Sample: OF 119, submitted on 3 February 1976

Material: wood: *Quercus* sp. – plank. The total number of rings counted was 79, with no sapwood. The sample consisted of a full section of 79 rings.

Initial comment: from BS, trench III, F312, postholes 830 and 847, layers 786 and 841; HAR-1851 is a substitute for HAR-1514 from the same context. No submission or certificate for HAR-1514 have been found. Group 9 (b).

Calibrated date: 1σ : cal AD 1020 – 1215
                     2σ : cal AD 970 – 1270

Final comments:
M Biddle: house XII, stone and timber; final phase 43 (P.ph. 712), mid to possibly late thirteenth-century. The radiocarbon date is early in relation to the phasing and the plank may be reused or residual.

A sample was taken for dendrochronology and measured, but not dated.

HAR-1852 1440 ± 70 BP

$\delta^{13}C$: −27.3 ‰

Sample: OF 1193, submitted on 11 August 1976

Material: wood: *Quercus* sp.. The total number of rings counted was 127, with 4 sapwood rings beginning immediately outside the sample. The sample consisted of c 75 rings from the outside of the trunk.

Initial comment: from BS, trench III (house XII), F778. Large timber-lined pit. HAR-288, HAR-878, and HAR-1279 also come from F778, but from different timbers. Group 5 (a).

Calibrated date: 1σ : cal AD 555 – 660
                     2σ : cal AD 440 – 680

Final comments:
M Biddle: residence, stone building [G]; final phase 4 (P.ph. 163), late eighth- to late ninth-century. Rephased as residence, stone building; date group 4 – 6 (P.ph. 163a), late eighth- to late ninth-century. The rings covered are from the outside of the timber. The radiocarbon date is early in relation to the phasing.

A sample was taken for dendrochronology and measured, but not dated.

Windsor Castle: St George's Chapel, Berkshire

Location: SU 9777 approx
              Lat. 51.28.59 N; Long. 00.36.10 W

Excavator: G Parnell (Department of the Environment), 1978

Site: two skeletons, one adult male and one juvenile aged 3 – 4 years, were found under the vestry floor during renovation work; both were aligned east – west, without coffins.

HAR-2896   450 ± 80 BP

$\delta^{13}C$: −20.0 ‰

Sample: 1, submitted on 27 October 1978

Material: human bone: left femora (robust).

Initial comment: from a shallow grave cut into a very dry deposit of chalk and clay.

Calibrated date: 1σ : cal AD 1410 – 1480
                     2σ : cal AD 1310 – 1640

Winklebury, Hampshire

Location: SU 61355290
              Lat. 51.16.17 N; Long. 01.07.14 W

Excavator: K Smith (Central Excavation Unit), 1975 – 6

Site: Iron Age hillfort.

References: Smith 1977, 82 – 3 (^{14}C)

Comments:
AML: one small sample, HAR-1777 (13692), has been withdrawn.

HAR-1764 2200 ± 60 BP

$\delta^{13}C$: −27.3 ‰

Sample: 13690, submitted on 10 October 1973

Material: charcoal.

Initial comment: from the remains of a charred post in a posthole, possibly forming part of the porch of an Iron Age round house (structure 3870).

Comment on uncalibrated date: slightly later than that suggested by the pottery, which belongs to the early phase, sixth to possibly fourth centuries BC.

Calibrated date: 1σ : cal BC 380 – 185
2σ : cal BC 400 – 100

Final comments:
Harwell: extensive rootlet contamination was separated as far as possible; excess benzene was burnt as HAR-1784 (2180 ± 70 BP).

References: Radiocarbon **27**, 83

HAR-1765   1930 ± 70 BP

$\delta^{13}C$: −25.0 ‰

Sample: 13646, submitted on 10 October 1973

Material: charcoal.

Initial comment: from the bottom layer but one in a pit which contained pottery of the sixth – fifth century BC (pit 3660, layer 3643).

Calibrated date: 1σ : cal BC 0 – 130 cal AD
2σ : cal BC 100 – 230 cal AD

Final comments:
Harwell: some modern rootlet contamination.

HAR-1778   1980 ± 90 BP

$\delta^{13}C$: −25.8 ‰

Sample: 13961, submitted on 10 October 1973

Material: charcoal.

Initial comment: from a deposit of burnt material (2628) in the top half of a beehive storage pit (2611); the layers above and below this produced saucepan pots dating to the third – first centuries BC.

Calibrated date: 1σ : cal BC 100 – 115 cal AD
2σ : cal BC 200 – 230 cal AD

References: Radiocarbon **27**, 83

HAR-1794   2020 ± 80 BP

$\delta^{13}C$: −25.6 ‰

Sample: 13988, submitted on 10 October 1973

Material: charcoal.

Initial comment: from a layer of burnt material (2133) in the top half of a storage pit (2129).

Comment on uncalibrated date: this date is consistent with the associated pottery.

Calibrated date: 1σ : cal BC 150 – 65 cal AD
2σ : cal BC 340 – 130 cal AD

References: Radiocarbon **27**, 83

Winterton, Humberside

Location: SE 911183
Lat. 53.39.11 N; Long. 00.37.17 W

Excavator: R Goodburn (Historic Buildings and Monuments Commission), 1968 – 85

Site: Roman villa excavated in advance of opencast mining.

References: Morgan 1976, 5 (^{14}C)

Objectives: to provide a date for the construction of the well, the timbers from which have been analysed dendrochronologically; to check their contemporaneity and felling season.

HAR-1605   1710 ± 60 BP

$\delta^{13}C$: −27.8 ‰

Sample: WIN1, submitted by R A Morgan on 3 February 1976

Material: wood: outermost 15 rings, all sapwood to the bark edge, from two timbers felled in the same year.

Initial comment: from a Roman well dug into sand and gravel, just above natural blue clay.

Comment on uncalibrated date: the ^{14}C date falls within the early part of the archaeological date range suggested on stratigraphical grounds.

Calibrated date: 1σ : cal AD 245 – 405
2σ : cal AD 145 – 440

Final comments:
R Goodburn: the stratigraphical dating of the feature would fit neatly with the calibrated range at one standard deviation. A date after AD 400 is not possible on any grounds.

Woodbury Castle, Devon

Location: SY 033875
Lat. 50.40.43 N; Long. 03.22.08 W

Excavator: H Miles (for the Department of the Environment), 1971

Site: a hillfort.

References: Miles 1975b, 201 – 2 (^{14}C)
Radiocarbon **19**, 401 – 2 (^{14}C)

Objectives: to date the constuction of the hillfort, which produced virtually no identifiable pottery or other finds.

HAR-235(S)   1930 ± 200 BP

$\delta^{13}C$: −24.0 ‰

Sample: WDC715835, submitted by S Limbrey in 1972

Material: charcoal: mainly *Quercus* sp., with one fragment of *Alnus* sp. and one of *Crataegus* sp. (C A Keepax).

Initial comment: from a pit which was apparently cut into the old land surface immediately before the construction of the rampart, and sealed by the rampart to a depth of *c* 0.45m; on the basis of the pottery and the nature of the earthwork, the expected date is fifth – fourth century BC, prior to the currency of Glastonbury pottery, which is fairly common in Devon.

Comment on uncalibrated date: this result is inconsistent with the expected age of the earthwork.

Calibrated date: 1σ : cal BC 180 – 330 cal AD
2σ : cal BC 400 – 540 cal AD

Final comments:
H Miles: the calibration at the two standard deviation level of confidence would provide a fit with other data; however this single date on a small sample should not be pressed too far.

Harwell: a small sample accounts for the larger than normal error term.

Wootton Wawen: Churchyard, Warwickshire

Location: SP 15296326
Lat. 52.16.01 N; Long. 01.46.33 W

Excavator: H James (Dyfed Archaeological Trust), 1974

Site: a medieval churchyard.

References: James 1982, 44 (^{14}C)
Radiocarbon **27**, 84 (^{14}C)

Objectives: to check the length of use of the cemetery, as there is some degree of superimposition; ^{14}C is the only means of dating the cemetery and the results are vital for establishing the age of the earliest priory buildings.

HAR-1820   790 ± 70 BP

$δ^{13}C$: −20.3 ‰

Sample: A62, submitted on 1 September 1976

Material: human bone.

Initial comment: from same phase as HAR-1822.

Calibrated date: 1σ : cal AD 1180 – 1275
2σ : cal AD 1045 – 1290

Final comments:
H James: selected for its stratigraphy: cuts early timber features and is cut by A61 (see below).

HAR-1821   790 ± 80 BP

$δ^{13}C$: −19.8 ‰

Sample: A61, submitted on 1 September 1976

Material: human bone.

Initial comment: from same context as HAR-1822.

Calibrated date: 1σ : cal AD 1170 – 1275
2σ : cal AD 1030 – 1375

Final comments:
H James: the date range supports the stratigraphic evidence for this grave being the latest in the sequence.

HAR-1822   900 ± 70 BP

$δ^{13}C$: −20.9 ‰

Sample: A21, submitted on 1 September 1976

Material: human bone.

Initial comment: from a grave cutting postholes and timber slots dug into the natural; sealed by medieval buildings.

Calibrated date: 1σ : cal AD 1025 – 1220
2σ : cal AD 1000 – 1270

Final comments:
H James: the date ranges allow this grave on the western edge of the cemetery to be the earliest of the three dated, but are close enough to the other two to uphold the excavator's conclusion of an eleventh- to thirteenth-century date range for the cemetery.

Worcester: 39 – 47 Sidbury Street, Hereford and Worcester

Location: SO 85155451
Lat. 52.11.18 N; Long. 02.13.02 W

Excavator: J Greig (University of Birmingham), 1975

Site: a medieval barrel latrine, set in natural gravel; very rich in plant remains, birds, insects, and parasite ova.

References: Carver 1980
Grieg 1981, 276 – 7 (^{14}C)

Objectives: to provide a date for the botanical remains; some cloth of medieval type was found, but no more precise dating evidence.

HAR-3100   510 ± 70 BP

$δ^{13}C$: −27.0 ‰

Sample: WS3, submitted on 9 February 1979

Material: organic material: very rich in the remains of plants, birds, and insects; also parasite ova and some cloth.

Initial comment: from the lower part of the main fill of the barrel (layer 2).

Calibrated date: 1σ : cal AD 1325 – 1445
2σ : cal AD 1290 – 1480

Final comments:
J Greig: this date shows the contents of the barrel date from the later medieval period.

Worcester: Sidbury, Hereford and Worcester

Location: SO 851545
Lat. 52.11.17 N; Long. 02.13.05 W

Excavator: M Carver (Birmingham University Field Archaeology Unit), 1976

Site: Roman road, three medieval tenements, post-medieval pits just outside the city wall.

References: Carver 1980, 209 (^{14}C)

Objectives: to locate the early medieval sequence.

HAR-1914   1130 ± 70 BP

$δ^{13}C$: −22.6 ‰

Sample: WS761274, submitted on 9 November 1976

Material: charcoal: *Quercus* sp. from large timbers (C A Keepax).

Initial comment: from fill of a cess pit with Chester type ware and limestone-tempered hand-made pottery: the expected date is Late Saxon.

Calibrated date: 1σ : cal AD 810 – 985
2σ : cal AD 715 – 1020

Final comments:
M Carver: this conforms with the archaeologist's date of *c* 900 AD.

Harwell: published by the excavator as HAR-1274.

HAR-1915 2030 ± 80 BP

$\delta^{13}C$: –25.8 ‰

Sample: WS761099, submitted on 9 November 1976

Material: charcoal: twiggy oak (*Quercus* sp.) with hazel (*Corylus* sp.) and cf blackthorn (*Prunus* sp.) and hawthorn type (Rosaceae, sub-family Pomoideae) (C A Keepax).

Initial comment: from a humic occupation layer which appears to be the latest in the Roman sequence (fourth-century), but which could be later (eighth- to eleventh-century).

Calibrated date: 1σ : cal BC 160 – 60 cal AD
2σ : cal BC 350 – 120 cal AD

Final comments:
M Carver: redeposited in the third or fourth century AD.

Harwell: published by the excavator as HAR-1099.

HAR-1916 7030 ± 70 BP

$\delta^{13}C$: unknown

Sample: WS761306, submitted on 9 November 1976

Material: charcoal: mainly *Quercus* sp. from large and twig-sized timbers with some *Corylus* sp. (C A Keepax).

Initial comment: from water pipe trench of possible fourth- to fifth-century date.

Calibrated date: 1σ : cal BC 5975 – 5805
2σ : cal BC 6075 – 5730

Final comments:
M Carver: reused bog-oak? The pipe is Late Roman.

York: 1 – 5 Aldwark, North Yorkshire

Location: SE 60585219
Lat. 53.57.43 N; Long. 01.04.36 W

Excavator: H Macgregor (York Archaeological Trust), 1977

Site: a rampart situated *c* 10m south-west of the north-east wall of the Roman fortress, which has either cut away Roman deposits or has been added to the Roman wall as a part of later defence works; the bank has been cut away by a large feature of unknown function and date which was backfilled in the thirteenth century.

References: MacGregor 1988, 65 (^{14}C)
Radiocarbon **29**, 83 (^{14}C)

Objectives: to help determine the evolution of the defences.

Comments:
H Macgregor: the ^{14}C measurements agree well with the artefactual evidence, which suggests that the rampart is probably of eleventh-century date.

HAR-2300 940 ± 70 BP

$\delta^{13}C$: –27.8 ‰

Sample: ALDW52, submitted by H Kenward on 1 June 1977

Material: wood, washed in distilled water and oven dried at 105°C: *Corylus/Alnus* sp. from twig-sized wood; *c* 25% identified (C A Keepax).

Initial comment: from brushwood at the base of the fortress rampart; possibly Roman, although the biological evidence suggests a medieval date.

Calibrated date: 1σ : cal AD 1015 – 1170
2σ : cal AD 970 – 1250

HAR-2301 950 ± 80 BP

$\delta^{13}C$: –27.3 ‰

Sample: ALDW49A, submitted by H Kenward on 1 June 1977

Material: wood: *Quercus* sp. from branch-sized and larger timber; *c* 25% identified.

Initial comment: from brushwood at the base of the fortress rampart; duplicate of HAR-2302.

Calibrated date: 1σ : cal AD 1005 – 1170
2σ : cal AD 900 – 1250

HAR-2302 910 ± 70 BP

$\delta^{13}C$: –27.3 ‰

Sample: ALDW49, submitted by H Kenward on 1 June 1977

Material: wood: *Quercus* sp. from branch-sized and larger timber; *c* 25% identified.

Initial comment: from the same context as HAR-2301.

Calibrated date: 1σ : cal AD 1025 – 1215
2σ : cal AD 990 – 1260

York: 16 – 22 Coppergate, North Yorkshire

Location: SE 60445168
Lat. 53.57.27 N; Long. 01.04.44 W

Excavator: R A Hall (York Archaeological Trust), 1976 – 81

Site: Late Saxon, Viking, and medieval settlement.

References: Hall 1984

Objectives: to aid the chronological interpretation of the site.

HAR-2915   770 ± 70 BP

$\delta^{13}C$: −27.3 ‰

Sample: CGT628, submitted by H Kenward

Material: charcoal and ash: Rosaceae, sub-family Pomoideae, and *Corylus/Alnus* sp. from twigs and large timbers (C A Keepax).

Initial comment: from layer 12600 associated with hearth 12500 in cut 12603; it is tentatively dated to the twelfth century.

Calibrated date: 1σ : cal AD 1215 – 1280
2σ : cal AD 1055 – 1375

Final comments:
R A Hall: the adjacent hearth 9241 has an archaeomagnetic date of 1175 – 1225.

HAR-2916   1080 ± 80 BP

$\delta^{13}C$: −26.4 ‰

Sample: CGT610, submitted by H Kenward on 27 October 1978

Material: charcoal-rich soil: *Quercus* sp. from mature timbers (C A Keepax).

Initial comment: from a layer (7826) of fine silt loam, interpreted as a destruction level; probably thirteenth-century.

Calibrated date: 1σ : cal AD 885 – 1020
2σ : cal AD 780 – 1155

Final comments:
R A Hall: the associated pottery is now known to be thirteenth century; charcoal from old timbers would be appropriate in this horizon.

HAR-3088   1110 ± 70 BP

$\delta^{13}C$: −27.1 ‰

Sample: CGT697, submitted by H Kenward on 9 February 1979

Material: charcoal: *Quercus* sp. from large timber, *Corylus/Alnus* sp. twigs, and *Fraxinus* sp. twigs (A R Hall and C A Keepax).

Initial comment: from context 7804, possibly twelfth-century.

Calibrated date: 1σ : cal AD 880 – 1000
2σ : cal AD 770 – 1030

Final comments:
R A Hall: the context is now known to be associated with the construction of buildings in the late tenth century; the date thus agrees well with this revised interpretation.

HAR-3089   1180 ± 70 BP

$\delta^{13}C$: −26.7 ‰

Sample: CGT646, submitted by H Kenward on 9 February 1979

Material: charcoal: *Quercus* sp., *Corylus* sp., and *Fraxinus* sp. (A R Hall and C A Keepax).

Initial comment: from context 7804, possibly eleventh- or twelfth-century destruction debris.

Calibrated date: 1σ : cal AD 770 – 955
2σ : cal AD 670 – 1000

Final comments:
R A Hall: as above.

York: 58 – 9 Skeldergate, Bishopshill 1, North Yorkshire

Location: SE 60215145
Lat. 53.57.20 N; Long. 01.04.56 W

Excavator: S Donaghey (York Archaeological Trust), 1973 – 5

Site: multiperiod urban site with a virtually uninterrupted sequence of occupation from the Roman period to the present day.

Objectives: to provide chronological fixed points in the sequence.

HAR-1412   1230 ± 80 BP

$\delta^{13}C$: −26.0 ‰

Sample: BH155, submitted by H Kenward on 19 December 1975

Material: charcoal: *Quercus* sp. and *Salix* sp. from fairly large timbers, *c* 20% identified (C A Keepax).

Initial comment: from occupation deposit (2131) above a Saxon (or Roman?) floor.

Comment on uncalibrated date: (R A Hall) the (uncalibrated) date is compatible with the eighth-century coin from this deposit, but the pottery from structure D was tenth-century, as was the beam in a slot marking one wall of the structure (HAR-1728); the ^{14}C result does not necessarily contradict the later date, as it reflects the age of the timber.

Calibrated date: 1σ : cal AD 675 – 890
2σ : cal AD 650 – 980

References: Moulden and Tweddle 1986, 45
Radiocarbon **29**, 80

HAR-1416   1840 ± 70 BP

$\delta^{13}C$: −27.2 ‰

Sample: BH198, submitted by H Kenward on 19 December 1975

Material: wood: mainly *Quercus* sp. with some diffuse porous fragments (not identifiable); *c* 20% identified (C A Keepax).

Initial comment: from the top part of the buried soil (2356).

Calibrated date: 1σ : cal AD 80 – 245
2σ : cal AD 10 – 340

Final comments:
S Donaghey: this confirms expectations.

References: Carver *et al* 1978, 13
Hall *et al* 1980, 105
Radiocarbon **29**, 80

HAR-1417 1820 ± 70 BP

$\delta^{13}C$: −26.7 ‰

Sample: BH201, submitted by H Kenward on 19 December 1975

Material: charcoal: all *Quercus* sp. from fairly large timbers; c 20% identified (C A Keepax).

Initial comment: from a charcoal-rich layer (2360) overlying the buried soil.

Comment on uncalibrated date: (P V Addyman) the (uncalibrated) results from HAR-1416 and HAR-1417 confirm the clearance of the area in the Early Roman period prior to primary occupation, and now allow the reconstruction of the local ecological conditions from the associated biological remains and soil evidence.

Calibrated date: 1σ : cal AD 110 – 315
2σ : cal AD 30 – 380

References: Carver *et al* 1978, 13
Hall *et al* 1980, 105
Radiocarbon **29**, 81

HAR-1418 1930 ± 70 BP

$\delta^{13}C$: −27.9 ‰

Sample: BH202, submitted by H Kenward on 19 December 1975

Material: charcoal: possibly *Corylus* sp., mainly from fairly large timbers, c 20% identified (C A Keepax).

Initial comment: from a layer associated with Roman destruction levels.

Comment on uncalibrated date: (P V Addyman) the (uncalibrated) result is surprisingly early as the deposit overlay third-century Roman levels; the charcoal was presumably derived from trees of considerable age.

Calibrated date: 1σ : cal AD 0 – 130 cal AD
2σ : cal BC 100 – 230 cal AD

References: Carver *et al* 1978, 13
Hall *et al* 1980, 105
Radiocarbon **29**, 81

HAR-1728 960 ± 70 BP

$\delta^{13}C$: −28.1 ‰

Sample: BH2046A, submitted by H Kenward on 1 February 1976

Material: wood: fragments with c 25 annual rings from a long beam, originally entire (may have been subject to contamination by humates from later organic layers).

Initial comment: from a beam slot (2046) forming part of Anglian structure D (see HAR-1412); the estimated date is eighth – ninth century AD.

Comment on uncalibrated date: (R A Hall) see HAR-1412.

Calibrated date: 1σ : cal AD 1005 – 1165
2σ : cal AD 960 – 1230

References: Moulden and Tweddle 1986; 45, 50
Radiocarbon **29**, 83

HAR-1729 1750 ± 80 BP

$\delta^{13}C$: −26.8 ‰

Sample: BH8068A, submitted by H Kenward on 1 September 1976

Material: wood.

Initial comment: from timber post 10 in the construction pit of a Roman well (8068).

Comment on uncalibrated date: (P V Addyman) the (uncalibrated) result accords well with the estimated date of construction in the second or third century AD.

Calibrated date: 1σ : cal AD 45 – 390
2σ : cal AD 80 – 440

References: *Radiocarbon* **29**, 81

HAR-1866 1840 ± 60 BP

$\delta^{13}C$: −27.0 ‰

Sample: BH220, submitted by H Kenward on 9 November 1976

Material: charcoal: too wet for identification (C A Keepax).

Initial comment: from the lowest fills of a Roman well; washed with distilled water.

Comment on uncalibrated date: this gives a very nice confirmation of the latest phase of the site and the beginning of the period of disuse.

Calibrated date: 1σ : cal AD 85 – 240
2σ : cal AD 30 – 335

References: Carver *et al* 1978, 25
Radiocarbon **29**, 81

HAR-1927 1830 ± 70 BP

$\delta^{13}C$: −26.4 ‰

Sample: BH300, submitted by H Kenward

Material: wood: *Quercus* sp., about 50 rings (H Kenward).

Initial comment: from the timber lining of a Roman well.

Comment on uncalibrated date: (P V Addyman) as HAR-1928.

Calibrated date: 1σ : cal AD 85 – 250
2σ : cal AD 20 – 375

References: Carver *et al* 1978, 25
Radiocarbon **29**, 81

HAR-1928 2150 ± 70 BP

$\delta^{13}C$: −27.7 ‰

Sample: BH301, submitted by H Kenward on 9 November 1976

Material: wood: *Quercus* sp., about 50 widely spaced rings present (H Kenward).

Initial comment: from the timber lining of a Roman well.

Comment on uncalibrated date: (P V Addyman) the early (uncalibrated) result suggests the reuse of old timbers.

Calibrated date: 1σ : cal BC 360 – 105
                   2σ : cal BC 390 – 10

Final comments:
Harwell: the difference in HAR-1927 and HAR-1928 is striking but nothing in experimental notes gives cause to doubt the results.

References: Carver *et al* 1978, 25
               Radiocarbon **29**, 81

HAR-2587   3410 ± 80 BP

$\delta^{13}C$: −26.2 ‰

Sample: BH211/1, submitted by H Kenward on 3 March 1978

Material: peat, washed in tap water through a 300μ sieve: botanical analysis shows heathland flora.

Initial comment: from what appear to be blocks of peat in the fill of a Roman well (as HAR-2588); a date is required to aid the interpretation of the enigmatic fill.

Calibrated date: 1σ : cal BC 1875 – 1625
                   2σ : cal BC 1930 – 1520

Final comments:
S Donaghey: what does this tell us about Roman resource exploitation?

HAR-2588   3500 ± 80 BP

$\delta^{13}C$: −27.4 ‰

Sample: BH278, submitted by H Kenward on 3 March 1978

Material: plant, residue from 10% NaOH soak sieved through a 300μ sieve; treatment and storage has not been ideal but the sample is believed to be uncontaminated.

Initial comment: from a peaty layer in the fill of a well (see HAR-2587).

Calibrated date: 1σ : cal BC 1935 – 1740
                   2σ : cal BC 2040 – 1640

Final comments:
S Donaghey: as above.

HAR-2753   2680 ± 70 BP

$\delta^{13}C$: −27.4 ‰

Sample: BH186, submitted by H Kenward on 3 March 1978

Material: humic soil.

Initial comment: from the upper fill of a Roman well.

Calibrated date: 1σ : cal BC 905 – 805
                   2σ : cal BC 990 – 780

York: Aldwark, Ebor Brewery, North Yorkshire

Location: SE 60655208
             Lat. 53.57.41 N; Long. 01.04.31 W

Excavator: J Magilton (York Archaeological Trust), 1974 and 1976

Site: an extensive cemetery and pre-Conquest church, extended in the twelfth century and widened in the thirteenth century (probably St Helen on the Walls).

References: Dawes and Magilton 1980; 10, 15, 18 (^{14}C)

Objectives: to elucidate the origins and growth of a York parish church of relatively low status and its cemetery.

Comments:
AML: one sample, HAR-6887 (EBR5556), was dated after 1981.

HAR-2898   780 ± 80 BP

$\delta^{13}C$: −19.1 ‰

Sample: EBR8013, submitted on 27 October 1978

Material: human bone.

Initial comment: from a possible Roman burial below the medieval cemetery.

Calibrated date: 1σ : cal AD 1180 – 1280
                   2σ : cal AD 1040 – 1380

Final comments:
J Magilton: this suggests that the burial is part of the medieval cemetery.

HAR-2899   720 ± 60 BP

$\delta^{13}C$: −20.7 ‰

Sample: EBR5795, submitted on 27 October 1978

Material: human bone.

Initial comment: from a possible Roman burial below the medieval cemetery.

Calibrated date: 1σ : cal AD 1260 – 1290
                   2σ : cal AD 1220 – 1390

Final comments:
J Magilton: as above.

HAR-2900   570 ± 70 BP

$\delta^{13}C$: −20.6 ‰

Sample: EBR5731, submitted on 27 October 1978

Material: human bone: the feet and ankles of an adult female.

Initial comment: from 5731, the only charcoal burial on the site; the rest of the body was lost when, or before, the north-west corner of the fourth church was constructed.

Calibrated date: 1σ : cal AD 1295 – 1425
                   2σ : cal AD 1280 – 1450

Final comments:
J Magilton: most charcoal burials are pre-twelfth century: this suggests a rather late example.

York: High Ousegate, North Yorkshire

Location: SE 60345174
             Lat. 53.57.29 N; Long. 01.04.49 W

Excavator: D Brinklow (York Archaeological Trust), 1977

Site: a watching brief of underpinning of the wall.

References: Addyman 1991, 186 (^{14}C)

Objectives: to establish whether the material is Late Roman or later.

HAR-2708   1480 ± 80 BP

$δ^{13}C$: −27.8 ‰

Sample: HO256, submitted by H Kenward on 3 March 1978

Material: humic soil.

Initial comment: from featureless deposits overlying Roman levels.

Calibrated date: 1σ : cal AD 460 – 650
        2σ : cal AD 410 – 670

Final comments:
D Brinklow: significant for future work in this part of York, since it suggests post-Roman dereliction in Roman buildings.

York: Parliament Street, North Yorkshire

Location: SE 603518
      Lat. 53.57.31 N; Long. 01.04.51 W

Excavator: R A Hall (York Archaeological Trust), 1976

Site: a watching brief on the mechanical exposure of the deeply buried Roman fortress, south-east wall.

Objectives: to provide dating for a tree-ring sequence.

HAR-2627   1990 ± 70 BP

$δ^{13}C$: −24.5 ‰

Sample: PARL2, submitted by J Hillam on 21 February 1978

Material: wood, waterlogged; fungicide used: *Quercus* sp., years 55 – 74 from a 101-year sequence (J Hillam).

Initial comment: as above.

Calibrated date: 1σ : cal BC 95 – 75 cal AD
        2σ : cal BC 180 – 130 cal AD

Final comments:
R A Hall: as above, indicating the use of mature timbers.

Harwell: the wood was treated with fungicide prior to submission. The cellulose fraction was therefore extracted and used for dating.

HAR-2628   1980 ± 70 BP

$δ^{13}C$: −23.3 ‰

Sample: PARL3, submitted by J Hillam on 21 February 1978

Material: wood, waterlogged; fungicide used: *Quercus* sp. from years 56 – 75 of a 106-year sequence (J Hillam).

Initial comment: as above.

Calibrated date: 1σ : cal BC 90 – 80 cal AD
        2σ : cal BC 170 – 140 cal AD

Final comments:
R A Hall: as above.

Harwell: the wood was treated with fungicide prior to submission. The cellulose fraction was therefore extracted and used for dating.

HAR-2629   2030 ± 70 BP

$δ^{13}C$: −23.8 ‰

Sample: PARL1, submitted by J Hillam on 21 February 1978

Material: wood, waterlogged; fungicide used: *Quercus* sp., years 86 – 105 from a 102-year sequence (J Hillam).

Initial comment: from stakes beneath the wall of the Roman fortress.

Calibrated date: 1σ : cal BC 150 – 50 cal AD
        2σ : cal BC 330 – 110 cal AD

Final comments:
R A Hall: this conforms to the likely date range of the wall's erection.

Harwell: wood treated with fungicide prior to submission. Years 86 – 105 from a 142 sequence.

York: Pavement, Lloyd's Bank, North Yorkshire

Location: SE 604518
      Lat. 53.57.30 N; Long. 01.04.30 W

Excavator: M Harrison (York Archaeological Trust), 1972 – 3

Site: the early medieval town.

References: Addyman 1991, 186 (^{14}C)
      Radiocarbon **19**, 413 (^{14}C)

Objectives: three samples from 50-year intervals of a 180-year tree-ring sequence were submitted to provide dates for the botanical and environmental studies.

Comments:
R A Morgan: the (uncalibrated) results fit the expected site chronology; the extreme values are not inconsistent with the dendrochronology when the standard deviations are properly analysed.

HAR-548   1090 ± 60 BP

$δ^{13}C$: −26.2 ‰

Sample: SAMPLE1, submitted by R Morgan

Material: wood: *Quercus* sp., rings 40 – 60 (R Morgan).

Initial comment: from planks at level 23.

Calibrated date: 1σ : cal AD 890 – 1010
        2σ : cal AD 790 – 1030

HAR-549   1170 ± 80 BP

$δ^{13}C$: −26.2 ‰

Sample: SAMPLE2, submitted by R Morgan

Material: wood: *Quercus* sp., rings 90 – 110 (R Morgan).

Initial comment: from planks at level 23.

Calibrated date: 1σ : cal AD 770 – 970
2σ : cal AD 670 – 1020

HAR-550 1130 ± 60 BP

$\delta^{13}C$: −26.4 ‰

Sample: SAMPLE3, submitted by R Morgan

Material: wood: *Quercus* sp., rings 140 – 60 (R Morgan).

Initial comment: from planks at levels 23(2) and 21(1).

Calibrated date: 1σ : cal AD 830 – 980
2σ : cal AD 770 – 1020

York: The Minster, North Yorkshire

Location: SE 603524
Lat. 53.57.50 N; Long. 01.04.51 W

Excavator: D Phillips (York Minster Archaeology Office), 1967 – 73

References: RCHME 1985
RCHME forthcoming

HAR-551 840 ± 60 BP

$\delta^{13}C$: −26.1 ‰

Sample: SAMPLEIV, submitted on 1 March 1974

Material: wood: rings 40 – 6 of a large beam.

Initial comment: from the substructure of the Norman cathedral crossing.

Calibrated date: 1σ : cal AD 1160 – 1260
2σ : cal AD 1030 – 1280

Final comments:
D Phillips: the range at two standard deviations of confidence fits best with the other evidence. The Norman cathedral was begun *c* AD 1080 and finished by c 1100.

York: The Minster, North Yorkshire

Location: SE 603524
Lat. 53.57.50 N; Long. 01.04.51 W

Excavator: D Phillips (York Minster Archaeology Office), 1972

Site: Roman legionary headquarters, Saxon graveyard, Norman minster constructed *c* 1080.

References: RCHME forthcoming

HAR-2105 1780 ± 60 BP

$\delta^{13}C$: −25.0 ‰

Sample: XL131, submitted by C Shorter on 16 May 1977

Material: charcoal.

Initial comment: from a pit (XL 137) filled with XL 131 and covered with charcoal; one of the earliest features in the Saxon graveyard outside the minster building.

Calibrated date: 1σ : cal AD 140 – 335
2σ : cal AD 90 – 400

Final comments:
D Phillips: clearly redeposited Roman charcoal.

HAR-2111 1040 ± 70 BP

$\delta^{13}C$: −25.5 ‰

Sample: XL125, submitted by C Shorter on 16 May 1977

Material: charcoal.

Initial comment: from a charcoal burial (125) in the part of the graveyard outside the minster building.

Calibrated date: 1σ : cal AD 900 – 1025
2σ : cal AD 880 – 1160

Final comments:
D Phillips: this results agrees well with those from the other charcoal burials.

HAR-2113 990 ± 80 BP

$\delta^{13}C$: −25.5 ‰

Sample: XL126, submitted by C Shorter on 16 May 1977

Material: charcoal.

Initial comment: from a charcoal burial (126) in the part of the graveyard outside the minster.

Calibrated date: 1σ : cal AD 980 – 1155
2σ : cal AD 890 – 1220

Final comments:
D Phillips: this is the latest of the charcoal burials sampled.

HAR-2114 110 ± 80 BP

$\delta^{13}C$: unknown

Sample: XK336, submitted by C Shorter on 16 May 1977

Material: charcoal.

Initial comment: from industrial activity inside the Roman annexe, after the Roman occupation and before the destruction of the buildings; outside the minster.

Comment on uncalibrated date: clearly redeposited Roman charcoal.

Final comments:
D Phillips: a disappointing result from an important context, which is Late Roman at the earliest.

AML: too recent to calibrate meaningfully.

HAR-2118 1820 ± 60 BP

$\delta^{13}C$: −24.9 ‰

Sample: S33, submitted by C Shorter on 16 May 1977

Material: charcoal.

Initial comment: from burnt roofing timbers in a spread of Roman tiles, contemporary with the destruction of the legionary headquarters; sealed by a graveyard under buildings dated to 1080; should be contemporary with HAR-2326.

Calibrated date: 1σ : cal AD 115 – 250
2σ : cal AD 60 – 340

Final comments:
D Phillips: an original late first- or early second-century roofing timber, reused in the fourth-century headquarters building. It was found in a demolition context.

HAR-2122 1070 ± 80 BP

$δ^{13}C$: –25.0 ‰

Sample: S224, submitted by C Shorter on 16 May 1977

Material: charcoal.

Initial comment: from an early charcoal burial (IX) in the graveyard under the minster, cut into a wall constructed of Roman tile and ashlar; date should be pre-1080.

Calibrated date: 1σ : cal AD 890 – 1020
2σ : cal AD 780 – 1155

Final comments:
D Phillips: this turned out to belong to the same charcoal burial as HAR-2234 below.

HAR-2234 1070 ± 70 BP

$δ^{13}C$: –26.3 ‰

Sample: S28, submitted by C Shorter

Material: charcoal.

Initial comment: from charcoal burial II in the graveyard under the minster, which lies against and is cut into a Roman column base; the date should be pre-1080.

Calibrated date: 1σ : cal AD 890 – 1020
2σ : cal AD 790 – 1150

Final comments:
D Phillips: this result agrees well with those from the other charcoal burials.

HAR-2235 1160 ± 70 BP

$δ^{13}C$: –26.4 ‰

Sample: S132, submitted by C Shorter on 24 April 1977

Material: charcoal.

Initial comment: from charcoal burial I in the graveyard under the minster; the date should be pre-1080.

Calibrated date: 1σ : cal AD 780 – 970
2σ : cal AD 680 – 1010

Final comments:
D Phillips: a good result. This provides the earliest date for the commencement of the burials.

HAR-2236 1900 ± 100 BP

$δ^{13}C$: –25.0 ‰

Sample: S62, submitted by C Shorter on 16 May 1977

Material: charcoal.

Initial comment: from a spread of fallen Roman roofing tiles and collapsed columns; this result should be contemporary with HAR-2118.

Calibrated date: 1σ : cal AD 0 – 230
2σ : cal BC 150 – 340 cal AD

Final comments:
D Phillips: this agrees reasonably with HAR-2118.

HAR-2237 1130 ± 70 BP

$δ^{13}C$: –26.2 ‰

Sample: S26, submitted by C Shorter on 16 May 1977

Material: charcoal.

Initial comment: from charcoal burial IV in the graveyard under the minster, stratigraphically the highest, but not necessarily the latest charcoal burial; the date should be pre-1080.

Calibrated date: 1σ : cal AD 810 – 985
2σ : cal AD 715 – 1020

Final comments:
D Phillips: this agrees well with the results from other charcoal burials.

York: Walmgate, North Yorkshire

Location: SE 60965149
Lat. 51.57.21 N; Long. 01.04.15 W

Excavator: D Brinklow (York Archaeological Trust), 1978

Site: domestic occupation and industrial activity on street front in the Anglo-Scandinavian and medieval periods.

Objectives: to assist chronological analysis of a sequence of features from which artefactual evidence was poor.

HAR-3756 1020 ± 70 BP

$δ^{13}C$: –27.3 ‰

Sample: WLM125, submitted by H Kenward on 21 April 1980

Material: wood: *Salix* sp., *Alnus* sp., and *Quercus* sp., young branches (A R Hall).

Initial comment: from an extensive floor deposit with much burnt material, possibly eleventh- or twelfth-century; the artefactual evidence is poor.

Calibrated date: 1σ : cal AD 970 – 1035
2σ : cal AD 890 – 1170

Final comments:
D Brinklow: no comments since the material awaits post-excavation analysis.

HAR-3757 1160 ± 70 BP

$δ^{13}C$: –27.4 ‰

Sample: WLM164, submitted by H Kenward on 21 April 1980

Material: wood: *Salix* sp. and possibly *Alnus* sp. (A R Hall).

Initial comment: from possible wall destruction debris; the estimated date is probably tenth century.

Calibrated date: 1σ : cal AD 780 – 970
2σ : cal AD 680 – 1010

Final comments:
D Brinklow: as above.

HAR-3758 1050 ± 70 BP

$\delta^{13}C$: –27.2 ‰

Sample: WLM8005, submitted by H Kenward on 21 April 1980

Material: wood: *Quercus* sp., probably inner sapwood and outer heartwood.

Initial comment: from a possible pile, context 3433.

Calibrated date: 1σ : cal AD 895 – 1025
2σ : cal AD 830 – 1155

Final comments:
D Brinklow: as above.

HAR-3790 1190 ± 70 BP

$\delta^{13}C$: –26.7 ‰

Sample: WLM8007, submitted by H Kenward on 21 April 1980

Material: wood, bark removed, the outer layers of 100 – 20mm diameter washed and rinsed in distilled water and dried at 60°C: *Quercus* sp. (A R Hall).

Initial comment: from the earliest 'post-Roman' structure in the front part of the site, context 3471.

Calibrated date: 1σ : cal AD 725 – 895
2σ : cal AD 670 – 990

Final comments:
D Brinklow: as above.

HAR-3844 990 ± 60 BP

$\delta^{13}C$: –29.0 ‰

Sample: WLM8011, submitted by H Kenward

Material: wood, washed and rinsed in distilled water, dried at room temperature: *Corylus* sp. (A R Hall).

Initial comment: from a wattle-lined water cistern (3450); possibly Late Anglo-Scandinavian, although the artefactual evidence is sparse.

Calibrated date: 1σ : cal AD 990 – 1150
2σ : cal AD 900 – 1170

Final comments:
D Brinklow: as above.

HAR-3881 980 ± 80 BP

$\delta^{13}C$: unknown

Sample: WLM91, submitted by H Kenward on 21 April 1980

Material: soil and charcoal.

Initial comment: from a charcoal surface.

Calibrated date: 1σ : cal AD 985 – 1160
2σ : cal AD 890 – 1230

Final comments:
D Brinklow: as above.

HAR-3907 1040 ± 70 BP

$\delta^{13}C$: –30.3 ‰

Sample: WLM162, submitted by H Kenward

Material: organic soil.

Initial comment: from the fill of the earliest pit in area III (3475), presumably refuse; the estimated date is eleventh century.

Calibrated date: 1σ : cal AD 900 – 1025
2σ : cal AD 880 – 1160

Final comments:
D Brinklow: as above.

HAR-3910 1080 ± 80 BP

$\delta^{13}C$: –30.0 ‰

Sample: WLM139, submitted by H Kenward on 21 April 1980

Material: peat.

Initial comment: from context 3426; a date is required since the pottery spans a long date range; the estimated date is eleventh century.

Calibrated date: 1σ : cal AD 885 – 1020
2σ : cal AD 780 – 1155

Final comments:
D Brinklow: as above.

HAR-3916 960 ± 70 BP

$\delta^{13}C$: –30.0 ‰

Sample: WLM150, submitted by H Kenward on 21 April 1980

Material: organic soil.

Initial comment: from a floor or post-abandonment build-up of peat.

Calibrated date: 1σ : cal AD 1005 – 1165
2σ : cal AD 960 – 1230

Final comments:
D Brinklow: as above.

Bibliography

Addyman, P V, 1991   Lloyds Bank Pavement, in *Urban structures and defences* (eds P V Addyman and R A Hall), Archaeol York, **8/3**

Allen, D, 1981   The excavation of a Beaker burial monument at Ravenstone, Buckinghamshire, *Archaeol J*, **138**, 72 – 117

anon, 1970   Pewsey: Black Patch Field, in *Excavations and fieldwork in Wiltshire, 1969, Wiltshire Archaeol Natur Hist Mag*, **65**, 204 – 9

——, 1971   Pewsey: Black Patch Field, in *Excavations and fieldwork in Wiltshire, 1970, Wiltshire Archaeol Natur Hist Mag*, **66**, 188 – 91

——, 1972   Early medieval, in *Wiltshire Archaeological Register for 1971, Wiltshire Archaeol Natur Hist Mag*, **67**, 167 – 78

——, 1973   Early medieval, in *Wiltshire Archaeological Register for 1972, Wiltshire Archaeol Natur Hist Mag*, **68**, 126 – 39

ApSimon, A M, 1973   Tregiffian Barrow, *Archaeol J*, **130**, 241 – 3

——, 1985   The carbon dates for the collared urn burials, in Taylor and Woodward 1985, 120

Ashbee, P, 1979 – 80   Amesbury Barrow 39, Excavations 1960, *Wiltshire Archaeol Natur Hist Mag*, **74/75**, 3 – 34

Atkin, M W, Ayers, B S, and Jennings, S, 1983   Thetford-Type ware production in Norwich, *E Anglian Archaeol Rep*, **17**, 61 – 97

Atkin, M W, and Sutermeister, H, 1980   Excavations in Norwich 1977/8: The Norwich survey – seventh interim report, *Norfolk Archaeol*, **37**, 19 – 55

Atkinson, R J C, Vatcher F de M, and Vatcher, H L, 1976   Radiocarbon dates for the Stonehenge Avenue, *Antiquity*, **50**, 239 – 40

Austin, D, 1978   Excavations in Okehampton Park, Devon, 1976 – 8, *Devon Archaeol Soc Proc*, **36**, 191 – 239

Austin, D, Daggett, R H, and Walker, M J C, 1980   Farms and fields in Okehampton Park, Devon: the problems of studying medieval landscape, *Landscape Hist*, **2**, 39 – 58

Ayers, B S, and Murphy, P, 1983   A waterfront excavation at Whitefriars Street car park, Norwich, 1979, *E Anglian Archaeol Rep*, **17**, 1 – 60

Baker, D, Baker, E, Hassall, J, and Simco, A, 1979   Excavations in Bedford 1967 – 77, *Bedfordshire Archaeol J*, **13**

Balaam, N, Smith, K, and Wainwright, G J, 1982   The Shaugh Moor project: fourth report – environment, context, and conclusion, *Proc Prehist Soc*, **48**, 203 – 78

Bamford, H M, 1985   *Briar Hill excavation 1974 – 78*, Northampton Dev Corp Archaeol Monogr **3**

Barrett, J, 1976   Deverel-Rimbury: problems of chronology and interpretation, *Settlement and economy in the third and second millennia BC* (eds C B Burgess and R Miket), BAR, **33**, 289 – 307

——, 1980   The pottery of the later Bronze Age in lowland England, *Proc Prehist Soc*, **46**, 297 – 319

Bascombe, K N, 1987   Two charters of King Suebred of Essex, *An Essex tribute* (ed K Neale), 85 – 96

Beckett, S C, 1979   The Palaeobotanical background to the Meare Lake village sites, *Somerset Levels Pap*, **5**, 18 – 24

Bedwin, O, 1978   Excavations inside Harting Beacon hill-fort, West Sussex, 1976, *Sussex Archaeol Collect*, **116**, 225 – 40

——, 1979   Excavations at Harting Beacon, West Sussex; second season 1977, *Sussex Archaeol Collect*, **117**, 21 – 35

——, 1980   Excavations at Chanctonbury Ring, Wiston, West Sussex, 1977, *Britannia*, **11**, 173 – 222

——, 1981   Excavations at the Neolithic enclosure on Bury Hill, Houghton, West Sussex 1979, *Proc Prehist Soc*, 69 – 86

Bedwin, O, and Holgate, R, 1985   Excavations at Copse Farm, Oving, West Sussex, *Proc Prehist Soc*, **551**, 215 – 45

Bedwin, O, and Pitts, M W, 1978   The excavation of an Iron Age settlement at North Bersted, Bognor Regis, West Sussex 1975 – 6, *Sussex Archaeol Collect*, **116**, 293 – 346

Bell, M, 1977   Excavations at Bishopstone, Sussex, *Sussex Archaeol Collect*, **115**

Bell, R D, Beresford, M W, and Thorn, J C, 1986   *Wharram Percy: the church of St Martin*, Soc Medieval Archaeol Monogr Ser, **11**

Beresford, G, 1977   Excavations in 1977, *Medieval Village Res Group Rep*, **25**, 28 – 36

Beswick, W R, 1978   A note on early iron-making in Sussex, *Sussex Industrial History*, **8**, 23 – 4

——, 1979   Ironmaking origins and their early impact on the English Weald, *Sussex Industrial History*, **9**, 7 – 14

Biddle, M, 1970   Excavations at Winchester, 1969, eighth interim report, *Antiq J*, **50**, 277 – 326 ——, 1972   Excavations at Winchester, 1970, ninth interim report, *Antiq J*, **52**, 93 – 131

Bidwell, P T, 1979   *The legionary bath-house and basilica and forum at Exeter*, Exeter Archaeol Rep, **1**

Biek, L, and Kay, P J, 1982   Evidence of glass melting, in Leech 1982, 132 – 3

Bond, D, 1988   Excavation at the North Ring, Mucking, Essex: a Late Bronze Age enclosure, *E Anglian Archaeol Rep*, **43**

Bradley, R, Lobb, S, Richards, J, and Robinson, M, 1980   Two Late Bronze Age settlements on the Kennet Gravels: excavations at Aldermaston Wharf and Knight's Farm, Burghfield, Berkshire, *Proc Prehist Soc*, **46**, 217 – 95

Bradley, R, and Richards, J, 1979 – 80   The excavation of two ring ditches at Heron's House, Burghfield, *Berkshire Archaeol J*, **70**, 1 – 7

Butcher, S A, 1978   Excavations at Nornour, Isles of Scilly, 1969 – 73: the pre-Roman settlement, *Cornish Archaeol*, **17**, 29 – 112

Carver, M O H, 1979   The excavation of three Saxo-Norman tenements in Durham City, *Medieval Archaeol*, **23**, 1 – 80

——, 1980   The excavation of three medieval craftsmen's tenements in Sidbury, Worcester in 1976, in *Medieval Worcester: an Archaeological Framework*, (ed M O H Carver), *Trans Worcestershire Archaeol Soc*, 3 ser, **7**, 155 – 219

Carver, M O H, Donaghey, S, and Sumpter, A B, 1978   *Riverside structures and a will in Skeldergate and buildings in Bishophill*, Archaeol York, **4/1**

Carr, R D, Tester, A, and Murphy, P, 1988   The Middle Saxon settlement at Staunch Meadow, Brandon, *Antiquity*, **62**, 371 – 7

Chambers, R A, 1973a   A cemetery site at Beacon Hill, near Lewknor, *Oxoniensia*, **38**, 138 – 45

——, 1973b   Beacon Hill cemetery, in *Archaeology and the M40 motorway* (eds T Rowley and M Davies), 31 – 4

——, 1976a   A cemetery site at Beacon Hill, near Lewknor, Oxon, 1972 (M40 Site 12): an inventory of the inhumations and a reappraisal, *Oxoniensia*, **41**, 77 – 85

——, 1976b   A Romano-British settlement at Curbridge, *Oxoniensia*, **41**, 38 – 55

——, 1978   Two radiocarbon dates from the Romano-British cemetery at Curbridge, Oxon, *Oxoniensia*, **43**, 252 – 3

——, 1986   A Roman timber bridge at Ivy Farm, Fencott with Murcott, Oxon, 1979, *Oxoniensia*, **51**, 31 – 6

Chapman, J, 1984   Animal and human bone, in *Excavations in Staines, 1975 – 6: the Friends' burial ground site* (ed K R Crouch and S A Shanks), Joint Publ London Middlesex Archaeol Soc/Surrey Archaeol Soc, **2**, 115 – 23

Chowne, P, 1978   Billingborough Bronze Age settlement: an interim note, *Lincolnshire Hist Archaeol*, **13**, 15 – 21

——, 1979   Billingborough, *Curr Archaeol*, **7**, 246 – 8

——, 1980   Bronze Age settlement in South Lincolnshire, in *Settlement and society in the Later Bronze Age* (eds J C Barrett and R J Bradley), BAR **83**, 295 – 305

——, 1988 Later prehistoric settlement in Lincolnshire: a study of the western fen margin and the Bain Valley, unpubl PhD thesis, Univ Nottingham

Christie, P M L, 1966 Carn Euny: a brief note on the 1965 excavations, *Cornish Archaeol*, **5**, 17 – 19

——, 1973 Excavation news: Carn Euny, Sancreed, *Cornish Archaeol*, **12**, 58

——, 1976 Carn Euny: interim report on the final seasons 1970 and 1972, *Cornish Archaeol*, **15**, 68 – 72

——, 1978 The excavation of an Iron Age souterrain and settlement at Carn Euny, Sancreed, Cornwall, *Proc Prehist Soc*, **44**, 309 – 433

——, 1983 Carn Euny, HMSO

——, 1985 Barrows on the North Cornish Coast: wartime excavations by C K Croft Andrew 1939 – 44, *Cornish Archaeol*, **24**, 23 – 121

Clark, A J, 1985 Results of radiocarbon analysis, *E Anglian Archaeol Rep*, **26**, 62

Clark, A J, Tarling, D H, and Noël, M, 1988 Developments in archaeomagnetic dating in Britain, *J Archaeol Sci*, **15**, 645 – 67

Clark, R M, 1975 A calibration curve for radiocarbon dates, *Antiquity*, **49**, 251 – 66

Clark, R M, and Morgan, R A, 1983 An alternative statistical approach to the calibration of floating tree-ring chronologies: two sequences from the Somerset Levels, *Archaeometry*, **25**, 3 – 15

Clarke, A, 1993 *Excavations at Mucking. Volume 1: the site atlas*, Engl Heritage Archaeol Rep, **20**

Clarke, D L, 1970 *Beaker pottery of Great Britain and Ireland*, Cambridge

Clay, P, 1981a *Two multiphase barrow sites at Sproxton and Eaton, Leicestershire*, Leicestershire Museums, Art Galleries & Record Service Archaeol Rep, **2**

——, 1981b The excavation of a composite round barrow at Sproxton, Leicestershire, in Clay 1981a, 1 – 26

——, 1981c The excavation of a multiphase barrow site at Piper House Farm, Eaton, Leicestershire, in Clay 1981a, 27 – 46

Coggins, D, Fairless, K J, and Batey, C E, 1983 Simy Folds: an early medieval settlement site in Upper Teesdale, Co Durham, *Medieval Archaeol*, **27**, 1 – 26

Coles, B J, and Dobson, M J, 1989 Calibration of radiocarbon dates from the Somerset Levels, *Somerset Levels Pap*, **15**, 64 – 9

Coles, B J, Rouillard, S E, and Backway, C, 1986 The 1984 excavations at Meare, *Somerset Levels Pap*, **12**, 30 – 57

Coles, B P L, and Funnell, B M, 1981 Holocene paleoenvironment of Broadland, England, in *Holocene marine sedimentation in the North Sea basin* (eds S-D Nio, R T E Stüttenhelm, and Tj C E Van Werring, Int Ass Sedimentologists Spec Publ, **5**, 123 – 31

Coles, J M, 1972 Later Bronze Age activity in the Somerset Levels, *Antiq J*, **52**, 269 – 75

——, 1979 Radiocarbon dates: third list, *Somerset Levels Pap*, **5**, 101

——, 1989 Prehistoric settlement in the Somerset Levels, *Somerset Levels Pap*, **15**, 14 – 33

Coles, J M, and Coles, B J, 1988 Radiocarbon dates: sixth list, *Somerset Levels Pap*, **14**, 91

Coles, J M, and Coles, M M, 1975 Check-list of radiocarbon dates relating to archaeological sites in the Levels, *Somerset Levels Pap*, **1**, 54 – 5

Coles, J M, and Fordham, S M, 1977 Radiocarbon dates: second list, *Somerset Levels Pap*, **3**, 89

Coles, J M, and Hibbert, A F, 1975 The Honeygore complex, *Somerset Levels Pap*, **1**, 11 – 19

Coles, J M, and Orme, B J, 1976a The Meare Heath trackway: excavation of a Bronze Age structure in the Somerset Levels, *Proc Prehist Soc*, **42**, 293 – 318

——, 1976b The Sweet Track, railway site, *Somerset Levels Pap*, **2**, 34 – 65

——, 1976c The Meare Heath trackway: excavation of a Bronze Age structure in the Somerset Levels, *Proc Prehist Soc*, **42**, 293 – 318

——, 1977a Neolithic hurdles from Walton Heath, Somerset, *Somerset Levels Pap*, **3**, 6 – 29

——, 1977b Garvin's tracks, *Somerset Levels Pap*, **3**, 73 – 81

——, 1978a The Meare Heath track, *Somerset Levels Pap*, **4**, 11 – 39

——, 1978b Multiple trackways from Tinney's Ground, *Somerset Levels Pap*, **4**, 47 – 81

——, 1978c Structures south of Meare Island, *Somerset Levels Pap*, **4**, 90 – 100

——, 1978d Bronze Age implements from Skinner's Wood, Shapwick, *Somerset Levels Pap*, **4**, 114 – 21

——, 1979 The Sweet Track: drove site, *Somerset Levels Pap*, **5**, 43 – 64

——, 1980 Tinney's Ground, 1978 – 9, *Somerset Levels Pap*, **6**, 61 – 8

——, 1981 The Sweet Track 1980, *Somerset Levels Pap*, **7**, 6 – 12

——, 1984 Ten excavations along the Sweet Track (3200 bc), *Somerset Levels Pap*, **10**, 5 – 45

——, 1985 Radiocarbon dates: fifth list, *Somerset Levels Pap*, **11**, 85

Coles, J M, Caseldine, A E, and Morgan, R A, 1982 The Eclipse Track 1980, *Somerset Levels Pap*, **8**, 26 – 39

——, 1988 Some Neolithic brushwood structures 1984 – 5, *Somerset Levels Pap*, **14**, 34 – 43

Coles, J M, Fleming, A M, and Orme, B J, 1980 The Baker Site: a Neolithic platform, *Somerset Levels Pap*, **6**, 6 – 23

Coles, J M, Hibbert, A F, and Clements, C F, 1970 Prehistoric roads and tracks in Somerset, England: 2, Neolithic, *Proc Prehist Soc*, **36**, 125 – 51

Coles, J M, Orme, B J, and Hibbert, F A, 1975 The Eclipse Track, *Somerset Levels Pap*, **1**, 20 – 8

Coles, J M, Orme, B J, Caseldine, A E, and Morgan, R A, 1985a A Neolithic jigsaw: the Honeygore complex, *Somerset Levels Pap*, **11**, 51 – 61

——, 1985b Godwin's Track: a Bronze Age structure at Sharpham, *Somerset Levels Pap*, **11**, 69 – 79

Coles, J M, Orme, B J, Hibbert, F A, and Jones, R A, 1975a Withy Bed Copse, 1974, *Somerset Levels Pap*, **1**, 29 – 42

——, 1975b Tinney's Ground, 1974, *Somerset Levels Pap*, **1**, 43 – 53

Coles, J M, Orme, B J, Morgan, R A, and Caseldine, A E, 1988 The Meare Heath Track, 1985, *Somerset Levels Pap*, **14**, 6 – 33

Colledge, S M, 1978 *An interim environmental report; the King's Pool, Stafford, (1977 – 8)*, Anc Mon Lab Rep, **2525**

Colyer, C, and Jones, M T, 1979 Excavations at Lincoln: second interim report: excavations in the lower town 1972 – 8, *Antiq J*, **59**, 50 – 91

Coombs, D G, 1976 Callis Wold round barrow, Humberside, *Antiquity*, **50**, 130 – 1

Cramp, R, 1969 Excavations at the Saxon monastic sites of Wearmouth and Jarrow, Co Durham, *Medieval Archaeol*, **13**, 21 – 66

——, 1976 Jarrow Church, *Archaeol J*, **133**, 220 – 8

Crummy, P, 1974 *Colchester: recent excavations and research*, Colchester Excavation Committee

——, 1984 *Excavations at Lion Walk, Balkerne Lane, and Middleborough, Colchester, Essex*, Colchester Archaeol Rep, **3**

Crummy, P, Hillam, J, and Crossan, C, 1982 Mersea Island: the Anglo-Saxon causeway, *Essex Archaeol Hist*, **14**, 77 – 86

Crump, R W, 1981 Excavation of a buried wooden structure at Foulness, *Essex Archaeol Hist*, **13**, 69 – 71

Cunliffe, B W, 1984 *Danebury: an Iron Age hillfort in Hampshire, Volumes 1 and 2*, CBA Res Rep, **52**

Dacre, M, and Ellison, A, 1981 A Bronze Age urn cemetery at Kimpton, Hampshire, *Proc Prehist Soc*, **47**, 147 – 203

Damon, P E, Long, A, and Wallick, E I, 1972 Dendrochronological calibration of the carbon-14 time scale, vol 1 of *Proceedings of the eighth international radiocarbon dating conference*, 2 vols (eds T A Rafter and T Grant-Taylor), 44 – 59

Davies, S M, 1981 Excavations at Old Down Farm, Andover; part 2: prehistoric and Roman, *Proc Hampshire Fld Club Archaeol Soc*, **37**, 81 – 163

Davidson, A, and Evans, D H, 1985 Excavations on 49 – 63 Botolph Street (Site 281N), *E Anglian Archaeol Rep*, **26**, 114 – 43

Dawes, J D, and Magilton, J R, 1980 *The cemetery of St Helen-on-the-Walls, Aldwark*, Archaeol York, **12/1**

De Brisay, K, 1979 The excavation of a Red Hill at Peldon, Essex, with notes on some other sites, *Antiq J*, **58**, 31 – 60

Dean, M, and Hammerson, M, 1980 Three inhumation burials from Southwark, *London Archaeol*, **4**, 17 – 22

Dent, J S, 1978 Wetwang Slack, *Curr Archaeol*, **6**, 46 – 50

——, 1979 Bronze Age burials from Wetwang Slack, *Archaeol J*, **51**, 23 – 39

——, 1982 Cemeteries and settlement patterns of the Iron Age on the Yorkshire Wolds, *Proc Prehist Soc*, **48**, 437 – 57

——, 1983 A summary of the excavations carried out in Garton and Wetwang Slack 1964 – 80, *E Riding Archaeol*, **7**, 1 – 14

Devoy, R J N, 1979 Flandrian sea level changes and vegetational history of the Lower Thames estuary, *Phil Trans R Soc London*, B ser, **285**, 355 – 407

Dix, B, 1980 Excavations at Harold Pit, Odell, 1974 – 8: a preliminary report, *Bedfordshire Archaeol J*, **14**, 15 – 18

Donaldson, P, 1977 The excavation of a multiple round barrow at Barnack, Cambridgeshire 1976, *Antiq J*, **57**, 197 – 231

Down, A, 1978 *Chichester excavations III*, Chichester

——, 1981 *Chichester excavations V*, Chichester

Drewett, P, 1975 The excavation of an oval burial mound of the third millenium BC at Alfriston, East Sussex, 1974, *Proc Prehist Soc*, **41**, 119 –52

——, 1976 The excavation of four round barrows of the second millenium BC at West Heath, Harting, 1973 – 5, *Sussex Archaeol Coll*, **114**, 126 –50

——, 1982a Later Bronze Age downland settlement and economy at Black Patch, East Sussex, *Proc Prehist Soc*, **48**, 321 –400

——, 1982b *The archaeology of Bullock Down, Eastbourne, East Sussex: the development of a landscape*, Sussex Archaeol Soc Monogr, **1**

Drury, P J, 1978 *Excavations at Little Waltham 1970 – 71*, CBA Res Rep, **26**, Chelmsford Excavation Committee Report, **1**

Durham, B, 1977 Archaeological investigations in St Aldates, Oxford, *Oxoniensia*, **42**, 83 – 203

Dyson, T (ed), 1986 *The Roman quay at St Magnus House, London*, London Middlesex Archaeol Soc Spec Pap, **8**

Ellis, P, 1981 – 2 Excavations at Silver Street, Glastonbury, 1978, *Somerset Archaeol Natur Hist*, **126**, 17 – 31

Ellis, R, 1982 Excavations at Grim's Dyke, Harrow, 1979, *Trans Lond Middlesex Archaeol Soc*, **33**, 173 – 6

Ellison, A, and Rahtz, P, 1987 Excavations at Hog Cliff Hill, Maiden Newton, Dorset, *Proc Prehist Soc*, **53**, 223 – 69

Evans, J G, 1984 Excavations at Bar Point, St Mary's, Isles of Scilly, 1979 – 80, *Cornish Stud*, , 7 – 32

Evans, J G, and Simpson, D D A, 1986 Radiocarbon dates for the Giant's Hill long barrow, Skendleby, Lincolnshire, in *Archaeological results from accelerator dating* (ed J A J Gowlett and R E M Hodges), Oxford Univ Comm Archaeol Monogr, **11**, 125 – 31

——, 1991 Giant's Hill 2 Long Barrow, Skendleby, Lincolnshire, *Archaeologia*, **109**, 1 – 45

Everson, P, 1977 Excavations in the Vicarage garden at Brixworth, 1972, *J Brit Archaeol Ass*, **130**, 55 – 122

Fasham, P J, 1978 The excavation of a triple barrow in Micheldever Wood, Hampshire, *Proc Hampshire Fld Club Archaeol Soc*, **35**, 5 – 40

——, 1979 Excavations on Bridget's and Burntwood Farms, Itchen Valley Parish, Hampshire, 1974 (Marc 3 sites R5 and R6), *Proc Hampshire Fld Club Archaeol Soc*, **36**, 37 – 86

——, 1981 Fieldwork and excavations at East Stratton along the Roman road from Winchester to Silchester (Marc 3 sites R1 and R3), *Proc Hampshire Fld Club Archaeol Soc*, **37**, 165 – 88

——, 1982 The excavation of four ring ditches in central Hampshire, *Proc Hampshire Fld Club Archaeol Soc*, **38**, 19 – 56

——, 1983 Fieldwork in and around Micheldever Wood, Hampshire, 1973 – 1980, *Proc Hampshire Fld Club Archaeol Soc*, **39**, 5 – 45

——, 1985 *The Prehistoric settlement at Winnall Down, Winchester*, Hampshire Fld Club Archaeol Soc Monogr, **2**, M3 Archaeol Rescue Comm Rep, **8**

Fasham, P J, and Ross, J M, 1978 A Bronze Age flint industry from a barrow site in Micheldever Wood, Hampshire, *Proc Prehist Soc*, **44**, 47 – 67

Fasham, P J, and Whinney, R J B, 1991 *Archaeology and the M3*, Hampshire Fld Club Archaeol Soc Monogr, **7**

Fawn, A J, Evans, K A, McMaster, I, and Davies, G M R, 1990 *The Red Hills of Essex, salt-making in antiquity*, Colchester Archaeological Group

Fenwick, V, 1984 Insula de Burgh: excavations at Burrow Hill, Butley, Suffolk, 1978 – 1981, in vol 3 of *Anglo-Saxon studies in archaeology and history*, 4 vols (eds S C Hawkes, J Campbell, and D Brown), 35 – 54

Field, D, and Cotton, J, 1987 Neolithic Surrey: a survey of the evidence, in *The Archaeology of Surrey to 1540* (eds J Bird and D J Bird), 71 – 96

Field, N, 1985 A multiphase barrow and possible henge monument at West Ashby, Lincolnshire, *Proc Prehist Soc*, **51**, 103 – 36

Fletcher, J, 1981 Roman and Saxon dendro dates, *Curr Archaeol*, **7**, 150 – 2

Fulford, M, 1984 *Silchester: excavations on the defences 1974 – 80*, Britannia Monogr Ser, **5**

Garrod, A P, and Heighway, C M, 1984 *Garrod's Gloucester: archaeological observations 1974 – 81*, Western Archaeological Trust

Gates, T, Lobb, S, and Richards, J, 1980 The other subsites, in Bradley *et al* 1980, 263 – 5

Gibson, A M, and McCormick, A, 1985 Archaeology at Grendon Quarry, Northamptonshire. Part 1: Neolithic and Bronze Age sites excavated in 1974 – 5, *Northamptonshire Archaeol*, **20**, 23 – 66

Gilmour, B J J, and Stocker, D A, 1986 *St Mark's church and cemetery*, The archaeology of Lincoln, **13/1**

Girling, M A, 1985 An 'Old Forest' beetle fauna from a Neolithic and Bronze Age peat deposit at Stileway, *Somerset Levels Pap*, **11**, 80 – 4

Godwin, H, 1960 Prehistoric wooden trackways of the Somerset Levels: their construction, age, and relation to climatic change, *Proc Prehist Soc*, **26**, 1 – 36

Graham, A H, 1978 The geology of North Southwark and its topographical development in the post-Pleistocene period, in *Southwark Excavations 1972 – 4* (ed anon), 501 – 17

Green, C J S, 1971 Interim report on excavations at Poundbury, Dorchester, 1971, *Dorset Natur Hist Archaeol Soc Proc*, **93**, 154 – 6

——, 1973 Interim report on excavations at Poundbury, Dorchester, 1973, *Dorset Natur Hist Archaeol Soc Proc*, **95**, 97 – 100

——, 1976 Dorchester, in *Archaeology in Dorset in 1976*, *Dorset Natur Hist Archaeol Soc Proc*, **98**, 55 – 6

——, 1982 The excavation of a Romano-British Christian community at Poundbury, Dorchester, Dorset, in *The early Church in western Britain and Ireland* (ed S M Pearce), BAR, **102**, 61 – 76

——, 1987 *Excavations at Poundbury, Dorchester, Dorset, 1966 – 82. Volume 1: the settlements*, Dorset Natur Hist Archaeol Soc Monogr Ser, **7**

Green, H S, and Sofranoff, S, 1985 A Neolithic settlement at Stacey Bushes, Milton Keynes, *Rec Buckinghamshire*, **27**, 10 – 37

Gregory, V L, 1973 Caerwent, *Archaeol Wales*, **13**, 51 – 2

―――, 1976   Excavations at Becket's Barn, Pagham, West Sussex, 1974, *Sussex Archaeol Collect*, **114**, 207 – 17

Grieg, J R A, 1981   The investigation of a medieval barrel-latrine from Worcester, *J Archaeol Sci*, **8**, 265 – 82

―――, 1982   Forest clearance and the barrow builders at Butterbump, Lincolnshire, *Lincolnshire Hist Archaeol*, **17**, 11 – 4

Griffith, F M, 1984   Archaeological investigations at Colliford Reservoir, Bodmin Moor, 1977 – 8, *Cornish Archaeol*, **23**, 49 – 140

Guilbert, G, 1975a   Planned hillfort interiors, *Proc Prehist Soc*, **41**, 203 – 21

―――, 1975b   Moel y Gaer, 1973: an area excavation on the defences, *Antiquity*, **49**, 109 – 17

―――, 1976   Moel y Gaer (Rhosemor) 1972 – 3: an area excavation in the interior, in *Hillforts: later prehistoric earthworks in Britain and Ireland* (ed D W Harding), 303 – 17

HMSO, 1974   *Archaeological excavations 1973*, London

Hadfield, J I, 1981   The excavation of a medieval kiln at Barnett's Mead, Ringmer, East Sussex, *Sussex Archaeol Collect*, **119**, 89 – 106

Hall, A R, Kenward, H K, and Williams, D, 1980   *The past environment of York: environmental evidence from Roman deposits in Skeldergate*, Archaeol York **14/3**

Hall, D, and Woodward, P J, 1977   Radwell excavations, 1974 – 5: the Bronze Age ring ditches, *Bedfordshire Archaeol J*, **12**, 1 – 16

Hall, R A, 1984   *The Viking dig*, London

Hall, R A, forthcoming   An observation of the fortress wall in Parliament Street, in *Excavations and observations on the defences and adjacent sites, 1971 – 90*, Archaeol York, **3/3**

Hamerow, H, 1993   *Excavations at Mucking. Volume 2: the Anglo-Saxon settlement*, Engl Heritage Archaeol Rep, **21**

Harris, D, 1979   Poldowrian, St Keverne; a Beaker mound on the Gabbro of the Lizard Peninsula, *Cornish Archaeol*, **18**, 13 – 32

―――, 1980   Excavation of a Romano British round at Shortlanesend, Kenwyn, Truro, *Cornish Archaeol*, **19**, 63 – 75

Haslam, J, 1980   A Middle Saxon iron smelting site at Ramsbury, Wiltshire, *Medieval Archaeol*, **24**, 1 – 68

Hassall, J, 1979a   Midland Road, in Baker *et al* 1979, 79 – 95

―――, 1979b   St John's Street in Baker *et al* 1979, 97 – 125

―――, 1983   Excavations in Bedford 1977 and 1978, *Bedfordshire Archaeol J*, **16**, 37 – 64

Hassall, T G, with Durham, B, and Woods, H, 1974   Excavations at Oxford 1973 – 4: sixth and final interim report, *Oxoniensia*, **39**, 53 – 61

Healey, H, and Hurcombe, L, 1989   A Bronze Age barrow group in Walcott, Lincolnshire, *Fenland Res*, **6**, 16 – 20

Healy, F, 1982   A round barrow at Trowse: Early Bronze Age burials and medieval occupation, *E Anglian Archaeol Rep*, **14**, 1 – 34

―――, 1988   *The Anglo-Saxon cemetery at Spong Hill, North Elmham, Part VI: occupation during the seventh to second millennia BC*, E Anglian Archaeol Rep, **39**

Heighway, C M, 1983   *The east and north gates of Gloucester and associated sites: excavations 1974 – 81*, Western Archaeol Trust Excav Monogr, **4**

Heighway, C M, Garrod, P, and Vince, A G, 1979   Excavations at 1 Westgate Street, Gloucester 1975, *Medieval Archaeol*, **23**, 159 – 213

Hill, C, 1975   The Roman riverside wall in the City, *London Archaeol*, **2**, 260 – 1

Hill, C, Millet, M, and Blagg, T, 1980   *The Roman riverside wall and monumental arch in London*, London Middlesex Archaeol Soc Spec Pap, **3**

Hillam, J, Groves, C M, Brown, D M, Baillie, M G L, Coles, J M, and Coles, B P L, 1990   Dendrochronology of the English Neolithic, *Antiquity*, **64**, 210 – 20

Hillam, J, and Morgan, R M, 1986   Tree-ring analysis of Roman timbers, in Dyson 1986, 75 – 85

Hinton, P (ed), 1988   *Excavations in Southwark 1973 – 6, Lambeth 1973 – 9*, Joint Publ London Middlesex Archaeol Soc/Surrey Archaeol Soc, **3**

Hinton, P, Orton, C, and Yule, B, 1988   Mark Brown's Wharf, in Hinton 1988, 133 – 74

Hobley, B and Schofield, J, 1977   Excavations in the City of London; first interim report 1974 – 5, *Antiq J*, **57**, 31 – 66

Horsey, I P, 1981   Poole, in *Waterfront archaeology in Britain and northern Europe* (eds G Milne and B Hobley), CBA Res Rep, **41**, 145 – 6

Horsey, I P, and Shackley, M, 1980   The excavation of a Bronze Age round barrow on Canford Heath, Poole, Dorset, *Dorset Natur Hist Archaeol Soc Proc*, **102**, 33 – 42

Horsey, I P, and Winder, J M, 1991   Late Saxon and Conquest-period oyster middens at Poole, Dorset, in *Waterfront archaeology* (eds G L Good, R H Jones, and M W Ponsford), CBA Res Rep, **74**

Howard, R, Laxton, R R, Litton, C D, and Simpson, W G, 1985   Tree-ring dates for some East Midland buildings: 3, *Trans Thoroton Soc Nottinghamshire*, **89**, 30 – 6

Huggins, P J, 1978   Excavation of Belgic and Romano-British farm with Middle Saxon cemetery and churches at Nazeingbury, Essex, 1975 – 6, *Essex Archaeol Hist*, **10**, 29 – 117

―――, 1988   Excavations on the north side of Sun Street, Waltham Abbey, Essex 1974 – 5: Saxon burials, precinct wall and south-east transept, *Essex Archaeol Hist*, **19**, 117 – 53

Hunter, K, and Foley, K, 1987   The Lincoln hanging bowl, in *From pinheads to hanging bowls: the identification, deterioration, and conservation of applied enamel and glass decoration on archaeological artefacts* (eds L Bacon and B Knight), UKIK Occas Pap, **7**, 16 – 18

Hurst, H, 1972   Excavations at Gloucester 1968 – 71: first interim report, *Antiq J*, **52**, 24 – 69

Hurst, J G, 1986   The Wharram Percy research project: results to 1983, *Medieval Archaeol*, **28**, 77 – 111

Jackson, D A, 1976   The excavation of Neolithic and Bronze Age sites at Aldwinkle, Northants 1967 – 71, *Northants Archaeol*, **11**, 12 – 70

―――, 1977   Further excavations at Aldwinkle, Northamptonshire 1969 – 71, *Northants Archaeol*, **12**, 9 – 54

―――, 1980a   Roman burials at Ringstead, Northamptonshire, *Northants Archaeol*, **15**, 12 – 34

―――, 1980b   An earthwork at Harringworth, Northamptonshire, *Northants Archaeol*, **15**, 158 – 60

―――, 1982   Great Oakley and other Iron Age sites in the Corby area, *Northants Archaeol*, **17**, 3 – 23

Jackson, D A, and Ambrose, T M, 1976   A Roman timber bridge at Aldwinkle, Northamptonshire, *Britannia*, **7**, 39 – 72

Jackson, D A, and Dix, B, 1986 – 7   Late Iron Age and Roman settlement at Weekley, Northants, *Northants Archaeol*, **21**, 41 – 94

Jackson, D A, and Knight, D, 1985   An Early Iron Age and Beaker site near Gretton, Northamptonshire, *Northants Archaeol*, **20**, 67 – 86

James, H, 1982   Excavations in Wooten Wawen churchyard, 1974 and 1975, *Birmingham Warwickshire Archaeol Soc Trans*, **90**, 37 – 48

Jarvis, K, 1982   *Excavations in Christchurch 1969 – 80*, Dorset Natur Hist Archaeol Soc Monogr Ser, **5**

Jobey, G, 1977   Iron Age and later farmsteads on Belling Law, Northumberland, *Archaeol Aeliana*, 5 ser, **5**, 1 – 38

Johnson, S, 1983   Burgh Castle, excavations by Charles Green 1958 – 61, *E Anglian Archaeol Rep*, **20**

Jones, M U, and Bond, D, 1980   Later Bronze Age settlement at Mucking, Essex, in *Settlement and society in the British Later Bronze Age* (eds J C Barrett and R J Bradley), BAR **83**, 471 – 82

Keen, L, 1982   The Umfravilles, the castle and the barony of Prudhoe, Northumberland, *Anglo-Norman Stud*, **5**, 165 – 84

Kirkham, B, 1981   The excavation of a prehistoric salten at Hogsthorpe, Lincolnshire, *Lincolnshire Hist Archaeol*, **16**, 5 – 10

Lambrick, G H, 1984   Pitfalls and possibilites in Iron Age pottery studies – experiences in the Upper Thames Valley, in *Aspects of the Iron Age in central southern Britain* (eds B Cunliffe and D Miles), Oxford Univ Comm Archaeol Monogr, **2**, 162 – 77

Lambrick, G H, and Robinson, M, 1979   *Iron Age and Roman riverside settlements at Farmoor, Oxfordshire*, CBA Res Rep, **32**

Lawson, A J, 1976a   The excavation of a round barrow at Harpley, *E Anglian Archaeol Rep*, **2**, 45 – 64

——, 1976b   Excavations at Whey Curd Farm, Wighton, *E Anglian Archaeol Rep*, **2**, 65 – 100

——, 1986a   Barrow excavation in Norfolk 1950 – 82, *E Anglian Archaeol Rep*, **29**

——, 1986b   The excavation of a round barrow at Little Cressingham 1977, in Lawson 1986a, 5 – 19

——, 1986c   The excavation of a ring ditch at Bowthorpe, Norwich 1979, in Lawson 1986a, 20 – 49

Lawson, A J, Martin, E A, and Priddy, D, 1981   The barrows of East Anglia, *E Anglian Archaeol Rep*, **12**

Lawson, A J, and Le Hegarat, R, 1986   The excavation of a mound on Gallows Hill, Thetford, 1978 – 9, in Lawson 1986a, 65 – 9

Leach, P (ed), 1983   *The archaeology of Taunton: excavation and fieldwork to 1980*, Western Archaeol Trust Excav Monogr, **8**

Leech, R, 1982   *Excavations at Catsgore 1970 – 3: a Romano-British village*, Western Archaeol Trust Excav Monogr, **2**

——, 1986   The excavation of a Romano-Celtic temple and a later cemetery on Lamyatt Beacon, Somerset, *Britannia*, **17**, 259 – 328

Longley, D, 1976   Excavations on the site of a Late Bronze Age settlement at Runnymede Bridge, Egham, *London Archaeol*, **3**, 10 – 17

——, 1980   *Runnymede Bridge 1976: excavations on the site of a Late Bronze Age settlement*, Res Vol Surrey Archaeol Soc, **6**

Longworth, I H, 1984   *Collared urns of the Bronze Age in Great Britain and Ireland*, Cambridge

Losco-Bradley, P M, and Salisbury, C R, 1979   A medieval fish weir at Colwick, Nottinghamshire, *Trans Thoroton Soc Nottinghamshire*, **83**, 15 – 22

Losco-Bradley, S, and Wheeler, H M, 1984   Anglo-Saxon settlement in the Trent valley: some aspects, in *Studies in late Anglo-Saxon settlement* (ed M Faull), 101 – 14

MacGregor, H, 1988   Structures adjacent to 1 – 5 Aldwark, in *Medieval tenements in Aldwark, and other sites* (eds R A Hall, H MacGregor, and M Stockwell), Archaeol York, **10/2**, 63 – 88

MacPherson-Grant, N, 1980   Archaeological work along the A2: 1966 – 74, *Archaeol Cantiana*, **96**, 133 – 84

Manby, T G, 1980   Excavation of barrows at Grindale and Boynton, East Yorkshire, 1972, *Yorkshire Archaeol J*, **52**, 19 – 47

Maltby, E, and Caseldine, C J, 1982   Prehistoric soil and vegetation development on Bodmin Moor, southwestern England, *Nature*, **297**, 397 – 400

Martin, E A, 1976   The excavation of two tumuli on Waterhall Farm, Chippenham, Cambridgeshire, 1973, *Proc Cambridge Antiq Soc*, **66**, 1 – 14

——, 1980   Suffolk Archaeological Unit excavations 1978, *Proc Suffolk Inst Archaeol Hist*, **3**, 218 – 20

——, 1988   Swales Fen, Suffolk: a Bronze Age cooking pit?, *Antiquity*, **62**, 358 – 9

Martin, E A, and Murphey, P, 1988   West Row Fen, Suffolk: a Bronze Age fen-edge settlement site, *Antiquity*, **62**, 353 – 8

McAvoy, F, Morris, E L, and Smith, G H, 1980   The excavation of a multi-period site at Cargoon Bank, Lizard, Cornwall, 1979, *Cornish Archaeol*, **19**, 31 – 62

McWhirr, A, Viner, L, and Wells, C, 1982   Romano-British cemeteries at Cirencester, *Cirencester Excavations*, **2**

Mercer, R J, 1980   *Hambledon Hill, a Neolithic landscape*, Edinburgh

——, 1985   A Neolithic fortress and funerary center, *Scientific American*, **252/3**, 76 – 83

Miles, D (ed), 1984   *Archaeology at Barton Court Farm, Abingdon, Oxon*, CBA Res Rep, **50**, Oxford Archaeol Unit Rep, **3**

Miles, H, 1975a   Barrows on the St Austell Granite, Cornwall, *Cornish Archaeol*, **14**, 5 – 82

——, 1975b   Excavations at Woodbury Castle, East Devon 1971, *Devon Archaeol Soc Proc*, **33**, 183 – 208

Miles, P, forthcoming   *Silver Street 1973*, The Archaeology of Lincoln

Miles, P, Young, J, and Wacher, J, 1989   *A late Saxon kiln site at Silver Street, Lincoln*, The Archaeology of Lincoln, **17/3**

Miller, L, and Schofield, J, 1986   The excavations at New Fresh Wharf, 1974 – 8, in Dyson 1986, 25 – 60

Millett, M, 1983   The history, architecture and archaeology of Johnson's Corner, Alton, *Proc Hampshire Fld Club Archaeol Soc*, **39**, 77 – 109

Millett, M, and James, S, 1983   Excavations at Cowdery's Down, Basingstoke, Hants, 1978 – 81, *Archaeol J*, **140**, 151 – 279

Milne, G, and Milne, C, 1982   *Medieval waterfront development at Trig Lane, London*, London Middlesex Archaeol Soc Spec Pap, **5**

Money, J H, 1977   The Iron Age hill-fort and Romano-British iron-working settlement at Garden Hill, Sussex: interim report on excavations 1968 – 76, *Britannia*, **8**, 339 – 50

Morgan, R A, 1976   *Tree-ring analysis of timbers from Winterton, Lincs*, Anc Mon Lab Rep, **1492**

——, 1977 Tree-ring dating of the London waterfronts, *London Archaeol*, **3**, 40 – 5

——, 1978a   Tree-ring studies in the Somerset Levels: the Meare Heath Track, *Somerset Levels Pap*, **4**, 40 – 1

——, 1978b   Tree-ring studies in the Somerset Levels: Tinney's Ground, *Somerset Levels Pap*, **4**, 82 – 5

——, 1979   Tree-ring studies in the Somerset Levels: floating oak tree-ring chronologies from the trackways and their radiocarbon dating, *Somerset Levels Pap*, **5**, 98 – 100

——, 1980a   Tree-ring studies in the Somerset Levels: Tinney's Ground, *Somerset Levels Pap*, **6**, 69 – 72

——, 1980b   The carbon 14 and dendrochronology, in Hill *et al* 1980, 88 – 94

——, 1982a   Tree-ring studies in the Somerset Levels: the Meare Heath Track 1974 – 80, *Somerset Levels Pap*, **8**, 39 – 45

——, 1982b   Further information on the Bradbourne Mill timbers, *Derbyshire Archaeol J*, **102**, 101

——, 1983   Further information on the Bradbourne Mill timbers – correction, *Derbyshire Archaeol J*, **103**, 6

——, 1988   Tree-ring studies in the Somerset Levels: bog oaks from the Brue valley and Sedgemoor, *Somerset Levels Pap*, **14**, 51 – 3

Morgan, R A, and Schofield, J, 1978   Tree-rings and the archaeology of the Thames waterfront in the City of London, in *Dendrochronology in Europe* (ed J Fletcher), BAR, **S51**, 223 – 33

Morgan, R A, Wildgoose, M, and Collis, J, 1980   Some post-medieval timbers from Bradbourne, Derbyshire, *Derbyshire Archaeol J*, **100**, 43 – 8

Moulden, J, and Tweddle, D, 1986   *Anglo-Scandinavian York: settlement south-west of the Ouse*, Archaeol York, **8/1**

Musson, C R, 1970   The Breddin, 1969, *Curr Archaeol*, **19**, 215 – 8

——, 1972   Two winters at the Breddin, *Curr Archaeol*, **33**, 263 – 7

——, 1976   Excavations at the Breddin 1969 – 73, in *Hillforts: later prehistoric earthworks in Britain and Ireland* (ed D W Harding), 293 – 302

——, 1991   *The Breddin hillfort: a later prehistoric settlement in the Welsh Marches*, CBA Res Rep, **76**

Mynard, D C, and Zeepvat, R J, 1978   Great Linford, Buckinghamshire, in *CBA Newsletter and Calendar*, **1.9**, 115

Neal, D S, 1977   Northchurch, Boxmoor, and Hemel Hempstead station: the excavation of three Roman buildings in the Bulbourne valley, *Hertfordshire Archaeol*, **4**, 1 – 136

——, 1979 Bronze Age, Iron Age, and Roman settlement sites at Little Somborne and Ashley, Hampshire, *Proc Hampshire Fld Club Archaeol Soc*, **36**, 91 – 143

——, 1983 Excavations on a settlement at Little Bay, Isles of Scilly, *Cornish Archaeol*, **22**, 47 – 80

——, 1987 Excavations at Magiovinium, Buckinghamshire, 1978 – 80, *Rec Buckinghamshire*, **29**, 1 – 124

Neal, D S, Wardle, A, and Hunn, J, 1990 *Excavation of the Iron Age, Roman, and medieval settlement at Gorhambury, St Albans*, Engl Heritage Archaeol Rep, **14**

Needham, S P, 1991 *Excavation and salvage at Runnymede Bridge, 1978: the Late Bronze Age waterfront Site*, London

Norman, C, and Clements, C F, 1979 Prehistoric timber structures on King's Sedgemoor: some recent discoveries, *Somerset Archaeol Nat Hist*, **123**, 5 – 18

O'Connor, T P, 1976 The excavation of a round barrow and cross-ridge dyke at Alfriston, East Sussex, 1975, *Sussex Archaeol Collect*, **144**, 151 – 63

Orme, B J, 1982 The use of radiocarbon dates from the Somerset Levels, *Somerset Levels Pap*, **8**, 9 – 25

Orme, B J, Caseldine, A E, and Morgan, R A, 1982 Recent discoveries on Walton Heath: Garvin's, Bisgrove's, and Jones' Tracks, *Somerset Levels Pap*, **8**, 51 – 64

Orme, B J, Coles, J M, Caseldine, A E, and Bailey, G N, 1981 Meare Village West 1979, *Somerset Levels Pap*, **7**, 12 – 69

Orme, B J, Coles, J M, Caseldine, A E, and Morgan, R A, 1985a Third millennium structures on Walton Heath, *Somerset Levels Pap*, **11**, 62 – 8

——, 1985b A Later Bronze Age complex at Stileway, *Somerset Levels Pap*, **11**, 75 – 9

Orme, B J, Coles, J M, and Sturdy, C R, 1979 Meare Lake Village West: a report on recent work, *Somerset Levels Pap*, **5**, 6 – 17

Orme, B J, Sturdy, C R, and Morgan, R A, 1980 East Moors 1979, *Somerset Levels Pap*, **6**, 52 – 9

Orton, C R, 1983 A statistical technique for integrating C14 dates with other forms of dating evidence, in *Computer applications and quantitative methods in archaeology* (ed J G B Haigh), 115 – 22

Palmer, N, 1980 A Beaker burial and medieval tenements in the Hamel, Oxford, *Oxoniensia*, **45**, 124 – 225

Parnell, G, 1977 Excavations at the Tower of London, 1976 – 7, *London Archaeol*, **3**, 97 – 9

Parrington, M, 1978 *The excavation of an Iron Age settlement, Bronze Age ring-ditches, and Roman features at Ashville Trading Estate, Abingdon, (Oxfordshire) 1974 – 6*, CBA Res Rep, **28**, Oxford Archaeol Unit Rep **1**

Pearson, G W, Pilcher, J R, Baillie, M G L, Corbett, D M, and Qua, F, 1986 High-precision ^{14}C measurement of Irish oaks to show the natural ^{14}C variations from AD 1840 to 5210 BC, *Radiocarbon*, **28**, 911 – 34

Penhallurick, R D, 1986 *Tin in antiquity*, London

Pitts, M W, 1982 On the road to Stonehenge: report on investigations beside the A344 in 1968, 1979, and 1980, *Proc Prehist Soc*, **48**, 75 – 132

RCHME, 1985 *Excavations at York Minster: Volume II. The Cathedral of Archbishop Thomas of Bayeux*, D Phillips, Royal Commission on the Historical Monuments of England

RCHME, forthcoming *Excavations at York Minster: Volume I*, Royal Commission on the Historical Monuments of England

Rahtz, P, and Meeson, R, 1992 *An Anglo-Saxon watermill at Tamworth: excavations in the Bolebridge Street area of Tamworth, Staffordshire, in 1971 and 1978*, CBA Res Rep, **83**

Ralph, E K, Michael, H N, and Han, M C, 1973 Radiocarbon dates and reality, *MASCA Newsletter*, **9**, 1 – 20

Reynolds, N M, 1979 Saltergate, in Colyer and Jones 1979, 84 – 9

Richardson, B, 1978 Excavation round-up 1977, in *London Archaeol*, **3**, 159 – 63

Richmond, H, Taylor, R, and Wade-Martins, P, 1982 Nos 28 – 34 Queen Street, Kings Lynn, *E Anglian Archaeol Rep*, **14**, 108 – 24

Robertson-Mackay, M E, 1980 A 'head and hooves' burial beneath a round barrow, with other Neolithic and Bronze Age sites, on Hemp Knoll, near Avebury, Wiltshire, *Proc Prehist Soc*, **46**, 123 – 76

Rodwell, W, 1976 The archaeological investigation of Hadstock Church, Essex: an interim report, *Antiq J*, **56**, 55 – 71

Rodwell, W, and Rodwell, K A, 1982 St Peter's Church, Barton-upon-Humber: excavation and structural study 1978 – 81, *Antiq J*, **62**, 283 – 315

——, 1985 – 6 *Rivenhall: investigations of a villa, church, and village, 1950 – 77*, CBA Res Rep, **55**, Chelmsford Archaeol Trust Rep, **4**

Rogerson, A, 1976 Excavations on Fuller's Hill, Great Yarmouth, *E Anglian Archaeol Rep*, **2**, 131 – 246

Rose, E, 1978 Wayford Bridge, Smallburgh, *E Anglian Archaeol Rep*, **8**, 23 – 8

Rose, J, 1976 The date of the buried channel deposits at Sproughton, *E Anglian Archaeol Rep*, **3**, 11 – 15

Salisbury, C R, Whitley P J, Litton, C D, and Fox, J L, 1984 Flandrian courses of the River Trent at Colwick, Nottingham, *The Mercian Geologist*, **9**, 189 – 207

Saville, A, 1978 Condicote Henge Monument, *Trans Bristol Gloucestershire Archaeol Soc*, **96**, 85

——, 1979a *Excavations at Guiting Power Iron Age site, Gloucestershire, 1974*, Committee for Rescue Archaeol in Avon, Gloucestershire, and Somerset Occas Pap, **7**

——, 1979b *Recent work at Cow Common Bronze Age cemetery, Gloucestershire*, Committee for Rescue Archaeol in Avon, Gloucestershire, and Somerset Occas Pap, **6**

——, 1983 Excavations at Condicote Henge Monument, Gloucestershire, 1977, *Trans Bristol Gloucestershire Archaeol Soc*, **101**, 21 – 47

——, 1985 Salvage recording of Romano-British, Saxon, medieval and post-medieval remains at North Street, Winchcombe, Gloucestershire, *Trans Bristol Gloucestershire Archaeol Soc*, **103**, 101 – 39

Saville, A, and Ellison, A, 1983 Excavations at Uley Bury hillfort, Gloucestershire, 1976, in *Uley Bury and Norbury hillforts: rescue excavations at two Gloucestershire Iron Age sites* (ed A Saville), Western Archaeol Trust Excav Monogr, **5**, 1 – 24

Shackley, M, and Hunt, S-A, 1984 – 5 Paleoenvironment of a mesolithic peat bed from Austin Friars, Leicester, *Leicestershire Archaeol Hist Soc Trans*, **59**, 1 – 12

Shoesmith, R, 1980 *Excavations at Castle Green*, CBA Res Rep, **36**, Hereford City Excavations, **1**

——, 1982 *Excavations on and close to the defences*, CBA Res Rep, **46**, Hereford City Excavations, **2**

Simmons, B B, 1975 Salt-making sites in the Silt Fens of Lincolnshire in the Iron Age and Roman periods, in *Salt: the study of an ancient industry* (ed K W de Brisay and K A Evans), 33 – 6

Smith, C (ed), 1979 *Fisherwick: the reconstruction of an Iron Age landscape*, BAR, **61**

Smith, G H, 1978 Excavations near Hadrian's Wall at Tarraby Lane 1976, *Britannia*, **9**, 19 – 56

Smith, G H, and Harris, D, 1982 The excavation of Mesolithic, Neolithic, and Bronze Age settlements at Poldowrian, St Keverne, 1980, *Cornish Archaeol*, **21**, 23 – 66

Smith, K, 1977 The excavation of Winklebury Camp, Basingstoke, Hampshire, *Proc Prehist Soc*, **43**, 31 – 130

Smith, K, Coppen, J, Wainwright, G J, and Beckett, S, 1981 The Shaugh Moor Project: third report – settlement and environmental investigations, *Proc Prehist Soc*, **47**, 205 – 74

Stanford, S C, 1982 Bromfield, Shropshire – Neolithic, Beaker, and Bronze Age sites 1966 – 79, *Proc Prehist Soc*, **48**, 279 – 320

Stead, I M, 1976 La Tène burials between Burton Fleming and Rudston, North Humberside, *Antiq J*, **56**, 217 – 26

Steane, K, 1991 St Paul-in-the-Bail: a dated sequence, in *Lincoln Archaeology 1990 – 91* (ed M J Jones), **3**, 28 – 31

Suess, H E, 1970 Bristlecone pine calibration of the radiocarbon timescale 5200 BC to the present, in *Radiocarbon variations and absolute chronology* (ed I U Olsson), 303 – 11

Tatton-Brown, T, 1974 Excavations at the Custom House site, City of London, 1973, *Trans London Middlesex Archaeol Soc*, **25**, 117 – 219

Taylor, A F, and Woodward, P J, 1975 Cainhoe Castle excavations, 1973, *Bedfordshire Archaeol J*, **10**, 41 – 52

——, 1983 Excavations at Roxton, Bedfordshire, 1972 – 4: The post-Bronze Age settlement, *Bedfordshire Archaeol J*, **16**, 7 – 28

——, 1985 A Bronze Age barrow cemetery and associated settlement at Roxton, Bedfordshire, *Archaeol J*, **142**, 73 – 149

Tebbutt, C F, 1982 A Middle-Saxon iron-smelting site at Millbrook, Ashdown Forest, Sussex, *Sussex Archaeol Collect*, **120**, 19 – 35

Thompson, F H, 1979 Three Surrey hillforts: excavations at Anstiebury, Holmbury, and Hascombe 1972 – 7, *Antiq J*, **59**, 245 – 318

Treen, C, and Atkin, M, forthcoming *Wharram: a study of settlement on the Yorkshire Wolds, VIII. Water utilization*, York Univ Archaeol Publ

Trudgian, P, 1977 Excavations at Tregileder, St Kew, 1975 – 6, *Cornish Archaeol*, **16**, 122 – 8

Trussler, R E, 1974 Recovery of ship's timbers at Sandwich, Kent, *Kent Archaeol Rev*, **No 36**, 166 – 9

Turnbull, P, 1986 Gayle Lane earthwork, Wensleydale, in *Archaeology in the Pennines* (eds T Manby and P Turnbull), BAR, **158**, 205 – 11

Tyers, I, 1988 The prehistoric peat layers (Tilbury IV), in Hinton 1988, 5 – 17

VCH Bucks IV, 1927 *The Victoria history of the county of Buckingham: Volume IV*, ed W Page, London

Wacher, J S, 1979 Silver Street, in Colyer and Jones 1979, 81 – 4

Wade, K, 1974 The Anglo-Saxon settlement at Bonhunt, Essex, an interim note, in *Anglo-Saxon settlement and landscape* (ed T Rowley), BAR, **6**, 74 – 7

——1980 A settlement site at Bonhunt Farm, Wicken Bonhunt, Essex, in *Archaeology in Essex to AD 1500* (ed D G Buckley), CBA Res Rep, **34**, 96 – 102

——1988 Ipswich, in *The rebirth of towns in the west AD 700 – 1050* (eds R Hodges and B Hobley), CBA Res Rep, **68**, 93 – 100

Wade-Martins, P, 1980 Excavations in North Elmham Park 1967 – 72, *E Anglian Archaeol Rep*, **9**, Part 1

Wainwright, G J, 1980 A pit burial at Lower Ashmore Farm, Rose Ash, Devon, *Devon Archaeol Soc Proc*, **38**, 13 – 15

Wainwright, G J, Fleming, A, and Smith, K, 1979 The Shaugh Moor project: first report, *Proc Prehist Soc*, **45**, 1 – 33

Wainwright, G J, and Smith, K, 1980 The Shaugh Moor project: second report – the enclosure, *Proc Prehist Soc*, **46**, 65 – 122

Walker, J S F, 1978 Excavations in medieval tenements on the Quilters Vaults site in Southampton, *Proc Hampshire Fld Club Archaeol Soc*, **35**, 183 – 216

Ward, A H, 1978 The excavation of a Bronze Age composite mound and other features on Pentre Farm, Pontardulais, West Glamorgan, *Archaeol Cambrensis*, **127**, 40 – 74

Ward, G K, and Wilson, S R, 1978 Procedures for comparing and combining radiocarbon age determinations: a critique, *Archaeometry*, **20**, 19 – 31

Watkins, J G, and Williams, R A H, 1983 An excavation in Highgate, Beverley, *E Riding Archaeol*, **7**, 71 – 84

Webster, L E, and Cherry, J, 1980 Medieval Britain in 1979, *Medieval Archaeol*, **24**, 218 – 64

West, S E, 1985 West Stow, the Anglo-Saxon village; Volume 1: text, *E Anglian Archaeol Rep*, **24**

Wheeler, H, 1979 Excavations at Willington, Derbyshire 1970 – 72, *Derbyshire Archaeol J*, **99**, 58 – 220

Whimster, R, 1977 Harlyn Bay reconsidered: the excavations of 1900 – 1905 in the light of recent work, *Cornish Archaeol*, **16**, 61 – 88

Williams, J H, 1979 *St Peter's Street, Northampton, excavations 1973 – 6*, Northampton Devel Corp Monogr, **2**

Williams, J H, and Shaw, M, 1981 Excavations in Chalk Lane, Northampton 1975 – 8, *Northamptonshire Archaeol*, **16**, 87 – 135

Williams, J H, Shaw, M, and Denham, V, 1985 *Middle Saxon palaces at Northampton*, Northampton Devel Corp Monogr, **4**

Wilmott, T, and Rahtz, S P Q, 1985 An Iron Age and Roman settlement outside Kenchester (Magnis), Herefordshire, excavations 1977 – 9, *Trans Woolhope Natur Fld Club*, **45**, 36 – 185

Wilson, D R, Wright, R P, and Hassall, M W C, 1973 Roman Britain in 1972, *Britannia*, **4**, 271 – 337

Wilson, D R, Wright, R P, Hassall, M W C, and Tomlin, R S O, 1975 Roman Britain in 1974, *Britannia*, **6**, 221 – 94

Woodward, P J, 1978 Flint distribution, ring ditches and Bronze Age settlement patterns in the Great Ouse valley, *Archaeol J*, **135**, 32 – 56

Wymer, J J, 1975 Two barbed points from Devil's Wood Pit, Sproughton, *E Anglian Archaeol Rep*, **1**, 1 – 4

——, 1976 A long blade industry from Sproughton, Suffolk, *E Anglian Archaeol Rep*, **3**, 1 – 10

Yule, B, 1976 A Roman burial from Southwark, *London Archaeol*, **2**, 359

# Index 1: general index

by Lesley and Roy Adkins

The index presents a guide to the excavated sites which have been subject to radiocarbon dating. It consists of the name of the excavator(s), secondary names of sites (not main names which are arranged in alphabetical order in the text), type of site (as described in each text entry under Site), and main periods (as originally defined by the submitter) with a list of relevant sites (usually as discussed in the text entries under Site).

1 Westgate Street 60–2
1-5 Aldwark 235
3-5 Lobster Lane, 336N 124
5 Cantilupe St 77
10 Lower Quay Street 62
10 Market Street 5
11-17 Southgate Street, Bell Hotel 62
16-22 Coppergate 235–6
19 Berkeley Street 62
20-24 St Johns Street 18
24 Hamwih Six Dials 187
29-39 St Johns Street 18–19
34-8 Eastgate Street 63
39-47 Sidbury Street 234
49-63 Botolph Street 125
58-9 Skeldergate, Bishopshill 1 236–8

Abbey (Romsey) 145
abbeys 60; see also monasteries, priories
Adams, S 140
Aldwark, Ebor Brewery 238
Allen, D 142
Allen and Hanbury's 200–1
All Saints Church, Oxford 132
Ancliffe, V 200
Andrews, P E 187
Andrews, R D 80
Anglo-Saxon, see also Saxon
    Abingdon 2
    Aldwincle 4
    Alfriston 4
    Barrow 10
    Barton-on-Humber 11
    Barton-under-Needwood 12
    Beacon Hill 15
    Bedford 19
    Bishopstone 22
    Brandon 26
    Brixworth 26
    Cowdery's Down 40
    Hadstock 68
    Mucking 115
    North Elmham 119
    North Elmham Park 119
    Pagham 133
    Pewsey 135
    Rivenhall 143
    Thirlings 196
    West Stow 204
    Wicken Bonhunt 209
Anglo-Scandinavian
    York 241
Annable, F K 135
ApSimon, A 151
Ashbee, P 5
Ashcott Heath 165
Ashcott Heath, Rowlands Track 165–6
Ashcott Heath, Signal Pole Ground 166
Ashville Trading Estate 1–2

Austin, D 129
Austin Friars 88
Ayers, B S 125, 126
Balkwill, C 8
Bamford, H 120
banjo enclosure 106
Barnard, J 85
barrows 4, 5, 6, 8, 24, 25, 29, 30, 31, 32, 36, 65, 67, 72, 73, 77, 80, 86, 92, 104, 105, 126, 127, 137, 152, 153, 164, 190, 192, 198, 199, 200, 203; see also cairns
Barton Court Farm 2
basilica 54
Batchelor, D 52
baths, Roman 35, 52
Baynard's Castle 93–5
beacon 27
Beaker
    Amesbury 5
    Barnack 8
    Bromfield 27
    Chippenham 36
    Marc 3 104
    Octon Wold 127
    Oxford 133
    Poldowrian 136
    Ravenstone 142
    Wetwang Slack 206
Bedwin, O 35, 73, 76, 81, 131
Beeby, B M 30, 31
Bell, M 22
bell pit 147
Berrington Street 77–8
Beswick, W R 76
Betts, T 71, 92
Bewell House 78
Bidwell, P 54
Blacka Brook 156–7
Blackfriars 133
Blacknall Field 135
boat 165
Bolebridge Street 193–4
Bond, D 117
Bowthorpe 126
Breage 140
Breiddin 114
Brett, D W 102
Brewster, T C M 57, 127
Briar Hill 120–2
Bridge bypass 32
Bridge, M C 141
bridges 3, 21, 56, 193
Bridge Street West 134–5
Bridget's Farm, R5 103–5
Brinklow, D 238, 241
Britnell, W 15
Broadfields 41
Broads Barrage Bores 64

Broad Street, City Arms 78
Bronze Age
    Alfriston 4
    Ardleigh 6
    Barham 8
    Billingborough Fen 21
    Bishopstone 22
    Black Patch 23, 24
    Bromfield 27
    Burghfield 28
    Butterbump 30
    Canterbury 32
    Carngoon Bank 34
    Chanctonbury Ring 35
    Chippenham 36
    Christchurch 36
    Eaton 54
    Fingrinhoe 56
    Garton Slack 57
    Grendon 65
    Harlyn Bay 71
    Harpley 72
    Hemp Knoll 77
    Kimpton 84
    Lambourn 86
    Levington 88
    Little Cressingham 92
    London 100
    Marc 3 104, 105
    Mildenhall 110, 111
    Milton Keynes 112
    Mucking 117
    Nazeingbury 118
    North Molton 120
    Norwich 126
    Poldowrian 137
    Pontardulais 137
    Poundbury 138
    Poundisford Park 140
    Radwell 141
    Rose Ash 1459, 110
    Roxton 146
    Runnymede 148
    St Neot 152
    St Stephen-in-Brannel 153
    Scilly Isles 154
    Seamer Carr 156
    Shaugh Moor 158, 161
    Somerset Levels 174
    Sproughton 189
    Sproxton 190
    Staines 191
    Thwing 197
    Upper Lambourn 199
    West Heath Common 203
    Wetwang Slack 206
Brown, M, 73
Bulls Head Yard 2

250

burials 3, 91, 96, 133, 145, 146, 195; see also cemeteries
burials (animal) 25
Burleigh, G R 92
burnt flint 110, 205; see also potboiler deposit
burnt mound 136
Burntwood Farm, R6 104
Burrow Hill 30
Bury Hill 81–2
Butcher, S 154

Cainhoe Castle 38
The Cairn field, site 10 161–2
cairns 120, 161; see also barrows
The Camery 202
Canford Heath 137–8
Canham, R 193
Car Dyke 22
Carr, R 26, 209
Carter, A 124
Carver, M 53, 191, 234
castles 33, 38, 86, 118, 122, 140, 189, 195
    Stamford 191–2
    Berkhamsted 20
    Castle Green 78–80
    Prudhoe 140–1
    Taunton 195–6
Cathedral Close, Exeter 54–5
Catholme 11–14
causeway (of timber piles) 204
causewayed enclosures 69, 71, 120
cemeteries 3, 10, 15, 26, 27, 28, 29, 30, 31, 36, 37, 41, 54, 57, 63, 71, 73, 74, 78, 84, 86, 115, 118, 119, 128, 135, 138, 202, 206, 208, 209, 210, 238; see also burials, graveyard
Chalk Lane 122–3
Challands, A 134
chambered tomb 151; see also barrows
Chambers, R A 15, 41, 56
chapels 80, 202
Cholwich Town 157–8
Chowne, P 21, 76
Christchurch Cathedral, Oxford 133
Christie, P 33
churches 10, 11, 26, 32, 68, 89, 90, 118, 125, 143, 145, 208, 212, 238
churchyard 234
Clack, P 32
Clark, R 197
Clay, P 54, 190
Clipson, J 87
Coles, J 165, 166, 167, 168, 169, 171, 174, 175, 176, 177, 180, 183, 184, 185, 186
Colledge, S M 17, 190
Colliford Reservoir, site II 152–3
Colliford Reservoir, site IV 153
Collins, D 95
Colwick Hall Gravel Pit 39
Colyer, C 89
Coombs, D 31
Coral Springs 41–2
corn-drying ovens 27
Courtney, T 198
Cow Common 192–3
Cramp, R 83
Crouch, K R 191

Crummy, P 109, 110, 136, 204
Crump, R 57
Cunliffe, B 42

Dacre, M 84
Dark Age
    Lamyatt Beacon 86
    Wensleydale 203
Darrah, R 205
Davies, S M 5
Davison, B 103
de Brisay, K 134
defences 193
Dennis, G 99
Dent, J 206
deserted medieval villages 87, 208
Devil's Wood 189–90
ditches 66, 192; see also enclosures, ring ditches
ditches (boundary) 201
ditches (defensive) 31, 63, 78, 125, 153
Dix, B 128
Dolby, M 21
Donaghey, S 236
Donaldson, A 9, 191, 199
Donaldson, P 8
Douch, H L 140
Down, A 35, 36
Drewett, P 4, 23, 24, 203
Drury, P 93
Dunmore, S 209
Durham, B 131, 132

earthwork enclosure 89
earthworks 72, 164, 203
East Moors, Ashcott Heath 166
Easton Down 104–5
Eddy, M 85
Edington Burtle, Chilton Moor 166–7
Ellis, P 60
Ellis, R 72
Ellison, A 198
Elmhirst, L 88
enclosures 5, 6, 10, 23, 56, 72, 81, 89, 92, 106, 111, 117, 138, 152, 158, 209, 212
Evans, J 164
Evans, J G 155
Everson, P 26
Ewart 196–7

farms 210
farmsteads 19, 128, 131, 138
Fasham, P 103, 104, 105, 106, 107
Fenwick, V 30, 153
field systems 23, 155
fish trap 39
Flaxengate 89
Ford, D 3
fortress 239
forum 62
Freke, D 89
Friar Street 52
Frog Hall Farm 56
Frost Hill 27
Fulford, M 164
Fuller's Hill 64–5
furnaces 6, 41, 76, 141

Garden Hill 72–3

Gates, T 28
Gibson-Hill, J 40
Gillibrand, 85
Gilmour, B 89, 90
Gloucester Cathedral, Church House 63
Goodburn, R 233
Gosling, P 33
Grapes Lane 32–3
graveyard 240; see also cemeteries
Green, C 27
Green, C J S 138
Green, H J M 63
Green, H S 111, 112
Greene, P 147
Gregory, V L 31, 133
Greig, J 2, 7, 21, 31, 190, 234
Griffith, F 152, 153
Grim's Dyke 72
Guilbert, G 33, 113
gully 28; see also ditches

Hadfield, J 143
Hall, R A 235, 239
The Hamel 133
Hammerson, M 98
Hampstead, West Heath Spa 95–6
Hamwih 187–9
Hannan, A 196
Harris, D 136, 163
Harrison, M 239
Hartigan's Gravel Pit, MK-19 111–12
Hartigan's Gravel Pit, MK-23 112
Hartigan's Gravel Pit, MK-223 112
Haslam, J 141
Hassall, J 18, 19
Hassall, T 131, 132, 133
Hazel Road 24–5
hearths 6, 76, 81, 95, 146, 198
Heighway, C 60, 62, 63
henge 39, 54
    Condicote 39
Heron's House 28
High Easton Farm 25
Highgate 20
High Ousegate 238–9
Hill, C 94, 96
hillforts 7, 35, 42, 73, 74, 81, 113, 114, 136, 138, 197, 198, 232, 233
Hills, C 119
Hinchliffe, J 6, 74
Hirst, S 20
Hodder, I 87
Hodgson's Court 33
Holdsworth, P 187, 189
Holm Castle, Windmill Hill 196
Hope-Taylor, B 130
Horsey, I P 137, 138
house platforms 34
Huggins, P J 118, 200
Hunt, A 52
hurdles 185; see also trackways
Hurst, H 62
Hurst, J G 208
hut platforms 23
huts 19

Iron Age
    Abingdon 1, 2
    Andover 5
    Balksbury 7

Barham 8
Barnham 10
Beckford 15
Belling Law 19
Billingborough Fen 21
Bishopstone 22
Bognor 24
Brandon 26
Burton Fleming 29
Carn Euny 34
Carngoon Bank 34
Chanctonbury Ring 35
Christchurch 36
Coddenham 38
Crawley 41
Danebury 42
Droitwich 52
Farmoor 55
Fingringhoe 56
Fisherwick 56
Garton Slack 57
Godmanchester 63
Gretton 66
Guiting Power 67
Harlyn Bay 71
Hartfield 73
Harting Beacon 73
Hascombe 74
Helpringham Fen 76
Hog Cliff Hill 81
Hogsthorpe 81
Ledston 87
Little Somborne 92
Little Waltham 93
London 98, 100
Marc 3 104, 107
Milton Keynes 112
Moel y Gaer 113
Montgomery 114
Mucking 117
North Elmham 119
Oakley 127
Odell 128
Oving 131
Peldon 134
Pewsey 135
Pitchbury Ramparts 136
Poundbury 138
Ringstead 143
St Kew 152
Scilly Isles 154
Somerset Levels 171
Staines 191
Uley Bury 198
Weekley 201
West Stow 204
Wetwang Slack 206
Willington 210
Wilmington 210
Winklebury 232
Woodbury Castle 233
iron smelting 6, 76, 141
ironworking settlement 41, 73
Ivy Farm 56

Jackson, D 3, 4, 66, 72, 127, 143, 201
James, H 234
Jarvis, K 36
Jenkins, F 32
Jobey, G 19

Jones, M U 115, 117
Jones, T 117

Kalis Corner 84
Keen, L 140
Keighley, J 87
Kenward, H 193
kilns 63, 91, 124, 143, 147, 191, 201
King's Pool 190-1
Kirkham, B 81
Knight's Farm 28-9

Lackford Bridge 205-6
lake 88
Lambrick, G 55
latrine 234
Lawson, A J 57, 72, 92, 126, 209
Leach, P 195
Leech, R 34, 86
Limbrey, S 39
linear earthworks 72, 164
Llanstephen Castle 33
Lloyd's Bank 21
Longley, D 148
Losco-Bradley, S 12
Lower Ashmore Farm 145
Lower Brook Street 212-31
Ludgate Hill 96

McAvoy, F 34
McCormick, A G 65
Macgregor, H 235
Mackreth, D 134
Maclagan, H 21
Macpherson-Grant, N 32
McWhirr, A 37
Magilton, J 238
Magiovinium 24
Mahany, C 191
Manby, T G 25, 67, 197
Martin, E A 8, 10, 36, 110, 111, 189
Meare Heath 167
Meare Heath Field, site 4 167
Meare Heath, Diffords Site 1 167-8
Meare Heath, Eclipse Track 168
Meare Heath, Eclipse Track (peat sequence) 168-9
Meare Heath, Meare Heath Track 169-70
Meare Lake Village West 171-4
Meare, Meare Heath Field 12.3 174
Meare, Stileway 174-5
Meare Village, West Meare 174
medieval, see also Norman
    Alton 5
    Andover 5
    Barton-on-Humber 11
    Bedford 18, 19
    Belling Law 19
    Bilby 21
    Brixworth 26
    Carlisle 32, 33
    Carmarthen 33
    Colwick 39
    Droitwich 52
    Durham 53
    Great Linford 64
    Great Yarmouth 64
    Hartlepool 74
    Hereford 77, 78
    Heysham 80

    Jarrow 83
    King's Lynn 84
    Kingston-upon-Thames 85
    Kirkham 86
    Layton 87
    Lincoln 89, 90, 91
    London 94, 96, 99, 100, 101
    Middleborough 110
    Nantwich 118
    Northampton 122, 123
    Norwich 126
    Okehampton 129
    Peterborough 135
    Poole 138
    Prudhoe 140
    Ringmer 143
    Runcorn 147
    Silchester 164
    Southampton 189
    Tamworth 193
    Taunton 195
    Wells Cathedral 202
    Wharram Percy 208
    Winchester 212
    Wootton Wawen 234
    Worcester 234
    York 235, 238, 239, 241
Meeson, R 193
Meldon Quarry 129-30
Mellor, J E 88
Mercer, R 69, 71
Mesolithic
    Carngoon Bank 34
    London 95
    Poldowrian 137
    Unstone 198
    Waltham Abbey 200
Micheldever Wood 105-6
Micheldever Wood 106
Midland Road, Trench II 19
Miket, R 196
The Mile Ditches 92
Miles, D 2
Miles, H 120, 153, 233
Millbrook 6
Miller, L 96
Millett, M 5, 40
mills 25, 27, 64, 130, 193
Mills, P 102
minster 240
The Minster 240-1
monasteries 26, 83, 200; see also abbeys, priories
Money, J H 73
Moor Hall Gravel Pit 71
mortar mixers 123
Morton, A D 187
mortuary enclosure 3
Moss Mire 9-10
mound 57; see also barrows
Murphy, P 64, 155, 205
Musson, C 114
Mynard, D 25

Neal, D 6, 24, 63, 92, 124, 154
Needham, S 148
Neolithic,
    Abingdon 2
    Aldwincle 3
    Andover 5

Index 1: general index

Bishopstone 22
Boynton 25
Bromfield 27
Butterbump 30
Callis Wold 31
Chanctonbury Ring 35
Christchurch 36
Elton 54
Garton Slack 57
Grindale 67
Hambledon Hill 69, 71
Houghton 82
Milton Keynes 112
Northampton 120
Poldowrian 137
Poundbury 138
Ringstead 143
St Buryan 151
Seamer Carr 156
Skendleby 164
Somerset Levels 177, 184
Sproughton 189
Tewkesbury 196
Thirlings 196
Willington 210
Newson, M 140
New Fresh Wharf 96–7
New Fresh Wharf, St Magnus House 97–8
New Market Tavern 110
Norman
    Romsey 145
    York 240
Nornour 154
Norton Priory 147–8
Nursery Road 118–19

O'Connor, T P 4
Old Bowling Green 52
Old Down Farm 5
Old Gayle Lane 203
Old Wall, north-west Shelford 57
ovens 27
Owles, E 38

Pacitto, A 20, 82
Paddock Hill 197
Palmer, N 133
Park Farm 199
Park Lane 63
Park Lodge Quarry 66–7
Parliament Street 239
Parnell, G 101, 232
Parrington, M 1
Partridge, C 200
Pavement, Lloyd's Bank 239–40
Pearce, T 88
peat bogs 2, 176, 183, 199
peat deposits 99, 100, 129, 155, 200, 205
peat (monolith) 156
Pentre Barrow 137
Pex Marine 138
Phillips, D 240
Philp, B 56, 210
pit alignments 66, 155
pits 7, 28, 104, 112, 138, 196, 234
Pitts, M 24
ponds 28, 56, 88, 208
postholes 192, 198
post-medieval

Bedford 18, 19
Bradwell Bury 25
Droitwich 52
Gallows Hill 57
London 100
Worcester 234
post-mills 27, 64
post-Roman 60
    Poundbury 138
potboiler deposit 111; see also burnt flint
Potter, T W 80
priories 86, 147, 195; see also abbeys, monasteries
Priory (Kirkham) 85–6

Queen Street (King's Lynn) 84–5
Queen Street (Kingston-upon-Hull) 85
Quilter's Vaults 189

Rahtz, P 80, 83, 193
rampart 235
Red Hill, Site 117
Reynolds, N M 91
Richards, J C 28, 80, 86, 199
ring cairns 120, 161
ring ditches 28, 36, 54, 88, 141, 142, 145, 146, 155
Ring Ditch II 142–3
roads 98, 107, 234
Roberts, J P 125
Robertson-Mackay, M E 77
Rodwell, W 11, 68, 143, 202
Rogerson, A 64
Roman, see also Romano-British
    Abingdon 1
    Alcester
    Aldwincle
    Andover 5
    Ashley 6-7
    Beacon Hill 15
    Bullock Down Farm 27
    Caerwent 31
    Carlisle 32, 33
    Chichester 35, 36
    Coddenham 38
    Dorchester 52
    Droitwich 52
    Exeter 54
    Fencott 56
    Gallows Hill 57
    Garton Slack 57
    Gloucester 62, 63
    Godmanchester 63
    Gorhambury 63
    Hartlepool 74
    Kenchester 83
    Lincoln 90, 91
    Little Waltham 93
    London 94, 95, 96, 98, 99, 100
    Marc 3 104, 107
    Northchurch 124
    North Elmham 119
    Odell 128
    Pagham 133
    Poundbury 138
    Roxton 146
    Scilly Isles 154
    Silchester 164
    Staines 191
    Swindon 193

    Tarraby 194
    Ware 200
    Weekley 201
    Wells Cathedral 202
    Winchcombe 211
    Winchester 212
    Winterton 233
    Worcester 234
    York 235, 236, 239, 240
Romano-British, see also Roman
    Abingdon 2
    Barton-under-Needwood 12
    Belling Law 19
    Bishopstone 22
    Bletchley 24
    Carngoon Bank 34
    Catsgore 34
    Chanctonbury Ring 35
    Cirencester 37
    Crawley 41
    Curbridge 41
    Hartfield 73
    Lamyatt Beacon 86
    Oving 131
    Peldon 134
    Shortlanesend 163
    Willington 210
Rookery Hill 22–3
Rose, E 165
round houses 19, 56, 71, 92, 113, 154
rounds 163
Rudling, D 27

Saddler Street, Sutton Sale Rooms 52–4
Saddlesborough Main Reave, site 208 161
St Chad's, Barrow 10–11
St George's Chapel, Windsor 232
St Mark's, Lincoln 89–90
St Martin's, Little Bay 154
St Mary's, Bar Point 155
St Mary's, Porthellick 155
St Pancras, Canterbury 32
St Pancras Priory, Southover 89
St Patrick's Chapel, Heysham 80
St Paul-in-the-Bail, Lincoln 90–1
St Paul's, Jarrow 83
St Peter's Church, Barton-on-Humber 11
St Peter's Street 123–4
Salisbury, C R 39
Saltergate 91
saltern 76
saltmaking hearth 81
salt production 52
saltworks 134
Saunders, A D 86
Saville, A 39, 67, 192, 198, 211
Sawle, J 52
Saxon, see also Anglo-Saxon
    Alfriston 4
    Ashdown Forest 6
    Avebury 7
    Bedford 18
    Burgh Castle 27
    Butley 30
    Canterbury 32
    Christchurch 36
    Clophill 38
    Glastonbury 60
    Harting Beacon 73

Hartlepool 73
Hereford 77, 78
Ipswich 82
Jarrow 83
Kingston-upon-Thames 85
Lewes 89
Lincoln 91
London 99
Marc 3 107
Northampton 122, 123
Norwich 125, 126
Odell 128
Old Windsor 130
Praa Sands 140
Ramsbury 142
Romsey 145
Southampton 187, 189
Stafford 191
Swindon 193
Tamworth 193
Wells Cathedral 202
West Mersea 204
Willington 210
Winchester 212
York 235, 240
Saxo-Norman
   Bedford 18, 19
   Brixworth 26
   Droitwich 52
Scaife, R G 155
Schadla-Hall, T 155, 156
Schofield, J 97
Scotts Barn 141
Sedgemoor, Chedzoy Tracks 175
Shallowmead 120
Shapwick Heath, Decoy Pool Wood 176
Shapwick Heath, Skinners Wood 176
Shapwick Heath, Sweet Track 176–7
Shapwick Heath, Withy Bed Copse 177
Shapwick, Sweet Track Heath 177–80
Shapwick, Sweet Track Terminal Site 180
Shapwick Terminal Site 1, Shapwick Heath 177
Sharpham, Durston's Works 180
Sharpham, Tinney's Ground 180–3
Sheldon, H 98, 99, 100
shell midden 138
Shoesmith, R 77, 78
Sidbury 234-5
Siddaway, R 200
Silver Street (Glastonbury) 60
Silver Street (Lincoln) 91–2
Simmons, B B 22, 76, 81
Simpson, D 164
Simy Folds Bog 199–200
smelting, see iron smelting
Smith, C 56
Smith, G 137, 194

Smith, K 156, 157, 158, 161, 162, 163, 232
Southwark, Elephant and Castle Leisure Centre 99
Southwark, Hays Lane Junction Box 99
Southwark, Hibernia Wharf 99
Southwark, Mark Brown's Wharf 99–100
Southwark, 124 Borough High Street 98
Southwark, Pilgrimage Street, Chaucer House 100
Southwark, Tabard Street, Chaucer House 100
Southwark, 213 Borough High Street 98–9
Southwark, Willson's Wharf 100–1
Spong Hill 119-20
Springs Bridge 25
Stacey Bushes, MK-228 112-13
Stanford, S C 27
Stepleton Enclosure 71
Stead, I M 29
Stratton Park, R1 107
street frontages 5, 19, 123, 212
The Strood 204
Stubbs, K 145
sunken-featured buildings 193

Taylor, A F 38, 54, 145, 146
Tebbutt, F C 6
temples 35, 86, 212
tenements 189, 234
Thackray, D 140
Thetford 57
Thompson, F H 74
Thompson, R G 189
threshing floor 27
Tipping Street 191
Tower of London 101
towns 19, 53, 60, 82, 83, 89, 91, 135, 187, 189, 190, 191, 239
trackways/tracks (wooden) 165, 166, 167, 168, 169, 174, 175, 176, 177, 183, 186
Tregiffian 151–2
Tregilders 152
Trig Lane 101–2
Trowlesworthy Cross Dyke 162
Trowlesworthy Warren 162
Trudgian, P 152
Turnball, P 203
Turner's Green 76

Upper Bugle Street 189

Vatcher, F J 7, 192
Vatcher, H L 192
Viking
   York 235
villages 12, 40, 87, 208
villas 63, 124, 201, 232

Wacher, J 91
Wade, K 82
Wade-Martins, P 84, 119
Wainwright, G J 7, 145, 156, 157, 158, 161, 162, 163
walls (town/city) 63, 77, 91, 94, 95, 234, 235
Walmgate 241-2
Walton Heath 183
Walton Heath, Bisgrove 183
Walton Heath, Garvin's Tracks 183-4
Walton Heath, Jones' Track 184
Walton Heath, Walton Meare 185
Warbleton 76
Ward, A 137
Watch Hill 153
watercourse 93
waterfronts 62, 84, 94, 96, 97, 101, 126, 138
Water Hall Farm 36
water mill 193
Wayford Bridge 165
weir 39
wells 4, 38, 200, 209
West, S E 204
Westgate Street 189
Westhay Level, Baker Platform 185–6
Westhay Level, Baker Track 186
Westhay Level, Honeygore Complex 186-7
Westminster, Cromwell Green 102
Westminster, Jewel Tower 102-3
Westminster, New Palace Yard 103
West Row Fen, Gravel Drove, MNL-124 110–11
West Row Fen, MNL-130 111
West Row Fen, MNL-137 111
Wheeler, H 210
Whimster, R 71
Whitefriars 126-7
Whitwell, B 20
Whitwell, J B 10
Wildgoose, M 25
Willcox, J 95
Williams, J 122, 123
Williams, R 85
Wills, J 15
Winnall Down R17 107–9
Winton Hill 4-5
Wollaston House 52
Woodward, P 38
Woodward, P J 141, 145, 146
Wotter Common, site 69 163
Wotter Playground, site 201 163

Yule, B 99, 100

Index 2: HAR numbers index

by Lesley and Roy Adkins

This index enables the reader to find the entries for individual HAR numbers without necessarily knowing the relevant site or excavator. The page references refer to the main date list.

HAR	Page	HAR	Page	HAR	Page	HAR	Page
H79/85	131	HAR-475	33	HAR-711	145–6	HAR-947	181
HAR-125	131	HAR-476	33	HAR-715	38	HAR-948	181–2
HAR-190(S)	133	HAR-477	33	HAR-717	31	HAR-949	12
HAR-191	133	HAR-483	26	HAR-718	131–2	HAR-950	12
HAR-209	131	HAR-484	26	HAR-728	188	HAR-951	12
HAR-234	81	HAR-485	27	HAR-729	132	HAR-952	12
HAR-235(S)	233–4	HAR-486	72	HAR-730	132	HAR-953	12
HAR-237	34	HAR-487	30	HAR-748	215–16	HAR-954	12
HAR-238	34	HAR-488	30	HAR-749	216	HAR-956	210
HAR-266	67	HAR-489	30	HAR-750	216	HAR-957	210
HAR-267	67	HAR-490	30	HAR-751	216	HAR-958	137
HAR-268	25	HAR-491	30–1	HAR-752	216	HAR-959	137
HAR-269	67	HAR-492	31	HAR-753	216	HAR-960	83
HAR-288	213	HAR-493	31	HAR-754	217	HAR-961	83
HAR-289	213	HAR-494	31	HAR-755	217	HAR-962	140
HAR-290	213	HAR-495	31	HAR-757	217	HAR-963	42–3
HAR-291	214	HAR-496	31	HAR-758	217	HAR-964	43
HAR-292	214	HAR-497	31	HAR-759	119	HAR-965	43
HAR-328	187	HAR-506	15	HAR-760	119	HAR-966	43
HAR-329	103	HAR-507	15	HAR-763	119	HAR-968	43
HAR-330	103	HAR-508	38	HAR-826	53	HAR-969	153–4
HAR-331	103	HAR-509	38	HAR-827	53	HAR-970	41
HAR-332	103	HAR-510	38	HAR-828	53	HAR-971	41
HAR-333	100	HAR-512	209	HAR-829	53	HAR-972	41
HAR-334	34	HAR-513	209	HAR-830	53	HAR-973	41
HAR-335	34	HAR-548	239	HAR-831	53–4	HAR-974	41
HAR-339	112	HAR-549	239–40	HAR-842	115	HAR-975	41
HAR-354	214	HAR-55O	240	HAR-843	115	HAR-976	19
HAR-362	214	HAR-551	240	HAR-844	196	HAR-978	86
HAR-363	214	HAR-552	39	HAR-845	196	HAR-979	87
HAR-366	215	HAR-568	189	HAR-846	39	HAR-980	87
HAR-367	215	HAR-569	187–8	HAR-847	20	HAR-981	87
HAR-368	215	HAR-570	188	HAR-855	112	HAR-983	87
HAR-369	215	HAR-572	188	HAR-856	112	HAR-984	87
HAR-413	79	HAR-573	188	HAR-857	112	HAR-985	79
HAR-414	79	HAR-599	53	HAR-858	113	HAR-986	79
HAR-418	132	HAR-601	53	HAR-860	112	HAR-987	18–19
HAR-419	132	HAR-602	53	HAR-863	91	HAR-988	79
HAR-442	8	HAR-603	113	HAR-865	92	HAR-992	37
HAR-443	8	HAR-604	113	HAR-872	111–12	HAR-993	139
HAR-444	8	HAR-605	113	HAR-873	112	HAR-994	139
HAR-445	8	HAR-606	113	HAR-876	217	HAR-995	139
HAR-446	8	HAR-607-I	38	HAR-877	217–18	HAR-996	139
HAR-447	91–2	HAR-607-II	38	HAR-878	218	HAR-997	146
HAR-448	124	HAR-607-III	38	HAR-879	218	HAR-998	146
HAR-449	30	HAR-645	203	HAR-880	218	HAR-999	146
HAR-450	115	HAR-646	203	HAR-881	218	HAR-1000	146–7
HAR-451	116	HAR-647	203–4	HAR-882	218–19	HAR-1001	147
HAR-452	136	HAR-648	204	HAR-883	219	HAR-1002	147
HAR-453	136	HAR-649	167	HAR-884	219	HAR-1003	147
HAR-455	192	HAR-650	176	HAR-885	219	HAR-1004	147
HAR-456	192	HAR-651	187	HAR-886	219	HAR-1006	37
HAR-457	154	HAR-652	187	HAR-887	219–20	HAR-1009	37
HAR-459	154	HAR-653	187	HAR-888	220	HAR-1010	37
HAR-460	154	HAR-654	153	HAR-889	220	HAR-1011	28-9
HAR-466-I	132	HAR-655	153	HAR-940	4	HAR-1012	29
HAR-466-II	132	HAR-680	168	HAR-942	4	HAR-1013	29
HAR-467	115	HAR-681	181	HAR-943	170	HAR-1021	104
HAR-468	115	HAR-682	184	HAR-944	177	HAR-1023	104
HAR-469	115	HAR-683	169	HAR-945	181	HAR-1024	89
HAR-470	115	HAR-684	181	HAR-946	181	HAR-1025	89

HAR-1038 128	HAR-1162 15	HAR-1384 178	HAR-1515 226
HAR-1039 104	HAR-1163 190	HAR-1393 20	HAR-1516 226
HAR-1040 104	HAR-1164 188	HAR-1394 20	HAR-1517 226
HAR-1041 105	HAR-1165 188	HAR-1398 197	HAR-1518 226
HAR-1042 105	HAR-1166 188	HAR-1410 25–6	HAR-1519 226
HAR-1043 105	HAR-1167 188	HAR-1411 3–4	HAR-1520 227
HAR-1044 105–6	HAR-1185 4	HAR-1412 236	HAR-1521 227
HAR-1047 93	HAR-1186 3	HAR-1416 236	HAR-1531 227
HAR-1057 29	HAR-1191 188	HAR-1417 237	HAR-1534 227
HAR-1058 29	HAR-1192 196	HAR-1418 237	HAR-1537 227
HAR-1060 220	HAR-1195 114	HAR-1420 141	HAR-1551 227
HAR-1061 220	HAR-1196 114	HAR-1421 98	HAR-1561 227–8
HAR-1062 220	HAR-1197 114	HAR-1422 98	HAR-1563 228
HAR-1063 220–1	HAR-1201 94	HAR-1425 43	HAR-1564 228
HAR-1064 221	HAR-1204 71	HAR-1426 45	HAR-1565 228
HAR-1065 221	HAR-1205 9	HAR-1427 128	HAR-1573 228
HAR-1066 221	HAR-1206 9	HAR-1428 128	HAR-1574 228
HAR-1067 221	HAR-1207 9	HAR-1430 9	HAR-1580 228
HAR-1068 221	HAR-1219 184	HAR-1431 124	HAR-1582 229
HAR-1069 221–2	HAR-1220 185	HAR-1432 102	HAR-1583 229
HAR-1070 222	HAR-1221 175	HAR-1433 102–3	HAR-1584 229
HAR-1075 222	HAR-1222 184	HAR-1437 124	HAR-1587 229
HAR-1076 222	HAR-1225 123	HAR-1440 43-4	HAR-1588 229
HAR-1077 222	HAR-1226 210	HAR-1442 44	HAR-1590 94
HAR-1078 222	HAR-1227 58	HAR-1443 62	HAR-1591 13
HAR-1079 64	HAR-1228 58	HAR-1444 62	HAR-1603 229
HAR-1080 65	HAR-1234 210	HAR-1446 62	HAR-1604 229
HAR-1081 93	HAR-1235 58	HAR-1448 31–2	HAR-1605 233
HAR-1082 93	HAR-1236 58	HAR-1451 196–7	HAR-1606 142
HAR-1083 95	HAR-1237 5	HAR-1452 124	HAR-1607 142
HAR-1084 222	HAR-1244 123	HAR-1454 124	HAR-1608 142
HAR-1085 133	HAR-1245 123	HAR-1456 94	HAR-1609 142
HAR-1086 22	HAR-1246 123	HAR-1457 94	HAR-1610 230
HAR-1087 93	HAR-1247 1	HAR-1464 94	HAR-1611 . . . . . . 54 5
HAR-1088 93	HAR-1248 1	HAR-1465 174–5	HAR-1612 9
HAR-1089 134	HAR-1249 1	HAR-1467 185	HAR-1613 55
HAR-1090 134	HAR-1257 223	HAR-1468 185	HAR-1614 55
HAR-1091 134	HAR-1259 223	HAR-1469 178	HAR-1620 77
HAR-1092 134	HAR-1260 78	HAR-1470 185	HAR-1621 13
HAR-1096 128	HAR-1261 210–11	HAR-1471 185	HAR-1626 142
HAR-1100 1	HAR-1271 223–4	HAR-1472 178–9	HAR-1627 170
HAR-1101 223	HAR-1274 58	HAR-1473 179	HAR-1630 117
HAR-1102 223	HAR-1275 58	HAR-1475 179	HAR-1632 116
HAR-1103 223	HAR-1277 224	HAR-1476 179	HAR-1633 116
HAR-1116 37	HAR-1278 224	HAR-1477 179	HAR-1634 117–18
HAR-1117 223	HAR-1279 224	HAR-1478 179	HAR-1636 62
HAR-1118 196	HAR-1282 58	HAR-1479 179–80	HAR-1638 26
HAR-1119 196	HAR-1283 58	HAR-1480 180	HAR-1639 230
HAR-1120 93	HAR-1284 58–9	HAR-1486 188–9	HAR-1645 9
HAR-1121 135	HAR-1289 75	HAR-1488 224	HAR-1646 204
HAR-1122 113–14	HAR-1290 75	HAR-1489 170	HAR-1648 130
HAR-1123 114	HAR-1296 59	HAR-1491 224–5	HAR-1649 130
HAR-1125 114	HAR-1318 99	HAR-1492 32	HAR-1652 60–1
HAR-1126 114	HAR-1320 68	HAR-1493 32	HAR-1653 100
HAR-1127 114	HAR-1323 68	HAR-1494 170	HAR-1655 61
HAR-1129 29	HAR-1325 193	HAR-1495 66	HAR-1656 61
HAR-1130 29–30	HAR-1326 193	HAR-1497 66	HAR-1657 61
HAR-1142 210	HAR-1329 208	HAR-1498 66	HAR-1658 61
HAR-1143 210	HAR-1332 1	HAR-1500 12–13	HAR-1662 22–3
HAR-1145 65	HAR-1333 1–2	HAR-1501 13	HAR-1663 23
HAR-1147 65	HAR-1334 2	HAR-1502 13	HAR-1664 143
HAR-1148 65	HAR-1335 2	HAR-1503 13	HAR-1665 206
HAR-1149 65	HAR-1337 208	HAR-1506 13	HAR-1666 118–19
HAR-1150 65	HAR-1339 63	HAR-1507 13	HAR-1673 189
HAR-1153 65	HAR-1342 2	HAR-1508 225	HAR-1676 130
HAR-1154 65–6	HAR-1374 55	HAR-1509 225	HAR-1677 230
HAR-1155 66	HAR-1375 78	HAR-1510 225	HAR-1678 230
HAR-1156 9	HAR-1378 4–5	HAR-1511 225	HAR-1680 230
HAR-1158 9	HAR-1379 178	HAR-1512 225	HAR-1681 119
HAR-1159 176	HAR-1383 166	HAR-1513 226	HAR-1685 211

HAR-1686 230–1	HAR-1875 79–80	HAR-2118 240–1	HAR-2347 13
HAR-1687 231	HAR-1876 110–1	HAR-2122 241	HAR-2368 69–70
HAR-1688 231	HAR-1878 206	HAR-2157 15	HAR-2371 70
HAR-1689 57	HAR-1879 206	HAR-2158 195	HAR-2372 70
HAR-1690 57	HAR-1882 69	HAR-2184 13	HAR-2375 70
HAR-1695 103	HAR-1885 69	HAR-2185 189	HAR-2377 70
HAR-1696 7	HAR-1886 69	HAR-2194 107	HAR-2378 70
HAR-1698 75	HAR-1894 33	HAR-2195 107–8	HAR-2379 70
HAR-1699 75	HAR-1895 33	HAR-2196 108	HAR-2387 2
HAR-1700 75	HAR-1896 18	HAR-2201 108	HAR-2388 2
HAR-1701 75	HAR-1897 18	HAR-2202 108	HAR-2389 121
HAR-1702 152	HAR-1899 201	HAR-2207 73	HAR-2390 134
HAR-1703 107	HAR-1908 194	HAR-2208 208	HAR-2398 119
HAR-1704 142	HAR-1909 194	HAR-2209 200	HAR-2399 211
HAR-1708 118	HAR-1910 55	HAR-2213 161	HAR-2404 144
HAR-1715 154	HAR-1913 97	HAR-2214 161–2	HAR-2407 211
HAR-1717 96	HAR-1914 234–5	HAR-2216 162	HAR-2408 211
HAR-1719 165	HAR-1915 235	HAR-2219 162	HAR-2409 211
HAR-1720 124	HAR-1916 235	HAR-2220 162	HAR-2410 211
HAR-1724 94–5	HAR-1917 97	HAR-2221 162	HAR-2411 73
HAR-1725 201	HAR-1918 97	HAR-2222 93	HAR-2412 140
HAR-1726 154	HAR-1922 71	HAR-2223 6–7	HAR-2416 101
HAR-1728 237	HAR-1923 71–2	HAR-2224 167	HAR-2417 101–2
HAR-1729 237	HAR-1925 55	HAR-2227 152	HAR-2418 102
HAR-1735 78	HAR-1926 55	HAR-2234 241	HAR-2419 102
HAR-1737 231	HAR-1927 237	HAR-2235 241	HAR-2425 102
HAR-1738 231	HAR-1928 237–8	HAR-2236 241	HAR-2426 102
HAR-1739 231	HAR-1929 18	HAR-2237 241	HAR-2427 144–5
HAR-1740 231	HAR-1930 18	HAR-2239 101	HAR-2428 174
HAR-1741 232	HAR-1931 63	HAR-2243 182	HAR-2429 182
HAR-1749 81	HAR-1954 135	HAR-2251 108	HAR-2446 13–14
HAR-1750 81	HAR-1961 89–90	HAR-2252 108	HAR-2448 14
HAR-1764 232–3	HAR-2005 42	HAR-2255 31	HAR-2449 14
HAR-1765 233	HAR-2006 42	HAR-2256 7	HAR-2456 14
HAR-1778 233	HAR-2007 202	HAR-2257 2	HAR-2457 14
HAR-1779 201	HAR-2008 202	HAR-2258 7	HAR-2458 14
HAR-1787 61	HAR-2010 90	HAR-2259 7	HAR-2459 14
HAR-1788 61	HAR-2011 90	HAR-2260 25	HAR-2460 208
HAR-1794 233	HAR-2012 90	HAR-2261 21	HAR-2462 208
HAR-1801 44	HAR-2013 192	HAR-2262 85	HAR-2466 74
HAR-1811 4	HAR-2015 143–4	HAR-2263 52	HAR-2467 74
HAR-1820 234	HAR-2016 144	HAR-2264 52	HAR-2468 85
HAR-1821 234	HAR-2017 144	HAR-2265 56	HAR-2469 56
HAR-1822 234	HAR-2018 144	HAR-2266 85	HAR-2470 56–7
HAR-1823 232	HAR-2019 144	HAR-2274 192	HAR-2471 57
HAR-1830 156	HAR-2021 144	HAR-2275 192	HAR-2472 159
HAR-1831 165	HAR-2024 194–5	HAR-2276 24–5	HAR-2473 159
HAR-1832 134	HAR-2025 195	HAR-2277 25	HAR-2474 159
HAR-1833 148	HAR-2027 107	HAR-2278 138	HAR-2475 159
HAR-1834 148	HAR-2028 44	HAR-2279 147–8	HAR-2482 155
HAR-1837 89	HAR-2029 44	HAR-2280 76	HAR-2483 21–2
HAR-1838 128	HAR-2030 44	HAR-2281 139	HAR-2484 206
HAR-1841 15	HAR-2031 44	HAR-2282 120	HAR-2486 59
HAR-1842 168	HAR-2032 44–5	HAR-2283 120	HAR-2488 59
HAR-1843 176	HAR-2033 45	HAR-2285 162	HAR-2489 59
HAR-1844 201–2	HAR-2034 45	HAR-2289 198	HAR-2490 59
HAR-1850 164–5	HAR-2035 45	HAR-2300 235	HAR-2491 59
HAR-1851 232	HAR-2036 45	HAR-2301 235	HAR-2492 59
HAR-1852 232	HAR-2037 45	HAR-2302 235	HAR-2493 59
HAR-1853 189	HAR-2038 45	HAR-2326 144	HAR-2497 85
HAR-1854 168	HAR-2039 45	HAR-2336 193	HAR-2498 85
HAR-1855 180	HAR-2040 45–6	HAR-2337 116	HAR-2499 98
HAR-1856 183	HAR-2041 69	HAR-2338 116	HAR-2501 98
HAR-1857 176–7	HAR-2073 134	HAR-2339 116	HAR-2502 56
HAR-1864 96–7	HAR-2085 46	HAR-2340 116	HAR-2504 100
HAR-1865 97	HAR-2090 189	HAR-2341 116	HAR-2506 100
HAR-1866 237	HAR-2105 240	HAR-2342 116	HAR-2507 14
HAR-1867 97	HAR-2111 240	HAR-2343 116–17	HAR-2508 14
HAR-1868 97	HAR-2113 240	HAR-2344 117	HAR-2510 111
HAR-1869 165	HAR-2114 240	HAR-2346 99	HAR-2516 111

HAR-2517 111	HAR-2673 162	HAR-2846 186	HAR-3027 48
HAR-2523 22	HAR-2674 195–6	HAR-2851 129	HAR-3039 191
HAR-2524 98	HAR-2676 157	HAR-2853 129	HAR-3041 74
HAR-2527 145	HAR-2689 191	HAR-2856 52	HAR-3046 157–8
HAR-2530 95	HAR-2690 111	HAR-2858 194	HAR-3056 74
HAR-2531 83–4	HAR-2692 102	HAR-2860 194	HAR-3058 71
HAR-2532 95	HAR-2693 106	HAR-2861 194	HAR-3060 71
HAR-2534 95	HAR-2694 157	HAR-2863 11	HAR-3061 70–1
HAR-2535 64	HAR-2696 102	HAR-2864 11	HAR-3062 71
HAR-2536 5	HAR-2697 69	HAR-2865 11	HAR-3064 39
HAR-2538 182	HAR-2698 98	HAR-2892 136	HAR-3065 86
HAR-2539 84–5	HAR-2700 125	HAR-2893 117	HAR-3066 86
HAR-2541 92	HAR-2701 125	HAR-2896 232	HAR-3067 39
HAR-2542 97	HAR-2702 125	HAR-2897 30	HAR-3069 21
HAR-2544 182	HAR-2703 35	HAR-2898 238	HAR-3073 9–10
HAR-2545 135	HAR-2708 239	HAR-2899 238	HAR-3074 10
HAR-2548 97	HAR-2732 3	HAR-2900 238	HAR-3075 10
HAR-2549 135	HAR-2733 99	HAR-2901 119–20	HAR-3078 184
HAR-2559 68	HAR-2734 193	HAR-2902 10	HAR-3079 140
HAR-2560 124	HAR-2736 20	HAR-2903 120	HAR-3080 140
HAR-2564 46	HAR-2745 104	HAR-2905 57	HAR-3081 140
HAR-2567 46	HAR-2749 28	HAR-2907 37	HAR-3083 129
HAR-2568 46	HAR-2753 238	HAR-2910 83	HAR-3084 35
HAR-2571 46	HAR-2754 28	HAR-2911 117	HAR-3085 35–6
HAR-2572 35	HAR-2756 80	HAR-2913 129	HAR-3086 36
HAR-2573 46	HAR-2757 80	HAR-2915 236	HAR-3088 236
HAR-2577 191	HAR-2760 66	HAR-2916 236	HAR-3089 236
HAR-2578 191	HAR-2761 66–7	HAR-2917 87	HAR-3090 82
HAR-2580 35	HAR-2762 109	HAR-2919 186	HAR-3091 82
HAR-2581 46	HAR-2763 82	HAR-2920 186	HAR-3092 81
HAR-2582 191	HAR-2764 82	HAR-2929 28	HAR-3093 15–16
HAR-2585 46–7	HAR-2765 103	HAR-2930 76	HAR-3094 16
HAR-2586 47	HAR-2766 103	HAR-2932 76	HAR-3095 16
HAR-2587 238	HAR-2768 80	HAR-2935 24	HAR-3096 16
HAR-2588 238	HAR-2769 107	HAR-2937 109	HAR-3097 16
HAR-2589 198–9	HAR-2770 106	HAR-2938 109	HAR-3100 234
HAR-2590 193	HAR-2771 106	HAR-2939 23	HAR-3101 22
HAR-2591 108	HAR-2772 177	HAR-2940 23	HAR-3102 76–7
HAR-2592 108–9	HAR-2773 182–3	HAR-2941 23	HAR-3103 96
HAR-2593 86	HAR-2774 138	HAR-2959 72	HAR-3104 96
HAR-2594 68	HAR-2775 138	HAR-2960 159	HAR-3105 96
HAR-2595 68	HAR-2776 207	HAR-2968 159	HAR-3106 11
HAR-2599 20	HAR-2777 207	HAR-2969 47	HAR-3107 136
HAR-2600 20–1	HAR-2778 82–3	HAR-2970 47	HAR-3108 136
HAR-2602 156	HAR-2780 106	HAR-2971 47	HAR-3109 40
HAR-2604 106	HAR-2781 83	HAR-2972 47	HAR-3111 54
HAR-2606 68–9	HAR-2795 106	HAR-2973 47	HAR-3112 148
HAR-2607 121	HAR-2799 106	HAR-2974 47	HAR-3113 148
HAR-2612 156	HAR-2800 106	HAR-2975 47	HAR-3114 148–9
HAR-2614 7	HAR-2802 128–9	HAR-2976 159	HAR-3115 149
HAR-2616 174	HAR-2803 75	HAR-2978 160	HAR-3116 149
HAR-2617 152	HAR-2804 195	HAR-2979 160	HAR-3117 149
HAR-2619 170	HAR-2805 87	HAR-2980 109	HAR-3118 149
HAR-2620 171	HAR-2806 195	HAR-2983 160	HAR-3119 149
HAR-2622 152	HAR-2809 75	HAR-2986 160	HAR-3120 149
HAR-2624 153	HAR-2810 22	HAR-2987 160	HAR-3121 64
HAR-2625 121	HAR-2812 60	HAR-2989 160	HAR-3122 64
HAR-2627 239	HAR-2813 60	HAR-2991 153	HAR-3123 10
HAR-2628 239	HAR-2814 60	HAR-2992 145	HAR-3124 10
HAR-2629 239	HAR-2815 195	HAR-2994 153	HAR-3125 10
HAR-2631 208–9	HAR-2816 73	HAR-2997 77	HAR-3126 10
HAR-2652 109	HAR-2817 75	HAR-2998 77	HAR-3127 11
HAR-2653 109	HAR-2818 76	HAR-3000 142–3	HAR-3128 11
HAR-2654 171	HAR-2819 73	HAR-3014 67	HAR-3129 190
HAR-2657 199	HAR-2823 156	HAR-3015 67	HAR-3130 190
HAR-2668 171	HAR-2825 88	HAR-3017 76	HAR-3131 190
HAR-2669 163	HAR-2829 120	HAR-3021 48	HAR-3132 190
HAR-2670 86	HAR-2843 185–6	HAR-3022 48	HAR-3133 190
HAR-2671 156	HAR-2844 186	HAR-3023 74	HAR-3140 62
HAR-2672 209	HAR-2845 186	HAR-3026 48	HAR-3174 24

HAR-3195 167	HAR-3493 5–6	HAR-3752 149–50	HAR-4005 161
HAR-3197 34–5	HAR-3494 6	HAR-3756 241	HAR-4008 158
HAR-3208 121	HAR-3495 6	HAR-3757 241–2	HAR-4013 161
HAR-3235 191	HAR-3496 6	HAR-3758 242	HAR-4017 162
HAR-3264 110	HAR-3521 172	HAR-3759 150	HAR-4033 137
HAR-3265 198	HAR-3535 172	HAR-3760 145	HAR-4044 62
HAR-3268 198	HAR-3546 172	HAR-3761 150	HAR-4052 137
HAR-3269 198	HAR-3575 209	HAR-3762 150	HAR-4054 205
HAR-3270 203	HAR-3584 209	HAR-3764 40	HAR-4055 205
HAR-3290 203	HAR-3585 125	HAR-3765 145	HAR-4057 121
HAR-3291 187	HAR-3590 158	HAR-3767 40	HAR-4058 121
HAR-3313 118	HAR-3591 163	HAR-3768 40	HAR-4064 127
HAR-3344 105	HAR-3592 161	HAR-3790 242	HAR-4065 121
HAR-3347 118	HAR-3593 157	HAR-3791 199	HAR-4066 121
HAR-3353 101	HAR-3594 157	HAR-3794 27	HAR-4067 121–2
HAR-3358 160	HAR-3595 82	HAR-3795 27–8	HAR-4071 122
HAR-3359 156	HAR-3596 82	HAR-3804 28	HAR-4072 122
HAR-3360 156–7	HAR-3599 80	HAR-3808 204	HAR-4073 122
HAR-3362 200	HAR-3607 80	HAR-3812 163	HAR-4074 122
HAR-3363 101	HAR-3608 80	HAR-3816 163	HAR-4075 122
HAR-3368 118	HAR-3610 8	HAR-3818 86	HAR-4076 199–200
HAR-3369 204	HAR-3611 126	HAR-3838 168	HAR-4078 183
HAR-3374 202	HAR-3616 143	HAR-3844 242	HAR-4084 52
HAR-3375 202	HAR-3617 143	HAR-3852 126–7	HAR-4086 26
HAR-3376 202	HAR-3618 143	HAR-3864 173	HAR-4087 26
HAR-3377 157	HAR-3620 59–60	HAR-3877 127	HAR-4089 122
HAR-3379 157	HAR-3624 17	HAR-3878 127	HAR-4092 122
HAR-3380 157	HAR-3629 129	HAR-3880 36	HAR-4093 205
HAR-3381 204	HAR-3630 126	HAR-3881 242	HAR-4111 205
HAR-3382 204–5	HAR-3633 172	HAR-3883 199	HAR-4115 95–6
HAR-3386 184–5	HAR-3634 172	HAR-3884 199	HAR-4116 90
HAR-3387 184	HAR-3653 36	HAR-3885 148	HAR-4117 6
HAR-3388 183	HAR-3654 36	HAR-3891 173	HAR-4120 90
HAR-3390 187	HAR-3655 36	HAR-3892 173	HAR-4121 90
HAR-3391 110	HAR-3656 125	HAR-3896 174	HAR-4130 176
HAR-3393 110	HAR-3657 200	HAR-3898 199	HAR-4131 91
HAR-3397 202	HAR-3658 200–1	HAR-3899 48–9	HAR-4143 91
HAR-3398 202	HAR-3686 201	HAR-3901 49	HAR-4145 205
HAR-3409+HAR3410 133	HAR-3687 126	HAR-3906 130	HAR-4146 205
HAR-3417 105	HAR-3688 123	HAR-3907 242	HAR-4147 205
HAR-3418 160–1	HAR-3689 123	HAR-3908 6	HAR-4177 91
HAR-3419 161	HAR-3693 172	HAR-3910 242	HAR-4181 163
HAR-3422 164	HAR-3694 155	HAR-3916 242	HAR-4187 63
HAR-3423 102	HAR-3695 155	HAR-3925 101	HAR-4191 205
HAR-3424 163–4	HAR-3706 88	HAR-3926 101	HAR-4194 205
HAR-3427 164	HAR-3707 125–6	HAR-3927 101	HAR-4203 56
HAR-3428 164	HAR-3710 32	HAR-3931 99	HAR-4206 49
HAR-3429 164	HAR-3712 34	HAR-3935 123	HAR-4207 49
HAR-3430 164	HAR-3719 172–3	HAR-3937 140–1	HAR-4208 49
HAR-3432 118	HAR-3720 40	HAR-3938 141	HAR-4240 158
HAR-3433 3	HAR-3721 40	HAR-3939 141	HAR-4243 49
HAR-3434 3	HAR-3722 126	HAR-3941 54	HAR-4244 49
HAR-3436 19	HAR-3723 155	HAR-3942 54	HAR-4248 158
HAR-3437 19	HAR-3724 155	HAR-3944 16	HAR-4250 127
HAR-3438 19	HAR-3726 48	HAR-3945 16	HAR-4251 127–8
HAR-3443 129–30	HAR-3733 48	HAR-3947 16	HAR-4252 131
HAR-3444 130	HAR-3735 23	HAR-3950 16	HAR-4255 205
HAR-3446 177	HAR-3736 23	HAR-3951 16	HAR-4257 150
HAR-3447 166	HAR-3737 24	HAR-3952 17	HAR-4260 88
HAR-3448 167	HAR-3740 173	HAR-3953 17	HAR-4262 211
HAR-3449 167	HAR-3741 88	HAR-3954 17–18	HAR-4263 211–12
HAR-3452 21	HAR-3742 89	HAR-3955 17	HAR-4264 150
HAR-3456 21	HAR-3743 48	HAR-3957 141	HAR-4265 150
HAR-3462 138	HAR-3744 173	HAR-3968 27	HAR-4266 150
HAR-3463 138	HAR-3745 173	HAR-3970 27	HAR-4267 150
HAR-3483 155	HAR-3747 72	HAR-3971 63	HAR-4268 150
HAR-3484 64	HAR-3748 203	HAR-3976 24	HAR-4269 150
HAR-3485 92	HAR-3749 32	HAR-3977 24	HAR-4270 151
HAR-3489 171	HAR-3750 149	HAR-4001 17	HAR-4272 151
HAR-3492 171–2	HAR-3751 159	HAR-4003 161	HAR-4273 151

HAR-4274 151	HAR-4325 50	HAR-4374 175	HAR-4468 51
HAR-4275 151	HAR-4327 50	HAR-4375 175	HAR-4470 51–2
HAR-4277 151	HAR-4328 50	HAR-4413 151	HAR-4477 175
HAR-4278 49	HAR-4329 50	HAR-4425 207	HAR-4494 127
HAR-4279 50	HAR-4330 50	HAR-4426 207	HAR-4541 180
HAR-4281 91	HAR-4331 50	HAR-4427 207	HAR-4542 168–9
HAR-4282 197	HAR-4337 50–1	HAR-4428 207	HAR-4543 169
HAR-4283 197	HAR-4339 51	HAR-4439 17	HAR-4544 169
HAR-4284 197	HAR-4340 151	HAR-4440 17	HAR-4739 166
HAR-4285+HAR-4530 197	HAR-4341 151	HAR-4442 17	HAR-5921 212
HAR-4316 84	HAR-4343 51	HAR-4447 40–1	HAR-5921+HAR-4352 212
HAR-4317 84	HAR-4352 212	HAR-4449 41	HAR-5922 212
HAR-4319 84	HAR-4366 51	HAR-4464 51	HAR-5922+HAR-4263 212
HAR-4320 84	HAR-4372 51	HAR-4466 51	

Index 3: Period index

by Alex Bayliss

This index presents the radiocarbon results in the order of true calendrical date. Time is divided into 500-year bands. All results whose maximum-intercept calibrated date range at two standard deviations overlaps a band are listed under that section. A result which spans several bands appears more than once. Results are listed in four columns within each section:

1) **Sample**: the laboratory sample number

2) **Period**: a period definition based on the calibrated date range at two standard deviations. A date range which spans mre than one period is given a compound definition. We have adapted the periods nomenclature used by RCHME for the National Archaeological Record, but have added chronological limits for prehistoric periods.

PA	Palaeolithic	until 10,000 BP
MME	Mesolithic	10,000 BP–4,000 cal BC
NE	Neolithic	4,000–2,500 cal BC
BA	Bronze Age	2,500–600 cal BC
IA	Iron Age	cal BC 600–43 cal AD
RO	Roman	43–410 cal AD
EM	early medieval	410–1066 cal AD
MD	medieval	1066–1540 cal AD
PM	post medieval	1540–1955 cal AD

See the Introduction for an explanation of 'modern' dates.

This column is not intended to imply anything about the material culture associated with a sample. It is intended as a rough guide so that, in conjunction with the other indexes provided, readers can find all the results from a particular class of site (eg Bronze Age from this column, barrows from the general index).

3) **Date**: the expected date of the sample as defined by the submitter before dating. These are divided into the same broad periods used above, although the terms do not have the same closely defined chronological implications.

4) **Page**: the page upon which a date appears in the main text.

Sample	Period	Date	Page

Results older than 7000 cal BC

Sample	Period	Date	Page
HAR-1039		BA	104
HAR-1702		NE	152
HAR-2590	MME	MME	193
HAR-2762		PA	109
HAR-2903		MME/NE	120
HAR-2917		PA	87
HAR-3360		PA	156–7
HAR-3380			157
HAR-4260			88
HAR-455	PA/MME		192
HAR-456	PA/MME		192
HAR-492		NE/BA	31
HAR-645	PA/MME	BA	203
HAR-844	MME		196
HAR-998	MME	BA	146

Results 7000–6500 cal BC

Sample	Period	Date	Page
HAR-2535	MME		64
HAR-2590	MME	MME	193
HAR-455	PA/MME		192
HAR-456	PA/MME		192
HAR-645	PA/MME	BA	203
HAR-844	MME		196
HAR-998	MME	BA	146

Results 6500–6000 cal BC

Sample	Period	Date	Page
HAR-1043	MME	NE/BA	105
HAR-1916	MME	RO/EM	235
HAR-2407	MME		211
HAR-2535	MME		64
HAR-2590	MME	MME	193
HAR-2673	MME		162
HAR-844	MME		196
HAR-998	MME	BA	146

Results 6000–5500 cal BC

Sample	Period	Date	Page
HAR-1043	MME	NE/BA	105
HAR-1320	MME	IA	68
HAR-1646	MME	BA	204
HAR-1685	MME		211
HAR-1855	MME		180
HAR-1916	MME	RO/EM	235
HAR-2407	MME		211
HAR-2671	MME		156
HAR-2673	MME		162
HAR-844	MME		196

Results 5500–5000 cal BC

Sample	Period	Date	Page
HAR-1043	MME	NE/BA	105

Sample	Period	Date	Page	Sample	Period	Date	Page
HAR-1320	MME	IA	68	HAR-1118	MME/NE		196
HAR-1685	MME		211	HAR-1226	NE		210
HAR-1855	MME		180	HAR-1261	MME/NE		210–11
HAR-2676	MME		157	HAR-1384	MME/NE	NE	178
HAR-3695	MME		155	HAR-1411	NE	NE	3–4
HAR-4076	MME		199–200	HAR-1469	MME/NE	NE	178
HAR-844	MME		196	HAR-1472	MME/NE	NE	178–9
HAR-956	MME	BA/IA	210	HAR-1473	MME/NE	NE	179
				HAR-1475	MME/NE	NE	179

Results 5000–4500 cal BC

Sample	Period	Date	Page
HAR-1831	MME		165
HAR-1856	MME		183
HAR-2282	MME	NE	120
HAR-2676	MME		157
HAR-3590	MME		158
HAR-3594	MME		157
HAR-3695	MME		155
HAR-4072	MME	NE	122
HAR-4076	MME		199–200
HAR-4092	MME	NE	122
HAR-4541	MME		180
HAR-956	MME	BA/IA	210

Sample	Period	Date	Page
HAR-1476	MME/NE	NE	179
HAR-1478	NE	NE	179
HAR-1479	NE	NE	179–80
HAR-1480	NE	NE	180
HAR-1497	NE		66
HAR-1498	NE		66
HAR-1501	NE	EM	13
HAR-1850	NE	NE	164–5
HAR-1857	MME/NE		176–7
HAR-1869	MME/NE	NE	165
HAR-1882	NE	NE	69
HAR-1885	NE	NE	69
HAR-1886	NE	NE	69
HAR-2196	NE		108
HAR-2201	NE		108
HAR-2202	NE		108
HAR-2224	NE	NE	167

Results 4500–4000 cal BC

Sample	Period	Date	Page
HAR-1010	MME/NE	RO	37
HAR-1087	MME/NE	NE	93
HAR-1116	MME/NE	RO	37
HAR-1118	MME/NE		196
HAR-1261	MME/NE		210–11
HAR-1384	MME/NE	NE	178
HAR-1469	MME/NE	NE	178
HAR-1472	MME/NE	NE	178–9
HAR-1473	MME/NE	NE	179
HAR-1475	MME/NE	NE	179
HAR-1476	MME/NE	NE	179
HAR-1831	MME		165
HAR-1856	MME		183
HAR-1857	MME/NE		176–7
HAR-1869	MME/NE	NE	165
HAR-2258	MME/NE		7
HAR-2282	MME	NE	120
HAR-2616	MME/NE		174
HAR-3133	MME/NE	BA	190
HAR-3195	MME/NE		167
HAR-3590	MME		158
HAR-3594	MME		157
HAR-4072	MME	NE	122
HAR-4092	MME	NE	122
HAR-4541	MME		180

Sample	Period	Date	Page
HAR-2258	MME/NE		7
HAR-2371	NE	NE	70
HAR-2375	NE	NE	70
HAR-2377	NE	NE	70
HAR-2378	NE	NE	70
HAR-2399	NE		211
HAR-2408	NE		211
HAR-2409	NE		211
HAR-2410	NE		211
HAR-2428	NE	BA	174
HAR-2612	NE		156
HAR-2616	MME/NE		174
HAR-267	NE		67
HAR-268	NE	NE	25
HAR-269	NE		67
HAR-2843	NE		185–6
HAR-2844	NE		186
HAR-2845	NE		186
HAR-2919	NE		186
HAR-2997	NE	NE	77
HAR-3058	NE	NE	71
HAR-3060	NE	NE	71
HAR-3061	NE	NE	70–1
HAR-3062	NE	NE	71
HAR-3078	NE	NE	184
HAR-3096	NE	IA	16
HAR-3133	MME/NE	BA	190
HAR-3195	MME/NE		167

Results 4000–3500 cal BC

Sample	Period	Date	Page
HAR-1010	MME/NE	RO	37
HAR-1087	MME/NE	NE	93
HAR-1116	MME/NE	RO	37

Sample	Period	Date	Page
HAR-3208	NE	BA	121
HAR-3484	NE	IA	64
HAR-3595	NE	NE	82

Sample	Period	Date	Page
HAR-3596	NE	NE	82
HAR-3883	NE	BA/EM	199
HAR-3884	NE	BA/EM	199
HAR-3898	NE	BA/EM	199
HAR-3968	NE	NE	27
HAR-4052	NE	MME/NE	137
HAR-4071	NE	NE	122
HAR-4075	NE	NE	122
HAR-4078	NE		183
HAR-4375	NE		175
HAR-4544	NE		169
HAR-4739	NE		166
HAR-649	NE		167

Results 3500–3000 cal BC

Sample	Period	Date	Page
HAR-1219	NE		184
HAR-1220	NE/BA		185
HAR-1222	NE		184
HAR-1226	NE		210
HAR-1234	NE		210
HAR-1379	NE	NE	178
HAR-1383	NE		166
HAR-1411	NE	NE	3–4
HAR-1465	NE		174–5
HAR-1467	NE		185
HAR-1468	NE		185
HAR-1470	NE		185
HAR-1471	NE		185
HAR-1473	MME/NE	NE	179
HAR-1478	NE	NE	179
HAR-1479	NE	NE	179–80
HAR-1480	NE	NE	180
HAR-1495	NE		66
HAR-1497	NE		66
HAR-1662	NE	NE	22–3
HAR-1850	NE	NE	164–5
HAR-1882	NE	NE	69
HAR-1885	NE	NE	69
HAR-1886	NE	NE	69
HAR-1954	NE/BA	NE/BA	135
HAR-2196	NE		108
HAR-2201	NE		108
HAR-2202	NE		108
HAR-2224	NE	NE	167
HAR-2255	NE		31
HAR-2368	NE	NE	69–70
HAR-2371	NE	NE	70
HAR-2372	NE	NE	70
HAR-2375	NE	NE	70
HAR-2377	NE	NE	70
HAR-2378	NE	NE	70
HAR-2379	NE	NE	70
HAR-2399	NE		211
HAR-2408	NE		211
HAR-2410	NE		211
HAR-2428	NE	BA	174

Sample	Period	Date	Page
HAR-2625	NE	NE	121
HAR-266	NE		67
HAR-267	NE		67
HAR-268	NE	NE	25
HAR-269	NE		67
HAR-2843	NE		185–6
HAR-2844	NE		186
HAR-2846	NE		186
HAR-2919	NE		186
HAR-2920	NE		186
HAR-2997	NE	NE	77
HAR-3058	NE	NE	71
HAR-3060	NE	NE	71
HAR-3061	NE	NE	70–1
HAR-3062	NE	NE	71
HAR-3078	NE	NE	184
HAR-3096	NE	IA	16
HAR-3208	NE	BA	121
HAR-3386	NE	NE	184–5
HAR-3387	NE	NE	184
HAR-3484	NE	IA	64
HAR-3592	NE		161
HAR-3595	NE	NE	82
HAR-3596	NE	NE	82
HAR-3883	NE	BA/EM	199
HAR-3884	NE	BA/EM	199
HAR-3898	NE	BA/EM	199
HAR-3968	NE	NE	27
HAR-4052	NE	MME/NE	137
HAR-4057	NE	NE	121
HAR-4071	NE	NE	122
HAR-4074	NE	NE	122
HAR-4075	NE	NE	122
HAR-4078	NE		183
HAR-4130	NE	NE	176
HAR-4374	NE		175
HAR-4375	NE		175
HAR-4428	NE	BA/IA	207
HAR-4543	NE		169
HAR-4544	NE		169
HAR-4739	NE		166
HAR-649	NE		167
HAR-651	NE	NE	187
HAR-652	NE	NE	187
HAR-653	NE	NE	187
HAR-682	NE		184
HAR-940	NE	BA	4

Results 3000–2500 cal BC

Sample	Period	Date	Page
HAR-1090	NE/BA		134
HAR-1158	NE/BA	BA	9
HAR-1219	NE		184
HAR-1220	NE/BA		185
HAR-1222	NE		184
HAR-1234	NE		210
HAR-1284	NE/BA		58–9

Sample	Period	Date	Page
HAR-1323	NE/BA	IA	68
HAR-1383	NE		166
HAR-1451	NE/BA	NE	196–7
HAR-1465	NE		174–5
HAR-1467	NE		185
HAR-1468	NE		185
HAR-1470	NE		185
HAR-1471	NE		185
HAR-1477	NE/BA	NE	179
HAR-1495	NE		66
HAR-1662	NE	NE	22–3
HAR-1882	NE	NE	69
HAR-1885	NE	NE	69
HAR-1954	NE/BA	NE/BA	135
HAR-2041	NE/BA	NE	69
HAR-2224	NE	NE	167
HAR-2255	NE		31
HAR-2368	NE	NE	69–70
HAR-2372	NE	NE	70
HAR-2379	NE	NE	70
HAR-2387	NE/BA	NE	2
HAR-2388	NE/BA	NE	2
HAR-2482	NE/BA		155
HAR-2484	NE/BA	BA?	206
HAR-2607	NE/BA	NE	121
HAR-2625	NE	NE	121
HAR-266	NE		67
HAR-267	NE		67
HAR-2844	NE		186
HAR-2846	NE		186
HAR-2907	NE	NE	37
HAR-2919	NE		186
HAR-2920	NE		186
HAR-3060	NE	NE	71
HAR-3108	NE/BA	NE?	136
HAR-3111	NE/BA	NE	54
HAR-3379	NE/BA	BA	157
HAR-3386	NE	NE	184–5
HAR-3387	NE	NE	184
HAR-3447	NE/BA		166
HAR-3592	NE		161
HAR-3976	NE/BA	BA	24
HAR-4033	NE/BA	MME	137
HAR-4057	NE	NE	121
HAR-4058	NE/BA	BA	121
HAR-4066	NE/BA	NE?	121
HAR-4073	NE/BA	NE	122
HAR-4074	NE	NE	122
HAR-4130	NE	NE	176
HAR-4248	NE/BA		158
HAR-4251	NE/BA	BA	127–8
HAR-4374	NE		175
HAR-4426	NE/BA	BA	207
HAR-4428	NE	BA/IA	207
HAR-4542	NE/BA		168–9
HAR-4543	NE		169
HAR-490	NE/BA	NE/BA	30

Sample	Period	Date	Page
HAR-651	NE	NE	187
HAR-652	NE	NE	187
HAR-653	NE	NE	187
HAR-682	NE		184
HAR-858	NE/BA	NE	113
HAR-940	NE	BA	4
HAR-957	NE/BA	BA/IA	210
HAR-999	NE/BA	BA	146

Results 2500–2000 cal BC

Sample	Period	Date	Page
HAR-1000	BA	BA	146–7
HAR-1002	BA	BA	147
HAR-1042	BA	BA	105
HAR-1089	BA		134
HAR-1090	NE/BA		134
HAR-1092	BA		134
HAR-1155	BA	BA	66
HAR-1158	NE/BA	BA	9
HAR-1195	BA	IA	114
HAR-1205	BA	BA	9
HAR-1220	NE/BA		185
HAR-1236	BA		58
HAR-1237	BA	NE	5
HAR-1248	BA	IA	1
HAR-1282	BA	BA	58
HAR-1284	NE/BA		58–9
HAR-1323	NE/BA	IA	68
HAR-1448	BA	NE	31–2
HAR-1451	NE/BA	NE	196–7
HAR-1477	NE/BA	NE	179
HAR-1645	BA	BA	9
HAR-1695	BA	BA	103
HAR-1750	BA		81
HAR-1843	BA		176
HAR-1876	BA	BA	110–1
HAR-1878	BA	BA?	206
HAR-1899	BA	IA/EM	201
HAR-1922	BA	BA	71
HAR-1923	BA	BA	71–2
HAR-1954	NE/BA	NE/BA	135
HAR-2013	BA		192
HAR-2041	NE/BA	NE	69
HAR-2216	BA	BA	162
HAR-2220	BA	BA	162
HAR-2243	BA		182
HAR-2387	NE/BA	NE	2
HAR-2388	NE/BA	NE	2
HAR-2389	BA	NE/BA	121
HAR-2474	BA	BA	159
HAR-2482	NE/BA		155
HAR-2484	NE/BA	BA?	206
HAR-2497	BA	NE/BA/IA	85
HAR-2498	BA		85
HAR-2510	BA	BA	111
HAR-2516	BA	BA	111
HAR-2541	BA	BA	92

Sample	Period	Date	Page
HAR-2588	BA	RO?	238
HAR-2607	NE/BA	NE	121
HAR-2617	BA	BA?	152
HAR-2622	BA	BA?	152
HAR-2624	BA	BA?	153
HAR-2669	BA		163
HAR-2690	BA	BA	111
HAR-2892	BA	BA	136
HAR-2901	BA	BA	119–20
HAR-2991	BA		153
HAR-2994	BA		153
HAR-2998	BA	BA	77
HAR-3000	BA	BA	142–3
HAR-3064	BA	BA	39
HAR-3067	BA	BA	39
HAR-3108	NE/BA	NE?	136
HAR-3111	NE/BA	NE	54
HAR-3129	BA	BA	190
HAR-3265	BA	BA	198
HAR-3268	BA	BA	198
HAR-3269	BA	BA	198
HAR-3270	BA	BA	203
HAR-3290	BA	BA	203
HAR-3379	NE/BA	BA	157
HAR-3388	BA		183
HAR-3409+HAR-3410	BA	BA	133
HAR-3447	NE/BA		166
HAR-3448	BA		167
HAR-3449	BA		167
HAR-3607	BA	BA	80
HAR-3611	BA	BA	126
HAR-3630	BA	BA	126
HAR-3818	BA	BA	86
HAR-3838	BA		168
HAR-3880	BA	BA	36
HAR-3908	BA	BA	6
HAR-3954	BA		17–18
HAR-3976	NE/BA	BA	24
HAR-4013	BA		161
HAR-4033	NE/BA	MME	137
HAR-4058	NE/BA	BA	121
HAR-4066	NE/BA	NE?	121
HAR-4067	BA	NE	121–2
HAR-4073	NE/BA	NE	122
HAR-4089	BA	NE	122
HAR-4181	BA		163
HAR-4248	NE/BA		158
HAR-4250	BA	BA	127
HAR-4251	NE/BA	BA	127–8
HAR-4285+HAR-4530	BA	BA	197
HAR-4316	BA	BA	84
HAR-4320	BA	BA	84
HAR-4426	NE/BA	BA	207
HAR-4427	BA	BA	207
HAR-450	BA		115
HAR-4542	NE/BA		168–9
HAR-486	BA	BA	72
HAR-488	BA	NE/BA	30
HAR-490	NE/BA	NE/BA	30
HAR-491	BA	NE/BA	30–1
HAR-605	BA	NE/BA	113
HAR-647	BA	BA	203–4
HAR-654	BA	BA	153
HAR-858	NE/BA	NE	113
HAR-950	BA	EM	12
HAR-957	NE/BA	BA/IA	210
HAR-958	BA	BA	137
HAR-966	BA	IA	43
HAR-997	BA	BA	146
HAR-999	NE/BA	BA	146

Results 2000–1500 cal BC

Sample	Period	Date	Page
HAR-1000	BA	BA	146–7
HAR-1001	BA	BA	147
HAR-1002	BA	BA	147
HAR-1003	BA	BA	147
HAR-1013	BA	IA	29
HAR-1023	BA	BA	104
HAR-1040	BA	BA	104
HAR-1041	BA	BA	105
HAR-1042	BA	BA	105
HAR-1044	BA	NE/BA	105–6
HAR-1047	BA	IA	93
HAR-1082	BA	IA	93
HAR-1089	BA		134
HAR-1090	NE/BA		134
HAR-1092	BA		134
HAR-1145	BA	BA	65
HAR-1147	BA		65
HAR-1148	BA		65
HAR-1149	BA		65
HAR-1150	BA	BA	65
HAR-1153	BA	BA	65
HAR-1154	BA	BA	65–6
HAR-1155	BA	BA	66
HAR-1156	BA	BA	9
HAR-1158	NE/BA	BA	9
HAR-1159	BA	BA	176
HAR-1163	BA	BA	190
HAR-1195	BA	IA	114
HAR-1205	BA	BA	9
HAR-1207	BA	BA	9
HAR-1227	BA	IA	58
HAR-1236	BA		58
HAR-1237	BA	NE	5
HAR-1248	BA	IA	1
HAR-1282	BA	BA	58
HAR-1323	NE/BA	IA	68
HAR-1325	BA	BA	193
HAR-1326	BA	BA	193
HAR-1430	BA	BA	9
HAR-1448	BA	NE	31–2
HAR-1489	BA		170

Index 3: Period index

Sample	Period	Date	Page
HAR-1494	BA		170
HAR-1591	BA	EM	13
HAR-1612	BA	BA	9
HAR-1645	BA	BA	9
HAR-1715	BA	BA	154
HAR-1750	BA		81
HAR-1811	BA	BA	4
HAR-1843	BA		176
HAR-1876	BA	BA	110–1
HAR-1878	BA	BA?	206
HAR-1879	BA		206
HAR-1899	BA	IA/EM	201
HAR-1922	BA	BA	71
HAR-1923	BA	BA	71–2
HAR-2013	BA		192
HAR-2213	BA	BA	161
HAR-2214	BA	BA	161–2
HAR-2216	BA	BA	162
HAR-2219	BA	BA	162
HAR-2220	BA	BA	162
HAR-2221	BA	BA	162
HAR-2243	BA		182
HAR-2278	BA	BA	138
HAR-2285	BA	BA	162
HAR-2339	BA		116
HAR-2340	BA	BA	116
HAR-2342	BA	BA	116
HAR-2389	BA	NE/BA	121
HAR-2474	BA	BA	159
HAR-2475	BA	BA	159
HAR-2491	BA		59
HAR-2492	BA		59
HAR-2493	BA		59
HAR-2497	BA	NE/BA/IA	85
HAR-2498	BA		85
HAR-2510	BA	BA	111
HAR-2516	BA	BA	111
HAR-2517	BA	BA	111
HAR-2541	BA	BA	92
HAR-2587	BA	RO?	238
HAR-2588	BA	RO?	238
HAR-2617	BA	BA?	152
HAR-2622	BA	BA?	152
HAR-2624	BA	BA?	153
HAR-2669	BA		163
HAR-2690	BA	BA	111
HAR-2754	BA	BA	28
HAR-2772	BA	BA	177
HAR-2829	BA	BA	120
HAR-2892	BA	BA	136
HAR-2901	BA	BA	119–20
HAR-2960	BA	BA	159
HAR-2968	BA	BA	159
HAR-2979	BA	BA	160
HAR-2983	BA	BA	160
HAR-2986	BA	BA	160
HAR-2987	BA	BA	160
HAR-2989	BA	BA	160
HAR-2991	BA		153
HAR-2994	BA		153
HAR-2998	BA	BA	77
HAR-3000	BA	BA	142–3
HAR-3064	BA	BA	39
HAR-3067	BA	BA	39
HAR-3107	BA	BA	136
HAR-3116	BA	BA	149
HAR-3129	BA	BA	190
HAR-3130	BA	BA	190
HAR-3131	BA	BA	190
HAR-3132	BA	BA	190
HAR-3265	BA	BA	198
HAR-3268	BA	BA	198
HAR-3270	BA	BA	203
HAR-3290	BA	BA	203
HAR-3344	BA	BA	105
HAR-3358	BA	BA	160
HAR-3409+HAR-3410	BA	BA	133
HAR-3417	BA	BA	105
HAR-3418	BA	BA	160–1
HAR-3448	BA		167
HAR-3449	BA		167
HAR-3599	BA	BA	80
HAR-3607	BA	BA	80
HAR-3608	BA	BA	80
HAR-3611	BA	BA	126
HAR-3630	BA	BA	126
HAR-3687	BA	BA	126
HAR-3694	BA		155
HAR-3736	BA	BA	23
HAR-3741	BA	BA	88
HAR-3812	BA		163
HAR-3818	BA	BA	86
HAR-3838	BA		168
HAR-3880	BA	BA	36
HAR-3908	BA	BA	6
HAR-3941	BA	BA	54
HAR-3942	BA	BA	54
HAR-3951	BA	IA	16
HAR-3954	BA		17–18
HAR-4003	BA	BA	161
HAR-4005	BA	BA	161
HAR-4013	BA		161
HAR-4058	NE/BA	BA	121
HAR-4065	BA	BA	121
HAR-4067	BA	NE	121–2
HAR-4073	NE/BA	NE	122
HAR-4089	BA	NE	122
HAR-4181	BA		163
HAR-4250	BA	BA	127
HAR-4282	BA	BA	197
HAR-4283	BA	BA	197
HAR-4284	BA	BA	197
HAR-4285+HAR-4530	BA	BA	197
HAR-4316	BA	BA	84

Index 3: Period index

Sample	Period	Date	Page
HAR-4319	BA	BA	84
HAR-4320	BA	BA	84
HAR-450	BA		115
HAR-486	BA	BA	72
HAR-488	BA	NE/BA	30
HAR-489	BA	NE/BA	30
HAR-490	NE/BA	NE/BA	30
HAR-491	BA	NE/BA	30–1
HAR-605	BA	NE/BA	113
HAR-646	BA	BA	203
HAR-647	BA	BA	203–4
HAR-648	BA	BA	204
HAR-654	BA	BA	153
HAR-655	BA	BA	153
HAR-680	BA		168
HAR-683	BA		169
HAR-858	NE/BA	NE	113
HAR-950	BA	EM	12
HAR-958	BA	BA	137
HAR-966	BA	IA	43
HAR-993	BA	BA	139
HAR-994	BA	BA	139
HAR-997	BA	BA	146
HAR-999	NE/BA	BA	146

Results 1500–1000 cal BC

Sample	Period	Date	Page
HAR-1001	BA	BA	147
HAR-1003	BA	BA	147
HAR-1011	BA	IA	28–9
HAR-1013	BA	IA	29
HAR-1023	BA	BA	104
HAR-1040	BA	BA	104
HAR-1041	BA	BA	105
HAR-1044	BA	NE/BA	105–6
HAR-1047	BA	IA	93
HAR-1082	BA	IA	93
HAR-1145	BA	BA	65
HAR-1147	BA		65
HAR-1150	BA	BA	65
HAR-1153	BA	BA	65
HAR-1154	BA	BA	65–6
HAR-1156	BA	BA	9
HAR-1159	BA	BA	176
HAR-1163	BA	BA	190
HAR-1204	BA	IA	71
HAR-1221	BA	BA	175
HAR-1227	BA	IA	58
HAR-1248	BA	IA	1
HAR-1249	BA	IA	1
HAR-1398	BA	BA	197
HAR-1420	BA	BA	141
HAR-1430	BA	BA	9
HAR-1489	BA		170
HAR-1492	BA	BA	32
HAR-1493	BA	BA	32
HAR-1494	BA		170

Sample	Period	Date	Page
HAR-1591	BA	EM	13
HAR-1612	BA	BA	9
HAR-1627	BA		170
HAR-1630	BA	BA/IA	117
HAR-1634	BA	BA/IA	117–8
HAR-1708	BA	BA/IA	118
HAR-1715	BA	BA	154
HAR-1726	BA	BA	154
HAR-1749	BA		81
HAR-1811	BA	BA	4
HAR-1834	BA	BA	148
HAR-1879	BA		206
HAR-1923	BA	BA	71–2
HAR-1931	BA	IA	63
HAR-2214	BA	BA	161–2
HAR-2278	BA	BA	138
HAR-2337	BA		116
HAR-2339	BA		116
HAR-2340	BA	BA	116
HAR-2342	BA	BA	116
HAR-2343	BA		116–7
HAR-2429	BA	BA	182
HAR-2472	BA	BA	159
HAR-2473	BA	BA	159
HAR-2475	BA	BA	159
HAR-2493	BA		59
HAR-2502	BA	IA	56
HAR-2538	BA		182
HAR-2544	BA		182
HAR-2589	BA/IA	MME?	198–9
HAR-2619	BA		170
HAR-2745	BA	BA	104
HAR-2749	BA	BA	28
HAR-2754	BA	BA	28
HAR-2772	BA	BA	177
HAR-2773	BA		182–3
HAR-2829	BA	BA	120
HAR-2893	BA/IA	BA	117
HAR-2911	BA	BA	117
HAR-2929	BA	BA	28
HAR-2939	BA	BA	23
HAR-2940	BA	BA	23
HAR-2941	BA	BA	23
HAR-2960	BA	BA	159
HAR-2968	BA	BA	159
HAR-2976	BA	BA	159
HAR-2979	BA	BA	160
HAR-2983	BA	BA	160
HAR-2986	BA	BA	160
HAR-2987	BA	BA	160
HAR-2989	BA	BA	160
HAR-2992	BA		145
HAR-3046	BA		157–8
HAR-3114	BA	BA	148–9
HAR-3115	BA	BA	149
HAR-3116	BA	BA	149
HAR-3118	BA	BA	149

Sample	Period	Date	Page
HAR-3119	BA/IA	BA	149
HAR-3120	BA	BA	149
HAR-3130	BA	BA	190
HAR-3132	BA	BA	190
HAR-3235	BA	BA/IA	191
HAR-332	BA		103
HAR-333	BA	BA/IA	100
HAR-3344	BA	BA	105
HAR-3358	BA	BA	160
HAR-339	BA	BA	112
HAR-3417	BA	BA	105
HAR-3418	BA	BA	160–1
HAR-3419	BA	BA	161
HAR-3521	BA	IA	172
HAR-3599	BA	BA	80
HAR-3694	BA		155
HAR-3712	BA	BA	34
HAR-3735	BA	BA	23
HAR-3736	BA	BA	23
HAR-3737	BA	BA	24
HAR-3740	BA	IA	173
HAR-3741	BA	BA	88
HAR-3750	BA	BA	149
HAR-3751	BA	BA	159
HAR-3752	BA	BA	149–50
HAR-3925	BA	BA	101
HAR-3926	BA	BA/IA	101
HAR-3951	BA	IA	16
HAR-4003	BA	BA	161
HAR-4005	BA		161
HAR-4008	BA		158
HAR-4065	BA	BA	121
HAR-4207	BA/IA	IA	49
HAR-4240	BA		158
HAR-4268	BA	BA	150
HAR-4272	BA	BA	151
HAR-4273	BA	BA	151
HAR-4274	BA	BA	151
HAR-4275	BA	BA	151
HAR-4277	BA	BA	151
HAR-4282	BA	BA	197
HAR-4283	BA	BA	197
HAR-4284	BA	BA	197
HAR-4285+HAR-4530	BA	BA	197
HAR-4316	BA	BA	84
HAR-4317	BA	BA	84
HAR-4319	BA	BA	84
HAR-4340	BA	BA	151
HAR-4341	BA	BA	151
HAR-4413	BA	BA	151
HAR-442	BA/IA	IA	8
HAR-4477	BA	BA	175
HAR-457	BA	BA/IA	154
HAR-460	BA	BA/IA	154
HAR-488	BA	NE/BA	30
HAR-489	BA	NE/BA	30
HAR-646	BA	BA	203
HAR-648	BA	BA	204
HAR-681	BA		181
HAR-683	BA		169
HAR-684	BA		181
HAR-860	BA	BA	112
HAR-865	BA		92
HAR-943	BA		170
HAR-944	BA		177
HAR-945	BA		181
HAR-946	BA		181
HAR-947	BA		181
HAR-948	BA		181–2
HAR-994	BA	BA	139

Results 1000–500 cal BC

Sample	Period	Date	Page
HAR-1011	BA	IA	28–9
HAR-1057	BA/IA	IA	29
HAR-1058	BA/IA	IA	29
HAR-1081	BA/IA	IA	93
HAR-1123	BA/IA	IA	114
HAR-1125	BA/IA	IA	114
HAR-1126	BA/IA	IA	114
HAR-1127	BA	IA	114
HAR-1130	BA/IA/RO	IA	29–30
HAR-1150	BA	BA	65
HAR-1154	BA	BA	65–6
HAR-1162	BA/IA	IA	15
HAR-1192	BA/IA	NE/BA	196
HAR-1196	BA/IA	IA	114
HAR-1197	BA/IA	IA	114
HAR-1204	BA	IA	71
HAR-1235	BA/IA	IA	58
HAR-1247	BA/IA	IA	1
HAR-1249	BA	IA	1
HAR-1283	BA/IA		58
HAR-1374	BA/IA	IA	55
HAR-1398	BA	BA	197
HAR-1420	BA	BA	141
HAR-1492	BA	BA	32
HAR-1493	BA	BA	32
HAR-1630	BA	BA/IA	117
HAR-1634	BA	BA/IA	117–8
HAR-1708	BA	BA/IA	118
HAR-1726	BA	BA	154
HAR-1833	BA/IA	BA	148
HAR-1834	BA	BA	148
HAR-1841	BA/IA	BA	15
HAR-1909	IA	EM/MD	194
HAR-1931	BA	IA	63
HAR-2029	BA/IA	IA	44
HAR-2032	BA/IA	IA	44–5
HAR-2033	BA/IA	IA	45
HAR-2039	BA/IA	IA	45
HAR-2085	BA/IA	IA	46
HAR-209	BA/IA		131
HAR-2157	BA		15

Index 3: Period index

Sample	Period	Date	Page
HAR-2222	BA/IA	IA	93
HAR-2251	BA/IA	IA	108
HAR-2337	BA		116
HAR-2338	BA/IA	BA/IA	116
HAR-234	BA/IA	BA/IA	81
HAR-2343	BA		116–7
HAR-238	BA/IA	IA	34
HAR-2429	BA	BA	182
HAR-2468	BA/IA	NE/BA/IA	85
HAR-2473	BA	BA	159
HAR-2483	BA/IA		21–2
HAR-2502	BA	IA	56
HAR-2506	BA	BA/IA	100
HAR-2523	BA/IA		22
HAR-2564	BA/IA	IA	46
HAR-2585	BA/IA	IA	46–7
HAR-2586	BA/IA	IA	47
HAR-2589	BA/IA	MME?	198–9
HAR-2604	BA/IA	IA	106
HAR-2619	BA		170
HAR-2620	BA/IA	IA	171
HAR-2653	BA/IA	IA	109
HAR-2689	BA/IA		191
HAR-2694	BA		157
HAR-2703	BA/IA	IA	35
HAR-2745	BA	BA	104
HAR-2753	BA	RO?	238
HAR-2760	BA/IA	IA	66
HAR-2773	BA		182–3
HAR-2799	IA	IA	106
HAR-2893	BA/IA	BA	117
HAR-2911	BA	BA	117
HAR-2937	IA		109
HAR-2939	BA	BA	23
HAR-2941	BA	BA	23
HAR-2975	BA/IA	IA	47
HAR-2976	BA	BA	159
HAR-2978	BA	BA	160
HAR-3015	BA/IA	IA	67
HAR-3026	BA/IA	IA	48
HAR-3046	BA		157–8
HAR-3069	IA	NE/BA	21
HAR-3092	BA/IA	IA	81
HAR-3093	BA/IA		15–16
HAR-3097	BA/IA	IA	16
HAR-3101	BA/IA	BA	22
HAR-3102	BA/IA	IA	76–7
HAR-3112	BA	BA	148
HAR-3113	BA	BA	148
HAR-3114	BA	BA	148–9
HAR-3115	BA	BA	149
HAR-3117	BA	BA	149
HAR-3118	BA	BA	149
HAR-3119	BA/IA	BA	149
HAR-3120	BA	BA	149
HAR-3235	BA	BA/IA	191
HAR-332	BA		103
HAR-333	BA	BA/IA	100
HAR-3362	BA/IA		200
HAR-3377	BA/IA		157
HAR-339	BA	BA	112
HAR-3419	BA	BA	161
HAR-3446	BA/IA		177
HAR-3521	BA	IA	172
HAR-3546	BA/IA	IA	172
HAR-3610	BA	BA/IA	8
HAR-3633	BA	IA	172
HAR-3723	BA/IA		155
HAR-3724	BA/IA		155
HAR-3735	BA	BA	23
HAR-3737	BA	BA	24
HAR-3740	BA	IA	173
HAR-3744	IA	IA	173
HAR-3750	BA	BA	149
HAR-3751	BA	BA	159
HAR-3759	BA/IA	BA	150
HAR-3761	BA/IA	BA	150
HAR-3762	BA/IA	BA	150
HAR-3791	BA/IA		199
HAR-3816	BA/IA		163
HAR-3864	BA/IA	IA	173
HAR-3926	BA	BA/IA	101
HAR-3927	BA/IA	IA	101
HAR-3931	BA/IA	NE/BA/IA	99
HAR-3945	BA/IA	IA	16
HAR-3950	BA/IA	IA	16
HAR-3951	BA	IA	16
HAR-4008	BA		158
HAR-4064	BA/IA	IA	127
HAR-4206	BA/IA	IA	49
HAR-4207	BA/IA	IA	49
HAR-4208	BA/IA	IA	49
HAR-4240	BA		158
HAR-4257	BA	BA	150
HAR-4264	BA	BA	150
HAR-4265	BA	BA	150
HAR-4267	BA	BA	150
HAR-4268	BA	BA	150
HAR-4269	BA	BA	150
HAR-4270	BA/IA	BA	151
HAR-4272	BA	BA	151
HAR-4273	BA	BA	151
HAR-4274	BA	BA	151
HAR-4275	BA	BA	151
HAR-4277	BA	BA	151
HAR-4278	BA/IA	IA	49
HAR-4284	BA	BA	197
HAR-4317	BA	BA	84
HAR-4325	BA/IA	IA	50
HAR-4328	BA/IA	IA	50
HAR-4329	BA/IA	IA	50
HAR-4330	BA/IA	IA	50
HAR-4331	BA/IA	IA	50
HAR-4339	BA/IA	IA	51

Sample	Period	Date	Page
HAR-4340	BA	BA	151
HAR-4341	BA	BA	151
HAR-4343	BA/IA	IA	51
HAR-4366	BA/IA	IA	51
HAR-4372	BA/IA	IA	51
HAR-4413	BA	BA	151
HAR-442	BA/IA	IA	8
HAR-4425	BA/IA	IA	207
HAR-4439	BA/IA	IA	17
HAR-446	BA/IA/RO	IA	8
HAR-4464	BA/IA	IA	51
HAR-4468	BA/IA	IA	51
HAR-4477	BA	BA	175
HAR-4494	BA/IA	IA	127
HAR-453	BA/IA	PA/IA	136
HAR-457	BA	BA/IA	154
HAR-467	BA/IA	IA	115
HAR-470	BA/IA	IA	115
HAR-475	BA/IA	IA/RO/EM	33
HAR-476	BA/IA	IA/RO/EM	33
HAR-477	BA/IA	IA/RO/EM	33
HAR-487	BA/IA	NE/BA	30
HAR-604	BA/IA	IA	113
HAR-606	BA/IA		113
HAR-646	BA	BA	203
HAR-650	BA/IA		176
HAR-842	BA/IA	IA	115
HAR-855	BA/IA	IA	112
HAR-856	BA/IA	IA	112
HAR-860	BA	BA	112
HAR-865	BA		92
HAR-872	BA/IA		111-12
HAR-942	BA/IA	BA	4
HAR-944	BA		177
HAR-946	BA		181
HAR-947	BA		181
HAR-996	BA/IA	EM	139

Results 500–1 cal BC

Sample	Period	Date	Page
HAR-1012	IA	IA	29
HAR-1021	IA/RO	RO	104
HAR-1058	BA/IA	IA	29
HAR-1076	IA/RO	EM/MD	222
HAR-1077	IA/RO	EM/MD	222
HAR-1081	BA/IA	IA	93
HAR-1086	IA	IA	22
HAR-1088	IA	IA	93
HAR-1091	IA/RO		134
HAR-1100	IA	IA	1
HAR-1120	IA/RO	IA	93
HAR-1121	IA	IA	135
HAR-1122	IA	IA	113–14
HAR-1123	BA/IA	IA	114
HAR-1125	BA/IA	IA	114
HAR-1126	BA/IA	IA	114
HAR-1129	IA/RO	IA	29
HAR-1130	BA/IA/RO	IA	29–30
HAR-1143	IA/RO	RO	210
HAR-1162	BA/IA	IA	15
HAR-1186	IA/RO	RO	3
HAR-1191	IA/RO/EM	EM	188
HAR-1192	BA/IA	NE/BA	196
HAR-1196	BA/IA	IA	114
HAR-1197	BA/IA	IA	114
HAR-1228	IA	IA	58
HAR-1235	BA/IA	IA	58
HAR-1247	BA/IA	IA	1
HAR-1274	IA/RO		58
HAR-1275	IA/RO		58
HAR-1283	BA/IA		58
HAR-1289	IA/RO	IA	79
HAR-1290	IA/RO	IA	79
HAR-1332	IA/RO	IA	1
HAR-1333	IA/RO	IA	1–2
HAR-1334	IA/RO	IA	2
HAR-1335	IA	IA	2
HAR-1374	BA/IA	IA	55
HAR-1394	IA/RO	RO	20
HAR-1418	IA/RO	RO	237
HAR-1425	IA/RO	IA	43
HAR-1440	IA	IA	43–4
HAR-1442	IA/RO	IA	44
HAR-1632	IA/RO		116
HAR-1633	IA/RO		116
HAR-1664	IA	NE/IA	143
HAR-1665	IA/RO	IA	206
HAR-1698	IA	IA	75
HAR-1699	IA	IA	75
HAR-1700	IA/RO	IA	75
HAR-1701	IA/RO	IA	75
HAR-1725	IA/RO	IA	201
HAR-1764	IA	IA	232–3
HAR-1765	IA/RO	IA	233
HAR-1778	IA/RO	IA	233
HAR-1779	IA/RO	IA	201
HAR-1794	IA/RO	IA	233
HAR-1801	IA/RO	IA	44
HAR-1832	IA/RO	RO	134
HAR-1841	BA/IA	BA	15
HAR-1844	IA/RO	IA	201–2
HAR-1895	IA/RO		33
HAR-1909	IA	EM/MD	194
HAR-1910	IA/RO	IA	55
HAR-1913	IA/RO	RO	97
HAR-1915	IA/RO	RO/EM	235
HAR-1925	IA	IA	55
HAR-1926	IA/RO	IA	55
HAR-1928	IA	RO	237–8
HAR-2007	IA	IA	202
HAR-2008	IA/RO	IA	202
HAR-2025	IA/RO	RO	195
HAR-2028	IA/RO	IA	44
HAR-2029	BA/IA	IA	44

Index 3: Period index

Sample	Period	Date	Page
HAR-2030	IA	IA	44
HAR-2031	IA/RO	IA	44
HAR-2032	BA/IA	IA	44–5
HAR-2033	BA/IA	IA	45
HAR-2034	IA	IA	45
HAR-2035	IA	IA	45
HAR-2036	IA/RO	IA	45
HAR-2037	IA/RO	IA	45
HAR-2038	IA/RO	IA	45
HAR-2039	BA/IA	IA	45
HAR-2085	BA/IA	IA	46
HAR-209	BA/IA		131
HAR-2158	IA/RO	IA/RO	195
HAR-2194	IA	IA	107
HAR-2195	IA/RO	RO	107–8
HAR-2208	IA/RO	IA?	208
HAR-2222	BA/IA	IA	93
HAR-2227	IA/RO	IA	152
HAR-2236	IA/RO	RO	241
HAR-2239	IA/RO		101
HAR-2251	BA/IA	IA	108
HAR-2252	IA	IA	108
HAR-2256	IA/RO		7
HAR-2263	IA/RO	RO	52
HAR-2276	IA/RO	IA	24–5
HAR-2277	IA/RO	IA	25
HAR-2280	IA	IA	76
HAR-2289	IA	IA	198
HAR-2338	BA/IA	BA/IA	116
HAR-234	BA/IA	BA/IA	81
HAR-2346	IA	BA	99
HAR-235(S)	IA	IA	233–4
HAR-238	BA/IA	IA	34
HAR-2390	IA/RO	RO	134
HAR-2411	IA	IA	73
HAR-2459	IA/RO	EM	14
HAR-2468	BA/IA	NE/BA/IA	85
HAR-2469	IA/RO	IA	56
HAR-2470	IA/RO	IA	56–7
HAR-2471	IA/RO	IA	57
HAR-2483	BA/IA		21–2
HAR-2486	IA		59
HAR-2490	IA/RO	IA	59
HAR-2499	IA/RO	IA/RO	98
HAR-2504	IA/RO	RO	100
HAR-2523	BA/IA		22
HAR-2531	IA/RO	EM	83–4
HAR-2532	IA/RO	RO	95
HAR-2534	IA/RO	RO	95
HAR-2564	BA/IA	IA	46
HAR-2567	IA	IA	46
HAR-2568	IA	IA	46
HAR-2571	IA/RO	IA	46
HAR-2573	IA/RO	IA	46
HAR-2581	IA	IA	46
HAR-2585	BA/IA	IA	46–7
HAR-2586	BA/IA	IA	47
HAR-2589	BA/IA	MME?	198–9
HAR-2591	IA	IA	108
HAR-2592	IA/RO	IA	108–9
HAR-2602	IA		156
HAR-2604	BA/IA	IA	106
HAR-2620	BA/IA	IA	171
HAR-2627	IA/RO	RO	239
HAR-2628	IA/RO	RO	239
HAR-2629	IA/RO	RO	239
HAR-2653	BA/IA	IA	109
HAR-2654	IA	IA	171
HAR-2668	IA/RO	IA	171
HAR-2689	BA/IA		191
HAR-2693	IA/RO	IA	106
HAR-2698	IA/RO	IA?	98
HAR-2703	BA/IA	IA	35
HAR-2760	BA/IA	IA	66
HAR-2761	IA	IA	66–7
HAR-2770	IA	IA	106
HAR-2771	IA	IA	106
HAR-2777	IA/RO	IA	207
HAR-2780	IA/RO	IA	106
HAR-2799	IA	IA	106
HAR-2803	IA/RO	IA	75
HAR-2805	IA/RO	IA	87
HAR-2809	IA	IA	75
HAR-2816	IA	IA	73
HAR-2817	IA	IA	75
HAR-2818	IA/RO	IA	76
HAR-2819	IA/RO	IA	73
HAR-2823	IA	BA	156
HAR-2825	IA	IA	88
HAR-2851	IA/RO	IA	129
HAR-2853	IA/RO	IA	129
HAR-2893	BA/IA	BA	117
HAR-2902	IA/RO	IA	10
HAR-2913	IA/RO	IA	129
HAR-2932	IA/RO	EM	76
HAR-2937	IA		109
HAR-2938	IA/RO	IA	109
HAR-2969	IA	IA	47
HAR-2970	IA/RO	IA	47
HAR-2971	IA	IA	47
HAR-2972	IA	IA	47
HAR-2973	IA/RO	IA	47
HAR-2974	IA/RO	IA	47
HAR-2975	BA/IA	IA	47
HAR-2980	IA	IA	109
HAR-3014	IA	IA	67
HAR-3015	BA/IA	IA	67
HAR-3017	IA/RO	EM	76
HAR-3021	IA	IA	48
HAR-3022	IA	IA	48
HAR-3026	BA/IA	IA	48
HAR-3027	IA	IA	48
HAR-3069	IA	NE/BA	21
HAR-3084	IA/RO	RO	35

Sample	Period	Date	Page	Sample	Period	Date	Page
HAR-3086	IA/RO	RO	36	HAR-3977	IA/RO	BA	24
HAR-3092	BA/IA	IA	81	HAR-4064	BA/IA	IA	127
HAR-3093	BA/IA		15–16	HAR-4120	IA/RO	EM	90
HAR-3094	IA	IA	16	HAR-4147	IA/RO	EM	205
HAR-3095	IA/RO	IA	16	HAR-4191	IA/RO	EM	205
HAR-3097	BA/IA	IA	16	HAR-4206	BA/IA	IA	49
HAR-3101	BA/IA	BA	22	HAR-4207	BA/IA	IA	49
HAR-3102	BA/IA	IA	76–7	HAR-4208	BA/IA	IA	49
HAR-3103	IA/RO	RO	96	HAR-4243	IA	IA	49
HAR-3105	IA/RO	RO	96	HAR-4244	IA/RO	IA	49
HAR-329	IA		103	HAR-4252	IA	IA	131
HAR-334	IA/RO	IA	34	HAR-4270	BA/IA	BA	151
HAR-335	IA/RO	IA	34	HAR-4278	BA/IA	IA	49
HAR-3362	BA/IA		200	HAR-4279	IA	IA	50
HAR-3377	BA/IA		157	HAR-4325	BA/IA	IA	50
HAR-3456	IA/RO		21	HAR-4327	IA	IA	50
HAR-3483	IA	BA	155	HAR-4328	BA/IA	IA	50
HAR-3485	IA/RO		92	HAR-4329	BA/IA	IA	50
HAR-3489	IA	IA	171	HAR-4330	BA/IA	IA	50
HAR-3492	IA	IA	171–2	HAR-4331	BA/IA	IA	50
HAR-3493	IA/RO	IA	5–6	HAR-4337	IA	IA	50–1
HAR-3494	IA/RO	IA	6	HAR-4339	BA/IA	IA	51
HAR-3495	IA/RO	IA	6	HAR-4343	BA/IA	IA	51
HAR-3496	IA/RO	IA	6	HAR-4366	BA/IA	IA	51
HAR-3535	IA	IA	172	HAR-4372	BA/IA	IA	51
HAR-3546	BA/IA	IA	172	HAR-442	BA/IA	IA	8
HAR-3591	IA/RO	NE	163	HAR-4425	BA/IA	IA	207
HAR-3620	IA/RO	IA	59–60	HAR-4439	BA/IA	IA	17
HAR-3634	IA		172	HAR-444	IA	IA	8
HAR-3693	IA	IA	172	HAR-4440	IA/RO	IA	17
HAR-3706	IA/RO	BA	88	HAR-4442	IA	IA	17
HAR-3719	IA	IA	172–3	HAR-445	IA/RO	IA	8
HAR-3723	BA/IA		155	HAR-446	BA/IA/RO	IA	8
HAR-3724	BA/IA		155	HAR-4464	BA/IA	IA	51
HAR-3726	IA	IA	48	HAR-4466	IA	IA	51
HAR-3733	IA	IA	48	HAR-4468	BA/IA	IA	51
HAR-3743	IA	IA	48	HAR-4470	IA	IA	51–2
HAR-3744	IA	IA	173	HAR-452	IA/RO	IA	136
HAR-3745	IA/RO	IA	173	HAR-453	BA/IA	PA/IA	136
HAR-3747	IA/RO	IA/EM	72	HAR-467	BA/IA	IA	115
HAR-3759	BA/IA	BA	150	HAR-468	IA	IA	115
HAR-3761	BA/IA	BA	150	HAR-469	IA	IA	115
HAR-3791	BA/IA		199	HAR-470	BA/IA	IA	115
HAR-3816	BA/IA		163	HAR-475	BA/IA	IA/RO/EM	33
HAR-3864	BA/IA	IA	173	HAR-476	BA/IA	IA/RO/EM	33
HAR-3891	IA	IA	173	HAR-477	BA/IA	IA/RO/EM	33
HAR-3892	IA/RO	IA	173	HAR-508	IA/RO	IA	38
HAR-3896	IA	IA	174	HAR-509	IA	IA	38
HAR-3899	IA/RO	IA	48–9	HAR-510	IA	IA	38
HAR-3901	IA/RO	IA	49	HAR-603	IA	IA	113
HAR-3927	BA/IA	IA	101	HAR-604	BA/IA	IA	113
HAR-3944	IA	IA	16	HAR-607-I	IA/RO	IA	38
HAR-3945	BA/IA	IA	16	HAR-607-II	IA/RO	IA	38
HAR-3947	IA	IA	16	HAR-607-III	IA/RO	IA	38
HAR-3950	BA/IA	IA	16	HAR-650	BA/IA		176
HAR-3952	IA/RO	IA	17	HAR-842	BA/IA	IA	115
HAR-3955	IA/RO	IA	17	HAR-855	BA/IA	IA	112

Sample	Period	Date	Page
HAR-856	BA/IA	IA	112
HAR-857	IA	IA	112
HAR-872	BA/IA		111–12
HAR-873	IA/RO		112
HAR-942	BA/IA	BA	4
HAR-960	IA/RO	EM	83
HAR-963	IA	IA	42–3
HAR-964	IA	IA	43
HAR-965	IA	IA	43
HAR-968	IA	IA	43
HAR-970	IA/RO	IA/RO	41
HAR-971	IA	IA/RO	41
HAR-973	IA/RO	IA/RO	41
HAR-974	IA/RO	IA/RO	41
HAR-975	IA/RO	IA/RO	41
HAR-995	IA/RO	EM	139
HAR-996	BA/IA	EM	139

Results 1–500 cal AD

Sample	Period	Date	Page
HAR-1004	RO/EM	RO/EM	147
HAR-1006	RO/EM	RO	37
HAR-1009	RO/EM	RO	37
HAR-1025	RO/EM	IA/EM	89
HAR-1066	RO/EM	EM/MD	221
HAR-1076	IA/RO	EM/MD	222
HAR-1077	IA/RO	EM/MD	222
HAR-1083	RO/EM	RO	95
HAR-1091	IA/RO		134
HAR-1102	IA/RO/EM	EM/MD	223
HAR-1119	EM		196
HAR-1120	IA/RO	IA	93
HAR-1129	IA/RO	IA	29
HAR-1130	BA/IA/RO	IA	29–30
HAR-1142	RO/EM	RO	21025
HAR-1166	EM	EM	188
HAR-1167	RO/EM	EM	188
HAR-1186	IA/RO	RO	3
HAR-1228	IA	IA	58
HAR-1289	IA/RO	IA	79
HAR-1290	IA/RO	IA	79
HAR-1318	RO/EM		99
HAR-1332	IA/RO	IA	1
HAR-1333	IA/RO	IA	1–2
HAR-1334	IA/RO	IA	2
HAR-1339	RO/EM	RO	63
HAR-1342	IA/RO	IA	2
HAR-1393	RO/EM	RO	20
HAR-1394	IA/RO	RO	20
HAR-1416	IA/RO	RO?	236
HAR-1417	IA/RO	RO?	237
HAR-1421	RO/EM	RO	98
HAR-1425	IA/RO	IA	43
HAR-1426	RO/EM	IA	45
HAR-1442	IA/RO	IA	44
HAR-1456	RO/EM	RO	94
HAR-1457	RO/EM	RO	94

Sample	Period	Date	Page
HAR-1464	RO/EM	RO	94
HAR-1590	RO/EM	RO	94
HAR-1605	RO/EM	RO	233
HAR-1613	EM	EM	55
HAR-1614	RO/EM	EM	55
HAR-1632	IA/RO		116
HAR-1633	IA/RO		116
HAR-1648	EM	EM	130
HAR-1652	RO/EM	RO/EM	60–1
HAR-1653	RO/EM		100
HAR-1663	RO/EM	EM	23
HAR-1665	IA/RO	IA	206
HAR-1699	IA	IA	75
HAR-1700	IA/RO	IA	75
HAR-1703	RO/EM	EM	107
HAR-1719	RO/EM	RO?	165
HAR-1724	RO/EM	RO	94–5
HAR-1725	IA/RO	IA	201
HAR-1729	RO/EM	RO	237
HAR-1739	RO/ME	EM/MD	231
HAR-1794	IA/RO	IA	233
HAR-1801	IA/RO	IA	44
HAR-1832	IA/RO	RO	134
HAR-1837	RO/EM	EM	89
HAR-1842	RO/EM		168
HAR-1844	IA/RO	IA	201–2
HAR-1852	EM	EM/MD	232
HAR-1854	RO/EM		168
HAR-1864	RO/EM	RO	96–7
HAR-1865	RO	RO	97
HAR-1866	IA/RO	RO	237
HAR-1867	IA/RO	RO	97
HAR-1868	RO	RO	97
HAR-1895	IA/RO		33
HAR-1908	RO/EM	EM	194
HAR-1910	IA/RO	IA	55
HAR-1913	IA/RO	RO	97
HAR-1915	IA/RO	RO/EM	235
HAR-1917	IA/RO	RO	97
HAR-1925	IA	IA	55
HAR-1926	IA/RO	IA	55
HAR-1927	IA/RO	RO	237
HAR-2005	IA/RO	RO/EM	42
HAR-2006	RO/EM	RO/EM	42
HAR-2008	IA/RO	IA	202
HAR-2024	RO	RO	194–5
HAR-2025	IA/RO	RO	195
HAR-2027	RO/EM	EM	107
HAR-2028	IA/RO	IA	44
HAR-2031	IA/RO	IA	44
HAR-2036	IA/RO	IA	45
HAR-2037	IA/RO	IA	45
HAR-2038	IA/RO	IA	45
HAR-2040	IA/RO	IA	45–6
HAR-2073	RO	RO	134
HAR-2105	RO	EM	240
HAR-2118	RO	RO	240–1

Index 3: Period index

Sample	Period	Date	Page
HAR-2158	IA/RO	IA/RO	195
HAR-2195	IA/RO	RO	107–8
HAR-2207	RO/EM		73
HAR-2208	IA/RO	IA?	208
HAR-2223	RO/EM	BA	6–7
HAR-2227	IA/RO	IA	152
HAR-2239	IA/RO		101
HAR-2252	IA	IA	108
HAR-2256	IA/RO		7
HAR-2257	RO	RO	2
HAR-2263	IA/RO	RO	52
HAR-2276	IA/RO	IA	24–5
HAR-2277	IA/RO	IA	25
HAR-2281	RO/EM	EM	139
HAR-2283	RO/EM	EM	120
HAR-2341	EM	EM	116
HAR-2344	EM	EM	117
HAR-235(S)	IA	IA	233–4
HAR-237	RO/EM	IA	34
HAR-2390	IA/RO	RO	134
HAR-2398	RO/EM	RO/EM	119
HAR-2459	IA/RO	EM	14
HAR-2466	RO/EM	EM	74
HAR-2469	IA/RO	IA	56
HAR-2470	IA/RO	IA	56–7
HAR-2471	IA/RO	IA	57
HAR-2486	IA		59
HAR-2488	RO/EM		59
HAR-2489	RO/EM		59
HAR-2499	IA/RO	IA/RO	98
HAR-2501	RO/EM	IA?	98
HAR-2504	IA/RO	RO	100
HAR-2508	EM	EM	14
HAR-2530	IA/RO	RO	95
HAR-2532	IA/RO	RO	95
HAR-2534	IA/RO	RO	95
HAR-2548	RO/EM	EM	97
HAR-2568	IA	IA	46
HAR-2571	IA/RO	IA	46
HAR-2572	RO/EM	RO	35
HAR-2573	IA/RO	IA	46
HAR-2580	RO/EM	RO	35
HAR-2582	RO/EM		191
HAR-2592	IA/RO	IA	108–9
HAR-2614	RO/EM		7
HAR-2629	IA/RO	RO	239
HAR-2652	IA/RO	IA	109
HAR-2668	IA/RO	IA	171
HAR-2670	EM	EM	86
HAR-2693	IA/RO	IA	106
HAR-2698	IA/RO	IA?	98
HAR-2708	EM	RO?	239
HAR-2734	EM	EM	193
HAR-2765	RO/EM	EM	103
HAR-2766	RO/EM	EM	103
HAR-2771	IA	IA	106
HAR-2776	RO	IA	207
HAR-2777	IA/RO	IA	207
HAR-2780	IA/RO	IA	106
HAR-2803	IA/RO	IA	75
HAR-2805	IA/RO	IA	87
HAR-2809	IA	IA	75
HAR-2810	RO/EM		22
HAR-2813	EM	EM	60
HAR-2814	EM	EM	60
HAR-2818	IA/RO	IA	76
HAR-2851	IA/RO	IA	129
HAR-2853	IA/RO	IA	129
HAR-2856	RO/EM	RO	52
HAR-2861	EM	EM	194
HAR-2902	IA/RO	IA	10
HAR-2905	RO/EM	BA	57
HAR-2913	IA/RO	IA	129
HAR-2930	RO	EM	76
HAR-2935	RO/EM	MD	24
HAR-2969	IA	IA	47
HAR-2970	IA/RO	IA	47
HAR-2971	IA	IA	47
HAR-2973	IA/RO	IA	47
HAR-2974	IA/RO	IA	47
HAR-2980	IA	IA	109
HAR-3041	EM	EM	74
HAR-3073	RO/EM		9–10
HAR-3074	EM		10
HAR-3079	RO/EM	EM	140
HAR-3080	RO/EM	EM	140
HAR-3081	RO/EM	EM	140
HAR-3084	IA/RO	RO	35
HAR-3085	RO/EM	RO	35–6
HAR-3090	EM	EM	82
HAR-3095	IA/RO	IA	16
HAR-3103	IA/RO	RO	96
HAR-3104	RO/EM	RO	96
HAR-3105	IA/RO	RO	96
HAR-3174	RO/EM	MD	24
HAR-3197	IA/RO	RO	34–5
HAR-331	RO/EM	EM/MD	103
HAR-334	IA/RO	IA	34
HAR-335	IA/RO	IA	34
HAR-3353	RO/EM	RO	101
HAR-3363	IA/RO	RO	101
HAR-3369	EM	RO	204
HAR-3381	RO/EM	IA	204
HAR-3424	IA/RO	IA/RO	163–4
HAR-3427	RO	IA/RO	164
HAR-3428	IA/RO	IA/RO	164
HAR-3429	IA/RO/ME	IA/RO	164
HAR-3430	RO	IA/RO	164
HAR-3438	RO/EM	MD	19
HAR-3456	IA/RO		21
HAR-3485	IA/RO		92
HAR-3493	IA/RO	IA	5–6
HAR-3494	IA/RO	IA	6
HAR-3495	IA/RO	IA	6

Sample	Period	Date	Page
HAR-3496	IA/RO	IA	6
HAR-3591	IA/RO	NE	163
HAR-3620	IA/RO	IA	59–60
HAR-3629	RO/EM	EM	129
HAR-3653	RO/EM	RO	36
HAR-3654	RO/EM	RO	36
HAR-3655	RO/EM	RO	36
HAR-3657	RO/EM	RO/EM	200
HAR-3658	RO/EM	RO/EM	200–1
HAR-3686	RO/EM	RO/EM	201
HAR-3688	RO/EM	EM	123
HAR-3689	EM	EM	123
HAR-3706	IA/RO	BA	88
HAR-3720	EM	EM	40
HAR-3721	RO/EM	EM	40
HAR-3743	IA	IA	48
HAR-3745	IA/RO	IA	173
HAR-3747	IA/RO	IA/EM	72
HAR-3749	RO/EM	RO	32
HAR-3764	RO/EM	EM	40
HAR-3767	RO/EM	EM	40
HAR-3768	RO/EM	EM	40
HAR-3892	IA/RO	IA	173
HAR-3901	IA/RO	IA	49
HAR-3947	IA	IA	16
HAR-3952	IA/RO	IA	17
HAR-3955	IA/RO	IA	17
HAR-3970	RO/EM	RO	27
HAR-3977	IA/RO	BA	24
HAR-4054	RO/EM	EM	205
HAR-4055	RO/EM	EM	205
HAR-4084	RO/EM	RO	52
HAR-4087	IA/RO		26
HAR-4093	RO/EM	EM	205
HAR-4111	EM	EM	205
HAR-4116	EM	EM	90
HAR-4120	IA/RO	EM	90
HAR-4131	EM	EM	91
HAR-4143	RO/EM	EM	91
HAR-4145	IA/RO	EM	205
HAR-4146	RO/EM	EM	205
HAR-4147	IA/RO	EM	205
HAR-4177	RO/EM	EM	91
HAR-4191	IA/RO	EM	205
HAR-4194	RO/EM	EM	205
HAR-4203	RO	RO	56
HAR-4244	IA/RO	IA	49
HAR-4255	EM	EM	205
HAR-4327	IA	IA	50
HAR-4352	RO/EM	EM	212
HAR-444	IA	IA	8
HAR-4440	IA/RO	IA	17
HAR-4447	RO/EM	EM	40–1
HAR-4449	RO/EM	EM	41
HAR-445	IA/RO	IA	8
HAR-446	BA/IA/RO	IA	8
HAR-447	EM	EM	91-2
HAR-448	RO	RO/PM	124
HAR-459	IA/RO	BA/IA	154
HAR-469	IA	IA	115
HAR-494	RO/EM	RO	31
HAR-495	EM	RO	31
HAR-497	EM	RO	31
HAR-508	IA/RO	IA	38
HAR-509	IA	IA	38
HAR-5921+HAR-4352	EM	EM	212
HAR-607-I	IA/RO	IA	38
HAR-607-II	IA/RO	IA	38
HAR-607-III	IA/RO	IA	38
HAR-711	EM	RO/EM	145–6
HAR-715	EM	EM	38
HAR-749	RO/EM	EM/MD	216
HAR-753	EM	EM/MD	216
HAR-831	RO/EM	EM	53–4
HAR-857	IA	IA	112
HAR-873	IA/RO		112
HAR-878	EM	EM/MD	218
HAR-949	RO/EM	EM	12
HAR-951	EM	EM	12
HAR-953	EM	EM	12
HAR-954	EM	EM	12
HAR-959	EM	BA	137
HAR-960	IA/RO	EM	83
HAR-961	RO/EM	EM	83
HAR-968	IA	IA	43
HAR-970	IA/RO	IA/RO	41
HAR-971	IA	IA/RO	41
HAR-972	IA/RO	IA/RO	41
HAR-973	IA/RO	IA/RO	41
HAR-974	IA/RO	IA/RO	41
HAR-975	IA/RO	IA/RO	41
HAR-984	RO/EM	MD	87
HAR-992	RO/EM	RO	37
HAR-995	IA/RO	EM	139

Results 500–1000 cal AD

Sample	Period	Date	Page
H79/85	EM	EM?	131
HAR-1004	RO/EM	RO/EM	147
HAR-1006	RO/EM	RO	37
HAR-1009	RO/EM	RO	37
HAR-1024	EM	IA/EM	89
HAR-1025	RO/EM	IA/EM	89
HAR-1038	EM	EM	128
HAR-1060	EM	EM/MD	220
HAR-1061	EM/MD	EM/MD	220
HAR-1062	EM	EM/MD	220
HAR-1063	EM/MD	EM/MD	220–1
HAR-1064	EM	EM/MD	221
HAR-1065	EM/MD	EM/MD	221
HAR-1066	RO/EM	EM/MD	221
HAR-1067	EM	EM/MD	221
HAR-1069	EM/MD	EM/MD	221–2
HAR-1070	EM	EM/MD	222

Sample	Period	Date	Page	Sample	Period	Date	Page
HAR-1080	EM/MD	EM/MD	65	HAR-1564	EM	EM/MD	228
HAR-1083	RO/EM	RO	95	HAR-1582	EM/MD	EM/MD	229
HAR-1085	EM	EM/MD	133	HAR-1587	EM/MD	EM/MD	229
HAR-1096	EM	EM	128	HAR-1605	RO/EM	RO	233
HAR-1101	EM/MD	EM/MD	223	HAR-1606	EM	EM	142
HAR-1117	EM/MD	EM/MD	223	HAR-1607	EM	EM	142
HAR-1119	EM		196	HAR-1608	EM/MD	EM	142
HAR-1164	EM	EM	188	HAR-1609	EM	EM	142
HAR-1165	EM/MD	EM	188	HAR-1610	EM/MD	EM/MD	230
HAR-1166	EM	EM	188	HAR-1613	EM	EM	55
HAR-1167	RO/EM	EM	188	HAR-1614	RO/EM	EM	55
HAR-1185	EM	EM	4	HAR-1620	EM/MD	EM	77
HAR-1225	EM	EM	123	HAR-1626	EM	EM	142
HAR-1244	EM	EM	123	HAR-1636	EM	EM	62
HAR-1245	EM	EM	123	HAR-1639	EM/MD	EM/MD	230
HAR-1246	EM	EM	123	HAR-1648	EM	EM	130
HAR-125	EM/MD	EM?	131	HAR-1649	EM	EM	130
HAR-1257	EM/MD	EM/MD	223	HAR-1652	RO/EM	RO/EM	60–1
HAR-1259	EM/MD	EM/MD	223	HAR-1653	RO/EM		100
HAR-1271	EM/MD	EM/MD	223–4	HAR-1655	EM	EM	61
HAR-1277	EM/MD	EM/MD	224	HAR-1656	EM	EM/MD	61
HAR-1278	EM	EM/MD	224	HAR-1658	EM/MD	EM	61
HAR-1279	EM/MD	EM/MD	224	HAR-1663	RO/EM	EM	23
HAR-1296	EM	IA	59	HAR-1666	EM	EM	118–19
HAR-1318	RO/EM		99	HAR-1673	EM	EM	189
HAR-1329	EM	MD	208	HAR-1676	EM	EM	130
HAR-1337	EM	MD	208	HAR-1677	EM/MD	EM/MD	230
HAR-1339	RO/EM	RO	63	HAR-1678	EM/MD	EM/MD	230
HAR-1375	EM/MD	EM	78	HAR-1680	EM/MD	EM/MD	230
HAR-1378	EM/MD	EM?	4–5	HAR-1681	EM	EM	119
HAR-1393	RO/EM	RO	20	HAR-1687	EM/MD	EM/MD	231
HAR-1412	EM	EM/MD	236	HAR-1688	EM/MD	EM/MD	231
HAR-1421	RO/EM	RO	98	HAR-1696	EM	BA	7
HAR-1422	EM/MD	EM	98	HAR-1703	RO/EM	EM	107
HAR-1427	EM	EM	128	HAR-1704	EM/MD	EM	142
HAR-1428	EM	EM	128	HAR-1717	EM/MD		96
HAR-1433	EM	MD	102–3	HAR-1720	EM	EM	124
HAR-1443	EM	EM	62	HAR-1728	EM/MD	EM	237
HAR-1444	EM	EM	62	HAR-1738	EM	EM/MD	231
HAR-1446	EM	EM	62	HAR-1787	EM/MD	EM	61
HAR-1452	EM	EM	124	HAR-1788	EM	EM	61
HAR-1454	EM/MD	EM	124	HAR-1837	RO/EM	EM	89
HAR-1456	RO/EM	RO	94	HAR-1838	EM	EM	128
HAR-1464	RO/EM	RO	94	HAR-1842	RO/EM		168
HAR-1486	EM	EM	188–9	HAR-1851	EM/MD	EM/MD	232
HAR-1488	EM	EM/MD	224	HAR-1852	EM/MD	EM/MD	232
HAR-1500	EM/MD	EM	12–13	HAR-1853	EM	EM	189
HAR-1502	EM	EM	13	HAR-1864	RO/EM	RO	96–7
HAR-1503	EM		13	HAR-1875	EM/MD	EM	79–80
HAR-1506	EM/MD	EM	13	HAR-1894	EM	RO	33
HAR-1507	EM	EM	13	HAR-1896	EM/MD	EM/MD	18
HAR-1508	EM	EM/MD	225	HAR-1897	EM	EM/MD	18
HAR-1509	EM	EM/MD	225	HAR-1908	RO/EM	EM	194
HAR-1511	EM/MD	EM/MD	225	HAR-190(S)	EM	EM	133
HAR-1513	EM/MD	EM/MD	226	HAR-1914	EM	EM	234–5
HAR-1518	EM/MD	EM/MD	226	HAR-2006	RO/EM	RO/EM	42
HAR-1519	EM	EM/MD	226	HAR-2010	EM/MD	EM	90

Index 3: Period index

Sample	Period	Date	Page	Sample	Period	Date	Page
HAR-2011	EM/MD	EM	90	HAR-2600	EM	EM	20–1
HAR-2012	EM	EM	90	HAR-2614	RO/EM		7
HAR-2015	EM/MD	EM	143–4	HAR-2670	EM	EM	86
HAR-2016	EM/MD	EM	144	HAR-2672	EM/MD	EM	209
HAR-2017	EM/MD	EM	144	HAR-2674	EM	EM	195–6
HAR-2019	EM/MD	EM	144	HAR-2692	EM		102
HAR-2021	EM/MD	EM	144	HAR-2696	EM		102
HAR-2090	EM	EM	189	HAR-2700	EM	EM	125
HAR-2111	EM/MD	EM	240	HAR-2701	EM	EM	125
HAR-2113	EM/MD	EM	240	HAR-2702	EM	EM	125
HAR-2122	EM/MD	EM	241	HAR-2708	EM	RO?	239
HAR-2184	EM	EM	1313	HAR-2732	EM/MD	EM/MD	3
HAR-2185	EM/MD	MD	189	HAR-2734	EM	EM	193
HAR-2207	RO/EM		73	HAR-2736	EM/MD	EM	20
HAR-2209	EM	EM	200	HAR-2756	EM/MD	EM/MD	80
HAR-2223	RO/EM	BA	6–7	HAR-2757	EM/MD	EM/MD	80
HAR-2234	EM/MD	EM	241	HAR-2763	EM	EM	82
HAR-2235	EM	EM	241	HAR-2764	EM	EM	82
HAR-2237	EM	EM	241	HAR-2765	RO/EM	EM	103
HAR-2274	EM	BA	192	HAR-2766	RO/EM	EM	103
HAR-2275	EM	BA	192	HAR-2768	EM/MD	EM/MD	80
HAR-2281	RO/EM	EM	139	HAR-2769	EM	EM	107
HAR-2283	RO/EM	EM	120	HAR-2774	EM	EM/MD	138
HAR-2300	EM/MD	EM/MD	235	HAR-2775	EM	EM/MD	138
HAR-2301	EM/MD	EM/MD	235	HAR-2778	EM/MD	EM	82–3
HAR-2302	EM/MD	EM/MD	235	HAR-2781	EM	EM	83
HAR-2341	EM	EM	116	HAR-2802	EM	EM	128–9
HAR-2344	EM	EM	117	HAR-2806	EM/MD	MD	195
HAR-235(S)	IA	IA	233–4	HAR-2812	EM	EM	60
HAR-2398	RO/EM	RO/EM	119	HAR-2813	EM	EM	60
HAR-2404	EM	EM	144	HAR-2814	EM	EM	60
HAR-2412	EM/MD	BA	140	HAR-2856	RO/EM	RO	52
HAR-2425	EM/MD	MD	102	HAR-2858	EM	EM	194
HAR-2427	EM/MD	EM/MD	144–5	HAR-2860	EM	EM	194
HAR-2446	EM	EM	13–14	HAR-2861	EM	EM	194
HAR-2449	EM/MD	EM	14	HAR-288	EM	EM	213
HAR-2456	EM	EM	14	HAR-289	EM	EM	213
HAR-2457	EM	EM	14	HAR-2897	EM	EM	30
HAR-2458	EM	EM	14	HAR-290	EM	EM	213
HAR-2460	EM/MD	EM	208	HAR-2905	RO/EM	BA	57
HAR-2462	EM/MD	EM	208	HAR-291	EM	EM	214
HAR-2466	RO/EM	EM	74	HAR-2910	EM	EM	83
HAR-2467	EM	EM	74	HAR-2916	EM/MD	MD	236
HAR-2489	RO/EM		59	HAR-292	EM/MD	EM/MD	214
HAR-2501	RO/EM	IA?	98	HAR-2935	RO/EM	MD	24
HAR-2507	EM	EM	14	HAR-2959	EM/MD	NE/BA/IA	72
HAR-2508	EM	EM	14	HAR-3023	EM	EM	74
HAR-2527	EM/MD	EM	145	HAR-3039	EM	EM	191
HAR-2539	EM/MD	MD	84–5	HAR-3041	EM	EM	74
HAR-2542	EM/MD	EM	97	HAR-3056	EM	EM	74
HAR-2548	RO/EM	EM	97	HAR-3065	EM/MD	MD	86
HAR-2572	RO/EM	RO	35	HAR-3066	EM/MD	MD	86
HAR-2577	EM/MD		191	HAR-3073	RO/EM		9–10
HAR-2582	RO/EM		191	HAR-3074	EM		10
HAR-2593	EM	EM	86	HAR-3079	RO/EM	EM	140
HAR-2594	EM/MD	EM	68	HAR-3080	RO/EM	EM	140
HAR-2599	EM/MD	EM	20	HAR-3081	RO/EM	EM	140

Index 3: Period index

Sample	Period	Date	Page
HAR-3083	EM	EM	129
HAR-3085	RO/EM	RO	35–6
HAR-3088	EM	MD	236
HAR-3089	EM	MD	236
HAR-3090	EM	EM	82
HAR-3091	EM	EM	82
HAR-3104	RO/EM	RO	96
HAR-3106	EM/MD	EM	1111
HAR-3109	EM		40
HAR-3123	EM/MD	EM	10
HAR-3125	EM	EM	10
HAR-3126	EM	EM	10
HAR-3127	EM/MD	EM	11
HAR-3128	EM	EM	11
HAR-3140	EM/MD	EM	62
HAR-3174	RO/EM	MD	24
HAR-328	EM	EM	103
HAR-3291	EM	EM	187
HAR-330	EM/MD		103
HAR-331	RO/EM	EM/MD	103
HAR-3313	EM	MD	118
HAR-3347	EM/MD	MD	118
HAR-3369	EM	RO	204
HAR-3374	EM/MD	EM	202
HAR-3375	EM/MD	EM	202
HAR-3376	EM/MD	EM	202
HAR-3381	RO/EM	IA	204
HAR-3382	EM	IA/EM	204–5
HAR-3390	EM	EM	187
HAR-3397	EM	EM	202
HAR-3422	EM/MD	IA/RO/EM	164
HAR-3423	EM		102
HAR-3438	RO/EM	MD	19
HAR-3444	EM		130
HAR-3452	EM		21
HAR-3462	EM/MD	EM/MD	138
HAR-3463	EM	EM/MD	138
HAR-354	EM	EM/MD	214
HAR-3575	EM/MD	EM	209
HAR-3584	EM	EM	209
HAR-3585	EM	EM	125
HAR-3593	EM		157
HAR-362	EM/MD	EM/MD	214
HAR-3624	EM/MD		17
HAR-3629	RO/EM	EM	129
HAR-363	EM/MD	EM/MD	214
HAR-3653	RO/EM	RO	36
HAR-3654	RO/EM	RO	36
HAR-3655	RO/EM	RO	36
HAR-3656	EM	EM	125
HAR-3657	RO/EM	RO/EM	200
HAR-3658	RO/EM	RO/EM	200–1
HAR-366	EM	EM	215
HAR-367	EM	EM	215
HAR-368	EM	EM/MD	215
HAR-3686	RO/EM	RO/EM	201
HAR-3688	RO/EM	EM	123
HAR-3689	EM	EM	123
HAR-369	EM	EM/MD	215
HAR-3707	EM	EM	125–6
HAR-3710	EM	EM	32
HAR-3720	EM	EM	40
HAR-3721	RO/EM	EM	40
HAR-3722	EM	EM	126
HAR-3742	EM/MD	BA	89
HAR-3748	EM	BA/IA/EM	203
HAR-3749	RO/EM	RO	32
HAR-3756	EM/MD	EM/MD	241
HAR-3757	EM	EM	241–2
HAR-3758	EM/MD		242
HAR-3760	EM/MD	EM	145
HAR-3764	RO/EM	EM	40
HAR-3765	EM	EM	145
HAR-3767	RO/EM	EM	40
HAR-3790	EM	EM?	242
HAR-3794	EM/MD	EM	27
HAR-3795	EM	EM	27–8
HAR-3804	EM	EM	28
HAR-3808	EM	RO	204
HAR-3844	EM/MD	EM	242
HAR-3852	EM/MD	EM	126–7
HAR-3877	EM/MD	EM	127
HAR-3878	EM/MD	EM	127
HAR-3881	EM/MD		242
HAR-3907	EM/MD	EM/MD	242
HAR-3910	EM/MD	EM/MD	242
HAR-3916	EM/MD		242
HAR-3935	EM	EM	123
HAR-3953	EM	IA	17
HAR-3970	RO/EM	RO	27
HAR-3971	EM/MD	EM/MD	63
HAR-4001	EM	IA	17
HAR-4054	RO/EM	EM	205
HAR-4055	RO/EM	EM	205
HAR-4086	EM		26
HAR-4093	RO/EM	EM	205
HAR-4111	EM	EM	205
HAR-4115	EM/MD	EM	95–6
HAR-4116	EM	EM	90
HAR-4117	EM	IA/EM	6
HAR-4121	EM	EM	90
HAR-413	EM/MD	EM	79
HAR-4131	EM	EM	91
HAR-414	EM/MD	EM	79
HAR-4143	RO/EM	EM	91
HAR-4146	RO/EM	EM	205
HAR-4177	RO/EM	EM	91
HAR-418	EM/MD	MD	132
HAR-4187	EM	EM/MD	63
HAR-419	EM/MD	EM	132
HAR-4194	RO/EM	EM	205
HAR-4255	EM	EM	205
HAR-4262	EM/MD	EM/MD	211
HAR-4263	EM	EM?	211–12

Sample	Period	Date	Page
HAR-4281	EM	EM	91
HAR-4352	RO/EM	EM	212
HAR-443	EM	IA	8
HAR-4447	RO/EM	EM	40–1
HAR-4449	RO/EM	EM	41
HAR-447	EM	EM	91–2
HAR-451	EM	EM	116
HAR-466-I	EM/MD	EM	132
HAR-466-II	EM/MD	EM	132
HAR-483	EM	IA/EM	26
HAR-484	EM	EM	26
HAR-485	EM	EM	27
HAR-493	EM	RO	31
HAR-494	RO/EM	RO	31
HAR-495	EM	RO	31
HAR-496	EM	RO	31
HAR-497	EM	RO	31
HAR-506	EM	RO/EM	15
HAR-507	EM/MD	RO/EM	15
HAR-512	EM	EM	209
HAR-513	EM	EM	209
HAR-548	EM	EM	239
HAR-549	EM	EM	239–40
HAR-550	EM	EM	240
HAR-568	EM/MD	EM	189
HAR-569	EM	EM	187–8
HAR-570	EM	EM	188
HAR-572	EM	EM	188
HAR-573	EM/MD	EM	188
HAR-5921	EM	EM	212
HAR-5921+HAR-4352	EM	EM	212
HAR-5922	EM	EM	212
HAR-5922+HAR-4263	EM	EM	212
HAR-599	EM/MD	MD	53
HAR-601	EM/MD	MD	53
HAR-602	EM/MD	EM	53
HAR-711	EM	RO/EM	145–6
HAR-715	EM	EM	38
HAR-718	EM	EM?	131–2
HAR-728	EM	EM	188
HAR-748	EM/MD	EM/MD	215–16
HAR-749	RO/EM	EM/MD	216
HAR-750	EM	EM/MD	216
HAR-752	EM/MD	EM/MD	216
HAR-753	EM	EM/MD	216
HAR-754	EM	EM/MD	217
HAR-755	EM	EM/MD	217
HAR-757	EM/MD	EM/MD	217
HAR-758	EM	EM/MD	217
HAR-759	EM	EM	119
HAR-760	EM/MD	EM	119
HAR-763	EM	EM	119
HAR-826	EM/MD	EM	53
HAR-827	EM/MD	EM	53
HAR-829	EM/MD	EM	53
HAR-831	RO/EM	EM	53–4
HAR-845	EM		196
HAR-863	EM	EM	91
HAR-876	EM/MD	EM/MD	217
HAR-877	EM	EM/MD	217–18
HAR-878	EM	EM/MD	218
HAR-879	EM/MD	EM/MD	218
HAR-880	EM	EM/MD	218
HAR-881	EM/MD	EM/MD	218
HAR-882	EM	EM/MD	218–19
HAR-883	EM	EM/MD	219
HAR-884	EM	EM/MD	219
HAR-885	EM	EM/MD	219
HAR-886	EM	EM/MD	219
HAR-887	EM/MD	EM/MD	219–20
HAR-888	EM/MD	EM/MD	220
HAR-889	EM	EM/MD	220
HAR-949	RO/EM	EM	12
HAR-951	EM	EM	12
HAR-952	EM	EM	12
HAR-953	EM	EM	12
HAR-954	EM	EM	12
HAR-959	EM	BA	137
HAR-961	RO/EM	EM	83
HAR-962	EM	BA	140
HAR-976	EM/MD	MD	19
HAR-979	EM/MD	MD	87
HAR-980	EM/MD	EM	87
HAR-981	EM	EM	87
HAR-983	EM/MD	EM	87
HAR-984	RO/EM	MD	87
HAR-985	EM	EM	79
HAR-986	EM/MD	EM	79
HAR-992	RO/EM	RO	37

Results 1000–1500 cal AD

Sample	Period	Date	Page
HAR-1024	EM	IA/EM	89
HAR-1060	EM	EM/MD	220
HAR-1061	EM/MD	EM/MD	220
HAR-1062	EM	EM/MD	220
HAR-1063	EM/MD	EM/MD	220–1
HAR-1064	EM	EM/MD	221
HAR-1065	EM/MD	EM/MD	221
HAR-1067	EM	EM/MD	221
HAR-1068	MD	EM/MD	221
HAR-1069	EM/MD	EM/MD	221–2
HAR-1070	EM	EM/MD	222
HAR-1075	EM/MD	EM/MD	222
HAR-1078	MD	EM/MD	222
HAR-1079	EM/MD	MD	64
HAR-1080	EM/MD	EM/MD	65
HAR-1084	MD	EM/MD	222
HAR-1085	EM	EM/MD	133
HAR-1101	EM/MD	EM/MD	223
HAR-1103	EM/MD	EM/MD	223
HAR-1117	EM/MD	EM/MD	223
HAR-1165	EM/MD	EM	188
HAR-1201	EM/MD	MD	94

Sample	Period	Date	Page	Sample	Period	Date	Page
HAR-1206	MD/PM	BA	9	HAR-1639	EM/MD	EM/MD	230
HAR-1244	EM	EM	123	HAR-1657	EM/MD	MD	61
HAR-125	EM/MD	EM?	131	HAR-1658	EM/MD	EM	61
HAR-1257	EM/MD	EM/MD	223	HAR-1677	EM/MD	EM/MD	230
HAR-1259	EM/MD	EM/MD	223	HAR-1678	EM/MD	EM/MD	230
HAR-1260	EM/MD	MD	78	HAR-1680	EM/MD	EM/MD	230
HAR-1271	EM/MD	EM/MD	223–4	HAR-1681	EM	EM	119
HAR-1277	EM/MD	EM/MD	224	HAR-1686	EM/MD	EM/MD	230–1
HAR-1278	EM	EM/MD	224	HAR-1687	EM/MD	EM/MD	231
HAR-1279	EM/MD	EM/MD	224	HAR-1688	EM/MD	EM/MD	231
HAR-1375	EM/MD	EM	78	HAR-1689	MD	MD	57
HAR-1378	EM/MD	EM?	4–5	HAR-1690	MD/PM	MD	57
HAR-1422	EM/MD	EM	98	HAR-1704	EM/MD	EM	142
HAR-1431	MD	EM/MD	124	HAR-1717	EM/MD		96
HAR-1432	MD	MD	102	HAR-1728	EM/MD	EM	237
HAR-1437	EM/MD	EM	124	HAR-1735	MD	MD	78
HAR-1444	EM	EM	62	HAR-1740	MD	EM/MD	231
HAR-1452	EM	EM	124	HAR-1741	MD	MD	232
HAR-1454	EM/MD	EM	124	HAR-1787	EM/MD	EM	61
HAR-1488	EM	EM/MD	224	HAR-1788	EM	EM	61
HAR-1500	EM/MD	EM	12–13	HAR-1820	EM/MD	EM/MD	234
HAR-1502	EM	EM	13	HAR-1821	EM/MD	EM/MD	234
HAR-1506	EM/MD	EM	13	HAR-1822	EM/MD	EM/MD	234
HAR-1508	EM	EM/MD	225	HAR-1830	MD/PM		156
HAR-1510	EM/MD	EM/MD	225	HAR-1851	EM/MD	EM/MD	232
HAR-1511	EM/MD	EM/MD	225	HAR-1875	EM/MD	EM	79–80
HAR-1512	MD	EM/MD	225	HAR-1894	EM	RO	33
HAR-1513	EM/MD	EM/MD	226	HAR-1896	EM/MD	EM/MD	18
HAR-1515	EM/MD	EM/MD	226	HAR-1897	EM	EM/MD	18
HAR-1516	EM/MD	EM/MD	226	HAR-190(S)	EM	EM	133
HAR-1517	EM/MD	EM/MD	226	HAR-191	EM/MD	MD	133
HAR-1518	EM/MD	EM/MD	226	HAR-1914	EM	EM	234–5
HAR-1520	MD	EM/MD	227	HAR-1929	MD	MD	18
HAR-1521	MD	EM/MD	227	HAR-1930	MD/PM	MD	18
HAR-1531	MD	EM/MD	227	HAR-1961	EM/MD	EM	89–90
HAR-1534	MD/PM	EM/MD	227	HAR-2010	EM/MD	EM	90
HAR-1537	EM/MD	EM/MD	227	HAR-2011	EM/MD	EM	90
HAR-1551	MD/PM	EM/MD	227	HAR-2012	EM	EM	90
HAR-1561	MD/PM	EM/MD	227–8	HAR-2015	EM/MD	EM	143–4
HAR-1563	EM/MD	EM/MD	228	HAR-2016	EM/MD	EM	144
HAR-1565	MD	MD	228	HAR-2017	EM/MD	EM	144
HAR-1573	MD	EM/MD	228	HAR-2018	EM/MD	EM/MD	144
HAR-1574	MD	MD	228	HAR-2019	EM/MD	EM	144
HAR-1580	EM/MD	EM/MD	228	HAR-2021	EM/MD	EM	144
HAR-1582	EM/MD	EM/MD	229	HAR-2111	EM/MD	EM	240
HAR-1583	MD	EM/MD	229	HAR-2113	EM/MD	EM	240
HAR-1584	EM/MD	MD	229	HAR-2122	EM/MD	EM	241
HAR-1587	EM/MD	EM/MD	229	HAR-2185	EM/MD	MD	189
HAR-1603	MD	EM/MD	229	HAR-2207	RO/EM		73
HAR-1604	EM/MD	EM/MD	229	HAR-2209	EM	EM	200
HAR-1606	EM	EM	142	HAR-2234	EM/MD	EM	241
HAR-1608	EM/MD	EM	142	HAR-2235	EM	EM	241
HAR-1610	EM/MD	EM/MD	230	HAR-2237	EM	EM	241
HAR-1611	EM/MD	EM	54–5	HAR-2259	MD/PM		7
HAR-1620	EM/MD	EM	77	HAR-2261	MD	MD	21
HAR-1626	EM	EM	142	HAR-2262	MD/PM	PM	85
HAR-1636	EM	EM	62	HAR-2264	EM/MD	EM/MD	52

Index 3: Period index

Sample	Period	Date	Page	Sample	Period	Date	Page
HAR-2265	MD	MD	56	HAR-2865	MD	MD	11
HAR-2266	MD/PM	PM	85	HAR-2896	MD/PM	MD	232
HAR-2275	EM	BA	192	HAR-2897	EM	EM	30
HAR-2279	MD	MD	147–8	HAR-2898	EM/MD	RO	238
HAR-2300	EM/MD	EM/MD	235	HAR-2899	MD	RO	238
HAR-2301	EM/MD	EM/MD	235	HAR-2900	MD	EM?	238
HAR-2302	EM/MD	EM/MD	235	HAR-291	EM	EM	214
HAR-2326	EM/MD	EM	144	HAR-2910	EM	EM	83
HAR-2336	MD	EM	193	HAR-2915	EM/MD	MD	236
HAR-2404	EM	EM	144	HAR-2916	EM/MD	MD	236
HAR-2412	EM/MD	BA	140	HAR-292	EM/MD	EM/MD	214
HAR-2416	MD	MD	101	HAR-2959	EM/MD	NE/BA/IA	72
HAR-2417	MD	MD	101–2	HAR-3023	EM	EM	74
HAR-2418	MD	MD	102	HAR-3039	EM	EM	191
HAR-2419	MD	MD	102	HAR-3065	EM/MD	MD	86
HAR-2425	EM/MD	MD	102	HAR-3066	EM/MD	MD	86
HAR-2426	MD	MD	102	HAR-3075	MD/PM		10
HAR-2427	EM/MD	EM/MD	144–5	HAR-3088	EM	MD	236
HAR-2449	EM/MD	EM	14	HAR-3100	MD	EM/MD	234
HAR-2460	EM/MD	EM	208	HAR-3106	EM/MD	EM	1111
HAR-2462	EM/MD	EM	208	HAR-3121	MD	MD	64
HAR-2507	EM	EM	14	HAR-3122	MD	MD	64
HAR-2524	EM/MD	IA?	98	HAR-3123	EM/MD	EM	10
HAR-2527	EM/MD	EM	145	HAR-3124	EM/MD	EM	10
HAR-2536	MD	MD	5	HAR-3125	EM	EM	10
HAR-2539	EM/MD	MD	84–5	HAR-3126	EM	EM	10
HAR-2542	EM/MD	EM	97	HAR-3127	EM/MD	EM	11
HAR-2545	EM/MD	MD	135	HAR-3128	EM	EM	11
HAR-2549	MD	MD	135	HAR-3140	EM/MD	EM	62
HAR-2559	EM/MD	EM/MD	68	HAR-3264	MD		110
HAR-2560	EM/MD	MD	124	HAR-328	EM	EM	103
HAR-2577	EM/MD		191	HAR-3291	EM	EM	187
HAR-2578	EM/MD		191	HAR-330	EM/MD		103
HAR-2594	EM/MD	EM	68	HAR-3313	EM	MD	118
HAR-2595	EM/MD	EM	68	HAR-3347	EM/MD	MD	118
HAR-2599	EM/MD	EM	20	HAR-3359	MD		156
HAR-2606	MD	EM	68–9	HAR-3368	MD	MD	118
HAR-2631	EM/MD	EM	208–9	HAR-3374	EM/MD	EM	202
HAR-2672	EM/MD	EM	209	HAR-3375	EM/MD	EM	202
HAR-2674	EM	EM	195–6	HAR-3376	EM/MD	EM	202
HAR-2697	EM/MD	EM	69	HAR-3391	MD/PM	PM	110
HAR-2701	EM	EM	125	HAR-3393	MD/PM	MD	110
HAR-2732	EM/MD	EM/MD	3	HAR-3398	EM/MD	EM	202
HAR-2736	EM/MD	EM	20	HAR-3422	EM/MD	IA/RO/EM	164
HAR-2756	EM/MD	EM/MD	80	HAR-3432	EM/MD	MD	118
HAR-2757	EM/MD	EM/MD	80	HAR-3433	MD	EM/MD	3
HAR-2764	EM	EM	82	HAR-3434	EM/MD	EM/MD	3
HAR-2768	EM/MD	EM/MD	80	HAR-3436	EM/MD	EM/MD	19
HAR-2778	EM/MD	EM	82–3	HAR-3437	EM/MD	MD	19
HAR-2795	EM/MD	IA	106	HAR-3444	EM		130
HAR-2800	EM/MD	IA	106	HAR-3462	EM/MD	EM/MD	138
HAR-2804	EM/MD	MD	195	HAR-354	EM	EM/MD	214
HAR-2806	EM/MD	MD	195	HAR-3575	EM/MD	EM	209
HAR-2815	EM/MD	MD	195	HAR-3593	EM		157
HAR-2860	EM	EM	194	HAR-3616	EM/MD	MD	143
HAR-2863	MD	MD	11	HAR-3617	EM/MD	MD	143
HAR-2864	EM/MD	MD	11	HAR-3618	MD	MD	143

Sample	Period	Date	Page
HAR-362	EM/MD	EM/MD	214
HAR-3624	EM/MD		17
HAR-363	EM/MD	EM/MD	214
HAR-369	EM	EM/MD	215
HAR-3710	EM	EM	32
HAR-3722	EM	EM	126
HAR-3742	EM/MD	BA	89
HAR-3748	EM	BA/IA/EM	203
HAR-3756	EM/MD	EM/MD	241
HAR-3757	EM	EM	241–2
HAR-3758	EM/MD		242
HAR-3760	EM/MD	EM	145
HAR-3765	EM	EM	145
HAR-3794	EM/MD	EM	27
HAR-3844	EM/MD	EM	242
HAR-3852	EM/MD	EM	126–7
HAR-3877	EM/MD	EM	127
HAR-3878	EM/MD	EM	127
HAR-3881	EM/MD		242
HAR-3885	EM/MD	MD	148
HAR-3906	MD		130
HAR-3907	EM/MD	EM/MD	242
HAR-3910	EM/MD	EM/MD	242
HAR-3916	EM/MD		242
HAR-3937	MD	MD	140–1
HAR-3938	EM/MD	MD	141
HAR-3939	MD	MD	141
HAR-3953	EM	IA	17
HAR-3957	MD/PM	PM	141
HAR-3971	EM/MD	EM/MD	63
HAR-4001	EM	IA	17
HAR-4017	EM/MD		162
HAR-4115	EM/MD	EM	95–6
HAR-413	EM/MD	EM	79
HAR-414	EM/MD	EM	79
HAR-418	EM/MD	MD	132
HAR-419	EM/MD	EM	132
HAR-4262	EM/MD	EM/MD	211
HAR-466-I	EM/MD	EM	132
HAR-466-II	EM/MD	EM	132
HAR-484	EM	EM	26
HAR-493	EM	RO	31
HAR-506	EM	RO/EM	15
HAR-507	EM/MD	RO/EM	15
HAR-548	EM	EM	239
HAR-549	EM	EM	239–40
HAR-550	EM	EM	240
HAR-551	EM/MD	MD	240
HAR-552	EM/MD	MD	39
HAR-568	EM/MD	EM	189
HAR-570	EM	EM	188
HAR-572	EM	EM	188
HAR-573	EM/MD	EM	188
HAR-5921	EM	EM	212
HAR-599	EM/MD	MD	53
HAR-601	EM/MD	MD	53
HAR-602	EM/MD	EM	53
HAR-717	EM/MD	EM?	31
HAR-718	EM	EM?	131–2
HAR-728	EM	EM	188
HAR-729	EM/MD	MD	132
HAR-730	MD	MD	132
HAR-748	EM/MD	EM/MD	215-16
HAR-752	EM/MD	EM/MD	216
HAR-754	EM	EM/MD	217
HAR-757	EM/MD	EM/MD	217
HAR-760	EM/MD	EM	119
HAR-826	EM/MD	EM	53
HAR-827	EM/MD	EM	53
HAR-828	MD	MD	53
HAR-829	EM/MD	EM	53
HAR-830	EM/MD	EM	53
HAR-846	EM/MD	MD	39
HAR-847	EM/MD		20
HAR-863	EM	EM	91
HAR-876	EM/MD	EM/MD	217
HAR-877	EM	EM/MD	217–18
HAR-879	EM/MD	EM/MD	218
HAR-881	EM/MD	EM/MD	218
HAR-883	EM	EM/MD	219
HAR-884	EM	EM/MD	219
HAR-886	EM	EM/MD	219
HAR-887	EM/MD	EM/MD	219–20
HAR-888	EM/MD	EM/MD	220
HAR-889	EM	EM/MD	220
HAR-969	MD	MD	153–4
HAR-976	EM/MD	MD	19
HAR-978	EM/MD	MD	86
HAR-979	EM/MD	MD	87
HAR-980	EM/MD	EM	87
HAR-981	EM	EM	87
HAR-983	EM/MD	EM	87
HAR-986	EM/MD	EM	79
HAR-987	EM/MD	MD	18–19
HAR-988	EM/MD	MD?	79

Results after 1500 cal AD

Sample	Period	Date	Page
HAR-1206	MD/PM	BA	9
HAR-1534	MD/PM	EM/MD	227
HAR-1551	MD/PM	EM/MD	227
HAR-1561	MD/PM	EM/MD	227–8
HAR-1621	PM	EM	13
HAR-1638	PM	MD/PM	26
HAR-1690	MD/PM	MD	57
HAR-1830	MD/PM		156
HAR-1930	MD/PM	MD	18
HAR-2259	MD/PM		7
HAR-2260	PM	MD	25
HAR-2262	MD/PM	PM	85
HAR-2266	MD/PM	PM	85
HAR-2347	PM	EM	13
HAR-2448	MD/PM	EM	14
HAR-2896	MD/PM	MD	232

Sample	Period	Date	Page
HAR-3075	MD/PM		10
HAR-3391	MD/PM	PM	110
HAR-3393	MD/PM	MD	110
HAR-3443	MD/PM	MD	129–30
HAR-3957	MD/PM	PM	141
HAR-843	PM	IA	115